Practical Systems Programming in Go

A hands-on guide to designing and building real-world systems software in Go

Mihalis Tsoukalos

<packt>

Practical Systems Programming in Go

Portfolio Director: Kunal Chaudhari
Relationship Lead: Denim Pinto
Project Manager: K. Loganathan
Content Engineer: Srishty Goyal
Technical Editor: Irfa Ansari
Copy Editor: Safis Editing
Indexer: Hemangini Bari
Proofreader: Srishty Goyal
Production Designer: Ponraj Dhandapani
Growth Lead: Vinishka Kalra

First published: March 2026
Production reference: 1260326
Published by Packt Publishing Ltd.
Grosvenor House
11 St Paul's Square
Birmingham
B3 1RB, UK.

ISBN 978-1-80611-219-7
`www.packtpub.com`

I would like to dedicate this book to my nephew, Vassilis

– Mihalis Tsoukalos

Contributors

About the author

Mihalis Tsoukalos is a UNIX Systems Engineer and a Technical Writer. He is the author of *Go Systems Programming, Time Series Indexing, and Mastering Go*. He holds a BSc in Mathematics from the University of Patras (Greece) and an MSc in IT from the University College London (UK). He has written more than 300 technical articles for magazines, including *Sys Admin*, *MacTech*, *Linux User and Developer*, USENIX; login:, *Linux Format*, and *Linux Journal*. His research interests include time series, data mining, machine learning, and indexing.

You can reach him at https://www.mtsoukalos.eu/ and @mactsouk.

As writing a book is a team effort, I would like to thank the people at Packt Publishing for helping me write this book, including Denim Pinto, Srishty Goyal, K. Loganathan, and Alexander Powell, as well as Natan Streppel and Gautam Rege, the technical reviewers of the book, for their excellent work, including finding logical code errors.

Finally, I would like to thank you, the reader, for choosing this book. I hope you find it helpful and that it will keep you engaged on your Go journey.

About the reviewers

Natan Streppel has been working in backend systems since 2011 and has been developing with Go since 2017. He is a strong advocate for the language's simplicity, clarity, and effectiveness in building reliable systems. His main interests lie in distributed systems and database internals, particularly in the design and operation of scalable data-intensive applications.

Gautam Rege is the Co-Founder of Josh Software and a technologist who still codes while building a company. With over 25 years of hands-on software experience, he works closely with banks, fintech companies, and product teams across the BFSI ecosystem. His work sits where strong engineering meets everyday behavior. An avid programmer, he codes mainly Go and Ruby and has written a couple of books, including *Ruby and MongoDB Web Developer's Guide*, *Learning Mongoid*, and *Hands-On Microservices with Go and MongoDB.*

He is also a regular sportsperson, playing squash, field hockey, and basketball — his mantra being, "one sport a day, seven days a week."

About the reviewers

Table of Contents

Preface xvii

Free benefits with your book ... xxii

Part 1: A quick introduction to Go 1

Chapter 1: Essential Go 3

Why use Go? ... 4

Go versus Rust versus Zig versus C ... 5

How to run Go code ... 6

Fundamental data types ... 8

Variables and constants • 9

Public and private (exported and unexported) • 9

Printing values • 10

Numeric data types • 10

Strings and runes • 12

Learning about strings.Builder • 16

Error handling ... 18

Arrays and slices ... 22

Arrays • 23

Slices • 23

Slicing • 24

Functions ... 27

Iterator functions • 29

Learning how to use regular expressions ... 31

Working with command-line arguments ... 35

The viper and cobra packages ... 38

The viper package • 38

The cobra package • 39

Implementing which(1) 39

Implementing basename(1) 42

Summary 44

Exercises 45

Additional resources 45

Chapter 2: Data Collections and Functions 47

Understanding and using maps 48

Understanding the versatility of structures 57

Pointers 84

Summary 89

Exercises 90

Additional resources 90

Chapter 3: Go Concurrency 91

Learning about goroutines 92

Creating goroutines • 93

Waiting for goroutines to finish their jobs • 95

WaitGroup.Go – new in Go 1.25 • 98

Learning about channels 99

Learning about the select statement • 99

Handling multiple channels with select • 100

Exchanging data with channels • 102

Buffered and unbuffered channels • 104

Timing out goroutines with channels • 108

Implementing worker pools • 110

Signal channels • 115

Monitor goroutines • 116

Catching deadlocks and race conditions 119

Race conditions • 120

Concurrent matrix multiplication in Go • 125

Deadlocks • 129

Summary 132

Exercises 132

Additional resources 133

Chapter 4: Advanced Go 135

The Go program execution process 136

Common misconceptions about Go 137

Go is slow because it has garbage collection • 137

Channels are the best way to do all concurrency in Go • 137

Go does not need profiling as it is already fast • 138

The Go compiler does not optimize much • 138

Goroutines are just like threads • 138

Go does not support fine-grained control over memory • 138

Go is just another general-purpose language • 138

The Go garbage collector 139

Learning about the GOGC environment variable • 140

Memory leaks • 143

Pointers and references creating memory leaks • 143

Goroutines creating memory leaks • 145

The Go scheduler 147

Learning about the effects of GOMAXPROCS • 148

Profile-Guided Optimization (PGO) 151

make and new 153

Workspaces 153

Interfaces 154

The empty interface • 154

The uses of the empty interface • 155

Reflection 159

Inspecting structures with reflection • 160

Generics 163

Packages and modules 165

Testing Go code 166

Testing ch01/basename.go • 167

The synctest package • 168

Understanding how dates and times work 170

Benchmarking Go code 172

Benchmarking ch04/jsonReflection.go • 173

Benchmarking PGO gains • 176

Profiling applications • 176

Summary 178

Exercises 179

Additional resources 179

Part 2: Systems Programming Essentials 181

Chapter 5: Working with File I/O 183

When learning, implement what you need or like 184

stdin, stdout, and stderr 184

Checking whether a file path exists 185

Reading files 186

File seeking • 187

Unbuffered reading • 189

Buffered reading • 190

Benchmarking buffered and unbuffered reading • 192

Profiling buffered and unbuffered reading • 192

Reading a file line by line • 197

Reading a file word by word • 198

Reading a file character by character • 199

Writing files 201

Creating new files • 202

Creating a file if it does not exist • 203

Appending to files • 205

System logging and logging to files • 207

Unbuffered writing • 211

Buffered writing • 212

Benchmarking buffered and unbuffered writing • 213

Benchmarking buffer size in buffered writing • 214

Benchmarking file copying 215

Converting tabs to spaces and vice versa 217

Developing wc(1) 219

Summary 220

Exercises 221

Additional resources 221

Chapter 6: UNIX Signals and File Systems 223

A story 224

Handling UNIX signals 224

Differentiating between file types 227

Finding more information about files 229

The io/fs package 230

Traversing directory trees 231

Embedding static assets in Go binaries 236

A utility for finding empty directories • 239

Creating the tree(1) utility in Go • 240

Copying a single file into multiple directories 251

Creating the dd(1) utility in Go 255

Summary 257

Exercises 257

Additional resources 258

Chapter 7: Working with Structured Data and Databases 259

Working with JSON data 260

Working with a stream of JSON records • 260

JSON benchmarking • 261

Converting from JSON to XML • 264

JSON's evolution: json/v2 • 266
Solving the traveling salesman problem 268
Creating sample graphs • 269
Implementing the traveling salesman algorithm • 271
Implementing the Dijkstra algorithm 275
Working with SQLite3 280
The use of external Go modules • 280
Demonstrating SQLite3 interactions • 280
Storing JSON data in a SQLite3 database • 285
Working with PostgreSQL 286
Using a Docker image for PostgreSQL • 288
Creating database reports 290
Summary 294
Exercises 295
Additional resources 295

Chapter 8: Programming TCP/IP Services 297

A story 297
Developing a TCP server 298
Testing the TCP server • 300
Making the TCP server concurrent • 301
Developing a TCP client • 302
Developing a UDP server 305
Developing a UDP client • 308
Collecting TCP/IP metrics 311
Containerizing the server • 316
Storing TCP/IP metrics • 317
Running Prometheus and the Go server as Docker images • 318
Summary 320
Exercises 320
Additional resources 320
Subscribe to Deep Engineering 320

Chapter 9: Creating Web Services 323

The net/http package 323
Creating a simple HTTP server with middleware 324
Creating an HTTP client • 330
Profiling HTTP applications • 333
Testing HTTP applications • 336
The context package 339
Creating a proxy server 343
Developing a web service 344
Developing a client for the web service 350
Implementing the commands • 351
Reading data from Prometheus 354
Creating sample data for Prometheus • 354
Implementing the utility • 356
Summary 360
Exercises 360
Additional resources 360

Part 3: Applications 363

Chapter 10: Writing a Programming Language 365

Why create a new programming language? 365
Defining the syntax of SMALL 366
The components of a programming language • 368
The lexer 368
Reading code from external files • 380
The parser 383
The evaluator 395
Using SMALL 405
Summary 406
Exercises 407

Additional resources ... 407

Chapter 11: Adding New Features to SMALL 409

Why do we need to extend a programming language ... 409
New features in SMALL ... 410
Implementing the updated version of SMALL ... 414
The lexer • 414
The parser • 415
The evaluator • 418
Using the language • 421
Writing tests for SMALL ... 424
Summary ... 433
Exercises ... 433
Additional resources ... 433

Chapter 12: Time Series Distances 435

If you only work for money, you will become miserable ... 436
Introduction to time series ... 436
Reading time series • 437
Getting information about a time series • 438
Time series distances ... 440
About the Euclidean distance • 440
About the Chebyshev distance • 440
About the Manhattan distance • 441
About LCSS • 441
About DTW • 441
About MPdist • 442
Creating a summary of a time series • 443
Creating a Go package ... 444
Working with workspaces • 444
Documenting the package • 447
How to see the documentation • 448

Publishing the Go package on GitHub • 449
Benchmarking the distances • 451
Finding the nearest neighbor of a time series 452
Using TigerBeetle for financial accounting 453
Connecting to TigerBeetle • 456
Writing data to TigerBeetle • 457
Reading the data back • 462
Summary 464
Exercises 464
Additional resources 465

Chapter 13: Time Series Data Mining 467

Classification 468
Classification implementation • 468
Clustering 479
Clustering methodology • 479
Clustering implementation • 479
Outlier analysis 487
Trying the Green Tea garbage collector 495
New in Go 1.26: Goroutine metrics 497
New in Go 1.26: Goroutine leak profile 499
Summary 502
Exercises 502
Additional resources 502

Chapter 14: Creating an Index for Unix Files 505

Understanding Binary Trees 506
A sweet improvement to new() • 506
Understanding Radix Trees 513
Creating a filesystem index service 520
The server code • 521
Using the service • 534

Creating a command-line client 535

About fsnotify • 535

New in Go 1.26: log to multiple targets 543

Summary 545

Exercises 546

Additional resources 546

Chapter 15: Unlock Your Exclusive Benefits 547

Unlock this Book's Free Benefits in 3 Easy Steps 548

Other Books You May Enjoy 552

Subscribe to Deep Engineering 554

Index 557

Preface

Welcome to the 1st Edition of *Practical Systems Programming in Go*! As the Go programming language continues to evolve and gain popularity, it has emerged as a language of choice for building scalable, performant, and maintainable systems software. Whether you are a seasoned Go developer looking to deepen your expertise or a newcomer eager to master the intricacies of the language, this book is your comprehensive guide.

While there are many books that teach Go as a general-purpose language, systems programming demands a different depth of understanding. Writing software that interacts directly with the operating system, manages files and signals, communicates over networks, processes structured data at scale, and squeezes performance out of concurrent workloads requires both a firm grasp of Go internals and a practical understanding of how modern UNIX systems work. Go is particularly well-suited for this domain — its standard library is rich, its concurrency model is powerful, and its compiled nature makes it fast enough for low-level work without sacrificing the readability and simplicity that developers love. Yet these topics are rarely treated together in a single, focused resource. This book fills that gap.

There are many exciting topics in this edition, including working with file I/O, Unix signals and file systems, programming TCP/IP services and web services, working with structured data and databases, and exploring time series distances and data mining. The book also features a particularly unique and rewarding journey into writing your own programming language from scratch and extending it with new features.

In the tradition of foundational texts like *The UNIX Programming Environment* and *The C Programming Language*, this book adopts a deliberate and detailed explanatory style. Rather than offering a superficial overview of syntax, we prioritize the logic behind every architectural decision. Systems programming is as much about understanding the constraints of the machine as it is about writing code; therefore, we pause frequently to examine the *why*. By engaging with these deep-dives, you are not merely learning a language but internalizing a philosophy of systems construction. We treat the code as a vehicle for understanding broader engineering trade-offs, from the durability of a Write-Ahead Log to the resource limits of filesystem watchers. While this level of detail requires a more patient reading experience, the reward is a mental model that remains stable long after specific library versions have evolved. Setting this expectation upfront ensures that our journey through the stack is both rewarding and practical, transforming abstract concepts into the intuitive tools of a master craftsman.

Thank you for choosing *Practical Systems Programming in Go*. Let's dive in and unlock the full potential of Go together! Happy coding!

Soli Deo gloria

Who this book is for

This book is for amateur and intermediate Go programmers who want to take their Go knowledge to the next level, as well as developers in other programming languages who want to learn systems programming in UNIX using Go.

If this is your first systems programming book, some sections may challenge you, and a second reading will often reveal details that were not immediately obvious the first time around. Do not be discouraged by this — it is perfectly normal.

Throughout the book, you will find practical examples and exercises designed to ground abstract concepts in real, working code. The best way to learn systems programming is to actually do it, so resist the temptation to skip them.

Finally, be prepared to struggle. You will write code that does not work, chase bugs that make no sense, and revisit ideas you thought you had already understood. That is not a sign that you are doing something wrong — it is the process. Push through it, and the rewards are well worth the effort.

What this book covers

Chapter 1, Essential Go, introduces the Go programming language, covering its core syntax, basic types, control flow, functions, and the tools you need to write, build, and run Go programs. In this chapter, we present arrays and slices and implement two traditional UNIX command line tools: `which(1)` and `basename(1)`.

Chapter 2, Data Collections and Functions, explores maps and structures alongside a deeper treatment of pointers, functions, closures, and variadic parameters. By the end of this chapter, you will be comfortable organizing and manipulating data in idiomatic Go.

Chapter 3, Go Concurrency, covers goroutines, channels, `select`, the `sync` package, and the patterns that make concurrent Go programs correct and efficient. We examine how to avoid race conditions and deadlocks, and how to coordinate work across multiple goroutines.

Chapter 4, Advanced Go, dives into interfaces, reflection, generics, and other language features that separate competent Go programmers from expert ones, as well as working with dates and times, testing and benchmarking Go code, and creating your own package. This chapter equips you with the tools to write flexible, reusable, and robust code while knowing what happens behind the scenes.

Chapter 5, *Working with File I/O*, is about reading from and writing to files, working with the `io.Reader` and `io.Writer` interfaces, buffered I/O, and the standard library packages that make file handling in Go both powerful and ergonomic. In this chapter, we create a `wc(1)` clone.

Chapter 6, *UNIX Signals and File Systems*, covers how Go programs interact with the operating system at a deeper level, including handling UNIX signals gracefully, navigating and manipulating the file system, and understanding the implications of these operations in long-running system processes. In *Chapter 6*, we develop a version of `tree(1)` and `dd(1)` in Go.

Chapter 7, *Working with Structured Data and Databases*, discusses parsing and producing structured data formats such as JSON and CSV, as well as interacting with relational and other databases. We build practical utilities that store, retrieve, and process data reliably, and a utility that creates reports. The database of choice is going to be SQLite3, but we are also going to create an example using PostgreSQL.

Chapter 8, *Programming TCP/IP Services*, explores the `net` package and the TCP and UDP protocols, developing practical client and server applications that communicate over the network at a low level. You learn how to collect metrics about TCP and UDP connections and make these metrics accessible to Prometheus.

Chapter 9, *Creating Web Services*, discusses the `net/http` package, the development of web servers and web services, the creation of web clients, and the timing out of HTTP connections while demonstrating how to build production-ready services. We show how to read data from Prometheus.

Chapter 10, *Writing a Programming Language*, takes an exciting detour into language design and implementation. We build a small interpreted programming language called SMALL from scratch in Go, covering lexing, parsing, and evaluation.

Chapter 11, *Adding New Features to SMALL*, continues the work of the previous chapter by extending SMALL with new capabilities, reinforcing how a real language evolves and how its interpreter must grow to accommodate it.

Chapter 12, *Time Series Distances*, introduces the concept of time series data and the algorithms used to measure similarity and distance between sequences, implementing a practical Go package along the way. *Chapter 12* concludes by showing how to work with TigerBeetle, a high-performance distributed database designed for financial accounting.

Chapter 13, *Time Series Data Mining*, builds on the previous chapter to explore data mining techniques applied to time series, including classification, clustering, and outlier detection, all implemented in Go.

Chapter 14, Creating an Index for Unix Files, brings the book to a close with a substantial systems programming project: building a utility that indexes UNIX files, combining File I/O, data structures, and performance considerations into a complete, practical tool.

To get the most out of this book

This book requires a modern computer with a relatively recent Go version installed, which includes any machine running Mac OS X, macOS, or Linux, as well as familiarity with your operating system, its filesystem, and `git(1)`. Most of the presented code also runs on Microsoft Windows machines without any changes.

As you embark on your journey to mastering Go, I encourage you to experiment, ask questions, and engage with the material actively. The Go programming language offers a refreshing blend of simplicity and power, and I am confident that this book will provide you with the knowledge and skills needed to become a proficient Go developer.

Download the example code files

The code bundle for the book is hosted on GitHub at `https://github.com/mactsouk/goSP`. We also have other code bundles from our rich catalog of books and videos available at `https://github.com/PacktPublishing/`. Check them out!

Download the color images

We also provide a PDF file that has color images of the screenshots and diagrams used in this book. You can download it here: `https://packt.link/gbp/9781806112197`.

Conventions used

There are a number of text conventions used throughout this book.

`CodeInText`: Indicates code words in text, database table names, folder names, filenames, file extensions, pathnames, dummy URLs, user input, and Twitter handles. For example: "Mount the downloaded `WebStorm-10*.dmg` disk image file as another disk in your system."

A block of code is set as follows:

```
package main
import "fmt"
func doubleSquare(x int) (int, int) {
return x * 2, x * x
}
```

Any command-line input or output is written as follows:

```
$ go run namedReturn.go 1 -2
-2 1
-2 1
```

Bold: Indicates a new term, an important word, or important information. For instance, words in menus or dialog boxes appear in the text like this. For example: "The next subsection illustrates the use of `sync.WaitGroup` for **goroutine synchronization**. "

> **Note**
>
> Warnings or important notes appear like this

> **Tip**
>
> Tips and tricks appear like this

Get in touch

Feedback from our readers is always welcome.

General feedback: Email `feedback@packtpub.com` and mention the book's title in the subject of your message. If you have questions about any aspect of this book, please email us at `questions@packtpub.com`.

Errata: Although we have taken every care to ensure the accuracy of our content, mistakes do happen. If you have found a mistake in this book, we would be grateful if you reported this to us. Please visit , click **Submit Errata**, and fill in the form.

Piracy: If you come across any illegal copies of our works in any form on the internet, we would be grateful if you would provide us with the location address or website name. Please contact us at `copyright@packtpub.com` with a link to the material.

If you are interested in becoming an author: If there is a topic that you have expertise in and you are interested in either writing or contributing to a book, please visit `http://authors.packtpub.com`.

Join us on Discord!

Read this book alongside other users, developers, experts, and the author himself.

Ask questions, provide solutions to other readers, chat with the authors via Ask Me Anything sessions, and much more. Scan the QR code or visit the link to join the community.

`https://packt.link/deep-engineering-golang`

Free benefits with your book

This book comes with free benefits to support your learning. Activate them now for instant access (see the "*How to unlock*" section for instructions).

Here's a quick overview of what you can instantly unlock with your purchase:

Share your thoughts

Once you've read *Practical Systems Programming in Go*, we'd love to hear your thoughts! Scan the QR code below to go straight to the Amazon review page for this book and share your feedback.

https://packt.link/r/1806112191

Your review is important to us and the tech community and will help us make sure we're delivering excellent quality content.

Part 1

A quick introduction to Go

In this first part of the book, you will develop a solid understanding of the Go programming language through the lens of a systems engineer. We begin by establishing the core syntax and philosophy, moving quickly into the data collections and patterns that underpin efficient software. The logic behind this section is to treat concurrency not as an advanced add-on but as a fundamental building block of the language, introduced early to ensure you can think in terms of parallel execution from the outset. By the end of this part, you will have mastered the advanced Go features necessary to build robust abstractions that remain performant under the pressures of a modern operating system.

This part of the book includes the following chapters:

- *Chapter 1, Essential Go*
- *Chapter 2, Data Collections and Functions*
- *Chapter 3, Go Concurrency*
- *Chapter 4, Advanced Go*

1

Essential Go

In the world of computing, simplicity is often mistaken for weakness, yet time and experience reveal that simplicity is where strength truly lies. **Go**, a modern programming language designed for simplicity, efficiency, and scalability, embraces this truth with conviction. It forgoes ornamentation in favor of clarity and avoids magic in favor of transparency. Born out of Google's need for a fast, reliable language to handle large-scale systems, Go combines the performance of a compiled language with the ease of use of a dynamic one. Whether you are building web servers, cloud applications, or complex command-line tools that support multiple commands and options, the straightforward syntax of Go, the powerful concurrency model, and the robust standard library make it an excellent choice.

In this chapter, we begin by exploring the core concepts and features that define Go, before talking about Go variables, data types, and error handling, giving you the foundation needed to write clean, efficient, and maintainable code. However, when building real-world programs, working with single values quickly becomes limiting. Most applications need to handle groups of related data — whether that is a list of usernames, a mapping of configuration keys to values, or a fixed set of numerical measurements. Go provides several powerful collection types to meet these needs; each is designed with simplicity and performance in mind. In this chapter, we present **arrays** that offer a fixed-size, contiguous block of elements and **slices** that build on arrays to provide a flexible, resizable view of data. Lastly, we implement two traditional Unix command-line tools.

This chapter equips you with the essential knowledge to start programming in Go, covering the following topics:

- The reasons for using Go
- Go versus Rust versus Zig versus C
- Executing Go code

- Go data types
- Error handling
- Regular expressions
- Arrays and slices
- Working with command-line arguments
- The `viper` and `cobra` packages
- Implementing `which(1)`
- Implementing `basename(1)`

Without further ado, let us begin learning Go for Unix systems programming!

> Note
>
> **Your purchase includes a free PDF copy + exclusive extras**
>
> Your purchase includes a DRM-free PDF copy of this book, 7-day trial to the Packt+ library (no credit card required), and additional exclusive extras. See the *Free benefits with your book* section in the *Preface* to unlock them instantly and maximize your learning.

Why use Go?

Go comes with some important advantages for developers, starting with the fact that it was designed by the legends of the software industry: Rob Pike, Robert Griesemer, and Ken Thompson, who is the co-creator of Unix and the father of the C programming language. Go is also easy to learn, especially if you are already familiar with programming languages such as C, Python, or Java. On top of that, Go code is good-looking, which is great when you are programming applications for a living and you must look at code daily. Go also offers support for Unicode out of the box, which means that you can make changes to existing Go code easily. Go has only 25 reserved keywords, which makes it much easier to remember the language. Can you say that about C++?

Go comes with concurrency capabilities using a simple concurrency model implemented using **goroutines** and **channels**. Go manages OS threads for you and has a powerful runtime that allows you to spawn lightweight units of work (goroutines) that, among other things, can communicate with each other and coordinate using channels. Although Go comes with a rich standard library, handy Go packages such as `cobra` and `viper` allow the Go developer to create complex command-line utilities such as `docker` and `hugo`. This is greatly supported by the fact that executable binaries are typically *statically linked*, which means that once they are generated, they do not depend on any shared libraries and include all required information.

Due to its simplicity, Go code is predictable and does not have strange side effects, and although Go supports pointers, it does not support **pointer arithmetic** like C – unless you use the `unsafe` package – which can be the root of many bugs and security holes. Although Go is not an object-oriented programming language, Go **interfaces** are very versatile and allow you to mimic some of the capabilities of object-oriented languages, such as polymorphism, encapsulation, and composition.

> **Note**
>
> Although the official name of the language is Go, it is sometimes (wrongly) referred to as Golang. The official reason for this is that `go.org` was not available for registration, and `golang.org` was chosen instead; however, nowadays, the official Go website is `https://go.dev/`. Keep in mind that when you are querying a search engine for Go-related information, the word *Go* is usually interpreted as a verb. Additionally, the official X hashtag for Go is `#golang`.

Go can help you develop the following kinds of applications and utilities:

- Professional web services
- Networking tools and servers, such as Kubernetes and Istio
- Backend systems
- System utilities
- Powerful command-line utilities such as `docker` and `hugo`
- Applications that exchange data in JSON format
- Applications that process data from relational databases, NoSQL databases, or other popular data storage systems
- Compilers and interpreters for your own programming languages
- Database systems such as CockroachDB and key/value stores such as `etcd`

Having examined the reasons for choosing Go, it is useful to place these strengths in a broader context. No programming language exists in isolation, and Go is often considered alongside other systems-oriented languages that address similar problem spaces in different ways. In the next section, we compare Go with Rust, Zig, and C.

Go versus Rust versus Zig versus C

Go, C, Rust, and Zig are all systems-oriented languages, but each strikes a different balance between control, safety, and productivity. C remains the foundation of low-level programming, offering minimal abstraction and maximum performance, but at the cost of manual memory management and risks such as memory leaks and buffer overflows. Rust takes a different path, combining performance with safety through its ownership model and borrow checker, preventing entire classes of memory bugs at compile time — though with a steeper learning curve. Go emphasizes simplicity and concurrency with goroutines and garbage collection, making it highly productive for scalable backend and cloud services, but less suitable for fine-grained systems programming due to garbage collection overhead. Zig positions itself as a modern alternative to C, providing manual memory management alongside optional safety checks, compile-time code execution, and smooth C interoperability, appealing to developers who want low-level control without the complexity of Rust. In practice, C remains essential for embedded systems and kernels, Go shines in high-concurrency applications, Rust dominates security-sensitive and performance-critical software, and Zig offers a middle ground for those seeking modern safety features with manual control.

As expected, the choice between these languages depends on specific project requirements, team expertise, performance constraints, and safety requirements. Each language represents different trade-offs between control, safety, performance, and developer productivity that should be evaluated beforehand.

With a clearer understanding of where Go fits among other systems languages, the next step is to move from theory to practice. Before writing larger programs or exploring advanced features, it is important to know how Go code is built and executed using the Go toolchain. So next, we focus on the practical mechanics of compiling and running Go programs, introducing the essential commands and workflows that turn source files into working executables.

How to run Go code

Running Go code is intentionally simple and designed to streamline both experimentation and production workflows. At its core, you use the `go run` command to compile and execute a Go source file directly, which is especially convenient for testing small programs or experimenting with snippets. For larger projects, you typically organize your code into **modules** and **packages**, using `go build` to produce executable binaries that you need to run in a subsequent step. The Go toolchain handles compilation, linking, and dependency management in a single unified workflow, so you do not need separate build scripts or external tools. In this section, we will walk through the different ways of running Go code.

> **Note**
>
> When we say *the Go toolchain*, we refer to the complete set of tools that comes with the Go distribution and is responsible for compiling, running, testing, and managing Go code. At the heart of it is the go command, which acts as the frontend interface for the

> developer. The toolchain includes the compiler (which translates Go source code into machine code), the linker (which assembles compiled code into an executable binary), the runtime (which provides garbage collection, concurrency support, and other core services at execution time), and the package manager (which resolves and manages dependencies through modules). Additionally, the toolchain integrates utilities for testing (go `test`), benchmarking, formatting (`gofmt`), and static analysis (go `vet`), all working together in a cohesive workflow. This self-contained ecosystem is one of the strengths of Go, as it eliminates the need for third-party build systems and ensures a consistent developer experience across platforms.

We are going to practice the execution of Go code using the famous `Hello World!` program (saved as `ch01/hw.go`), which contains the following code – this is the simplest Go program that creates output:

```
package main

import (
	"fmt"
)

func main() {
	fmt.Println("Hello World!")
}
```

This simple Go program prints `Hello World!` to the console and serves as a minimal example to introduce the structure of a Go application. The first line, `package main`, declares that this file belongs to the `main` package, which is special in Go because it defines an executable program rather than a reusable library. Execution always begins in the `main()` function within this package. Next, the `import "fmt"` statement brings in the `fmt` package from the standard library, which provides functions for formatted input and output. Inside `main()`, the call to `fmt.Println("Hello World!")` invokes the `Println()` function from the `fmt` package, passing it the `"Hello World!"` string as an argument. This causes the string to be printed to the console, followed by a newline. When you run the program using the Go toolchain with a command such as `go run hello.go`, the Go compiler compiles the code, links necessary components, and executes the `main()` function, resulting in the output appearing on your terminal. Even though the program is short, it demonstrates essential Go concepts: declaring a package, importing libraries, defining functions, and using the standard library for output — all of which form the foundation for writing more complex Go applications.

> **Note**
>
> One of the most valuable design choices of Go is its strict prohibition of **cyclic imports**. A cyclic import occurs when, for example, package *A* depends on *B*, *B* depends on *C*, and *C* depends back on *A*. Cyclic imports create spaghetti-like dependencies on the scale of an entire code base, making projects fragile and difficult to reason about. While many package managers discourage these patterns, most mainstream programming languages still allow them within a project. Go takes a different, opinionated approach: it completely forbids import cycles. If an import cycle exists, the code simply will not compile.

Here is the first way that you can run `ch01/hw.go` on your machine:

```
$ go run ./ch01/hw.go
Hello World!
```

And here is the second way:

```
$ go build ./ch01/hw.go
$ ./hw
$ Hello World!
```

As a rule of thumb, go `run` is ideal for rapid testing and prototyping, whereas go `build` is more appropriate for production use, repeated executions, and deployment scenarios.

Remember that Go code is organized in packages. The `main` package is required for executable programs. Execution always starts in `main()` within the `main` package, and functions are declared with `func`. Let us now continue by learning about Go data types.

Fundamental data types

Go offers a strong, yet straightforward type system designed to be efficient, predictable, and expressive. This chapter explores the fundamental data types, including numeric types, Boolean values, strings, arrays, and slices. But first, let us discuss variables and constants.

Variables and constants

In Go, **variables** and **constants** are fundamental building blocks for managing data, but they serve different purposes. Variables are declared using the `var` keyword or the short declaration operator (`:=`) and can hold values that may change during program execution. Go is **statically typed**, but it also supports **type inference**, meaning the compiler can deduce the variable type from the assigned value when using `:=`. For example, `x := 10` automatically infers `x` as an `int` type. On the other hand, constants are declared using the `const` keyword and represent immutable values known at compile time. They must be assigned a value that the compiler can determine before runtime, making them ideal for fixed values such as mathematical constants, configuration keys, or buffer sizes. Constants can be **typed** or **untyped**; untyped constants are more flexible because they can be assigned to variables of compatible types without explicit conversion.

In Go, every variable you declare is automatically initialized with a zero value if you do not explicitly assign one. This behavior eliminates the risk of using uninitialized variables, a common source of bugs in other languages. The zero value depends on the type: numeric types such as `int` and `float64` default to `0`, Booleans to `false`, strings to an empty string (`""`), and pointers, slices, maps, channels, interfaces, and functions default to `nil`. For example, declaring `var x int` without assigning a value sets `x` to `0` automatically. This feature is tightly coupled with the Go philosophy of simplicity and safety — you can start using variables right away without worrying about undefined states. When you need explicit initialization, you can use short variable declarations (`x := 42`), standard `var` assignments, or composite literals for more complex types such as slices, structs, and maps.

Public and private (exported and unexported)

In Go, the concepts of **public** and **private** visibility are determined by the *capitalization* of identifiers rather than using explicit keywords such as `public` or `private` found in other languages. If a name — such as a variable, constant, function, type, or struct field — starts with an uppercase letter, it is exported, meaning it is publicly accessible from other packages. Conversely, if the name begins with a lowercase letter, it is unexported and thus private to the package in which it is defined. For example, a function named `PrintMessage()` can be called from outside its package, while a function named `printMessage()` cannot. This simple and consistent rule applies uniformly across all identifiers, making the Go visibility model straightforward and easy to follow. However, it also encourages developers to think carefully about which parts of their code should form a public API and which should remain internal implementation details. This rule does not apply to package names.

Printing values

At its core, printing is about making the invisible visible. Whether debugging low-level behavior, tracing execution paths, or formatting structured output, the ability to display data clearly and precisely is essential in systems programming. The Go `fmt` package offers a powerful and flexible toolkit for printing — from basic strings and values to complex, formatted diagnostics. In this section, we explore how to use `fmt` effectively: to write readable output, reveal program state, and build tools that communicate their internals as clearly as their interfaces. You can get the documentation of the `fmt` package by typing `go doc fmt` on your Unix shell (the same applies to all packages of the Go standard library). You will see printing examples throughout the entire chapter.

Numeric data types

When writing systems software in Go, working directly with numerical data is fundamental. Whether you are managing memory offsets, working with binary protocols, or implementing performance-critical algorithms, choosing the right numeric type matters. Go provides a rich set of numerical data types, including signed and unsigned integers of various sizes, floating-point numbers, and complex numbers. Each type is designed with clear size guarantees and predictable behavior, making Go well-suited for low-level and performance-sensitive tasks.

For integers, Go offers both signed (`int8`, `int16`, `int32`, and `int64`) and unsigned (`uint8`, `uint16`, `uint32`, and `uint64`) variants, along with the machine-dependent `int` and `uint` types, whose size matches the target architecture (typically 32 or 64 bits). Floating-point support includes IEEE-754-compliant `float32` and `float64`, while complex numbers are represented using `complex64` and `complex128`. Go also includes aliases such as `byte` (an alias for `uint8`) and `rune` (an alias for `int32`) to improve code clarity when working with binary data and Unicode code points, respectively.

The example Go code that follows demonstrates the complete set of built-in numeric types, organized into four categories: integers, floating-point numbers, complex numbers, and type aliases. The part that presents integer data types comes with the following code:

```
// Signed integers
var a int8 = -128
var b int16 = -32768
var c int32 = -2147483648
var d int64 = -9223372036854775808

// Unsigned integers
var ua uint8 = 255
```

```
var ub uint16 = 65535
var uc uint32 = 4294967295
var ud uint64 = 18446744073709551615

// Machine-dependent integers
var e int = -42   // int (32-bit or 64-bit depending on architecture)
var f uint = 42  // uint
```

The `int` and `uint` types are shown here. These are machine-dependent types, meaning their size is either 32 or 64 bits, depending on the target architecture. They are suitable for general-purpose counters, indexes, and loop variables where maximum performance is desired.

The example code concerning floating-point numbers is the following:

```
// Floating-point numbers
var g float32 = 3.14159
var h float64 = 2.718281828459045
```

`float32` and `float64` conform to the IEEE 754 standard for binary floating-point arithmetic. `float32` offers approximately 6 to 7 decimal digits of precision and is typically used in performance-sensitive contexts or where memory is constrained, whereas `float64` offers higher precision (approximately 15 to 17 decimal digits) and is the default floating-point type in Go for most numerical work. These types are essential for scientific purposes but must be used more cautiously in systems-level tasks due to rounding and determinism concerns.

Here is the example code for creating complex numbers:

```
// Complex numbers
var i complex64 = complex(1.5, -2.5)
var j complex128 = complex(3.0, 4.0)
```

This example demonstrates the use of built-in type aliases in Go. The `byte` and `rune` identifiers are not new types but aliases for existing types. Using these aliases does not change the underlying type or behavior; it simply makes the code clearer and more expressive:

```
// Aliases
var k byte = 0xFF   // byte is alias for uint8
var l rune = 'λ'      // rune is alias for int32 (Unicode code point)
```

`byte` is used to emphasize operations on raw binary data, such as file I/O buffers or encoded formats. On the other hand, `rune` is used to represent Unicode code points, aligning with Go native UTF-8 string representation and providing clarity when working with individual characters.

The remaining implementation of `main()` contains additional code for printing all these numeric values; feel free to look at the code on your own to better understand printing.

Running `numeric.go` produces the following output:

```
$ go run ch01/numeric.go
Signed Integers:
int8: -128 int16: -32768 int32: -2147483648 int64: -9223372036854775808
Unsigned Integers:
uint8: 255 uint16: 65535 uint32: 4294967295 uint64: 18446744073709551615
Machine-Dependent Integers:
int: -42 uint: 42
Floating-Point Numbers:
float32: 3.14159 float64: 2.718281828459045
Complex Numbers:
complex64: (1.5-2.5i) complex128: (3+4i)
Aliases:
byte: 255 (0xFF)
rune: λ (U+03BB)
```

Most printing operations are straightforward and need no further explanation, which is not true for `byte` and `rune`. As `byte` is an alias for `uint8` and `rune` is an alias for `int32`, the `fmt.Printf()` functions are used to display these values both in numeric and formatted output (e.g., hexadecimal and Unicode) – these are the last two lines of the output.

In systems programming, selecting the appropriate numeric type is critical for correctness, performance, and interoperability with hardware, binary protocols, and memory layouts. We continue by presenting strings and runes in more detail.

Strings and runes

In Go, strings and runes are tightly integrated into the language and designed to handle modern text processing needs; thus, there is full support for Unicode. A string in Go is a read-only slice of bytes that represents a UTF-8 encoded sequence. This design offers compatibility with standard encoding formats and efficient handling of raw data, but it also means that indexing a string yields individual bytes, not characters or runes.

As discussed earlier, to work with actual Unicode code points, Go introduces the `rune` type, which is an alias for `int32` and represents a single Unicode scalar value. Since UTF-8 is a variable-length encoding, characters may span multiple bytes; therefore, iterating over strings byte by byte can lead to incorrect interpretation of characters. To address this, Go provides tools such as `for ... range`, which decodes UTF-8 sequences into runes automatically, ensuring the correct traversal of multi-byte characters.

The `stringsRunes.go` Go program provides a comprehensive demonstration of how strings, bytes, and runes interact in the language. It begins with the `import` block:

```
package main

import (
    "fmt"
    "unicode/utf8"
)

func main() {
    str := "Go ♥ Zig"
    fmt.Println("Original string:", str)
    fmt.Println("Length in bytes:", len(str))

    fmt.Println("*** Byte-wise iteration:")
    for i := 0; i < len(str); i++ {
        fmt.Printf("Byte %d: 0x%X (%q)\n", i, str[i], str[i])
    }

    fmt.Println("*** Rune-wise iteration using range:")
    for i, r := range str {
        fmt.Printf("Rune at byte %d: %c (U+%04X)\n", i, r, r)
    }

    // Convert to []byte and []rune
    bytes := []byte(str)
    runes := []rune(str)

    fmt.Println("Converted to []byte:", bytes)
    fmt.Println("Converted to []rune:", runes)

    fmt.Println("Number of runes:", utf8.RuneCountInString(str))
    fmt.Println("First rune:", string(runes[0]), "| Uni:", runes[0])
}
```

The code begins by declaring a string, `str := "Go ♥ Zig"`, which contains both ASCII and a Unicode character (♥). In Go, strings are *immutable sequences* of bytes encoded in UTF8, so while the string visually contains 8 characters, its length in bytes is 10 due to the 3-byte encoding of the heart symbol. The program first prints the string and its byte length using `len(str)`, which reflects the raw storage size rather than the number of characters. It then performs a byte-wise iteration over the string using indexing, where each byte is printed individually. This highlights an important aspect of UTF8: characters such as ♥ are split across multiple bytes (`0xE2`, `0x99`, `0xA5`) when accessed this way, and when printed, these individual bytes no longer represent valid or meaningful characters on their own.

To correctly interpret characters, the program uses a `for ... range` loop, which decodes UTF-8 sequences into runes. In this loop, Go correctly identifies each Unicode character in the string, including the multibyte heart symbol, and prints its position, character representation, and Unicode code point. The program also demonstrates how to convert a string to a `[]byte` slice to view its raw byte representation, and to a `[]rune` slice to access the decoded Unicode code points. This distinction is crucial in systems programming: `[]byte` provides precise control over encoding and memory layout, while `[]rune` enables character-level manipulation. Finally, the program uses the `utf8.RuneCountInString()` function to compute the actual number of characters and prints the first rune both as a character and as a code point.

Running `stringsRunes.go` produces the following output – think about the expected output before looking at it. What do you expect to get?

```
$ go run ch01/stringsRunes.go
Original string: Go ♥ Zig
Length in bytes: 10
*** Byte-wise iteration:
Byte 0: 0x47 ('G')
Byte 1: 0x6F ('o')
Byte 2: 0x20 (' ')
Byte 3: 0xE2 ('â')
Byte 4: 0x99 ('\u0099')
Byte 5: 0xA5 ('¥')
Byte 6: 0x20 (' ')
Byte 7: 0x5A ('Z')
Byte 8: 0x69 ('i')
Byte 9: 0x67 ('g')
*** Rune-wise iteration using range:
Rune at byte 0: G (U+0047)
Rune at byte 1: o (U+006F)
```

```
Rune at byte 2:   (U+0020)
Rune at byte 3: ♥ (U+2665)
Rune at byte 6:   (U+0020)
Rune at byte 7: Z (U+005A)
Rune at byte 8: i (U+0069)
Rune at byte 9: g (U+0067)
Converted to []byte: [71 111 32 226 153 165 32 90 105 103]
Converted to []rune: [71 111 32 9829 32 90 105 103]
Number of runes: 8
First rune: G | Uni: 71
```

The output of the program demonstrates the fundamental difference between bytes and runes in Go, particularly when working with UTF-8 encoded strings. The `"Go ♥ Zig"` string appears simple but contains a multibyte Unicode character: the heart symbol ♥ (U+2665), which occupies three bytes in UTF-8 (`0xE2 0x99 0xA5`). When the program prints the length of the string using `len(str)`, it reports `10`, which reflects the number of bytes, not characters. This distinction is critical because Go strings are sequences of bytes, and indexing into them gives individual bytes, not full Unicode characters. The byte-wise iteration loop shows this clearly: each character is printed as a single byte. ASCII characters such as `'G'` and `'o'` are represented in one byte, but the heart symbol is split across three separate byte values (`0xE2`, `0x99`, and `0xA5`), none of which represent the character meaningfully on their own.

In contrast, the `for...range` loop iterates over runes (Unicode code points) by decoding each UTF-8 sequence correctly. This loop identifies ♥ as a single character starting at byte index 3 and prints its correct code point, `U+2665`. The same happens for all other characters in the string, including ASCII and Unicode symbols. When converting the string to a byte slice (`[]byte`), the output shows the underlying byte values used for UTF-8 encoding. Converting it to a rune slice (`[]rune`), however, yields an array of integers representing the Unicode code points, making each character a first-class value regardless of byte length. Finally, the program uses `utf8.RuneCountInString()` to count the number of runes, reporting 8, which matches the actual number of visible characters in the string. The difference between the 10 bytes and 8 runes emphasizes why systems programmers must be careful when handling strings at the byte level. Go gives you precise control over both representations — byte sequences for performance and I/O and runes for correctness in Unicode processing.

Now, let's learn how to construct strings in Go with `strings.Builder`.

Learning about strings.Builder

`strings.Builder` is a powerful and efficient way to construct strings in Go. Introduced in Go 1.10, it helps you build strings incrementally without creating many intermediate string values, which would otherwise cause repeated allocations and memory copying.

The most used method is `WriteString(s string)`, which appends a string to its internal buffer without creating a new string allocation. For working with raw binary data, `Write(p []byte)` appends a slice of bytes, while `WriteByte(b byte)` appends a single byte, making it ideal for ASCII-heavy string construction. To handle Unicode characters correctly, `WriteRune(r rune)` appends a single UTF-8 encoded code point, allowing you to mix ASCII and multibyte characters seamlessly. After building your content, you can retrieve the result using the `String()` method, which returns the current contents as a standard Go string. To inspect the state of the builder, `Len()` reports the number of bytes currently in the buffer, and `Cap()` returns the buffer's total capacity. If you know in advance how much data you will write, calling `Grow(n int)` can preallocate enough space to reduce memory copying and improve performance. Finally, if you wish to reuse a `strings.Builder` instance, `Reset()` clears the buffer so it can be used again from scratch. You can learn more about `strings.Builder` by typing `go doc strings.Builder` on your Unix shell.

This Go program (`stringOperations.go`) demonstrates how to efficiently build and manipulate strings using the `strings.Builder` type, along with various functions from the `strings` package and formatted output from the `fmt` package:

```
package main

import (
    "fmt"
    "strings"
)

func main() {
    var builder strings.Builder
    builder.Grow(128)
    // Write plain strings
    builder.WriteString("Go is ")
    builder.WriteString("fast!\n")
    // Append formatted data
    language := "Go"
    version := 1.25
```

```
    fmt.Fprintf(&builder, "Language: %s - ", language)
    fmt.Fprintf(&builder, "Version: %.2f\n", version)

    cores := 12
    fmt.Fprintf(&builder, "Running on %d logical CPU cores\n", cores)
    final := builder.String()
    fmt.Print("Final output: ")
    fmt.Print(final)

    // Report internal statistics
    fmt.Printf("Length: %d bytes, Capacity: %d bytes\n", builder.Len(),
builder.Cap())

    // Original string
    s := "Go is powerful!"
    // Count occurrences
    fmt.Println("Count of 's':", strings.Count(s, "s"))
    // Convert to uppercase and lowercase
    fmt.Println("Upper:", strings.ToUpper(s))
    fmt.Println("Lower:", strings.ToLower(s))
    // Replace words
    replaced := strings.ReplaceAll(s, "powerful", "fast")
    fmt.Println("REPLACED:", replaced)

    // Split into words
    words := strings.Fields(s)
    fmt.Println("Words:", words)
    // Join words with dashes
    dashed := strings.Join(words, "-")
    fmt.Println("Dashed:", dashed)
    // Index of a substring
    index := strings.Index(s, "powerful")
    fmt.Println("Index of 'powerful':", index)
}
```

The program starts by importing the necessary packages and creating a `strings.Builder` instance, which provides an efficient way to construct large strings without repeatedly allocating memory. The program *preallocates* 128 bytes of capacity using `builder.Grow(128)` to reduce memory reallocations. It then appends strings using `WriteString()` and adds formatted content via `fmt.Fprintf()`. After building the final string, it retrieves its value using `builder.String()`

and prints it, along with internal statistics such as its current length and capacity, using `builder.Len()` and `builder.Cap()`, respectively (you will learn more about length, capacity, and their relationship when we talk about arrays and slices later in this chapter).

The program then demonstrates several string operations using the `strings` package. It counts occurrences of a specific character with `strings.Count()`, converts the string to uppercase and lowercase with `strings.ToUpper()` and `strings.ToLower()`, respectively, and replaces a word using `strings.ReplaceAll()`. It also splits a string into words using `strings.Fields()`, joins them back together with dashes via `strings.Join()`, and finds the index of a substring using `strings.Index()`. Together, these examples show how Go combines efficient string building with powerful manipulation utilities, giving you precise control over string operations while keeping memory usage optimized.

Run `stringOperations.go` on your machine to get the following output:

```
$ go run stringOperations.go
Final output: Go is fast!
Language: Go - Version: 1.25
Running on 12 logical CPU cores
Length: 75 bytes, Capacity: 128 bytes
Count of 's': 1
Upper: GO IS POWERFUL!
Lower: go is powerful!
REPLACED: Go is fast!
Words: [Go is powerful!]
Dashed: Go-is-powerful!
Index of powerful: 6
```

Now that you have learned the fundamentals of the core Go data types, it is time to shift our focus to a crucial aspect of writing reliable Go programs: **error handling**. In Go, *errors are treated as values*, making them easy to create, return, and manage consistently. Unlike exceptions in other languages, Go encourages developers to handle errors explicitly at every step, which leads to more predictable and maintainable code. In the next section, we will dive into the Go error-handling philosophy, explore built-in types such as `error`, and learn how to propagate and wrap errors.

Error handling

Error handling in Go is explicit, simple, and predictable, reflecting the design philosophy of clarity over hidden complexity. Unlike many other languages that rely on exceptions, Go uses

error values to signal failure, making error handling an integral part of normal program flow. As Go functions can have multiple return values, when they fail, they typically return an `error` as an *additional result*, and it is the caller function's responsibility to inspect and handle it. This design encourages developers to check errors early and often, leading to more robust and maintainable systems. Go also provides tools such as the `errors` and `fmt` packages for creating, wrapping, and formatting errors, as well as the `errors.Is()` and `errors.As()` helpers for advanced inspection. With Go 1.13, error wrapping became idiomatic, allowing developers to preserve context while still enabling comparisons.

The following program illustrates errors and error handling in Go, beginning with the definition of a new custom error type as a structure:

```
package main

import (
    "errors"
    "fmt"
    "os"
)

// Custom error type for division errors
type DivideError struct {
    A, B float64
}

func (e *DivideError) Error() string {
    return fmt.Sprintf("cannot divide %.2f by %.2f", e.A, e.B)
}

// divide performs division and demonstrates basic error handling
func divide(a, b float64) (float64, error) {
    if b == 0 {
        return 0, &DivideError{A: a, B: b}
    }
    return a / b, nil
}
```

The code defines a custom error type called `DivideError`, represented as a struct with two floating-point fields, `A` and `B`. These fields store the numbers involved in a division operation. To make this struct behave like a standard Go error, it implements the `Error()` method, which satisfies the built-in `error` interface, and returns a formatted string describing the error. The `divide()` function performs the division and demonstrates how to return an error when something goes wrong. It takes two `float64` values, `a` and `b`, and returns both the result and an `error`. If the `b` divisor is zero, the function does not attempt division but instead creates a new `DivideError` struct and returns it as an error. Otherwise, it safely performs the division and returns the result along with `nil` to indicate the absence of an error. Interfaces are explained in more detail in *Chapter 4, Advanced Go.*

The `riskyFileOperation()` function attempts to open a file and handles potential critical failures gracefully, which will create a panic situation:

```
func riskyFileOperation(filename string) {
    defer func() {
        // Recover from panic if it occurs
        if r := recover(); r != nil {
            fmt.Println("Recovered from panic:", r)
        }
    }()

    // Try to open a file that may not exist
    f, err := os.Open(filename)
    if err != nil {
        // Wrapping the error with additional context
        panic(fmt.Errorf("critical failure opening %q: %w", filename, err))
    }
    defer f.Close()

    fmt.Println("Successfully opened file:", filename)
}
```

This code demonstrates *panic and recover* mechanisms through a simulated risky file operation. Inside the function, a deferred anonymous function is defined at the very start. This deferred function uses the built-in `recover()` mechanism to intercept and handle any panic that might occur during the function execution. If a panic is triggered, `recover()` captures its value, and the program prints a message.

After setting up the deferred recovery block, the code attempts to open the specified file using `os.Open()`. If the file does not exist or cannot be opened for any reason, an error is returned. Instead of handling the error directly, the code uses `panic()` to escalate the failure into a runtime panic. The panic wraps the original error using `fmt.Errorf()` with the `%w` verb, adding extra context about the failure — a best practice when propagating critical errors. If the file opens successfully, the function defers `f.Close()` to ensure that the file handle is properly released, and then prints a success message.

Next, we have the `main()` function implementation:

```
func main() {
    fmt.Println("=== Basic Error Handling ===")
    result, err := divide(10, 0)
    if err != nil {
        fmt.Println("Error:", err)

        // Using errors.As to check for custom error type
        var divErr *DivideError
        if errors.As(err, &divErr) {
            fmt.Printf("Info: A=%.2f, B=%.2f\n", divErr.A, divErr.B)
        }
    } else {
        fmt.Println("Result:", result)
    }

    fmt.Println("\n=== Using errors.Is ===")
    // Simulate file handling and check against known sentinel errors
    _, err = os.Open("/tmp/nonexistent.txt")
    if errors.Is(err, os.ErrNotExist) {
        fmt.Println("The file does not exist.")
    }

    fmt.Println("\n=== Panic, Recover, and Defer ===")
    // Attempt a risky file operation
    riskyFileOperation("/tmp/nonexistent.txt")
    fmt.Println("Program continues normally after recover.")
}
```

The `main()` function begins by printing a header for basic error handling and then calls the `divide()` function with `10` and `0` as arguments. Since dividing by zero is invalid, the function returns an error of the `*DivideError` type. The program checks for errors and, if one is found, prints it. It then uses `errors.As()` to determine whether the returned error is of the custom `*DivideError` type. If so, it extracts additional details about the operands and displays them, helping the developer understand exactly why the error occurred. Next, the program demonstrates `errors.Is()` to handle sentinel errors, which represent well-known, predefined error conditions. It tries to open a non-existent file called `/tmp/nonexistent.txt`. Since the file does not exist, `os.Open()` returns an error. By using `errors.Is(err, os.ErrNotExist)`, the code checks whether the specific error matches `os.ErrNotExist` and, if `true`, prints a user-friendly message indicating that the file is missing. Finally, the program transitions to demonstrating panic recovery by calling `riskyFileOperation()` with a missing file. Inside `riskyFileOperation()`, a panic occurs due to a critical failure, but the deferred recovery mechanism intercepts it, preventing the program from crashing. After recovering, the program prints a confirmation message showing that it continues running normally despite the panic.

Run `errorHandling.go` on your machine to produce the following output:

```
$ go run ch01/errorHandling.go
=== Basic Error Handling ===
Error: cannot divide 10.00 by 0.00
Info: A=10.00, B=0.00

=== Using errors.Is ===
The file does not exist.

=== Panic, Recover, and Defer ===
Recovered from panic: critical failure opening "/tmp/nonexistent.txt": open /tmp/
nonexistent.txt: no such file or directory
Program continues normally after recover.
```

Having explored errors and error handling in Go, you now have the tools to write programs that fail safely, recover gracefully, and communicate problems clearly.

Arrays and slices

Memory layout matters in systems programming, and in Go, arrays and slices give you two tightly related tools to work with contiguous memory. Arrays offer predictability and fixed-size precision, while slices provide flexibility and idiomatic power without sacrificing performance. Understanding the relationship between them — how slices reference underlying arrays, how capacity and length interact, and how sharing memory can lead to subtle bugs — is key to writing robust and efficient Go programs. In this section, we explore how to use arrays and slices effectively, with an eye toward performance, memory safety, and control over data representation.

Arrays

Arrays in Go are fixed-size, indexed collections of elements of the same type. They serve as the most fundamental data structure for storing sequences in contiguous memory, offering deterministic performance and predictable layout. You define an array by specifying its size and element type, such as `var a [3]int`, which declares an array of three integers, each initialized to zero. You can also use a composite literal, for example, `a := [3]int{10, 20, 30}`. Array elements are accessed using zero-based indexing, so `a[0]` refers to the first element, `a[1]` the second, and so on. Assignment and access use the standard `[]` operator syntax. Arrays in Go are value types. Therefore, assigning one array to another array *copies all its elements.*

Unlike slices, which are covered next, arrays in Go carry their size as part of their type, which means `[4]int` and `[8]int` are distinct and incompatible types. This explicitness promotes safer and more controlled memory usage, especially in low-level contexts where size constraints and performance overheads must be tightly managed.

Slices

Slices in Go are dynamic, flexible views into arrays. They provide a more convenient and expressive way to work with sequences of data without sacrificing the performance benefits of contiguous memory. A slice does not store data itself, but rather it describes a segment of an underlying array, through three components: a pointer to the first element, a length (the number of accessible elements), and a capacity (the number of elements from the start to the end of the backing array). You can define a slice directly using a composite literal, such as `s := []int{1, 2, 3}`, or by slicing an array, such as `s := a[1:3]`, which selects elements from index `1` up to (but not including) index `3`. Elements are accessed just like arrays, using `s[i]`, and slices can be safely passed to functions *without copying the underlying data.* Slices grow and shrink through operations such as `append()`, and their behavior is tightly coupled with the Go memory model and garbage collector.

The length of a slice represents the number of elements it currently holds, which you can retrieve with `len(slice)`. The capacity shows how much a slice can be expanded *without the need to allocate more memory* and change the underlying array; you can check it with `cap(slice)`. Although after slice creation, the capacity of a slice is handled by Go, we can define the capacity of a slice at creation time using the `make()` function — after that, the capacity of the slice doubles each time the length of the slice is about to become bigger than its current capacity. The first argument of `make()` is the data type of the slice, the second is its initial length, and the third, which is optional, is the capacity of the slice. For example, `numbers := make([]int, 3, 5)` creates a slice of integers with a length of `3` and a capacity of `5`. When you use `append()` and the new size does not exceed the current capacity, the slice reuses the same underlying array, meaning other slices sharing that array will see changes, too. However, if appending exceeds the capacity, Go automatically allocates a new array, copies the existing data, and assigns it to the slice. From that point on, the new slice becomes independent of the old one.

Slicing

In Go, *slicing* refers to the creation of a new view (slice) into an existing array or slice without copying the underlying data. Both arrays and slices support slicing using the syntax `a[start:end]`, where `start` is the inclusive starting index, and end is the exclusive ending index. For example, if you have `arr := [5]int{10, 20, 30, 40, 50}`, then `sub := arr[1:4]` creates a slice containing the elements `{20, 30, 40}`. Importantly, the resulting slice still references the same underlying array as the original, meaning that modifying elements in the slice also changes them in the original array. Go also provides shorthand forms such as `a[:end]` to slice from the beginning, `a[start:]` to slice until the end, and `a[:]` to create a slice of the entire array. For slices, the behavior is the same, but slices additionally track their length and capacity. While the length is the number of accessible elements, the capacity is determined by the size of the underlying array starting from the slice's first element. This means you can often extend a slice within its capacity using `append()` without reallocating memory.

As slices are backed by arrays, they share the same underlying memory *until their capacity is exceeded.* Therefore, when you create a new slice from an existing array, both structures will point to the same underlying array, so modifying one will affect the other. However, if you use `append()` and the resulting slice grows beyond its current capacity, Go automatically allocates a *new underlying array* large enough to hold the expanded data. The existing elements are copied into this new array, and the returned slice now references it independently. From this point forward, changes to the new slice do not affect the original array or any other slices based on the old array. This automatic reallocation makes slicing both flexible and safe, as it seamlessly switches between shared and independent storage based on capacity limits without requiring manual memory management.

Now, let us consolidate our understanding of arrays, slices, and slicing using a code example, which demonstrates how Go handles arrays and slices, focusing on how they share memory and what happens when a slice grows beyond its capacity:

```
package main

import (
    "fmt"
)

func main() {
```

```
    arr := [5]int{10, 20, 30, 40, 50}
    fmt.Println("Original array:", arr)

    // Create two slices from the same array.
    slice1 := arr[1:4]
    slice2 := arr[2:]
    fmt.Println("Slice1:", slice1)
    fmt.Println("Slice2:", slice2)

    fmt.Println("\n--- Modifying slice1 ---")
    slice1[1] = 999
    fmt.Println("Slice1 after modification:", slice1)
    fmt.Println("Slice2 after modification:", slice2)
    fmt.Println("Array after modification:", arr)
    fmt.Printf("\nSlice1 length: %d, capacity: %d\n", len(slice1), cap(slice1))

    fmt.Println("\n--- Appending within capacity ---")
    slice1 = append(slice1, 888) // Still fits in the original array.
    fmt.Println("Slice1 after append:", slice1)
    fmt.Println("Array after append:", arr)
    fmt.Println("\n--- Appending beyond capacity ---")
    slice1 = append(slice1, 777) // Now we exceed the capacity.
    fmt.Println("Slice1 after exceeding capacity:", slice1)
    fmt.Println("Array after exceeding capacity:", arr)
    slice1[0] = 12345
    fmt.Println("Slice1 after independent modification:", slice1)
    fmt.Println("Array remains unchanged:", arr)
}
```

The code starts by creating an array and forming two slices from it, showing that slices are simply views into the same underlying data. Because of this, modifying one slice also changes the original array and any other slices referencing the same data. The program then illustrates how slices manage their length and capacity: as long as new elements fit within the existing capacity, appending updates the original array. However, when the capacity is exceeded, Go automatically creates a new, independent array to store the expanded slice, meaning subsequent changes no longer affect the original data (not understanding this fact could create some nasty bugs!).

Execute `slicing.go` on your machine to see what happens:

```
$ go run ch01/slicing.go
Original array: [10 20 30 40 50]
```

```
Slice1: [20 30 40]
Slice2: [30 40 50]

--- Modifying slice1 ---
Slice1 after modification: [20 999 40]
Slice2 after modification: [999 40 50]
Array after modification: [10 20 999 40 50]

Slice1 length: 3, capacity: 4

--- Appending within capacity ---
Slice1 after append: [20 999 40 888]
Array after append: [10 20 999 40 888]

--- Appending beyond capacity ---
Slice1 after exceeding capacity: [20 999 40 888 777]
Array after exceeding capacity: [10 20 999 40 888]
Slice1 after independent modification: [12345 999 40 888 777]
Array remains unchanged: [10 20 999 40 888]
```

Initially, we start with an array of `[10 20 30 40 50]` and create two slices: `slice1 := arr[1:4]`, which gives `[20 30 40]`, and `slice2 := arr[2:]`, which gives `[30 40 50]`. When we set `slice1[1] = 999`, the change propagates to the array and to `slice2`, producing `[10 20 999 40 50]` in the array and updating `slice2` to `[999 40 50]`.

Next, we examine the length and capacity of `slice1`. Its length is `3` because it spans three elements, while its capacity is 4 because it starts at index 1 of the array and can extend up to index `5` (the end of the array). When we append an element within this capacity using `slice1 = append(slice1, 888)`, Go simply writes the new element into the existing array. As a result, both `slice1` and the original array reflect this addition, and the array becomes `[10 20 999 40 888]`. However, when we append another element beyond this capacity with `slice1 = append(slice1, 777)`, Go can no longer fit the new value into the original array. At this point, it automatically allocates a new, larger array, copies the existing slice elements into it, and appends the new value. From now on, `slice1` no longer shares the same underlying array as the original `arr`.

This separation becomes evident when we modify the first element of `slice1` by setting `slice1[0] = 12345`. Because `slice1` now resides on a new array, the original `arr` remains unchanged at `[10 20 999 40 888]`, while `slice1` becomes `[12345 999 40 888 777]`. The key takeaway is that *slices act as views into arrays and share data until an append operation exceeds their capacity*. When that happens, Go seamlessly switches the slice to a new, independent array, making further modifications isolated from the original data. This behavior makes slicing both efficient and flexible, as Go minimizes allocations when possible but transparently creates new storage when needed.

Now that you understand arrays, slices, and how slicing works under the hood, it is time to see how these data structures interact with *functions* in Go. Functions are a core building block of any Go program, and they allow you to organize logic, reuse code, and work with data more effectively. When working with arrays and slices, functions play an important role in transforming, filtering, or aggregating data. It is also important to understand how Go passes these values to functions: *arrays are passed by value*, meaning a full copy is made, while *slices are passed by reference*, sharing the same underlying array. This distinction has significant implications for performance and side effects, making it an ideal time to dive into Go's approach to defining, calling, and working with functions.

Functions

Functions in Go are first-class citizens as they can be assigned to variables, passed as arguments, and returned from other functions. At the core, a function in Go is defined using the `func` keyword, followed by its name, parameter list, and return types. Go enforces strict type declarations for both parameters and return values, promoting explicit, type-safe design. Multiple return values are supported natively and are often used to return a value along with an error, following the idiomatic error-handling model of Go. Unlike some languages, Go functions do not support default parameters or overloading; each function must have a unique name and signature. Function literals, or anonymous functions, can be declared inline and are commonly used as closures, capturing local state for later execution. Additionally, Go supports variadic functions (e.g., `func sum(nums ...int)`) and allows methods to be attached to types, enabling a clear and composable design without full object orientation. Look at the following example code that demonstrates several important aspects of functions in Go:

```
package main

import (
    "fmt"
    "strings"
)

func greet(name string) string {
    return "Hello, " + name + "!"
```

```
}

func divide(a, b float64) (float64, error) {
    if b == 0 {
        return 0, fmt.Errorf("cannot divide by zero")
    }
    return a / b, nil
}

func rectangleStats(length, width float64) (area, perimeter float64) {
    area = length * width
    perimeter = 2 * (length + width)
    return // Uses named returns
}

func joinStrings(separator string, words ...string) string {
    return strings.Join(words, separator)
}

func applyTwice(fn func(int) int, value int) int {
    return fn(fn(value))
}

func main() {
    // 1. Basic function call.
    fmt.Println(greet("Mihalis"))

    // 2. Function returning multiple values.
    result, err := divide(10, 2)
    if err != nil {
        fmt.Println("Error:", err)
    } else {
        fmt.Println("Division result:", result)
    }

    // 3. Named return values.
    area, perimeter := rectangleStats(5, 3)
    fmt.Printf("Rectangle → A: %.2f, P: %.2f\n", area, perimeter)

    // 4. Variadic function.
    joined := joinStrings("-", "Go", "is", "fast", "and", "fun")
```

```
    fmt.Println("Joined string:", joined)

    // 5. Higher-order function.
    double := func(x int) int { return x * 2 }
    fmt.Println("Applying double twice to 5:", applyTwice(double, 5))
}
```

The program begins with a simple function, `greet()`, which takes a string parameter and returns a greeting, showing the most basic form of function declaration. The `divide()` function illustrates multiple return values, a powerful Go feature: it returns both a `float64` result and an `error`, encouraging explicit error handling instead of exceptions. The `rectangleStats()` function uses *named return values*, allowing us to define and return variables directly without specifying them in the `return` statement. Next, the `joinStrings()` function introduces *variadic functions*, which can accept any number of arguments — here, multiple strings are joined using the chosen separator. Finally, the `applyTwice()` function demonstrates higher-order functions by accepting another function as an argument and applying it twice to a value. In `main()`, we call each function to showcase its behavior, including error handling, formatted printing, and flexible function passing.

Run `functions.go` on your machine to get the following output:

```
$ go run ch01/functions.go
Hello, Alice!
Division result: 5
Rectangle → Area: 15.00, Perimeter: 16.00
Joined string: Go-is-fast-and-fun
Applying double twice to 5: 20
```

Having explored the fundamentals of functions in Go, including parameters, multiple return values, variadic functions, and higher-order functions, we are now ready to dive into a more advanced and powerful concept: **iterator functions**.

Iterator functions

Introduced in Go version 1.23, iterator functions allow you to create lazy, on-demand sequences of values without allocating intermediate slices or arrays. Instead of returning all results at once, an iterator yields one value at a time and pauses execution until the next value is requested, thus enabling you to use the range keyword directly over functions that yield values. This makes them particularly efficient for processing large datasets, streaming information, or generating sequences such as the Fibonacci numbers. Look at the following example code that illustrates the concept by implementing a lazy Fibonacci sequence generator:

```
package main
import (
    "fmt"
)

func fibonacci(limit int) func(yield func(int) bool) {
    return func(yield func(int) bool) {
        a, b := 0, 1
        for i := 0; i < limit; i++ {
            if !yield(a) {
                return
            }
            a, b = b, a+b
        }
    }
}

func main() {
    fmt.Println("First 10 Fibonacci numbers:")

    for num := range fibonacci(10) {
        fmt.Print(num, " ")
    }
    fmt.Println()
}
```

The program defines a higher-order function called `Fibonacci()` that accepts a limit parameter and returns an iterator function. This returned function follows the Go iterator protocol by accepting a `yield` function as its parameter, which the iterator calls to produce each value in the sequence. The core logic initializes two variables, `a` and `b`, with values of `0` and `1`, respectively, representing consecutive Fibonacci numbers. The function then enters a loop that runs for the specified limit, calling the `yield` function with the current Fibonacci number `a` on each iteration. The `yield` function returns a Boolean value that indicates whether the consumer wants to continue receiving values; if it returns `false`, the iterator terminates early by returning from the function. After each `yield` call, the code updates the Fibonacci sequence by setting `a` to the previous value of `b` and `b` to the sum of the previous `a` and `b` values using the multiple assignment syntax. Notice that `yield` is a conventional function name, not a Go keyword.

The `main()` function demonstrates this lazy iterator by using the range-over-function syntax to iterate through the first 10 Fibonacci numbers. When the `range` loop encounters the iterator function returned by `fibonacci(10)`, Go automatically calls it with an appropriate `yield` function that feeds values back to the loop variable `num`. The program prints each number as it receives it, showcasing how the Fibonacci sequence generates lazily, computing each value only when the consumer requests it rather than precomputing the entire sequence. This approach provides memory efficiency and allows for early termination if the consumer stops iterating before reaching the limit.

Running the program generates the following output:

```
$ go run ch01/functionIterators.go
First 10 Fibonacci numbers:
0 1 1 2 3 5 8 13 21 34
```

With this foundation, it is time to shift our focus to a powerful tool for working with textual data: regular expressions. A **regular expression**, or **regex**, allows you to define a flexible search pattern to match, extract, or transform text with precision. Go provides built-in support for regular expressions via the `regexp` package, offering efficient compilation and execution of patterns. In the upcoming section, we will learn how to define regex patterns, compile them, perform matches, extract subgroups, and replace text dynamically.

Learning how to use regular expressions

Pattern matching is a technique for searching a string for some set of characters based on a specific search pattern expressed in terms of regular expressions and grammar. A *regular expression* is a sequence of characters that defines a search pattern. Regular expressions and pattern matching are illustrated in `ch01/regularExp.go`. Here is a part of `main()` that starts with a simple matching example:

```
package main

import (
	"fmt"
	"regexp"
)

func main() {
```

```
// 1. Simple matching using MatchString
fmt.Println("=== Simple Matching ===")
pattern := `Go`
re := regexp.MustCompile(pattern)
text := "Go is expressive, concise, clean, and efficient."
fmt.Printf("Does the text contain '%s'? %v\n", pattern, re.MatchString(text))
```

First, the program defines a pattern as the string `` `Go` ``, which represents the exact text we want to search for – backticks in Go denote *raw string literals* and they are particularly useful when working with regular expressions because, unlike interpreted string literals (double-quoted strings), raw string literals do not process escape sequences, meaning characters such as backslashes are treated literally. Then, it compiles this pattern into a regular expression object using `regexp.MustCompile(pattern)`. Unlike `regexp.Compile()`, `regexp.MustCompile()` panics immediately if the pattern is invalid, making it a convenient choice when you are confident that the regular expression is correct. After that, it defines the `text` string. The program uses the `MatchString()` method on the compiled regular expression to check whether the pattern "Go" appears anywhere within the text. Finally, it prints the result using `fmt.Printf()`, showing both the pattern being searched for and whether it was found.

In the next part of the program, the focus is on *finding all matches* of a regular expression within a given string using the `regexp` package:

```
// 2. Finding all matches
fmt.Println("=== Finding All Matches ===")
pattern = `[A-Z][a-z]+`
re = regexp.MustCompile(pattern)
text = "Go Rust Python Zig C C++"
matches := re.FindAllString(text, -1)
fmt.Printf("Capitalized words: %v\n", matches)
```

The code defines the pattern `` `[A-Z][a-z]+` ``, which matches any word that starts with a single uppercase letter followed by one or more lowercase letters. Using `regexp.MustCompile(pattern)`, the regular expression is compiled and applied to the string `"Go Rust Python Zig C C++"`. The `re.FindAllString(text, -1)` function is then used to locate all substrings matching the pattern, with the `-1` argument indicating that there is no limit on the number of matches returned. The resulting matches are stored in a slice named `matches` and printed to the console. Given the input string, the output includes capitalized words such as `["Go", "Rust", "Python", "Zig"]`, while `"C"` and `"C++"` are excluded because they do not satisfy the lowercase-letter requirement. This example illustrates how Go can efficiently extract structured information from unstructured text by combining regular expressions with built-in string matching functions.

In the next part of the program, the focus is on **extracting submatches** — also known as **capturing groups** — from a string using `regexp`:

```
// 3. Extracting submatches (groups)
fmt.Println("=== Extracting Submatches ===")
pattern = `(\w+)@(\w+\.\w+)`
re = regexp.MustCompile(pattern)
email := "contact us at support@example.com"
submatches := re.FindStringSubmatch(email)
if len(submatches) > 0 {
    fmt.Printf("Full match: %s\n", submatches[0])
    fmt.Printf("Username: %s\n", submatches[1])
    fmt.Printf("Domain: %s\n", submatches[2])
}
```

Note

In regular expressions, the `\w` symbol represents any "word character," which, in Go and most modern regex engines, means letters (both uppercase and lowercase), digits, and the underscore character. In other words, `\w` matches the same set as `[A-Za-z0-9_]`. Alongside `\w`, there are several other special shorthand character classes worth remembering. For instance, `\d` matches any digit (`[0-9]`). Similarly, `\s` matches any whitespace character, such as space, tab, or newline, and `\S` matches any non-whitespace character. The dot (`.`) is also important — it matches any single character except a newline by default. Anchors such as `^` and `$` are also crucial: `^` asserts that a match must start at the beginning of a string, while `$` asserts that it must occur at the end.

The `` `(\w+)@(\w+\.\w+)` `` regular expression pattern is defined to match email-like structures. Here, the first capturing group, `(\w+)`, matches the username portion before the @ symbol, while the second group, `(\w+\.\w+)`, matches the domain name after the @ symbol. Using `regexp.MustCompile(pattern)`, the regular expression is compiled, and the `re.FindStringSubmatch(email)` method is applied to the `"contact us at support@example.com"` string. This function returns a slice where the first element is the full match (`support@example.com`), followed by the captured groups: the username (`support`) and the domain (example.com). The program checks whether submatches contains results and then prints the full match along with the extracted components.

In the next part of the program, the focus is on *replacing all matching patterns* in a string using regexp:

```
    // 4. Replacing matches
    fmt.Println("=== Replacing Matches ===")
    pattern = `\d+`
    re = regexp.MustCompile(pattern)
    text = "Order IDs: 1234, 5678, 91011"
    replaced := re.ReplaceAllString(text, "XXXX")
    fmt.Println("Replaced IDs:", replaced)
```

The \d+ regular expression pattern matches one or more consecutive digits, which represent order IDs in the given text. The regexp.MustCompile(pattern) function compiles the regular expression, and then re.ReplaceAllString(text, "XXXX") is used to replace every sequence of digits in the "Order IDs: 1234, 5678, 91011" string with the "XXXX" string. The result is stored in the replaced variable and printed, producing the output: "Order IDs: XXXX, XXXX, XXXX". So regular expressions can be used not only for matching and extracting patterns but also for *sanitizing* or *masking sensitive data* in strings.

In the final part of the program, the focus is on *validating user input* with regexp, specifically, checking whether email addresses follow a proper format:

```
    // 5. Validating input
    fmt.Println("=== Validating Input ===")
    pattern = `^[a-zA-Z0-9._%+-]+@[a-zA-Z0-9.-]+\.[a-zA-Z]{2,}$`
    re = regexp.MustCompile(pattern)
    emails := []string{"user@example.com", "invalid-email@",
"hello.world@ziglang.org"}
    for _, e := range emails {
        if re.MatchString(e) {
            fmt.Printf("%s is a valid email\n", e)
        } else {
            fmt.Printf("%s is NOT a valid email\n", e)
        }
    }
}
```

The `` `^[a-zA-Z0-9._%+-]+@[a-zA-Z0-9.-]+\.[a-zA-Z]{2,}$` `` regular expression defines the rules for a standard simple email. It ensures that the string starts and ends with the correct structure by using `^` and `$` anchors. The `[a-zA-Z0-9._%+-]+` part matches one or more valid characters for the username portion of the email, followed by an @ symbol. After that, `[a-zA-Z0-9.-]+` matches one or more valid characters for the domain name, and `\.[a-zA-Z]{2,}` enforces the presence of a dot followed by at least two alphabetic characters for the top-level domain, such as `.com` or `.org`. The program compiles this pattern with `regexp.MustCompile()` and iterates over a list of sample email addresses, checking each with `re.MatchString(e)`. If the email conforms to the pattern, it is marked as valid; otherwise, it is flagged as invalid.

Execute `ch01/regularExp.go` on your machine to see the results of the code:

```
$ go run ch01/regularExp.go
=== Simple Matching ===
Does the text contain 'Go'? true
=== Finding All Matches ===
Capitalized words: [Go Rust Python Zig]
=== Extracting Submatches ===
Full match: support@example.com
Username: support
Domain: example.com
=== Replacing Matches ===
Replaced IDs: Order IDs: XXXX, XXXX, XXXX
=== Validating Input ===
user@example.com is a valid email
invalid-email@ is NOT a valid email
hello.world@ziglang.org is a valid email
```

Now that we have explored how to harness the power of regular expressions for matching, extracting, and transforming textual data, it is time to shift our focus to another essential aspect of building real-world Go programs: working with command-line arguments. In the next section, we will explore how to read command-line arguments, parse options, and build flexible, user-friendly command-line utilities.

Working with command-line arguments

Many Go utilities and system tools rely on parameters passed at runtime to control their behavior, making it crucial to understand how to access and process these inputs effectively. Go provides built-in support through the `os` and `flag` packages, enabling you to retrieve raw arguments, define structured flags, and validate user input with ease. The simplest way to access arguments passed to a program is through `os.Args`, a slice of strings where `os.Args[0]` holds the program name, and the remaining elements represent the arguments themselves. However, for more robust and user-friendly handling, Go provides the `flag` package, which lets you define options, default values, and parse user input seamlessly. This dual approach gives you flexibility: you can quickly grab raw arguments when simplicity is enough, or you can build fully featured CLI tools with proper flags and usage messages.

Consider the following example code, found in `ch01/cla.go`, that demonstrates the reading and the handling of command-line arguments and options:

```
package main

import (
    "flag"
    "fmt"
    "os"
    "path/filepath"
)

func main() {
    fmt.Println("=== Raw Command-Line Arguments ===")
    programName := filepath.Base(os.Args[0])
    fmt.Printf("Program name: %s\n", programName)

    if len(os.Args) > 1 {
        fmt.Println("Arguments:")
        for i, arg := range os.Args[1:] {
            fmt.Printf("  Arg %d: %s\n", i+1, arg)
        }
    } else {
        fmt.Println("No additional arguments provided.")
    }
```

This Go code demonstrates how to access and process raw command-line arguments using the built-in `os.Args` slice. As expected, the program begins by importing the necessary packages. The `main()` function starts by extracting and displaying the program executable name using `filepath.Base(os.Args[0])`, where `os.Args[0]` contains the full path to the running program and `filepath.Base()` extracts just the filename portion without the directory path. The program then checks whether additional command-line arguments were provided by examining the length of `os.Args`. When arguments are present (indicated by `len(os.Args) > 1`), the code iterates through them using a range loop over os.Args[1:], which creates a slice starting from the second element to skip the program name. The loop uses both the index and value from the range operation, printing each argument with a numbered label starting from 1. If no additional arguments are provided, the program simply displays a message indicating that no arguments were passed.

Next, the code demonstrates the use of the flag package for structured command-line argument parsing with named flags and default values:

```
    fmt.Println("=== Using the flag Package ===")
    port := flag.Int("port", 8080, "Port to listen on")
    host := flag.String("host", "localhost", "Hostname or IP")
    debug := flag.Bool("debug", false, "Enable debug mode")

    // Parse the flags from os.Args.
    flag.Parse()

    fmt.Printf("Server will start at %s:%d\n", *host, *port)
    fmt.Printf("Debug mode: %v\n", *debug)

    // Show remaining non-flag arguments, if any.
    remaining := flag.Args()
    if len(remaining) > 0 {
        fmt.Println("Non-flag arguments:", remaining)
    } else {
        fmt.Println("No non-flag arguments provided.")
    }
}
```

In this part, the program defines three command-line flags: flag.Int() creates a port flag with a default value of 8080, flag.String() creates a host flag defaulting to "localhost", and flag.Bool() creates a debug flag that defaults to false. Each flag definition includes the flag name, default value, and a usage description that the flag package can display in help messages. The crucial flag.Parse() call processes the actual command-line arguments from os.Args, matching them against the defined flags and parsing their values according to their specified types. This function handles the complex parsing logic, including flag syntax recognition (supporting both -flag and --flag formats), type conversion, and error handling. After parsing, the code accesses the flag values by dereferencing the pointers returned by the flag definition functions, using *host, *port, and *debug to get the actual values that were either provided by the user or set to their defaults. The program then demonstrates how to handle non-flag arguments using `flag.Args()`, which returns a slice of any remaining command-line arguments that were not recognized as flags or flag values. This allows programs to accept both structured flags (such as `--port=8080` or `--debug`) and positional arguments simultaneously. The `flag` package automatically handles common command-line conventions, provides built-in help generation with `-h` or `--help`, and offers robust error handling for invalid flag formats or type mismatches, making it significantly more powerful than manually parsing raw `os.Args` elements.

Run `ch01/cla.go` on your machine and try different values. The expected output should be analogous to the following:

```
$ go run ch01/cla.go
=== Raw Command-Line Arguments ===
Program name: cla
No additional arguments provided.
=== Using the flag Package ===
Server will start at localhost:8080
Debug mode: false
No non-flag arguments provided.
```

As your command-line tools grow in complexity, parsing arguments and flags using the `os` and `flag` packages can become cumbersome and error-prone. This is where the `cobra` and `viper` packages come into play, offering a higher-level and more structured approach to building feature-rich CLI applications. `cobra` simplifies the creation of commands, subcommands, and help menus, while `viper` handles configuration management seamlessly, supporting environment variables, configuration files, and command-line flags. Together, they form a powerful ecosystem for developing professional-grade Go utilities. In the next section, we will explore the capabilities of these two packages.

The viper and cobra packages

When `os` and `flag` are not powerful enough for a complex command-line tool such as `docker` or `hugo`, we can turn to the `viper` and `cobra` packages.

The viper package

`viper` is a powerful configuration management package in Go designed to simplify the process of handling application settings from multiple sources in a unified way. It allows you to load configuration values from JSON, TOML, YAML, HCL, INI, or environment variables, as well as directly from command-line flags. It supports default values, live watching of configuration files, and automatic environment variable binding, making it ideal for both simple applications and complex, production-grade systems.

It integrates seamlessly with the `cobra` package, enabling developers to build CLI applications where configuration can come from various layers without additional boilerplate code. Internally, `viper` maintains a *key-value store* and provides methods such as `Set()`, `Get()`, `BindEnv()`, and `BindPFlag()` to manage configuration hierarchies efficiently. This flexibility allows developers to centralize configuration logic, reduce duplication, and improve maintainability while keeping the codebase clean and scalable.

The cobra package

`cobra` is a widely used Go package for building powerful and user-friendly command-line interfaces. It provides a structured way to define commands, subcommands, and associated flags, making it easier to create complex command-line applications with minimal boilerplate. Each command in `cobra` is represented as a `*cobra.Command` struct, which defines its name, description, arguments, and behavior via a `Run()` function. It also offers built-in support for hierarchical commands, meaning you can organize related functionality under parent commands, improving usability and clarity for end users. Additionally, it automatically generates robust and customizable help and usage messages, reducing the need for manual documentation.

`cobra` integrates seamlessly with the `viper` package, allowing command-line flags to be directly bound to configuration values from files or environment variables. Its combination of flexibility, modularity, and automation makes `cobra` an industry-standard tool for developing Go-based CLI applications.

We shall be revisiting both `cobra` and `viper` later in the book. Now, however, in the final two sections of this chapter, we are going to implement simplified versions of two classic Unix utilities: `which(1)` and `basename(1)`.

Implementing which(1)

In this section, we will implement in Go the `which(1)` utility, a classic Unix command that locates the executable file associated with a given command by searching through the directories listed in the `PATH` environment variable. This exercise introduces working with *environment variables* and *executable file detection* in Go. We will leverage the os and `path/filepath` packages to inspect directories, combine paths, and verify permissions.

Note

When we say *idiomatic Go,* we mean writing Go code in the style and spirit that the Go community has collectively embraced as natural, clear, and efficient. Every programming language has its own set of unwritten rules and conventions beyond mere syntax, and in Go, these idioms emphasize *simplicity*, *readability*, and *explicitness*. For example, idiomatic Go favors using short variable names in small scopes (`i`, `n`, `err`), handling errors immediately rather than deferring them, and returning multiple values instead of exceptions. It also encourages leveraging the powerful abstractions of the standard library (such as `io.Reader` and `io.Writer`), using slices and maps instead of reinventing data structures, and embracing the concurrency model of Go with goroutines and channels.

To call code *idiomatic Go* is to say it looks like it belongs in the language — that another Go programmer could read it easily, understand its intent, and see that it follows the design philosophy of Go itself. In practice, this often means prioritizing clarity over cleverness, explicit error handling over hidden control flow, and minimalism over abstraction-heavy designs. The phrase is a reminder that Go is not just about what the compiler accepts, but about writing code that fits well with the ecosystem and communicates effectively with other developers.

Here is a Go implementation of the `which(1)` utility, in which the `which()` function does most of the job:

```
package main

import (
    "fmt"
    "os"
    "path/filepath"
    "strings"
)

func which(command string) (string, error) {
    pathEnv := os.Getenv("PATH")
    paths := strings.Split(pathEnv, string(os.PathListSeparator))

    for _, dir := range paths {
        fullPath := filepath.Join(dir, command)
```

```
        fileInfo, err := os.Stat(fullPath)
        if err != nil {
            if os.IsNotExist(err) {
                continue
            }
            return "", err
        }

        // Check if the file is executable
        if fileInfo.Mode().Perm()&0111 != 0 {
            return fullPath, nil
        }
    }

    return "", fmt.Errorf("%s not found in PATH", command)
}

func main() {
    if len(os.Args) < 2 {
        fmt.Fprintf(os.Stderr, "Usage: %s <command>\n", os.Args[0])
        os.Exit(1)
    }

    command := os.Args[1]
    path, err := which(command)
    if err != nil {
        fmt.Fprintf(os.Stderr, "Error: %v\n", err)
        os.Exit(1)
    }

    fmt.Println(path)
}
```

The core `which()` function begins by retrieving the `PATH` environment variable using `os.Getenv("PATH")`, which contains a delimited list of directories where the system searches for executable files. The function then splits this `PATH` string using `os.PathListSeparator`, which automatically provides the correct delimiter for the operating system (colon on Unix-like systems, semicolon on Windows). For each directory in the `PATH`, the function constructs a potential full path to the command using `filepath.Join()`, which handles path separator differences across operating systems and ensures proper path construction regardless of platform. The file existence and executability checking logic uses `os.Stat()` to gather file information, handling the common case where files do not exist by checking for `os.IsNotExist(err)` and continuing to the next directory. When a file is found, the program examines its permissions using `fileInfo.Mode().Perm()&0111 != 0`, which performs a bitwise `AND` operation with octal `0111` to check whether any execute bits are set (owner, group, or other execute permissions). This permission check ensures that the found file is actually executable rather than just a regular file with the same name as the requested command. The `main()` function handles command-line argument validation and error reporting, checking that exactly one command name is provided and using `fmt.Fprintf(os.Stderr, ...)` to write error messages to standard error rather than to standard output. The program follows Unix conventions by returning appropriate exit codes: `1` for errors and `0` (implicit) for success. When the command is found, the program prints the full path to standard output, making it suitable for use in shell scripts and command pipelines where the output can be captured and used by other programs. Experiment with `ch01/which.go` on your own machine and see the way it works.

Having explored how to implement `which(1)`, a utility that locates executables by searching through the directories in the system `PATH`, we now turn our attention to another classic Unix command: `basename(1)`.

Implementing basename(1)

While `which(1)` focuses on locating files across multiple directories, `basename(1)` deals with extracting the final component of a single file path, optionally removing any specified suffixes. So, in this section, we will implement a Go version of the `basename(1)` utility, a classic Unix command-line tool that extracts the final component of a file path. This exercise will help you deepen your understanding of Go's string manipulation capabilities.

The first part of `ch01/basename.go` is about a function named `basename()` that takes a mandatory `path` parameter of the `string` type and a `suffixes` variadic parameter of the `string` type:

```
func basename(path string, suffixes ...string) string {
    // Handle root directory case:
    if path == "/" {
        return "/"
    }

    // Remove trailing slashes (except if the path is just "/")
    path = strings.TrimRight(path, "/")
    if path == "" { // Happens if input was something like "////"
```

```
        return "/"
    }
```

The `suffixes ...string` syntax means the caller can pass zero or more suffixes that the function might strip from the resulting base name. The function returns a single string. Inside the function, the first `if` block handles the special case where the provided path is exactly the root directory (`"/"`). In such cases, the function simply returns `"/"`, because the base name of the root path is the root itself. Next, the code removes any trailing slashes from the path using `strings.TrimRight(path, "/")`. This ensures that paths such as `/usr/local/bin/` are normalized to `/usr/local/bin` before further processing. However, if the original input contained only slashes (for example, `"////"`), then after trimming, the path becomes an empty string. The following `if` statement checks for this case and safely returns `"/"`, preserving the semantic meaning of the root directory. So, at this point, the code has normalized the path and handled edge cases.

The remaining part of the `basename()` function focuses on extracting the last component of the provided path and optionally removing any matching suffixes:

```
    // Extract the last component after the last '/'
    lastSlash := strings.LastIndex(path, "/")
    if lastSlash >= 0 {
        path = path[lastSlash+1:]
    }

    // Handle empty result (shouldn't happen due to earlier checks)
    if path == "" {
        return "/"
    }

    // Remove suffix if specified (exact match)
    if len(suffixes) > 0 {
        for _, suffix := range suffixes {
            if strings.HasSuffix(path, suffix) {
                path = strings.TrimSuffix(path, suffix)
                break
            }
        }
    }
```

```
    return path
}
```

First, it uses `strings.LastIndex(path, "/")` to find the position of the last forward slash in the path. If a slash exists (`lastSlash >= 0`), the code slices the string to keep only the portion after the slash, effectively isolating the base name. For example, given `/usr/local/bin/go`, this step extracts go. Next, the function includes a safety check to handle the unlikely case where the resulting path is an empty string. Although earlier trimming logic already guards against most such situations, this check ensures that if the computed base name is empty, the function still returns "/" to maintain correct semantics.

After that, the function deals with the optional `suffixes` parameter. If the caller provided one or more suffixes, it iterates over them and checks whether the current base name ends with any of the specified suffixes using `strings.HasSuffix()`. If a match is found, the code removes the matching suffix via `strings.TrimSuffix()` and immediately breaks out of the loop to avoid unnecessary work. This allows the function to handle use cases such as stripping `.txt` from `report.txt` or `.gz` from `archive.tar.gz`. Finally, after these transformations, the function returns the resulting path — now representing the cleaned-up base name, potentially with any requested suffix removed.

You can see the implementation of the `main()` function for yourself. Running `basename.go` produces the following kind of output:

```
$ go run ch01/basename.go /opt/homebrew/bin/go
go
$ go run ch01/basename.go ///opt////
opt
```

The output highlights the robustness of the implementation and reinforces how careful string handling leads to predictable, user-friendly command-line tools.

Summary

As we conclude this comprehensive journey through the foundational elements of Go, you have now encountered the building blocks that make Go both powerful and elegantly simple: from basic data types and control structures that form the backbone of logical flow to the rich data structures of arrays and slices. These core features work in harmony to embody the Go philosophy of doing more with less — where explicit is better than implicit, composition trumps inheritance, and simplicity enables scalability. However, we have only scratched the surface of what Go has to offer the systems programmer. As we progress through the book, we will continue to dive deeper into the language, uncovering more advanced features, patterns, and best practices. Each chapter will build on what you have learned so far, gradually expanding your understanding of Go and helping you develop the skills needed to write efficient, idiomatic, and production-grade systems software. As you continue your journey, remember that mastering Go is less about memorizing rules and more about embracing its philosophy: write clear, concise, and maintainable code.

With this solid grounding in the essentials of Go syntax and core concepts, you are ready to dive deeper into the advanced features of Go. These include building blocks that let us represent, organize, and manipulate data more effectively. In the next chapter, we bring together three essential features of the language: maps, structures, and functions. Maps provide a flexible way to associate keys with values, whereas structures allow us to design custom types that mirror real-world entities, and functions, meanwhile, enable us to encapsulate logic and reuse it across programs. Together, these elements form the backbone of practical Go programming, preparing us to solve more complex problems with clarity and efficiency, and unlock Go's full potential for building robust, high-performance systems.

Exercises

1. Write a Go program that converts a temperature from Celsius to Fahrenheit and vice versa. Use constants where appropriate and practice formatted output.
2. Write a program that accepts two numbers and an operator (+, -, *, /) from the command line, performs the calculation, and prints the result. Use `os.Args` for getting your input.
3. Create an empty slice and use a loop to append elements to it one by one. After each append, print the current length and capacity of the slice using the `len()` and `cap()` functions. Observe how the capacity grows as more elements are added.

Additional resources

- Go official site: `https://go.dev/`
- The Go standard library: `https://pkg.go.dev/std`
- The `viper` package: `https://github.com/spf13/viper`
- The `cobra` package: `https://github.com/spf13/cobra`
- The `regexp` package documentation: `https://pkg.go.dev/regexp`

Get this book's PDF version and more

Scan the QR code (or go to `packtpub.com/unlock`). Search for this book by name, confirm the edition, and then follow the steps on the page.

UNLOCK NOW

Note: Keep your invoice handy. Purchases made directly from Packt don't require an invoice.

2

Data Collections and Functions

Although arrays and slices are versatile and powerful, they cannot cover all our needs. This is where **maps** and **structures** come into play. Maps let you associate keys with values efficiently, and structs allow you to bundle related fields together into a custom type.

Building upon iterators and functional programming patterns, maps provide a handy and fundamental data structure that demonstrates the emphasis on simplicity and performance. Maps serve as the Go built-in associative array type, offering efficient key-value storage with a hash table implementation under the hood. Unlike the sequential nature of slices, maps provide constant-time average-case lookup operations and flexible key types, making them essential for tasks ranging from caching and indexing to building more complex data structures. Under the hood, Go implements maps as **hash tables**, providing average *O(1)* time (*constant*) complexity for insertions, deletions, and lookups. On the other hand, structures give you the ability to define your own composite data types by grouping related fields under a single name. Unlike basic types such as integers or strings, a struct lets you represent more complex real-world entities in code, such as a bank account, a person, or a network packet. Each field in a struct has its own type and name, making your programs more expressive and organized. By combining fields into meaningful units, structs become the foundation for modeling data in larger applications and for building more advanced concepts such as methods and interfaces.

This chapter covers the following:

- Maps
- Structures
- Pointers
- Functions

Without further ado, let us begin with learning about maps.

Understanding and using maps

Both arrays and slices limit you to using positive integers as indexes, which start from 0 and cannot have gaps in them – this means that even if you want to put data in the slice element at index 99 only, the slice is still going to occupy 100 elements in memory. Maps are more powerful data structures because they allow you to use indexes of various data types as keys to look up your data if these keys are *comparable* – if a type cannot be compared using == and !=, you cannot use it as a map key. The map syntax and behavior reflect the language design philosophy of making common operations straightforward while maintaining the performance characteristics that systems programming demands. Maps are illustrated with the following example code, which uses the `main()` function implementation to show the different ways to declare and initialize maps:

```
func main() {
    fmt.Println("=== Go Maps Comprehensive Example ===\n")
    fmt.Println("1. Map Declaration and Initialization:")
    // Various ways to create maps
    var grades map[string]int       // (nil map)
    scores := make(map[string]int) // Create empty map with make()
    inventory := map[string]int{   // Map literal with initial values
        "apples": 50, "bananas": 30, "oranges": 25,
    }

    grades = make(map[string]int)
```

You can declare a map without initialization, such as `var grades map[string]int`, which results in a *nil map* that cannot be used until it is initialized. Alternatively, you can create an empty map with `string` keys and `int` values, with `make` using `scores := make(map[string]int)`. Another way is to define a map literal with predefined values, as seen with `inventory := map[string]int{"apples": 50, "bananas": 30, "oranges": 25}`. If you start with a `nil` map, you must initialize it using `make` before adding elements.

The next code shows how to add and update key-value pairs:

```
    fmt.Printf("Empty scores map: %v\n", scores)
    fmt.Printf("Inventory map: %v\n", inventory)
    fmt.Println()

    fmt.Println("2. Adding and Updating Elements:")
```

```
grades["Marietta"] = 95
grades["Epifanios"] = 87
grades["Athina"] = 92
scores["Team A"] = 150
scores["Team B"] = 200
fmt.Printf("Grades after adding: %v\n", grades)
fmt.Printf("Scores after adding: %v\n", scores)

grades["Marietta"] = 98
fmt.Printf("Updated Marietta's grade: %v\n", grades)
fmt.Println()
```

You can assign values directly using the key, such as `grades["Marietta"] = 95` or `scores["Team A"] = 150`. Updating existing entries works the same way – assigning a new value to an existing key automatically replaces the old one. For instance, `grades["Marietta"] = 98` updates Marietta's grade.

The next code shows what happens if you try to read the value of a key that does not exist:

```
fmt.Println("3. Reading Values and Zero Values:")
mariettaGrade := grades["Marietta"]
nonExistentGrade := grades["David"] // Returns zero value
fmt.Printf("Marietta's grade: %d\n", mariettaGrade)
fmt.Printf("David's grade (doesn't exist): %d\n", nonExistentGrade)
fmt.Println()
```

When you access a value from a map using a key, Go returns the associated value if it exists. If the key is missing, Go returns the zero value *for the value type of the map.* For example, if `grades["David"]` does not exist, the returned value will be `0` since the map stores integers.

Next, we'll see how to distinguish between a missing key and an existing key with a zero value using the **comma ok idiom**.

```
fmt.Println("4. Checking if Key Exists:")
if grade, exists := grades["Marietta"]; exists {
    fmt.Printf("Marietta exists with grade: %d\n", grade)
}

if grade, exists := grades["David"]; exists {
    fmt.Printf("David exists with grade: %d\n", grade)
} else {
```

```
        fmt.Printf("David doesn't exist in grades map\n")
    }
    fmt.Println()
```

The `exists` Boolean tells you whether the key is present in the map, allowing you to handle missing data gracefully.

Maps in Go allow you to remove entries using the `delete()` function, which is presented next:

```
    fmt.Println("5. Deleting Elements:")
    fmt.Printf("Before deletion: %v\n", grades)
    delete(grades, "Epifanios")
    fmt.Printf("After deleting Epifanios: %v\n", grades)
    // Deleting non-existent key is safe (no-op)
    delete(grades, "NonExistent")
    fmt.Printf("After deleting non-existent key: %v\n", grades)
    fmt.Println()
```

For example, `delete(grades, "Epifanios")` removes the entry for `Epifanios`. Importantly, deleting a non-existent key is safe – Go simply ignores the request without throwing an error.

Next is the iteration over maps using the `range` keyword:

```
    fmt.Println("6. Iterating Over Maps:")
    fmt.Println("Iterating over key-value pairs:")
    for name, grade := range grades {
        fmt.Printf("  %s: %d\n", name, grade)
    }

    fmt.Println("Iterating over keys only:")
    for name := range grades {
        fmt.Printf("  Student: %s\n", name)
    }
    fmt.Println("Iterating over values only:")
    for _, grade := range grades {
        fmt.Printf("  Grade: %d\n", grade)
    }
    fmt.Println()
```

You can iterate over both keys and values simultaneously. You can also iterate over just keys or just values, depending on your needs. However, map iteration order in Go is randomized, so results are not deterministic unless you explicitly sort the keys.

After that, we see how to get the length of a map:

```
fmt.Println("7. Map Length:")
fmt.Printf("Number of students: %d\n", len(grades))
fmt.Printf("Number of inventory items: %d\n", len(inventory))
fmt.Println()
```

You can quickly find the number of key-value pairs in a map using the built-in `len()` function. So, `len(grades)` returns the number of students currently in the map.

Maps in Go are highly flexible when it comes to key types. Keys can be strings, integers, Booleans, and more, as long as they are comparable types. Here is the relevant code:

```
fmt.Println("8. Maps with Different Key Types:")
// String keys
cities := map[string]string{
    "NY": "New York",
    "CA": "California",
    "TX": "Texas",
}

// Integer keys
fibonacci := map[int]int{
    1: 1, 2: 1, 3: 2, 4: 3, 5: 5, 6: 8,
}

// Boolean keys
permissions := map[bool]string{true: "allowed", false: "denied"}

fmt.Printf("Cities: %v\n", cities)
fmt.Printf("Fibonacci: %v\n", fibonacci)
fmt.Printf("Permissions: %v\n", permissions)
fmt.Println()
```

The previous code shows examples of maps with string keys (`cities`), integer keys (`fibonacci`), and even Boolean keys (`permissions`).

You can also nest maps inside other maps to represent hierarchical data:

```
fmt.Println("9. Nested Maps:")
studentGrades := map[string]map[string]int{
    "Alice": {"Math": 95, "Science": 92, "English": 88},
    "Bob":   {"Math": 87, "Science": 90, "English": 85},
}

fmt.Printf("Student grades: %v\n", studentGrades)
fmt.Printf("Alice Math: %d\n", studentGrades["Alice"]["Math"])
fmt.Println()
```

The `studentGrades` structure allows you to store multiple subject grades for each student in a structured, organized way.

Maps in Go are reference types, meaning assigning one map to another *does not create a deep copy*. Instead, both variables point to the same underlying data. Modifying one map affects the other, as shown when adding new keys to the copy map also updates the `original`. This is illustrated in the following example code:

```
fmt.Println("10. Maps are Reference Types:")
original := map[string]int{"a": 1, "b": 2}
copy := original // This creates a reference, not a copy
fmt.Printf("Original: %v\n", original)
fmt.Printf("Copy: %v\n", copy)

copy["c"] = 3 // Modifying copy affects original
fmt.Printf("After modifying copy:\n")
fmt.Printf("Original: %v\n", original)
fmt.Printf("Copy: %v\n", copy)
fmt.Println()
```

The next code shows how to sort map keys for deterministic iteration – however, when order really matters, you can use a slice of keys to control iteration order:

```
fmt.Println("11. Sorting Map Keys for Deterministic Iteration:")
products := map[string]float64{
    "laptop": 999.99, "mouse": 29.99, "keyboard": 79.99, "monitor": 299.99,
}

// Get keys and sort them
```

```
keys := make([]string, 0, len(products))
for key := range products {
    keys = append(keys, key)
}
sort.Strings(keys)
fmt.Println("Products sorted by name:")
for _, key := range keys {
    fmt.Printf("  %s: $%.2f\n", key, products[key])
}
fmt.Println()
```

To achieve deterministic output, the code extracts the keys into a slice, sorts them using `sort.Strings()`, and then iterates over the sorted keys to access the map values in a predictable order.

Go lacks a built-in set type, but you can simulate one using a map where the keys represent unique items and the values are empty structs to save memory:

```
fmt.Println("12. Using Maps as Sets:")
// Map with empty struct values to simulate a set
uniqueWords := make(map[string]struct{})
words := []string{"hello", "world", "hello", "go", "world", "programming"}

for _, word := range words {
    uniqueWords[word] = struct{}{}
}

fmt.Printf("Original words: %v\n", words)
fmt.Print("Unique words: ")
for word := range uniqueWords {
    fmt.Printf("%s ", word)
}
fmt.Printf("\nNumber of unique words: %d\n", len(uniqueWords))
fmt.Println()
```

Adding words to the map automatically removes duplicates, making it a set. This is also a memory-efficient way to track unique elements.

The example code concludes by showing how maps can power small analytics.

```
fmt.Println("13. Map Operations Summary:")
summary := map[string]interface{}{
```

```
        "total_students": len(grades),
        "average_grade":  calculateAverage(grades),
        "highest_grade":  findHighestGrade(grades),
        "map_size_bytes": "varies by implementation",
    }

    for key, value := range summary {
        fmt.Printf("  %s: %v\n", key, value)
    }
}

// Helper function to calculate average grade
func calculateAverage(grades map[string]int) float64 {
    if len(grades) == 0 {
        return 0
    }

    total := 0
    for _, grade := range grades {
        total += grade
    }

    return float64(total) / float64(len(grades))
}

// Helper function to find highest grade
func findHighestGrade(grades map[string]int) int {
    highest := 0
    for _, grade := range grades {
        if grade > highest {
            highest = grade
        }
    }
    return highest
}
```

Using helper functions such as `calculateAverage()` and `findHighestGrade()`, we derive insights such as total students, average grades, and the highest grade achieved. This demonstrates how maps integrate seamlessly with functions to create reusable, modular programs.

If you execute `maps.go` on your machine, you will obtain the following output:

```
$ go run ch02/maps.go
=== Go Maps Comprehensive Example ===

1. Map Declaration and Initialization:
Empty scores map: map[]
Inventory map: map[apples:50 bananas:30 oranges:25]

2. Adding and Updating Elements:
Grades after adding: map[Athina:92 Epifanios:87 Marietta:95]
Scores after adding: map[Team A:150 Team B:200]
Updated Marietta's grade: map[Athina:92 Epifanios:87 Marietta:98]

3. Reading Values and Zero Values:
Marietta's grade: 98
David's grade (doesn't exist): 0

4. Checking if Key Exists:
Marietta exists with grade: 98
David doesn't exist in grades map

5. Deleting Elements:
Before deletion: map[Athina:92 Epifanios:87 Marietta:98]
After deleting Epifanios: map[Athina:92 Marietta:98]
After deleting non-existent key: map[Athina:92 Marietta:98]

6. Iterating Over Maps:
Iterating over key-value pairs:
  Marietta: 98
  Athina: 92
Iterating over keys only:
  Student: Marietta
  Student: Athina
Iterating over values only:
  Grade: 92
  Grade: 98

7. Map Length:
Number of students: 2
Number of inventory items: 3
```

```
8. Maps with Different Key Types:
Cities: map[CA:California NY:New York TX:Texas]
Fibonacci: map[1:1 2:1 3:2 4:3 5:5 6:8]
Permissions: map[false:denied true:allowed]

9. Nested Maps:
Student grades: map[Alice:map[English:88 Math:95 Science:92] Bob:map[English:85
Math:87 Science:90]]
Alice Math: 95

10. Maps are Reference Types:
Original: map[a:1 b:2]
Copy: map[a:1 b:2]
After modifying copy:
Original: map[a:1 b:2 c:3]
Copy: map[a:1 b:2 c:3]

11. Sorting Map Keys for Deterministic Iteration:
Products sorted by name:
  keyboard: $79.99
  laptop: $999.99
  monitor: $299.99
  mouse: $29.99

12. Using Maps as Sets:
Original words: [hello world hello go world programming]
Unique words: hello world go programming
Number of unique words: 4

13. Map Operations Summary:
  map_size_bytes: varies by implementation
  total_students: 2
  average_grade: 95
  highest_grade: 98
```

As your Go programs grow in complexity, you will often need to represent real-world entities that consist of multiple related pieces of data. While maps are great for key-value storage, they are not always ideal for modeling structured information. This is where **structures** (or **structs** in Go) come in. *Structs allow you to group fields of different types under a single, cohesive unit, making your data easier to manage, pass around, and reason about.* In the next section, we will explore how to define, initialize, and work with structs to create richer and more organized representations of data.

Understanding the versatility of structures

Structures in Go are both powerful and widely used for organizing and grouping related data under a single type. They are among the most versatile constructs in the language, as they can also have associated functions — called methods — which allow behavior to be attached directly to data. While JSON can be parsed without using structs, defining structs with appropriate field tags makes encoding and decoding JSON significantly more convenient and type-safe. **Struct tags** allow encoding libraries to map JSON fields directly onto struct fields, simplifying data validation and improving readability when working with structured data.

As structures are an important part of Go, in this section, we present, bit by bit, an extended code example that illustrates the multiple uses and personalities of structures. The first portion of code establishes the foundation for a comprehensive exploration of struct functionality by importing essential packages and defining a basic struct type:

```
package main

import (
    "encoding/json"
    "fmt"
    "reflect"
    "strings"
    "time"
    "unsafe"
)

// 1. Basic Struct Definition
type Person struct {
    Name string
    Age  int
    City string
}
```

The program imports six key packages that enable different aspects of struct manipulation: `encoding/json` for converting structs to and from JSON format, `fmt` for formatted input/output operations, `reflect` for runtime type inspection and manipulation, `strings` for string processing utilities, `time` for working with temporal data within structs, and `unsafe` for low-level memory operations and size calculations. The code then demonstrates the most fundamental aspect of Go structs by defining a `Person` type using the `struct` keyword. This `Person` struct contains *three fields with different basic types*: `Name` as a string for textual data, `Age` as an integer for numeric data, and `City` as another string field. In the struct definition, each field is declared with its name followed by its type, creating a composite data type that groups related information together. This basic pattern establishes the foundation for more complex struct usage patterns, where structs serve as the primary mechanism for creating custom data types that model real-world entities and organize related data into cohesive, type-safe units that can be passed between functions, stored in collections, and extended with methods to create object-oriented programming patterns within the Go composition-based paradigm.

The next code portion demonstrates a more sophisticated struct definition that showcases Go's ability to combine multiple data types within a single composite structure.

```
// 2. Struct with Different Field Types
type Product struct {
    ID        int
    Name      string
    Price     float64
    InStock   bool
    Tags      []string
    CreatedAt time.Time
}
```

The struct contains six fields that collectively demonstrate different categories of data types commonly used in Go programming. The `ID` field uses an integer for unique identification, while `Name` employs a string for textual representation. The `Price` field utilizes `float64` for precise decimal number handling, which is essential for financial calculations, and `InStock` uses a Boolean to represent binary state information. The `Tags` field introduces a slice type `[]string`, demonstrating how structs can contain collections of data, allowing a single product to be associated with multiple categorical labels or keywords. Finally, the `CreatedAt` field uses `time.Time` from the imported `time` package, showing how structs can incorporate specialized types to handle complex data such as timestamps, dates, and durations. This structure design pattern reflects the Go philosophy of explicit typing and composition, where each field serves a specific purpose and the aggregate structure models a complete business entity. The combination of primitive types (`int`, `string`, `float64`, `bool`), collection types (`[]string`), and standard library types (`time.Time`) within a single struct demonstrates how Go enables developers to create rich, type-safe data models that accurately represent complex real-world objects while maintaining the emphasis on clarity and performance.

The code that follows demonstrates one of the most powerful features of Go: **struct embedding**, which implements composition-based *inheritance* as an alternative to the traditional class-based inheritance found in other object-oriented languages.

```
// 3. Struct with Embedded Fields (Composition)
type Address struct {
    Street  string
    City    string
    State   string
    ZipCode string
}

type Employee struct {
    Person     // Embedded struct (anonymous field)
    Address    // Embedded struct
    ID         int
    Department string
    Salary     float64
    IsManager  bool
}
```

The code first defines an `Address` struct with four string fields (`Street`, `City`, `State`, and `ZipCode`) that collectively represent a complete mailing address, establishing a reusable component that can be embedded in other structs rather than duplicated. The `Employee` struct includes both `Person` and `Address` as anonymous fields without explicit field names. This embedding syntax allows the `Employee` struct to automatically inherit all the fields from both embedded structs, meaning an `Employee` instance can directly access `Name`, `Age`, and `City` from the `Person` struct, as well as `Street`, `State`, and `ZipCode` from the `Address` struct, without requiring dot notation to traverse through intermediate struct names. The `Employee` struct also defines its own specific fields (`ID`, `Department`, `Salary`, and `IsManager`) that are unique to the employee concept.

When embedding structs, each embedded type retains its own identity and can always be accessed explicitly through qualification (for example, `employee.Person.City` or `employee.Address.City`). This becomes especially important when multiple embedded structs contain fields with the same name. If both `Person` and `Address` define a `City` field, the promoted name `employee.City` becomes ambiguous and cannot be used directly. In such cases, explicit access is required to disambiguate which field is intended. Although Go supports automatic field promotion for convenience (for example, `employee.Name`), you must know that explicit qualification is necessary whenever name collisions occur.

Next, we demonstrate how *structs can be extended with methods using receiver functions,* which is the Go approach to implementing object-oriented behavior without traditional classes.

```
// 4. Struct with Methods (Receiver Functions)
type Rectangle struct {
    Width  float64
    Height float64
}

// Value receiver - doesn't modify the struct
func (r Rectangle) Area() float64 {
    return r.Width * r.Height
}

// Value receiver
func (r Rectangle) Perimeter() float64 {
    return 2 * (r.Width + r.Height)
}

// Pointer receiver - can modify the struct
func (r *Rectangle) Scale(factor float64) {
    r.Width *= factor
    r.Height *= factor
}

// Pointer receiver
func (r *Rectangle) SetDimensions(width, height float64) {
    r.Width = width
    r.Height = height
}
```

The `Rectangle` struct defines a simple geometric shape with two `float64` fields for `Width` and `Height`, serving as the foundation for demonstrating different types of method receivers and their behavioral implications. The code illustrates the critical distinction between *value receivers* and *pointer receivers* through four different methods. The `Area()` and `Perimeter()` methods use value receivers (`r Rectangle`), meaning *they operate on a copy of the struct and cannot modify the original instance.* These methods are purely computational, taking the current field values to calculate and return derived information without any side effects on the struct itself. The value receiver pattern is ideal for methods that need only to read data and perform calculations, as it provides immutability guarantees and allows the methods to be called on both struct values and pointers.

In contrast, the `Scale()` and `SetDimensions()` methods use pointer receivers (`r *Rectangle`), which *receive a memory address rather than a copy of the struct.* This enables these methods to directly modify the original struct field values, with `Scale()` multiplying both dimensions by a scaling factor and `SetDimensions()` completely replacing the width and height values. The pointer receiver pattern is essential when methods need to mutate the structure state, and Go automatic dereferencing allows these methods to access fields naturally using dot notation (`r.Width`) without explicit dereferencing syntax. This receiver system provides developers with clear control over whether methods should preserve immutability (value receivers) or enable state modification (pointer receivers), supporting both functional and imperative programming patterns within the same type system.

The next Go code demonstrates encapsulation and data hiding principles through the Go visibility rules and the constructor pattern commonly used to create well-designed APIs.

```
// 5. Struct with Private and Public Fields
type BankAccount struct {
    AccountNumber string  // Public (exported)
    balance       float64 // Private (unexported)
    ownerName     string  // Private
}

// Constructor function (common Go pattern)
func NewBankAccount(accountNumber, ownerName string, initialBalance float64)
*BankAccount {
    return &BankAccount{
        AccountNumber: accountNumber,
        balance:       initialBalance,
        ownerName:     ownerName,
    }
}

// Getter method for private field
func (b *BankAccount) Balance() float64 {
    return b.balance
}

// Setter method for private field with validation
```

```
func (b *BankAccount) Deposit(amount float64) error {
    if amount <= 0 {
        return fmt.Errorf("deposit amount must be positive")
    }
    b.balance += amount
    return nil
}

func (b *BankAccount) Withdraw(amount float64) error {
    if amount <= 0 {
        return fmt.Errorf("withdrawal amount must be positive")
    }
    if amount > b.balance {
        return fmt.Errorf("insufficient funds")
    }
    b.balance -= amount
    return nil
}
```

The `BankAccount` struct showcases the simple but effective approach of Go to access control, where field names beginning with uppercase letters (`AccountNumber`) are exported (*public*) and accessible from other packages, while field names beginning with lowercase letters (`balance` and `ownerName`) are unexported (*private*) and only accessible within the same package. This visibility mechanism protects sensitive data such as account balance and owner information from direct external manipulation while still allowing controlled access through the public account number field.

The `NewBankAccount` constructor function follows the Go idiomatic pattern for creating properly initialized structs, accepting the necessary parameters and returning a pointer to a new `BankAccount` instance. Because Go does not provide built-in constructors, such `New`-prefixed functions serve as conventional entry points for creating valid instances. The associated methods then expose a controlled API around the unexported fields. Instead of allowing direct mutation, operations such as retrieving the balance or modifying it are performed through methods that encapsulate validation and business rules, reinforcing the principle of encapsulation and ensuring the struct's internal state remains consistent.

The next Go code demonstrates *interface implementation and polymorphism* through the Go implicit interface satisfaction system, which differs fundamentally from explicit interface implementation found in languages such as Java or C#.

```
// 6. Interface Implementation
type Shape interface {
    Area() float64
    Perimeter() float64
}

type Circle struct {
    Radius float64
}

func (c Circle) Area() float64 {
    return 3.14159 * c.Radius * c.Radius
}

func (c Circle) Perimeter() float64 {
    return 2 * 3.14159 * c.Radius
}
```

The `Shape` interface defines a contract by specifying two method signatures that any implementing type must provide: `Area()` and `Perimeter()`, both returning `float64` values. This interface establishes a common behavioral contract for geometric shapes without dictating how each shape should calculate these properties, enabling polymorphic behavior where different shape types can be treated uniformly. The `Circle` struct represents a concrete implementation with a single `Radius` field of type `float64`, providing the data necessary to perform geometric calculations for circular shapes. The struct itself makes no explicit declaration of implementing the `Shape` interface, demonstrating the Go implicit interface satisfaction philosophy, where types automatically satisfy interfaces simply by *implementing the required methods with matching signatures*. The two methods `Area()` and `Perimeter()` complete the interface implementation by providing the concrete mathematical calculations specific to circles. The `Area()` method implements the formula πr^2 using an approximation of pi (`3.14159`), while the `Perimeter()` method calculates the circumference using $2\pi r$. Both methods use value receivers (`c Circle`) since they only need to read the radius value without modifying the struct. By implementing these two methods with the exact signatures specified in the `Shape` interface, the `Circle` type implicitly satisfies the interface contract, allowing `Circle` instances to be used anywhere a `Shape` is expected, such as in slices of `Shape` types or as parameters to functions that accept `Shape` interfaces.

Next, the `User` struct showcases how struct tags, which are *string literals enclosed in backticks* following field declarations, provide a declarative way to specify how fields should be handled by different systems without cluttering the struct definition with imperative code. Each field contains multiple tags separated by spaces, with each tag consisting of a key-value pair that instructs specific libraries or frameworks on how to process that field.

```
// 7. Struct with Tags (for JSON, database mapping, etc.)
type User struct {
    ID       int    `json:"id" db:"user_id" validate:"required"`
    Username string `json:"username" db:"username" validate:"required,min=3"`
    Email    string `json:"email" db:"email" validate:"required,email"`
    Password string `json:"-" db:"password_hash"`    // "-" excludes from JSON
    FullName string `json:"full_name,omitempty" db:"name"` // omitempty excludes
if empty
}
```

The struct tags illustrate various serialization control mechanisms that the `encoding/json` package recognizes and respects during marshaling and unmarshaling operations – marshaling is the process of converting a data structure into a format suitable for storage or transmission (such as JSON or bytes) while unmarshaling is the reverse operation. The `ID`, `Username`, and `Email` fields use straightforward mappings that specify the JSON field names, allowing Go conventional `PascalCase` field names to be converted to more typical `snake_case` or `camelCase` JSON representations. The `Password` field demonstrates data protection using the special `json:"-"` tag, which completely excludes the field from JSON serialization, ensuring that sensitive information never appears in API responses or log files. The `FullName` field uses the `omitempty` directive, which instructs the JSON encoder to exclude the field from output when it contains the zero value for its type, reducing JSON payload size and avoiding unnecessary null fields. The additional `db` and `validate` tags demonstrate how struct tags enable multi-purpose metadata that different libraries can interpret for their specific needs. The `db` tags specify database column names, allowing the struct to serve as both a Go data model and a database schema representation. The `validate` tags provide declarative validation rules that validation libraries can process, specifying requirements such as mandatory fields (`required`), minimum string lengths (`min=3`), and format validation (`email`) without requiring separate validation logic.

The Go code that follows demonstrates anonymous structs, which are struct types defined inline without being given a separate type name. They provide a convenient way to create nested data structures for specific use cases such as configuration management.

```
// 8. Anonymous Structs
type Config struct {
    Database struct {
        Host     string `json:"host"`
        Port     int    `json:"port"`
        Username string `json:"username"`
        Password string `json:"password"`
    } `json:"database"`
    Server struct {
        Port int    `json:"port"`
        Host string `json:"host"`
    } `json:"server"`
}
```

The `Config` struct contains two fields, `Database` and `Server`, but instead of referencing separately defined struct types, each field uses an anonymous struct definition that appears directly within the field declaration. This approach creates a hierarchical structure where the configuration data is organized into logical groupings without requiring the overhead of defining separate named types for each subsection. The `Database` field uses an anonymous struct containing four fields (`Host`, `Port`, `Username`, and `Password`) that collectively represent database connection parameters. Similarly, the `Server` field defines its own anonymous struct with `Port` and `Host` fields for server configuration. Each anonymous struct is treated as a distinct type, even though they both happen to contain `Port` and `Host` fields, demonstrating how the Go type system maintains strict type safety even with inline definitions. The anonymous structs also include JSON tags that specify how the nested structures should be serialized, with the outer fields tagged as `"database"` and `"server"` to create properly nested JSON objects.

This pattern is particularly useful for configuration files, API responses, and other scenarios where the nested structure is specific to a single use case and does not warrant creating separate named types that would clutter the package namespace. Anonymous structs provide the benefits of strong typing and structured data access (allowing code such as `config.Database.Host` or `config.Server.Port`) while keeping the type definitions localized and focused. This approach balances the Go preference for explicit typing with pragmatic brevity, especially when the nested structures are unlikely to be reused elsewhere in the code base or when the hierarchical relationship is more important than the individual component types.

Next, the code defines a simple structure named `Point` with two `int` fields named `X` and `Y`:

```
// 9. Struct Comparison and Copying
type Point struct {
    X, Y int
}
```

Next, we have the `main()` function, which begins by showcasing different struct initialization patterns using the previously defined `Person` struct, illustrating how Go provides flexibility in struct creation while maintaining type safety and clear semantics.

```
func main() {
    fmt.Println("=== Go Structures Comprehensive Example ===\n")

    // 1. Basic Struct Usage
    fmt.Println("1. Basic Struct Declaration and Initialization:")

    // Different ways to create structs
    var p1 Person                            // Zero value initialization
    p2 := Person{}                           // Empty initialization
    p3 := Person{"Alice", 30, "New York"} // Positional initialization
    p4 := Person{                            // Named field initialization
        Name: "Bob",
        Age:  25,
        City: "Boston",
    }

    fmt.Printf("p1 (zero value): %+v\n", p1)
    fmt.Printf("p2 (empty): %+v\n", p2)
    fmt.Printf("p3 (positional): %+v\n", p3)
    fmt.Printf("p4 (named): %+v\n", p4)
    fmt.Println()
```

The first initialization method, `var p1 Person`, demonstrates Go **zero value initialization**, *where declaring a variable without explicit initialization automatically sets all fields to their respective zero values* (empty string for strings, `0` for integers). The second method, `p2 := Person{}`, uses the **short variable declaration syntax** with an empty struct literal, which produces the same result as zero value initialization but makes the intent more explicit. These two approaches are functionally equivalent but differ in their declarative style, with the first being a more traditional variable declaration and the second being more explicit about creating a struct instance. The third and fourth initialization methods show the two ways to provide initial values during struct creation. The positional initialization `p3 := Person{"Alice", 30, "New York"}` assigns values to fields based on their declaration order in the struct definition, requiring all fields to be specified and in the correct sequence. The named field initialization for `p4` uses field names explicitly (`Name: "Bob", Age: 25, City: "Boston"`), allowing fields to be initialized in any order and enabling partial initialization where only some fields are set while others receive zero values. The code uses `fmt.Printf()` with the `%+v` formatting verb to display each struct with both field names and values, providing clear output that shows how each initialization method affects the final struct contents.

Next, the code demonstrates the straightforward field access and modification syntax that makes structs intuitive to work with in Go programming.

```
// 2. Accessing and Modifying Fields
fmt.Println("2. Accessing and Modifying Fields:")

p1.Name = "Charlie"
p1.Age = 35
p1.City = "Chicago"

fmt.Printf("Modified p1: %+v\n", p1)
fmt.Printf("p1.Name: %s, p1.Age: %d\n", p1.Name, p1.Age)
fmt.Println()
```

The code takes the previously declared `p1` variable, which was initialized with zero values, and shows how individual struct fields can be accessed and modified using dot notation. Each assignment statement (`p1.Name = "Charlie"`, `p1.Age = 35`, `p1.City = "Chicago"`) directly assigns a new value to the corresponding field, transforming the initially empty struct into a fully populated `Person` instance. The field modification syntax illustrates the clean and predictable approach to struct manipulation of Go, where the dot operator provides direct access to struct members without requiring special getter or setter methods. This direct field access pattern works because the struct fields are exported (capitalized field names), making them accessible for both reading and writing operations. The assignments demonstrate type safety in action, as each field receives a value of its declared type (`string` for `Name` and `City`, `int` for `Age`), and the Go compiler catches any type mismatches at compile time. The subsequent `fmt.Printf()` statements show two different approaches to displaying struct data: the first uses `%+v` to print the entire struct with field names and values in a structured format, whereas the second demonstrates selective field access by reading individual fields (`p1.Name` and `p1.Age`) and formatting them with type-specific format specifiers (`%s` for string, `%d` for integer).

Next, we'll demonstrate **struct pointers** and Go's convenient automatic dereferencing feature that simplifies pointer-based struct manipulation.

```
// 3. Struct Pointers
fmt.Println("3. Struct Pointers:")

p5 := &Person{"David", 40, "Denver"} // Pointer to struct
fmt.Printf("p5 pointer: %p\n", p5)
fmt.Printf("p5 value: %+v\n", *p5)

// Go automatically dereferences struct pointers
fmt.Printf("p5.Name (auto-dereference): %s\n", p5.Name)

// Explicit dereferencing - not recommended but available
fmt.Printf("(*p5).Name (explicit): %s\n", (*p5).Name)

// Modifying through pointer
p5.Age = 41
fmt.Printf("Modified through pointer: %+v\n", *p5)
```

The code creates `p5` as a pointer to a `Person` struct using the address-of operator (&) combined with struct literal initialization, resulting in a variable that holds the memory address of the struct rather than the struct value itself. The subsequent `fmt.Printf()` statements illustrate the distinction between the pointer (displayed as a hexadecimal memory address using `%p`) and the actual struct value (accessed through explicit dereferencing with `*p5`). The Go **automatic dereferencing** feature is showcased through the comparison between `p5.Name` and `(*p5).Name`, both of which produce identical results but demonstrate different syntax approaches. The automatic dereferencing allows developers to access struct fields through pointers using the same dot notation as with direct struct values, eliminating the need for explicit dereferencing syntax in most cases. This syntactic convenience makes pointer-based struct operations as natural and readable as value-based operations, reducing cognitive overhead and potential syntax errors while maintaining the performance benefits of pointer usage. The field modification example (`p5.Age = 41`) demonstrates how automatic dereferencing works for both reading and writing operations, allowing the code to modify the original struct through the pointer without requiring explicit dereferencing syntax. The final `fmt.Printf()` statement shows the modified struct by explicitly dereferencing the pointer (`*p5`), confirming that the change was made to the original struct instance rather than a copy. This pointer behavior is crucial for understanding Go memory management and performance characteristics, as pointers enable efficient passing of large structs to functions and methods while avoiding expensive copy operations, particularly important when working with substantial data structures or when functions need to modify the original struct rather than working with copies.

The code that follows demonstrates **struct embedding**, showing how composition creates powerful data structures that combine multiple types into cohesive entities.

```
// 4. Embedded Structs (Composition)
fmt.Println("4. Embedded Structs (Composition):")

emp := Employee{
    Person: Person{
        Name: "Emily",
        Age:  28,
        City: "Seattle",
    },
    Address: Address{
        Street:  "123 Main St",
        City:    "Seattle",
        State:   "WA",
        ZipCode: "98101",
    },
    ID:         1001,
    Department: "Engineering",
    Salary:     75000,
    IsManager:  false,
}
fmt.Printf("Employee: %+v\n", emp)

// Accessing embedded fields directly
fmt.Printf("Employee name: %s\n", emp.Name) // From embedded Person
fmt.Printf("Employee street: %s\n", emp.Street) // From embedded Address
fmt.Printf("Employee department: %s\n", emp.Department)

// Accessing embedded fields explicitly
fmt.Printf("Person info: %+v\n", emp.Person)
fmt.Printf("Address info: %+v\n", emp.Address)
```

The `Employee` initialization uses named field syntax to explicitly populate both the embedded structs (`Person` and `Address`) and the `Employee`-specific fields. The embedded `Person` struct is initialized with Emily's personal information, while the embedded `Address` struct contains the location details, and the remaining fields (`ID`, `Department`, `Salary`, `IsManager`) represent employment-specific data that belongs directly to the `Employee` type. The field access examples illustrate the *automatic field promotion feature,* where fields from embedded structs become directly accessible through the containing struct without requiring intermediate navigation. When the code accesses `emp.Name` and `emp.Street`, Go automatically promotes these fields from the embedded `Person` and `Address` structs, respectively, making them appear as if they were direct fields of the `Employee` struct. This promotion mechanism provides convenient shorthand access while maintaining the logical separation of concerns, as `Name` conceptually belongs to the person aspect of the employee, and `Street` belongs to the address aspect. The explicit access examples demonstrate that embedded structs maintain their identity and can be accessed as complete units when needed. By accessing `emp.Person` and `emp.Address`, the code retrieves the entire embedded struct instances, which is useful when you need to pass the embedded data to functions that expect the specific embedded type or when you want to work with the embedded data as a cohesive unit. This dual access pattern – both direct field promotion and explicit struct access – gives developers flexibility in how they interact with composed types, allowing them to treat the composite structure as either a flattened set of fields or as a hierarchical composition of distinct components depending on the specific requirements of their code.

The next Go code demonstrates the practical application of methods with different receiver types, showcasing how value receivers and pointer receivers behave differently during method execution.

```
// 5. Methods on Structs
fmt.Println("5. Methods on Structs:")

rect := Rectangle{Width: 10, Height: 5}
fmt.Printf("Rectangle: %+v\n", rect)
fmt.Printf("Area: %.2f\n", rect.Area())
fmt.Printf("Perimeter: %.2f\n", rect.Perimeter())

// Method with pointer receiver
fmt.Printf("Before scaling: %+v\n", rect)
rect.Scale(2)
fmt.Printf("After scaling by 2: %+v\n", rect)

rect.SetDimensions(15, 8)
fmt.Printf("After setting new dimensions: %+v\n", rect)
fmt.Println()
```

The code creates a `Rectangle` instance with specific dimensions and then calls the `Area()` and `Perimeter()` methods, both of which use value receivers and perform read-only calculations without modifying the original struct. These methods demonstrate how value receivers work with copies of the struct data, making them safe for concurrent access and ensuring that the original struct remains unchanged regardless of what happens inside the method. The scaling operation illustrates the fundamental difference between value and pointer receivers through a before-and-after comparison that shows the state change of the structure. When `rect.Scale(2)` is called, the method uses a pointer receiver that directly modifies the original field values of the structure, multiplying both `Width` and `Height` by the scaling factor. This modification is *persistent* because the pointer receiver operates on the memory location of the original struct rather than a copy, demonstrating how pointer receivers enable methods to have lasting effects on the structure's state. The `SetDimensions(15, 8)` call further demonstrates pointer receiver mutation by completely replacing the rectangle dimensions with new values. The sequential `fmt.Printf()` statements show how the struct state evolves through each method call: the initial state, the unchanged state after read-only method calls, the scaled state after the `Scale()` method, and finally the state with completely new dimensions after `SetDimensions()`.

After that, we demonstrate practical implementation of encapsulation and data protection through the constructor pattern and controlled access methods:

```
// 6. Private Fields and Constructor Pattern
fmt.Println("6. Private Fields and Constructor Pattern:")

account := NewBankAccount("ACC-001", "John Doe", 1000.0)
fmt.Printf("New account: %+v\n", account)
fmt.Printf("Initial balance: $%.2f\n", account.Balance())

// Deposit money
err := account.Deposit(500)
if err != nil {
    fmt.Printf("Deposit error: %v\n", err)
} else {
    fmt.Printf("After deposit: $%.2f\n", account.Balance())
}

// Withdraw money
err = account.Withdraw(300)
if err != nil {
    fmt.Printf("Withdrawal error: %v\n", err)
} else {
```

```
        fmt.Printf("After withdrawal: $%.2f\n", account.Balance())
    }

    // Try invalid operations
    err = account.Withdraw(2000)
    if err != nil {
        fmt.Printf("Invalid withdrawal: %v\n", err)
    }
    fmt.Println()
```

The code begins by calling `NewBankAccount()` with initial parameters, creating a properly initialized bank account instance where sensitive fields such as balance and owner name are protected from direct external access. The constructor ensures that the account starts in a valid state with all required information, and the subsequent calls to `account.Balance()` show how the getter method provides read-only access to the private balance field without exposing it for direct access. Each financial operation returns an `error` value that the code checks before proceeding, demonstrating how methods can enforce business rules while providing clear feedback about operation success or failure. The successful deposit increases the account balance through the controlled `Deposit()` method, which includes validation to ensure only positive amounts can be deposited, while the successful withdrawal demonstrates how the `Withdraw()` method checks both for positive amounts and sufficient funds before modifying the balance. The invalid withdrawal attempt showcases the protective nature of the encapsulated design, where the `Withdraw()` method detects an attempt to withdraw more money than available in the account and returns an appropriate error message without modifying the account state. This error handling pattern prevents the account from entering an invalid state (negative balance) while providing clear feedback about why the operation failed. The systematic error checking after each operation demonstrates the Go error handling philosophy, where potential failure conditions are acknowledged and handled at each step rather than being ignored or handled through exception mechanisms. This philosophy results in more predictable and maintainable financial software that protects data integrity through controlled access.

Next, we demonstrate **polymorphism** through interface usage, showing how different concrete types can be treated uniformly when they satisfy the same interface contract.

```
    // 7. Interface Implementation
    fmt.Println("7. Interface Implementation:")
    shapes := []Shape{
        Rectangle{Width: 10, Height: 5},
        Circle{Radius: 3},
    }
```

```
    for i, shape := range shapes {
        fmt.Printf("Shape %d:\n", i+1)
        fmt.Printf("  Type: %T\n", shape)
        fmt.Printf("  Area: %.2f\n", shape.Area())
        fmt.Printf("  Perimeter: %.2f\n", shape.Perimeter())
    }
    fmt.Println()
```

The code creates a slice of `Shape` interfaces containing instances of both `Rectangle` and `Circle` types, which can coexist in the same collection because both types implicitly implement the `Shape` interface by providing `Area()` and `Perimeter()` methods with matching signatures. This heterogeneous collection showcases the interface system of Go, where the compiler automatically recognizes that both types satisfy the interface requirements without any explicit declarations or inheritance relationships. The `range` loop iterates over the `shape` collection, treating each element as a `Shape` interface regardless of its underlying concrete type. The `%T` format verb in the `fmt.Printf()` statement reveals the actual runtime type of each shape (`main.Rectangle` and `main.Circle`), demonstrating how Go maintains type information even when working through interfaces. This type information is crucial for debugging and understanding program behavior, as it shows that interface variables retain knowledge of their concrete types while presenting a uniform interface for method calls. The `shape.Area()` and `shape.Perimeter()` method calls demonstrate runtime polymorphism, where the same method names invoke different implementations depending on the concrete type stored in the interface variable. When called on the `Rectangle`, these methods use the rectangular calculation formulas, while the same method calls on the `Circle` use the circular calculation formulas. This polymorphic behavior enables powerful design patterns where algorithms can work with collections of different types through common interfaces, promoting code reuse and flexibility while maintaining type safety and performance.

The next Go code snippet demonstrates the practical application of struct tags for JSON serialization and metadata inspection through the reflection capabilities of Go.

```
    // 8. Struct Tags and JSON
    fmt.Println("8. Struct Tags and JSON:")

    user := User{
        ID:       1,
        Username: "johndoe",
        Email:    "john@example.com",
        Password: "secret123",
```

```
        FullName: "John Doe",
    }

    // Convert to JSON
    jsonData, err := json.Marshal(user)
    if err != nil {
        fmt.Printf("JSON marshal error: %v\n", err)
    } else {
        fmt.Printf("JSON representation: %s\n", string(jsonData))
    }

    // Reflect on struct tags
    userType := reflect.TypeOf(user)
    for i := 0; i < userType.NumField(); i++ {
        field := userType.Field(i)
        jsonTag := field.Tag.Get("json")
        dbTag := field.Tag.Get("db")
        fmt.Printf("Field %s: json='%s', db='%s'\n", field.Name, jsonTag, dbTag)
    }
    fmt.Println()
```

The code creates a `User` instance with complete field data and then uses `json.Marshal()` to convert the struct into JSON format, where the `struct` tags control the serialization behavior. The resulting JSON output will show how the tags transform `PascalCase` field names into JSON-appropriate formats, exclude the `Password` field entirely due to its `json:"-"` tag, and include the `FullName` field as `"full_name"` because it contains a non-empty value that passes the `omitempty` check. The **JSON marshaling** process illustrates how struct tags provide declarative control over serialization without requiring imperative code or custom serialization methods. The `json.Marshal()` function automatically reads and interprets the JSON tags, applying the specified transformations and exclusions to produce JSON that conforms to external API expectations while keeping the Go struct fields named according to Go conventions. The reflection section demonstrates Go's runtime type inspection capabilities, using `reflect.TypeOf()` to examine the metadata programmatically. The code iterates through each field using `NumField()` and `Field()` methods, then extracts specific tag values using `Tag.Get()` for both `json` and `db` tags. This reflection-based tag inspection shows how Go programs can programmatically discover and utilize struct metadata, which is essential for building frameworks and validation libraries that need to understand struct definitions at runtime. The output displays the name of each field alongside its tag values, revealing how the same struct can carry multiple sets of metadata for different purposes, enabling a single Go structure to serve as both a data model for JSON APIs and a database entity mapping. We will revisit reflection in *Chapter 4, Advanced Go.*

The next code snippet demonstrates the practical application of anonymous structs for creating lightweight, purpose-specific data structures without the overhead of formal type definitions.

```
// 9. Anonymous Structs
fmt.Println("9. Anonymous Structs:")

// Inline anonymous struct
settings := struct {
    Theme    string
    Language string
    Debug    bool
}{
    Theme:    "dark",
    Language: "en",
    Debug:    true,
}
fmt.Printf("Settings: %+v\n", settings)

// Anonymous struct in slice
people := []struct {
    Name string
    Role string
}{
    {"Alice", "Developer"},
    {"Bob", "Designer"},
    {"Charlie", "Manager"},
}

fmt.Println("People:")
for _, person := range people {
    fmt.Printf("  %s - %s\n", person.Name, person.Role)
}
fmt.Println()
```

The first example shows an inline anonymous struct for application settings, where the struct type definition and initialization are combined in a single expression. The anonymous struct contains three fields (`Theme`, `Language`, and `Debug`) that collectively represent configuration data, and the initialization immediately provides values using named field syntax. This pattern is particularly useful for local data organization, where creating a separate named type would be overkill, such as temporary data structures, configuration objects, or data that is only relevant within a specific function scope.

The second example demonstrates anonymous structs within slice declarations, creating a collection of person records where each element has `Name` and `Role` fields. The slice initialization uses both named field syntax for the struct type definition and a mix of named and positional initialization for the individual elements, showing the flexibility available when working with anonymous structs. The positional initialization (`{"Alice", "Developer"}`) provides a more concise syntax when the field order is clear and the struct is simple, while maintaining type safety and field access through dot notation.

The iteration over the `people` slice illustrates how anonymous structs integrate seamlessly with standard control structures and operations. Despite not having a named type, the **anonymous struct** elements support all the same field access patterns as named structs, allowing the code to access `person.Name` and `person.Role` naturally within the `range` loop. This demonstrates how anonymous structs provide the benefits of structured data organization and type safety without requiring formal type declarations, making them ideal for scenarios such as API response parsing, temporary data transformations, test data creation, and situations where the structure usage is localized, and its reusability outside the immediate context is unlikely.

The next Go code demonstrates the practical usage of **nested anonymous structs** for creating hierarchical configuration data with clean field access patterns.

```
// 10. Nested Anonymous Structs
fmt.Println("10. Nested Anonymous Structs:")

config := Config{}
config.Database.Host = "localhost"
config.Database.Port = 5432
config.Database.Username = "admin"
config.Database.Password = "secret"
config.Server.Host = "0.0.0.0"
config.Server.Port = 8080
fmt.Printf("Config: %+v\n", config)
fmt.Println()
```

The code creates an instance of the previously defined `Config` type and populates its nested anonymous struct fields using dot notation that traverses the structural hierarchy. The field assignments, such as `config.Database.Host` and `config.Server.Port`, show how the dot operator naturally navigates through the nested anonymous struct layers, providing intuitive access to deeply nested fields without requiring complex dereferencing or intermediate variable declarations. The configuration population process illustrates how nested anonymous structs create logical groupings of related settings while maintaining type safety and clear namespace separation. The database-related settings (`Host`, `Port`, `Username`, `Password`) are all accessed through the `config.Database` path, whereas server-related settings (`Host`, `Port`) are accessed through `config.Server`, even though both sections contain fields with identical names, such as `Host` and `Port`. This **namespace isolation** prevents naming conflicts and creates self-documenting code where the field access path clearly indicates the context and purpose of each setting.

We continue by demonstrating struct comparison and copying behavior, illustrating the value semantics of Go and how structs with comparable fields support direct equality operations.

```
// 11. Struct Comparison and Copying
fmt.Println("11. Struct Comparison and Copying:")

point1 := Point{X: 1, Y: 2}
point2 := Point{X: 1, Y: 2}
point3 := Point{X: 3, Y: 4}
fmt.Printf("point1: %+v\n", point1)
fmt.Printf("point2: %+v\n", point2)
fmt.Printf("point3: %+v\n", point3)
fmt.Printf("point1 == point2: %t\n", point1 == point2)
fmt.Printf("point1 == point3: %t\n", point1 == point3)

// Copying structs (value semantics)
point4 := point1 // Creates a copy
point4.X = 10
fmt.Printf("Original point1: %+v\n", point1)
fmt.Printf("Modified copy point4: %+v\n", point4)
fmt.Println()
```

The code creates three `Point` instances with different coordinate values and then performs equality comparisons using the == built-in operator. The comparison `point1 == point2` returns `true` because both structs contain identical field values (`X=1, Y=2`), while `point1 == point3` returns `false` due to differing coordinates, showing how Go performs field-by-field comparison for structs containing only comparable types such as integers, strings, and Booleans. The struct comparison capability works because the `Point` struct contains only `int` fields, which are comparable types in Go. Go automatically generates comparison logic that compares each corresponding field between the two struct instances, returning `true` only when all fields match exactly. This built-in comparison behavior eliminates the need for custom equality methods in many cases, making struct comparisons straightforward and efficient while maintaining type safety. The Boolean format verb `%t` clearly displays the comparison results, demonstrating how the comparison operators integrate naturally with struct types.

The copying demonstration reveals value semantics for struct assignment, where `point4 := point1` creates a complete independent copy of all field values rather than a reference to the same memory location. It should be noted that only primitive data types are copied. In practice, this means that if you have *a slice or pointer to a struct, it will reference that same location and will not be a copy*.

When the code modifies `point4.X = 10`, only the copy is affected while the original `point1` remains unchanged, as evidenced by the final `fmt.Printf()` statements showing different values for the two variables. This copying behavior is crucial to understanding the memory model of Go and data ownership, as it ensures that struct assignments create isolated instances that can be modified independently without unintended side effects. This value semantics approach promotes safer concurrent programming and reduces bugs related to shared mutable state, though developers should be aware of the performance implications when copying large structs frequently.

The next Go code demonstrates how structs can incorporate complex field types such as slices and specialized types from the Standard Library, creating rich data models that accurately represent real-world entities.

```
// 12. Struct with Slice and Map Fields
fmt.Println("12. Struct with Complex Fields:")

product := Product{
    ID:         101,
    Name:       "Laptop",
    Price:      999.99,
    InStock:    true,
    Tags:       []string{"electronics", "computer", "portable"},
    CreatedAt: time.Now(),
}

fmt.Printf("Product: %+v\n", product)
fmt.Printf("Tags: %s\n", strings.Join(product.Tags, ", "))
fmt.Printf("Created: %s\n", product.CreatedAt.Format("2006-01-02 15:04:05"))
fmt.Println()
```

The `Product` initialization showcases a struct that combines primitive types (`ID` as `int`, `Name` as `string`, `Price` as `float64`, and `InStock` as `bool`) with more sophisticated field types, including a string slice (`Tags`) and a time value (`CreatedAt`). The tags slice contains multiple categorical labels that demonstrate how structs can hold collections of related data, while the `time.Now()` call captures the *current timestamp*, showing how structs can integrate with Standard Library types for specialized data handling. The `strings.Join(product.Tags, ", ")` statement demonstrates accessing and processing the slice field, converting the array of tags into a comma-separated string for display purposes. This shows how slice fields within structs support all standard slice operations and can be passed to functions that expect slice parameters, maintaining full functionality while being part of a larger composite data structure. The time formatting example reveals how specialized types within structs retain their full method sets and capabilities. The `product.CreatedAt.Format("2006-01-02 15:04:05")` call uses the Go reference time formatting system to convert the timestamp into a human-readable string, demonstrating that embedded complex types do not lose any functionality when incorporated into struct definitions.

The next code demonstrates the specialized use of **empty structs** as a memory-efficient solution for implementing set data structures and signaling mechanisms.

```
// 13. Empty Struct Usage
fmt.Println("13. Empty Struct Usage:")
// Empty struct as signal
type Signal struct{}

// Using empty struct as set values (memory efficient)
visited := make(map[string]struct{})
items := []string{"apple", "banana", "apple", "cherry", "banana"}

for _, item := range items {
    visited[item] = struct{}{}
}

fmt.Printf("Original items: %v\n", items)
fmt.Print("Unique items: ")
for item := range visited {
    fmt.Printf("%s ", item)
}
fmt.Printf("\nEmpty struct size: %d bytes\n", unsafe.Sizeof(struct{}{}))
fmt.Println()
```

The code defines a `Signal` struct with no fields, illustrating how empty structs serve as zero-cost type markers that provide semantic meaning without consuming memory. The primary example shows how empty structs work as map values to create a *set-like data structure*, where the map keys represent the set elements and the empty struct values indicate presence without wasting memory on unnecessary data storage. The set implementation uses `map[string]struct{}` where the empty struct values serve purely as existence markers, allowing the code to leverage map key uniqueness to automatically handle duplicate elimination. The loop that populates the `visited` map assigns `struct{}{}` (an empty struct literal) to each key, creating entries that indicate membership in the set without storing any actual value data. This pattern transforms a slice with duplicates into a set of unique elements, demonstrating a common Go idiom for deduplication and membership testing that's both memory-efficient and performant.

The memory efficiency demonstration using `unsafe.Sizeof(struct{}{})` reveals that *empty structs consume zero bytes of memory*, making them ideal for scenarios where only the presence or absence of a key matters rather than any associated value data. The iteration over the map keys (`for item := range visited`) shows how to extract the unique elements from the set, ignoring the empty struct values entirely since they contain no meaningful information. This empty struct pattern is widely used in Go for implementing sets, signal channels, and other scenarios where a type is needed for semantic purposes, but no actual data storage is required.

The next code demonstrates automatic method receiver handling and the flexible method set system that allows both struct values and struct pointers to call methods regardless of receiver type:

```
    // 14. Method Sets and Value vs Pointer Receivers
    fmt.Println("14. Method Sets Summary:")
    rect1 := Rectangle{Width: 5, Height: 3}
    rect2 := &Rectangle{Width: 7, Height: 4}
    // Both value and pointer can call value receiver methods
    fmt.Printf("rect1.Area(): %.2f\n", rect1.Area())
    fmt.Printf("rect2.Area(): %.2f\n", rect2.Area())

    // Both value and pointer can call pointer receiver methods
    // (Go automatically takes address of value or dereferences pointer)
    rect1.Scale(1.5)
    rect2.Scale(2.0)
    fmt.Printf("After scaling - rect1: %+v\n", rect1)
    fmt.Printf("After scaling - rect2: %+v\n", *rect2)
}
```

The code creates two `Rectangle` instances using different approaches: `rect1` as a direct struct value and `rect2` as a pointer to a struct, establishing the foundation for showing how the Go method dispatch system works uniformly across both value and pointer contexts. The value receiver method calls illustrate automatic dereferencing behavior, where both the struct value (`rect1.Area()`) and struct pointer (`rect2.Area()`) can call methods with value receivers without any special syntax. When called on a pointer such as `rect2`, Go automatically dereferences the pointer to access the struct value before passing it to the value receiver method. The pointer receiver method calls demonstrate an automatic address-taking feature, where both struct values and pointers can call methods with pointer receivers through the same uniform syntax. When `rect1.Scale(1.5)` is called, Go automatically takes the address of the struct value to satisfy the pointer receiver requirement, while `rect2.Scale(2.0)` uses the existing pointer directly. Under the hood, the compiler rewrites the expression as `(&rect1).Scale(1.5)`, implicitly taking the address of the value so that it matches the required receiver type. This transformation happens at compile time and introduces no runtime overhead. The key requirement is that the value must be addressable — that is, it must have a stable memory location, such as a local variable or struct field. Temporary values, such as composite literals, are not addressable and therefore cannot benefit from this implicit conversion. The reverse rule also applies: if a method has a value receiver and you call it on a pointer, the compiler automatically dereferences the pointer.

The final output shows the results of the scaling operations, with `rect1` displaying its modified state directly and `rect2` requiring explicit dereferencing (`*rect2`) to show the modified struct contents.

Execute `ch02/structures.go` on your machine to see what it does – expect lots of output:

```
$ go run ch02/structures.go
=== Go Structures Comprehensive Example ===

1. Basic Struct Declaration and Initialization:
p1 (zero value): {Name: Age:0 City:}
p2 (empty): {Name: Age:0 City:}
p3 (positional): {Name:Alice Age:30 City:New York}
p4 (named): {Name:Bob Age:25 City:Boston}

2. Accessing and Modifying Fields:
Modified p1: {Name:Charlie Age:35 City:Chicago}
p1.Name: Charlie, p1.Age: 35

3. Struct Pointers:
```

```
p5 pointer: 0x14000108150
p5 value: {Name:David Age:40 City:Denver}
p5.Name (auto-dereference): David
(*p5).Name (explicit): David
Modified through pointer: {Name:David Age:41 City:Denver}

4. Embedded Structs (Composition):
Employee: {Person:{Name:Emily Age:28 City:Seattle} Address:{Street:123 Main St
City:Seattle State:WA ZipCode:98101} ID:1001 Department:Engineering Salary:75000
IsManager:false}
Employee name: Emily
Employee street: 123 Main St
Employee department: Engineering
Person info: {Name:Emily Age:28 City:Seattle}
Address info: {Street:123 Main St City:Seattle State:WA ZipCode:98101}

5. Methods on Structs:
Rectangle: {Width:10 Height:5}
Area: 50.00
Perimeter: 30.00
Before scaling: {Width:10 Height:5}
After scaling by 2: {Width:20 Height:10}
After setting new dimensions: {Width:15 Height:8}

6. Private Fields and Constructor Pattern:
New account: &{AccountNumber:ACC-001 balance:1000 ownerName:John Doe}
Initial balance: $1000.00
After deposit: $1500.00
After withdrawal: $1200.00
Invalid withdrawal: insufficient funds

7. Interface Implementation:
Shape 1:
  Type: main.Rectangle
  Area: 50.00
  Perimeter: 30.00
Shape 2:
  Type: main.Circle
  Area: 28.27
  Perimeter: 18.85
```

```
8. Struct Tags and JSON:
JSON representation:
{"id":1,"username":"johndoe","email":"john@example.com","full_name":"John Doe"}
Field ID: json='id', db='user_id'
Field Username: json='username', db='username'
Field Email: json='email', db='email'
Field Password: json='-', db='password_hash'
Field FullName: json='full_name,omitempty', db='name'

9. Anonymous Structs:
Settings: {Theme:dark Language:en Debug:true}
People:
  Alice - Developer
  Bob - Designer
  Charlie - Manager

10. Nested Anonymous Structs:
Config: {Database:{Host:localhost Port:5432 Username:admin Password:secret}
Server:{Port:8080 Host:0.0.0.0}}

11. Struct Comparison and Copying:
point1: {X:1 Y:2}
point2: {X:1 Y:2}
point3: {X:3 Y:4}
point1 == point2: true
point1 == point3: false
Original point1: {X:1 Y:2}
Modified copy point4: {X:10 Y:2}

12. Struct with Complex Fields:
Product: {ID:101 Name:Laptop Price:999.99 InStock:true Tags:[electronics computer
portable] CreatedAt:2025-09-05 16:31:59.138822 +0300 EEST m=+0.000454876}
Tags: electronics, computer, portable
Created: 2025-09-05 16:31:59

13. Empty Struct Usage:
Original items: [apple banana apple cherry banana]
Unique items: apple banana cherry
Empty struct size: 0 bytes

14. Method Sets Summary:
```

```
rect1.Area(): 15.00
rect2.Area(): 28.00
After scaling - rect1: {Width:7.5 Height:4.5}
After scaling - rect2: {Width:14 Height:8}
```

Having explored structures as a way to group related data into cohesive units, the next natural step is to understand how Go manages memory and references. While structures let us organize complex data, working efficiently with them often requires **pointers**, which allow direct access to the memory address of a variable. Pointers enable functions to modify structures without copying them, reduce memory overhead, and support dynamic data manipulation. By combining structures with pointers, Go programmers gain fine-grained control over data, bridging the gap between high-level abstractions and low-level memory management. This sets the stage for a deeper exploration of pointers, their syntax, and practical use cases in systems programming.

Pointers

Pointers are a fundamental feature in Go that allow you to directly reference and manipulate memory locations. Unlike some higher-level languages that abstract away memory management, Go gives you controlled access to pointers, enabling more efficient and flexible code without sacrificing safety. This subsection explores how pointers work in Go, including how to declare them, dereference them, and use them to modify data indirectly. You will also learn how Go handles memory allocation with the `new` and `make` functions, and how pointers interact with structs, functions, and slices.

The first example of the use of pointers is a simple one, as it demonstrates pointer usage for passing variables by reference to enable functions to modify the original variable's value.

```
package main

import "fmt"

func main() {
    x := 10
    fmt.Println("Before:", x)

    // Pass the address of x to the function
    updateValue(&x)
    fmt.Println("After:", x)
}

// Takes a pointer to an int as an argument
```

```
func updateValue(ptr *int) {
    *ptr = *ptr + 5 // Dereference the pointer and modify the value
}
```

The program declares an integer variable x with value `10` and prints its initial state before calling the `updateValue()` function. The key operation occurs when the code passes `&x` to the `updateValue()` function, where the ampersand operator `&` *retrieves the memory address* of variable x rather than its value. This address gets passed as an argument to the function, allowing it to access and modify the original variable location in memory. The `updateValue()` function accepts a parameter `ptr` of type `*int`, which is a pointer type that can hold the memory address of an integer variable. Inside the `updateValue()` function, the code uses the dereference operator `*` twice in the expression `*ptr = *ptr + 5`. The right side `*ptr` dereferences the pointer to read the current value stored at that memory address (which is `10`), adds `5` to it, and then the left side `*ptr` dereferences the pointer again to write the new value (`15`) back to that same memory location. This direct memory modification changes the original variable x in the `main()` function. After the function call completes, the program prints the updated value of `x`, which now shows `15` instead of the original `10`. The pointer mechanism provides an efficient way to avoid copying large data structures while enabling functions to modify their arguments directly.

The second example is about creating a **linked list** in Go. In this example, pointers to structures are also illustrated. The program begins by defining the foundation of a **singly linked list** using structures.

```
package main

import "fmt"

// Node defines a node in a singly linked list
type Node struct {
    Value int
    Next  *Node
}
// LinkedList represents the linked list
type LinkedList struct {
    Head *Node
}
```

The first struct, `Node`, represents an individual element in the list. Each node contains two fields: `Value`, which holds the data of type `int`, and `Next`, which is a pointer to the next node in the list. If

`Next` is `nil`, it means the node is the last element. The second struct, `LinkedList`, serves as a container for the entire linked list. It has a single field, `Head`, which points to the first node in the list. If `Head` is `nil`, the entire list is empty. Together, these two structs define the basic data structure needed to create, traverse, and manipulate a singly linked list.

Next, we present the `Insert()` and `Delete()` methods.

```
func (l *LinkedList) Insert(value int) {
    newNode := &Node{Value: value}
    if l.Head == nil {
        l.Head = newNode
        return
    }
    current := l.Head
    for current.Next != nil {
        current = current.Next
    }
    current.Next = newNode
}

func (l *LinkedList) Delete(value int) {
    if l.Head == nil {
        return
    }
    if l.Head.Value == value {
        l.Head = l.Head.Next
        return
    }
    prev := l.Head
    curr := l.Head.Next
    for curr != nil {
        if curr.Value == value {
            prev.Next = curr.Next
            return
        }
        prev = curr
        curr = curr.Next
    }
}
```

The `Insert()` method appends a new node to the end of the list. It first creates a new node using the given `value`. If the list is empty (i.e., `Head` is `nil`), the new node becomes the head of the list. Otherwise, the method traverses the list by iterating through each node until it reaches the last node — identified when `current.Next` is `nil`. At that point, it links the new node by setting the `Next` field of the last node to point to it, effectively extending the list.

The `Delete()` method removes the first occurrence of a node that matches the given `value`. It begins by checking if the list is empty; if so, there is nothing to delete. If the head node contains the target value, the head is simply moved to the next node, effectively removing the first element. Otherwise, the function uses two pointers: `prev` to track the previous node and `curr` to scan the list. As it traverses, if it finds a node where `curr.Value` equals the target value, it bypasses the node by setting `prev.Next = curr.Next`, effectively unlinking it from the list. If the value is not found, the traversal continues until the end. Together, these methods make the linked list dynamic, allowing efficient addition and removal of elements without reallocating or shifting underlying data.

After that, we present the implementation of the `Sort()` method:

```
func (l *LinkedList) Sort() {
    if l.Head == nil || l.Head.Next == nil {
        return
    }
    swapped := true
    for swapped {
        swapped = false
        curr := l.Head
        for curr.Next != nil {
            if curr.Value > curr.Next.Value {
              // Swap values
              curr.Value, curr.Next.Value = curr.Next.Value, curr.Value
              swapped = true
            }
            curr = curr.Next
        }
    }
}

func (l *LinkedList) Print() {
    current := l.Head
    for current != nil {
```

```
        fmt.Print(current.Value, " -> ")
        current = current.Next
    }
    fmt.Println("nil")
}
```

The `Sort()` method arranges the list values in ascending order using the bubble sort algorithm. It starts by checking if the list is empty or contains only one element; in either case, no sorting is needed, so the function returns early. Otherwise, it enters a loop controlled by the `swapped` flag, which tracks whether any swaps occurred in a pass. Inside the loop, it iterates through the list from the head node, comparing each node's value with the value of the next node. If the current node value is greater than the next node's, the two values are swapped, and the `swapped` flag is set to `true`. This process continues until a complete pass occurs with no swaps, meaning the list is fully sorted. The `Print()` method displays the contents of the list in a readable format. It starts from the head node and traverses the list sequentially, printing each node's value followed by " -> " to represent the link to the next node. When it reaches the end of the list (`current` becomes `nil`), it prints `"nil"` to indicate termination.

The `main()` function demonstrates how to create, manipulate, and display a singly linked list using the methods defined earlier:

```
func main() {
    list := &LinkedList{}

    // Insert values
    list.Insert(5)
    list.Insert(3)
    list.Insert(8)
    list.Insert(1)
    fmt.Println("Original list:")
    list.Print()
    // Delete a value
    list.Delete(3)
    fmt.Println("After deleting 3:")
    list.Print()
    // Sort the list
    list.Sort()
    fmt.Println("After sorting:")
    list.Print()
}
```

The function begins by creating a new, empty linked list using `&LinkedList{}`. Next, it inserts several integer values into the list using the `Insert()` method, which appends each new value to the end of the list. After populating the list, the program prints its original state by calling `list.Print()`, which traverses the nodes and outputs their values in sequence. It then demonstrates the `Delete()` method by removing the node containing the value 3. After deletion, it prints the list again to confirm that the value has been successfully removed while the rest of the list remains intact. Finally, the program calls the `Sort()` method to arrange the remaining values in ascending order. Once sorting is complete, it prints the list one last time to show the updated, ordered sequence of nodes.

Run `linkedList.go` on your machine. You should get the following output:

```
$ go run ch02/linkedList.go
Original list:
5 -> 3 -> 8 -> 1 -> nil
After deleting 3:
5 -> 8 -> 1 -> nil
After sorting:
1 -> 5 -> 8 -> nil
```

The output illustrates the behavior of the linked list operations step by step. Initially, the list contains the elements `5 -> 3 -> 8 -> 1`, reflecting the insertion order. After deleting the value 3, the list is correctly updated to `5 -> 8 -> 1`, demonstrating how node removal adjusts the internal links without affecting the remaining elements. Finally, the sorted output `1 -> 5 -> 8 -> nil` confirms that the sorting logic successfully rearranges the nodes in ascending order while preserving the integrity of the list structure. By performing insertion, deletion, and sorting operations, we saw how dynamic data structures rely on explicit pointer management and careful link updates.

Summary

In this chapter, we explored four essential building blocks of Go programming: maps, structures, functions, and pointers. Pointers provide precise memory control and reference semantics. Maps give us a way to store and retrieve data using keys, enabling fast lookups and flexible data organization. Structures allow us to design custom types that group related fields together, making our programs more expressive and easier to manage. Functions provide the foundation for organizing logic, reusing code, and building abstractions that keep programs modular and maintainable. Pointers introduce reference semantics and fine-grained control over memory, allowing us to share data efficiently and modify values without unnecessary copying. Together, these concepts form a strong toolkit for writing clear, efficient, and well-structured Go applications.

It is now time to explore one of the most distinctive and powerful features of Go: concurrency. Go was designed from the ground up with modern, concurrent systems in mind, and its concurrency model – built around lightweight goroutines and channels – sets it apart from many other programming languages. In the next chapter, we will dive deep into how Go enables you to write programs that can perform multiple tasks at once, and how to communicate safely between them and scale efficiently across multi-core architectures.

Exercises

1. Create an empty map and use a loop to add elements to it one by one. After each new element, print the current length of the map using the `len()` function.

Additional resources

- Hash tables: `https://dl.acm.org/doi/10.5555/2830286.2830288`

3

Go Concurrency

Modern computing is not sequential – it pulses with **parallelism**, reacts in real time, and scales across cores and networks. To write programs that thrive in this environment, we must embrace concurrency not as an optimization but as a model of thought. Go offers us a powerful, pragmatic approach to concurrency – one that is rooted in the simplicity of goroutines and channels, yet expressive enough to model complex interactions with grace. Concurrency is one of the most powerful and distinctive features of Go, enabling developers to write efficient, scalable programs that can handle multiple tasks simultaneously. Unlike traditional threading models, which are often cumbersome and error-prone, Go embraces lightweight **goroutines** along with **channels** for safe communication between them. This approach simplifies concurrent programming while helping to avoid common pitfalls such as race conditions and deadlocks. In this chapter, we will explore goroutines, channels, synchronization primitives, and best practices for writing clean, performant concurrent code in Go. Concurrency in Go invites us to think like the mind thinks: to isolate responsibilities, communicate through clear channels, and trust that well-designed systems can manage many things at once without falling apart.

This chapter covers the following:

- Learning about goroutines
- Learning about channels
- Various uses of channels and goroutines
- The `select` statement
- Catching deadlocks and race conditions

Understanding these individual components is essential, but their true power lies in how they harmonize to build resilient, high-performance systems. To see this orchestration in action, it is time to begin exploring the building block that makes Go concurrency possible: goroutines. Goroutines are lightweight, independently executing functions that allow us to break down complex tasks into smaller, concurrent units of work that form the foundation of the Go concurrency model. We will begin by understanding the fundamentals of goroutines, then explore channels as the communication mechanism, before diving into practical patterns and common pitfalls.

Learning about goroutines

Everything in Go is executed as a goroutine, either transparently or intentionally. To create a new goroutine, we use the go keyword followed by a function call or an anonymous function – the two methods are equivalent. Each executable Go program has at least one goroutine, which is used for running the `main()` function of the `main` package. For a goroutine or a function to terminate the entire Go application, it should call `os.Exit()` instead of `return`. However, most of the time, we exit a goroutine or a function using `return` because what we really want is to exit that specific goroutine or function and not stop the entire application. Each goroutine is executed on a single OS thread according to the instructions of the **Go scheduler**, which is responsible for the execution of goroutines – the developer has no control over the amount of memory allocated to a goroutine.

The Go runtime scheduler, rather than the OS, manages the creation of threads. It does so by using a specific constraint, `GOMAXPROCS`, which defines the maximum number of logical processors available to execute user-level code simultaneously. While the runtime may spawn many more OS threads than this limit — particularly to handle goroutines blocked on system calls or I/O — it will only allow a number of threads equal to `GOMAXPROCS` to be actively running Go code at any one time. This ensures that the application maintains its intended level of CPU parallelism without being stalled by individual blocking operations.

As goroutines *cannot communicate with each other directly*, data sharing in Go is implemented using either channels or shared memory. However, in Go, there is no shared memory in the traditional way that is used in Java or C++ unless we are dealing with global variables. According to the Go philosophy, do not communicate by sharing memory; instead, share memory by communicating! Based on that, channels act as the glue that can connect multiple goroutines. However, channels serve as conduits for data — they can send data to goroutines, receive data from goroutines, or serve special purposes in coordination. While a goroutine is the unit of execution, the channel is the medium of synchronization. They do not process information themselves; instead, they act as the connective tissue that allows independent threads of execution to exchange state safely and predictably without the need for complex manual locking. Let us now learn how to create our own goroutines.

Creating goroutines

When you prefix a function or method call with the go keyword, Go schedules that call to run asynchronously as a goroutine. Under the hood, the runtime uses a work-stealing scheduler and a pool of system threads to multiplex thousands of goroutines efficiently.

Look at the following example code that illustrates goroutines. The program accepts a single command-line argument, which specifies the number of goroutines to create:

```
package main

import (
    "fmt"
    "os"
    "strconv"
    "time"
)

func worker(id int) {
    fmt.Printf("Worker %d starting\n", id)
    time.Sleep(time.Millisecond)
    fmt.Printf("Worker %d done\n", id)
}

func main() {
    if len(os.Args) < 2 {
        fmt.Println("Usage: go run main.go <number_of_goroutines>")
        return
    }

    n, err := strconv.Atoi(os.Args[1])
    if err != nil || n <= 0 {
        fmt.Println("Please provide the number of goroutines.")
        return
    }
    fmt.Printf("Starting %d goroutines...\n", n)
    // Launch goroutines without any synchronization.
    for i := 1; i <= n; i++ {
        go worker(i)
    }
```

```
    fmt.Println("Main function is exiting without waiting!")
}
```

> **Note**
>
> In Go, goroutines capture variables by reference, not by value. This means that when you launch a goroutine inside a `for` loop, the goroutine does not get its own copy of the loop variable – instead, it refers to the memory location used by the loop. As a result, by the time the goroutine executes, the loop may have advanced, and the variable value might have changed. This leads to unexpected and inconsistent results, such as all goroutines printing the same value. The common solution is variable shadowing: creating a new local variable inside the loop that holds the current iteration value. Before Go 1.22, this was the recommended approach. Starting with Go 1.22, however, the compiler automatically introduces a new variable for each loop iteration in `for ... range` loops, effectively resolving this issue.

Inside the program, a simple `worker()` function prints a message when it starts, simulates some quick work by sleeping for a short time, and then prints another message when it finishes. In `main()`, a `for` loop launches the specified number of goroutines using the go keyword. However, there is no mechanism to coordinate or wait for their completion. As a result, the `main()` function may exit before some or even all goroutines have finished running. When you execute the program, you might see partial output, or in some cases no output, depending on how quickly the program terminates compared to the execution speed of the goroutines. This behavior highlights why synchronization tools such as channels and the `sync.WaitGroup` type are essential in concurrent Go programs to ensure that all goroutines complete their work before the program ends. The output of the program is not deterministic. A possible output could be as follows:

```
$ go run ch03/goroutines.go 20
Starting 20 goroutines...
Worker 3 starting
Main function is exiting without waiting!
Worker 20 starting
Worker 1 starting
```

In this example, the program launches 20 goroutines but does not use any form of synchronization to wait for them to finish. When you run the go `run ch03/goroutines.go 20` command, the program prints `Starting 20 goroutines` and immediately begins creating goroutines. Each goroutine executes the `worker()` function, which prints a message when it starts. However, since the `main()` function does not wait for the goroutines to complete, it quickly reaches the end of its execution and prints `Main function is exiting without waiting!` before most of the workers have had a chance to run. In the sample output, only three workers – worker 3, worker 20, and worker 1 – managed to start before the program terminated, while the remaining 17 goroutines never got the opportunity to execute. So, remember that goroutines run independently, and that without any proper synchronization using tools such as channels or `sync.WaitGroup`, the `main()` function may exit before goroutines finish their work, resulting in incomplete or unpredictable output. The next subsection illustrates the use of `sync.WaitGroup` for **goroutine synchronization**.

Waiting for goroutines to finish their jobs

When working with multiple goroutines, it is often necessary to ensure that they complete their tasks before the main program continues or exits. Go provides several mechanisms for synchronizing goroutines, with `sync.WaitGroup` being the most common and efficient tool for this purpose. `WaitGroup` lets you track the number of active goroutines, wait until all of them finish, and avoid premature termination of your program. This example code (`ch03/syncGoroutines.go`) demonstrates the use of `sync.WaitGroup`:

```
package main

import (
    "fmt"
    "sync"
)

func main() {
    var wg sync.WaitGroup
    tasks := []string{"task1", "task2", "task3"}

    for _, t := range tasks {
        wg.Add(1) // Manually increment the counter
        go func(task string) {
            defer wg.Done() // Must remember to call Done()
            fmt.Println("Processing:", task)
        }(t)
    }

    wg.Wait()
```

```
    fmt.Println("All tasks completed!")
}
```

The program begins by creating a slice of tasks containing three strings: "task1", "task2", and "task3". A WaitGroup named wg is then declared to keep track of the goroutines. Inside the for loop, the program iterates over each task, calls wg.Add(1) to increment the counter for the new goroutine, and then launches a goroutine to process that task. Each goroutine takes the current task as an argument, prints a message indicating it is processing the task, and uses defer wg.Done() to ensure the counter is decremented once the goroutine finishes. After all the goroutines have been launched, the main() function calls wg.Wait(), which blocks until the counter returns to zero – meaning all goroutines have finished executing. Finally, when all tasks are complete, the program prints "All tasks completed!" to confirm that the work has finished.

In the previous program, we see the defer keyword, which we also saw in ch01/errorHandling.go. In Go, the defer keyword is used to postpone the execution of a function call until the surrounding function returns. Deferred calls are placed on a stack, meaning they are executed in **last-in, first-out (LIFO)** order. This feature is particularly useful for cleanup tasks, such as closing files, unlocking mutexes, or signaling the completion of a goroutine, because it guarantees that the deferred function will run no matter how the surrounding function exits – whether it ends normally, returns early, or even panics. For example, when working with goroutines and sync.WaitGroup, you often write defer wg.Done() at the beginning of the goroutine. This ensures that the Done() call will always be executed when the goroutine finishes, even if the code inside the goroutine has multiple return paths. By using defer, you make your code safer, cleaner, and easier to maintain, since it reduces the risk of forgetting to release resources or signal completion in all execution paths.

Lastly, remember that when using sync.WaitGroup, it is crucial that every call to wg.Add() has a matching call to wg.Done(). If the numbers do not agree, the program behavior will be incorrect and may even deadlock. For example, if you call wg.Add(5), which is a valid call, but only four goroutines call wg.Done(), the wg.Wait() in the main() goroutine will block forever because the counter never reaches zero. On the other hand, if you call wg.Done() more times than wg.Add(), the program will panic at runtime with the negative WaitGroup counter error, since the internal counter cannot go below zero. This makes it important to ensure that the Add() and Done() calls are balanced and carefully placed, typically by calling wg.Add(1) before launching each goroutine and deferring wg.Done() inside the goroutine itself. If you run the example code on your machine, the output will show that the three tasks were processed, but not in the order in which they were defined in the slice:

```
$ go run ch03/syncGoroutines.go
Processing: task2
Processing: task3
Processing: task1
All tasks completed!
```

This happens because each task is handled by a separate goroutine, and goroutines run concurrently. The Go scheduler decides when each goroutine executes, so their outputs may interleave or appear in a different sequence each time you run the program. Despite the unpredictable order of processing, `sync.WaitGroup` ensures that the `main()` function waits for all goroutines to complete before proceeding. That is why the final message, `"All tasks completed!"`, is always printed last, once every task has finished processing.

> **Note**
>
> The ease with which goroutines can be spawned often leads to their overuse, creating programs that are structurally complex and difficult to debug. A critical rule of thumb for deciding whether a task should be offloaded to a goroutine is the concept of **idempotency**. An operation is idempotent if it can be performed multiple times while yielding the same result, a property that inherently suggests the task is self-contained. By ensuring a goroutine is idempotent, you guarantee that it does not depend on shifting global variables or mutable references from an outer scope that could change during its execution. This discipline prevents the subtle inconsistencies that arise when concurrent tasks collide over shared state. Rather than using goroutines for every asynchronous need, treating idempotency as a prerequisite ensures that your concurrency is a tool for performance rather than a source of non-deterministic behavior.

While `sync.WaitGroup` has traditionally required you to call `Add()` before launching a goroutine and `Done()` inside the goroutine, Go 1.25 introduced a more convenient method called `WaitGroup.Go`. This method simplifies the process by combining the counter increment, goroutine launch, and deferred `Done()` call into a single step. Instead of managing these pieces manually, you can pass a function directly to `WaitGroup.Go`, and it takes care of the bookkeeping for you. This not only reduces boilerplate code but also lowers the risk of common mistakes, such as forgetting to call `Done()` or mismatching `Add()` and `Done()` calls. In the following subsection, we will explore how `WaitGroup.Go` works in practice and see how it can make concurrent code safer and easier to read.

WaitGroup.Go – new in Go 1.25

Starting with Go 1.25, the sync package introduces a new method called `WaitGroup.Go`, which simplifies launching goroutines while automatically managing the life cycle of the `WaitGroup`. Traditionally, you had to explicitly call `Add(1)` before starting a goroutine and ensure that `Done()` was called inside it, and forgetting either step could lead to deadlocks or subtle bugs. With `WaitGroup.Go`, you can pass a function directly, and the method handles both incrementing and decrementing the counter under the hood. Consider the following `main()` function that illustrates `WaitGroup.Go`:

```
func main() {
    var wg sync.WaitGroup
    tasks := []string{"task1", "task2", "task3"}

    for _, t := range tasks {
        wg.Go(func() {
            fmt.Println("Processing:", t)
        })
    }

    wg.Wait() // Wait for all goroutines to finish
    fmt.Println("All tasks completed!")
}
```

The two programs achieve the same goal – processing a list of tasks concurrently and waiting for all goroutines to finish – but they differ in how they use `sync.WaitGroup`. In the first version, the program must explicitly call `wg.Add(1)` before starting each goroutine and place a `defer wg.Done()` call inside the goroutine to ensure the counter is decremented when the task is complete. This approach works well but requires careful bookkeeping, as forgetting either call can cause deadlocks or runtime panics. In contrast, the second version takes advantage of the new `WaitGroup.Go` method, which automates this process. Instead of managing the counter manually, you simply pass the task function to `wg.Go()`, which increments the counter, launches the goroutine, and ensures `Done()` is called when the function exits. As a result, the second program is shorter, cleaner, and less error-prone, while still preserving the same concurrency behavior as the first. Execute `ch03/waitGroupGo.go` on your own machine to see its output.

Now that you understand how to create and manage goroutines, the next step is learning how these independent execution units can communicate and coordinate with each other. Running code concurrently is powerful, but without a safe way to share data, you risk introducing race conditions and inconsistent state. This is where *channels* come in. Channels provide a simple, built-in mechanism for passing data between goroutines safely and synchronizing their execution without relying on explicit locks or shared memory. By combining goroutines with channels, you can build highly concurrent, efficient, and maintainable programs in Go.

Learning about channels

In concurrent systems, coordination matters. Channels provide a built-in way for goroutines to exchange data safely by communicating directly, without relying on shared memory or explicit locking. A channel creates a synchronization point: a sender will block until a receiver is ready, and vice versa, enabling deterministic interaction between independently executing routines.

When working with channels in Go, it is important to understand how they behave once closed. If you *read from a closed channel*, the operation does not block; instead, it immediately returns the channel's zero value along with a Boolean indicator (`ok`) set to `false`, which you can use to detect that the channel has been closed. This makes it safe to keep receiving from a channel in a loop until it is closed. On the other hand, *if you write to a closed channel*, Go panics at runtime with the `"send on closed channel"` error. This behavior enforces the rule that channels should only be closed by the sender, and only when no further values will be sent. Misusing channel closure is a common source of bugs in concurrent programs, so it is essential to handle closure carefully.

In many real-world programs, a goroutine may need to *listen to multiple channels at once* or react differently depending on which channel is ready. This is where the `select` statement comes in. In the next section, we will dive into the `select` statement and see how it gives Go programs more flexibility and control in concurrent workflows.

Learning about the select statement

The `select` keyword matters because it allows a goroutine to listen to several channels at once. It works much like a `switch` statement but for communication; `select` waits for multiple channel operations and proceeds with whichever one becomes available first. A `select` block can have multiple cases and an optional default case, which mimics the `switch` statement. It is good for `select` blocks to have a timeout option just in case. Last, a `select` without any cases (`select{}`) waits forever.

> **Note**
>
> In practice, `select` allows a goroutine to wait on multiple communication operations. So, `select` gives you the power to listen to multiple channels using a single `select`

> block. Consequently, you can have nonblocking operations on channels if you have implemented your `select` blocks appropriately.

A `select` statement is *not evaluated sequentially,* as all its channels are examined simultaneously. If none of the channels in a `select` statement are ready, the `select` statement blocks (waits) until one of the channels is ready. If multiple channels of a `select` statement are ready, then the Go runtime makes a random selection from the set of these ready channels.

Handling multiple channels with select

Communication is what makes complexity manageable – both in minds and in programs. Just as our thoughts coordinate through signals, attention, and choice, Go programs synchronize through channels and `select` statements. While not strictly necessary for every concurrent operation, channels provide a safe, structured pathway for data and intent. They offer a high-level orchestration layer that allows independent goroutines to collaborate without needing to know the intimate details of each other's internal state. The `select` statement, in turn, resembles focused attention – it listens for multiple possible signals and reacts to the one that arrives first. In this section, we explore how to model concurrency not with brute force or locks, but with expressive, responsive design.

Look at the following example code (`ch03/select.go`) that illustrates `select`. The code creates two workers who work at random speeds and uses `select` to handle their responses as they arrive, regardless of order:

```
package main

import (
    "fmt"
    "math/rand"
    "time"
)

func worker(name string, ch chan<- string) {
    delay := time.Duration(rand.Intn(1000)) * time.Millisecond
    time.Sleep(delay)
    ch <- fmt.Sprintf("%s finished after %v", name, delay)
}

func main() {
    ch1 := make(chan string)
```

```
    ch2 := make(chan string)
    go worker("Worker 1", ch1)
    go worker("Worker 2", ch2)

    for i := 0; i < 2; i++ {
        select {
        case msg1 := <-ch1:
            fmt.Println("Received:", msg1)
        case msg2 := <-ch2:
            fmt.Println("Received:", msg2)
        }
    }
    fmt.Println("All workers reported back!")
}
```

The `select` statement is like having a receptionist who can answer multiple phone lines and takes whichever call comes in first. Each worker sleeps for a random duration between 0 and 1,000 milliseconds, then sends a completion message to their own dedicated channel. Worker 1 sends to `ch1` and Worker 2 sends to `ch2`, and since they are working with random delays, you never know which one will finish first. The `worker()` function uses a channel with a direction (`chan<- string`), which means *it can only send data, not receive it* – this is a safety feature that prevents accidental misuse that also supports channels that you can only read from (`read <-chan string`). The magic happens in the `main()` function's `select` statement inside the `for` loop. Instead of checking `ch1` first and then `ch2` (which would always prioritize Worker 1), the `select` statement *simultaneously listens to both channels* and immediately processes whichever message arrives first. If Worker 2 finishes before Worker 1, it will handle Worker 2's message first, and vice versa. The loop runs twice because we know that we are expecting exactly two messages, one from each worker.

When you run this program, the output will vary each time because the two workers sleep for random amounts of time before sending their results. For example, you might see `Received: Worker 2 finished after 327ms` followed by `Received: Worker 1 finished after 812ms`, but in another run, the order could be reversed. The key point is that `select` allows the program to handle whichever channel becomes ready first, rather than waiting on one channel at a time. Once both workers have reported back, the program prints `All workers reported back!` to confirm that all concurrent tasks are done. Try it on your own machine; the output will look as follows:

```
$ go run ch03/select.go
Received: Worker 2 finished after 53ms
Received: Worker 1 finished after 270ms
All workers reported back!
```

Now that we have seen how channels can work with the `select` statement, it is time to focus on their primary purpose: exchanging data among goroutines. Channels provide a safe and structured way for concurrent tasks to communicate without the need for explicit locks or shared variables. By sending and receiving values through channels, goroutines can coordinate their work, pass results, or signal completion in a straightforward manner.

Exchanging data with channels

Channels can be used for many purposes, one of them being the collection and exchange of data (remember that goroutines cannot communicate directly with each other). This is illustrated in `./ch03/sendReceive.go`, which demonstrates a classic concurrency pattern where two functions work together at the same time, like two friends passing notes through a mailbox:

```
package main

import (
    "fmt"
    "time"
)

func sender(ch chan int, count int) {
    for i := 1; i <= count; i++ {
        fmt.Printf("Sender: sending %d\n", i)
        ch <- i // Send data to the channel.
        time.Sleep(time.Millisecond * 300)
    }
    fmt.Println("Sender: closing channel")
    close(ch) // Signal that no more data will be sent.
}

// receiver reads numbers from the channel until it is closed.
func receiver(ch chan int, done chan bool) {
    for num := range ch { // Automatically stops when channel is closed.
```

```
        fmt.Printf("Receiver: received %d\n", num)
        time.Sleep(time.Millisecond * 500)
    }
    fmt.Println("Receiver: no more data, stopping")
    done <- true
}

func main() {
    ch := make(chan int)     // Unbuffered channel for exchanging data.
    done := make(chan bool) // Used to signal completion.

    // Start sender and receiver goroutines.
    go sender(ch, 5)
    go receiver(ch, done)

    // Wait for the receiver to finish.
    <-done
    fmt.Println("Main: all done!")
}
```

The program creates two **mailboxes** (channels): one called `ch` for passing numbers between functions, and another called `done` for signaling when everything is finished. The `sender()` function generates numbers 1 through 5, puts each one in the mailbox using `ch <- i`, and waits 300 milliseconds between each note. When it is done with all five numbers, the function closes the mailbox to signal that no more notes are coming. Meanwhile, the receiver function acts as if it is reading those notes, continuously checking the mailbox using `for num := range ch`, taking out each number as it arrives, and then spending 500 milliseconds processing each one. When the mailbox closes, it automatically stops checking and sends a completion signal through the done channel.

The `main()` function supervises this entire process by starting both goroutines at the same time using the go keyword, which creates goroutines that run concurrently. Then it waits for the completion signal by reading from the done channel with `<-done`. When you run this program, you will see the sender and receiver messages interleaved in the output, showing how they are working simultaneously at their own speeds. `sender()` quickly puts numbers in the channel, while `receiver()` takes them out more slowly, and the Go channel system automatically handles this coordination, just as a real mailbox handles the timing differences between when mail is delivered and when you check it. This pattern is fundamental in Go programming and appears everywhere: web servers processing requests, file readers feeding data to analyzers, or any situation where you need different parts of your program to work together concurrently at their own natural pace. Running the program produces the following kind of output:

```
$ go run ch03/sendReceive.go
Sender: sending 1
Receiver: received 1
Sender: sending 2
Receiver: received 2
Sender: sending 3
Receiver: received 3
Sender: sending 4
Receiver: received 4
Sender: sending 5
Receiver: received 5
Sender: closing channel
Receiver: no more data, stopping
Main: all done!
```

In our mailbox example, we used what is called an **unbuffered channel**. Imagine a mailbox that can only hold one note at a time, so that we must wait for someone to pick up each note before we can deliver the next one. This creates a direct handoff between the sender and receiver, ensuring they stay synchronized. But Go also offers **buffered channels**, which are like mailboxes with multiple slots capable of storing several notes at once, thereby allowing us to drop off multiple notes even when the receiver is not immediately available to read them. Understanding the difference between these two types of channels is crucial because it affects how your concurrent programs behave, when goroutines block or continue running, and how you design systems goroutines that work at different speeds.

Buffered and unbuffered channels

As you already know, Go provides buffered and unbuffered channels. Both unbuffered and buffered channels are created using the built-in `make()` function, but they differ in how you define their capacity and how they synchronize data exchange. An unbuffered channel is created by omitting the capacity argument, for example, `ch := make(chan int)`. Since it has no internal buffer, every send operation blocks until another goroutine receives the value, and every receive blocks until a value is sent. This enforces strict synchronization between the sender and the receiver, making unbuffered channels ideal when you need to coordinate actions tightly. In contrast, a buffered channel is created by providing a second argument to `make()`, which specifies its capacity, such as `ch := make(chan string, 3)`. In this case, the sender can place up to three values into the channel without waiting, and only when the buffer is full does a send operation block. Similarly, a receiver blocks only when the buffer is empty. Buffered channels are useful when you want to decouple senders and receivers, allowing data to flow asynchronously up to the defined capacity. The key distinction lies in how the capacity affects synchronization: unbuffered channels require both parties to be ready simultaneously, while buffered channels provide flexibility by allowing multiple values to be queued.

Look at the following code example (`ch03/bufUnbuf.go`) that demonstrates buffered and unbuffered channels inside `main()`:

```
package main

import (
	"fmt"
	"time"
)

// sendNumbers sends a sequence of numbers to the provided channel.
func sendNumbers(ch chan int, count int) {
	for i := 1; i <= count; i++ {
		fmt.Printf("Sending %d...\n", i)
		ch <- i
		fmt.Printf("Sent %d!\n", i)
		time.Sleep(time.Millisecond * 200)
	}
	fmt.Println("Closing channel")
	close(ch)
}

// receiveNumbers reads numbers from the channel until it is closed.
func receiveNumbers(ch chan int) {
	for num := range ch {
		fmt.Printf("Received %d\n", num)
		time.Sleep(time.Millisecond * 400)
	}
	fmt.Println("Receiver done")
}

func main() {
	fmt.Println("=== Unbuffered Channel Example ===")
	unbuffered := make(chan int)
	go sendNumbers(unbuffered, 3)
```

```
    receiveNumbers(unbuffered) // Blocks until all values are consumed.

    fmt.Println("\n=== Buffered Channel Example ===")
    buffered := make(chan int, 3) // Capacity of 3

    go func() {
        sendNumbers(buffered, 5)
    }()
    receiveNumbers(buffered)
}
```

The code starts by defining the `sendNumbers()` function, which sends a sequence of numbers to a channel. Inside the function, a `for` loop iterates from `1` up to a given count. For each value, it prints a message indicating that it is sending the number, writes the number to the channel using `ch <- i`, and prints a confirmation message when the value is sent. A short sleep of 200 milliseconds simulates processing time, which is a common technique. After all values are sent, the function prints a closing message and calls `close(ch)` to signal the receiver that no more data will arrive. Next, we define the `receiveNumbers()` function, which continuously reads values from the channel until it is closed. This function uses a `for ... range` loop to iterate over the channel, printing each received value and sleeping for 400 milliseconds to simulate slower processing. When the channel is closed, the loop exits, and a final message confirms that the receiver has finished.

In the `main()` function, we first demonstrate an unbuffered channel by creating one with `unbuffered := make(chan int)`. We launch a goroutine that calls `sendNumbers(unbuffered, 3)`, and then call `receiveNumbers(unbuffered)` in the `main()` goroutine. Because the channel is unbuffered, the sender must wait for the receiver to read each value before sending the next one, enforcing strict synchronization between them. After that, we demonstrate a buffered channel by creating one with `buffered := make(chan int, 3)`, giving it a capacity of 3. This time, we launch an anonymous goroutine that calls `sendNumbers(buffered, 5)`, and again, we call `receiveNumbers(buffered)` in `main()`. Unlike the unbuffered example, the sender can place up to three values into the channel without blocking. Once the buffer is full, any further sends will block until the receiver consumes a value, allowing bursts of data to flow more smoothly.

Execute `ch03/bufUnbuf.go` on your own machine:

```
$ go run ch03/bufUnbuf.go
=== Unbuffered Channel Example ===
Sending 1...
Sent 1!
```

```
Received 1
Sending 2...
Received 2
Sent 2!
Sending 3...
Received 3
Sent 3!
Closing channel
Receiver done

=== Buffered Channel Example ===
Sending 1...
Sent 1!
Received 1
Sending 2...
Sent 2!
Received 2
Sending 3...
Sent 3!
Sending 4...
Sent 4!
Received 3
Sending 5...
Sent 5!
Closing channel
Received 4
Received 5
Receiver done
```

This output beautifully illustrates the fundamental difference between unbuffered and buffered channels by showing how they handle the timing of sending and receiving data. In the unbuffered channel example, notice the strict alternating pattern: `'Sending 1... Sent 1! Received 1'` shows that the sender must wait for the receiver to actually pick up each value before it can continue. It is like handing someone a note directly – you cannot let go of the note until they grab it from your hand. The sender blocks (waits) on each send operation until the receiver is ready, creating a synchronized handshake where both sides must be ready at the same time.

The buffered channel example tells a completely different story. Here, you can see the sender racing ahead; `'Sending 1... Sent 1! Received 1 Sending 2... Sent 2! Received 2`

`Sending 3... Sent 3! Sending 4... Sent 4! Received 3'` shows the sender successfully dropping off multiple values (1, 2, 3, 4) before the receiver has even processed the third one. The sender only blocks when the buffer fills up, which happens when it tries to send the fifth value while the buffer (which appears to hold 3-4 items) is full. The key insight is that buffered channels decouple the timing between producers and consumers, allowing them to work at different speeds and providing a cushion for temporary mismatches in processing rates, while unbuffered channels create tight synchronization where both parties must be ready simultaneously.

While channels are handy, they do not resolve the risk of a consumer or producer becoming indefinitely stalled by a slow dependency. To prevent a single delayed operation from hanging a goroutine and leaking resources, we must introduce a temporal dimension to our communication using timeouts.

Timing out goroutines with channels

In a production environment, an indefinite wait is indistinguishable from a failure. There are times when a goroutine may take longer than expected to complete its work, whether due to heavy computation, slow I/O, or waiting indefinitely on a resource. Timeouts are the fundamental mechanism for ensuring system resilience, preventing a single sluggish dependency from cascading into a resource exhaustion event where every worker goroutine is trapped waiting for a response that may never arrive.

To keep your program responsive and prevent it from hanging, Go provides mechanisms for applying timeouts to goroutines. By combining channels with the `time.After()` function, you can enforce deadlines and ensure that a goroutine's work is either completed within a given timeframe or safely abandoned.

Consider the following example code when implementing the timing out of goroutines. This is a program that demonstrates how to use the `select` statement with `time.After()` to implement timeouts when working with goroutines:

```
package main

import (
    "fmt"
    "time"
)

// Simulates a long-running task (5 seconds).
func longTask(done chan<- string) {
    time.Sleep(5 * time.Second)
```

```
    done <- "Long task finished"
}

// Simulates a short-running task (1 second).
func shortTask(done chan<- string) {
    time.Sleep(1 * time.Second)
    done <- "Short task finished"
}

func main() {
    longDone := make(chan string)
    shortDone := make(chan string)
    go longTask(longDone)
    go shortTask(shortDone)
    // Handle the short task with a 2-second timeout.
    select {
    case result := <-shortDone:
        fmt.Println("Short:", result)
    case <-time.After(2 * time.Second):
    fmt.Println("Short: Timeout! Took too long.")
    }

    // Handle the long task with a 2-second timeout.
    select {
    case result := <-longDone:
        fmt.Println("Long:", result)
    case <-time.After(2 * time.Second):
        fmt.Println("Long: Timeout! Took too long.")
    }
}
```

It defines two tasks: `longTask()`, which simulates a time-consuming operation by sleeping for five seconds, and `shortTask()`, which sleeps for only one second. Both functions send a message to their respective channels once they finish. In `main()`, two channels are created, and both tasks are launched concurrently as goroutines. The program then waits for the result of the short task using a `select` block, but it also sets a two-second timeout using `time.After()`. Since the short task completes in one second, its result is printed before the timeout triggers. The program then repeats the process for the long task, which takes five seconds to complete. However, because the timeout is only two seconds, the `time.After()` case is selected, and the program reports that the long task took too long. Execute `ch03/timeOut.go` on your machine to get the following output:

```
$ go run ch03/timeOut.go
Short: Short task finished
Long: Timeout! Took too long.
```

The output confirms how the timeouts influence the execution of the two concurrent tasks. Because of this, the `time.After()` branch of the `select` statement is triggered, and the program prints `Long: Timeout! Took too long.` instead of waiting for the actual task result. This behavior demonstrates how timeouts allow you to gracefully handle slow or stuck goroutines without blocking the rest of the program.

Now that you have seen how goroutines can run tasks independently and how timeouts prevent them from blocking progress, the next step is to explore how these tasks can communicate and coordinate their work. So, in the following subsection, we will focus on **worker pools**.

Implementing worker pools

In concurrent programming, a worker pool is a common pattern used to manage and distribute workloads efficiently across multiple goroutines. Instead of creating a new goroutine for every task, which can quickly become resource-intensive, a worker pool uses a fixed number of goroutines (the "workers") to process a stream of jobs from a shared channel. The main program sends tasks into the channel, and each worker retrieves and processes them concurrently. This approach limits the number of active goroutines, reduces scheduling overhead, and provides better control over resource usage. In Go, worker pools are typically implemented using channels for task distribution and synchronization, making worker pools a powerful and idiomatic way to handle large volumes of work while maintaining efficiency and scalability.

Consider the following example code (`ch03/workerPool.go`) for worker pools, the first part of which sets up the foundational types for implementing a worker pool:

```
package main

import (
    "fmt"
    "os"
    "strconv"
    "sync"
    "time"
)
```

```go
// Job represents a unit of work.
type Job struct {
    ID int
}

// Result represents the outcome of processing a job.
type Result struct {
    JobID  int
    Output string
}
```

Two simple structures define the workflow: `Job`, which represents a unit of work identified by an integer ID, and `Result`, which represents the outcome of processing a job. Each `Result` stores the `JobID` value it corresponds to and a string describing the output of that job. These types provide a clean way to separate input tasks from their processed results, making it easier to build a system where multiple workers can handle jobs concurrently and report their results back in a structured manner.

Next, we implement the functionality of each worker as a function:

```go
func worker(id int, jobs <-chan Job, results chan<- Result) {
    for job := range jobs {
        // Simulate some work.
        fmt.Printf("Worker %d processing job %d\n", id, job.ID)
        time.Sleep(time.Millisecond * 500)

        // Send the result back.
        results <- Result{
            JobID:  job.ID,
            Output: fmt.Sprintf("Job %d - worker %d", job.ID, id),
        }
    }

    fmt.Printf("Worker %d exiting\n", id)
}
```

The `worker()` function defines how individual workers in the pool process incoming jobs and report results. Each worker is assigned an ID to distinguish its activity in the output. The function continuously listens on the `jobs` channel, receiving tasks until the channel is closed. For every job, it simulates work by printing a message and pausing for half a second using `time.Sleep()`.

Once the simulated work is complete, the worker constructs a `Result` containing the job ID and a string noting which worker processed it, and then sends this result back on the `results` channel. When there are no more jobs to process, the `for ... range` loop exits, and the worker prints a final message indicating that it is shutting down. This design allows multiple workers to operate concurrently, each taking jobs as they become available and returning their results in a structured way.

The `main()` function ties the worker pool together, handling the input, setup, and coordination of jobs and workers:

```
func main() {
    if len(os.Args) < 3 {
        fmt.Println("Usage: ./<exe> <num_workers> <num_jobs>")
        os.Exit(1)
    }
    numWorkers, err := strconv.Atoi(os.Args[1])
    if err != nil || numWorkers <= 0 {
        fmt.Println("Please provide a positive integer for the number of
workers.")
        os.Exit(1)
    }

    numJobs, err := strconv.Atoi(os.Args[2])
    if err != nil || numJobs <= 0 {
        fmt.Println("Provide a positive integer for number of jobs.")
        os.Exit(1)
    }

    jobs := make(chan Job, numJobs)
    results := make(chan Result, numJobs)
    var wg sync.WaitGroup

    fmt.Printf("%d workers for %d jobs...\n", numWorkers, numJobs)
    for w := 1; w <= numWorkers; w++ {
        workerID := w
        wg.Go(func() {
            worker(workerID, jobs, results)
        })
    }
    // Send jobs to the workers in a separate goroutine.
```

```
    wg.Go(func() {
        for j := 1; j <= numJobs; j++ {
            jobs <- Job{ID: j}
        }
        close(jobs)
    })

    // Wait for all workers and close results channel when done.
    go func() {
        wg.Wait()
        close(results)
    }()

    for result := range results {
        fmt.Println("Result:", result.Output)
    }
    fmt.Println("All jobs processed!")
}
```

`main()` begins by checking the command-line arguments to ensure that the user provides both the number of workers and the number of jobs; if not, the program prints usage instructions and exits. It then parses these values, validating that both are positive integers. Next, two buffered channels are created: one for `jobs`, sized to hold all incoming tasks, and one for `results`, sized to hold all processed outputs. `sync.WaitGroup` is declared to track active goroutines. The program then launches the specified number of workers using `WaitGroup.Go`, passing each a unique ID along with the `jobs` and `results` channels. Another goroutine is responsible for feeding jobs into the `jobs` channel and closing it when all tasks have been sent. Meanwhile, a separate goroutine waits for all workers to finish, then closes the `results` channel to signal that no further outputs will arrive. Finally, the `main()` goroutine iterates over the `results` channel, printing each result as it becomes available. Once all results are consumed, it prints a confirmation message, `"All jobs processed!"`, indicating the successful completion of the worker pool workload.

Run `ch03/workerPool.go` on your machine:

```
$ go run ch03/workerPool.go 2 5
2 workers for 5 jobs...
Worker 2 processing job 2
Worker 1 processing job 1
Worker 1 processing job 3
Worker 2 processing job 4
```

```
Result: Job 1 - worker 1
Result: Job 2 - worker 2
Worker 2 processing job 5
Worker 1 exiting
Result: Job 4 - worker 2
Result: Job 3 - worker 1
Worker 2 exiting
Result: Job 5 - worker 2
All jobs processed!
```

This example illustrates a pool of two workers processing a sequence of five jobs through a shared input channel. The logic relies on multiple goroutines competing for work; as soon as a worker completes a task, it immediately attempts to retrieve the next available job from the queue. Because these workers operate independently, the order of the output reflects the timing of task completion rather than the sequence of assignment. This asynchronous behavior means the results for job 4 may appear before those of job 3, effectively decoupling task submission from task completion. Once the shared channel is exhausted and all results have been collected by the main goroutine, the workers terminate gracefully, and the program confirms the finalization of the batch.

> **Note**
>
> The decision to use a worker pool versus simply spawning goroutines hinges on the nature of the task's resource consumption. You should opt for a worker pool when dealing with heavy resource constraints — such as high memory usage in image processing or strict rate limits on external APIs — as this allows you to set a deliberate cap on concurrent execution. Conversely, for lightweight or CPU-bound tasks where complexity outweighs the need for throttling, the spawn-away approach keeps your code simple.

Having seen how worker pools can efficiently distribute tasks across multiple goroutines, we now turn to another important aspect of concurrency: coordination. While worker pools focus on dividing and processing work, sometimes goroutines need a simple way to signal events such as completion, shutdown, or cancellation. This is where signal channels come into play. Instead of carrying data, these channels are often used purely for synchronization, letting one part of the program notify others that something has happened. In the next subsection, we will explore how signal channels can help orchestrate goroutines and ensure clean, predictable program behavior.

Signal channels

Channels in Go are mostly introduced as a way to synchronize goroutines or to pass data safely between them, but their usefulness goes far beyond these basic patterns. Once you become comfortable with their semantics, you can apply channels to implement powerful constructs such as signaling mechanisms, task distribution pipelines, rate limiting, resource pools, and graceful shutdown sequences. In this subsection, we explore how to use channels for signaling.

Consider the following program (`ch03/signalChannels.go`) that shows signal channels:

```
package main

import (
	"fmt"
	"time"
)

func worker(done chan struct{}) {
	fmt.Println("Worker: starting work")
	time.Sleep(2 * time.Second)
	fmt.Println("Worker: done with work")
	// Signal completion by sending an empty struct
	done <- struct{}{}
}

func main() {
	// Channel used only for signaling
	done := make(chan struct{})
	go worker(done)
	// Wait for the signal before exiting
	<-done
	fmt.Println("Main: received signal, exiting")
}
```

The `worker()` function begins by printing a message, simulating two seconds of work with `time.Sleep()`, and then signaling that it has finished by sending an empty struct (`struct{}{}`) into the done channel. Using an empty struct is a common Go idiom for signaling, since it carries no data and requires no extra memory. In the `main()` function, the done channel is created and passed to the worker goroutine. The main goroutine then blocks on `<-done`, waiting until the worker sends its signal. Once the signal is received, `main()` prints a confirmation message and exits. This design ensures that the main program does not terminate before the worker completes its task, demonstrating how channels can be used for synchronization without transferring actual data.

Execute `ch03/signalChannels.go` on your machine to get the following output:

```
$ go run ch03/signalChannels.go
Worker: starting work
Worker: done with work
Main: received signal, exiting
```

The output confirms the sequence of events and shows how the signal channel synchronizes the goroutines. First, the worker goroutine begins its task and prints `'Worker: starting work'`, then it pauses for two seconds to simulate doing some work. After the pause, the worker prints `'Worker: done with work'` and sends a signal into the done channel. At this point, the main goroutine, which has been blocked waiting on `<-done`, is unblocked. It then prints `'Main: received signal, exiting'` before the program terminates. The next subsection combines signal channels with goroutines to create **monitor goroutines**.

Monitor goroutines

While worker pools provide the engine for high-throughput processing, they inevitably create a coordination problem: as multiple workers finish their tasks, they often need to update a shared counter, a cache, or a database. A monitor goroutine is a useful design pattern in Go, where a single goroutine is dedicated to managing access to shared state, ensuring that no two goroutines can modify it at the same time. Instead of protecting the shared resource with explicit locks such as `sync.Mutex`, the monitor goroutine takes ownership of the state and interacts with other goroutines exclusively through channels. This means all requests to read or update the state are sent as messages, and the monitor goroutine processes them one at a time. By centralizing control, this pattern avoids race conditions, simplifies reasoning about the program, and often reduces the need for complex synchronization mechanisms. It is a powerful example of the concurrency philosophy of Go: *do not communicate by sharing memory; share memory by communicating*. Consider the following example code (`ch03/monitor.go`) when working with monitor goroutines:

```
package main

import (
    "fmt"
    "sync"
    "time"
```

```
)

type Request struct {
    Increment int
    Reply     chan int
}

func counterMonitor(requests <-chan Request) {
    count := 0
    for req := range requests {
        count += req.Increment
        req.Reply <- count
    }
    fmt.Println("Monitor exiting")
}

func main() {
    requests := make(chan Request)
    var wg sync.WaitGroup
    numWorkers := 3
    numIncrements := 2

    // Start worker goroutines
    for i := 0; i < numWorkers; i++ {
        wg.Go(func() {
            reply := make(chan int)
            for j := 0; j < numIncrements; j++ {
                requests <- Request{Increment: 1, Reply: reply}
                fmt.Printf("Worker %d sees counter = %d\n", i, <-reply)
                time.Sleep(time.Millisecond * 200)
            }
        })
    }

    // Start monitor goroutine separately
    monitorDone := make(chan struct{})
    go func() {
        counterMonitor(requests)
        close(monitorDone) // signal monitor has exited
    }()
```

```
    wg.Wait()         // Wait for all workers to finish
    close(requests) // Now it is safe to close requests
    <-monitorDone     // Wait for monitor to exit
    fmt.Println("All workers and monitor finished.")
}
```

The `Request` struct represents messages sent to the monitor, carrying both an `Increment` value and a `Reply` channel so that the monitor can return the updated counter. The `counterMonitor()` function owns the counter state and processes incoming requests sequentially, updating the counter and sending the new value back through the reply channel. In `main()`, several worker goroutines are started using `sync.WaitGroup`. Each worker creates a private reply channel, sends increment requests to the monitor goroutine, and prints the counter values it receives. The monitor runs in its own goroutine, ensuring safe updates without requiring a mutex. After all workers finish, the `requests` channel is closed, signaling the monitor to exit cleanly. A `monitorDone` channel is used to notify `main()` that the monitor has shut down. This design avoids race conditions by centralizing state management in a single goroutine while allowing workers to run concurrently. Run `ch03/monitor.go` on your machine:

```
$ go run ch03/monitor.go
Worker 0 sees counter = 1
Worker 1 sees counter = 2
Worker 2 sees counter = 3
Worker 2 sees counter = 4
Worker 0 sees counter = 6
Worker 1 sees counter = 5
Monitor exiting
All workers and monitor finished.
```

The output shows how the monitor goroutine controls access to the shared counter and how concurrency affects the order of events. Each worker sends increment requests to the monitor, which processes them sequentially. That is why the counter increases consistently: first 1, then 2, then 3, and so on. However, the order in which workers receive and print these updates is not deterministic, since multiple workers run concurrently and compete to send requests. For example, worker 2 prints the fourth increment before worker 1 prints the fifth, and worker 0 reports the sixth before worker 1's fifth value appears. Despite this interleaving, the counter itself never skips or duplicates values because only the monitor goroutine modifies it. Finally, `main()` reports that all workers and the monitor have finished, showing that both the work and state management completed without deadlocks or race conditions.

Up to this point, we have focused on building concurrent programs that coordinate work through goroutines, channels, and worker pools. While these patterns unlock powerful ways to structure parallel tasks, they also introduce risks if not managed carefully. Two of the most common pitfalls in concurrency are **deadlocks** and **race conditions**. Both can cause subtle bugs that are hard to reproduce and debug. In the next section, we will explore how these issues arise, examine code examples that demonstrate them, and learn how to detect and prevent them in Go.

Catching deadlocks and race conditions

Deadlocks (goroutines waiting forever on each other) and race conditions (multiple goroutines accessing shared data in unpredictable ways) are among the most challenging concurrency bugs in Go programs, because they often appear only under specific timing or workload conditions. A deadlock occurs when goroutines wait on each other in a cycle, preventing the program from making progress, while a race condition arises when multiple goroutines access shared memory without proper synchronization, leading to unpredictable results. In this section, we will learn how to detect these issues early, using the built-in race detector of Go and runtime deadlock checks, as well as how to design our programs to minimize the risk of encountering them in the first place.

The good thing is that the Go toolchain provides built-in support for detecting common concurrency issues such as race conditions and deadlocks, helping developers write safer programs. The Go race detector is a powerful tool built into the Go toolchain that helps developers identify race conditions in their programs. By running a program with the `-race` flag, the race detector instruments the binary and monitors all memory accesses during execution. If it finds conflicting accesses – where multiple goroutines read and write the same variable without proper synchronization – it reports detailed information, including stack traces and the locations of the conflicting operations. While the race detector adds runtime overhead and increases memory usage, it is invaluable during development and testing because it can expose subtle, hard-to-reproduce bugs that would otherwise go unnoticed until they cause unpredictable behavior in production. To catch race conditions, you can use the `-race` flag when running or building a program. This enables the race detector, which monitors memory accesses at runtime and reports any situation where multiple goroutines access the same variable concurrently and at least one of the accesses is a write. For deadlocks, the Go runtime automatically detects when all goroutines are blocked and no further progress is possible, such as when two goroutines are each waiting to send or receive on channels with no corresponding receivers or senders. In such cases, the runtime automatically panics and prints a stack trace showing which goroutines are stuck. Let us begin by working with race conditions.

Race conditions

The following small program (`ch03/raceF1.go`) demonstrates a classic race condition. Examine the code and try to understand where the problem is:

```
package main

import (
	"fmt"
	"sync"
)

var counter int

func main() {
	fmt.Println("=== Demonstrating a Race Condition ===")
	counter = 0
	var wg sync.WaitGroup

	for i := 0; i < 5; i++ {
		wg.Add(1)
		go func(id int) {
			defer wg.Done()
			for j := 0; j < 1000; j++ {
				// Multiple goroutines update counter
						// at the same time.
				counter++
			}
		}(i)
	}
	wg.Wait()
	fmt.Println("Final counter value (expected 5000):", counter)
}
```

First, a shared `counter` variable is declared. Then, `main()` launches five goroutines, each tasked with incrementing `counter` 1,000 times. Ideally, with 5 × 1,000 increments, the final value of `counter` should be 5,000. However, because multiple goroutines are updating the same variable at the same time without synchronization, the increments often overlap, and some updates are lost. `sync.WaitGroup` ensures that the `main()` function waits for all goroutines to finish before printing the result, but it does not prevent the race itself.

Execute `ch03/raceF1.go` on your machine to see the issue:

```
$ go run ch03/raceF1.go
=== Demonstrating a Race Condition ===
Final counter value (expected 5000): 3282
```

The program typically prints a value less than 5,000, as it happens in the previous output, clearly illustrating the dangers of unsynchronized access to shared memory in concurrent programs. This example highlights why race conditions occur and why proper synchronization techniques, such as **mutexes** or **atomic operations**, are necessary when multiple goroutines work on shared data. Use the `-race` flag to examine `ch03/raceF1.go` for potential race conditions:

```
$ go run -race ch03/raceF1.go
=== Demonstrating a Race Condition ===
==================
WARNING: DATA RACE
Read at 0x000104f2b0d0 by goroutine 8:
  main.main.func1()
      ~/go/src/github.com/mactsouk/goSP2/ch03/raceF1.go:21 +0x88
  main.main.gowrap1()
      ~/go/src/github.com/mactsouk/goSP2/ch03/raceF1.go:23 +0x40

Previous write at 0x000104f2b0d0 by goroutine 9:
  main.main.func1()
      ~/go/src/github.com/mactsouk/goSP2/ch03/raceF1.go:21 +0xa0
  main.main.gowrap1()
      ~/go/src/github.com/mactsouk/goSP2/ch03/raceF1.go:23 +0x40

Goroutine 8 (running) created at:
  main.main()
      ~/go/src/github.com/mactsouk/goSP2/ch03/raceF1.go:17 +0xc8

Goroutine 9 (finished) created at:
  main.main()
      ~/go/src/github.com/mactsouk/goSP2/ch03/raceF1.go:17 +0xc8
==================
==================
WARNING: DATA RACE
Write at 0x000104f2b0d0 by goroutine 10:
  main.main.func1()
      ~/go/src/github.com/mactsouk/goSP2/ch03/raceF1.go:21 +0xa0
```

```
  main.main.gowrap1()
      ~/go/src/github.com/mactsouk/goSP2/ch03/raceF1.go:23 +0x40

Previous write at 0x000104f2b0d0 by goroutine 8:
  main.main.func1()
      ~/go/src/github.com/mactsouk/goSP2/ch03/raceF1.go:21 +0xa0
  main.main.gowrap1()
      ~/go/src/github.com/mactsouk/goSP2/ch03/raceF1.go:23 +0x40

Goroutine 10 (running) created at:
  main.main()
      ~/go/src/github.com/mactsouk/goSP2/ch03/raceF1.go:17 +0xc8

Goroutine 8 (running) created at:
  main.main()
      ~/go/src/github.com/mactsouk/goSP2/ch03/raceF1.go:17 +0xc8
==================
Final counter value (expected 5000): 4000
Found 2 data race(s)
exit status 66
```

The output demonstrates how the Go race detector identifies and reports unsafe concurrent access to shared memory. The program begins by printing `=== Demonstrating a Race Condition ===`, and as multiple goroutines increment a shared counter, the race detector intervenes with detailed warnings. Each `WARNING: DATA RACE` message points to a memory address being accessed by more than one goroutine at the same time. The log shows exactly where in the source code the race occurred – in this case, line 21 of `raceF1.go`, where `counter` is incremented. The messages distinguish between reads and writes and list the goroutines involved, making it clear that two or more goroutines are modifying the counter concurrently without synchronization. At the end, the program prints `Final counter value (expected 5000): 4000`, which highlights the effect of the race condition: the result is lower than expected because some increments were lost due to overlapping updates. The final line confirms that the race detector caught multiple instances of unsafe access.

The fixed version of the program (`ch03/raceF1mutex.go`) is the following:

```
package main

import (
    "fmt"
```

```
    "sync"
)

var counter int
var mu sync.Mutex

func main() {
    fmt.Println("=== Fixed Race Condition ===")
    counter = 0
    var wg sync.WaitGroup

    for i := 0; i < 5; i++ {
        wg.Add(1)
        go func(id int) {
            defer wg.Done()
            for j := 0; j < 1000; j++ {
                mu.Lock()
                counter++ // Protect access with a mutex.
                mu.Unlock()
            }
        }(i)
    }

    wg.Wait()
    fmt.Println("Final counter value (expected 5000):", counter)
}
```

Just like in the previous example, five goroutines are launched, each incrementing a shared counter 1,000 times, so the expected final value is 5,000. However, instead of directly incrementing `counter`, which previously led to race conditions, the program now protects access with a `sync.Mutex()`. A **mutex**, short for **mutual exclusion**, ensures that only one goroutine at a time can execute a critical section of code. In this case, every increment operation is wrapped between `mu.Lock()` and `mu.Unlock()`. When a goroutine calls `Lock()`, it acquires ownership of the mutex, preventing other goroutines from entering the critical section until it calls `Unlock()`. This guarantees that increments to `counter` happen in sequence, without overlapping, thereby preserving correctness. Once all goroutines finish, the final counter value reliably matches the expected 5,000, showing how mutexes are a straightforward and effective solution for synchronizing shared memory in Go.

In addition to the standard `sync.Mutex`, Go provides `sync.RWMutex`, which is designed for scenarios where multiple goroutines frequently read shared data but only occasionally write to it. `RWMutex` allows multiple readers to hold the lock simultaneously, if no goroutine is writing. When a goroutine needs to modify the shared data, it must acquire a write lock, which is exclusive, blocking both other writers and readers until the write is complete. This makes `RWMutex` especially useful when reads are far more common than writes, since it reduces contention and improves performance by letting many readers work in parallel. However, if writes are frequent, the advantage of `RWMutex` over a regular `Mutex` diminishes, because writers must still wait until all readers have released their locks.

When a goroutine acquires a lock with `mu.Lock()` or `rwmu.Lock()` but fails to call the corresponding `Unlock()`, the *lock remains held indefinitely*. This effectively blocks all other goroutines that attempt to acquire the same lock, leading to a deadlock. Deadlocks are tricky because the program does not crash immediately, but simply stops making progress, appearing to *hang*. For example, if one goroutine locks a shared resource and forgets to unlock it, all other goroutines trying to access that resource will wait forever. This is why it is a best practice in Go to pair `Lock()` calls with `Unlock()` using `defer`, which ensures that the lock is released even if the function returns early due to an error or other logic. By consistently using `defer mu.Unlock()`, you significantly reduce the risk of forgetting to unlock and introducing subtle deadlocks into your program.

However, this approach is most effective when the function holding the lock is relatively short. The reason is that `defer` statements are executed only *when the surrounding function returns*, meaning the lock is held for the entire duration of the function. If the function performs a large amount of work or has complex logic, keeping the lock held until the very end can unnecessarily block other goroutines that need access to the same resource. In such cases, it is better to manually call `Unlock()` as soon as the protected section of code is complete, allowing other goroutines to proceed sooner. This trade-off highlights the importance of balancing safety and performance when working with `defer` in synchronization.

Having explored how goroutines, channels, and synchronization primitives such as mutexes help us manage concurrency safely, we can now move to a more practical example: **matrix multiplication**. The next section presents a case where proper program design can often prevent deadlocks and race conditions without relying solely on locks or complex synchronization. So, when possible, carefully structuring how goroutines access shared data and communicate ensures that no two goroutines block each other indefinitely and that shared state is updated safely.

Concurrent matrix multiplication in Go

Matrix multiplication is a fundamental operation that appears in many areas of computing, science, and engineering. In computer graphics, it is used to apply transformations such as rotation, scaling, and translation to 3D models. In scientific computing and simulations, matrices model complex systems such as physical interactions, electrical circuits, and fluid dynamics. Machine learning and data science rely heavily on matrix multiplication for operations such as computing weighted sums in neural networks, covariance matrices, and linear regression solutions. It also appears in cryptography, signal processing, and graph algorithms, where adjacency matrices and transition matrices are multiplied to analyze networks and compute probabilities. Because it is so widely used, optimizing matrix multiplication can significantly improve the performance of applications in these domains. The Go concurrency model makes it easy to divide the work across multiple goroutines, allowing different elements of the result matrix to be computed in parallel. In this section, we explore how to implement matrix multiplication using goroutines, showing how careful structuring of concurrent operations can prevent race conditions while dramatically improving performance. Put simply, proper program design can help you solve many problems, so think carefully before getting help from mutexes, channels, or `select` blocks. Here is example code (`ch03/matrix.go`) that implements matrix multiplication. As expected, the program begins with an `import` block that brings in several standard library packages before defining the `randomMatrix()` function:

```
package main

import (
    "fmt"
    "math/rand"
    "os"
    "strconv"
    "sync"
)

func randomMatrix(rows, cols int) [][]int {
    mat := make([][]int, rows)
    for i := range mat {
        mat[i] = make([]int, cols)
        for j := range mat[i] {
                // Random value: -1, 0, or 1
            mat[i][j] = rand.Intn(3) - 1
        }
    }
```

```
    return mat
}
```

`randomMatrix()` constructs a two-dimensional integer slice with a given number of rows and columns. For each row, it allocates a slice of integers representing the columns, then assigns each element a random value of either -1, 0, or 1. This is achieved by calling `rand.Intn(3)` to generate a random integer between 0 and 2 and then subtracting 1 to shift the range into negative and positive values. The function returns the completed matrix, which can later be used in computations such as matrix multiplication or testing concurrent operations.

Functions such as `randomMatrix()` are particularly useful in programming because they generate test data automatically, saving time and effort when building or experimenting with algorithms. For example, if you are implementing matrix multiplication, graph algorithms, or statistical computations, you need sample matrices to verify that your code works correctly. Instead of manually creating large datasets, a helper function such as this can quickly provide matrices of any size with varied values. Using random values also introduces unpredictability, which is valuable in testing and simulation. It helps uncover edge cases and behaviors that might not appear with fixed, hand-crafted data. Beyond testing, randomness is central in many fields: it drives simulations in physics and finance, underpins randomized algorithms that improve efficiency, and plays a role in machine learning for tasks such as shuffling datasets or initializing neural network weights. In short, random values add diversity, robustness, and realism to both experiments and real-world applications.

Let us now continue with the rest of the program that has to do with reading the dimensions of the matrices and performing the multiplication:

```
func main() {
    if len(os.Args) < 4 {
        fmt.Println("Usage: ./<program name> <n> <m> <k>")
        os.Exit(1)
    }
    // Parse matrix dimensions
    n, _ := strconv.Atoi(os.Args[1])
    m, _ := strconv.Atoi(os.Args[2])
    k, _ := strconv.Atoi(os.Args[3])

    // Generate matrices
    A := randomMatrix(n, m)
    B := randomMatrix(m, k)

    // Initialize result matrix
```

```
result := make([][]int, n)
for i := range result {
    result[i] = make([]int, k)
}
```

In matrix multiplication, the dimensions of the two matrices must satisfy a key rule: *the number of columns in the first matrix must equal the number of rows in the second matrix.* This ensures that each element in a row of the first matrix can be paired with the corresponding element in a column of the second matrix to compute the dot product. In the example from `main()`, the first matrix, `A`, has dimensions nm, and the second matrix, `B`, has dimensions mk. Because both matrices share the middle dimension `m`, they can be multiplied together. The resulting matrix will have dimensions nk, with `n` rows inherited from the first matrix and `k` columns inherited from the second. Choosing dimensions that violate this rule would make multiplication mathematically invalid and would require the program to handle the error. So, `main()` begins by checking that the user has provided three arguments, which represent the dimensions of the matrices: `n` rows, `m` columns for the first matrix, and `k` columns for the second matrix. If insufficient arguments are supplied, the program prints a usage message and exits. The program then parses the arguments into integers using `strconv.Atoi()`.

Using the previously defined `randomMatrix()` function, it generates two matrices: `A` of size nm and `B` of size mk, populated with random values of `-1`, `0`, or `1`. Finally, it prepares the result matrix for storing the product of `A` and `B`. The result is allocated as a slice of `n` rows, and each row is a slice of `k` integers, initialized to zero. This setup provides the framework needed to perform matrix multiplication, either sequentially or concurrently.

The next code snippet demonstrates **concurrent matrix multiplication** using goroutines and `sync.WaitGroup`:

```
// Perform matrix multiplication concurrently
var wg sync.WaitGroup
for i := 0; i < n; i++ {
    for j := 0; j < k; j++ {
        wg.Add(1)
        go func(row, col int) {
            defer wg.Done()
            sum := 0
            for l := 0; l < m; l++ {
                sum += A[row][l] * B[l][col]
            }
                                // Safe: each goroutine
```

```
                // writes to a unique cell
                result[row][col] = sum
            }(i, j)
        }
    }
    wg.Wait()
```

It iterates over every cell in the resulting matrix, with `i` representing the row and `j` the column. For each cell `(i, j)`, the program increments the wait group counter with `wg.Add(1)` and launches a goroutine that computes the dot product for that cell. Inside the goroutine, a local variable, `sum`, accumulates the sum of element-wise products from the corresponding row of `A` and column of `B`. After the computation, the goroutine writes the result to `result[row][col]`. This is safe because each goroutine writes to a unique cell in the result matrix, so there is no risk of race conditions between goroutines. The use of `defer wg.Done()` ensures that the wait group counter is decremented when the goroutine finishes, even if an error occurs. Finally, `wg.Wait()` blocks the main goroutine until all worker goroutines have completed, guaranteeing that the result matrix is fully computed before the program proceeds. This approach effectively parallelizes the computation of each cell, leveraging concurrency to speed up matrix multiplication for large matrices. The rest of the code, which is not presented here, prints the results on screen. Run `ch03/matrix.go` on your machine:

```
$ go run ch03/matrix.go 2 3 2
Matrix A:
[0 1 -1]
[0 0 0]
Matrix B:
[0 0]
[0 1]
[-1 0]
Result Matrix (A x B):
[1 1]
[0 0]
```

After exploring concurrent matrix multiplication and seeing how Go can harness multiple goroutines to speed up computationally intensive tasks, it is important to address another risk that comes with concurrency. While dividing work among goroutines can improve performance, poor coordination or misuse of synchronization mechanisms can lead to situations where goroutines block each other indefinitely. Understanding how deadlocks arise, why they occur, and how to avoid them is essential for writing safe and reliable concurrent Go programs.

Deadlocks

A deadlock occurs when goroutines become permanently stuck, each waiting for a condition that can never be satisfied. In Go, this often happens with channels, for example, if a goroutine tries to send on a channel but no other goroutine is receiving, or if all goroutines are waiting to receive with no one sending. When every goroutine in a program is blocked and no progress can be made, the Go runtime detects the situation and reports a deadlock, terminating the program with an error message. Consider the following example code that illustrates a deadlock situation:

```
package main

import (
    "fmt"
    "time"
)

func main() {
    fmt.Println("=== Demonstrating a Deadlock ===")
    ch := make(chan int)

    // Worker goroutine sends a value, but no one is receiving.
    go func() {
        fmt.Println("Goroutine: sending value...")
        ch <- 42 // This blocks forever
        fmt.Println("Goroutine: done")
    }()

    // Main goroutine also tries to send instead of receiving.
    time.Sleep(time.Second)
    fmt.Println("Main: also sending value...")
    ch <- 99 // Deadlock occurs here

    // This line is never reached.
    fmt.Println("End of program")
}
```

The program begins by creating an unbuffered channel and launching a worker goroutine. Inside the goroutine, the code tries to send the value `42` into the channel, but because unbuffered channels require a matching receiver to proceed, the goroutine blocks indefinitely at the send statement. Meanwhile, the main goroutine waits for a second, then also tries to send the value `99` into the same channel. At this point, both the worker goroutine and the main goroutine are stuck, each attempting to send into the channel with no corresponding receiver. This creates a deadlock situation where neither side can continue and the program stalls. As a result, the final statement, `fmt.Println("End of program")`, is never executed. The issue arises from misunderstanding the rules of unbuffered channels: every send must have a matching receive, and vice versa. Here, both goroutines are sending, but no code is ever receiving from the channel, which guarantees a deadlock. The problem could be fixed by ensuring that at least one goroutine performs a receive operation – for example, by having the main goroutine read from the channel instead of sending its own value. Running `ch03/deadlock.go` generates the following kind of output:

```
$ go run ch03/deadlock.go
=== Demonstrating a Deadlock ===
Goroutine: sending value...
Main: also sending value...
fatal error: all goroutines are asleep - deadlock!

goroutine 1 [chan send]:
main.main()
        ~/go/src/github.com/mactsouk/goSP2/ch03/deadlock.go:22 +0xf0

goroutine 35 [chan send]:
main.main.func1()
        ~/go/src/github.com/mactsouk/goSP2/ch03/deadlock.go:15 +0x64
created by main.main in goroutine 1
        ~/go/src/github.com/mactsouk/goSP2/ch03/deadlock.go:13 +0xa0
exit status 2
```

The `fatal error: all goroutines are asleep - deadlock!` message shows the root of the problem. Here is an improved version of the program (`ch03/deadlockFixed.go`) that resolves the deadlock situation:

```
package main

import (
    "fmt"
    "time"
)

func main() {
    fmt.Println("=== Fixed Deadlock Example ===")
```

```
    ch := make(chan int)

    go func() {
        fmt.Println("Goroutine: sending value...")
        ch <- 42
        fmt.Println("Goroutine: done")
    }()
    time.Sleep(time.Second)
    fmt.Println("Main: receiving value...")
    val := <-ch
    fmt.Println("Main: received", val)
    fmt.Println("End of program")
}
```

This program demonstrates how to avoid a deadlock by ensuring that a send operation on an unbuffered channel has a corresponding receive. The program starts by creating an unbuffered channel and launching a goroutine that sends the value 42 into the channel. In this case, the goroutine blocks at the send statement until another goroutine is ready to receive the value. After a short pause, the main goroutine steps in to perform the receive operation with `val := <-ch`. This action unblocks the goroutine, allowing the value 42 to be successfully transferred, after which the goroutine prints `"Goroutine: done"`. The goroutine of the `main()` function then continues by printing the received value and ends the program gracefully. The key difference from the deadlock example is that here we properly *pair one sender with one receiver*. In unbuffered channels, such matching is essential because neither the sender nor the receiver can complete without the other. By coordinating the goroutines so that one sends and the other receives, we avoid a situation where both sides are waiting forever.

The new version is executed without any issues:

```
$ go run ch03/deadlockFixed.go
=== Fixed Deadlock Example ===
Goroutine: sending value...
Main: receiving value...
Main: received 42
End of program
```

The output illustrates a successful synchronization between the main execution thread and a background worker. By launching the sending operation in its own goroutine, the program ensures that the channel send — which is a blocking operation — does not halt the main thread before the receiver is ready. This specific sequence where the goroutine prints its `"sending"` message followed by the "received" confirmation demonstrates that the two independent execution paths have met at the channel's synchronization point, exchanged data, and proceeded to completion without hanging.

The key takeaway from this section is that concurrency requires a rendezvous. A deadlock occurs when every path of execution is blocked waiting for an event that only a blocked path can provide. Successful concurrency is less about "fixing" bugs and more about designing communication flows where no one is left waiting forever.

Summary

Our minds are inherently concurrent. At any moment, we juggle memory, intention, perception, and action – parallel processes that somehow compose a unified experience. Writing software that behaves in the same way is deceptively difficult. This chapter explored the essence of concurrent programming in Go by cultivating a mindset of coordination, isolation, and communication. In doing so, we learn to write programs that not only run faster but also operate in harmony with the world around them.

In the next chapter, the focus shifts from learning concurrency and synchronization basics to mastering the tools and internal concepts that make Go such a practical language for production systems. We will start by addressing common misconceptions and then dive into core runtime features such as the garbage collector and the scheduler. From there, we will explore concepts such as reflection, interfaces, and generics, while also learning how to organize and structure code effectively with packages and workspaces. Practical skills such as logging, testing, benchmarking, and handling dates and times will round out the chapter.

Exercises

1. Write a program that launches a goroutine to send a string through a channel, and the main goroutine receives and prints it. Extend it to send multiple messages and close the channel.
2. Build a three-stage pipeline using Go channels. The first stage generates a sequence of numbers and sends them through a channel. The second stage receives these numbers, squares them, and forwards the results to the next stage. The third and final stage consumes the squared numbers and computes their sum. Print the sum and then exit.
3. The `sync/atomic` package provides low-level primitives for performing *atomic memory operations on shared variables.* These operations are crucial when you need to safely update values that might be accessed by multiple goroutines without the overhead of traditional locking mechanisms such as `sync.Mutex`. Functions such as `atomic.AddInt32()`, `atomic.LoadInt64()`, `atomic.CompareAndSwapInt64()`, and

`atomic.StoreUint32()` let you increment, read, write, or conditionally update values in a way that is guaranteed to be atomic, meaning no other goroutine can interrupt the operation. This makes `atomic` ideal for counters, flags, or other small shared states where performance is critical and lock contention would be costly. However, as atomic operations operate at a very low level, they should be used carefully; for more complex coordination, higher-level synchronization primitives are usually preferable. Write a program that starts 5 goroutines, each incrementing a shared counter 1,000 times. Use `atomic.AddInt64()` to safely update the counter and print the final value. Compare what happens if you remove the `atomic` call and use a plain `counter++`.

4. Implement a simple program where multiple goroutines (the number of goroutines being given as a command-line argument) try to set a shared flag (an integer value starting at 0) to `1` using `atomic.CompareAndSwapInt32()`. Make sure only one goroutine succeeds in setting the flag and print which goroutine won the "race."

Additional resources

- The `sync` package: `https://pkg.go.dev/sync`
- Data Race Detector: `https://go.dev/doc/articles/race_detector`
- The `os` package documentation: `https://pkg.go.dev/os`

Get this book's PDF version and more

Scan the QR code (or go to `packtpub.com/unlock`). Search for this book by name, confirm the edition, and then follow the steps on the page.

UNLOCK NOW

Note: Keep your invoice handy. Purchases made directly from Packt don't require an invoice.

Additional resources

Get this book's PDF version and more

4

Advanced Go

In this chapter, we shift from learning the language to understanding it. The novice asks what a language can do; the experienced developer begins to ask why it behaves the way it does. Advanced Go is about common Go misconceptions, the Go garbage collector and scheduler, `GOGC`, `GOMAXPROCS`, profile-guided optimization, reflection, interfaces, and generics. In this chapter, we also discuss dates, times, workspaces, modules, and packages. These topics are not merely a collection of features but the essential machinery that governs how Go programs interact with the OS and memory. By exploring *why* the scheduler distributes work across processors or *why* a specific interface implementation incurs overhead, we transform our intuition into a precise engineering discipline. Understanding the *why* behind these components allows a developer to predict how a system will behave under load, turning the runtime from a black box into a controllable environment. So, this chapter covers the following:

- The Go program execution process
- Common misconceptions about Go
- The Go garbage collector and the Go scheduler
- Profile-guided optimization
- `make` and `new`
- Interfaces, reflection, and generics
- Working with dates and times
- Workspaces
- Packages
- Testing and benchmarking Go code

Let's begin by presenting the way a Go program is executed.

The Go program execution process

The Go program execution process begins with Go source code, which is then compiled and linked using go `build`. This creates a statically linked binary. The OS loader then executes this binary, which in turn triggers the Go runtime initialization. Once the Go runtime is set up, it starts the `main()` function. From here, the runtime system manages several key components. Let's look at *Figure 4.1*, which shows the progression starting from Go source code files at the top and moving down to the runtime system:

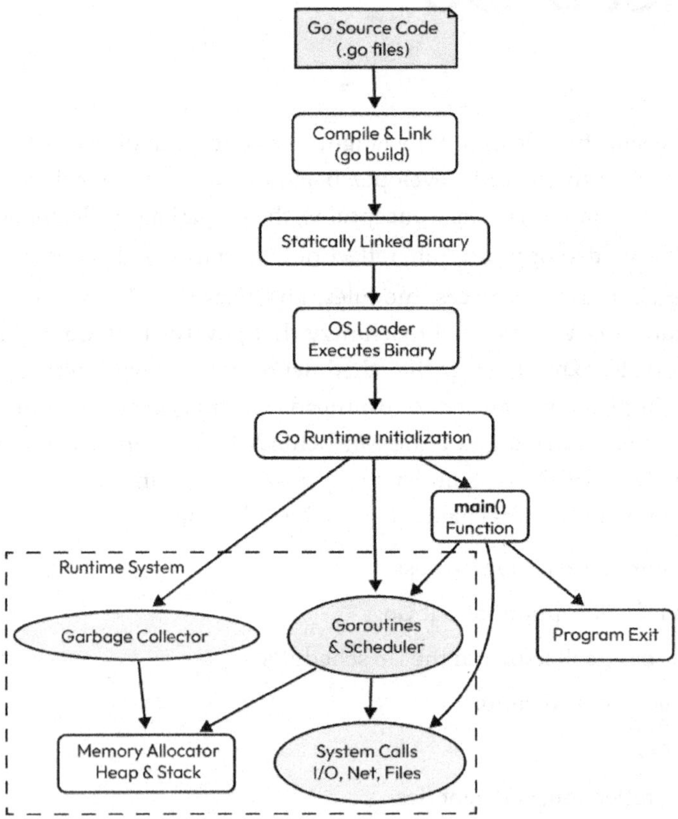

Figure 4.1 – How a Go program is executed

The *garbage collector* is responsible for memory management and works with the *memory allocator* to handle the heap and stack. *Goroutines* and the *scheduler* manage concurrent execution, allowing for efficient use of system resources. Goroutines can interact with the *system calls* layer to perform I/O operations, network communication, and file access. `main()` can also directly interact with goroutines and the system calls layer. The program concludes with a *program exit*, either by `main()` returning or via an explicit call to `os.Exit()` from another function.

Now that we have covered the foundational principles of Go execution, it is important to address the common misunderstandings that new and experienced developers alike may encounter. While the Go philosophy of simplicity and efficiency is a significant strength, it can also lead to several myths and incorrect assumptions about its capabilities and performance. By examining these misconceptions, we can replace assumptions with the technical precision required for high-performance systems.

Common misconceptions about Go

There are quite a few misconceptions about the performance characteristics of Go and associated tooling, especially from developers who are experienced in languages such as C++, Java or Python. These misconceptions often come from projecting expectations based on other ecosystems, or from treating Go as either a scripting language or a systems programming language without fully appreciating its unique design philosophy. Let us examine these misconceptions one by one.

Go is slow because it has garbage collection

This is one of the most persistent myths. But is this genuinely a real concern? While it is true that garbage collection can introduce an overhead, the Go GC has become extremely efficient. With sub-millisecond pause times, concurrent sweeping, and intelligent allocation strategies, the runtime manages memory very effectively for a wide range of workloads. What many developers miss is that *Go trades off a small amount of GC overhead for massive gains in developer productivity and runtime safety*, and in many real-world services, the GC overhead is far smaller than people expect – often in the range of *1–2% CPU usage* under load. Where performance really matters, reducing allocations and managing object lifetimes more explicitly (e.g., using object pools) is usually more than enough to get great results. For most server-side applications, Go offers performance that is within reach of C++ but with a fraction of the complexity. To sum up: Go is sufficient for most use cases, and its performance is usually better than expected. However, for cases where memory or processing capabilities are limited, choose Rust, Zig, or C.

Channels are the best way to do all concurrency in Go

Channels are a first-class feature of the language, and they shine in certain scenarios, especially when you need coordination or communication between goroutines. But *not all concurrency in Go needs channels* – overusing channels could lead to trouble, but the Go philosophy is not to blame for that. Sometimes simple `sync.Mutex`, `sync.WaitGroup`, or even `sync/atomic` operations are more appropriate. Overusing channels can reduce clarity and performance if they are forced into situations where shared memory or state mutation is more natural. Go gives you both shared-memory and message-passing concurrency. *Use the option that best fits the problem*, not just the idiomatic one.

Go does not need profiling as it is already fast

This is a dangerous myth. Go does have great performance out of the box, but every system has bottlenecks. Without profiling, it is impossible to know where the real issues are. Developers sometimes assume their service is slow because of the Go runtime, when in reality the problem is excessive allocations, blocking I/O, or inefficient algorithms. *Go tooling makes it easy to profile*, with built-in support for CPU, memory, and goroutine profiles via `pprof` and deeper inspection with `trace`.

The Go compiler does not optimize much

This may have been true in early Go versions, but it is outdated today. The Go compiler has become significantly more sophisticated, especially with the introduction of escape analysis, inlining improvements, register allocation enhancements, and now **Profile-Guided Optimization** (**PGO**). Developers coming from C/C++ sometimes expect the Go compiler to perform magic-level optimizations at the cost of long compile times. Go deliberately avoids some of the deepest optimizations to preserve fast, predictable builds – but it still performs many effective optimizations.

Goroutines are just like threads

Not quite. Goroutines are *much lighter* than OS threads, and they are multiplexed onto a smaller number of threads by the Go scheduler. You can spawn tens of thousands of goroutines without any issues, something that would bring a traditional thread-based program to its knees. However, this leads to another misconception: that goroutines are free. *Goroutines are cheap but not free*. They still require stack space, scheduler overhead, and coordination. If you leak goroutines or over-parallelize, performance will degrade.

Go does not support fine-grained control over memory

It is true that Go abstracts a lot of the low-level memory and CPU management you would have in C or Rust. But that does not mean you are flying blind. Go provides *great visibility into runtime behavior*: you can tune garbage collection (`GOGC`), track allocations (`-memprofile`), monitor goroutine behavior, and analyze lock contention. With tools such as go `tool trace`, `pprof`, and runtime metrics via Prometheus, Go gives you *enough insight to make data-driven decisions*, without micromanaging every byte.

Go is just another general-purpose language

The biggest misconception about the Go performance model is to assume it behaves like another language when, in fact, Go offers a distinctive *balance of speed, simplicity, and safety*. It is not the fastest language in raw benchmarks, but it often wins in real-world performance, especially when you consider factors such as build time, memory safety, debugging ease, and observability. Once developers embrace Go's tooling – especially profiling, tracing, and modern compiler features such as PGO – they often find it not just "fast enough" but *remarkably efficient for building scalable, production-grade systems.*

After clearing up these common misconceptions about Go, let's turn our attention to one of the most debated and often misunderstood components of Go: the garbage collector. Many of the assumptions that developers make are closely tied to how the Go GC works. By understanding the design and behavior of the GC, we can see how the language balances developer productivity with runtime efficiency.

The Go garbage collector

Garbage collection is the process of freeing up memory space that is not being used. In other words, the Go **garbage collector (GC)** sees which objects are out of scope and cannot be referenced anymore and frees the memory space they consume. This process happens in a concurrent way while a Go program is running and not before or after the execution of the program. The GC is a **concurrent**, non-generational (does not divide objects by age), **mark-and-sweep** collector designed to provide low-latency memory management while keeping application throughput high. Unlike traditional stop-the-world collectors, the Go GC runs concurrently with application code, significantly reducing pause times and making it suitable for latency-sensitive systems. The collector operates in cycles, alternating between an active marking phase and a background reclamation phase known as **lazy sweeping**: it marks all live objects by tracing from root pointers, then sweeps and reclaims memory that is no longer reachable. Recent versions of Go have optimized the GC to keep pause times consistently below a millisecond, even for applications managing large heaps. Additionally, the GC dynamically adjusts its pacing based on allocation rates and available memory, providing an adaptive balance between CPU usage for garbage collection and memory efficiency.

At the start of a collection, all objects in the heap are considered *white*, meaning they are candidates for reclamation. The collector then identifies the set of **roots**, which includes active variables on goroutine stacks, global variables, and references held by the runtime, and colors them *gray*. Gray objects represent memory that is reachable but not yet fully scanned. The collector repeatedly processes gray objects by scanning their pointers: any referenced objects are moved from white to gray, while the original gray object is marked *black*, meaning it has been fully processed and will not be revisited. This process continues until no gray objects remain, at which point all remaining white objects are unreachable and can be safely freed during the **sweep phase**. The logic behind this bit-marking system is to provide a high-performance tracking mechanism that the runtime can query and update with minimal overhead. Once the lazy sweeping phase completes the reclamation of memory, these bit-marks are reset across the heap.

Because this work happens concurrently with program execution, Go uses a **write barrier** to intercept pointer writes: whenever a black object gains a reference to a white object, that white object is immediately shaded gray to ensure it is not missed. The algorithm therefore guarantees that no live object is accidentally collected, while minimizing pause times by performing most of the heavy work alongside the running program.

Let's look at a little descriptive example now: imagine a program where a `User` object lives on the heap and contains references to `Profile` and `Settings` objects. At runtime, the stack holds a pointer to the `User`, so the GC begins by marking it gray. During scanning, the collector sees that `User` references `Profile` and `Settings`, so those two objects are marked gray as well. Once the collector fully inspects `User`, it becomes black. The process continues: `Profile` points to a `Photo` object, which is marked gray and eventually processed, while `Settings` has no additional references, so it turns black immediately. At the end of marking, `User`, `Profile`, `Settings`, and `Photo` are black, showing they are all live. Suppose an old `Cache` object existed in memory but was not referenced anywhere in this chain; it would remain white and be reclaimed during the sweeping phase. Having explored how the GC works in principle and practice, it is time to look at how developers can influence its behavior. While the GC is designed to run automatically and efficiently without intervention, Go exposes a powerful control knob through the `GOGC` environment variable. This setting allows you to control how aggressively or conservatively the collector reclaims memory, directly affecting the trade-off between memory usage and CPU overhead.

Learning about the GOGC environment variable

The `GOGC` environment variable influences the frequency of garbage collection. When `GOGC` is set to a low value (e.g., 2 or 20), the GC runs very aggressively, which means that while memory usage is kept under tighter control, the program spends more CPU time on garbage collection. When set to a higher value (e.g., 100 or 200), the GC is less aggressive, which can improve CPU efficiency since fewer GC pauses happen, but this is at the cost of higher memory consumption. The `main()` function of `ch04/GOGC.go` will help understand `GOGC`:

```
func main() {
    fmt.Println("GOGC:", os.Getenv("GOGC"))
    var data [][]byte

    for i := 0; i < 15; i++ {
        chunk := make([]byte, 50<<20) // Allocate 50 MB chunks
        data = append(data, chunk)
```

```
        if (i+1)%3 == 0 && len(data) > 2 {
            data = data[len(data)-2:]
        }

        var m runtime.MemStats
        runtime.ReadMemStats(&m)
        fmt.Printf("After iter %d: HeapAlloc = %d MB, NumGC = %d\n",
            i+1, m.HeapAlloc/1024/1024, m.NumGC)
        time.Sleep(500 * time.Millisecond) // give GC time to run
    }
}
```

Inside the `for` loop, the program allocates a 50 MB chunk of memory in each iteration and appends it to the data slice, keeping a reference to it so that it will not be immediately garbage-collected. However, at iterations 3, 6, 9, 12, and 15, once there are more than two elements in the slice, the code trims data so that only the last two chunks remain, dropping older references and making that memory eligible for collection. After each allocation, it reads memory statistics using `runtime.ReadMemStats()` and prints out the current heap size in megabytes along with the number of garbage collection cycles (`NumGC`) that have occurred. The short sleep at the end of each iteration gives the GC a chance to run in the background, ensuring more consistent reporting.

Execute `ch04/GOGC.go` with various `GOGC` values and watch the different outputs:

```
$ GOGC=5 go run ch04/GOGC.go
GOGC: 5
After iter 1: HeapAlloc = 50 MB, NumGC = 1
After iter 2: HeapAlloc = 100 MB, NumGC = 2
After iter 3: HeapAlloc = 150 MB, NumGC = 3
After iter 4: HeapAlloc = 200 MB, NumGC = 4
After iter 5: HeapAlloc = 250 MB, NumGC = 5
After iter 6: HeapAlloc = 300 MB, NumGC = 6
After iter 7: HeapAlloc = 300 MB, NumGC = 8
After iter 8: HeapAlloc = 350 MB, NumGC = 8
After iter 9: HeapAlloc = 400 MB, NumGC = 9
After iter 10: HeapAlloc = 300 MB, NumGC = 11
After iter 11: HeapAlloc = 350 MB, NumGC = 12
After iter 12: HeapAlloc = 250 MB, NumGC = 13
After iter 13: HeapAlloc = 300 MB, NumGC = 14
After iter 14: HeapAlloc = 350 MB, NumGC = 15
After iter 15: HeapAlloc = 250 MB, NumGC = 16
```

```
$ GOGC=50 go run ch04/GOGC.go
GOGC: 50
After iter 1: HeapAlloc = 50 MB, NumGC = 0
After iter 2: HeapAlloc = 100 MB, NumGC = 2
After iter 3: HeapAlloc = 150 MB, NumGC = 2
After iter 4: HeapAlloc = 200 MB, NumGC = 3
After iter 5: HeapAlloc = 250 MB, NumGC = 3
After iter 6: HeapAlloc = 300 MB, NumGC = 4
After iter 7: HeapAlloc = 350 MB, NumGC = 4
After iter 8: HeapAlloc = 400 MB, NumGC = 4
After iter 9: HeapAlloc = 400 MB, NumGC = 5
After iter 10: HeapAlloc = 450 MB, NumGC = 5
After iter 11: HeapAlloc = 500 MB, NumGC = 5
After iter 12: HeapAlloc = 550 MB, NumGC = 5
After iter 13: HeapAlloc = 300 MB, NumGC = 6
After iter 14: HeapAlloc = 350 MB, NumGC = 6
After iter 15: HeapAlloc = 250 MB, NumGC = 7
```

With `GOGC=5`, the GC is extremely aggressive, running very frequently and reclaiming memory as soon as the heap grows slightly. This is why the number of collections (`NumGC`) climbs rapidly – by iteration 2, there have already been 2 collections, and by iteration 15, the count reaches 16. The memory usage shows a clear sawtooth pattern where `HeapAlloc` oscillates between growth and dramatic drops (such as iteration 10 dropping from 400 MB to 300 MB and iteration 12 plummeting to 250 MB), demonstrating that the aggressive GC is constantly working to reclaim freed memory. With `GOGC=50`, the collector is less aggressive, allowing the heap to grow more substantially before triggering collections. Here, `NumGC` increases more slowly – by iteration 5, only 3 garbage collections have occurred, compared to 5 with `GOGC=5`. The heap usage (`HeapAlloc`) grows steadily, reaching 550 MB by iteration 12 before the GC finally catches up with the cleanup operations, resulting in a sharp drop to 300 MB at iteration 13. This demonstrates a more relaxed balance between allocations and collections, where memory can accumulate longer before being reclaimed, though the eventual cleanup is more dramatic when it does occur.

Now that we have explored how the GC manages memory allocation and reclamation, it is important to turn our attention to situations where *memory is not released as expected*. Even in a language with automatic memory management such as Go, *improper coding practices can lead to memory leaks* – cases where memory remains allocated but is no longer useful to the application *memory leak*).

Memory leaks

Even with this automated system, *memory leaks can still occur*, usually when references to objects are inadvertently retained, preventing the GC from reclaiming them. In this section, we will explore two common sources of memory leaks in Go.

Pointers and references creating memory leaks

Pointers and references are powerful tools in Go, giving you direct control over memory and enabling efficient data sharing without costly copies. However, this same power can easily lead to subtle memory leaks if not managed carefully. When a pointer or reference to a large object is kept around (whether intentionally or accidentally), the GC cannot reclaim that memory, even if the program no longer needs the data. Over time, such lingering references accumulate and inflate the memory footprint of your application.

The program that follows (`ch04/leaksRef.go`) demonstrates how memory leaks can occur in Go, not by bypassing the GC but by holding on to references that prevent it from freeing unused memory. This is a classic example of an application-level memory leak in Go: the memory is technically reachable, so the runtime considers it live, but from the program's perspective, it is wasted, leading to persistent and unnecessary memory growth. The code that generates the leaks is the following:

```
// A simple struct to simulate memory usage
type Data struct {
    payload [1024 * 1024]byte
}

func leakyFunction(data *Data) {
        ch := make(chan bool)
        go func() {
                ch <- true
        }()
}

func main() {
        fmt.Println("Memory leak example (stuck goroutines)...")
        printMemUsage()

        for i := 0; i < 10; i++ {
                d := &Data{}
                leakyFunction(d)
                printMemUsage()
```

```
            time.Sleep(500 * time.Millisecond)
        }

        fmt.Printf("# goroutines: %d (should be 11: main + 10 stuck)\n",
            runtime.NumGoroutine())

        fmt.Println("\nForcing 3 GC cycles to try to clean up...")
        for i := 0; i < 3; i++ {
            runtime.GC()
            time.Sleep(100 * time.Millisecond)
            printMemUsage()
        }
}
```

The program demonstrates a common memory leak pattern in Go caused by stuck goroutines that inadvertently retain references to large objects. The code defines a `Data` struct containing a 1 MB byte array as payload and implements a `leakyFunction()` that creates an unbuffered channel and launches a goroutine that attempts to send a Boolean value into that channel. Since the channel is unbuffered and no receiver ever reads from it, the goroutine blocks forever on the send operation, remaining alive indefinitely. Because the goroutine closure captures the `data` parameter, it maintains a reference to the `Data` object, preventing the GC from reclaiming that memory even though the main program has no direct access to it after `leakyFunction()` returns. The `main()` function creates a baseline memory measurement, then enters a loop that allocates ten 1 MB `Data` objects, passing each to `leakyFunction()` while printing memory statistics after each allocation. Execute `ch04/leaksRef.go` on your machine to see the issue:

```
$ go run ch04/leaksRef.go
Memory leak example (stuck goroutines)...
Alloc = 0 MB, TotalAlloc = 0 MB, NumGC = 0
Alloc = 1 MB, TotalAlloc = 1 MB, NumGC = 0
Alloc = 2 MB, TotalAlloc = 2 MB, NumGC = 0
Alloc = 3 MB, TotalAlloc = 3 MB, NumGC = 0
Alloc = 4 MB, TotalAlloc = 4 MB, NumGC = 0
Alloc = 2 MB, TotalAlloc = 5 MB, NumGC = 1
Alloc = 3 MB, TotalAlloc = 6 MB, NumGC = 1
Alloc = 1 MB, TotalAlloc = 7 MB, NumGC = 2
Alloc = 2 MB, TotalAlloc = 8 MB, NumGC = 2
Alloc = 3 MB, TotalAlloc = 9 MB, NumGC = 2
Alloc = 1 MB, TotalAlloc = 10 MB, NumGC = 3
# of goroutines: 11 (should be 11: main + 10 stuck)
```

```
Forcing 3 GC cycles to try to clean up...
Alloc = 0 MB, TotalAlloc = 10 MB, NumGC = 4
Alloc = 0 MB, TotalAlloc = 10 MB, NumGC = 5
Alloc = 0 MB, TotalAlloc = 10 MB, NumGC = 6
```

The output reveals the memory leak through several patterns that become increasingly evident as the program progresses. Starting from a baseline of 0 MB allocated memory, the program shows steady growth in both `Alloc` (currently allocated heap memory) and `TotalAlloc` (cumulative allocations) as each 1 MB object is created. During the allocation phase, the `Alloc` value exhibits a sawtooth pattern, climbing from 1 MB to 3 MB before dropping back to 1 MB when the GC triggers, which happens three times during the 10 iterations, as indicated by `NumGC` reaching 3. However, the critical evidence of the leak becomes apparent when examining `TotalAlloc`, which climbs steadily to 10 MB without ever decreasing, because this metric tracks all allocations regardless of whether they have been freed. The goroutine count of 11 confirms that 10 goroutines remain blocked and alive, each holding a reference to its respective 1 MB data object. The most critical evidence appears in the final section where three forced garbage collection cycles drive `Alloc` down to 0 MB (showing the GC is working properly and can reclaim temporary objects), yet `TotalAlloc` remains at 10 MB and the goroutine count stays at 11, proving that approximately 10 MB of memory is being held by reachable but inaccessible references within the stuck goroutines. This demonstrates that while the GC is functioning correctly by not collecting reachable memory, the program has inadvertently created a leak through goroutines that will never terminate and objects that will never be released, illustrating why proper goroutine lifecycle management is essential for preventing memory leaks in concurrent Go programs.

Sometimes memory leaks in Go arise not from holding on to data, but from leaving work unfinished. After examining how pointers and references can trap memory, we now turn our attention to goroutines, which introduce a different kind of leak.

Goroutines creating memory leaks

Goroutines are lightweight and efficient, designed to scale into the thousands, but if they are left running indefinitely or are blocked waiting on resources that never arrive, they accumulate and consume memory over time. Unlike data leaks, which are visible in retained objects, goroutine leaks are subtler: they tie up both stack space and runtime bookkeeping, gradually degrading performance. The included code example highlights a key pitfall in systems programming with Go: *goroutines are cheap but not free*, and if they are not managed carefully with cancellation or exit conditions, they can silently leak memory and resources. The example code of `ch04/`

`leaksGoroutines.go` illustrates goroutines-related memory leaks. Here is the `main()` function implementation:

```
func main() {
    for i := 0; i < 50; i++ { // Launch 50 goroutines quickly
        go func(id int) {
            data := make([]byte, 5*1024*1024)
            for {
                _ = data // Keep reference alive
                time.Sleep(500 * time.Millisecond)
            }
        }(i)
        time.Sleep(50 * time.Millisecond)
        if i%5 == 0 {
            printMemUsage()
        }
    }
    fmt.Println("All goroutines launched-memory continues to grow.")
    time.Sleep(5 * time.Second)
}
```

In the `main()` function, 50 goroutines are launched in quick succession. Each goroutine allocates a 5 MB slice of bytes and then enters an infinite loop where it keeps the reference alive by reusing `_ = data` and repeatedly sleeping for half a second. Because the reference to the slice never goes out of scope, the memory cannot be garbage collected. The small delay (`time.Sleep(50 * time.Millisecond)`) in the launching loop staggers the allocations slightly, while `printMemUsage()` periodically shows the memory consumption increasing. The issue here is twofold. First, each goroutine permanently consumes 5 MB of memory, so with 50 goroutines, the program allocates around 250 MB that can never be reclaimed. Second, the goroutines themselves are also leaked: they remain blocked in their infinite loops without any mechanism to stop or clean them up. Over time, this can put increasing pressure on the runtime, leading to high memory usage, degraded performance, or even exhaustion of system resources.

Execute `ch04/leaksGoroutines.go` on your machine to see the issue:

```
$ go run ch04/leaksGoroutines.go
Alloc = 0 MB, TotalAlloc = 5 MB, NumGoroutine = 2
Alloc = 10 MB, TotalAlloc = 30 MB, NumGoroutine = 7
Alloc = 0 MB, TotalAlloc = 55 MB, NumGoroutine = 12
Alloc = 5 MB, TotalAlloc = 80 MB, NumGoroutine = 17
```

```
Alloc = 5 MB, TotalAlloc = 105 MB, NumGoroutine = 22
Alloc = 5 MB, TotalAlloc = 130 MB, NumGoroutine = 27
Alloc = 5 MB, TotalAlloc = 155 MB, NumGoroutine = 32
Alloc = 5 MB, TotalAlloc = 180 MB, NumGoroutine = 37
Alloc = 10 MB, TotalAlloc = 205 MB, NumGoroutine = 42
Alloc = 10 MB, TotalAlloc = 230 MB, NumGoroutine = 47
All goroutines launched-memory continues to grow.
```

At the start, the program reports `Alloc = 0 MB`, meaning no memory is currently in active use, but `TotalAlloc = 5 MB` indicates that the runtime has already allocated and freed some memory since the program began, and there are two goroutines running (the main goroutine plus one background runtime goroutine). As the loop progresses, new goroutines are created, each holding a 5 MB slice. The `Alloc` value fluctuates between 0 MB, 5 MB, and 10 MB because the Go GC occasionally reclaims some memory buffers, but `TotalAlloc` steadily increases, reflecting the cumulative amount of memory ever requested. The `NumGoroutine` count steadily climbs from two up to 47, showing that goroutines are being launched and never exiting. Each of these goroutines holds onto its slice in an infinite loop, preventing the GC from reclaiming that memory. Although `Alloc` does not show a dramatic increase at every step, the overall trend of `TotalAlloc` and the rising goroutine count make the problem clear: memory consumption is continuously growing, and more goroutines are leaking.

Having seen how goroutines can create both opportunities for concurrency and pitfalls such as memory leaks, it is natural to ask how Go manages such a vast number of lightweight threads so efficiently. The answer lies in the Go runtime itself, which orchestrates the execution of goroutines behind the scenes. This brings us to the **Go scheduler**, a critical part of the runtime that makes concurrency practical in real-world systems.

The Go scheduler

The Go scheduler is responsible for mapping goroutines onto OS threads, ensuring fair execution, balancing workload across CPU cores, and keeping context-switching overhead low. Unlike traditional thread-based models, the scheduler is designed to be lightweight and scalable, allowing Go programs to spin up thousands – or even millions – of goroutines without overwhelming system resources. Technically speaking, the scheduler operates as part of the runtime and is responsible for deciding which goroutines run, when they run, and on which OS threads they execute. It is built around the **G-M-P model**, where **G** represents **goroutines**, **M** represents **machine threads**, and **P** represents **processors**, which are logical resources that schedule goroutines onto threads. Each goroutine is a lightweight abstraction that *holds only a stack and execution context,* while machine threads map to actual OS threads. The scheduler ensures that runnable goroutines (*G*) are assigned to available processors (*P*), which in turn are executed by threads (*M*). This design allows Go to multiplex thousands of goroutines over a much smaller pool of OS threads, reducing overhead and context-switching costs. The scheduler uses techniques such as **work stealing**, where *idle processors take tasks from others,* to balance the load and keep CPUs busy. It also cooperates with the GC and system calls, ensuring that blocking operations do not stall the entire program. The result is a *highly efficient concurrency system that feels lightweight for the programmer* but is carefully orchestrated under the hood to maximize CPU utilization and scalability. Understanding the Go scheduler sets the stage for exploring one of its most important tuning knobs: `GOMAXPROCS`. While the scheduler decides how goroutines are executed, `GOMAXPROCS` directly influences how much of the underlying hardware Go is allowed to use.

Learning about the effects of GOMAXPROCS

`GOMAXPROCS` determines the maximum number of OS threads that can run Go code simultaneously, effectively controlling how many CPU cores the runtime will exploit. By default, it matches the number of available cores, but it can be adjusted to limit or expand concurrency based on workload characteristics. Consider the following example code (`ch04/GOMAXPROCS.go`) for understanding `GOMAXPROCS`; all the important code is in the `main()` function. The program compares single-threaded execution against multi-threaded execution across all available CPU cores.

```
func main() {
    fmt.Printf("Number of CPUs: %d\n", runtime.NumCPU())
    fmt.Printf("Default GOMAXPROCS: %d\n\n", runtime.GOMAXPROCS(0))

    // Test with GOMAXPROCS = 1 (single-threaded)
    fmt.Println("=== Testing with GOMAXPROCS = 1 ===")
    runtime.GOMAXPROCS(1)

    start := time.Now()
    var wg sync.WaitGroup

    // Start 4 goroutines
    for i := 0; i < 4; i++ {
        wg.Add(1)
        go func(id int) {
            defer wg.Done()
            doWork(id, 1000000)
        }(i)
    }
```

```
    wg.Wait()
    sThreadT := time.Since(start)
    fmt.Printf("Time with GOMAXPROCS=1: %v\n\n", sThreadT)

    // Test with GOMAXPROCS = NumCPU (multi-threaded)
    maxProcs := runtime.NumCPU()
    fmt.Printf("=== Testing with GOMAXPROCS = %d ===\n", maxProcs)
    runtime.GOMAXPROCS(maxProcs)

    start = time.Now()
    // Start 4 goroutines again
    for i := 0; i < 4; i++ {
        wg.Add(1)
        go func(id int) {
            defer wg.Done()
            doWork(id, 1000000)
        }(i)
    }

    wg.Wait()
    mThreadT := time.Since(start)
    fmt.Printf("Time with GOMAXPROCS=%d: %v\n\n", maxProcs, mThreadT)

    // Show the performance difference
    if sThreadT > mThreadT {
        speedup := float64(sThreadT) / float64(mThreadT)
        fmt.Printf("Multi-threaded was %.2fx faster!\n", speedup)
    } else {
        fmt.Println("Single-threaded was faster!")
    }
    // Show current settings
    fmt.Printf("\nFinal GOMAXPROCS: %d\n", runtime.GOMAXPROCS(0))
    fmt.Printf("Number of goroutines: %d\n", runtime.NumGoroutine())
}
```

The code begins by printing the number of logical CPUs and the default `GOMAXPROCS` value. The program first sets `GOMAXPROCS` to 1, forcing all goroutines to execute on a single operating system thread. It then launches four goroutines, each performing a CPU-intensive task via the `doWork()` function, and measures the total execution time. Because only one thread is available, the goroutines effectively run sequentially, resulting in a longer runtime. Next, `GOMAXPROCS` is set to the number of available CPU cores, allowing the scheduler to execute goroutines in parallel across multiple threads. The same four goroutines are launched, and the program measures the new, shorter runtime. It then calculates and prints the speedup factor achieved by multi-threading. Finally, the program reports the current GOMAXPROCS and the total number of active goroutines.

The output shows the results of running a Go program that experiments with the effect of GOMAXPROCS. On a Mac Mini M4 with 14 CPU cores, the output looks as follows:

```
$ go run ch04/GOMAXPROCS.go
Number of CPUs: 14
Default GOMAXPROCS: 14

=== Testing with GOMAXPROCS = 1 ===
Worker 3 finished (sum: 333332833333500000)
Worker 0 finished (sum: 333332833333500000)
Worker 1 finished (sum: 333332833333500000)
Worker 2 finished (sum: 333332833333500000)
Time with GOMAXPROCS=1: 1.20325ms

=== Testing with GOMAXPROCS = 14 ===
Worker 3 finished (sum: 333332833333500000)
Worker 1 finished (sum: 333332833333500000)
Worker 2 finished (sum: 333332833333500000)
Worker 0 finished (sum: 333332833333500000)
Time with GOMAXPROCS=14: 369.208µs

Multi-threaded was 3.26x faster!

Final GOMAXPROCS: 14
Number of goroutines: 1
```

The program first detects that the machine has 14 CPU cores, and by default, GOMAXPROCS is set to 14, meaning Go can fully utilize all available cores. When the program is tested with GOMAXPROCS=1, only one core is used, so *all worker goroutines run sequentially*, producing identical sums but taking longer to complete – about 1.2 milliseconds. When tested with GOMAXPROCS=14, the same four workers finish the computation much faster, in about 0.37 milliseconds, because they can run in parallel across multiple cores. This demonstrates a speedup of 3.26× when using multiple threads compared to a single thread. At the end, the program confirms that GOMAXPROCS was restored to its original value (14) and that only one goroutine remains running, showing proper cleanup. The output illustrates the performance benefits of the Go concurrency model when allowed to use multiple CPU cores. The speedup is not 14×, even though the machine has 14 cores, because *parallel performance is limited by several practical factors*. First, the work is split across only four goroutines in the example, not 14, so even with all CPUs available, the maximum parallelism is capped by the number of workers. Second, the Go scheduler and runtime *introduce overhead when managing goroutines*, synchronizing threads, and coordinating CPU usage, which *reduces the theoretical maximum speedup*. Third, memory access patterns can become a bottleneck: all workers repeatedly perform additions, which are fast but compete for access to shared caches and memory bandwidth, preventing perfectly linear scaling. Finally, not all tasks scale linearly; some amount of work – such as setting up goroutines, starting timers, or collecting results – must still be done sequentially.

We have explored how `GOMAXPROCS` can be tuned to optimize the utilization of available CPU cores. While this setting helps us manage the Go scheduler's interaction with the operating system, it is just one piece of the performance puzzle. *The next logical step is to look into the compilation process itself*. We can ask, what if the compiler could make smarter decisions about our code by understanding how it behaves in the real world? This leads us to **Profile-Guided Optimization (PGO)**, a powerful technique that takes a data-driven approach to performance, allowing the compiler to produce a more efficient binary tailored to your application's typical workload.

Profile-Guided Optimization (PGO)

Profile-Guided Optimization (PGO) is a powerful compiler optimization technique that uses real-world program execution data to make more intelligent decisions during the compilation process. Unlike traditional static compilation, which analyzes code without knowledge of its runtime behavior, PGO leverages a **profile**, which is a collection of data about which parts of the code are "hot" or most frequently executed. This data-driven approach allows the compiler to perform targeted optimizations, such as inlining functions, reordering code for better cache locality, and improving branch prediction, resulting in a binary that is significantly faster for its typical workload. The process is a two-step dance: first, you generate the profile by running an instrumented version of your program, and second, you use that profile to guide a subsequent, more effective compilation. Go has traditionally emphasized simplicity and fast compilation over deep compiler optimizations, but PGO changes that. It gives us a new way to fine-tune performance based on how our code actually runs in production. We are now going to present an example to illustrate the ideas behind PGO. Consider the following implementation of `main()`, as found in `ch04/pgoSimple.go` – feel free to look at the simplistic implementations of `hotPath()` and `coldPath()`.

```
func main() {
    rand.Seed(time.Now().UnixNano())
```

```
    total := 0

    // Simulate workload: hotPath() dominates
    for i := 0; i < 10_000; i++ {
        if rand.Intn(10000) == 0 { // very rare case
            total += coldPath()
        } else {
            total += hotPath()
        }
    }

    fmt.Println("Total:", total)
}
```

The provided code simulates a workload in which the `hotPath()` function is executed the vast majority of the time, while `coldPath()` is invoked only in a very rare case (`rand.Intn(10000) == 0`). Each iteration of the loop generates a random number between 0 and 9999, and only if this number is zero does the program execute the cold path; otherwise, it executes the hot path. *The performance issue arises from the compiler not knowing which branch is the "hot" one at compile time.* As a result, without additional guidance, it treats both paths as equally likely, potentially leading to inefficient instruction layout, suboptimal branch prediction, and unnecessary function call overhead. The hot path is executed thousands of times, so even small inefficiencies accumulate into significant runtime costs. This scenario is precisely where PGO can improve performance: by collecting runtime execution statistics, the compiler can recognize that `hotPath()` dominates and optimize it aggressively, for example, by *inlining it*, arranging code to favor the hot branch for the CPU branch predictor, and placing frequently executed instructions contiguously in memory to improve cache efficiency. For such a simple example, you might observe minimal performance differences, which is typical and expected for several interconnected reasons:

- The original code consists of relatively straightforward computational logic that the Go compiler *already optimizes* quite effectively, even without profile guidance, meaning there is limited room for additional improvement through PGO
- Additionally, small timing variations fall within normal **measurement noise** that occurs due to factors such as system load, memory layout variations, and other background processes affecting execution time
- Furthermore, the hot path in the code is essentially a simple arithmetic loop that modern compilers can already optimize near-optimally through standard techniques such as loop unrolling and vectorization, leaving few additional optimization opportunities that PGO could exploit

PGO tends to show more dramatic benefits in complex code bases with intricate control flow, indirect function calls, interface dispatch patterns, and sophisticated branching logic. In these cases, runtime profiling data can guide the compiler toward better optimization decisions that static analysis alone cannot determine. At the end of this chapter, you are going to see a PGO with benchmarking example.

While PGO and benchmarking help us optimize existing code, understanding Go's memory allocation primitives is essential for writing performant code from the ground up. Both `make()` and `new()` serve distinct roles in the Go memory model. Understanding the subtle differences between these allocation primitives, their performance characteristics, and their appropriate use cases is crucial for systems programming where memory layout, allocation patterns, and GC pressure directly impact application performance and resource utilization.

make and new

In Go, both `make` and `new` allocate memory, but they serve different purposes and reflect different design philosophies of the language. At first glance, they seem interchangeable – after all, both produce usable values – but their roles are distinct. The `new` built-in is minimalistic: it allocates zeroed memory for any type and *returns a pointer to it*, leaving initialization entirely to you. In contrast, `make` is specialized and opinionated: it works only with slices, maps, and channels, *allocating and initializing* the underlying data structures so they are immediately ready to use. Psychologically, you can think of `new` as giving you a blank sheet of paper, while `make` hands you a fully bound notebook, ready for writing.

For example, `p := new(int)` gives you a pointer to an integer initialized to `0`. Think of `new` as handing you an empty box, and you decide what to put inside it, whereas `s := make([]int, 5)` creates a slice of five integers initialized to zero, and `m := make(map[string]int)` gives you a fully functional empty map. Using `new` here would fail because the internal runtime structures for these composite types would not be set up correctly.

Having explored the fundamental memory allocation primitives of Go, we now shift our focus from low-level memory management to high-level project organization. As Go has evolved, its approach to dependency management and module isolation has changed significantly, introducing the concept of **workspaces** to make handling multi-module setups more intuitive. If you have ever struggled with juggling different versions of dependencies across related projects, then you will like the modern, structured solution that workspaces provide.

Workspaces

In Go, *Workspaces* provide a way to manage multiple modules and projects in a single development environment, enabling seamless code sharing and dependency management.

Technically, a workspace is defined via a `go.work` file, which lists the directories containing modules that you want to include in the workspace. This allows the Go toolchain to resolve module paths locally rather than always fetching dependencies from remote repositories, which is particularly useful when working on several interdependent modules simultaneously. The `go.work` file supports directives such as `use` for including module directories and `replace` for overriding module versions or paths. When you run commands such as go `build`, go `test`, or go `run` inside a workspace, tools automatically consider all modules listed in the workspace, allowing imports across these modules without requiring them to be published. Workspaces thus improve developer productivity, support complex multi-module projects, and simplify local testing and integration by creating a coherent, controlled environment for module resolution. In *Chapter 12, Time Series Distances*, we will revisit workspaces.

Next, we turn our attention to **Interfaces**, a fundamental language feature that enables polymorphism and flexible code design. Understanding interfaces is crucial for writing modular, reusable, and testable code, as they allow functions and methods to operate on values of different types without knowing the concrete implementations in advance. The next section introduces the concept of interfaces, demonstrates how to define and implement them, and shows how they interact with the Go type system to support abstraction and dynamic behavior.

Interfaces

An **interface** is a Go mechanism for defining behavior that is implemented using a set of methods. Interfaces should not be unnecessarily complex. If you decide to create your own interfaces, then you should *begin with a common behavior* that you want to be used by multiple data types. Additionally, you should not design your programs by defining interfaces. You should start designing your program, wait for common behaviors to reveal themselves, and then convert those common behaviors into interfaces. Last, if the use of interfaces does not make your code simpler, consider removing some or all your interfaces. Interfaces define none, a single, or multiple type methods that need to be implemented. *Once you implement the required type methods of an interface, that interface is satisfied implicitly.* In simpler terms, once you implement the methods of an interface for a given data type, that interface is satisfied automatically for that data type.

The empty interface

Do not confuse the concept of interfaces with the **empty interface data type**. The empty interface is defined as `interface{}` (or its type alias any, introduced in Go 1.18) and represents a fundamentally different use case from regular interfaces. Because the empty interface has no methods, it means that it is already satisfied by all data types automatically — every type in Go implements the empty interface without doing anything. This makes `interface{}` capable of holding values of any type, which is why functions such as `fmt.Println()` can accept arguments of arbitrary types. However, this flexibility comes at a cost: using the empty interface sacrifices compile-time type safety and requires type assertions or type switches to access the underlying concrete value. Let us now discuss the **empty interface** and its uses in more detail.

The uses of the empty interface

The empty interface, written as `interface{}`, serves as the universal container type that can *hold values of any type*, making it one of the most versatile yet performance-sensitive constructs in the language. It finds extensive use in generic programming scenarios where type flexibility is required, such as implementing heterogeneous collections, such as `[]interface{}` for storing mixed-type data, serving as function parameters that accept arbitrary types in utility functions such as `fmt.Printf()`, and acting as map values in configuration systems where `map[string]interface{}` can represent JSON-like structures with varying field types. The empty interface is fundamental to the Go reflection system, where `reflect.ValueOf()` accepts `interface{}` parameters to enable runtime type introspection and manipulation, and it is commonly used in serialization libraries, database drivers, and API frameworks that must handle unknown or dynamic data structures. However, this flexibility comes at a cost: storing concrete values in empty interfaces requires boxing (heap allocation) and type assertions or type switches for value extraction, which introduces both performance overhead and potential runtime panic if type assertions fail. That makes it essential for developers to understand when the convenience of `interface{}` justifies its runtime costs, versus using more specific types or generics for type-safe, performant alternatives.

The presented example (`ch04/interfaces.go`) illustrates all kinds of interfaces in action:

```
package main

import (
    "fmt"
    "math"
)

// 1. Define a regular interface
type Shape interface {
    Area() float64
    Perimeter() float64
}
```

In this code, we define an interface named Shape that represents the general behavior of geometric shapes. Recall that an interface specifies a set of methods that a type must implement to satisfy it. Here, the Shape interface requires only two methods: Area() float64 and Perimeter() float64. The next code snippet defines two concrete types, Rectangle and Circle, that implement the Shape interface:

```
// 2. Define concrete types
type Rectangle struct {
    Width, Height float64
}
func (r Rectangle) Area() float64 {
    return r.Width * r.Height
}
func (r Rectangle) Perimeter() float64 {
    return 2 * (r.Width + r.Height)
}

type Circle struct {
    Radius float64
}
func (c Circle) Area() float64 {
    return math.Pi * c.Radius * c.Radius
}
func (c Circle) Perimeter() float64 {
    return 2 * math.Pi * c.Radius
}
```

Each type has its own fields that describe its dimensions: Rectangle uses Width and Height, while Circle uses Radius. Both types provide implementations for the Area() and Perimeter() methods, which makes them valid Shape values.

Next, we present a function that works with any type implementing the Shape interface:

```
// 3. Generic function for Shape interface
func printShapeInfo(s Shape) {
    fmt.Printf("Area: %.2f ", s.Area())
    fmt.Printf("Perimeter: %.2f ", s.Perimeter())
    fmt.Println()
}
```

The `printShapeInfo()` function accepts a parameter `s` of type `Shape` and then calls the `Area()` and `Perimeter()` methods defined by the interface. Because `printShapeInfo()` depends only on the interface and not on any specific implementation, it can handle rectangles, circles, or any other type that provides `Area()` and `Perimeter()` methods. This demonstrates the power of interfaces in Go: you can write flexible, reusable functions that operate across many types without being tied to a single concrete implementation.

Next, we explore the empty interface:

```
// 4. Function demonstrating the use of empty interfaces
func printAnything(v interface{}) {
    fmt.Printf("Value: %v, Type: %T\n", v, v)
    // Using a type assertion
    if str, ok := v.(string); ok {
        fmt.Println("This is a string with length:", len(str))
    }

    // Using a type switch for multiple types
    switch val := v.(type) {
    case int:
        fmt.Println("It's an integer, doubled:", val*2)
    case float64:
        fmt.Println("It's a float, squared:", val*val)
    case Shape:
        fmt.Println("It's a Shape:")
        printShapeInfo(val)
    default:
        fmt.Println("Unknown type!")
    }
}
```

The `printAnything()` function demonstrates the flexibility of the empty interface (`interface{}`), which *can hold values of any type*. At the start, it prints both the value and its dynamic type. To handle specific cases, the function first uses a **type assertion**: if the value is a `string`, it prints its length. Then it applies a **type switch** to branch logic based on the actual type stored in `v`. For integers, it doubles the value; for floats, it squares the number; and if the value implements the `Shape` interface, it calls `printShapeInfo()` to display the area and perimeter. Any type that does not match these cases falls into the `default` branch, reporting an unknown type.

Next, we present the implementation of `main()` that ties together all the interface concepts demonstrated in the program:

```
func main() {
    rect := Rectangle{Width: 10, Height: 5}
    circle := Circle{Radius: 7}
    fmt.Println("Rectangle:")
    printShapeInfo(rect)
    fmt.Println("Circle:")
    printShapeInfo(circle)

    // Slice of Shape interfaces
    shapes := []Shape{
        Rectangle{3, 4},
        Circle{2.5},
        Rectangle{5, 8},
    }

    fmt.Println("Iterating over multiple shapes:")
    for i, s := range shapes {
        fmt.Printf("Shape %d:\n", i+1)
        printShapeInfo(s)
    }

    // 5. Using empty interfaces to hold mixed types
    fmt.Println("Working with empty interfaces:")
    items := []interface{}{
        "Go is awesome!",
        42,
        3.14,
        rect,
        circle,
        true,
    }

    for _, item := range items {
        printAnything(item)
    }
}
```

`main()` begins by creating a `Rectangle` and a `Circle` and then uses the `printShapeInfo()` function to display their area and perimeter, showing how concrete types can be handled through the `Shape` interface. Next, it defines a slice of `Shape` values *containing a mix of rectangles and circles*. Iterating through this slice emphasizes **polymorphism**: even though the elements are different concrete types, they are all accessed uniformly via the interface. Afterwards, the function introduces the empty interface with a slice of mixed types, including strings, integers, floats, shapes, and a Boolean value. Each item is passed to `printAnything()`, demonstrating how empty interfaces allow heterogeneous collections, and how type assertions and type switches enable type-specific handling at runtime. Run `ch04/interfaces.go` on your machine to see the generated output.

Having examined interfaces, we progress to another advanced feature: **reflection**. This is the runtime mechanism that enables programs to inspect and manipulate types and values dynamically. Reflection offers the tools to discover what those types actually are and interact with them programmatically. The Go reflection system, primarily embodied in the `reflect` package, builds upon the foundation of empty interfaces by providing a comprehensive API for runtime type introspection, value manipulation, and dynamic method invocation that would otherwise require compile-time knowledge of specific types. Reflection serves as the backbone for many of Go's powerful features, including JSON marshaling, template engines, dependency injection frameworks, and debugging tools, enabling developers to write highly generic code that can adapt to arbitrary data structures at runtime. However, this power comes with significant trade-offs: reflection sacrifices the Go compile-time type safety guarantees, introduces substantial performance overhead compared to statically typed operations, and can make code more complex and harder to reason about. Thus, careful consideration is required as to whether its *flexibility justifies these costs* in systems programming.

Reflection

You might be wondering how you can find out the names of the fields of a structure at execution time. In such cases, you need to use **reflection**. Reflection provides a powerful, albeit *low-level*, mechanism to inspect and manipulate program values at runtime. While systems programming often favors performance, determinism, and type safety, there are cases where runtime flexibility is not just useful but necessary – such as when building debuggers, serializers, or generic utilities. The Go `reflect` package offers access to the internal types of a program's metadata and value representations, enabling developers to write code that can adapt to types it has never seen before. Apart from enabling you to print the fields and the values of a structure, reflection allows you to explore and manipulate unknown structures, such as the ones created from decoding JSON data.

The most useful parts of the reflect package are two data types named reflect.Value and reflect.Type. reflect.Value is used for storing values of any type, whereas reflect.Type is used for representing Go types. There exist two functions named reflect.TypeOf() and reflect.ValueOf() that return reflect.Type and reflect.Value values, respectively. Note that reflect.TypeOf() returns the actual type of variable; if we are examining a structure, it returns the name of the structure. As structures are important in Go, the reflect package offers the reflect.NumField() method for listing the number of fields in a structure, as well as the Field() method for getting the reflect.Value value of a specific field of a structure. The reflect package also defines the reflect.Kind data type, which is used for representing the specific data type of a variable: int, struct, and so on. The documentation of the reflect package lists all possible values of the reflect.Kind data type. The Kind() function returns the kind of a variable. Lastly, the Int() and String() methods return the integer and string value of a reflect.Value, respectively. Keep in mind that *reflection code can look unpleasant and is sometimes hard to read.* Therefore, according to the Go philosophy, you should rarely use reflection unless it is necessary, because it does not create clean code.

Inspecting structures with reflection

The next program showcases the power and flexibility of the reflect package by inspecting types, modifying struct fields dynamically, and invoking functions at runtime.

```
package main

import (
    "fmt"
    "reflect"
)

type User struct {
    Name string
    Age  int
}

// A function to be called dynamically using reflection
func Greet(name string) {
    fmt.Printf("Hello, %s!\n", name)
}

func main() {
    // --- 1. Inspecting basic types ---
```

```
    fmt.Println("=== Inspecting Types and Values ===")
    var x float64 = 3.14

    v := reflect.ValueOf(x)
    t := reflect.TypeOf(x)
    fmt.Println("Type:", t)         // float64
    fmt.Println("Value:", v)        // 3.14
    fmt.Println("Kind:", v.Kind()) // float64

    // --- 2. Modifying struct fields dynamically ---
    fmt.Println("=== Modifying Struct Fields ===")
    u := User{Name: "Alice", Age: 30}
    fmt.Println("Before:", u)

    // Get a reflect.Value of the struct pointer
    rv := reflect.ValueOf(&u).Elem()

    // Modify the "Name" field
    nameField := rv.FieldByName("Name")
    if nameField.IsValid() && nameField.CanSet() {
        nameField.SetString("Bob")
    }

    // Modify the "Age" field
    ageField := rv.FieldByName("Age")
    if ageField.IsValid() && ageField.CanSet() {
        ageField.SetInt(42)
    }
    fmt.Println("After:", u)

    // --- 3. Calling a function dynamically ---
    fmt.Println("=== Calling Functions Dynamically ===")
    greetFunc := reflect.ValueOf(Greet)
    args := []reflect.Value{reflect.ValueOf("Charlie")}
    greetFunc.Call(args)
}
```

The code begins by declaring a simple `User` struct with `Name` and `Age` fields, as well as a standalone function, `Greet()`, that prints a greeting message. In the first part of `main()`, the program illustrates type inspection using reflection. A `float64` value is passed to `reflect.ValueOf()` and `reflect.TypeOf()`, allowing the program to print its type, value, and kind – demonstrating how reflection enables runtime introspection of variables.

In the second part, the program shows how reflection allows you to *modify struct fields dynamically*. A `User` instance is created and then wrapped in a `reflect.Value` using `reflect.ValueOf(&u).Elem()` to obtain a *modifiable reference to its fields*. The program retrieves the `Name` and `Age` fields using `FieldByName()` and checks whether they are valid and settable before updating their values to `"Bob"` and `42`, respectively. After the modification, the updated `struct` is printed, showing that the changes were applied successfully without directly accessing the fields in code. Finally, the third part demonstrates how to *call a function dynamically using reflection*. The `Greet()` function is converted to a `reflect.Value`, and an argument slice containing a `reflect.Value` of `"Charlie"` is prepared. Using the `Call()` method, the program invokes the `Greet()` function at runtime with the provided argument.

Now run `ch04/reflection.go` on your machine to see its code in action:

```
$ go run ch04/reflection.go
=== Inspecting Types and Values ===
Type: float64
Value: 3.14
Kind: float64
=== Modifying Struct Fields ===
Before: {Alice 30}
After: {Bob 42}
=== Calling Functions Dynamically ===
Hello, Charlie!
```

The generated output of the program clearly demonstrates the three main capabilities of reflection. In the first section, under `Inspecting Types and Values`, the program analyzes a `float64` variable at runtime. It prints its type as `float64`, its value as `3.14`, and its kind – a more general category in the Go type system – also as `float64`. In the second section, `Modifying Struct Fields`, the program prints the state of a `User` struct before and after modifying its fields using reflection. Initially, the struct is displayed as `{Alice 30}`, showing the original `Name` and `Age` values. After using `reflect.Value` to access and modify these fields dynamically, the struct updates to `{Bob 42}`. This demonstrates that reflection allows direct, runtime manipulation of struct fields without referencing them explicitly in code. Finally, the third section, `Calling Functions Dynamically`, highlights how reflection can be used to invoke functions at runtime. The program dynamically calls the `Greet()` function, passing in the string `Charlie`. As a result, the output displays `Hello, Charlie!`, confirming that the function was successfully invoked using `reflect.Value.Call()`.

So far, we have explored how reflection allows you to inspect types, manipulate struct fields dynamically, and even invoke functions at runtime. These capabilities become even more powerful when applied to practical tasks, such as serializing data into JSON. We now turn to a fundamentally different approach to type safety and code reuse: **generics**. While reflection provides powerful **runtime flexibility** at the cost of compile-time safety and performance overhead, generics, introduced in Go 1.18, offer a compile-time solution for writing type-safe, reusable code without sacrificing runtime performance.

Generics

Generics enable developers to create functions, types, and data structures that work across multiple types while maintaining full type checking and optimization opportunities that reflection-based approaches inherently cannot provide. This shift from runtime type discovery to compile-time type parameterization represents a significant evolution in Go's approach to abstraction, allowing systems programmers to build highly efficient, type-safe libraries and frameworks that previously required either code duplication or the performance penalties associated with `interface{}` and reflection.

Look at the following example code as found in `ch04/generics.go`:

```
type Numeric interface {
    ~int | ~int8 | ~int16 | ~int32 | ~int64 |
        ~uint | ~uint8 | ~uint16 | ~uint32 | ~uint64 |
        ~float32 | ~float64
}

func Sum[T Numeric](nums []T) T {
    var total T
    for _, v := range nums {
        total += v
    }
    return total
}
```

This code defines a **custom generic constraint** and a corresponding **generic function**. The `Numeric` interface acts as a **constraint** that restricts the types a generic function can accept. Using the ~ operator, it specifies that any type whose underlying type is one of the listed numeric types – signed integers (`int`, `int8`, `int16`, `int32`, `int64`), unsigned integers (`uint`, `uint8`, `uint16`, uint32, uint64), or floating-point numbers (float32, float64) – satisfies the Numeric constraint. The Sum() function is a generic function that takes a slice of any type T constrained by Numeric. Inside the function, it initializes a total variable of type T, iterates over the nums slice, and accumulates the sum of its elements. Finally, it returns total. This design ensures type safety while allowing the same function to operate on any numeric type, eliminating the need for multiple functions for integers, floats, or unsigned numbers.

Now, here is the version of Sum() that demonstrates a **non-generic approach** to summing numeric values using the empty interface, interface{}.

```
func SumInterface(nums []interface{}) interface{} {
    if len(nums) == 0 {
        return nil
    }
    switch nums[0].(type) {
    case int:
        total := 0
        for _, v := range nums {
            total += v.(int)
        }
        return total
    case float64:
        total := 0.0
        for _, v := range nums {
            total += v.(float64)
        }
        return total
    case uint:
        var total uint = 0
        for _, v := range nums {
            total += v.(uint)
        }
        return total
    default:
        // fallback for unsupported types
        fmt.Printf("Unsupported: %v\n", reflect.TypeOf(nums[0]))
        return nil
    }
}
```

`SumInterface()` takes a slice of `interface{}` elements, meaning it can *theoretically accept values of any type*. Since `interface{}` is not type-specific, the function must *inspect the type of elements at runtime* to perform type-safe operations. The function first checks whether the slice is empty and returns `nil` if so. Then it examines the type of the first element using a `switch` statement on `nums[0].(type)`. For each supported numeric type (`int`, `float64`, `uint`), it initializes an appropriate accumulator (`total`) and iterates over the slice, using **type assertions** such as `v.(int)` to safely convert each element back to its concrete type before adding it to the total. If an unsupported type is encountered, the `default` case prints a warning with `reflect.TypeOf(nums[0])` and returns `nil`. This approach is flexible but has several drawbacks compared to generics: runtime type checks introduce overhead, type assertions can panic if misused, and the function must manually handle each type, making it verbose and less maintainable. In contrast, generics allow compile-time type safety, eliminating the need for runtime checks and simplifying code for multiple numeric types. Run `ch04/generics.go` on your machine to see that both versions generate the same output.

Generics in Go are a powerful addition that allows you to write reusable, type-safe functions and data structures without duplicating code for each type. However, they should be used with care. Generics shine when you are implementing algorithms or data structures that truly operate on multiple types in the same way – functions such as `Sum()` or **generic containers** such as stacks, queues, or maps with custom behaviors. In these cases, generics help reduce code duplication and prevent bugs caused by inconsistent implementations across different types. On the other hand, *using generics everywhere* can make code harder to read and maintain, especially if the problem could be solved more simply with interfaces, concrete types, or plain duplication where clarity is more important than abstraction. Generics can also introduce additional complexity when debugging, as the type constraints may obscure what types are actually being used.

As you progress with Go, you will quickly notice that real-world applications are rarely contained in a single source file. Instead, they rely on a well-structured organization of code into reusable components. This is where **packages** and **modules** come in. Packages are the building blocks of Go programs, allowing you to group related functionality, promote code reuse, and maintain a clean separation of concerns. Understanding how to create, import, and manage packages is an essential step toward writing scalable and maintainable Go projects.

Packages and modules

In Go, **packages** are the building blocks of modular, maintainable, and reusable code. They allow you to organize related functionality into logical units, making complex systems easier to understand and evolve. Every Go program is made up of packages: from the built-in Standard Library that provides core capabilities such as networking, file handling, and concurrency, to custom packages you create to structure your own projects. While packages help you organize and reuse code within a project, modern Go development often extends beyond a single code base. Real-world systems rely on external libraries, and managing these dependencies efficiently is just as important as structuring your own code. That is where **Go modules** come in. Introduced to replace the older `GOPATH`-based workflow, modules provide a robust way to version, fetch, and track dependencies directly within your projects.

So, packages and modules are closely related but serve different purposes in organizing and managing code. A package is the smallest unit of code organization in Go. It consists of one or more `.go` source files located in the same directory, compiled together, and typically grouped because they serve a common purpose. For example, the Standard Library provides packages such as `fmt`, `net/http`, and `math`, each focused on a specific area of functionality. A module, on the other hand, is a higher-level concept introduced in Go 1.11 and made the default in Go 1.13. A module is a collection of related packages that are **versioned** and **managed** as a single unit. A module is defined by the presence of a `go.mod` file at its root, which specifies the module path and declares its dependencies. Unlike packages, modules handle semantic versioning and make it possible to manage external libraries reliably. Think of the hierarchy like files, folders, and projects: individual `.go` source files belong to a package (a directory), and one or more packages together form a module (a project). In *Chapter 12, Time Series Distances*, we will revisit packages.

Once you have a solid understanding of how to structure your code with packages and manage dependencies with modules, the next natural step is to ensure that your code actually works as intended. Organizing code into packages makes it easier to test specific parts of a program in isolation, and modules help guarantee consistency across environments. This brings us to *testing in Go*, a critical practice for building reliable software. In the following section, we will explore how to leverage the `testing` framework to validate functionality, catch regressions, and improve overall code quality.

Testing Go code

Testing is not merely an afterthought in systems programming, but rather it is a critical foundation that determines whether your software will reliably serve users or will catastrophically fail under production loads. Go treats testing as a first-class citizen, providing built-in testing tools and conventions that make it straightforward to verify code correctness, measure performance, and ensure that code behaves predictably under various conditions. The `testing` package offers a pragmatic approach that emphasizes simplicity and convention over configuration, allowing you to write comprehensive test suites without external dependencies or complex frameworks. In systems programming, where bugs can lead to data corruption, security vulnerabilities, or service outages affecting thousands of users, the testing capabilities of Go become your primary defense against catastrophic failures.

Testing in Go is built directly into the language through the `testing` package, which provides a simple yet powerful framework for writing and running unit tests, benchmarks, and examples. Test functions follow a strict naming convention: any function starting with `Test` and taking a single `*testing.T` parameter is recognized as a test by the Go toolchain. You run tests using the `go test` command, which automatically discovers and executes them across your packages. Within a test, you can use methods such as `t.Errorf()` or `t.Fatalf()` to report failures, and subtests can be created with `t.Run()` for organizing related checks. Go also supports table-driven testing, a common idiom where multiple test cases are expressed as rows in a slice and executed in a loop, improving readability and maintainability. Beyond unit tests, the `testing` package supports benchmarks (functions named `BenchmarkXxx`) for performance measurement, and example functions (named `ExampleXxx`) that serve as executable documentation. We continue by testing the functionality of `ch01/basename.go`.

Testing ch01/basename.go

In this section, we test `ch01/basename.go` by comparing its actual results with the expected results. In Go, the convention is that all test files must end with `_test.go` so the `go test` tool can find and run them. So, in our case, we have `ch04/basename.go` as copied from `ch01/` and `ch04/basename_test.go`, which is presented next:

```
package main

import (
    "testing"
)

func TestBasename(t *testing.T) {
    tests := []struct {
        path     string
        suffixes []string
        expected string
    }{
        // Basic filenames
        {"file.txt", nil, "file.txt"},
        {"file.txt", []string{".txt"}, "file"},
        {"file.txt", []string{".log"}, "file.txt"},
        {"/usr/local/bin/go", nil, "go"},
        {"/usr/local/bin/go", []string{"go"}, ""},
        {"/usr/local/bin/go1.20", []string{"1.20"}, "go"},
        {"/usr/local/bin/", nil, "bin"},
```

```
        {"////", nil, "/"}, // multiple slashes collapse to "/"
        {"/", nil, "/"},
        {".gitignore", nil, ".gitignore"},
        {".gitignore", []string{".gitignore"}, ""},
        {"myfile.go.txt", []string{".txt"}, "myfile.go"},
        {"myfile.go.txt", []string{".go.txt"}, "myfile"},
    }

    for _, tc := range tests {
        result := basename(tc.path, tc.suffixes...)
        if result != tc.expected {
            t.Errorf("basename(%q, %q) = %q; want %q",
                tc.path, tc.suffixes, result, tc.expected)
        }
    }
}
```

This test function is a **table-driven test**, a common Go idiom for checking a function against many inputs and expected outputs in a compact and maintainable way. Inside `TestBasename()`, a slice of anonymous structs defines a series of test cases, each containing a `path` string to process, optional `suffixes` to strip, and the `expected` result. The test cases cover a wide variety of scenarios: simple filenames, files with extensions, files in directories, edge cases such as root (`"/"`), and multiple slashes (`"////"`), as well as hidden files such as `.gitignore`. The loop then iterates over all test cases, calls the `basename()` function with the given arguments, and compares the result with the expected value. If they do not match, `t.Errorf()` reports a failure with a descriptive message showing what was received and what was expected.

Now execute the tests on your machine:

```
$ go test -v ch04/basename*
=== RUN   TestBasename
--- PASS: TestBasename (0.00s)
PASS
ok      command-line-arguments  0.219s
```

Everything is OK! Next, we discuss the `synctest` package for testing concurrent programs.

The synctest package

Testing concurrent programs is notoriously difficult because race conditions and timing issues rarely reveal themselves consistently. The `synctest` package in Go addresses this challenge by providing a controlled environment for testing code that relies on synchronization. Instead of leaving the execution order of goroutines to chance, `synctest` gives you deterministic control over scheduling, allowing you to reproduce tricky timing scenarios reliably. This makes it easier to uncover hidden deadlocks, subtle races, and other concurrency-related bugs that traditional testing might miss. The `ch04/synctest_test.go` file contains sample code that demonstrates `synctest` for making concurrent and time-based tests deterministic, reliable, and free from race conditions that often occur in real-world asynchronous code. Each test runs inside a `synctest.Run()` bubble, which isolates goroutines and replaces real time with a controlled fake clock, ensuring that events such as goroutine scheduling, timeouts, and network waits can be tested without depending on actual timing.

The first example, `TestAfterFunc()`, shows how `context.AfterFunc()` can be reliably tested: the test verifies that a function is not called before cancellation and then confirms that it executes after `cancel()` is invoked, with `synctest.Wait()` controlling the synchronization point. The second example, `TestWithTimeout()`, highlights how fake time makes time-based logic reliable and fast – sleeping for nearly the entire timeout and then a single nanosecond triggers the expected deadline without slowing the test. The third example, `TestHTTP100Continue()`, demonstrates protocol testing using `net.Pipe()` for in-memory network connections. It checks that a client waits for a `100 Continue` response before sending its request body, ensuring proper implementation of the HTTP/1.1 expectation mechanism. The fourth example, `TestChannelCommunication()`, verifies producer–consumer behavior over channels, ensuring that messages flow correctly and that goroutines complete deterministically. Finally, `TestBubbleIsolation()` illustrates how `synctest` distinguishes between goroutines and channels created inside the bubble (durably blocking and controlled) versus external resources (not controlled), making concurrency testing safer and more predictable. Now, execute the tests in `ch04/synctest_test.go` – use `GOEXPERIMENT=synctest` as this is currently an experimental feature:

```
$ GOEXPERIMENT=synctest go test ch04/synctest_test.go
ok      command-line-arguments    0.378s
```

It is important to notice that although the tests cover timeouts, sleeps, cancellations, and even protocol exchanges, they still finish quickly. That is because `synctest` uses virtualized time and goroutine control rather than making the program literally wait for five seconds or depend on unpredictable scheduling. Instead, `synctest.Wait()` advances the fake clock and ensures goroutines are synchronized deterministically. As a result, the suite looks as though it exercised real delays and concurrency, but from the outside, it runs in just a fraction of a second. Having explored how Go handles concurrency, memory, and testing, it is time to shift our focus to another essential aspect of systems programming: dealing with dates and times.

Understanding how dates and times work

Working with dates and times is a fundamental task in systems programming, yet it often hides a surprising amount of complexity. Programs need to represent points in time, measure durations, and format timestamps for both human readability and machine processing. In Go, the `time` package provides a powerful and consistent interface for handling these operations, from simple tasks such as getting the current time to more advanced ones such as parsing layouts, scheduling events, and working with time zones.

In Go, *custom date and time formatting* is handled in a way that is both unique and initially surprising. Instead of using placeholder symbols such as `%Y` or `%d` as in many other languages, Go uses a reference date – `Mon Jan 2 15:04:05 MST 2006` – to define layouts. Each component of this date corresponds to a specific part of the time format: `2006` represents the year, `01` the month, `02` the day, `15` the hour in 24-hour format, `03` the hour in 12-hour format, `04` the minutes, `05` the seconds, and `MST` the time zone. To create a custom format, you simply *rearrange and select the relevant portions* of this reference date. For example, a layout of `"2006-01-02 15:04:05"` produces a timestamp in the familiar `YYYY-MM-DD HH:MM:SS` style, while `"02 Jan 2006"` yields a more human-friendly date string. This design ensures that formatting and parsing are tightly linked: if you can define a layout to display a time, you can use the same layout to parse a string back into a `time.Time` object. While it may feel odd at first, this approach is both flexible and memorable. All these are demonstrated in the following `main()` function (`ch04/datesTimes.go`), starting with working with the current system time:

```
func main() {
    // 1. Get the current local time
    now := time.Now()
    fmt.Println("Current local time:", now)

    // 2. Format the current time in different layouts
    fmt.Println("Default format:", now.Format(time.RFC3339))
    fmt.Println("Custom format:", now.Format("Monday, 02-Jan-2006 15:04:05 MST"))
```

The code begins by calling `time.Now()`, which retrieves the current local time as a `time.Time` value. The result is stored in the `now` variable and printed to the console, showing the exact date and time when the program was executed. Next, the code illustrates how to format this time in different ways using the `Format()` method. The first example uses the predefined constant `time.RFC3339`, which outputs the time in a widely used, standardized layout (`YYYY-MM-DDTHH:MM:SSZ`). The second example shows a custom format string: `"Monday, 02-Jan-2006 15:04:05 MST"`. The next part demonstrates two important features of the `time` package: parsing strings into `time.Time` values and performing arithmetic with time durations:

```
// 3. Parse a time string into a time.Time value
layout := "2006-01-02 15:04:05"
input := "2025-09-03 14:30:00"
parsedTime, err := time.Parse(layout, input)
if err != nil {
    fmt.Println("Error parsing time:", err)
    return
}
fmt.Println("Parsed time:", parsedTime)
// 4. Add and subtract durations
twoHoursLater := now.Add(2 * time.Hour)
thirtyMinutesEarlier := now.Add(-30 * time.Minute)
fmt.Println("Two hours later:", twoHoursLater)
fmt.Println("Thirty minutes earlier:", thirtyMinutesEarlier)
```

First, the code defines a layout string: `"2006-01-02 15:04:05"`. The input string `"2025-09-03 14:30:00"` is then parsed using `time.Parse()`, producing a `time.Time` value that represents that exact date and time. If parsing fails, the error is handled gracefully. Next, the code shows how to manipulate time by adding and subtracting durations. By calling `now.Add(2 * time.Hour)`, it computes a new time two hours ahead of now, and with `now.Add(-30 * time.Minute)`, it calculates a time 30 minutes earlier. This final section demonstrates comparing times, handling time zones, and calculating durations:

```
// 5. Compare times
if parsedTime.After(now) {
    fmt.Println("Parsed time is in the future.")
} else {
    fmt.Println("Parsed time is in the past.")
}
// 6. Work with time zones
// Convert local time to UTC
utc := now.UTC()
fmt.Println("UTC time:", utc)
// Load a specific time zone
loc, err := time.LoadLocation("America/New_York")
```

```
    if err != nil {
        fmt.Println("Error loading location:", err)
        return
    }
    nyTime := now.In(loc)
    fmt.Println("Time in New York:", nyTime)
    // 7. Calculate duration between two times
    duration := parsedTime.Sub(now)
    fmt.Printf("Duration between now and parsed time: %v\n", duration)
}
```

The program first checks whether `parsedTime` is later than the current `now` value, printing whether the parsed timestamp lies in the future or the past. It then shows how to convert a local time to **Coordinated Universal Time** (**UTC**) using the `UTC()` method, which is essential for standardizing timestamps across different systems. Next, it illustrates working with custom time zones by calling `time.LoadLocation("America/New_York")`. If successful, the program converts the current time into that zone with `now.In(loc)` and prints it, allowing us to view the same moment from another region's perspective. Finally, the code calculates the exact duration between two time values by subtracting `now` from `parsedTime` using `Sub()`. The result is a `time.Duration` object that expresses the difference, which can be positive or negative depending on whether the parsed time is ahead of or behind the current time. Execute `ch04/datesTimes.go` on your machine to see its output and try to explain it.

Now that you have seen how to handle dates and times in Go, it is a good moment to shift our focus from correctness to performance. While working with time values is essential for scheduling, logging, and real-world applications, developers also need to understand how efficiently their code runs. This brings us to **benchmarking**, a process that allows us to measure execution speed and resource usage in a controlled and repeatable way.

Benchmarking Go code

Benchmarking in Go is a first-class feature of the testing framework that enables precise performance measurement and optimization validation. The Go benchmarking system leverages statistical analysis, automatic iteration scaling (a mechanism for running your benchmark the right number of times so that the timing data is accurate, stable, and statistically meaningful), and sub-nanosecond timing precision to provide reliable performance insights. The framework integrates deeply with the optimization pipeline and runtime profiling infrastructure of the compiler, allowing developers to correlate performance characteristics with actual code execution patterns and resource utilization.

Benchmarking in Go is not just about measuring speed: it is about collecting accurate, repeatable data to make informed engineering decisions. Always use the built-in testing framework by placing benchmarks in `*_test.go` files and leveraging the `testing.B` type, which integrates seamlessly with the toolchain. Running commands such as `go test -bench=. -benchmem` provides both execution time and memory allocation statistics, giving you a more complete performance profile. When writing benchmarks, focus on *isolating the code under test* and avoid unrelated computations, disk operations, or network calls that could distort results. Make sure to use representative datasets so that the measurements reflect real-world scenarios rather than idealized edge cases.

Benchmark functions follow a specific pattern: they receive a `*testing.B` parameter and typically include a `for` loop that iterates from `0` to `b.N`. This loop ensures that the operation being measured runs enough times for the benchmarking framework to collect reliable timing data. The value of `b.N` is *automatically adjusted by the Go testing framework* to achieve statistically meaningful measurements. Inside the loop, the code performs the operation under test so that the total runtime accurately reflects the cost of repeated executions.

Benchmarking ch04/jsonReflection.go

When working with features such as reflection, which inherently introduce runtime overhead, intuition alone is rarely sufficient to understand their impact. Benchmarks allow you to *measure execution time, memory usage, and allocation patterns* under realistic workloads, giving you a clear picture of how different implementations compare. In the case of custom JSON encoding versus the standard `encoding/json` package, benchmarking highlights the *trade-offs between flexibility and efficiency*. It helps you decide whether a specialized, reflection-based solution justifies its additional complexity or whether the built-in package already meets your performance needs. More broadly, this kind of benchmarking cultivates a performance-oriented mindset, ensuring that design decisions are driven by data rather than assumptions, which is an essential skill when building reliable, high-performance systems. Here is the example benchmarking code; feel free to look at the code of `ch04/jsonReflection.go`:

```
package main

import (
    "encoding/json"
    "testing"
)

var cfg = ServerConfig{
    Name: "api",
```

```
    Port: 8080,
    Tags: []string{"go", "prod"},
    Limits: map[string]uint32{
        "requests_per_min": 1200,
        "conn":             100,
    },
    TLS: &TLSConfig{
        Enabled: true,
        CertPEM: "-----BEGIN CERTIFICATE--------...",
    },
    Metadata: map[string]any{
        "region":   "eu-central-1",
        "revision": 42,
        "debug":    false,
    },
}

// Benchmark: Standard library JSON encoder (compact)
func BenchmarkStdJSONCompact(b *testing.B) {
    for i := 0; i < b.N; i++ {
        _, _ = json.Marshal(cfg)
    }
}

// Benchmark: Custom reflection-based encoder (compact)
func BenchmarkCustomJSONCompact(b *testing.B) {
    enc := &Encoder{} // no indentation, compact mode
    for i := 0; i < b.N; i++ {
        _ = enc.Marshal(cfg)
    }
}

// Benchmark: Standard library JSON encoder (pretty)
func BenchmarkStdJSONPretty(b *testing.B) {
    for i := 0; i < b.N; i++ {
        _, _ = json.MarshalIndent(cfg, "", "  ")
    }
}

// Benchmark: Custom reflection-based encoder (pretty)
func BenchmarkCustomJSONPretty(b *testing.B) {
```

```
    enc := &Encoder{Indent: "  ", SortMapKeys: true}
    for i := 0; i < b.N; i++ {
        _ = enc.Marshal(cfg)
    }
}
```

This code defines a set of benchmarks to measure JSON encoding performance in Go. The `cfg` variable represents a sample server configuration containing nested structures, slices, maps, pointers, and fields with heterogeneous types. The first benchmark, `BenchmarkStdJSONCompact()`, measures the performance of the `json.Marshal()` function when producing compact JSON without indentation. The second, `BenchmarkCustomJSONCompact()`, tests a custom reflection-based encoder in compact mode, iterating `b.N` times to produce JSON for the same configuration. Similarly, `BenchmarkStdJSONPretty()` uses `json.MarshalIndent()` to produce human-readable, indented JSON, while `BenchmarkCustomJSONPretty()` evaluates the custom encoder configured with indentation and key sorting for readability. By running these benchmarks, we can compare the efficiency of the built-in JSON serialization against a custom implementation under both compact and pretty-printed scenarios, gaining insights into performance trade-offs in encoding complex data structures:

```
$ go test -bench=. -benchmem ch04/jsonReflection*
goos: darwin
goarch: arm64
cpu: Apple M4 Pro
BenchmarkStdJSONCompact-14    1861180 629.3 ns/op 664 B/op  14 allocs/op
BenchmarkCustomJSONComact-14 935070   1289 ns/op   904 B/op 30 allocs/op
BenchmarkStdJSONPretty-14     778904   1478 ns/op  1145 B/op 5 allocs/op
BenchmarkCustomJSONPretty-14 633439   1850 ns/op  1670 B/op 44 allocs/op
PASS
ok      command-line-arguments    5.777s
```

In the first two benchmarks (`*Compact()`), we see that the Standard Library is significantly faster and more memory-efficient when producing compact JSON (that is, JSON without extra whitespace). The standard implementation processes about *1.86 million operations per second*, taking roughly 629.3 nanoseconds per operation, with 664 bytes allocated and 14 allocations per operation. In contrast, the custom reflection-based encoder handles only *935,070 operations per second* and takes roughly 1.29 microseconds per operation, while also using more memory (904 bytes per operation) and performing more than twice as many allocations (30 allocations per operation). After that, the next benchmarks (`*Pretty()`) measure the performance when generating **pretty-printed JSON** (formatted with indentation and line breaks). Again, the

Standard Library version performs better, averaging 1.48 microseconds per operation with 1145 bytes allocated and only 5 allocations per operation. The custom encoder is slower at around 1.85 microseconds per operation, and is less memory-efficient, requiring 1670 bytes and 44 allocations per operation.

Overall, these results highlight that the `encoding/json` package is highly optimized, both in terms of speed and memory usage, compared to a custom reflection-based solution. While writing your own JSON encoder with reflection provides flexibility and fine-grained control over serialization, it introduces a performance penalty and typically increases memory allocations. Therefore, unless you have very specific serialization requirements or need custom encoding rules that the built-in tools of Go cannot handle, the standard JSON encoder is the better choice for most production scenarios.

Benchmarking PGO gains

To better understand how PGO works in practice, let us work with a small Go example (found in `ch04/PGO/`) designed to highlight the difference between hot and cold execution paths. The code simulates a workload where one branch of a function is executed the vast majority of the time, while the other branch is rarely taken. By benchmarking this function, we can produce a profile that captures the frequency of each path. But first, let us discuss application profiling.

Profiling applications

Profiling applications is an essential practice in systems programming that allows developers to understand how their programs consume resources, identify performance bottlenecks, and optimize critical paths. In Go, profiling goes beyond simple benchmarking in that it provides detailed runtime information such as CPU usage, memory allocation, goroutine activity, and blocking operations. By instrumenting a program and analyzing its behavior under realistic workloads, developers can pinpoint inefficiencies, detect memory leaks, and make informed decisions to improve throughput, reduce latency, and enhance overall system performance. Profiling forms the foundation for advanced techniques such as **Profile-Guided Optimization (PGO)**, where observed execution patterns guide the compiler in generating faster, more efficient code.

From a technical perspective, Go provides several built-in tools for profiling applications. The `runtime/pprof` package enables CPU and memory profiling by instrumenting code to collect detailed runtime statistics, which can then be written to profile files and visualized using tools such as `go tool pprof`. CPU profiles record the amount of time spent in each function, highlighting hot paths that dominate execution, while memory profiles track allocations and object lifetimes, helping to identify leaks and inefficient memory usage. Additionally, Go supports block and mutex profiling, which reveals contention points and synchronization bottlenecks in concurrent programs. These profiles can be analyzed interactively (use `ch04/PGO/processData.go` to see how to collect profiling data).

We are not going to present any code here; you should adjust your own programs and make them suitable for benchmarking based on your code. What is important is to understand that PGO requires a **representative workload** during the profiling phase to be effective, meaning the profile data you collect should accurately reflect the typical usage patterns of the application at hand in production environments. The profiling run should exercise the same hot paths, branch patterns, and function call frequencies that your application encounters in real-world scenarios, as *PGO optimizations are only as good as the training data provided.* Additionally, you must ensure your code includes the necessary profiling instrumentation, either through benchmark functions in test files or by adding CPU profiling capabilities directly to your main application using the `runtime/pprof` package. The key insight is that PGO works best with applications that have clear performance bottlenecks, predictable execution patterns, and sufficient complexity to benefit from compiler optimizations. Simple programs with straightforward control flow may see minimal improvements, while complex applications with interface dispatch, branching logic, and hot loops typically experience the most significant performance gains from profile-guided compilation.

Go to the `ch04/PGO/` directory and run `go mod init` to create a module environment, which is needed for this project. Now execute the following commands on your machine:

```
$ go run processData.go -cpuprofile=cpu.prof
$ ls -l cpu.prof
-rw-r--r--  1 mtsouk  staff  699 Sep 22 21:18 cpu.prof
$ go test -bench=. -count=10 > before.txt
$ go test -pgo=cpu.prof -bench=. -count=10 > after.txt
```

We are also going to use the `benchstat` utility to analyze the differences between the benchmarks. You can download and install `benchstat` on `~/go/bin` by running the `go install golang.org/x/perf/cmd/benchstat@latest` command. Now, let us compare `before.txt` and `after.txt` using the handy `benchstat` utility:

```
$ ~/go/bin/benchstat before.txt after.txt
goos: darwin
goarch: arm64
pkg: github.com/mactsouk/goSP2/ch04/PGO
cpu: Apple M4 Pro
                    │ before.txt │              after.txt              │
                    │   sec/op   │    sec/op     vs base               │
```

```
DramaticWorkload-14      98.08n ± 1%    100.80n ± 1%  +2.78% (p=0.000 n=10)
InterfaceDispatch-14     13.23n ± 5%     12.52n ± 2%  -5.40% (p=0.014 n=10)
CalculateMetrics-14      25.13n ± 7%     24.46n ± 0%  -2.67% (p=0.003 n=10)
geomean                  31.95n          31.37n       -1.82%
```

The `benchstat` results reveal a picture of the PGO performance impact across different computational patterns, demonstrating both the benefits and limitations of profile-guided optimization on modern hardware. The `DramaticWorkload` benchmark shows a counterintuitive 2.78% performance regression (98.08ns to 100.80ns), which is statistically significant (`p=0.000`) and suggests that the optimization decisions of PGO may have inadvertently hurt performance for this complex mixed workload – possibly due to code layout changes, altered inlining decisions, or cache effects that negatively impact the overall execution flow. Conversely, the `InterfaceDispatch` benchmark demonstrates the primary strength of PGO, with a meaningful 5.40% improvement (`13.23ns` to `12.52ns`, `p=0.014`), indicating successful devirtualization in which the compiler eliminated interface call overhead by directly dispatching to the frequently used concrete type identified during profiling. The `CalculateMetrics` benchmark shows a modest 2.67% improvement (`25.13ns` to `24.46ns`, `p=0.003`), likely resulting from better function inlining decisions based on the profile data showing this function's frequent execution. The geometric mean of `-1.82%` suggests that, overall, PGO provided a small net benefit across all benchmarks combined, but these results highlight the inherent unpredictability of PGO optimizations. Improvements in specific areas can be offset by regressions elsewhere, which emphasizes the importance of comprehensive testing when deploying PGO-optimized binaries in production environments. The `p`-value indicates the statistical significance of an observed performance difference, representing the probability that the measured change occurred purely by chance rather than due to a real performance improvement or regression. A smaller `p`-value provides stronger evidence that the observed difference represents a genuine performance change rather than measurement noise.

In the next chapter, we are going to see more benchmarking examples as we examine file I/O techniques.

Summary

This chapter guided you through some of the most important aspects of Go's runtime and standard tooling. You learned how the GC operates, how its behavior can be tuned using the `GOGC` environment variable, and what trade-offs are involved in balancing memory usage and collection frequency. We also explored interfaces, empty interfaces, and generics, emphasizing when each approach makes sense and what pitfalls to avoid. A good rule of thumb is to reach for generics only when the logic is truly type-agnostic and will be reused across multiple types. For everyday business logic or domain-specific problems, sticking with concrete types or interfaces often keeps the code simpler, clearer, and more idiomatic. On the practical side, you saw how to test and benchmark Go applications effectively. Finally, we examined profiling and PGO. *Ultimately, effective benchmarking is about understanding trade-offs rather than chasing raw speed.*

The next chapter is about interacting with the external environment. The Go Standard Library provides robust and efficient tools for reading from and writing to files, which is a core requirement for almost any real-world application, from data processing pipelines to configuration management. So, we will shift our focus to the `os` and `io` packages, exploring the key concepts and practical patterns for handling file input and output, and ensuring that our applications can seamlessly store, retrieve, and manipulate data on disk.

Exercises

1. Create two different functions that reverse a string: one using `[]rune` and one using `byte` manipulation. Now compare their performance.
2. Extend the `Shape` interface example by adding a `Triangle` type. Implement its `Area()` and `Perimeter()` methods and verify that it works with the `printShapeInfo()` function.
3. Create tests for `ch04/basename.go` by comparing the output of `basename()` with the output the `filepath.Base()` function of the Standard Library.
4. Create a generic `Max()` function that returns the maximum value from a slice of numeric types. Test it with `[]int`, `[]float64`, and `[]uint`.
5. Write a program that allocates a large slice of integers inside a loop. Run the program with different values of `GOGC` (10, 100, 200) and record how `HeapAlloc` and `NumGC` change. Explain what you observe.
6. Write a program that generates prime numbers up to a large `n`. Enable CPU profiling and heap profiling using the `pprof` package and analyze where most time and memory are spent.

Additional resources

- Testing Time (and other asynchronicities): `https://go.dev/blog/testing-time`
- The `testing` package: `https://pkg.go.dev/testing`
- The `benchstat` utility: `https://pkg.go.dev/golang.org/x/perf/cmd/benchstat`
- The `runtime/pprof` package: `https://pkg.go.dev/runtime/pprof`

Part 2

Systems Programming Essentials

In the second part of the book, we transition from the language itself to the interface between Go and the underlying system. We explore the mechanics of high-performance file I/O and the nuances of Unix signals, ensuring your applications can interact gracefully with the kernel and handle asynchronous events with precision. The progression moves from local resource management to distributed systems, covering structured data persistence and the programming of TCP/IP services. By examining how Go handles TCP/IP networking and web service creation, you will gain the expertise required to build resilient backend infrastructure that scales effectively without sacrificing simplicity or safety.

This part of the book includes the following chapters:

- *Chapter 5, Working with File I/O*
- *Chapter 6, UNIX Signals and File Systems*
- *Chapter 7, Working with Structured Data and Databases*
- *Chapter 8, Programming TCP/IP Services*
- *Chapter 9, Creating Web Services*

5

Working with File I/O

In this chapter, you are going to learn how to perform file I/O operations. These play a key role in many Go applications, from reading configuration files to processing large datasets. The `os`, `io`, and `bufio` packages of the Go standard library provide robust tools for creating, reading, writing, and manipulating files efficiently. Whether you are dealing with text, binary data, or structured formats such as JSON or CSV, the simplicity and performance of Go make file operations straightforward. So, we are going to explore common file operations, error-handling best practices, and techniques for working with files effectively in Go, including how to read plain text files line by line, word by word, and character by character. These three approaches form the foundation of text processing and give you practical techniques to handle a wide variety of input scenarios, such as scanning large log files without overwhelming memory, counting words in a document, or analyzing text with high precision.

In Go, **byte slices** (`[]byte`) are the fundamental building blocks for file I/O operations. Whenever you read from or write to a file, the data is handled in terms of bytes, and slices provide a flexible container for that data. Functions such as `os.ReadFile()` return the entire file contents as a `[]byte` byte slice, while methods such as `File.Read()` and `File.Write()` operate on slices provided by you. This design gives you fine-grained control: you can decide the size of the slice (and therefore the chunk size of reads or writes), reuse slices to reduce allocations, or manipulate raw bytes directly before converting them into higher-level data types such as strings or structs.

Interfaces also play a central role in file I/O, providing a powerful abstraction that separates what operations are performed from their implementation. The `io.Writer` and `io.Reader` interfaces allow code to write to or read from any data source that implements these methods, whether it is a file on disk, standard output, a network connection or an in-memory buffer. This design enables highly flexible and reusable code: a single function can accept any `io.Reader` or `io.Writer` interface without knowing the underlying type, making it easy to compose file operations, buffers, and other streams in a uniform way.

This chapter covers the following main topics:

- Reading files
- Writing files
- Buffered and unbuffered file I/O operations
- Logging in Go
- Copying files
- Implementing `wc(1)`

But let us begin with some food for thought.

When learning, implement what you need or like

Building something that you need or like is one of the best ways to learn a new programming language, so it is good to implement something as soon as possible, but not sooner! This means you should spend some time learning the language or the libraries that you need, but make experimentation and implementation parts of the learning process. I usually begin by implementing traditional Unix command-line tools such as `wc(1)` and `cp(1)`, mainly because I like systems programming. Your tastes might vary, so you might like to implement a game, a REST client, or a productivity tool. Other good candidates include bots that fetch X tweets based on given keywords, utilities that post images to Instagram, or weather applications. If you want something more challenging, then you might try implementing a Unix service such as `cron(8)`, a programming language, or even a network traffic analyzer. *The choice is yours, and it mainly depends on your passion, your skill level, your time commitments, and your interests.* However, the benefits of such a task are enormous, as you learn how to use a programming language for real-world applications. And who knows, you just might end up starting a new company from such side projects!

stdin, stdout, and stderr

Every Unix operating system has three files open all the time for its processes. Unix uses file descriptors, which are positive integer values, as an internal representation for accessing open files. This is much prettier than using long paths. By default, all Unix systems support three special and standard filenames: `/dev/stdin`, `/dev/stdout`, and `/dev/stderr`, which can also be accessed using `0`, `1`, and 2 file descriptors, respectively. These three file descriptors are also called **standard input**, **standard output**, and **standard error**, respectively. Go uses `os.Stdin` for accessing standard input, `os.Stdout` for accessing standard output, and `os.Stderr` for accessing standard error. Although you can still use `/dev/stdin`, `/dev/stdout`, and `/dev/stderr`, it is safer and more portable to stick with `os.Stdin`, `os.Stdout`, and `os.Stderr`. While `stdin`, `stdout`, and stderr provide the standard channels for a process to communicate with its environment, most real-world applications eventually need to go beyond these transient streams and interact with persistent storage. The most fundamental step in this shift is verifying the environment before we attempt to manipulate it. With that in mind, let us learn how to tell whether a path exists or not.

Checking whether a file path exists

Checking whether a file path exists is a common task in Go programs that interact with the filesystem because the filesystem is an external dependency that is not under our direct control. Before reading, writing, or modifying a file, it is often necessary to verify that the given path points to a valid file or directory. Here is the `main()` function implementation of `ch05/doesItExist.go`, which determines whether a given filesystem path exists and reports the result to the user:

```
func main() {
    if len(os.Args) < 2 {
        fmt.Println("Usage:", os.Args[0], "<path>")
        os.Exit(1)
    }
    path := os.Args[1]

    _, err := os.Stat(path)
    if err == nil {
        fmt.Printf("Path %s exists.\n", path)
        return
    }

    if errors.Is(err, fs.ErrNotExist) {
        fmt.Printf("Path %s does not exist.\n", path)
        return
    }

    // Other possible errors (e.g., permission issues)
    fmt.Fprintf(os.Stderr, "Error checking path: %v\n", err)
    os.Exit(1)
}
```

The code calls `os.Stat()`, which attempts to retrieve information about the file or directory at the specified path. If `os.Stat()` succeeds without error, the program concludes that the path exists and prints a confirmation message. If the function returns an error, the program checks whether the error is of type `fs.ErrNotExist` using `errors.Is()`. In that case, it clearly reports that the path does not exist. For any other type of error – such as insufficient permissions or unexpected I/O issues – the program writes an error message to standard error and exits with a nonzero status code. Now, run the program to get information about Unix paths:

```
$ go run ch05/doesItExist.go /bin/ls
Path /bin/ls exists.
$ go run ch05/doesItExist.go /bin/doesNOTexist
Path /bin/doesNOTexist does not exist.
```

Once we have established that the resource is reachable and valid, we must then negotiate with the operating system to open a stream and pull the raw bytes into our application's memory. Reading files is the gateway to working with external information — transforming static bits on a disk into actionable data for analyzing logs or handling large datasets — and it is the necessary next step in our interaction with the filesystem.

Reading files

Reading files is one of the most common operations in Go, and the standard library offers multiple approaches you can use, according to your needs. For simple cases where you want the *entire content at once*, `os.ReadFile()` is the most convenient choice, returning the file contents as a byte slice. For streaming access, `os.Open()` combined with a `bufio.Scanner` instance lets you iterate line by line or even word by word, making it memory-efficient for large files. If you need lower-level control, `bufio.NewReader()` provides methods such as `ReadBytes()`, `ReadString()`, or `ReadRune()` for fine-grained reading. The next program (`ch05/readFile.go`) demonstrates the simplest way to read the contents of a file in Go:

```
func main() {
    if len(os.Args) < 2 {
        fmt.Println("Usage:", os.Args[0], "<filename>")
        os.Exit(1)
    }
    filename := os.Args[1]
    data, err := os.ReadFile(filename)
    if err != nil {
        fmt.Fprintf(os.Stderr, "Error reading file: %v\n", err)
        os.Exit(1)
    }
    fmt.Printf("Read %s: %d bytes\n", filename, len(data))
}
```

After checking that a filename has been provided as a command-line argument, the code uses `os.ReadFile()` to load the entire contents of the specified file into memory. The `os.ReadFile()` function is a convenience function in the Go standard library that handles opening the file, reading all its data into a byte slice, and then closing the file automatically. If an error occurs, the error is reported, and the program exits. Once the file data is successfully read, we print its length. *Although this approach is straightforward and efficient for small to medium-sized files, a streaming approach may be preferable to avoid high memory usage when dealing with very large files.* Additionally, although `os.Stat()` is useful for checking file properties, it does not give access to the file's data. The `os.ReadFile()` function is the right choice when you need the actual file data. If the file path does not exist, then `os.ReadFile()` will find that out, just as `os.Stat()` did. Let us now try `readFile.go`:

```
$ go run ch05/readFile.go README.md
Read README.md: 521 bytes
```

> **Note**
>
> If you try `go run ch05/readFile.go ch05/readFile.go`, the command will fail because Go interprets the second `ch05/readFile.go` as another source file to compile, not as a command-line argument for your program. In that case, you should `go build` your source code file first and use the binary executable.

Before we dive into writing file content, however, it is important to understand file seeking, which allows us to move the read/write cursor to arbitrary positions within a file.

File seeking

File seeking allows you to move the read or write cursor within an open file, giving you precise control over where data is accessed so that you can access just the parts you need. This is particularly useful for tasks such as resuming partial downloads, reading specific sections of large files, or updating records in place. Go provides this functionality through the `Seek()` method on `*os.File`, which takes an offset and a `whence` argument (`io.SeekStart`, `io.SeekCurrent`, or `io.SeekEnd`) to specify the reference point for the offset. For example, `file.Seek(0, io.SeekStart)` positions the cursor at *the beginning of the file,* while `file.Seek(-10, io.SeekEnd)` moves it *10 bytes before the end.* When combined with functions such as `Read()` or `ReadAt()`, seeking gives you random-access capabilities that go beyond simple sequential reading. Look at the example code of `seekAndRead()` as found in `ch05/fseek.go`, which demonstrates how to open a file, move the read pointer to a specific offset, and then read a given number of bytes:

```
func seekAndRead(fileName string, offset int64, length int) ([]byte, error) {
    // Open file
    f, err := os.Open(fileName)
    if err != nil {
        return nil, fmt.Errorf("error opening file: %w", err)
    }
    defer f.Close()

    // Seek to offset
    _, err = f.Seek(offset, io.SeekStart)
    if err != nil {
        return nil, fmt.Errorf("error seeking file: %w", err)
    }

    // Read requested bytes
    buf := make([]byte, length)
    n, err := f.Read(buf)
    if err != nil && err.Error() != "EOF" {
        return nil, fmt.Errorf("error reading file: %w", err)
    }
    return buf[:n], nil
}
```

The code begins by opening the file using `os.Open()`, and if this fails, it returns an error wrapped with context. With the file safely opened, it uses `f.Seek(offset, io.SeekStart)` to move the read pointer to the desired offset, where `0` indicates that the offset is measured from the beginning of the file. Next, it allocates a `buf` byte slice of the requested length and attempts to read data into it using `f.Read()`. The function then handles any read errors, making sure to allow `EOF` as a non-fatal condition, and finally returns the slice of bytes actually read. Observe how `os.Open()` and `os.ReadFile()` serve different purposes in Go, even though both are used to work with files. The `os.Open()` function opens a file and returns a file descriptor (`*os.File`), which you can then use for operations such as reading chunks of data, seeking within the file, or streaming large files. It gives you fine-grained control over how the file is accessed, making it suitable for very large files where you do not want to load everything into memory. The `os.ReadFile()` function, on the other hand, is a convenience function that opens the file internally, reads its entire contents into memory as a byte slice, and then closes the file for you.

This makes `os.ReadFile()` simpler to use when dealing with small to medium-sized files, where you just need the full contents at once; it is less efficient or even impractical for very large files.

Now, try `ch05/fseek.go` on your machine using the plain text file of your choice. The output is going to be similar to the following:

```
$ go run ch05/fseek.go /tmp/sample_large.txt 100 10
Read 10 bytes from offset 100:
e, and eff
```

Once we can open and seek within files, the next step is to explore unbuffered reading, where data is read directly from the file without any intermediate buffering.

Unbuffered reading

Unbuffered reading in Go refers to reading data directly from an input source, such as a file, network connection, or standard input, without the use of an intermediate buffer. This approach means that each read operation fetches data immediately from the underlying source and typically results in a smaller, more granular amount of data per read call. While unbuffered reading provides the simplest and most direct way to access data, it can be less efficient for high-throughput scenarios (because it involves more *frequent system calls*) and can increase latency. This approach gives you fine-grained control and is useful when you want to process binary data, partial records at a time, or when working with custom buffering strategies.

The following code snippet from `ch05/unbufRead.go` demonstrates *unbuffered file reading* in small chunks and illustrates how raw bytes can be processed as they are read:

```
    // Read the file unbuffered
    buffer := make([]byte, 16) // 16-byte buffer
    byteCount := 0

    for {
        n, err := file.Read(buffer)
        if n > 0 {
            byteCount++
            // Print first 16x bytes to show the reading process
            if byteCount <= 50 {
                if buffer[0] == '\n' {
                    fmt.Printf("\\n")
                } else if buffer[0] == '\t' {
                    fmt.Printf("\\t")
                } else if buffer[0] < 32 || buffer[0] > 126 {
```

```
                fmt.Printf(".")
            } else {
                fmt.Printf("%c", buffer[0])
            }
        }
    }
    if err != nil {
        break
    }
}
```

A slice of 16 bytes is created with `make([]byte, 16)`, which acts as a temporary buffer for each read operation. Inside the loop, the call to `file.Read(buffer)` attempts to fill the slice with data from the file and returns the number of bytes actually read (`n`). If any bytes are read, `byteCount` is incremented, and for the first 50 iterations, the program inspects the *first byte of the buffer* to print a representation of it. Special handling is included: newline characters are shown as `\n`, tabs as `\t`, and non-printable or out-of-ASCII-range bytes are replaced with a dot. Otherwise, the character itself is printed. The loop continues until an error occurs (typically `io.EOF`, meaning the *end of the file*), at which point the loop breaks. If we try `ch05/unbufRead.go`, we get the following output:

```
$ go run ch05/unbufRead.go /tmp/sample_large.txt
Reading file '/tmp/sample_large.txt' using unbuffered I/O:
Reading byte by byte...
=orlkuiiuspesit pmb tarresr2&"iyNhoes g dltenvymif...

Total bytes read: 655362
Each byte required a separate system call to the OS.
```

Let us now, in the next subsection, see how buffered reading works.

Buffered reading

Buffered reading in Go involves reading data through an intermediate buffer, which temporarily stores chunks of data from the input source before the program processes it. This technique reduces the number of direct read operations on the underlying source by fetching larger blocks of data at once, improving efficiency and performance – especially when dealing with slow or costly I/O such as disk files or network streams. The Go standard library provides convenient tools such as `bufio.Reader` that handle buffering transparently, letting you read data in smaller pieces while benefiting from fewer system calls. This makes buffered reading the preferred choice when working with text files or line-by-line processing, as it reduces overhead and provides higher-level abstractions, while unbuffered reading is more suitable for low-level or performance-sensitive tasks where control over the exact read size matters. The `bufio.Reader` tool defaults to an internal 4 KB buffer because this size strikes a balance between memory usage and system call efficiency. On most modern operating systems, disk and filesystem blocks are typically multiples of 4 KB, so aligning the buffer size with this block size reduces wasted reads and allows efficient interaction with the OS page cache. If you want a different size (say a 16 KB buffer), then you can write `reader := bufio.NewReaderSize(file, 16*1024)`.

The following code snippet (`ch05/bufRead.go`) shows how to use buffered I/O with the `bufio` package:

```
// Create a buffered reader with default buffer size (4KB)
reader := bufio.NewReader(file)
byteCount := 0

// Read the file using buffered I/O
for {
    b, err := reader.ReadByte()
    if err != nil {
        break
    }
    byteCount++
    if byteCount <= 50 {
        if b == '\n' {
            fmt.Printf("\\n")
        } else if b == '\t' {
            fmt.Printf("\\t")
        } else if b < 32 || b > 126 {
            fmt.Printf(".")
        } else {
            fmt.Printf("%c", b)
        }
    }
}
```

A `bufio.NewReader(file)` instance is created with the default buffer size of 4 KB. Inside the loop, the program calls `reader.ReadByte()`, which retrieves a single byte from the internal buffer. Only when the buffer runs out does `ReadByte()` trigger a system call to refill it, making it far more efficient than calling `file.Read()` for each byte. The `byteCount` and `readOperations` counters track how many bytes and read operations have been performed. As before, the first `50` bytes are printed, with special formatting for newlines (`\n`), tabs (`\t`), and non-printable characters (shown as a dot). Use `ch05/bufRead.go` on your machine to see the kind of output it creates.

Now that we have seen how buffered and unbuffered reading work in practice, the next step is to benchmark their performance side by side to measure the impact of buffering on speed and efficiency.

Benchmarking buffered and unbuffered reading

In this section, we will focus on *benchmarking buffered and unbuffered reading* to compare their performance characteristics. Instead of walking through code examples, which we have already explored in detail, we will concentrate on the results of running benchmarks under different conditions. The benchmarks can be found in `ch05/reading_test.go`, which creates a file at `/tmp/largefile.txt` for testing purposes:

```
$ go test -bench . ch05/reading_test.go
goos: darwin
goarch: arm64
cpu: Apple M4 Pro
BenchmarkUnbufferedRead-14                    1    3571846500 ns/op
BenchmarkBufferedRead-14                     58      20271705 ns/op
PASS
ok      command-line-arguments     5.226s
```

The benchmark results clearly highlight the dramatic difference between unbuffered and buffered file reading in Go. The unbuffered version (`BenchmarkUnbufferedRead`) took about `3.57` seconds to complete just a single iteration, which shows how inefficient it is to read a file 1 byte at a time. Every `Read()` system call incurs kernel overhead, and when repeated millions of times, this adds up quickly. In contrast, the buffered version (`BenchmarkBufferedRead`) ran `58` iterations at roughly `20` milliseconds per iteration. This makes buffered reads not just faster, but also more scalable as file sizes grow.

With the benchmark results in hand, we can now transition to profiling buffered and unbuffered reading, examining how CPU and memory resources are used by each method as well as timings.

Profiling buffered and unbuffered reading

Using the `runtime/pprof` package, we can capture detailed information about function call frequency, allocation patterns, and system interactions. The relevant program (`ch05/`

`profReading.go`) is long, so we are going to present just the most important parts of it, starting with the code for basic profiling setup:

```
import (
    "runtime/pprof"
    "os"
)

// Start CPU profiling
f, err := os.Create("cpu.prof")
if err != nil {
    log.Fatal(err)
}
defer f.Close()

if err := pprof.StartCPUProfile(f); err != nil {
    log.Fatal(err)
}
defer pprof.StopCPUProfile()

// Your I/O operations here...

// Write memory profile
runtime.GC() // Force GC for accurate memory profile
if err := pprof.WriteHeapProfile(memFile); err != nil {
    log.Fatal(err)
}
```

This code snippet demonstrates how to *enable and collect runtime profiling data* in Go using the `runtime/pprof` package. It begins by creating a file named `cpu.prof` where **CPU profiling** data will be written. The call to `pprof.StartCPUProfile(f)` activates CPU profiling, which records where the program spends time during execution, and the deferred call to `pprof.StopCPUProfile()` ensures that profiling stops and data is flushed when the program ends. You place the code you want to profile between these two calls. Unlike CPU profiling, **memory profiling** does not require starting and stopping a session with dedicated function calls. Go runtime is always tracking memory allocations in the background. To capture this information, you simply call `pprof.WriteHeapProfile()`, which writes the current heap statistics to the provided file, which must be created beforehand, such as `cpu.prof`. It is common to call `runtime.GC()` just before writing the profile to ensure that the data reflects the most recent state of the program. So, while CPU profiling requires actively starting and stopping, memory profiling is *always on* and only needs to be dumped at the right time using `WriteHeapProfile()`.

The following two functions demonstrate the fundamental difference between unbuffered and buffered file reading in Go, while maintaining identical high-level behavior but dramatically different performance characteristics:

```
// Unbuffered reading - shows the performance problem
func readUnbuffered(filename string) int64 {
    file, _ := os.Open(filename)
    defer file.Close()

    buffer := make([]byte, 1) // Single byte - the key issue!
    totalBytes := int64(0)

    for {
        n, err := file.Read(buffer)
        if n > 0 {
            totalBytes += int64(n)
        }
        if err == io.EOF {
            break
        }
    }
    return totalBytes
}

// Buffered reading - shows the solution
func readBuffered(filename string) int64 {
    file, _ := os.Open(filename)
    defer file.Close()

    reader := bufio.NewReader(file) // Key difference!
    totalBytes := int64(0)

    for {
        _, err := reader.ReadByte()
        if err == io.EOF {
            break
        }
```

```
        totalBytes++
    }
    return totalBytes
}
```

Both functions open the same file, read through it completely byte by byte, and count the total bytes read and return that count, making them functionally equivalent from the caller's perspective. However, the critical difference lies in their interaction with the filesystem interface. The `readUnbuffered()` function creates a single-byte buffer using `make([]byte, 1)` and calls `file.Read(buffer)` for every individual byte in the file. This approach means that for a 1 MB file, the function makes approximately 1 million separate system calls to the operating system kernel, with each call requesting just 1 byte of data. Every system call involves expensive context switching between user space and kernel space, along with the overhead of the kernel's filesystem operations, making this approach extremely inefficient despite its conceptual simplicity. In contrast, the `readBuffered()` function uses `bufio.NewReader(file)` to create a buffered reader that internally maintains a 4 KB buffer by default. When `reader.ReadByte()` is called, the buffered reader serves the byte from its *internal memory buffer*, only making system calls when the buffer needs to be refilled from the file. For the same 1 MB file, this approach might make only around 250 system calls (1 MB divided by 4 KB), dramatically reducing expensive kernel interactions while providing the same byte-by-byte interface to the application.

Next, we present a utility function named `generateSampleFile()`, which creates test files of specified sizes for benchmarking and profiling I/O operations. It demonstrates practical file-generation techniques as well as the application of *buffered writing* principles, which will be covered in the next section:

```
func generateSampleFile(size int64, filename string) {
    file, _ := os.Create(filename)
    defer file.Close()
    writer := bufio.NewWriter(file)
    defer writer.Flush()
    pattern := "The quick brown fox jumps over the lazy dog. "
    bytesWritten := int64(0)

    for bytesWritten < size {
        n, _ := writer.WriteString(pattern)
        bytesWritten += int64(n)
    }
}
```

The function begins by creating a new file using `os.Create()`, which truncates any existing file with the same name, then immediately defers its closure to ensure proper resource cleanup. It wraps the file with a `bufio.NewWriter` instance to employ buffered writing, which is crucial for performance when writing many small pieces of data, and defers the `Flush()` call to guarantee that any data remaining in the buffer is written to disk before the function exits. The core operation uses a simple but effective approach: it repeatedly writes a fixed text pattern until the desired file size is reached. The function tracks `bytesWritten()` to ensure precise size control, accumulating the return value from each `WriteString()` call, which reports how many bytes were written.

Besides its utility for file creation, this function serves as a handy tool for performance analysis and educational demonstrations. By generating files of controlled sizes (1 KB, 1 MB, 10 MB, etc.), developers can systematically study how I/O performance scales with file size and observe dramatic differences between buffered and unbuffered operations across various scenarios. The function itself exemplifies good, buffered writing practices, using `bufio.NewWriter` instead of writing directly to the file, which would be inefficient for the many small `WriteString()` operations. You will learn about writing operations in the **Writing files** section.

Run the following commands on your machine to create a sample file as well as profiling information. All commands use `ch05/profReading.go`:

```
$ go run ch05/profReading.go -generate=100MB # create file
$ go run ch05/profReading.go -file=/tmp/sample_custom_100MB.txt -
cpuprofile=cpu.prof -memprofile=mem.prof # get profile data
$ go tool pprof cpu.prof
File: profReading
Type: cpu
Time: 2025-09-29 19:58:56 EEST
Duration: 30.76s, Total samples = 27.69s (90.01%)
Entering interactive mode (type "help" for commands, "o" for options)
(pprof) top
Showing nodes accounting for 27.62s, 99.75% of 27.69s total
Dropped 12 nodes (cum <= 0.14s)
Showing top 10 nodes out of 14
      flat  flat%   sum%        cum   cum%
    27.62s 99.75% 99.75%     27.63s 99.78%  syscall.syscall
         0     0% 99.75%      0.14s  0.51%  bufio.(*Reader).ReadByte
         0     0% 99.75%      0.14s  0.51%  bufio.(*Reader).fill
         0     0% 99.75%     27.64s 99.82%  internal/poll.(*FD).Read
         0     0% 99.75%     27.63s 99.78%  internal/poll.ignoringEINTRIO (inline)
```

```
        0     0% 99.75%     27.64s 99.82%  main.main
        0     0% 99.75%      0.14s  0.51%  main.readBuffered
        0     0% 99.75%     27.50s 99.31%  main.readUnbuffered
        0     0% 99.75%     27.64s 99.82%  main.runBothProfiling
        0     0% 99.75%     27.64s 99.82%  os.(*File).Read
```

This CPU profile output reveals a critical performance bottleneck in the unbuffered I/O implementation by showing where the program spends its execution time. The most striking finding is that `syscall.syscall` consumed `27.62` seconds of the `27.69` total seconds, representing `99.75%` of the CPU time with a `flat` time measurement that indicates time spent directly in that function rather than in functions it called. This overwhelming dominance of `syscall` time demonstrates that the program was spending virtually *all its execution time performing system calls rather than actual application logic.* This is the hallmark of inefficient unbuffered I/O, where each byte read requires a separate transition from user space to kernel space and back. The cumulative time (`cum`) column shows the call-stack relationships and reinforces this conclusion: `main.readUnbuffered` has a cumulative time of `27.50` seconds, meaning nearly all program time flows through this function, while `main.readBuffered` shows only `0.14` seconds cumulative time. The zero `flat` times for most functions indicate they are not computationally expensive themselves but rather serve as conduits for expensive syscall operations. The `main.readUnbuffered -> os.(*File).Read -> internal/poll.(*FD).Read -> syscall.syscall` call chain shows the path of unbuffered reading, where each byte-by-byte read operation eventually triggers a system call. In contrast, `main.readBuffered` shows minimal time because `bufio.(*Reader).fill` only occasionally makes system calls to refill its buffer, with most `ReadByte` calls being served directly from memory. The program essentially spent 99.75% of its time *context-switching between user and kernel space* rather than performing useful work. The dramatic difference between 27.50 seconds for unbuffered reading and 0.14 seconds for buffered reading (*approximately 196x faster*) demonstrates why buffered I/O is critical for performance. The profile also shows that the actual I/O operations themselves are not slow – it is the overhead of making thousands or millions of individual system calls that creates the bottleneck.

The next subsections are going to present code that shows how to read plain text files line by line, word by word, and character by character. The reason we cover different levels of file reading is that each approach serves distinct needs.

Reading a file line by line

Reading a file line by line is one of the most common patterns when processing text data, as it allows programs to handle files of arbitrary size without loading the entire content into memory. In Go, this is typically achieved using `bufio.Scanner`. Its default split function (`ScanLines()`) is configured to split input on newlines, abstracting away the low-level details of detecting line endings. The following `readLines()` utility function that implements the functionality can be found in `ch05/lineByLine.go`:

```
func readLines(filename string) ([]string, error) {
    file, err := os.Open(filename)
    if err != nil {
        return nil, err
    }
    defer file.Close()

    var lines []string
    scanner := bufio.NewScanner(file)
    for scanner.Scan() {
        lines = append(lines, scanner.Text())
    }

    if err := scanner.Err(); err != nil {
        return nil, err
    }

    return lines, nil
}
```

The function reads a plain text file line by line and returns its contents as a **slice of strings**. It begins by opening the file specified by the `filename` argument using `os.Open()`, and if that fails, then the function immediately returns with an error. A `defer file.Close()` statement ensures that the file is properly closed once the function completes, preventing resource leaks. It then initializes a `bufio.Scanner` instance to read the file line by line. Inside a loop, each line is read with `scanner.Scan()` and appended to the `lines` slice using `scanner.Text()`. After reading all lines, the function checks for scanning errors via `scanner.Err()`, returning an error if one occurs. If no errors are encountered, the function returns the accumulated slice of lines and a `nil` error. Next, we consider reading a file word by word.

Reading a file word by word

Sometimes it is necessary to process a file at the word level rather than line by line, for example, in tasks such as text analysis, word frequency counting, or parsing structured input where individual tokens matter. The `bufio.Scanner` utility supports this word-level processing via the

ScanWords split function, which tokenizes the input on whitespace boundaries. Consider this code for reading a plain text file word by word:

```
func readWords(filename string) ([]string, error) {
    file, err := os.Open(filename)
    if err != nil {
        return nil, err
    }
    defer file.Close()
    var words []string
    scanner := bufio.NewScanner(file)
    scanner.Split(bufio.ScanWords) // Split by words

    for scanner.Scan() {
        words = append(words, scanner.Text())
    }
    if err := scanner.Err(); err != nil {
        return nil, err
    }
    return words, nil
}
```

The `readWords()` function reads the contents of a text file and returns them as a slice of words. The function uses a `bufio.Scanner` instance to process the file content and configures it with `scanner.Split(bufio.ScanWords)`, which instructs the scanner to break the input into words instead of lines (`bufio.ScanLines`). Inside a loop, each word is appended to the `words` slice. When scanning is complete, the function checks, with `scanner.Err()`, for any errors that may have occurred during scanning. If no errors are encountered, it returns the full slice of words and a `nil` error. Next, let's talk about reading a file character by character.

Reading a file character by character

For certain applications, such as *lexical analysis*, *syntax parsing*, or fine-grained text processing, reading a file character by character is essential. In Go, this can be achieved using `bufio.Reader` with `ReadRune()`, which properly handles Unicode characters while giving precise control over each character read. This method allows programs to inspect, transform, or validate text at the smallest meaningful unit, supporting tasks that require detailed parsing or incremental processing of both ASCII and non-ASCII content. Here is the code of the first part of ch05/charByChar.go, where the core functionality is implemented:

```
func readChars(file *os.File) ([]rune, error) {
    reader := bufio.NewReader(file)
    var chars []rune

    for {
        r, _, err := reader.ReadRune()
        if err != nil {
            if err == io.EOF {
                break
            }
            return nil, err
        }
        chars = append(chars, r)
    }

    return chars, nil
}
```

The `readChars()` function reads a text file character by character and returns its contents as a **slice of runes**. It takes an already opened `*os.File` instance as input and wraps it in a `bufio.NewReader()` function, which provides buffered reading for efficiency. Inside an infinite loop, it calls `reader.ReadRune()`, which reads the next UTF-8 encoded character from the file and returns it as a rune. If an error occurs, the function checks whether it is `io.EOF`, which signals the end of the file; in that case, the loop breaks cleanly. Any other error is returned immediately. Each successfully read rune is appended to the `chars` slice, ensuring that multi-byte characters are handled correctly. Once the loop completes, the function returns the slice of runes and a `nil` error, making this a reliable way to process files at the character level in Go.

The rest of the code of `ch05/charByChar.go` is about the implementation of `main()`:

```
func main() {
    var input *os.File
    var err error

    if len(os.Args) > 1 {
        input, err = os.Open(os.Args[1])
        if err != nil {
```

```
            fmt.Fprintf(os.Stderr, "Error opening: %v\n", err)
            os.Exit(1)
        }
        defer input.Close()
    } else {
        input = os.Stdin
    }

    chars, err := readChars(input)
    if err != nil {
        fmt.Fprintf(os.Stderr, "Error reading input: %v\n", err)
        os.Exit(1)
    }

    for i, c := range chars {
        fmt.Printf("%d: %c\n", i+1, c)
    }
}
```

The `main()` function provides a simple entry point for reading characters from *either a file or standard input*. It begins by checking whether a filename has been provided as a command-line argument. If a filename is given, the program attempts to open the file, handling any errors by printing an appropriate message to standard error and exiting. A `defer input.Close()` function ensures that the file is properly closed after use. If no filename is provided, the program defaults to reading from standard input, making it flexible enough to handle both files and piped input. Once the input source is determined, it calls `readChars()` to extract the contents as a slice of runes. Any error during this step is reported and causes the program to terminate. Finally, the program loops through the characters, printing each one along with its position. Execute `ch05/charByChar.go` to see it in action.

Now that we have seen how to read data from files in Go, it is time to turn our attention to the other half of file handling: **writing**. Reading gives us access to existing information, but most real-world programs also need to create new files, update existing ones, or log data as they run. Writing files involves different considerations than reading, such as choosing the correct file mode, handling overwrites, and managing buffered versus unbuffered output.

Writing files

Writing files is a fundamental operation in Go that allows programs to store data permanently on disk. Whether you need to save configuration settings, generate reports, or log application activity, the Go standard library provides straightforward and flexible tools for writing data to files. By choosing the right file-opening modes, you can control whether you overwrite existing content, append new data, or create files only if they do not already exist. Once you have a file handle, you can write data with methods such as `f.Write()`, which accepts a byte slice, or `f.WriteString()`, which accepts a string directly. For more efficient output, the `bufio.NewWriter()` type can wrap a file handle and perform buffer writes before flushing them with `w.Flush()`. Once you understand the basics of writing files in Go, the next step is to handle situations where you want to *add new data to an existing file without overwriting its current contents.* So, to kick things off, let's see how to create a new file.

Creating new files

Creating new files in Go is straightforward using functions such as `os.Create()` and `os.OpenFile()` that not only generate a file on disk but also return a file descriptor for immediate writing operations. The following `main()` function from `ch05/create.go` shows how to create empty files:

```
func main() {
    if len(os.Args) < 2 {
        fmt.Fprintf(os.Stderr, "Usage: %s <filename>\n", os.Args[0])
        os.Exit(1)
    }
    filename := os.Args[1]

    file, err := os.Create(filename)
    if err != nil {
        fmt.Println("Error creating file", filename, err)
        os.Exit(1)
    }
    err = file.Close()
    if err != nil {
        fmt.Println("Error creating file", filename, err)
        os.Exit(1)
    }
    // Check if the file was a new creation or an override
    fileInfo, err := os.Stat(filename)
    if err != nil {
        fmt.Fprintf(os.Stderr, "Error checking info: %v\n", err)
        os.Exit(1)
    }
    fmt.Printf("Successfully created empty file: %s\n", filename)
```

```
    fmt.Printf("File size: %d bytes\n", fileInfo.Size())
    fmt.Printf("File permissions: %v\n", fileInfo.Mode())
}
```

The core file operation uses `os.Create(filename)`, which is a wrapper around the lower-level `os.OpenFile()` function with `O_RDWR|O_CREATE|O_TRUNC` flags. This system call *either creates a new file or truncates an existing file to 0 bytes*, effectively overriding any existing content while maintaining the same *inode* (a data structure that describes a filesystem object, such as a file or a directory). The function returns both a file pointer and an `error` value, where the error is checked immediately after the operation. If file creation fails due to permissions, disk space, or other filesystem issues, the program prints an error message and exits with code `1`. The program immediately closes the file using `file.Close()`, since the goal is to create an empty file rather than write data, and since proper resource management requires explicit closure of file descriptors to avoid resource leaks. After closure, the program performs an `os.Stat()` call to retrieve filesystem metadata about the newly created file. Finally, the program provides user feedback by displaying the filename, file size (which should be `0` bytes for an empty file), and file permissions in their string representation format, confirming successful completion of the file creation operation, and providing verification that the file exists in the expected state. Run `ch05/create.go` on your machine to check those features, as demonstrated here:

```
$ go run ch05/create.go /tmp/test.txt
Successfully created empty file: /tmp/test.txt
File size: 0 bytes
File permissions: -rw-r--r--
```

While the previous examples demonstrated *creating and overriding files unconditionally*, many real-world scenarios require a more cautious approach in which files are created only if they do not already exist. That is what comes next.

Creating a file if it does not exist

When working with files in Go, you may often want to create a new file, but only if it does not already exist. This prevents overwriting valuable data by mistake and ensures your program behaves predictably in environments where files may already be present. The `os.OpenFile()` function provides the necessary control through specific flags that let you enforce exclusive creation. By combining these flags with proper error handling, you can build safe and reliable file operations that only write new data when the target file was previously absent. Consider the following `main()` function implementation that showcases the technique:

```
func main() {
    fn := "/tmp/unique.txt"

    // os.O_CREATE:  create file if not exists
    // os.O_EXCL:    fail if file already exists
    // os.O_WRONLY:  open for writing
    f, err := os.OpenFile(fn, os.O_CREATE|os.O_EXCL|os.O_WRONLY, 0644)
    if err != nil {
        if os.IsExist(err) {
            fmt.Printf("File %s already exists.\n", fn)
            return
        }
        fmt.Fprintf(os.Stderr, "Error creating file: %v\n", err)
        os.Exit(1)
    }
    defer f.Close()

    content := "This file was created only because it did not exist.\n"
    _, err = f.WriteString(content)
    if err != nil {
        fmt.Fprintf(os.Stderr, "Error writing to file: %v\n", err)
        os.Exit(1)
    }

    fmt.Printf("File %s created successfully.\n", fn)
}
```

The code defines the file path as `/tmp/unique.txt` and uses `os.OpenFile()` with a combination of flags: `os.O_CREATE` instructs Go to create the file if it is missing, `os.O_EXCL` forces the operation to fail if the file already exists, and `os.O_WRONLY` opens the file in write-only mode. Together, these flags ensure that the program will never overwrite an existing file. If the file already exists, the error is caught with `os.IsExist(err)` and a message is printed without modifying the file. If another error occurs, it is reported, and the program exits. When the file is created successfully, the program writes a short message into it using `f.WriteString()` and then confirms creation with a success message. The `defer f.Close()` statement guarantees that the file is properly closed before the program terminates. This approach makes file creation safe and prevents accidental data loss. Run `ch05/newFile.go` on your machine twice:

```
$ go run ch05/newFile.go
File /tmp/unique.txt created successfully.
$ go run ch05/newFile.go
File /tmp/unique.txt already exists.
```

The first time you run the program, it successfully creates the `/tmp/unique.txt` file because the file does not yet exist. On the second run, however, the file is already present in `/tmp`, so the `os.O_EXCL` flag prevents the file from being overwritten or truncated. This approach is a standard defensive programming pattern that ensures that the process of checking for a file and creating it happens as a single operation.

After learning how to create and write new files, the next step is to see how we can extend files without overwriting their contents.

Appending to files

Appending to a file means adding new data to the end of an existing file without overwriting its current contents. This operation is particularly useful for tasks such as logging, incremental data storage, or maintaining sequential records. The Go standard library provides straightforward ways to open files in append mode, automatically positioning the write cursor at the end of the file and creating the file if it does not already exist. The `ch05/append.go` utility demonstrates how to append text to a file in Go using input from command-line arguments. Here is its `main()` function:

```
func main() {
    if len(os.Args) < 3 {
        fmt.Println(os.Args[0], "<filename> <text to append>\n")
        os.Exit(1)
    }

    fn := os.Args[1]
    text := strings.Join(os.Args[2:], " ") + "\n"
    f, err := os.OpenFile(fn,os.O_APPEND|os.O_CREATE|os.O_WRONLY, 0644)
    if err != nil {
        fmt.Fprintf(os.Stderr, "Error opening file: %v\n", err)
        os.Exit(1)
    }
    defer f.Close()
```

```
    _, err = f.WriteString(text)
    if err != nil {
        fmt.Fprintf(os.Stderr, "Error writing to file: %v\n", err)
        os.Exit(1)
    }

    fmt.Printf("Successfully appended content to %s\n", fn)
}
```

The code begins by checking that at least two arguments are provided: the filename and the text to append. If not, it prints usage instructions and then exits. The filename is taken from the first argument, while the remaining arguments are joined into a single string of text, followed by a newline to ensure proper formatting. The program then opens the target file with `os.OpenFile()` using the `os.O_APPEND`, `os.O_CREATE`, and `os.O_WRONLY` flags, which together mean *append new content to the file if it exists, create it if it does not,* and *open it for writing.* If an error occurs at this stage, the program prints the error and exits. Once the file is successfully opened, it defers closing the file to release resources properly. It then writes the given text with `WriteString()`, checking again for errors. Finally, if all goes well, it prints a confirmation message to let the user know the content was successfully appended to the file.

Run `ch05/append.go` on your machine to add text to files:

```
$ go run ch05/append.go /tmp/test.txt "Adding text"
Successfully appended content to /tmp/test.txt
$ go run ch05/append.go /tmp/test.txt "Adding more text"
Successfully appended content to /tmp/test.txt
$ cat /tmp/test.txt
Adding text
Adding more text
```

When displaying the file contents with the `cat(1)` command, we see both lines, showing that the program appended data correctly.

Having seen how to create, write, and append data to files, the next logical step is to explore how these same techniques apply to **logging** – an essential feature in any real-world program. **System logging** and logging to files allow applications to record events, errors, and status updates for later *analysis* or *debugging*. Unlike simple file writing, logging requires consistent formatting, proper handling of concurrent writes, and sometimes integration with system-logging facilities.

System logging and logging to files

Go's logging ecosystem operates on a foundation of interface-driven design and zero-allocation principles (designing and using operations that do not produce unnecessary heap allocations during normal execution), providing simplicity for basic use cases with extensibility for complex systems. The `log` and `log/slog` packages implement structured logging with compile-time optimizations, while the interface-based architecture facilitates integration with high-performance third-party loggers. The `log` package provides a thread-safe logger built around a `sync.Mutex`-protected `io.Writer` instance. Each log operation acquires an exclusive lock, formats the message using `fmt.Sprintf()` style formatting, and performs a *single write syscall.* The package implements a global logger instance accessible through package-level functions and supports creating isolated logger instances with custom prefixes, flags, and output destinations. Go 1.21 introduced `log/slog`, a structured logging package designed around key-value pairs and hierarchical contexts. The implementation uses a `Handler` interface that enables pluggable backends while maintaining zero-allocation fast paths for disabled log levels through compile-time optimizations. This means that when `slog` processes log messages, it uses a `Handler` interface to allow different output backends, such as JSON files, syslog, or external logging services, to be plugged in easily. At the same time, the implementation is designed so that when a log level is disabled, such as `Debug` logs in a production build, Go can skip the logging call entirely without allocating memory or doing any formatting work. This is achieved through simple condition checks and compiler optimizations that remove the unused code paths. As a result, *disabled log statements have virtually zero performance cost: no allocations, no string building, and no unnecessary work.*

Let us see all these features in action in `ch05/logging.go`. The next code snippet defines a Go struct named `multiWriter` that holds a slice of `io.Writer` interfaces:

```
type multiWriter struct {
    writers []io.Writer
}
```

The purpose of this struct is to aggregate multiple writers so that the same data can be written to several destinations at once. Each element in the `writers` slice represents a target for output, which could be a file, standard output, a network connection, or any other type that implements the `io.Writer` interface.

The `Write()` method that follows is an implementation of the `io.Writer` interface for the `multiWriter` custom type we saw earlier:

```
func (m *multiWriter) Write(p []byte) (int, error) {
    var lastErr error
    for _, w := range m.writers {
        if _, err := w.Write(p); err != nil {
            lastErr = err
        }
    }

    return len(p), lastErr
}
```

The `Write()` method of the `multiWriter` struct is designed to broadcast a single byte slice to multiple output destinations. Unlike a strict sequential implementation that halts at the first sign of trouble, this version adopts a more resilient approach. By iterating through the entire slice of `io.Writer` objects, the method ensures that a failure in one destination does not prevent the remaining sinks from receiving the data. In this implementation, the loop continues regardless of whether an individual `Write()` call succeeds or fails. If an error occurs, it is captured locally so that it can be returned at the end of the operation, but it does not interrupt the broadcast to the other writers. The function ultimately returns the length of the `p` input slice to signal that the data has been processed by the broadcast logic, along with any errors encountered during the process. This design provides better consistency across logs, ensuring that critical telemetry reaches as many targets as possible even during partial system failures. In *Chapter 14, Creating an Index for Unix Files,* you are going to learn a better way to do so! Now, let us continue by presenting the `main()` function, where the program sets up multiple logging destinations by opening different writers:

```
func main() {
    // Open a JSON log file
    file, err := os.OpenFile("/tmp/app.log", os.O_CREATE|os.O_APPEND|os.O_WRONLY,
0644)
    if err != nil {
        panic(err)
    }
    defer file.Close()

    // Syslog writer
```

```
    syslogWriter, err := syslog.New(syslog.LOG_INFO|syslog.LOG_LOCAL0, "myapp")
    if err != nil {
        panic(err)
    }
    defer syslogWriter.Close()

    // Combine stdout, file, and syslog writers
    w := &multiWriter{
        writers: []io.Writer{
            file,
            os.Stdout,
            syslogWriter,
        },
    }
```

The code begins by creating or opening a log file at `/tmp/app.log` using `os.OpenFile()`. The file permissions are set to `0644`, meaning it is readable by everyone but writable only by the owner. Next, a syslog writer is initialized using `syslog.New()`, which connects the application to the *system logging facility*. The arguments specify the log priority (`LOG_INFO`) and facility (`LOG_LOCAL0`), as well as a `"myapp"` tag to identify log entries. Finally, the program combines the file writer, the standard output stream (`os.Stdout`), and the syslog writer into a single `multiWriter` instance. This allows subsequent log messages to be written simultaneously to all three destinations, ensuring consistent and redundant logging across different outputs.

In the remaining part of `main()`, the program sets up and uses Go's structured logging through the `slog` package:

```
    // Create JSON handler with empty HandlerOptions
    handler := slog.NewJSONHandler(w, &slog.HandlerOptions{})

    // Create logger
    logger := slog.New(handler)

    // Example logs
    logger.Info("Application started")
    logger.Debug("Processing request",
        "id", 12345,
        "user", "alice",
        "attempt", 1,
    )
```

```
    err = doSomething()
    if err != nil {
        logger.Error("Failed to process data",
            "error", err,
        )
    }

    logger.Info("Application finished successfully")
}
```

First, the code creates a *JSON log handler* with `slog.NewJSONHandler()`, passing in the custom `multiWriter` instance so that all log messages will be written simultaneously to the log file, standard output, and syslog. The `&slog.HandlerOptions{}` argument specifies default handler options, but could be customized to control log levels, timestamps, or formatting. Next, a `logger` instance is created with `slog.New(handler)`, which becomes the central logging instance for the application. The `logger` instance is then used to write several structured log entries. An informational message logs the application startup, while a debug log records details about a simulated request, attaching key-value pairs (`id`, `user`, and `attempt`) that make the log entries more *searchable* and *machine-friendly*. The code then calls a `doSomething()` function and, if it returns an error, logs the error with `logger.Error()`. Finally, the program logs a message indicating that the application finished successfully.

The implementation of `doSomething()` is simple, as it just returns `nil`:

```
// Simulate a function that may return an error
func doSomething() error {
    // For demonstration, return nil or a simple error
    return nil
}
```

Execute `ch05/logging.go` on your machine to see logging in action:

```
$ go run ch05/logging.go
{"time":"2025-09-29T07:29:25.397365+03:00","level":"INFO","msg":"Application
started"}
{"time":"2025-09-29T07:29:25.397726+03:00","level":"INFO","msg":"Application
finished successfully"}
```

The contents of `/tmp/app.log` are the same as the ones in the output. Keep in mind that *logging in JSON* format provides structured, machine-readable entries that make it easier to parse, search, and analyze logs with modern tools, while remaining human-readable.

Having established how to log information to multiple destinations using structured logging, we now return to the fundamentals of file I/O. It is important to understand unbuffered writing — the most direct way of sending data to a file.

Unbuffered writing

In **unbuffered writing**, data is written directly to the output destination without any intermediate buffering, the write operation being passed to the underlying system as soon as the write call completes. This can be crucial for certain real-time or synchronous operations where immediate output is required, and it can simplify the programming model, but in most scenarios, unbuffered writing is less efficient than buffered writing as it increases the number of system calls and overhead involved. This is especially the case when performing many small writes.

The part of `ch05/unbufWrite.go` that illustrates unbuffered writing, for the case of data being written *1 byte at a time*, is the following:

```
// Write the file byte by byte (unbuffered)
for i := 0; i < len(fullData); i++ {
    buffer := []byte{fullData[i]}
    n, err := file.Write(buffer)
    if err != nil {
        fmt.Fprintf(os.Stderr, "Error writing: %v\n", err)
        os.Exit(1)
    }
    bytesWritten += n
    systemCalls++
}
```

The loop iterates over each byte in the `fullData` slice and creates a `buffer` single-byte slice to pass to `file.Write()`. Each call to `Write()` sends a single byte directly to the operating system, meaning that there is a *separate system call for each byte*. The program checks for errors after each write and terminates with an error message if one occurs. It also keeps track of the total number of bytes written in `bytesWritten` and counts the number of system calls in `systemCalls`.

This approach is *highly inefficient for large data*, as each byte incurs the overhead of a system call. So, after understanding how *unbuffered writing* offers simplicity and direct control, let's see how and why buffered writing offers efficiency.

Buffered writing

As buffered reading reduces system calls on input, **buffered writing** does the same on output by using an intermediate memory buffer to accumulate data before sending it in larger chunks to the underlying output destination. The Go standard library offers the `bufio.Writer` type to facilitate buffered writing, allowing your program to write data efficiently by collecting it in memory and flushing it all at once or when the buffer is full. The following code is found in `ch05/bufWrite.go` and illustrates buffered writing:

```
bytesWritten := 0
// Write the file byte by byte using buffered I/O
for i := 0; i < len(fullData); i++ {
    err := writer.WriteByte(fullData[i])
    if err != nil {
        fmt.Fprintf(os.Stderr, "Error writing: %v\n", err)
        os.Exit(1)
    }
    bytesWritten++

}

// Flush the buffer to ensure all data is written
writer.Flush()
file.Sync() // Force data to be written to disk
```

Instead of writing directly to the file 1 byte at a time, the code uses a buffered writer (`writer`, which is initialized as `writer := bufio.NewWriter(file)`), which collects data in memory before performing fewer, larger system calls to the operating system. Inside the loop, `writer.WriteByte(fullData[i])` appends each byte from `fullData` into the writer's internal buffer, while `bytesWritten` counts the number of bytes successfully staged for writing. Unlike unbuffered I/O, *these calls do not immediately reach the filesystem but are accumulated in the buffer.* After the loop finishes, `writer.Flush()` is called to force any remaining buffered data to be written out to the file. Finally, `file.Sync()` ensures that the operating system flushes its own buffers to disk, making the data physically persistent.

The next code snippet from `ch05/bufWrite.go` shows how to write text data line by line using a buffered writer (`lineWriter := bufio.NewWriter(file)`):

```
linesWritten := 0
for _, line := range lines {
```

```
        n, err := lineWriter.WriteString(line + "\n")
        if err != nil {
            fmt.Fprintf(os.Stderr, "Error writing: %v\n", err)
            break
        }
        linesWritten++
        fmt.Printf("Wrote line %d (%d bytes)\n", linesWritten, n)
    }
```

The loop iterates over the `lines` slice, and for each string, it calls `lineWriter.WriteString(line + "\n")`. This writes the line along with a newline character, ensuring that each entry appears on a separate line in the output file. The method returns the number of bytes written (`n`) and an `error` value. If an error occurs, the program prints the error to standard error and exits the loop to avoid further writes. A counter, `linesWritten`, keeps track of how many lines were successfully written, and for each line, the program prints a confirmation message showing the line number and the number of bytes written. Now, use `ch05/bufWrite.go` on your machine to see its output.

With both unbuffered and buffered writing techniques in place, the next step is to benchmark their performance to see how they differ.

Benchmarking buffered and unbuffered writing

Information obtained by benchmarking to compare the impact of using a buffer versus writing data directly to the output destination is especially useful when working with large datasets, high-frequency writes, or performance-critical applications. It can help you decide whether the added complexity of buffering is justified for your specific use case, and you can modify the benchmarks to match your needs. Running the relevant code, found in `ch05/writing_test.go`, generates the following sort of output:

```
$ go test -bench=. ch05/writing_test.go
goos: darwin
goarch: arm64
cpu: Apple M4 Pro
BenchmarkUnbufferedWrite_1MB-14               2     901584062 ns/op
BenchmarkBufferedWrite_1MB-14               226       5323956 ns/op
BenchmarkUnbufferedWrite_10MB-14              1    9318937125 ns/op
BenchmarkBufferedWrite_10MB-14               20      54047833 ns/op
PASS
ok      command-line-arguments    15.472s
```

These benchmark results demonstrate *dramatic performance differences* between unbuffered and buffered writing in Go. For the 1 MB file, unbuffered writing takes roughly `901` milliseconds per operation, whereas buffered writing completes the same task in only about `5.3` milliseconds, highlighting how buffering drastically reduces *system call overhead*. The difference becomes even more pronounced with larger files: writing 10 MB unbuffered takes nearly `9.3` seconds, while buffered writing handles it in approximately 54 milliseconds. So, as a rule of thumb, unbuffered writing should be reserved for scenarios where *immediate data durability* is more critical than raw throughput.

With the performance benefits of buffered writing established, the next step is to examine how different buffer sizes impact efficiency, which will lead naturally into a discussion on benchmarking buffer size in buffered writing.

Benchmarking buffer size in buffered writing

Here, we focus on measuring how different *buffer sizes* affect the efficiency of writing data in Go. As we have seen, when using buffered writing, data is first collected in memory and then flushed to the output destination in chunks. The size of the memory buffer directly influences performance: smaller buffers may result in frequent flushes and more system calls, while overly large buffers can waste memory without offering significant speed improvements. By running benchmarks with varying buffer sizes, you can determine the most effective configuration for your specific workload and file size, achieving a balance between write performance, memory usage, and system overhead.

The relevant code can be found in `ch05/buffer_test.go`; using it generates the following kind of output:

```
$ go test -bench=. ch05/buffer_test.go
goos: darwin
goarch: arm64
cpu: Apple M4 Pro
BenchmarkBufferedWrite_1MB_512-14          162      7258326 ns/op
BenchmarkBufferedWrite_1MB_4KB-14          222      5387291 ns/op
BenchmarkBufferedWrite_1MB_32KB-14         236      5104669 ns/op
BenchmarkBufferedWrite_1MB_256KB-14        272      4614332 ns/op
BenchmarkBufferedWrite_10MB_512-14          16     71145104 ns/op
BenchmarkBufferedWrite_10MB_4KB-14          22     52635623 ns/op
BenchmarkBufferedWrite_10MB_32KB-14         26     48859393 ns/op
BenchmarkBufferedWrite_10MB_256KB-14        27     46614238 ns/op
PASS
ok      command-line-arguments    12.486s
```

The test was executed on an Apple M4 Pro processor with ARM64 architecture running macOS, and the benchmark framework automatically adjusted the number of iterations (shown in the second column) to ensure that each test ran for approximately 1 second to provide statistically meaningful measurements. The benchmarks systematically explore two file sizes (1 MB and 10 MB) with four different buffer sizes (512 bytes, 4 KB, 32 KB, and 256 KB) and reveal a clear performance improvement as buffer size increases. For the 1 MB file tests, execution time decreases from `7.26` milliseconds with a 512-byte buffer to `4.61` milliseconds with a 256 KB buffer, representing a 57% performance improvement. This pattern holds consistently for the 10 MB files as well, where performance improves from `71.1` milliseconds with 512-byte buffers to `46.6` milliseconds with 256 KB buffers – a 34% speedup. The diminishing returns between buffer sizes are also evident: the jump from 512 bytes to 4 KB provides substantial improvement, while the gains between 32 KB and 256 KB buffers are more modest, suggesting that beyond a certain buffer size, the benefit of reducing system calls will plateau while memory overhead increases. The iteration counts in the second column provide additional context about benchmark reliability and performance characteristics, the faster buffered operations (256 KB buffer) running more iterations (272 for 1 MB, 27 for 10 MB) compared to slower operations (162 and 16 iterations respectively for 512-byte buffers), as the benchmark framework automatically runs more iterations of faster operations to gather sufficient statistical data. The consistent 10x ratio in execution times between 1 MB and 10 MB tests across all buffer sizes (approximately `5` milliseconds to `50` milliseconds for similar buffer configurations) confirms that performance scales linearly with file size, indicating that the I/O operations are not hitting unexpected bottlenecks or non-linear behavior. This benchmark data illustrates that while buffering dramatically improves performance over unbuffered I/O, there is an *optimal buffer size range* (likely 32 KB-256 KB for this system) beyond which further increases yield diminishing returns.

Up to this point, we have explored buffered writing from a theoretical perspective, examining how different buffer sizes affect performance. Now, it is time to move from theory into practice. A natural next step is to apply what we have learned to a real-world task: copying files.

Benchmarking file copying

File copying is one of the most common operations in systems programming, and it gives us the opportunity to see in a practical setting how buffered writing strategies influence efficiency. When it comes to copying files in Go, there are several techniques you can use, each with its own trade-offs in terms of simplicity and performance. At a high level, the `io.Copy()` function offers a concise and reliable way to duplicate file contents, handling the details for you under the hood. For more control, you can use buffered copying with `bufio`, where you explicitly manage how much data is read and written at a time. Finally, the most granular method involves manually reading chunks of bytes with `Read()` and writing them with `Write()`, giving you full flexibility but requiring more code. In this section, we benchmark these approaches side by side to highlight how different strategies affect performance in real-world scenarios. The relevant source code file is `ch05/copy_bench_test.go`, which compares the performance of three different file-copying strategies in Go – `io.Copy()`, buffered copying with a fixed buffer size, and manual read-and-write loops – across files of two sizes, 1 MB and 10 MB:

```
func BenchmarkIOCopy_1MB(b *testing.B) {
	benchmarkCopy(b, 1<<20, copyFileIOCopy)
}
func BenchmarkIOCopy_10MB(b *testing.B) {
	benchmarkCopy(b, 10<<20, copyFileIOCopy)
}
func BenchmarkBuffer_1MB(b *testing.B) {
	benchmarkCopy(b, 1<<20, func(s, d string) error {
		return copyFileBuffer(s, d, 4096)
	})
}
func BenchmarkBuffer_10MB(b *testing.B) {
	benchmarkCopy(b, 10<<20, func(s, d string) error {
		return copyFileBuffer(s, d, 4096)
	})
}
func BenchmarkReadWrite_1MB(b *testing.B) {
	benchmarkCopy(b, 1<<20, copyFileReadWrite)
}
func BenchmarkReadWrite_10MB(b *testing.B) {
	benchmarkCopy(b, 10<<20, copyFileReadWrite)
}
```

The `BenchmarkIOCopy_1MB()` and `BenchmarkIOCopy_10MB()` functions use `io.Copy()`, which is *highly optimized for speed and minimal overhead.* The `BenchmarkBuffer_1MB()` and `BenchmarkBuffer_10MB()` functions measure performance when data is copied using a custom buffer of 4 KB, allowing us to see how buffer size affects throughput. Finally, `BenchmarkReadWrite_1MB()` and `BenchmarkReadWrite_10MB()` test a manual loop that explicitly reads from the source and writes to the destination, providing maximum control but often at the cost of efficiency. Together, these benchmarks highlight how implementation choices and file sizes influence performance, making it easier to identify trade-offs between convenience, control, and speed. Running `ch05/copy_bench_test.go` produces the following kind of output:

```
$ go test -bench=. ch05/copy_bench_test.go
goos: darwin
goarch: arm64
cpu: Apple M4 Pro
BenchmarkIOCopy_1MB-14              194           6405221 ns/op
BenchmarkIOCopy_10MB-14             100          10421437 ns/op
BenchmarkBuffer_1MB-14              170           9519117 ns/op
BenchmarkBuffer_10MB-14              80          14665059 ns/op
BenchmarkReadWrite_1MB-14          4150            295479 ns/op
BenchmarkReadWrite_10MB-14          486           2139259 ns/op
PASS
ok      command-line-arguments  12.198s
```

The benchmark results highlight clear performance differences among the three file-copying strategies. Using `io.Copy()` is consistently fast and efficient, completing the 1 MB file in roughly `6.4` milliseconds per operation and the 10 MB file in about `10.4` milliseconds, demonstrating its optimized handling and reasonable scaling with file size. Copying with a custom 4 KB buffer is slightly slower, taking around `9.5` milliseconds for 1 MB and `14.6` milliseconds for 10 MB, due to the overhead of manually managing the buffer and issuing repeated read and write calls. The manual read-and-write loop performs exceptionally well for the small 1 MB file, at only `295` milliseconds per operation, but its efficiency declines with larger files, taking `2.1` milliseconds for 10 MB. This reflects the cost of multiple system calls as the file grows. Overall, these results illustrate that `io.Copy()` generally offers the best combination of simplicity and performance for large files, buffered copying provides control over the buffer at a modest performance cost, and *manual read/write is advantageous for small files but less scalable for larger ones.*

Having explored file reading, writing, and copying, we now turn to a practical text-processing task: converting tabs to spaces and vice versa.

Converting tabs to spaces and vice versa

Text files often use tabs or spaces for indentation, but different projects and editors may have different conventions. *Converting tabs to spaces — or spaces to tabs —* is a common text-processing task to ensure consistent formatting and improve readability. This section explores a practical implementation of these conversions, showing how command-line arguments can control the number of spaces per tab and the direction of conversion. This `parseMode()` function – found in `ch05/t2s.go` – implements a *bidirectional parser* that interprets mode strings for **tab-to-space** and **space-to-tab** conversion operations, using the position of the numeric value relative to the word "`tabs`" to determine the conversion direction:

```
func parseMode(mode string) (direction string, count int, err error) {
    if strings.HasSuffix(mode, "tabs") {
        numStr := strings.TrimSuffix(mode, "tabs")
        count, err = strconv.Atoi(numStr)
        if err != nil {
            return "", 0, fmt.Errorf("invalid mode: %s", mode)
        }
        direction = "spaces-to-tabs"
        return
    } else if strings.HasPrefix(mode, "tabs") {
        numStr := strings.TrimPrefix(mode, "tabs")
        count, err = strconv.Atoi(numStr)
        if err != nil {
            return "", 0, fmt.Errorf("invalid mode: %s", mode)
        }
        direction = "tabs-to-spaces"
        return
    }
    return "", 0, fmt.Errorf("unknown mode: %s", mode)
}
```

The function code parses mode strings where the position of the number relative to "`tabs`" determines conversion direction: if the number comes before "`tabs`" (such as "`4tabs`"), it converts spaces to tabs using that tab width, while if the number comes after "`tabs`" (such as "`tabs4`"), it converts tabs to spaces using that number of spaces per tab. For example, `parseMode("4tabs")` returns `direction="spaces-to-tabs"` and `count=4` (meaning replace every four spaces with a tab), while `parseMode("tabs4")` returns `direction="tabs-to-spaces"` and `count=4` (meaning replace every tab with four spaces), and `parseMode("invalid")` returns an error because it does not match either pattern. Try `ch05/t2s.go` on your own machine with your own files.

While our indentation converter focused on the structural transformation of text, another fundamental aspect of file processing is the extraction of quantitative metrics. To explore these capabilities, we will now develop the classic Unix `wc(1)` utility in Go. This will demonstrate how to build a tool that efficiently scans a file once while simultaneously calculating line, word, and character counts, mirroring the performance and utility of standard system tools.

Developing wc(1)

The classic Unix `wc(1)` utility is a simple yet powerful tool that counts the number of lines, words, and characters in a text file. Recreating this functionality in Go provides an excellent exercise in file processing and text scanning, as it combines reading from files with efficient counting techniques. Rather than treating each count separately, a single pass through the file can update all three metrics at once, demonstrating how careful design can save time and resources. Creating three separate functions for counting lines, words, and characters independently would require opening and reading the same file three times, wasting I/O operations and CPU cycles.

The `count()` function serves as the core statistical analysis engine of the word count utility, accepting any `io.Reader` interface as input. This allows it to work seamlessly with files, standard input, network streams, or any other readable data source in Go:

```
func count(r io.Reader) (lines, words, bytes, runes int) {
    buf := bufio.NewReader(r)

    for {
        line, err := buf.ReadString('\n')
        if err != nil && err != io.EOF {
            fmt.Fprintf(os.Stderr, "read error: %v\n", err)
            break
        }
        if len(line) > 0 {
            lines++
            trimmed := strings.TrimRight(line, "\r\n")
            words += countWordsInLine(trimmed)
            bytes += len(line)
            runes += utf8.RuneCountInString(trimmed) + 1
        }
        if err == io.EOF {
            break
        }
    }
    return
}
```

The function returns four metrics using named return values: `lines`, `words`, `bytes` and `runes` (Unicode characters), which are accumulated over the course of the reading process. It begins by *wrapping the input reader* with `bufio.NewReader` to create a *buffered reader*, which significantly improves performance by reducing the number of system calls. The main logic of the function is within the infinite `for` loop that reads one line at a time using `buf.ReadString('\n')`, which returns both the line content (including the newline delimiter) and an `error` value. For each non-empty line, the function does the following:

- Increments the line counter
- Trims trailing carriage return and newline characters using `strings.TrimRight()` (handling both Unix and Windows line endings)
- Delegates word counting to the specialized `countWordsInLine` function
- Accumulates the byte count using `len(line)`, which returns the number of bytes in the string
- Calculates the rune count using `utf8.RuneCountInString()`, which properly counts Unicode characters that may span multiple bytes, adding one to account for the newline character itself

Not shown here is `printCounts()`, which handles the presentation layer. It formats the count results to match the `wc(1)` output style, with right-aligned seven-character-wide columns. It implements the default behavior (showing lines, words, and bytes when no flags are specified) and selectively displays only the requested metrics based on command-line flags. Using `ch05/wc.go` produces the following kind of output:

```
$ go run ch05/wc.go /tmp/test.txt /tmp/testFile
      2       5      29 /tmp/test.txt
      5      37     222 /tmp/testFile
      7      42     251 total
$ wc /tmp/test.txt /tmp/testFile
       2       5      29 /tmp/test.txt
       5      37     222 /tmp/testFile
       7      42     251 total
```

The fact that both `wc(1)` and `ch05/wc.go` produce the same output validates that the Go implementation correctly understands and replicates the specifications and behaviors of the original utility.

Summary

As we conclude this chapter on file I/O in Go, it becomes clear that the combination of *interfaces*, *buffers*, and robust standard library functions provides both power and flexibility when working with data. We have explored unbuffered and buffered reading and writing, file creation and appending, seeking within files, and techniques for efficiently processing text at the line, word, and character levels. By understanding the trade-offs between performance, memory usage, and simplicity, and by leveraging interfaces such as `io.Reader` and `io.Writer`, you can build reliable, reusable, and high-performance I/O routines.

In practice, *buffered reading* is almost always the preferred approach for file I/O due to its significant performance advantages. While *unbuffered reading* provides direct, predictable access to files through individual system calls, it becomes inefficient for larger files due to the overhead of frequent kernel interactions. Buffered reading through Go's `bufio` package dramatically reduces system call overhead by reading data in chunks and serving individual requests from memory, often improving performance by orders of magnitude. The minimal memory cost of maintaining a buffer is typically far outweighed by the performance benefits. Understanding both approaches helps developers make informed decisions about when rare cases requiring unbuffered access might be necessary, but in the vast majority of scenarios, embracing Go's buffered I/O capabilities will lead to more efficient and responsive applications.

For file-writing operations, buffered I/O through Go's `bufio` package is typically the optimal choice due to its substantial performance improvements over unbuffered alternatives. While *unbuffered writing* provides immediate, predictable system interaction with each write operation, it becomes prohibitively slow for applications that write substantial amounts of data due to system call overhead. *Buffered writing* accumulates data in memory and writes it in efficient chunks, often improving performance dramatically while providing convenient methods for writing strings and lines. The key consideration with buffered writing is remembering to flush the buffer to ensure data persistence, but this small additional responsibility is easily managed and far outweighed by the performance benefits.

The next chapter examines how Go programs can respond to signals and navigate the filesystem beyond basic reading and writing. By connecting I/O operations with system-level events and file management, the next chapter bridges the gap between high-level file processing and underlying mechanisms that govern program execution.

Exercises

1. Make `ch05/logging.go` accept the log file as a command-line argument
2. Change `ch05/newFile.go` so that it accepts the file as an argument

Additional resources

- io code: `https://github.com/golang/go/blob/master/src/io/io.go`

- `log/slog` documentation: `https://pkg.go.dev/log/slog`
- `log` package documentation: `https://pkg.go.dev/log`

6

UNIX Signals and File Systems

At the heart of every UNIX system lies a balance between structure and interruption. **File systems** embody order: they organize data into hierarchies, enforce permissions, and preserve information over time. **Signals**, by contrast, introduce disruption. A signal is an asynchronous notification sent by the operating system to a process to indicate that an event has occurred — for example, when a user presses *Ctrl* + *C* (`SIGINT`) or when the system requests termination (`SIGTERM`). Programs must be prepared to handle such events gracefully, even when they arrive unexpectedly. In this chapter, we begin by exploring how Go allows us to intercept and handle **UNIX signals** so that our programs can respond cleanly — printing progress information, releasing resources, or shutting down safely instead of terminating abruptly. From there, we shift our attention to file systems and the tools we can build to interact with them. You will implement utilities ranging from simple file-copy programs to tools that traverse entire directory trees and even virtual file systems, reporting useful metadata along the way. As you will see, the real complexity rarely lies in copying bytes or walking directories. Instead, it emerges from validating parameters, handling errors carefully, and ensuring that every operation leaves the system in a consistent state. Go provides several helpers for directory traversal. The older `filepath.Walk()` and `filepath.WalkDir()` functions remain useful for many scenarios, while the newer `fs.WalkDir()` operates directly on the `fs.FS` abstraction and returns `fs.DirEntry` values, offering greater flexibility and efficiency.

This chapter covers the following:

- Handling UNIX signals
- Differentiating between different file types
- Finding more information about files
- The `io/fs` package
- Working with `embed.FS`

- Traversing directory trees
- Finding empty directories
- Creating a version of `tree(1)`
- Creating a version of `dd(1)`

A story

On September 20, 2025, I sat down to tackle a nagging issue on my *Omarchy Linux* system: duplicate Go and Zig installations. I was determined to clean things up, and the process of figuring it out was surprisingly satisfying. The problem showed up when I ran `mise list`, which listed different versions of Go and Zig than the ones that were installed by Arch Linux itself — Omarchy Linux sits on top of *Arch Linux*. The happiness came from solving the puzzle. Finding the duplicates with `find(1)`, configuring `mise` properly, and tweaking `PATH` made my development environment clean and efficient. Linux simplicity and the power of the UNIX terminal made the process a rewarding win. Using tools such as `mise` and `find(1)` turned into a practical lesson in file system navigation, echoing the themes of this chapter that you are about to read.

Handling UNIX signals

In UNIX-like systems, a signal is a lightweight, asynchronous notification mechanism used by the operating system to inform a process that an event has occurred. Common examples include `SIGINT` (sent when the user presses *Ctrl* + *C*) and `SIGTERM` (a request to terminate gracefully).

UNIX signal handling in Go requires the use of a channel, as defined by the `signal.Notify()` function, which is used exclusively for this task. The capacity of this particular channel is `1` to be able to receive and keep *one signal at a time*. This makes perfect sense as a signal can terminate a program, and there is no need to try to handle another signal at the same time. There is usually an anonymous function that is executed as a goroutine and performs the signal handling, and nothing else. The main task of that goroutine is to listen to the channel for data. Once a signal is received, it is sent to that channel, read by the goroutine, and stored in a variable — at this point, the channel can receive more signals. That variable is processed by a `switch` statement.

The presented program handles `SIGINT`, which is called `syscall.SIGINT` in Go and `SIGINFO` separately, and uses a `default` case in a `switch` block for handling the remaining signals. The implementation of that `switch` block allows you to differentiate between the various signals according to your needs. Keep in mind that *some signals cannot be caught* and the operating system cannot ignore them: `SIGKILL` and `SIGSTOP` cannot be blocked, caught, or ignored, and the reason for this is that they allow privileged users, as well as the UNIX kernel, to terminate any process they desire.

The example code that showcases UNIX signal handling is found in `ch06/signals.go`. We begin by presenting a simple signal handling function:

```
func handleSignal(sig os.Signal) {
    fmt.Println("handleSignal() Caught:", sig)
}
```

`handleSignal()` accepts a parameter of type `os.Signal`, which represents the specific signal that triggered the function, such as `SIGINT` when the user presses *Ctrl* + *C*. The function just prints a message to standard output, indicating that a signal has been caught and showing its name or description. Although minimal, this function demonstrates the core idea of signal handling: detecting and reacting to *asynchronous events* generated by the operating system. In larger programs, such a handler could be extended to perform more meaningful tasks, such as cleaning up resources, saving progress, or shutting down gracefully when a termination signal is received.

The `main()` function serves as the entry point of the program and coordinates its overall behavior. In this example, it initializes signal handling, records the start time, and launches a goroutine dedicated to reacting to incoming UNIX signals. Once the setup is complete, `main()` enters a simple loop that keeps the process running, allowing signals to be delivered and handled asynchronously:

```
func main() {
    fmt.Printf("Process ID: %d\n", os.Getpid())
    sigs := make(chan os.Signal, 1)
    signal.Notify(sigs)
    start := time.Now()
    go func() {
        for {
            sig := <-sigs
            switch sig {
            case syscall.SIGINT:
                duration := time.Since(start)
                fmt.Println("Execution time:", duration)
            case syscall.SIGINFO:
                handleSignal(sig)
                os.Exit(0)
            default:
                fmt.Println("Caught:", sig)
```

```
            }
        }
    }()

    for {
        fmt.Print("+")
        time.Sleep(10 * time.Second)
    }
}
```

At the start of `main()`, the program prints its process ID, which is useful if you want to send signals manually with commands such as `kill(1)`. It then creates a buffered channel of type `os.Signal` and registers it with `signal.Notify()`, ensuring that any signals delivered to the process will be sent through this channel. A goroutine is launched to continuously receive signals from the channel and act on them. The `switch` statement checks which signal was caught: if it is `SIGINT` (commonly triggered with *Ctrl* + *C*), the program prints how long it has been running by comparing the current time with the start time. If it is `SIGINFO`, it calls the previously defined `handleSignal()` function and then exits. The `default` case ensures that all other signals are still acknowledged by printing their name, even if the program does not have explicit handling logic for them. It is worth noting that, in Go, you do not necessarily need to write separate signal handling functions such as `handleSignal()`; you can keep the logic inline within the goroutine and `switch` statement if the handling is short and simple. The choice depends on readability and maintainability: factoring out separate functions is cleaner for complex logic, while inline handling is perfectly fine for straightforward reactions. Meanwhile, the main goroutine simply prints a + every 10 seconds, keeping the process alive so you have time to send it signals and observe the behavior.

> **Note**
>
> On Linux machines, `syscall.SIGINFO` is not supported. So, another signal, such as `syscall.SIGUSR1` or `syscall.SIGUSR2`, should be used in its place (`https://github.com/golang/go/issues/1653`).

Now, execute `ch06/signals.go` on your machine. The initial output at the terminal window where `ch06/signals.go` is running should be similar to the following:

```
$ go run ch06/signals.go
Process ID: 85877
```

In this case, the process ID is 85877, so this is where we are going to send our signals to. While `ch06/signals.go` is running, use another terminal window to execute the following commands: first, `kill -SIGINT 85877`, then `kill -SIGHUP 85877`, and last, `kill -SIGINFO 85877`, which terminates the program.

After issuing these three `kill(1)` commands, the rest of the output from `ch06/signals.go` should look as follows:

```
+Execution time: 26.378074709s
+Caught: hangup
+handleSignal() Caught: information request
```

The + signs appear because the main goroutine continuously prints them every 10 seconds, serving as a heartbeat that shows the process is still alive. When you see `Execution time: 26.378074709s`, it means the process received a `SIGINT` signal and printed the total time it had been running since startup. The next line, `Caught: hangup`, shows that the process caught a `SIGHUP` signal, which was handled by the `default` branch of the `switch` statement, since no explicit case was defined for it. Finally, `handleSignal() Caught: information request` indicates that the process received a `SIGINFO` signal, which triggered a call to the separate `handleSignal()` function and `os.Exit(0)`, which terminates the entire program.

As we saw in the previous section, robust command-line utilities must remain responsive to their execution environment, reacting gracefully to signals such as interrupts or status requests. At the same time, these tools spend most of their time interacting with the file system, where understanding what kind of object they are operating on is just as important. Before we can build more advanced file system utilities, it is therefore essential to know how to differentiate between various file types — such as regular files, directories, symbolic links, and special device files — so that our programs can handle each appropriately.

Differentiating between file types

Each UNIX file system contains different types of files, including regular files, directories, symbolic links, UNIX pipes, and so on. Understanding how to identify these different file types is foundational because traversal operations, such as `fs.WalkDir()`, rely on this distinction to make decisions — whether to recurse into a directory, follow a symbolic link, or process a regular file. In this subsection, we are going to create a small command-line utility that can detect the file type of a path. The `fileType()` function found in `ch06/fileType.go` illustrates how to detect the file type of a file – remember that in UNIX *everything is a file*:

```
func fileType(info os.FileInfo) string {
    mode := info.Mode()
    switch {
    case mode.IsRegular():
        return "regular file"
    case mode.IsDir():
        return "directory"
    case mode&os.ModeSymlink != 0:
        return "symbolic link"
    case mode&os.ModeNamedPipe != 0:
        return "named pipe (FIFO)"
    case mode&os.ModeSocket != 0:
        return "socket"
    case mode&os.ModeDevice != 0:
        if mode&os.ModeCharDevice != 0 {
            return "character device"
        }
        return "block device"
    default:
        return "unknown"
    }
}
```

The `filetype()` function takes a Go `os.FileInfo` object and returns a human-readable description of the file type. Internally, it works with the `os.FileMode` value obtained from `info.Mode()`, which encodes both the file's permissions and its type. The function then uses a `switch` statement with Boolean conditions to check the file type in order. It first checks if the entry is a regular file using `mode.IsRegular()`, then if it is a directory with `mode.IsDir()`. For special types, it uses bitmask checks, for example, `mode & os.ModeSymlink != 0` identifies *symbolic links*, while similar checks detect *named pipes* (FIFOs) and *sockets*. When the `os.ModeDevice` bit is set, the function distinguishes between character devices (such as `/dev/tty`) and block devices (such as `/dev/sda`) by checking for the `os.ModeCharDevice` flag. If none of the conditions match, the function returns `"unknown"`.

Now execute `ch06/fileType.go` on your machine, trying it on multiple files. You should get output like the following:

```
$ go run ch06/fileType.go /tmp
Path: /tmp
Type: symbolic link
$ go run ch06/fileType.go /bin/ls
Path: /bin/ls
Type: regular file
```

So, the `ch06/fileType.go` utility works as expected. Having learned how to tell different file types apart, the next logical step is to go deeper into the *metadata* that the operating system exposes about each file.

Finding more information about files

Beyond knowing whether something is a regular file, directory, or symbolic link, we often need details such as its size, permissions, last modification time, or ownership. This additional information allows us to build richer utilities that can report on file properties, enforce security checks, or even drive decisions about data processing and storage. The relevant example code can be found in the `main()` function of `ch06/fileInfo.go`:

```
func main() {
    if len(os.Args) < 2 {
        fmt.Println(filepath.Base(os.Args[0]), "<file-path>")
        os.Exit(1)
    }
    path := os.Args[1]

    info, err := os.Stat(path)
    if err != nil {
        fmt.Fprintf(os.Stderr, "Error: %v\n", err)
        os.Exit(1)
    }

    fmt.Println("File:", path)
    fmt.Println("Name:", info.Name())
    fmt.Println("Size:", info.Size(), "bytes")
    fmt.Println("Permissions:", info.Mode())
    fmt.Println("Modified:", info.ModTime().Format(time.RFC1123))
    if info.IsDir() {
```

```
        fmt.Println("Type: Directory")
    } else {
        fmt.Println("Type: File")
    }
}
```

The code first checks whether the user has provided a file path; if not, it prints a usage message and exits with an error code of `1`. The file path is taken from the first argument and passed to `os.Stat()`, which retrieves metadata about the file. If an error occurs, such as the file not existing, the program writes an error message to standard error and terminates. When the file is successfully opened, the program prints several details: the full path, the base name, its size in bytes, its permission bits, and the last modification time formatted in RFC1123 style. Finally, it checks whether the entry is a directory with `info.IsDir()`; if so, it prints `"Type: Directory"`; otherwise, it reports `"Type: File"`. In essence, this code acts as a lightweight version of the UNIX `stat(1)` utility, giving the user key file properties in a straightforward way. Let us use it to find more information about the go binary itself:

```
$ go run ch06/fileInfo.go `which go`
File: /opt/homebrew/bin/go
Name: go
Size: 14099458 bytes
Permissions: -rwxr-xr-x
Modified: Wed, 27 Aug 2025 18:49:40 EEST
Type: File
```

The preceding output shows how much information the operating system exposes through basic file metadata. In this case, we can immediately see that the go executable is a regular file, can be executed by all users, and occupies roughly 14 MB on disk.

With a solid understanding of how to inspect individual files using `os.Stat()`, we are now ready to explore the `io/fs` package, which provides a more flexible and uniform way to work with entire file systems and virtual file hierarchies.

The io/fs package

The `io/fs` package, introduced in Go 1.16, defines a set of interfaces and types to work with file systems in a uniform and abstract way. Instead of relying on the operating system's file system directly, `io/fs` allows developers to write code that can access files and directories through any file system implementation that satisfies its interfaces. This abstraction makes it easier to write modular, testable, and flexible code that can handle a variety of file system sources, such as real disk files, in-memory files, or embedded files bundled within the application. The package includes essential types such as `fs.FS`, which represents a read-only file system and provides functions to open, read, and walk directories in a consistent manner. One of the most significant uses of the `io/fs` package is in conjunction with the `embed.FS` type from the `embed` package. `embed.FS` implements the `fs.FS` interface, providing access to these embedded files as a virtual file system. Using `embed.FS` with `io/fs` makes it possible to write code that treats embedded files the same way as regular files on disk, greatly simplifying the handling of static assets in Go applications. *This means that your applications can create their own internal file systems and work with their own files.*

We are going to revisit `io/fs` in a while and see it in practice. For now, we will continue building on the `io/fs` package by using it to traverse entire directory trees. This allows our programs to recursively inspect, list, and process files across complex filesystem hierarchies.

Traversing directory trees

Traversing directory trees is a core operation in systems programming that involves recursively visiting directories and their contained files to perform inspection, analysis, or transformation. In this section, we focus on programmatically navigating a hierarchical file system. Go offers `fs.WalkDir()` and `filepath.Walk()`, which both provide mechanisms for recursively traversing a directory tree, but they differ in their design and flexibility. `filepath.Walk()` delivers each visited file or directory as an `os.FileInfo`, requiring extra system calls to obtain detailed information about entries, whereas `fs.WalkDir()` provides an `fs.DirEntry`, which is lighter and allows you to check properties such as whether the entry is a directory without additional overhead. Moreover, `fs.WalkDir()` works with any `fs.FS` implementation, including virtual or embedded filesystems, while `filepath.Walk()` operates on real filesystems only. Both functions allow the user to handle errors for individual entries, but `fs.WalkDir()` emphasizes working with interfaces and abstracted filesystems, offering a more modern and efficient approach for traversing directories in Go. In more detail, while both `os.FileInfo` and `fs.DirEntry` provide information about files and directories, they differ in scope and efficiency. `os.FileInfo` is a concrete type that represents file metadata, including its name, size, permissions, modification time, and whether it is a directory or symbolic link. It provides methods such as `Name()`, `IsDir()`, and `Type()` to inspect basic file attributes without requiring a full `FileInfo` object or additional system calls. When more detailed metadata is needed, `fs.DirEntry` offers the `Info()` method to obtain an `os.FileInfo`. Overall, `fs.DirEntry` is more efficient for large directory traversals, while `os.FileInfo` provides a richer set of file metadata.

The relevant example code can be found in `ch06/walkTree.go`, which is going to be presented in three parts. The first part contains the following code, which can also be used as the foundation for a file system analysis program – it defines two custom struct types that serve as data containers for the program:

```
type Stats struct {
    Dirs  int
    Files int
    Bytes int64
}

type FileInfo struct {
    Path string
    Size int64
}
```

The first struct, `Stats`, is designed to accumulate summary statistics about a directory tree. It contains three fields: `Dirs` (an integer counting the number of directories encountered), `Files` (an integer counting the number of files), and `Bytes` (an `int64`, which is used for counting bytes because file sizes can easily exceed the range of a regular 32-bit integer, especially when summing up many files). The second struct, `FileInfo`, represents information about individual files. It has two fields: `Path` (a `string` storing the file location in the file system) and `Size` (an `int64` holding the file size in bytes). This struct is designed to collect detailed information about each file.

In the second part, the code logic of the program is presented as found in `main()`:

```
func main() {
    // Command-line flags
    topN := flag.Int("top", 5, "Number of largest files to display")
    flag.Parse()

    if flag.NArg() < 1 {
        fmt.Fprintf(os.Stderr, "Usage: %s [options] <directory>\n",
filepath.Base(os.Args[0]))
        flag.PrintDefaults()
        os.Exit(1)
    }
    root := flag.Arg(0)
    var stats Stats
    var files []FileInfo
```

```
    err := fs.WalkDir(os.DirFS(root), ".",
        func(path string, d fs.DirEntry, err error) error {
            if err != nil {
                fmt.Fprintf(os.Stderr, "Error accessing %s: %v\n", path, err)
                return nil
            }

            if d.IsDir() {
                stats.Dirs++
                return nil
            }

            info, err := d.Info()
            if err != nil {
                fmt.Fprintf(os.Stderr, "Error getting info for %s: %v\n", path,
err)
                return nil
            }

            stats.Files++
            stats.Bytes += info.Size()
            files = append(files,
                FileInfo{Path: filepath.Join(root, path), Size: info.Size()})
            return nil
        })

    if err != nil {
        fmt.Println("Error walking the directory:", err)
        os.Exit(1)
    }
```

The `main()` begins by defining a command-line flag called `topN` using `flag.Int()`, which allows users to specify how many of the largest files they want to see (defaulting to `5`). After calling `flag.Parse()` to process any command-line arguments, the function checks if the user provided at least one non-flag argument (the directory path to analyze). If no directory is specified, it prints a usage message to standard error showing the program name, displays the available options, and exits with a *status code of 1* to indicate an error.

Once validation passes, the function retrieves the directory path from the first argument using `flag.Arg(0)` and stores it in the `root` variable. It then initializes two variables: `stats` (an instance of the `Stats` struct to accumulate totals) and `files` (a slice to collect individual `FileInfo` records). The core of the function is the `fs.WalkDir()` call, which recursively traverses the directory tree. It uses `os.DirFS(root)` to create a file system interface rooted at the specified directory and then walks from `"."` (the current directory *within* that file system root). The *anonymous function* passed to `fs.WalkDir()` serves as a callback *that is invoked for each file and directory encountered.* If an error occurs accessing a path, it prints a warning but continues processing by returning `nil` rather than stopping the walk. When it encounters a directory as determined by `d.IsDir()`, it simply increments the directory counter and moves on. For files, it retrieves detailed file information using `d.Info()`, which returns a `fs.FileInfo` object. It then updates the statistics by incrementing the file count, adding the file size to the total bytes, and appending a new `FileInfo` struct to the files slice. The `filepath.Join(root, path)` call constructs the full absolute path by combining the root directory with the relative path. Finally, after the walk completes, the function checks if any fatal error occurred during the traversal and exits with an error code if so, though the error handling within the callback makes this unlikely since most errors are caught and logged individually.

In the last part, we compute and present some statistics about the files:

```
    // Sort files by size descending
    sort.Slice(files, func(i, j int) bool {
        return files[i].Size > files[j].Size
    })
    fmt.Printf("Directory statistics for %s:\n", root)
    fmt.Printf("Directories: %d\n", stats.Dirs)
    fmt.Printf("Files: %d\n", stats.Files)
    fmt.Printf("Total size: %d bytes\n\n", stats.Bytes)

    fmt.Printf("Top %d largest files:\n", *topN)
    for i, f := range files {
        if i >= *topN {
            break
        }
        fmt.Printf("%d. %s (%d bytes)\n", i+1, f.Path, f.Size)
    }
}
```

This code segment completes the directory analysis tool by sorting the collected files and displaying the results. It begins by using `sort.Slice()` to reorder the `files` slice in descending order by file size. The `sort.Slice()` function takes the slice and a comparison function that receives two indices, `i` and `j`, and returns `true` when the element at index `i` should come before the element at index `j`. By comparing `files[i].Size > files[j].Size`, the function ensures larger files appear first in the sorted list. After sorting, the function displays the accumulated statistics in a formatted output. It prints the root directory path being analyzed, followed by three key metrics from the `stats` struct: the total number of directories found, the total number of files encountered, and the cumulative size of all files in bytes. The final portion displays the largest files found during the scan. It prints a header indicating how many top files will be shown (using `*topN` to dereference the pointer and get the actual integer value from the command-line flag). The function then iterates through the sorted `files` slice using a `range` loop, which provides both the index `i` and the file information `f`. Inside the loop, there is a critical check: if the current index reaches or exceeds the requested number of top files, the loop breaks early to avoid displaying more files than requested. For each file that should be displayed, it prints a numbered line showing the rank (index plus one for human-readable numbering), the full file path, and the file size in bytes. This is useful for identifying what is consuming the most disk space. Now, let us see the directory analysis tool (`ch06/walkTree.go`) in action:

```
$ go run ch06/walkTree.go .
Directory statistics for .:
Directories: 220
Files: 479
Total size: 484954 bytes

Top 5 largest files:
1. ch05/profReading.go (12122 bytes)
2. ch02/structures.go (11118 bytes)
3. ch10/parser.go (10966 bytes)
4. ch06/tree.go (10650 bytes)
5. .git/index (10392 bytes)
```

The first section, `Directory statistics for .`, reports that under the current directory there are *220 directories, 479 files*, and the files together take up about 485 `KB`. The second section, `Top 5 largest files`, lists the five biggest files in descending order by size, showing both their relative paths and sizes in bytes. For example, `ch05/profReading.go` is the largest file with about 12 KB, followed by `ch02/structures.go` and others, including a non-source file, `.git/index`, from the Git repository.

Once we know how to work with files at runtime, a natural next step is to learn how to *package static assets directly into our Go binaries*, ensuring our programs remain *self-contained and easy to distribute*. This is explained in the section that follows, as well as how to apply `fs.WalkDir()` in these embedded file systems!

Embedding static assets in Go binaries

Embedding static assets in Go binaries is a powerful technique that allows developers to bundle files such as HTML templates, CSS stylesheets, JavaScript scripts, images, or other resources directly into the compiled executable. This approach simplifies deployment by eliminating the need to distribute and manage external asset files separately, ensuring that all necessary resources travel with the application. Therefore, embedding assets can improve portability, reduce runtime errors caused by missing files, and streamline the build and release process, making it ideal for creating self-contained, easy-to-distribute Go applications.

So, starting with Go 1.16, the **embed package** was introduced, offering a straightforward, type-safe way to include files or directories at compile time. By using the `//go:embed` directive, you can specify one or more files or patterns that get compiled into the binary and accessed as byte slices or `fs.FS` file systems during runtime. This eliminates the need for third-party tools and integrates seamlessly with the Standard Library. Before Go 1.16, developers often relied on external tools to generate Go source code from asset files, which then could be compiled into the application. File embedding is based on code that looks as follows:

```
//go:embed assets/*
var embeddedFiles embed.FS
```

This code uses the `embed` package to include external files directly in the compiled binary. The special comment `//go:embed assets/*` tells the compiler to take all files under the `assets` directory and *embed them into the binary at build time*. The `embeddedFiles` variable is of type `embed.FS`, which behaves like a *read-only virtual file system*. After compilation, you can access the embedded files using functions such as `embeddedFiles.Open("assets/file")` without needing the original files present on disk. This approach is especially useful for bundling configuration files, templates, or static web assets into a single self-contained executable. In this case, this means that `assets` should also be under the `ch06` directory; otherwise, you are going to get an error message telling you `no matching files found`.

The following snippet shows the beginning of the `main()` function implementation:

```
func main() {
    fileToRead := flag.String("file", "", "Specific embedded file")
    flag.Parse()
    // Create a sub-filesystem rooted at "assets"
```

```
    assetsFS, err := fs.Sub(embeddedFiles, "assets")
    if err != nil {
        log.Fatalf("failed to get sub FS: %v", err)
    }
```

The code first defines a command-line flag called `-file`, which lets the user optionally specify the name of a file to read from the embedded data; if no flag is given, the program will simply list or process files without reading one. After parsing the command-line arguments with `flag.Parse()`, the code creates a sub-filesystem rooted at the `"assets"` directory inside the embedded data by calling `fs.Sub(embeddedFiles, "assets")`. This effectively restricts the view of the embedded filesystem to just the `assets/` subtree, making file access simpler and more controlled. If an error occurs while creating this sub-filesystem, the program logs a fatal message and terminates, ensuring it does not continue with an invalid or incomplete filesystem reference. The next part of the program traverses the embedded filesystem to list all its contents.

```
    err = fs.WalkDir(assetsFS, ".", func(path string, d fs.DirEntry, err error)
error {
        if err != nil {
            fmt.Fprintf(os.Stderr, "Error accessing %s: %v\n", path, err)
            return nil
        }
        info, _ := d.Info()
        if d.IsDir() {
            fmt.Printf("[DIR]  %s\n", path)
        } else {
            fmt.Printf("[FILE] %s (%d bytes)\n", path, info.Size())
        }
        return nil
    })
    if err != nil {
        log.Fatalf("walk error: %v", err)
    }
```

Notice how the same traversal logic now applies to a virtual filesystem? The code still uses `fs.WalkDir()` to recursively walk through the directory tree starting at `"."`, which is the root of the sub-filesystem previously restricted to `assets/`. For each entry, the callback function receives the relative `path`, an `fs.DirEntry` object, `d`, and any error that occurred while accessing that entry. If there is an error, it prints a warning to *standard error* but continues the traversal by returning `nil`. For valid entries, it retrieves additional information such as file size by calling d.Info(). The code then checks whether the entry is a directory with d.IsDir() and prints either [DIR] followed by the directory path or [FILE] followed by the file path and its size in bytes. After the walk completes, the outer err variable is checked; if fs.WalkDir() itself encountered a fatal problem, the program logs the error and terminates.

In this final section of the program, the code checks whether the user provided a filename via the -file command-line flag.

```
    if *fileToRead != "" {
        content, err := fs.ReadFile(assetsFS, filepath.Clean(*fileToRead))
        if err != nil {
            fmt.Fprintf(os.Stderr, "Error reading file %s: %v\n", *fileToRead,
err)
            os.Exit(1)
        }
        fmt.Printf("\nContents of %s:\n", *fileToRead)
        fmt.Println(string(content))
    }
}
```

If a filename is specified, it attempts to read the file contents directly from the embedded filesystem using fs.ReadFile(), which takes the sub-filesystem, assetsFS, and the cleaned file path for safety. If reading the file fails, the program reports the error to standard error and terminates with a non-zero exit code to signal failure. Otherwise, it prints a header showing the name of the file followed by the file contents, converted from bytes to a string for readability.

Execute ch06/embedFS.go on your machine — please make sure that the ch06/assets directory exists and it contains files and, optionally, directories. Also, keep in mind that for this case, the assets directory should be in the same directory as the source code file.

```
$ go run ch06/embedFS.go
[DIR]  .
[DIR]  aDir
[FILE] aDir/emptyFile (0 bytes)
[FILE] file (16 bytes)
```

Presenting the contents of file requires executing go run ch06/embedFS.go -file file, which you can try on your machine. Having seen how to traverse an embedded filesystem and distinguish files from directories, we can now build a practical utility that identifies *directories containing no files*.

A utility for finding empty directories

When managing large directory trees, it is common to encounter folders that serve no real purpose because they are empty. These directories can accumulate over time due to incomplete cleanups, application behavior, or user oversight. For example, a build system may create per-run output directories, or a backup script may leave behind date-stamped folders after files are moved or deleted. Identifying and handling such directories is important for maintaining a tidy file system and freeing up space for meaningful data. In this subsection, we will learn how to write a Go program that locates empty directories. The logic of the utility is found in the following code, which can be found in `main()`, which demonstrates how to traverse a directory tree in Go using `fs.WalkDir()` while identifying and printing empty directories:

```
err := fs.WalkDir(os.DirFS(root), ".",
    func(path string, d fs.DirEntry, err error) error {
        if err != nil {
            fmt.Fprintf(os.Stderr, "Error accessing %s: %v\n", path, err)
            return nil
        }
        if d.IsDir() {
            entries, err := os.ReadDir(filepath.Join(root, path))
            if err != nil {
                fmt.Fprintf(os.Stderr,
                    "Error in directory %s: %v\n", path, err)
                    return nil
            }
            if len(entries) == 0 {
                fmt.Println(filepath.Join(root, path))
            }
        }
        return nil
    })
if err != nil {
    log.Fatalf("Error walking directory tree: %v\n", err)
}
```

The code starts by creating a filesystem rooted at `root` using `os.DirFS(root)` and begins walking from the current directory, `"."`. The traversal is performed via a **callback function** that is called for every entry in the tree. Inside the callback function, the code first checks if an error occurred while accessing the current path; if so, it prints an error message to standard error and continues. Next, it determines whether the current entry is a directory using `d.IsDir()`. If it is a directory, `os.ReadDir(filepath.Join(root, path))` reads its contents to obtain a list of entries. If reading the directory itself produces an error, that error is reported but does not stop the traversal. When the list of entries is empty, indicating that the directory contains no files or subdirectories, the program prints the full path of the empty directory. Finally, after the traversal completes, the outer `err` check ensures that any unexpected errors from `fs.WalkDir()` itself are handled, terminating the program with a fatal log message. Run `ch06/emptyDir.go` on your machine:

```
$ go run ch06/emptyDir.go .
.git/objects/info
.git/refs/tags
ch11
ch13
```

To take the ideas of this subsection further, we can now attempt a more ambitious project: re-implementing one of the classic UNIX utilities that combines traversal, formatting, and structured output into a single program.

Creating the tree(1) utility in Go

The `tree(1)` utility is a widely used command-line tool that displays a directory hierarchy in a human-readable tree structure. In this section, we will design and implement a simplified version of `tree(1)` that recursively explores directories, prints their contents with indentation, and distinguishes between files and subdirectories. The structure of the program follows a simple and deliberate flow. Command-line flags are first collected into an `options` structure, which is passed unchanged throughout the traversal. The `doTree()` function prepares each root path and decides whether recursion is needed, while `walkDir()` performs the actual directory traversal and output generation. Supporting helpers handle directory reading, entry formatting, and permission rendering, allowing the core traversal logic to remain readable and focused.

The first part of `ch06/tree.go` is the following:

```go
// options holds CLI options.
type options struct {
    all       bool
    dirsOnly  bool
    level     int
    dirsFirst bool
    fullPath  bool
    showPerm  bool
    showSize  bool
    human     bool
```

```
    noReport  bool
}
type stats struct {
    dirs  int
    files int
    bytes int64
}
```

This code snippet defines the foundation for the utility by declaring configuration options and statistics tracking. The `options` struct models the various command-line flags that control how the program behaves. For example, `all` corresponds to showing hidden files, `dirsOnly` to listing only directories, `level` to limiting the depth of traversal, `dirsFirst` to controlling sort order, and flags such as `fullPath`, `showPerm`, `showSize`, and `human` toggle additional display details such as absolute paths, file permissions, file sizes, and human-readable formats. The `noReport` flag likely disables the summary statistics normally shown at the end of the output. The second struct, `stats`, is used for collecting metrics during directory traversal. It maintains counters for the number of directories (`dirs`), the number of files (`files`), and the total size in bytes (`bytes`) of all encountered files. Together, these definitions establish the configuration and reporting backbone for the program: `options` dictates *how* the filesystem should be traversed and displayed, while `stats` keeps track of *what* has been discovered and measured during execution. Next, we see the implementation of `doTree()`, which is responsible for traversing and printing the directory tree while also collecting statistics about the traversal:

```
func doTree(root string, opt options) (stats, error) {
    var st stats

    // Resolve root printing name
    displayRoot := root
    if !opt.fullPath {
        if base, err := filepath.Abs(root); err == nil {
            // Show just the base name for the root when not full path
            displayRoot = filepath.Base(base)
        } else {
            displayRoot = filepath.Base(root)
        }
    } else {
        if abs, err := filepath.Abs(root); err == nil {
            displayRoot = abs
        }
```

```
    }
    fmt.Println(displayRoot)

    // If level is 0, do not list children.
    if opt.level == 0 {
        return st, nil
    }

    // We Lstat the root to decide if it's a file or directory.
    info, err := os.Lstat(root)
    if err != nil {
        return st, err
    }
```

`doTree()` takes two arguments: the starting directory path (`root`) and an `options` struct (`opt`) that defines how the traversal should behave. The function returns a `stats` struct with counts and sizes of files and directories, along with a possible error. The first step is to prepare the display name of the `root`. If the `fullPath` option is disabled, the program tries to resolve the absolute path of `root` and then reduces it to just the base name (the last component of the path). If resolution fails, it still falls back to the base name. If `fullPath` is enabled, the function instead uses the absolute path as the display name. This ensures that the `root` directory is always printed in a meaningful way according to user preferences. Next, the `root` is printed as the starting point of the tree. The function checks if the `level` option is set to zero, which acts as a stopping condition: in that case, the root is displayed but no child directories or files are listed and the function immediately returns. Finally, the code uses `os.Lstat()` to retrieve information about the root file system object. Unlike `os.Stat()`, `Lstat()` *does not follow symbolic links*, which allows the program to distinguish between symlinks and the actual files they may point to. This information is necessary to determine whether the root is a file or a directory, and it influences how the traversal proceeds in the remaining part of the function.

The second part of the `doTree()` function handles two possible cases: when the root is a single file and when it is a directory.

```
    if !info.IsDir() {
        // Single file: print details if requested and return.
        line := formatEntry(root, info, "", true, opt)
        if line != "" {
            fmt.Println(line)
        }
```

```
        st.files++
        st.bytes += info.Size()
        return st, nil
    }

    err = walkDir(root, "", 1, opt, &st)
    return st, err
}
```

If the root path points to a file, the program formats file information using `formatEntry()`, which applies the display options (such as showing size, permissions, or whether the full path should be printed). If the resulting line is not empty, it is printed. At the same time, the statistics are updated: since this is not a directory, the file count (`st.files`) is incremented and the total byte size (`st.bytes`) increases by the file size. `doTree()` then returns immediately because there are no children to traverse. If the `root` is a directory, the traversal continues by calling `walkDir()`, a helper function responsible for recursively walking the directory tree. It starts from the root with an initial prefix (used for formatting indentation in the tree view) and a depth level of `1`. The `stats` structure is passed by reference so it can be updated as files and directories are encountered. When `walkDir()` completes, the accumulated statistics and any error it returns are passed back up.

The `walkDir()` function is the core routine responsible for traversing a directory tree and printing its structure in the desired format. It begins by reading the directory contents with `readDir()`, which respects the options passed in (such as sorting or filtering). If reading fails, the function reports the error but continues, ensuring that one bad directory does not abort the entire traversal. Here is its implementation:

```
func walkDir(root, prefix string, depth int, opt options, st *stats) error {
    entries, err := readDir(root, opt)
    if err != nil {
        fmt.Fprintf(os.Stderr, "gotree: %s: %v\n", root, err)
        return nil // continue
    }

    for i, entry := range entries {
        last := i == len(entries)-1
        branch := "├── "
        nextPrefix := prefix + "│   "
        if last {
            branch = "└── "
```

```
            nextPrefix = prefix + "    "
        }

        // Fetch FileInfo via Lstat to avoid following symlinks.
        full := filepath.Join(root, entry.Name())
        info, err := os.Lstat(full)
        if err != nil {
            fmt.Fprintf(os.Stderr, "gotree: %s: %v\n", full, err)
            continue
        }

        if !opt.all && strings.HasPrefix(entry.Name(), ".") {
            continue
        }

        line := prefix + branch + formatEntry(full, info, root, false, opt)
        if line != "" {
            fmt.Println(line)
        }

        if info.IsDir() {
            st.dirs++
        } else {
            st.files++
            st.bytes += info.Size()
        }
        if info.IsDir() {
            if opt.level < 0 || depth < opt.level {
                if err := walkDir(full, nextPrefix, depth+1, opt, st); err != nil
{
                    return err
                }
            }
        }
    }
    return nil
}
```

For each entry in the directory, the function determines whether it is the last element in the list to decide how to draw the tree branch. This also controls the nextPrefix string, which maintains the visual alignment for child entries at deeper levels of the tree. The code then constructs the full path and calls `os.Lstat()` to get file information *without following symbolic links*. Using `Lstat()` instead of `Stat()` is important because following symbolic links could lead to cyclic structures — for example, a symbolic link that points back to a parent directory — which would cause an infinite loop during traversal. By examining the link itself rather than its target, the code can safely identify and handle symbolic links as distinct file types. Even worse, you can escape the current subtree and traverse into completely unintended parts of the file system! If the lookup fails, the error is printed, and the loop moves on to the next entry. Hidden files and directories (names starting with ".") are skipped unless the `-a` option (`opt.all`) is enabled. Next, the function formats the entry's display string using `formatEntry()`, prepending the proper branch and prefix, and prints it if not empty. Statistics are updated accordingly: directories increment the `dirs` counter, while files increment both the `files` counter and the cumulative bytes total. Finally, if the entry is a directory, the function checks whether recursion is allowed. This is controlled by the `level` option: if `level` is negative, recursion is unlimited, while a positive `level` restricts how deep the traversal goes. When allowed, the function calls itself recursively with the updated prefix and increased depth.

The `readDir()` function is a helper routine that reads the contents of a given directory and applies filtering and sorting rules based on the user options:

```
func readDir(path string, opt options) ([]fs.DirEntry, error) {
    entries, err := os.ReadDir(path)
    if err != nil {
        return nil, err
    }

    // Filter hidden unless -a; filter files if -d
    filtered := entries[:0]
    for _, e := range entries {
        name := e.Name()
        if !opt.all && strings.HasPrefix(name, ".") {
            continue
        }
        if opt.dirsOnly {
            if !e.IsDir() {
                continue
            }
        }
        filtered = append(filtered, e)
    }
    sort.Slice(filtered, func(i, j int) bool {
```

```
        ei, ej := filtered[i], filtered[j]
        // Optionally list directories first
        if opt.dirsFirst {
            if ei.IsDir() != ej.IsDir() {
                return ei.IsDir() && !ej.IsDir()
            }
        }
        return strings.ToLower(ei.Name()) < strings.ToLower(ej.Name())
    })

    return filtered, nil
}
```

The function begins with a call to `os.ReadDir()`, which retrieves a slice of `fs.DirEntry` values representing the files and subdirectories within the target path. Next, the function filters the entries. It skips hidden files and directories (those whose names begin with `"."`) unless the `-a` flag (`opt.all`) has been enabled. Similarly, if the `-d` (directories only) option is set, any non-directory entries are excluded. This filtering is performed by reusing the existing slice (`entries[:0]`) to avoid unnecessary allocations, and only the accepted entries are appended to it. This is an interesting and highly efficient construct, but it requires careful understanding. When you create `filtered := entries[:0]`, you are creating a new slice header that shares the same underlying array as `entries` but with a length of zero. As you append to `filtered`, you are overwriting elements in the shared underlying array that `entries` also references. This means that as the filtering progresses, the `entries` slice becomes corrupted — it still has its original length, but its contents are being rearranged and overwritten.

After filtering, the function *sorts the results.* The sorting logic respects the `dirsFirst` option: if enabled, directories are always listed before files. Within each group, entries are ordered alphabetically in a *case-insensitive manner* by converting their names to lowercase before comparison. This ensures consistent ordering regardless of filename capitalization. Finally, the filtered and sorted slice of entries is returned to the caller function.

The `formatEntry()` function is responsible for formatting how a single file or directory entry will appear in the tree output, based on the user options. It takes the full path of the entry, its `fs.FileInfo`, the root directory, a flag indicating whether it is the root file, and the set of options. The function ultimately returns a `string` that represents the entry in the tree display.

```
func formatEntry(fullPath string, info fs.FileInfo, root string, isRootFile bool,
opt options) string {
    name := info.Name()
```

```
    // Determine display name per -f
    display := name
    if opt.fullPath {
        var base string
        if isRootFile {
            base = ""
        } else {
            base = root
        }
        p := fullPath
        if base != "" {
            // Normalize absolute
            if abs, err := filepath.Abs(fullPath); err == nil {
                p = abs
            }
        }
        display = p
    }

    // Identify symlink and potential target
    if info.Mode()&os.ModeSymlink != 0 {
        if target, err := os.Readlink(fullPath); err == nil {
            display = fmt.Sprintf("%s -> %s", display, target)
        }
    }

    var meta []string
    if opt.showPerm {
        meta = append(meta, modeString(info.Mode()))
    }
    if opt.showSize {
        if opt.human {
            meta = append(meta, humanizeBytes(info.Size()))
        } else {
            meta = append(meta, fmt.Sprintf("%d", info.Size()))
        }
    }

    if len(meta) > 0 {
        return fmt.Sprintf("%s [%s]", display, strings.Join(meta, " "))
    }
```

```
    return display
}
```

The code begins by determining the name to display. By default, it shows only the file or directory name (`info.Name()`), but if the `-f` (*full path*) option is enabled, it adjusts the display. For the root entry, it may simply use the provided path, while for others it attempts to resolve an absolute path with `filepath.Abs()`. This ensures that the output reflects either relative names or full paths, depending on user preference. Next, the function checks whether the entry is a **symbolic link**. If so, it attempts to read the target of the link using `os.Readlink()`. If successful, it appends the target path to the display string using the `->` notation, making symlinks immediately recognizable in the tree. The function then builds a list of metadata fields to include, depending on options. If the `showPerm` flag is set, it appends a human-readable representation of the file permissions (via a helper, `modeString()`). If `showSize` is enabled, it appends the file size, either in raw bytes or in human-readable form, depending on whether the human option was requested. Finally, if any metadata has been collected, the function formats the display string as `<name> [<metadata>]`, with the metadata fields joined by spaces. Otherwise, it simply returns the display name.

Next, `modeString()` generates a human-readable string representing the file mode, like the output of the `ls -l` command in UNIX. It takes an `fs.FileMode` as input and returns a string such as `drwxr-xr-x` that encodes both the file type and its permission bits:

```
func modeString(m fs.FileMode) string {
    var b strings.Builder

    switch {
    case m.IsDir():
        b.WriteByte('d')
    case m&os.ModeSymlink != 0:
        b.WriteByte('l')
    case m&os.ModeSocket != 0:
        b.WriteByte('s')
    case m&os.ModeNamedPipe != 0:
        b.WriteByte('p')
    case m&os.ModeDevice != 0:
        if m&os.ModeCharDevice != 0 {
            b.WriteByte('c')
        } else {
            b.WriteByte('b')
```

```
        }
    default:
        b.WriteByte('-')
    }

    rwx := []fs.FileMode{0400, 0200, 0100, 0040, 0020, 0010, 0004, 0002, 0001}
    for i, bit := range rwx {
        if m&bit != 0 {
            switch i % 3 {
            case 0:
                b.WriteByte('r')
            case 1:
                b.WriteByte('w')
            case 2:
                b.WriteByte('x')
            }
        } else {
            b.WriteByte('-')
        }
    }

    // Setuid, setgid, sticky adjustments
    if m&os.ModeSetuid != 0 {
        // user execute position (index 3)
        replaceAt(&b, 3, 's', 'S')
    }
    if m&os.ModeSetgid != 0 {
        // group execute position (index 6)
        replaceAt(&b, 6, 's', 'S')
    }
    if m&os.ModeSticky != 0 {
        // others execute position (index 9)
        replaceAt(&b, 9, 't', 'T')
    }
    return b.String()
}
```

The function starts by identifying the file type. It examines the mode flags: directories are represented by `'d'`, symbolic links by `'l'`, sockets by `'s'`, named pipes by `'p'`, block or character devices by `'b'` or `'c'`, respectively, and regular files by `'-'`. This single character is written first in the string. Next, it encodes the standard UNIX permissions for user, group, and others. The `rwx` slice represents the read, write, and execute bits in order. The function loops over each bit, appending `'r'`, `'w'`, or `'x'` if the corresponding bit is set and `'-'` if not. The loop ensures the nine permission positions are filled sequentially.

After the basic permissions, the function adjusts for special mode bits: **setuid**, **setgid**, and **sticky**. If `os.ModeSetuid` is set, it replaces the `user execute` position with `'s'` if `execute` is enabled, or `'S'` if not. Similarly, `os.ModeSetgid` modifies the `group execute` position, and `os.ModeSticky` modifies the `others execute` position using `'t'` or `'T'`. The helper function, `replaceAt()`, performs these replacements in the string. Finally, the constructed string is returned, providing a concise, `ls(1)` style representation of both the file type and its permissions, suitable for inclusion in a tree listing or detailed file display.

The `sameFile()` function determines whether two `fs.FileInfo` values refer to the *same underlying file*. It first checks if either of the inputs is `nil` and returns `false` immediately if so, since a `nil` value cannot represent a valid file.

```
func sameFile(fi1, fi2 fs.FileInfo) bool {
    if fi1 == nil || fi2 == nil {
        return false
    }
    s1, ok1 := fi1.Sys().(*syscall.Stat_t)
    s2, ok2 := fi2.Sys().(*syscall.Stat_t)
    if ok1 && ok2 {
        return s1.Dev == s2.Dev && s1.Ino == s2.Ino
    }
    // Fallback: compare names & sizes if Stat_t unavailable
    return fi1.Name() == fi2.Name() && fi1.Size() == fi2.Size() && fi1.Mode() ==
fi2.Mode()
}
```

For platforms that support `syscall.Stat_t`, it retrieves the low-level file system information from the `Sys()` method of `fs.FileInfo`. This includes the **device ID** (`Dev`) and **inode number** (`Ino`), which *together uniquely identify a file on a given filesystem.* If both `fs.FileInfo` values provide valid `Stat_t` structures, the function compares these fields and returns `true` only if both the device and inode match, ensuring an accurate comparison even for files with the same name in different locations or hard links. If the platform does not support `Stat_t` or the `Sys()` call does not return a `Stat_t` structure, the function falls back to a simpler heuristic: it compares the names, sizes, and mode bits of the two entries. While not guaranteed to be unique (two different files could coincidentally have the same name, size, and permissions), this fallback provides a reasonable approximation for most practical purposes. Try `ch06/tree.go` on your machine, which is going to give the following kind of output:

```
$ go run ch06/tree.go ch07
ch07
├── data.json
├── datetime
│   ├── config.yaml
│   └── convert.go
├── Dijkstra.go
├── json.go
├── json2xml.go
├── jsonV2.go
├── postgres
│   └── postgres.go
├── sqlite
│   └── lite3.go
└── users.json

3 directories, 10 files
```

The code in this section demonstrated how option parsing, directory traversal, metadata inspection, and error handling come together to form a practical file system utility. Each function solves a narrow problem, but their composition enables a flexible traversal of complex directory trees. Now that we know how to walk directory trees and examine their contents, we can move on to practical tasks that build on these skills, such as distributing a single file across multiple directories.

Copying a single file into multiple directories

Copying a single file into multiple directories is a common task when deploying configuration files or assets to different locations in a system. In this section, we will explore how Go can efficiently replicate a file into several target directories, handling errors gracefully and ensuring that each copy is correctly written without overwriting existing files unintentionally. The implementation demonstrates an important architectural principle: *separation of validation from execution*. By using the `CopyResult` structure (`ch06/cpMultiple.go`) to track outcomes and delegating the actual copying work to helper functions, we create a clear boundary between error handling logic and file I/O operations:

```
type CopyResult struct {
    Directory string
    Success   bool
    Error     string
}
```

This snippet defines a simple Go struct named `CopyResult`, which is designed to capture the outcome of copying a file into a single target directory. The `Directory` field stores the path of the directory where the file was copied (or attempted to be copied). The `Success` Boolean indicates whether the copy operation completed without errors, making it easy to programmatically check the result. Finally, the `Error` field holds an error message, if one occurred, giving useful diagnostic information when the operation fails. After that, we implement the `copyFileToDirectories()` function, which is responsible for copying a single source file into multiple target directories, returning a slice of `CopyResult` values that summarize the outcome of each individual copy attempt.

```
func copyFileToDirectories(sourceFile string, targetDirs []string) []CopyResult {
    results := make([]CopyResult, len(targetDirs))

    sourceInfo, err := os.Stat(sourceFile)
    if err != nil {
        // If source doesn't exist, mark all operations as failed
        for i, dir := range targetDirs {
            results[i] = CopyResult{
                Directory: dir,
                Success:   false,
                Error:     fmt.Sprintf("source file error: %v", err),
            }
        }
        return results
    }

    if sourceInfo.IsDir() {
        for i, dir := range targetDirs {
            results[i] = CopyResult{
                Directory: dir,
                Success:   false,
```

```
                Error:     "source is a directory, not a file",
            }
        }
        return results
    }

    filename := filepath.Base(sourceFile)
    for i, targetDir := range targetDirs {
        results[i] = copyToSingleDirectory(sourceFile, targetDir, filename)
    }
    return results
}
```

The code begins by preparing a `results` slice with the same length as the list of target directories, so each directory gets its own status entry. Before copying, the function *checks whether the source file exists and is a regular file.* If `os.Stat()` fails, meaning the file does not exist or is not accessible, the function marks every copy attempt as failed, including the error message in each corresponding `CopyResult`. Similarly, if the source path is a directory, it returns a failure for each destination *since directories cannot be copied by this function.* Once those checks pass, the function extracts the filename without its path using `filepath.Base()`, ensuring that the file is copied into each destination directory with the correct name. Finally, it iterates over the list of target directories and delegates the actual copy operation to another helper function, `copyToSingleDirectory()`, storing the returned `CopyResult` for each case.

Next, we present the `copyToSingleDirectory()` implementation, which is responsible for copying a single file into one specific target directory – *most of its logic focuses on validating that all the required elements exist and are in a valid state before performing the actual copy.*

```
func copyToSingleDirectory(sourceFile, targetDir, filename string) CopyResult {
    result := CopyResult{Directory: targetDir}
    if _, err := os.Stat(targetDir); os.IsNotExist(err) {
        result.Success = false
        result.Error = "directory does not exist"
        return result
    }

    targetFile := filepath.Join(targetDir, filename)

    if _, err := os.Stat(targetFile); err == nil {
        result.Success = false
```

```
        result.Error = "file already exists in directory"
        return result
    }

    err := copyFile(sourceFile, targetFile)
    if err != nil {
        result.Success = false
        result.Error = fmt.Sprintf("copy failed: %v", err)
        return result
    }
    result.Success = true
    return result
}
```

The code starts by creating a `CopyResult` for the given target directory, which will later record whether the operation succeeded or failed. The function first checks whether the target directory exists using `os.Stat()`; if it does not, the operation is immediately marked as failed with an appropriate error message. Next, it builds the full target file path by joining the directory with the filename and checks whether a file with the same name already exists there. If it does, the function again records failure to avoid overwriting. Only when these conditions are satisfied does the function proceed with the actual file copy, delegated to a helper function, `copyFile()`. If this copy attempt fails, the error is captured in the `result`. Otherwise, the function marks the operation as successful. Feel free to see the implementation of `copyFile()` by looking at `ch06/cpMultiple.go`. Now, use `ch06/cpMultiple.go` on your machine:

```
$ go run ch06/cpMultiple.go README.md /tmp /Users/mtsouk /thisWillFail
Copying 'README.md' to 3 directories...
Results:
--------
/tmp - SUCCESS
/Users/mtsouk - SUCCESS
/thisWillFail - FAILED: directory does not exist
Summary:
--------
Total directories: 3
Successful copies: 2
Failed copies: 1
Note: Some operations failed. Check directory existence and permissions.
exit status 2
```

As `/thisWillFail` does not exist, it makes perfect sense that the operation failed. Building on the foundation of this section, we now turn to a more sophisticated and historically significant tool: the `dd(1)` utility.

Creating the dd(1) utility in Go

This Go program functions as a simple, signal-aware file copy utility, inspired by the behavior of `dd(1)`. It reads data from a specified input file (or standard input) and writes it to an output file (or standard output) in fixed-size blocks, with optional parameters for block size, block count, and output seek offset. Rather than using a command-line flag for progress reporting, it relies entirely on UNIX signals: sending `SIGUSR1` to the running process prints the current number of blocks and bytes copied along with the transfer speed, while sending `SIGINT` or `SIGTERM` prints a final progress report and exits gracefully. Internally, the program uses **atomic counters** to safely track blocks copied and total bytes across concurrent operations, and it ensures proper handling of errors such as missing input files, existing output files, read/write failures, and seek issues.

In programs such as `ch06/dd.go`, most of the code is dedicated not just to the actual data transfer but to *reading and validating user parameters, handling errors, and responding to signals.* Before any bytes are copied, the program checks that input and output files exist (or can be created), applies optional seek offsets, and ensures that provided flags such as block size or count are valid. During the copy loop, it carefully monitors read and write operations, handles end-of-file conditions, and updates progress counters in a thread-safe manner. Signal handling is integrated so that the program can report progress or terminate gracefully when requested. These supporting tasks — parameter validation, error handling, concurrency-safe bookkeeping, and signal management — often account for the majority of the code, while the core logic of reading from the input and writing to the output is comparatively straightforward. The actual copy loop, which implements the core functionality of `dd.go`, is part of `main()` and is just the following:

```
for {
    if count > 0&&blocksCopied>= int64(count) {
        break
    }
    n, readErr := io.ReadFull(in, buf)
    if n > 0 {
        _, writeErr := out.Write(buf[:n])
        if writeErr != nil {
            fmt.Fprintf(os.Stderr, "Write error: %v\n", writeErr)
            os.Exit(1)
        }
        atomic.AddInt64(&blocksCopied, 1)
```

```
        atomic.AddInt64(&totalBytes, int64(n))
    }
    if readErr == io.EOF || readErr == io.ErrUnexpectedEOF {
        break
    }
    if readErr != nil {
        fmt.Fprintf(os.Stderr, "Read error: %v\n", readErr)
        os.Exit(1)
    }
}
```

The code continuously reads data from the input file into a buffer and writes it to the output file, handling both partial reads and end-of-file conditions. The loop first checks whether a user-specified block count has been reached; if so, it exits. Using `io.ReadFull()`, the program attempts to fill the buffer completely from the input, returning the number of bytes read. If any bytes are read, they are immediately written to the output file, with write errors handled by printing an error message and terminating the program. After each successful write, the loop updates the atomic counters `blocksCopied` and `totalBytes` to track progress safely across goroutines. If the read operation signals the end of the input via `io.EOF` or `io.ErrUnexpectedEOF`, the loop breaks, completing the copy. Any other read errors are considered fatal. By using `atomic.AddInt64()`, the program ensures that each increment is performed as an indivisible operation, so the progress reporter always sees a consistent, accurate view of the copy operation. This is especially important for real-time monitoring, as any inconsistency could mislead the user about how much data has been processed.

We are now going to create a large file by running `go run ch05/profReading.go -generate=1000MB` – one of the most satisfying aspects of systems programming is using your own tools! The input file is `/tmp/sample_custom_1000MB.txt`, and we are about to use it with `dd.go` and a small buffer to slow down the process, which is going to give us enough time to send our signals:

```
$ go run ch06/dd.go -if /tmp/sample_custom_1000MB.txt -of /tmp/copy.dat -bs 2
Process ID: 13555
Progress: 2578481 blocks copied (5156962 bytes, 1.6 MB/s)
Progress: 4725073 blocks copied (9450146 bytes, 1.5 MB/s)
Progress: 8918330 blocks copied (17836660 bytes, 1.5 MB/s)
Interrupted, exiting.
exit status 1
```

The output shows the behavior of `dd.go` when copying a large 1 GB file with a *deliberately small block size* of 2 bytes, which is not usually the case. Using such a tiny block size was intentional to slow down the process so that we could observe signal-driven progress reporting in action. Each `Progress:` line reports the number of blocks copied, the total bytes processed, and the approximate speed. Here, you can see that copying a few million tiny 2-byte blocks results in only a few megabytes per second, which is far slower than usual — exactly what we wanted for demonstration purposes. Finally, `Interrupted, exiting.` shows that a `SIGINT` signal was sent to stop the program, triggering a graceful termination with a final report. If `/tmp/copy.dat` already exists, `dd.go` will exit with an `Output file /tmp/copy.dat already exists, not overwriting` message.

By combining file I/O operations from the `os` package, signal handling from `os/signal`, and atomic operations from `sync/atomic`, we can build utilities that behave like traditional UNIX tools while leveraging Go safety guarantees around concurrency and error handling.

Summary

We began this chapter by showing how to handle UNIX signals in Go. Then, we explored Go's capabilities for working with the filesystem in depth. We started with the basics of retrieving file information before moving on to traversing directory trees and gathering useful statistics about files and directories. We learned how to differentiate between file types, locate empty directories, and even embed static assets directly into Go binaries using the `embed` package. Along the way, we saw how the `io/fs` package provides a consistent abstraction for handling file and directory data, with tools such as `fs.WalkDir()` simplifying traversal. We also built practical utilities such as file statistics collectors, empty directory finders, a utility that copies a single file into multiple directories, and simplified `tree(1)` and `dd(1)` clones, demonstrating how Go code can replicate UNIX commands.

In the next chapter, we will move from unstructured bytes and directory hierarchies to the world of structured data. There, we will learn how to parse and manipulate formats such as JSON and XML, and extend our programs to interact with databases, enabling us to organize, query, and persist information in more powerful ways.

Exercises

1. Change `ch06/fileType.go` to support multiple command-line arguments.
2. Create a *File Size Histogram*: Traverse a directory and group files into size ranges (e.g., 0–1KB, 1–10KB, 10–100KB, etc.) and print a histogram.

Additional resources

- The `sort` package documentation: `https://pkg.go.dev/sort`
- The `io/fs` documentation: `https://pkg.go.dev/io/fs`
- The `embed` package documentation: `https://pkg.go.dev/embed`

7

Working with Structured Data and Databases

Most real-world programs do not just crunch numbers in memory; they need to handle information that comes from outside sources. That might be a JSON file with configuration values, a CSV export from another system, or an entire database full of records that your application needs to query and update. Working with structured data and databases is where your Go programs start to feel *real* as you are dealing with the same formats and systems that production software uses every day. In this chapter, we will explore how Go makes it easy to read and write structured data in JSON and how to interact with databases using the `database/sql` package. You will see how to parse data into Go types, transform it, and write it back out again. We will also use structured data to drive graph-processing tasks such as shortest-path computation and the **traveling salesman problem** (**TSP**) to show how real programs combine data handling with computation. Finally, we will step into the world of databases: connecting to them, running queries, and even generating simple reports. The database of choice is going to be SQLite3 for reasons of simplicity. However, we are also going to run through an example that uses PostgreSQL.

This chapter covers the following:

- Working with JSON data
- Working with graphs in JSON format
- Working with SQLite3 and PostgreSQL
- Creating database reports

Working with JSON data

JSON has become the standard format for exchanging structured data between systems, and Go provides excellent support for working with it. In this section, you will learn how to process JSON streams without loading everything into memory and how to convert JSON records to the XML format.

Working with a stream of JSON records

In this section, we will process streams of JSON records efficiently. Instead of reading it line by line or loading entire files into memory, we will use the `json.Decoder()` type, which reads and decodes one JSON object at a time directly from an **input stream**. Look at the following implementation of `main()` as found in `ch07/json.go`, which reads and processes a stream of JSON records from a file, decoding each record as it arrives, making it ideal for logs, event data, or network streams:

```
func main() {
    if len(os.Args) < 2 {
        fmt.Println("Usage:", os.Args[0], "<json-stream-file>")
        os.Exit(1)
    }
    f, err := os.Open(os.Args[1])
    if err != nil {
        fmt.Println("Error opening file:", err)
        os.Exit(1)
    }
    defer f.Close()
    dec := json.NewDecoder(f)
    for {
        var rec Record
        iferr:=dec.Decode(&rec); err != nil {
            // When the stream ends, json.Decoder returns io.EOF
            if err.Error() == "EOF" {
                break
            }
            fmt.Println("Skipping invalid JSON:", err)
            continue
        }
        fmt.Printf("ID: %d | Event: %s | Time: %s\n", rec.ID, rec.Event, rec.Time)
```

```
    }
}
```

After opening the input file, the program creates a JSON decoder that processes the data directly from the file stream, avoiding the need to load everything into memory at once. The decoder reads one JSON object at a time and attempts to unmarshal it into a `Record` structure. Malformed input is skipped with an error message, while reaching the end of the file cleanly terminates processing. Each successfully decoded record is immediately formatted and printed, displaying its ID, event type and timestamp. Now, let us try `ch07/json.go` using a sample JSON file (`ch07/data.json`):

```
$ go run ch07/json.go ch07/data.json
ID: 1 | Event: login | Time: 2025-09-25T10:00:00Z
ID: 2 | Event: upload | Time: 2025-09-25T10:05:00Z
ID: 3 | Event: logout | Time: 2025-09-25T10:10:00Z
```

This simple output illustrates how JSON records can be processed one at a time from a file stream. Beyond this example, such streaming patterns are particularly useful when handling large datasets, real-time event logs, or continuous data feeds, where loading the entire dataset into memory would be inefficient or impractical.

Let us now see how the processing of individual JSON records, which we saw in `ch02/structures.go`, is compared to the processing of continuous JSON streams.

JSON benchmarking

Let us now benchmark the process to compare it with the processing of a single JSON record at a time. The benchmarking code (`ch07/jsonProcess_test.go`) compares the performance of JSON encoding and decoding in Go when processing 1,000 records one by one versus a stream of many records, using identical data structures for fairness. This distinction is particularly important for real-world workloads such as log processing, event streams, telemetry pipelines, and large data exports, where applications must process continuous flows of JSON records efficiently without loading the entire dataset into memory. The program defines a simple `Record` struct with fields such as `ID`, `Name`, `Email`, and `Balance`:

```
type Record struct {
    ID      int     `json:"id"`
    Name    string  `json:"name"`
    Email   string  `json:"email"`
```

```
    Balance float64 `json:"balance"`
}
```

A helper function, generateRecords(), which is not presented here, creates a slice of Record values to simulate realistic input data. The first benchmark, BenchmarkSingleRecord(), encodes and decodes the generated 1,000 records one by one to measure the overhead of handling small, discrete JSON objects. It uses json.Marshal() and json.Unmarshal() to convert between Go structs and JSON data, resetting the timer right before the benchmarking loop to ensure accurate timing:

```
func BenchmarkSingleRecord(b *testing.B) {
    records := generateRecords(1000)
    b.ResetTimer()
    for i := 0; i < b.N; i++ {
        for _, rec := range records {
            data, _ := json.Marshal(rec)
            var decoded Record
            _ = json.Unmarshal(data, &decoded)
        }
    }
}
```

The b.ResetTimer() statement is used to ensure that only the actual code being measured contributes to the timing results. When a benchmark function begins, there is often setup work that prepares data structures, initializes input, or allocates resources — tasks that you do not want included in the performance measurement.

The second benchmark, BenchmarkStream(), tests how Go performs when reading a continuous stream of JSON records — a scenario common in log processing and data ingestion systems. Before the benchmark loop begins, it generates 1,000 records and encodes them sequentially into a bytes.Buffer to simulate a JSON stream. During benchmarking, it uses a json.Decoder() with an io.Reader to parse this stream one record at a time until it reaches the end of the input:

```
func BenchmarkStream(b *testing.B) {
    records := generateRecords(1000)
    buf := new(bytes.Buffer)
    enc := json.NewEncoder(buf)
    for _, r := range records {
        _ = enc.Encode(r)
    }
```

```
    streamData := buf.Bytes()
    b.ResetTimer()
    for i := 0; i < b.N; i++ {
        dec := json.NewDecoder(bytes.NewReader(streamData))
        var rec Record
        for {
            iferr:=dec.Decode(&rec); err == io.EOF {
                break
            } else if err != nil {
                b.Fatal(err)
            }
        }
    }
}
```

Run the benchmarks on your machine to get an output similar to the following:

```
$ go test -bench=. -benchmem ch07/jsonProcess_test.go
goos: darwin
goarch: arm64
cpu: Apple M4 Pro
BenchmarkSingleRecord-14   1897 656289 ns/op 416185 B/op 9000 allocs/op
BenchmarkStream-14         2562 465048 ns/op 23880 B/op  2009 allocs/op
PASS
ok      command-line-arguments    3.956s
```

In `BenchmarkSingleRecord()`, each iteration processes 1,000 JSON objects independently using `json.Marshal()` and `json.Unmarshal()`. This approach takes on average *656,289 nanoseconds per iteration*, performing *9,000 memory allocations* and consuming approximately *416 KB of heap memory*. These figures indicate that every encode and decode operation allocates new byte slices and temporary buffers, creating significant memory churn and increasing garbage collection overhead. The result is a relatively higher latency due to repeated heap activity and CPU cache misses associated with object creation and destruction. The `BenchmarkStream()` test, on the other hand, processes the same total number of records using a continuous JSON stream through `json.Encoder()` and `json.Decoder()`. It completes each iteration in *465,048 nanoseconds*, showing about a *30% improvement in execution time*, while allocating only *23.8 KB of memory* and performing *2,009 allocations*. The lower allocation count demonstrates that streaming reuses internal buffers and parses data incrementally, which reduces both heap usage and garbage collector work. From a technical standpoint, the streaming approach exhibits better cache locality, reduced allocation overhead, and improved scalability for large datasets or long-running services.

Let us now turn our attention to data format transformation — specifically, how to convert structured data from JSON to XML.

Converting from JSON to XML

Having seen how structured data can be read, processed, and stored, we can now look at how the same data can be reused across different formats. In this subsection, we present a small utility (`ch07/json2xml.go`) that takes JSON data as input and converts it into the XML format, demonstrating how Go makes it straightforward to transform structured data to meet the needs of different systems and interfaces. Such transformations are common in real systems where different services or legacy platforms rely on different data formats. We will begin by presenting the definition of the structures that hold the JSON and XML data:

```
type Record struct {
    ID    int    `json:"id" xml:"id"`
    Event string `json:"event" xml:"event"`
    Time  string `json:"timestamp" xml:"timestamp"`
}

type Records struct {
    XMLName xml.Name `xml:"records"`
    Items   []Record `xml:"record"`
}
```

This code defines two Go structs, `Record` and `Records`. The `Record` struct represents a single data entry with three fields: `ID`, `Event`, and `Time`. Each field includes **struct tags** that specify how it should be named when the data is encoded to or decoded from JSON or XML — for example, `ID` becomes `"id"` in both formats. The `Records` struct serves as a container for multiple `Record` entries. It includes an `XMLName` field that defines the root XML element (`<records>`) and an `Items` slice tagged as `<record>` elements inside it. This setup allows `encoding/json` and `encoding/xml` packages to easily convert between Go data structures and structured JSON or XML representations of the same data. Next, we present the implementation of `main()` as found in `ch07/json2xml.go`:

```
func main() {
    if len(os.Args) < 2 {
        fmt.Println("Usage:", os.Args[0], "<json-file>")
        os.Exit(1)
```

```
    }
    f, err := os.Open(os.Args[1])
    if err != nil {
        fmt.Println("Error opening file:", err)
        os.Exit(1)
    }
    defer f.Close()

    var records []Record
    scanner := bufio.NewScanner(f)
    for scanner.Scan() {
        line := strings.TrimSpace(scanner.Text())
        if line == "" {
            continue
        }

        var rec Record
        if err := json.Unmarshal([]byte(line),&rec); err != nil {
            fmt.Println("Skipping invalid JSON:", err)
            continue
        }

        records = append(records, rec)
    }
    if err := scanner.Err(); err != nil {
        fmt.Println("Error reading file:", err)
    }

    output := Records{Items: records}
    xmlData, err := xml.MarshalIndent(output, "", "  ")
    if err != nil {
        fmt.Println("Error generating XML:", err)
        os.Exit(1)
    }
    fmt.Println(xml.Header + string(xmlData))
}
```

This `main()` function reads a JSON file containing multiple JSON records — one per line — and converts them into an XML representation. It starts by checking that the user provided a filename as a command-line argument; if not, it prints a usage message and exits. The program then opens the specified file and ensures it is closed at the end using `defer f.Close()`. The file is read line by line using `bufio.Scanner`. Each line is trimmed of whitespace and empty lines are skipped. For every non-empty line, the program attempts to parse it into a `Record` struct using `json.Unmarshal()`. If parsing fails due to invalid JSON, it prints an error message and skips that line. Successfully parsed records are appended to a slice named `records`. Once all lines are processed, the program wraps the collected slice in a `Records` struct and converts it to formatted XML using `xml.MarshalIndent()`. If XML generation succeeds, it prints the XML header (`<?xml version="1.0" encoding="UTF-8"?>`) followed by the XML data.

Now, run `ch07/json2xml.go` on your machine using sample data from `ch07/data.json`:

```
$ go run ch07/json2xml.go ch07/data.json
<?xml version="1.0" encoding="UTF-8"?>
<records>
  <record>
    <id>1</id>
    <event>login</event>
    <timestamp>2025-09-25T10:00:00Z</timestamp>
  </record>
  <record>
    <id>2</id>
    <event>upload</event>
    <timestamp>2025-09-25T10:05:00Z</timestamp>
  </record>
  <record>
    <id>3</id>
    <event>logout</event>
    <timestamp>2025-09-25T10:10:00Z</timestamp>
  </record>
</records>
```

After exploring how to convert JSON data into other structured formats, such as XML, it is worth turning our attention back to JSON itself and how Go continues to improve its support for it. In the next section, we will look at `json/v2`, an evolution of the JSON package. This new version introduces a cleaner design and better performance while maintaining compatibility with existing code.

JSON's evolution: json/v2

The `encoding/json/v2` package, introduced as an experimental feature in Go 1.25, is a next-generation JSON library designed to improve both performance and strictness over the original `encoding/json`. The `json/v2` version enforces stricter compliance with the JSON standard (RFC 8259), rejects duplicate keys, and provides more precise error messages, helping to catch issues that might otherwise go unnoticed. From a performance perspective, `json/v2` reduces allocations during unmarshaling, which can significantly improve throughput when processing large datasets or streaming JSON records. Unlike the original package, the streaming API (`json.Decoder`) is currently not supported, so workflows involving large or continuous streams of JSON must rely on manual chunking, line-by-line scanning, or array-based unmarshaling. To enable `json/v2`, Go provides the `GOEXPERIMENT=jsonv2` build flag. Once enabled, existing code that uses `json.Unmarshal()` or `json.Marshal()` can often benefit from the stricter semantics and improved performance with minimal modification. Let us now present the JSON-related code of the `main()` function of `ch07/jsonV2.go`:

```
    scanner := bufio.NewScanner(f)
    var inArray bool
    var arrayBuffer strings.Builder
    for scanner.Scan() {
        line := strings.TrimSpace(scanner.Text())
        if line == "" {
            continue
        }

        // Detect start and end of a JSON array
        if strings.HasPrefix(line, "[") {
            inArray = true
            line = line[1:] // remove [
        }
        if strings.HasSuffix(line, "]") {
            inArray = false
            line = line[:len(line)-1] // remove ]
        }

        // Remove trailing commas
        line = strings.TrimSuffix(line, ",")
        if inArray {
            arrayBuffer.WriteString(line)
            // End of an object in the array?
            if strings.HasSuffix(line, "}") {
                processRecord(arrayBuffer.String())
                arrayBuffer.Reset()
            }
```

```
        } else {
            processRecord(line)
        }
    }

    if err := scanner.Err(); err != nil {
        fmt.Println("Error reading file:", err)
    }
```

While both programs (`ch07/jsonV2.go` and `ch07/json.go`) process multiple JSON records from a file, they differ mainly in how they read and interpret the input. The experimental `ch07/jsonV2.go` performs manual parsing, reading input line by line and using string manipulation to detect JSON object boundaries, including handling arrays by tracking brackets and trimming commas. This provides flexibility but adds complexity and increases the risk of subtle parsing errors. In contrast, `ch07/json.go` relies on the standard library streaming decoder (`json.NewDecoder`), which automatically handles whitespace, arrays, and object boundaries, resulting in simpler, more robust, and easier-to-maintain code. In short, the `json/v2` example demonstrates low-level control over mixed or array-based input and may be useful when dealing with irregular or non-standard JSON streams, while the `json.Decoder` approach showcases idiomatic, stream-oriented JSON processing in Go and is generally the preferred choice for well-formed, sequential JSON data.

Let us now see `ch07/jsonV2.go` in action:

```
$ GOEXPERIMENT=jsonv2 go run ch07/jsonV2.go ch07/data.json
ID: 1 | Event: login | Time: 2025-09-25T10:00:00Z
ID: 2 | Event: upload | Time: 2025-09-25T10:05:00Z
ID: 3 | Event: logout | Time: 2025-09-25T10:10:00Z
```

Having worked extensively with structured data formats such as JSON, we can now apply them to a more computational challenge — the TSP. In the next section, we represent a graph of cities and distances using JSON, where each node and edge is described as structured data. This format makes it easy to visualize, exchange, and manipulate graph information, whether it comes from a file, an API, or a database.

Solving the traveling salesman problem

The TSP is a classic problem in computer science and operations research. It asks the following question: *Given a list of cities and the distances between each pair of cities, what is the shortest possible route that visits each city exactly once and returns to the origin city?* In this section, we will use the

JSON format for storing the **weighted graph representation**, read it using Go, build the graph in memory, and implement the algorithm. This practical example shows how JSON can serve not just as a data exchange format but also as a flexible foundation for algorithmic problem solving.

A typical JSON representation for a weighted graph might look like this:

```
{
  "nodes": ["A", "B", "C", "D", "E"],
  "edges": {
    "A": { "B": 2, "C": 9, "D": 10, "E": 7 },
    "B": { "A": 2, "C": 6, "D": 4, "E": 3 },
    "C": { "A": 9, "B": 6, "D": 8, "E": 5 },
    "D": { "A": 10, "B": 4, "C": 8, "E": 6 },
    "E": { "A": 7, "B": 3, "C": 5, "D": 6 }
  }
}
```

The adjacency map JSON file represents a small **weighted directed graph** with five nodes labeled `A` through `E`. The `nodes` array lists all vertices, while the `edges` object defines the graph's connectivity by mapping each source node to a set of destination nodes and their associated weights. For example, the entry for node `A` specifies the cost of reaching nodes `B`, `C`, `D`, and `E`, and this same pattern applies uniformly to the remaining nodes. These mappings fully describe both the structure of the graph and the relative cost of moving between vertices. This representation is particularly well suited to problems such as the TSP, shortest-path algorithms, and general network analysis, where weighted edges are required to compute optimal paths. `ch07/graph05.json` provides a compact and human-readable encoding of a complete weighted graph.

Creating sample graphs

For the purposes of this chapter, we will develop a utility that creates weighted graphs, like the graphs that we are going to use as input to the TSP, as well as the Dijkstra algorithm, presented in the next section.

The `main()` function implementation of `ch07/generateGraph.go`, which generates a fully connected graph and writes it as a JSON file, is as follows:

```
func main() {
    if len(os.Args) < 3 {
        fmt.Println(os.Args[0], "<number-of-nodes> <output-file>")
        return
    }
    var n int
```

```
    fmt.Sscanf(os.Args[1], "%d", &n)
    outputFile := os.Args[2]
    //Initialize nodes
    nodes := make([]string, n)
    for i := 0; i < n; i++ {
        nodes[i] = string('A' + i)
    }
    // Initialize edges map
    edges := make(map[string]map[string]float64)
    for _, u := range nodes {
        edges[u] = make(map[string]float64)
        for _, v := range nodes {
            if u == v {
                continue
            }
            edges[u][v] = math.Round(rand.Float64()*9 + 1)
        }
    }

    graph := map[string]interface{}{
        "nodes": nodes,
        "edges": edges,
    }

    data, err := json.MarshalIndent(graph, "", " ")
    if err != nil {
        fmt.Println("Error generating JSON:", err)
        return
    }

    if err := os.WriteFile(outputFile, data, 0644); err != nil {
        fmt.Println("Error writing file:", err)
        return
    }

    fmt.Printf("Fully connected graph: %d nodes: %s\n", n, outputFile)
}
```

The code begins by checking the command-line arguments, expecting the number of nodes to create and the name of the output file. If these are missing, it prints a usage message and exits. Next, the program initializes the list of node names, assigning each node a single uppercase letter starting from `A`. It then seeds a random number generator with the current time to ensure that each run produces different weights. The main part of the program builds the `edges` map, which represents the node connections in the graph. For every pair of nodes `(u, v)`, it creates a random edge weight between 1 and 10, skipping self-loops where `u == v`. After constructing the data structure, it combines the `nodes` slice and the `edges` map into a single `graph` map. This graph is then marshaled into formatted JSON using `json.MarshalIndent()`, making the output easy to read. Finally, the program writes the JSON data to the specified file and prints a confirmation message. Let us now see `ch07/generateGraph.go` in action:

```
$ go run ch07/generateGraph.go 5 /tmp/fiveNodes.json
Generated fully connected graph with 5 nodes: /tmp/fiveNodes.json
```

Feel free to run it on your machine and see the contents of the output file. We can now move on to the practical part — implementing the traveling salesman algorithm in Go to find the most efficient route among a set of nodes.

Implementing the traveling salesman algorithm

With our sample data at hand, we are ready to proceed with the implementation of the traveling salesman algorithm, starting with the definition of the TSP, which is based on the **Hamiltonian cycle**. A Hamiltonian cycle (or Hamiltonian circuit) is a special kind of path in a graph that visits every vertex exactly once and returns to the starting vertex, forming a closed loop. The TSP is a weighted version of the Hamiltonian cycle problem: *Find the shortest Hamiltonian cycle in a weighted graph*. While the Hamiltonian cycle problem only asks whether such a cycle exists, the TSP asks for the optimal one. Both problems are *NP-complete*, meaning they are *computationally hard*, and no efficient algorithm is known to solve them for large graphs. In our implementation, we use **dynamic programming** (**DP**) because the problem involves exploring all possible paths between cities to find the shortest possible route that visits each city exactly once and returns to the starting point. DP is a problem-solving technique that breaks complex problems into smaller, overlapping subproblems, solving each subproblem only once and storing its result for future reuse. This approach avoids redundant computations, making it highly efficient for optimization problems where decisions depend on previously computed states. The **naive brute-force** approach has a factorial time complexity due to the exponential number of permutations. DP, on the other hand, uses the **principle of optimality** — the idea that an optimal solution contains optimal sub-solutions — to compute and reuse partial tour costs. Algorithms such as the **Held–Karp algorithm** use DP to reduce the complexity of the TSP, making it feasible for moderate-sized datasets while still guaranteeing the optimal solution. Let us begin by presenting the structure used for representing the graph:

```
type Graph struct {
    Nodes []string                    `json:"nodes"`
    Edges map[string]map[string]float64 `json:"edges"`
}
```

This Graph structure defines a weighted graph using JSON-friendly data types. The Nodes field is a slice of strings that lists all the nodes (or vertices) in the graph, such as cities or locations. The Edges field is a nested map that represents the connections between nodes and their corresponding weights. Each key in the outer map corresponds to a source node, and its value is another map that links destination nodes to their edge weights — typically distances or costs. For example, Edges["A"]["B"] = 4.5 means there is an edge from node A to node B with a weight of 4.5. This structure provides a flexible and intuitive way to represent and process graphs loaded from or stored as JSON data. Now, let us present the function that solves the TSP, which is called tspDP() and is going to be presented in multiple parts. Its first part is the following:

```
func tspDP(g Graph) (float64, []string) {
    n := len(g.Nodes)
    index := make(map[string]int)
    for i, node := range g.Nodes {
        index[node] = i
    }

size := 1 << n
    dp := make([][]float64, size)
    path := make([][]int, size)
    for i := range dp {
        dp[i] = make([]float64, n)
        path[i] = make([]int, n)
        for j := range dp[i] {
            dp[i][j] = math.Inf(1)
            path[i][j] = -1
        }
    }
```

This part of the tspDP() function initializes the data structures needed to solve the TSP using DP with bitmasking. The function takes a Graph as input and returns the minimum total distance and the optimal visiting order of nodes. It first determines the number of nodes, `n`, and creates a mapping `index` that assigns each node a unique integer index, which simplifies the use of bitmasks later in the algorithm. The `size` variable represents the total number of possible subsets of nodes, computed as (2^n), since each node can either be included or not in a subset. Two two-dimensional slices are then created: `dp`, which stores the minimal cost to reach a certain subset of nodes ending at a particular node, and `path`, which keeps track of the previous node used to reach that state for route reconstruction. Both are initialized with infinite costs (`math.Inf(1)`) and placeholder indices (`-1`) to indicate that no path has been set yet. This initialization lays the groundwork for filling in the DP table as the algorithm explores all possible node subsets. The next part contains the code that performs the core DP computation and explores all possible paths between nodes:

```
start := 0
dp[1<<start][start] = 0
for mask := 1; mask < size; mask++ {
    for u := 0; u < n; u++ {
        ifmask&(1<<u) == 0 {
            continue
        }
        for v := 0; v < n; v++ {
            ifmask&(1<<v) != 0 {
                continue
            }
            w, ok := g.Edges[g.Nodes[u]][g.Nodes[v]]
            if !ok {
                continue
            }
            newMask := mask | (1 << v)
            if dp[mask][u]+w < dp[newMask][v] {
                dp[newMask][v] = dp[mask][u] + w
                path[newMask][v] = u
            }
        }
    }
}
```

This part of `tspDP()` begins by defining the starting node, here set to index `0`, and initializes the cost of visiting only that node (`dp[1<<start][start] = 0`) as zero. The algorithm then iterates over all possible subsets of nodes represented by the `mask` bitmask variable. For each subset, it

examines each node, u, that is already included in the subset (mask&(1<<u) != 0). For every such node, u, it checks all other nodes, v, that are not yet included in the subset (mask&(1<<v) == 0). If there is a valid edge between u and v, it calculates a new subset (newMask) that includes node v as well. The DP table is updated if the cost of reaching v through u (dp[mask][u] + w) is smaller than the current stored value for dp[newMask][v]. The path table records u as the previous node leading to v in the optimal route. Through this process, the algorithm systematically builds up all possible tours by extending smaller subsets into larger ones while keeping track of the minimal total distance. The next part finalizes the computation by determining the optimal Hamiltonian cycle:

```
    endMask := size - 1
    bestCost := math.Inf(1)
    last := -1
    for u := 0; u < n; u++ {
        w, ok := g.Edges[g.Nodes[u]][g.Nodes[start]]
        if !ok {
            continue
        }
        if dp[endMask][u]+w < bestCost {
            bestCost = dp[endMask][u] + w
            last = u
        }
    }
```

The endMask variable represents the bitmask in which all nodes have been visited (size - 1 means all bits are set). The algorithm initializes bestCost to infinity and last to -1 to track the minimum total cost and the index of the last node in the optimal path. It then iterates through all nodes, u, checking whether there is an edge from node u back to the starting node. For each valid connection, it computes the total tour cost as the sum of the shortest path to u (dp[endMask][u]) and the edge weight back to the start (w). If this cost is lower than the current bestCost, the algorithm updates both bestCost and last. By the end of the loop, these values represent the minimal total distance for completing the full cycle and the node from which the path returns to the starting point, effectively identifying the most efficient tour through all nodes. This final section of the tspDP() function reconstructs the optimal route and returns the result:

```
    if last == -1 {
        return math.Inf(1), nil
    }
```

```
    // reconstruct path
    route := make([]string, n)
    mask := endMask
    for i := n - 1; i >= 0; i-- {
        route[i] = g.Nodes[last]
        prev := path[mask][last]
        mask ^= 1 << last
        last = prev
    }
    return bestCost, route
}
```

The code first checks whether a valid Hamiltonian cycle was found — `if last == -1`, if true, means no complete path exists that visits all nodes and returns to the start, so the function returns infinity and `nil`. Otherwise, the algorithm builds the actual route in reverse order using the `path` matrix, which stores the predecessor of each node during the DP process. Starting from the last node in the optimal cycle, it traces back through the recorded predecessors, updating the `mask` to remove each visited node (`mask ^= 1 << last`). Each node is placed into the route slice from the end to the beginning, effectively reconstructing the full tour. Once the loop completes, the function returns both the minimal total distance (`bestCost`) and the ordered list of node names (`route`), representing the most efficient round trip through all nodes in the graph.

Now, run `ch07/travelingSales.go` on your machine:

```
$ go run ch07/travelingSales.go /tmp/fiveNodes.json
Optimal path: [A D C B E]
Total cost: 14.00
```

With the TSP solved using DP, we now turn to another fundamental graph algorithm, the **Dijkstra algorithm.**

Implementing the Dijkstra algorithm

The Dijkstra algorithm is a well-known shortest-path algorithm that computes the minimum distance from a single source vertex to all other vertices in a weighted graph with non-negative edge weights. It is commonly used in GPS systems, network routing, and other applications where finding the shortest path is crucial. We are going to implement it in Go while representing the graph in JSON format as we did for the TSP. As the Dijkstra algorithm does not work with negative weights, if you want to work with negative weights, you can use the **Bellman-Ford algorithm** instead.

The algorithm begins by assigning a distance of zero to the source vertex and infinity to all others. Then, it repeatedly selects the unvisited vertex with the smallest known distance, explores its neighbors, and updates (or *relaxes*) their tentative distances if a shorter path is found through the current vertex. Once a vertex is visited, its shortest distance is finalized and never changes. This process continues until all vertices are visited or the shortest path to a target vertex has been determined. The algorithm's efficiency comes from using a **priority queue (PQ)**, typically implemented as a **min-heap**, which ensures that the next closest vertex is always processed first. We begin by showing the Go code for the implementation of a PQ as found in `ch07/Dijkstra.go`:

```
// Item for priority queue
type Item struct {
    node     string
    priority float64
    index    int
}

// PriorityQueue implements heap.Interface
type PriorityQueue []*Item
func (pq PriorityQueue) Len() int { return len(pq) }
func (pq PriorityQueue) Less(i, j int) bool {
    return pq[i].priority < pq[j].priority
}
func (pq PriorityQueue) Swap(i, j int) {
    pq[i], pq[j] = pq[j], pq[i]
    pq[i].index = i
    pq[j].index = j
}
func (pq *PriorityQueue) Push(x any) {
    n := len(*pq)
    item := x.(*Item)
    item.index = n
    *pq = append(*pq, item)
}
func (pq *PriorityQueue) Pop() any {
    old := *pq
    n := len(old)
    item := old[n-1]
    item.index = -1
    *pq = old[0 : n-1]
```

```
        return item
    }
```

The PQ is defined using the `container/heap` interface. By always allowing the algorithm to quickly extract the node with the smallest tentative distance, the PQ is essential for efficiency, reducing the overall complexity from `O(n²)` to `O((n + e) log n)` in a graph with `n` nodes and `e` edges. The choice of the right data structure directly improves the algorithm's performance.

The `Item` struct represents each element in the queue, storing the node name, its `priority` value (for Dijkstra, this would be the current tentative distance), and the `index` to track its position in the heap. The `PriorityQueue` type is a slice of pointers to `Item` and implements the required methods for a heap: `Len()`, `Less()`, and `Swap()` for maintaining the heap property, as well as `Push()` and `Pop()` for inserting and removing items. The `Less()` method ensures that the heap is a **min-heap**, so the item with the lowest priority (shortest distance) is always at the top. The advantages of a PQ include efficient retrieval of the element with the highest or lowest priority, typically in *O(log n)* time for insertions and removals, which is much faster than scanning an entire unsorted list. This makes PQs especially useful for graph algorithms such as Dijkstra, where repeatedly selecting the next node with the smallest tentative distance is required. PQ disadvantages include slightly higher memory overhead and added implementation complexity compared to simple slices or arrays. Additionally, updating priorities efficiently may require careful management of indices, as in this implementation. In the context of Dijkstra's algorithm, the PQ allows the algorithm to efficiently always select the unvisited node with the smallest distance, ensuring correctness while improving performance from `O(V²)` with a simple array scan to `O((V + E) log V)` using a min-heap.

Next, we present the implementation of the algorithm in the `dijkstra()` function:

```
func dijkstra(g Graph, source string) (map[string]float64, map[string]string) {
    dist := make(map[string]float64)
    prev := make(map[string]string)
    for _, node := range g.Nodes {
        dist[node] = math.Inf(1)
        prev[node] = ""
    }
    dist[source] = 0

    pq := &PriorityQueue{}
    heap.Init(pq)
    heap.Push(pq, &Item{node: source, priority: 0})
    for pq.Len() > 0 {
```

```
        u := heap.Pop(pq).(*Item)
        for v, w := range g.Edges[u.node] {
            alt := dist[u.node] + w
            if alt < dist[v] {
                dist[v] = alt
                prev[v] = u.node
                heap.Push(pq, &Item{node: v, priority: alt})
            }
        }
    }
    return dist, prev
}
```

The `dijkstra()` function takes a `Graph` and a `source` string as input and returns two maps: `dist`, which stores the shortest distance from the source to each node, and `prev`, which records the predecessor of each node along the shortest path. The code begins by initializing `dist` for all nodes to infinity and `prev` to an *empty string*, then sets the source node's distance to zero. A PQ is created and initialized using `heap.Init()`, with the source node pushed first at priority zero. This ensures that the next node to process is always the one with the smallest tentative distance. The main loop continues while the PQ is not empty. In each iteration, the node, `u`, with the smallest distance is popped from the queue. For each neighbor, `v`, of `u`, the algorithm calculates an alternative distance, `alt`, through `u`. If this new distance is smaller than the currently stored distance for `v`, the algorithm updates `dist[v]` and `prev[v]` and pushes a new `Item` for `v` into the PQ with the updated priority. Once all nodes are processed, `dist` contains the shortest distances from the source to every node, and `prev` allows reconstruction of the actual shortest paths. Last, we have a helper function named `reconstructPath()`:

```
func reconstructPath(prev map[string]string, target string) []string {
    path := []string{}
    for u := target; u != ""; u = prev[u] {
        path = append([]string{u}, path...)
    }
    return path
}
```

`reconstructPath()` rebuilds the shortest path from the source node to a given `target` node using the `prev` map produced by Dijkstra's algorithm. It initializes an empty `path` slice and then traces backward from the target node, following each node's predecessor stored in `prev`. At each step, the current node, `u`, is prepended to the `path` slice, ensuring that the final sequence starts with the source and ends with the target. The loop continues until it reaches an empty string, which indicates that the source has been reached. The function then returns the fully reconstructed path as a slice of node names, representing the exact route along the shortest path from the source to the target.

Running `Dijkstra.go` produces the following kind of output:

```
$ go run ch07/Dijkstra.go ch07/graph15.json A
Shortest distances from A:
A: 0.00
B: 2.00
C: 4.00
...
O: 4.00

Paths from source:
A -> B
Path: [A B]
A -> C
Path: [A J E C]
...
A -> O
Path: [A J O]
```

This output shows the (abbreviated) results of running the Dijkstra algorithm on the fully connected 15-node graph starting from node `A`. The first part, `Shortest distances from A`, lists the minimum total weights (or costs) required to reach each node from `A`. For example, the distance to `B` is `2.00`, meaning the smallest total weight from `A` to `B` is 2. Similarly, the distance to `C` is `4.00`, which indicates that the sum of edge weights along the shortest path from `A` to `C` is 4. The distance to the source node itself (`A`) is always `0` because no travel is needed. The second part, `Paths from source`, shows *the actual shortest path* for each node. Each path lists the sequence of nodes you need to traverse to achieve the minimum distance. For instance, the shortest path from `A` to `C` is `[A J E C]`, meaning the algorithm found that going from `A` to `J`, then `E`, and finally to `C` gives the smallest total weight (`4.00` in this case). Similarly, the path from `A` to `B` is simply `[A B]`, indicating that a direct edge exists with the minimal weight.

With a solid understanding of JSON processing and graph algorithms, we can now shift focus to persistent storage by exploring how to work with **SQLite3 databases** from Go.

Working with SQLite3

SQLite3 is one of the most convenient databases for Go developers: it is lightweight and serverless and stores data in a single file, making it ideal for prototyping, local testing, and embedded applications. In this section, you will learn how to connect to a SQLite3 database from Go, create tables, and insert and query data. We will also cover how to use prepared statements for efficient repeated queries and how to combine SQLite3 with the `database/sql` package for a clean design.

The use of external Go modules

When working with external packages such as those used for SQLite3 or PostgreSQL, it is a good practice to organize your Go code into separate directories for clarity and maintainability. Each directory can represent a small, self-contained module or program, making it easier to manage dependencies and avoid conflicts between projects. Before running your code, you should initialize the Go project in that directory by executing go `mod init`, which creates a go`.mod` file. Then, use go `mod tidy` to automatically download any required dependencies and clean up unused ones. This ensures your project has a consistent and reproducible build environment, especially when using third-party packages such as `github.com/mattn/go-sqlite3` or `github.com/jackc/pgx/v5`. It is important to note that `github.com/mattn/go-sqlite3` depends on CGO, which means that the resulting Go binary is not fully self-contained. Using this package requires a C compiler on the system, and cross-compilation may be more complex.

The go `mod init` command lists the dependencies your code requires. It acts as the manifest for your Go project, specifying which module versions are needed for successful builds. The file records not only the module paths but also the minimum required versions, ensuring that your project can be rebuilt consistently across environments and over time. Alongside it, the go`.sum` file is automatically generated when you download dependencies. It contains cryptographic hashes of the specific module versions that your project depends on. These hashes guarantee integrity and security — if a dependency's contents change unexpectedly, Go will detect the mismatch and refuse to build. Having discussed the use of external packages, we can now demonstrate practical interactions with SQLite3.

Demonstrating SQLite3 interactions

In this section, we will explore how to interact with a SQLite3 database from a Go program. You will learn how to establish a connection, insert records, retrieve data through queries, update existing entries, and remove records when needed. Each operation is encapsulated in a separate function to keep the code organized and reusable, providing a clear view of typical database workflows. We will start with the function that connects to a SQLite3 database as found in `ch07/`

`sqlite/lite3.go`. The importance of this function lies in its role as the *foundation of all database interactions*. It abstracts setup details, ensures that the database schema is ready, and provides a reliable connection object for use in other operations, such as inserting, querying, and updating records. By doing this setup once at the start, the rest of the program can safely perform data manipulation without worrying about connection management or table existence:

```
func connectDB(dbFile string) (*sql.DB, error) {
    db, err := sql.Open("sqlite3", dbFile)
    if err != nil {
        return nil, err
    }
    if _, err := db.Exec(`CREATE TABLE IF NOT EXISTS users (
        id INTEGER PRIMARY KEY AUTOINCREMENT,
        name TEXT,
        email TEXT
    )`); err != nil {
        return nil, err
    }
    return db, nil
}
```

`connectDB()` is responsible for connecting to a SQLite3 database and ensuring that the required table structure exists before any data operations begin. It takes the `dbFile` database filename as an argument and uses `sql.Open("sqlite3", dbFile)` to establish a connection through the `database/sql` package and the SQLite3 driver. If the file does not already exist, SQLite automatically creates it. The function then executes a SQL statement to create a `users` table if it is not already present. This table includes an auto-incrementing integer ID as the primary key, along with `name` and `email` fields for storing user data. If any part of this process fails, the function returns an error. Otherwise, it returns a ready-to-use database connection.

Then, we have a function for inserting a single record into the database:

```
func insertUser(db *sql.DB, name, email string) error {
    _, err := db.Exec(`INSERT INTO users (name, email) VALUES (?, ?)`, name,
email)
    return err
}
```

The `insertUser()` function is a concise utility for adding new user records to the `users` table. It takes an existing and open database connection, `db`, and two string parameters, `name` and `email`.

The function executes a SQL INSERT statement using placeholders (?) for parameterized queries, which are securely filled with the provided name and email values. This approach prevents SQL injection attacks and ensures safe data handling. If the Exec() operation fails — due to issues such as a locked database, invalid input, or schema mismatch — the resulting error is returned. After that, we present a technique for inserting multiple records using a **prepared statement**:

```
func insertUsersPrepared(db *sql.DB, users map[string]string) error {
    stmt, err := db.Prepare(`INSERT INTO users (name, email) VALUES (?, ?)`)
    if err != nil {
        return err
    }
    defer stmt.Close()
    for name, email := range users {
        if _, err := stmt.Exec(name, email); err != nil {
            return err
        }
    }
    return nil
}
```

The insertUsersPrepared() function is an improved and efficient way of inserting multiple user records into a SQLite3 database. It begins by preparing a SQL statement using db.Prepare(), which compiles the SQL query once and allows it to be reused multiple times. This prepared statement is then deferred for closure to ensure proper resource cleanup. The function takes a map of users, where each key is a name and each value is an email address, and iterates over this map to execute the prepared statement for each user. If any insertion fails, the function immediately returns the encountered error; otherwise, it completes successfully and returns nil. This function differs from the previous insertUser() implementation, which creates and executes a new SQL statement every time it is called. While that approach works well for single insertions, it becomes inefficient when inserting multiple records because each execution involves parsing and compiling the SQL statement again. In contrast, insertUsersPrepared() prepares the statement only once and reuses it in a loop, making it faster and more efficient for batch operations.

The queryUsers() function retrieves and prints all user records:

```
func queryUsers(db *sql.DB) error {
    rows, err := db.Query(`SELECT id, name, email FROM users ORDER BY id`)
    if err != nil {
        return err
```

```
    }
    defer rows.Close()
    fmt.Println("Current users:")
    for rows.Next() {
        var id int
        var name, email string
        iferr:=rows.Scan(&id,&name,&email); err != nil {
            return err
        }
        fmt.Printf("%d | %s | %s\n", id, name, email)
    }
    return rows.Err()
}
```

The queryUsers() function retrieves and displays all user records stored in the users table of a SQLite3 database. It begins by executing a SELECT statement using db.Query() to fetch the id, name, and email columns from all records, ordered by id for readability. If the query execution fails, the function immediately returns the resulting error. Upon a successful query, it defers the closing of the rows object to ensure that database resources are properly released after processing. The function then iterates over the returned rows using rows.Next(), which advances the cursor through each record. For each row, it declares local variables (id, name, and email) and uses rows.Scan() to copy the data from the current row into these variables. The user information is then printed to the console in a formatted manner, providing a simple and readable output of all stored users. Finally, the function returns rows.Err(), which checks for any iteration or scanning errors that might have occurred.

Next, we present updateUser(), which updates the email address of an existing user in the users table based on the user's name:

```
func updateUser(db *sql.DB, name, newEmail string) error {
    _, err := db.Exec(`UPDATE users SET email = ? WHERE name = ?`, newEmail, name)
    return err
}
```

updateUser() uses the db.Exec() method to execute a SQL UPDATE statement with two parameters: the new email value and the name of the user whose record should be updated. If the execution is successful, the database updates the corresponding record; otherwise, the function returns the encountered error. The code highlights the simplicity and safety of using parameterized queries for dynamic updates.

Lastly, we implement the `deleteUser()` function, which removes a specific user from the `users` table based on their name:

```
func deleteUser(db *sql.DB, name string) error {
    _, err := db.Exec(`DELETE FROM users WHERE name = ?`, name)
    return err
}
```

The code executes a SQL `DELETE` statement using `db.Exec()`, with the user's name provided as a parameter. If the deletion succeeds, the function completes silently; if an error occurs, it returns the error to the caller. Now, let us try `ch07/sqlite/lite3.go` on our machines:

```
$ cd ch07/sqlite
$ go mod init; go mod tidy
$ go run lite3.go
Inserting a few users individually...

Inserting multiple users using a prepared statement...
Current users:
1 | Alice | alice@example.c
. . .
5 | Eve | eve@example.com

Updating Bob's email...
Current users:
1 | Alice | alice@example.com
. . .
5 | Eve | eve@example.com

Deleting Alice...
Current users:
2 | Bob | bob@newdomain.com
. . .
5 | Eve | eve@example.com
```

Having explored how to perform basic **create, read, update, and delete** (**CRUD**) operations with SQLite3, we can now move on to a more advanced and practical task — storing structured JSON data directly in a SQLite3 database.

Storing JSON data in a SQLite3 database

This section demonstrates how Go can seamlessly parse, validate, and persist JSON records. The example code is stored in `ch07/storeJSON/storeJSON.go`. First, we present the `Record` structure, which represents a single JSON object in the stream:

```
type Record struct {
    ID        int    `json:"id"`
    Event     string `json:"event"`
    Timestamp string `json:"timestamp"`
}
```

The remaining code can be found inside `main()`. The interesting part of it is the following:

```
stmt, err :=
db.Prepare(`INSERT OR IGNORE INTO events(id, event, timestamp) VALUES (?, ?, ?)`)
if err != nil {
    fmt.Println("Error preparing insert statement:", err)
    os.Exit(1)
}
defer stmt.Close()
// Create JSON decoder for streaming
dec := json.NewDecoder(f)
for {
    var rec Record
    iferr:=dec.Decode(&rec); err != nil {
        if err == io.EOF {
            break
        }
        fmt.Println("Skipping invalid JSON:", err)
        continue
    }
    // Insert record into database
    _, err := stmt.Exec(rec.ID, rec.Event, rec.Timestamp)
    if err != nil {
        fmt.Println("Error inserting record:", err)
    } else {
        fmt.Printf("Inserted: ID=%d | Event=%s | Time=%s\n",
            rec.ID, rec.Event, rec.Timestamp)
```

```
    }
}
```

This code snippet begins by preparing a SQL statement using `db.Prepare()`. The use of `INSERT OR IGNORE` ensures that if a record with the same ID already exists, SQLite will silently skip the insertion instead of raising an error — a useful safeguard against duplicate entries.

Next, the program sets up a streaming JSON decoder with `json.NewDecoder(f)`, allowing it to process large JSON files record by record without loading the entire file into memory. Inside the loop, each JSON object is decoded into a `Record` struct. If decoding fails due to malformed JSON, the code skips the invalid record and continues. For valid records, the program executes the prepared statement with the extracted values, inserting them into the database. Finally, each successful insertion is acknowledged with a confirmation message printed to the console. Run `ch07/storeJSON/storeJSON.go` on your machine — but first go to the `ch07/storeJSON` directory:

```
$ cd ch07/storeJSON
$ go mod init; go mod tidy
$ go run storeJSON.go ../data.json /tmp/myJSON.db
Inserted: ID=1 | Event=login | Time=2025-09-25T10:00:00Z
Inserted: ID=2 | Event=upload | Time=2025-09-25T10:05:00Z
Inserted: ID=3 | Event=logout | Time=2025-09-25T10:10:00Z
```

After learning how to interact with SQLite3 for local data management, it is time to move toward a more scalable and production-ready database system, **PostgreSQL**.

Working with PostgreSQL

PostgreSQL is a powerful, production-grade relational database that offers advanced features such as transactions, indexing, and concurrency control. In this section, we will build on what you learned with SQLite3 to connect Go programs to PostgreSQL databases, execute queries, and perform CRUD operations. The PostgreSQL version of the Go program is very similar to the SQLite3 version in terms of overall structure and logic. Both programs define the same set of functions for connecting to the database — inserting, querying, updating, deleting, and using prepared statements — and they both rely on the `database/sql` interface. The main differences are localized to the `connectDB()` function and the connection string it uses. For PostgreSQL, the program connects to a server using either the `pgx` or `postgres` driver with a network-based URL including credentials and database name. Beyond this, minor adjustments may be needed in the table creation SQL to match the PostgreSQL type system (e.g., using `SERIAL` for auto-incrementing IDs), but the rest of the code — such as the insert, query, update, delete, and prepared statement functions — remains essentially identical. This demonstrates how Go's database abstraction allows the same application logic to work with different database backends by changing only the connection setup code. The implementation of `connectDB()` as found in `ch07/postgres/postgres.go` initializes the database connection using `pgx` and creates a table:

```
func connectDB() (*sql.DB, error) {
    connStr := "postgres://postgres:password@localhost:5432/testdb?
sslmode=disable"
    db, err := sql.Open("pgx", connStr)
    if err != nil {
        return nil, err
    }
    if err := db.Ping(); err != nil {
        return nil, err
    }
    createTable := `
    CREATE TABLE IF NOT EXISTS users (
        id SERIAL PRIMARY KEY,
        name TEXT NOT NULL,
           email TEXT UNIQUE NOT NULL
    )`
    if _, err := db.Exec(createTable); err != nil {
        return nil, err
    }
    return db, nil
}
```

This function establishes a connection between a Go program and a PostgreSQL database using the `pgx` driver. The **connection string** defines how to access the database — it includes the username (`postgres`), password (`password`), host (`localhost`), port (`5432`), database name (`testdb`), and an option to disable SSL for local development. The `sql.Open()` function initializes a database handle, but the connection is not verified until `db.Ping()` is called, ensuring that the database is reachable and the credentials are valid. After confirming connectivity, the function executes a SQL command that creates a table named `users` if it does not already exist. This table includes three fields: `id`, which is a `SERIAL` column that automatically increments for each new record; `name`, a text field that must be provided; and `email`, another text field that must be unique, preventing duplicate entries. The function returns the database handle for further operations or an error if any step fails. The remaining CRUD operations for PostgreSQL follow the same logic and structure as those used with SQLite3. Both databases are accessed through the `database/sql` package, which provides a unified interface for executing SQL commands regardless of the underlying driver. The only difference lies in the database connection setup — once connected, inserting, querying, updating, or deleting records uses the same `Exec()` and `Query()` functions with nearly identical SQL statements. We are not going to run `ch07/postgres/postgres.go` yet as we are going to use a Docker image for it, which is presented next.

Using a Docker image for PostgreSQL

In this section, we will explore how to use a Docker image to run PostgreSQL in a clean, isolated environment. Docker makes it easy to deploy and manage database instances without manually installing PostgreSQL on your system. By pulling the official PostgreSQL image, you can quickly start a containerized database, configure credentials and ports, and connect your Go applications for testing or development. Here is the `docker-compose.yaml` file that we are going to use for PostgreSQL:

```
services:
  postgres:
    image: postgres:15
    container_name: go_pg
    restart: unless-stopped
    environment:
      POSTGRES_USER: postgres
      POSTGRES_PASSWORD: password
      POSTGRES_DB: testdb
    ports:
      - "5432:5432"
```

This configuration launches a ready-to-use PostgreSQL 15 database named `testdb`, accessible via the username `postgres` and password `password`, running inside a container named go_pg. It will automatically restart if interrupted and listens for connections on your local port 5432. Given the previous `docker-compose.yaml` file, run the `docker-compose up -d` command from inside the `ch07/postgres` directory. This starts PostgreSQL in the background. You can check the logs with the `docker-compose logs -f` command. The connection string that should be used in the Go code is `connStr := "postgres://postgres:password@localhost:5432/testdb?sslmode=disable"`, which corresponds to the Docker image configuration. With that in mind and the PostgreSQL Docker image up and running, we are ready to execute the Go utility and interact with the PostgreSQL Docker image. Do not forget to run `go mod init` and `go mod tidy` first:

```
$ go run postgres.go
Inserting users...

Inserting multiple users using prepared statements...
Current users:
1 | Alice | alice@example.com
. . .
5 | Dave | dave@example.com

Updating Bob's email...
Current users:
. . .
5 | Dave | dave@example.com

Deleting Alice...
Current users:
2 | Bob | bob@newdomain.com
. . .
5 | Dave | dave@example.com
```

After successfully testing your PostgreSQL operations, it is often useful to reset the environment to ensure you start from a clean slate for the next run. The `docker-compose down -v` command does exactly that — it stops and removes all running containers defined in your `docker-compose.yaml` file and deletes the associated volumes where PostgreSQL stores its data. Since Docker volumes are designed to persist database files even after a container is removed, adding the `-v` flag ensures that those volumes are also deleted, effectively erasing all stored tables, records, and database schemas. This is particularly helpful during development or testing, where you frequently reinitialize databases, change schemas, or test data population scripts. By running this command, you guarantee that the next time you start the service with `docker-compose up`, PostgreSQL begins with a completely fresh database instance. If you do not delete the database files, which in some cases might be what you want, you may end up having issues related to duplicate entries and table keys, depending on your table definitions. In our case, `ch07/postgres.go` contains `email TEXT UNIQUE NOT NULL` when defining the `users` table, which means that you are going to have issues with duplicate keys.

In the next section, we will learn how to create database reports — both in human-readable form and as structured JSON output — to summarize and analyze stored information effectively. For reasons of simplicity, we are going to work with SQLite3.

Creating database reports

Data, by itself, is often raw, unstructured, and overwhelming. The true value of a database emerges when that data is transformed into meaningful, actionable insights — and this is where reports come in. A database report distills large volumes of stored information into organized summaries, highlighting patterns, trends, and exceptions that matter to your application or organization. Generating database reports require more than simple queries; you must structure your code to retrieve, format, and present information in a clear and reliable way. In this section, we will explore the techniques and best practices for building robust reporting functionality, ensuring your reports not only answer the right questions but do so efficiently and elegantly. In many real-world systems, these reports form the foundation of dashboards, analytics tools, and monitoring systems that help stakeholders make timely, data-driven decisions. We will begin by presenting the `parseCSV()` helper function as found in `ch07/reports/createReports.go`:

```
func parseCSV(input string) []string {
	if input == "" {
		return nil
	}
	parts := strings.Split(input, ",")
	for i := range parts {
		parts[i] = strings.TrimSpace(parts[i])
	}
	return parts
}
```

The `parseCSV()` function takes a comma-separated string and converts it into a slice of clean, individual values. It begins by checking whether the input string is empty — if so, it returns `nil`, indicating that there are no items to process. Otherwise, it splits the input using `strings.Split(input, ",")`, producing a slice where each element corresponds to one value separated by a comma. It then iterates through the resulting slice, using `strings.TrimSpace()` to remove any leading or trailing whitespace from each element. Finally, it returns the cleaned slice of strings. This function is useful for processing simple CSV-like input where fields are separated by commas, such as lists of names, email addresses, or tags. Next, we present another helper function named `saveJSON()`, which writes structured Go data into a JSON file in a readable, indented format:

```
func saveJSON(filename string, data interface{}) {
    file, err := os.Create(filename)
    if err != nil {
        log.Fatal("Failed to create JSON file:", err)
    }
    defer file.Close()
    enc := json.NewEncoder(file)
    enc.SetIndent("", "  ")
    if err := enc.Encode(data); err != nil {
        log.Fatal("Failed to write JSON:", err)
    }
    fmt.Println("JSON report saved to", filename)
}
```

`saveJSON()` begins by attempting to create a new file using `os.Create()`. If the file cannot be created, the program terminates with a fatal error message. The `defer file.Close()` statement ensures that the file is properly closed when the function finishes executing, preventing resource leaks. Next, a new JSON encoder is created using `json.NewEncoder(file)`, which is configured to produce pretty-printed output via `enc.SetIndent("", "  ")`. The `Encode()` method writes the provided data (of any type, thanks to the `interface{}` parameter) to the file. If any errors occur during encoding, the program exits with an error message. Finally, a confirmation message is printed to inform the user that the JSON file was successfully saved. This function is particularly useful for exporting structured data or reports in a clean, human-readable JSON format. After that, here is another helper function for populating the `customers` table with random data:

```
func populateCustomers(db *sql.DB, count int) {
    for i := 1; i <= count; i++ {
        name := fmt.Sprintf("Customer%d", i)
        email := fmt.Sprintf("customer%d@example.com", i)
        _, err := db.Exec(`INSERT INTO customers (name, email) VALUES (?, ?)`,
name, email)
        if err != nil {
            log.Fatal(err)
        }
    }
}
```

The `populateCustomers()` function automatically inserts a specified number of customer records into a database table named `customers`. It takes a database connection, `db`, and an integer, `count`, that determines how many records to create. Inside the loop, which runs from `1` to `count`, the function dynamically generates a name and email for each customer using `fmt.Sprintf()`, creating entries such as `"Customer1"` and `"customer1@example.com"`. Each record is then inserted into the table with an `INSERT` statement executed through `db.Exec()`. If any insertion fails, the program immediately terminates with `log.Fatal(err)` to prevent inconsistent data states. There exist two analogous helper functions for populating the `products` and `orders` tables, named `populateProducts()` and `populateOrders()`, respectively.

Next, the `randomDate()` helper function creates random dates:

```
func randomDate(startYear, endYear int) string {
    start := time.Date(startYear, 1, 1, 0, 0, 0, 0, time.UTC).Unix()
    end := time.Date(endYear, 12, 31, 23, 59, 59, 0, time.UTC).Unix()
    randTime := rand.Int63n(end-start) + start
    return time.Unix(randTime, 0).Format("2006-01-02")
}
```

The remaining program contains three functions for creating the reports. We show the code of the `reportSalesPerCustomer()` function here — the `reportOrdersPerMonth()` and `reportPopularProducts()` functions contain analogous code and generate the reports for orders per month and the most popular products, respectively. The first part of `reportSalesPerCustomer()` contains the following code:

```
func reportSalesPerCustomer(db *sql.DB, toJSON bool, customers []string) {
    type CustomerSales struct {
        Name  string  `json:"name"`
        Total float64 `json:"total_sales"`
    }
    query := `
    SELECT c.name, SUM(p.price * o.quantity) AS total_sales
    FROM orders o
    JOIN customers c ON o.customer_id = c.id
    JOIN products p ON o.product_id = p.id
    `
    var args []interface{}
    if len(customers) > 0 {
        query += "WHERE c.name IN (" + placeholders(len(customers)) + ") "
```

```
        for _, c := range customers {
            args = append(args, c)
        }
    }
    query += "GROUP BY c.name ORDER BY total_sales DESC"
```

`reportSalesPerCustomer()` is designed to generate a sales report that summarizes the total sales per customer, optionally returning the results in JSON format. It begins by defining an internal struct named `CustomerSales`, which represents each row of the report. This struct is annotated with JSON tags so that, if needed, the results can be serialized cleanly into JSON. The query is grouped by `c.name` and ordered by `total_sales` in descending order, ensuring the output lists the highest-spending customers first.

The rest of the code is responsible for executing the SQL query, processing the results, and optionally exporting them to a JSON file:

```
    rows, err := db.Query(query, args...)
    if err != nil {
        log.Fatal(err)
    }
    defer rows.Close()
    var report []CustomerSales
    fmt.Println("\n--- Total Sales per Customer ---")
    for rows.Next() {
        var cs CustomerSales
        iferr:=rows.Scan(&cs.Name,&cs.Total); err != nil {
            log.Fatal(err)
        }
        fmt.Printf("%-12s | $%.2f\n", cs.Name, cs.Total)
        report = append(report, cs)
    }
    if toJSON {
        saveJSON("/tmp/sales_per_customer.json", report)
    }
}
```

After dynamically constructing the query in the previous section, the function runs it using `db.Query(query, args...)`, safely passing in any user-supplied parameters. If the query execution fails, the program logs the error and terminates, ensuring that invalid database operations are handled immediately. The `defer rows.Close()` statement guarantees that the database resources are properly released once the function finishes executing. If the `toJSON` flag is set to `true`, the entire sales report is serialized and saved to `/tmp/sales_per_customer.json` using the `saveJSON()` helper function. Run `ch07/reports/createReports.go` on your machine:

```
$ cd ch07/reports
$ go mod init; go mod tidy
$ go run createReports.go
Database populated with random data.

--- Total Sales per Customer ---
Customer6     | $3425.65
. . .
Customer4     | $1317.21

--- Top 5 Most Popular Products ---
Product14     | 61 units
. . .
Product9      | 42 units

--- Orders per Month ---
2025-01 | 15 orders
. . .
2025-12 | 17 orders
```

The output shows key sales statistics generated from randomly populated database data and shows that the utility works as expected. The same reporting pattern can easily be extended to other datasets by adjusting the underlying queries and aggregation logic, making this approach suitable for analyzing logs, metrics, user activity, or any structured data where summary insights are needed.

Summary

As we conclude this chapter, it should be clear that mastering structured data and database interactions is essential for building practical, reliable Go applications. From parsing JSON files to designing queries, generating database reports, and even representing complex structures such as graphs in JSON, you have seen how Go enables you to move and process information across different sources. By exploring both single-record operations and flowing data streams, you have seen how Go provides tools for processing information at scale, whether using the classic `encoding/json` or the high-performance experimental `json/v2`. The chapter also highlighted how structured formats such as JSON underpin not only configuration and operational records but also algorithmic applications.

In the next chapter, we will shift our focus from data at rest to data in motion. You will learn how to build networked TCP/IP applications in Go, starting with simple TCP and UDP servers and clients and getting TCP/IP metrics, before progressing to storing data in Prometheus.

Exercises

1. Adding a date range filter to `ch07/reports/createReports.go` would make it fully dynamic for reporting purposes. Try to implement it.
2. Make `ch07/reports/createReports.go` work with a PostgreSQL database.
3. Make `ch07/reports/createReports.go` work with a MySQL database.
4. Similarly, make `ch07/storeJSON/storeJSON.go` work with PostgreSQL.
5. Write a Go program that converts a very large XML file into JSON using a streaming approach. Your implementation should process the input incrementally so that the program can transform a multi-gigabyte XML file while using no more than about 50 MB of RAM. Consider using streaming encoders and decoders to avoid loading the entire dataset into memory at once.
6. Estimate the memory requirements for solving the TSP using DP for different numbers of cities. For example, calculate the size of the `dp` table if `n = 30`, `n = 20`, and `n = 15`. Based on your calculations, discuss why this approach is only practical for *moderate-sized* datasets and explore alternative strategies for handling larger numbers of cities efficiently.

Additional resources

- SQLite3: `https://sqlite.org/index.html`
- PostgreSQL: `https://www.postgresql.org/`
- The `json/v2` package: `https://pkg.go.dev/encoding/json/v2`
- JSON evolution: `https://antonz.org/go-json-v2/`

Get this book's PDF version and more

Scan the QR code (or go to `packtpub.com/unlock`). Search for this book by name, confirm the edition, and then follow the steps on the page.

UNLOCK NOW

Note: Keep your invoice handy. Purchases made directly from Packt don't require an invoice.

8

Programming TCP/IP Services

The **Transmission Control Protocol/Internet Protocol** (**TCP/IP**) suite forms the foundational communication framework of the modern internet and most computer networks. Developed in the 1970s by Vint Cerf and Bob Kahn under Defense Advanced Research Projects Agency (DARPA) funding, TCP/IP emerged from the need to create a robust, scalable network architecture that could interconnect diverse computer systems. TCP/IP is not a single protocol but rather a comprehensive suite of protocols organized in a layered architecture. This modular design enables interoperability between different hardware platforms, operating systems, and network technologies while providing reliable end-to-end communication across complex internetworks. This chapter dives into the fundamentals of network programming in Go, guiding you through the creation of TCP/IP servers and clients. You will also learn how to collect information about TCP and UDP connections and make these metrics accessible to Prometheus.

This chapter covers the following topics:

- Creating TCP servers and clients
- Creating UDP servers and clients
- Getting TCP/IP metrics and storing them in Prometheus

Let us now begin with a story.

A story

This is a real story that happened to my brother. While he was working for a company as a network and systems administrator, the following situation came up: some computers could not connect to the company's network, although his own computer was OK. After investigating the problem, he found out that after a given time of the day, no computer could correctly connect to the company's network. Additionally, after a working computer was rebooted, it could not connect to the company's network anymore! It is easy to guess that there was a legitimate DHCP server running on the network that supplied IP addresses and the rest of the configuration information to all computers. Debugging the situation involved using **Wireshark** to capture network traffic and realizing that there were two DHCP servers running! After that, solving the issue was easy. It turned out that the second DHCP server was running on the operating system of a virtual machine. By mistake, the OS on the virtual machine had its own DHCP server, and that was the cause of the problem! So, the next time your network client is not behaving properly, look for multiple DHCP servers. However, most of the time, networking issues usually turn out to be **DNS** issues. DNS is the service that you need to troubleshoot when having networking issues. In general, the most difficult bugs to debug are the ones that include more than one error situation. In such cases, you should think out of the box and try to isolate the environment or the code that generates the error condition.

Developing a TCP server

Developing a TCP server is a fundamental step in understanding how networked systems communicate at a low level. The `net` package provides a simple yet powerful API for creating TCP listeners, accepting client connections, and exchanging data over sockets. The `main()` function implementation of `ch08/tcpServer.go` is the following; this is how a **non-concurrent TCP server**, which serves a single client at a time, is implemented:

```
func main() {
    listener, err := net.Listen("tcp", ":8080")
    if err != nil {
        panic(err)
    }
    defer listener.Close()
    fmt.Println("Non-concurrent TCP server listening on port 8080...")
    for {
        // Wait for a client to connect
        conn, err := listener.Accept()
        if err != nil {
            fmt.Println("Error accepting connection:", err)
            continue
        }

        fmt.Printf("Client: %s\n", conn.RemoteAddr().String())
        handleConnection(conn)
    }
}
```

The code begins by calling `net.Listen("tcp", ":8080")`, which tells the operating system to open a TCP listening socket on port `8080` and wait for incoming connections. The returned `listener` object represents the server's endpoint and `defer listener.Close()` ensures that the socket will be properly closed when the `main()` function exits, preventing resource leaks. Once the `listener` object is successfully created, the server prints a message to indicate that it is ready to accept client connections. The server then enters an **infinite loop**, repeatedly calling `listener.Accept()`. This function blocks until a new client attempts to connect; when a client connects, `Accept()` returns a `conn` object representing the established TCP connection between the server and that client. If an error occurs during acceptance, the server prints the error and continues listening for additional clients. For each accepted client, the server prints the remote address of the client using `conn.RemoteAddr().String()`, providing visibility into which client is connected. The connection is then passed to the `handleConnection(conn)` function, which contains the logic for communicating with that specific client. Because this server is non-concurrent, each client is handled sequentially: the server will not accept a new connection until `handleConnection()` returns, meaning that multiple clients must wait if one client session is still active. We are going to fix that in the next subsection.

Next is the implementation of `handleConnection()`, which defines how the server communicates with its clients:

```
func handleConnection(conn net.Conn) {
    defer conn.Close()
    scanner := bufio.NewScanner(conn)
    for scanner.Scan() {
        text := scanner.Text()
        fmt.Printf("Received: %s\n", text)

        if strings.TrimSpace(text) == "quit" {
            fmt.Println("Close connection request.")
            return
        }

        // Echo message back to client
        response := fmt.Sprintf("Echo: %s\n", text)
        conn.Write([]byte(response))
    }

    if err := scanner.Err(); err != nil {
        fmt.Println("Error reading from connection:", err)
```

```
    }
}
```

The function wraps the connection (conn) in bufio.Scanner, which provides a convenient way to read input from the client line by line, handling buffering automatically. The server enters a loop using scanner.Scan(), which reads each line sent by the client. For every received line, it retrieves the text with scanner.Text() and prints it to the console, allowing the server operator to monitor incoming messages. The function checks whether the client sent the "quit" string, ignoring leading and trailing whitespace with the help of strings.TrimSpace(). If so, it prints a message indicating that the client requested to close the connection and then returns, ending the session with that client. If the message is not "quit", the server constructs a simple echo response by prefixing the message with "Echo: " and writes it back to the client using conn.Write([]byte(response)). This creates an immediate, line-by-line echo behavior where the server repeats back whatever the client sent. After the loop ends — either because the client closed the connection or an error occurred — the function checks scanner.Err() for any read errors and prints them if present.

After developing a TCP server, the next crucial step is to verify that it operates correctly, even before creating your own clients. Testing ensures that the server can accept client connections and exchange data reliably.

Testing the TCP server

In this section, we will focus on testing the TCP server using the nc(1) (**Netcat**) utility, a versatile command-line tool commonly used for debugging and interacting with network services. Netcat allows you to connect to the server, send custom messages, and observe its responses directly, making it ideal for quick manual testing.

First, execute ch08/tcpServer.go on one terminal window. Then, execute the following nc(1) commands on another terminal:

```
$ nc localhost 8080
Hi!
Echo: Hi!
quit
```

The output of ch08/tcpServer.go is going to be similar to the following:

```
$ go run ch08/tcpServer.go
Non-concurrent TCP server listening on port 8080...
Client: 127.0.0.1:50469
```

```
Received: Hi!
Received: quit
Close connection request.
```

When a client connects, the server logs the remote address — in this case, `127.0.0.1:50469`. This output verifies that the TCP server is working correctly: it accepts a client connection, receives and processes incoming messages, and gracefully closes the connection when the `"quit"` command is sent. The server itself continues running and remains ready to accept new clients until it is manually stopped by pressing *Ctrl* + *C* on your Unix terminal. After having a working TCP server, it is time to make it handle multiple clients at the same time. In the next section, we will transform our single-connection server into a concurrent one by using goroutines.

Making the TCP server concurrent

Developing a concurrent TCP server is a cornerstone of network programming, showcasing how to handle multiple client connections efficiently and safely. A concurrent TCP server listens for incoming connections, spawns a new goroutine for each client, and handles bidirectional communication — reading requests and writing responses — while maintaining isolation between connections. In this case, the only difference is in the endless `for` loop as found in `ch08/concTCP.go`:

```
for {
    conn, err := listener.Accept()
    if err != nil {
        logWithTime("Error accepting connection: %v", err)
        continue
    }
    go handleConnection(conn)
}
```

In this version, each client connection is handled in its own goroutine by invoking `handleConnection(conn)` concurrently. This *per-connection goroutine pattern* allows the server to scale naturally: slow or long-lived clients no longer block others, and multiple connections can be served in parallel with minimal coordination. However, spawning an unrestricted number of goroutines can also expose the server to resource-exhaustion attacks such as slowloris-style denial-of-service attempts, where many clients keep connections open without sending data. In production systems, this is often mitigated by introducing limits on active connections — for example, by using a worker-pool pattern or other forms of connection throttling. The `logWithTime()` helper complements this design by adding timestamps to log messages, making it easier to observe how multiple client interactions overlap in time and execute independently.

Let us now test that server using `nc(1)`. The generated output is the following:

```
$ go run ch08/concTCP.go
[2025-10-18 18:55:57] Concurrent TCP server listening on port 8080...
[2025-10-18 18:55:59] Client connected: 127.0.0.1:50474
[2025-10-18 18:56:03] [127.0.0.1:50474] Received: Hello there!
[2025-10-18 18:56:16] Client connected: 127.0.0.1:50475
[2025-10-18 18:56:23] [127.0.0.1:50475] Received: Hello from another client!
[2025-10-18 18:56:35] [127.0.0.1:50474] Received: First client is about to quit.
[2025-10-18 18:56:36] [127.0.0.1:50474] Received: quit
[2025-10-18 18:56:36] [127.0.0.1:50474] Disconnected by client
[2025-10-18 18:56:40] [127.0.0.1:50475] Received: quit
[2025-10-18 18:56:40] [127.0.0.1:50475] Disconnected by client
```

The first client (`127.0.0.1:50474`) exchanges several messages before signaling termination with `quit`, while a second client (`127.0.0.1:50475`) connects independently and sends its own message stream. Each `quit` results in a clean, logged disconnection tied to the client IP. This interaction pattern — *multiple clients operating independently and disconnecting gracefully* — is fundamental to real-world networked systems such as chat servers, APIs, and microservices, where concurrency and orderly connection life cycle management are essential for reliability and scalability.

With our concurrent TCP server in place, the next step is to create a TCP client that can connect, send messages, and receive responses. Having a client allows us to interact with the server in a controlled way and verify that the concurrent design behaves correctly when handling incoming requests.

Developing a TCP client

In this section, we will build a TCP client designed to interact with a simple echo server, emphasizing bidirectional communication and user-driven input. Rather than issuing a single request, the client keeps the connection open, repeatedly sending lines typed by the user and processing server responses until a graceful shutdown is requested.

A TCP client begins by dialing a server using `net.Dial("tcp", address)`, which returns a `net.Conn` representing the connection. Once connected, the client can read from and write to the server using standard I/O calls, such as `conn.Write([]byte(message))` to send data and `bufio.NewScanner(conn)` or `io.ReadFull()` to receive responses. This pattern of reading and writing over the same TCP connection enables bidirectional communication and is common in many real systems, including chat clients, streaming services, and other interactive network protocols. By combining these calls with basic user input handling via `os.Stdin` or command-line flags, you build a flexible client capable of sending messages, receiving replies, and gracefully closing the connection when finished. Here is the example code of `main()` as found in `ch08/tcpClient.go`, which defines the behavior of the TCP client:

```
func main() {
    host := flag.String("host", "localhost", "Server")
    port := flag.String("port", "8080", "Server TCP port number")
    flag.Parse()
    address := fmt.Sprintf("%s:%s", *host, *port)
    conn, err := net.Dial("tcp", address)
    if err != nil {
        fmt.Println("Error connecting to server at", address, err)
        os.Exit(1)
    }
    defer conn.Close()
    logWithTime("Connected to server at %s", address)
    fmt.Println("Type messages to send. Type 'quit' to exit.")

    // Channel to receive messages from the server
    go func() {
        serverScanner := bufio.NewScanner(conn)
        for serverScanner.Scan() {
            fmt.Printf("Server: %s\n", serverScanner.Text())
        }
        if err := serverScanner.Err(); err != nil {
            logWithTime("Error reading from server: %v", err)
        }
        os.Exit(0)
    }()
```

The code begins by defining two command-line flags using the `flag` package: `host`, which defaults to `"localhost"`, and `port`, which defaults to `"8080"`. After parsing the flags, the program combines the host and port into a single address string using `fmt.Sprintf()`. The client then attempts to establish a TCP connection to that address with `net.Dial("tcp", address)`. If the connection fails, it prints an error message and exits. If the connection succeeds, it defers a call to `conn.Close()`. A timestamped message is logged using a helper function, `logWithTime()`, to confirm the connection, and the user is prompted to type messages to send to the server. Next, there is a twist: the client launches a goroutine that continuously listens for messages from the server (*bidirectional communication pattern*). Inside this goroutine, a `bufio.Scanner` reads incoming text lines from the connection, printing each one to the console prefixed with "Server:". If an error occurs while reading, it is logged with a timestamp, and the program terminates. This design allows the client to simultaneously send and receive data, ensuring responsive, bidirectional communication with the TCP server!

The second part of `main()` handles user input and message transmission from the client to the TCP server:

```
    // Read user input and send to the server
    inputScanner := bufio.NewScanner(os.Stdin)
    for {
        fmt.Print("> ")
        if !inputScanner.Scan() {
            break
        }
        text := inputScanner.Text()
        _, err := fmt.Fprintln(conn, text)
        if err != nil {
            logWithTime("Error sending message: %v", err)
            break
        }
        if strings.TrimSpace(text) == "quit" {
            logWithTime("Disconnected from server.")
            break
        }
    }
}
```

So, after starting the goroutine that listens for server messages, the program creates a `bufio.Scanner` to read lines of text entered by the user from standard input (`os.Stdin`). Inside an infinite loop, it prompts the user with a `">  "` symbol and waits for input. When the user types a line and presses *Enter*, the scanner retrieves the text. The client then sends the message to the server using `fmt.Fprintln(conn, text)`, which writes the text followed by a newline character over the TCP connection. If an error occurs while sending, it logs the error using `logWithTime()` and exits the loop gracefully. The program also checks whether the user typed `"quit"` (ignoring surrounding spaces). If so, it logs a disconnection message and breaks out of the loop.

Run `ch08/tcpClient.go` on your machine to interact with `ch08/tcpServer.go`, which should be running in a different terminal:

```
$ go run ch08/tcpClient.go localhost 8080
[2025-10-18 18:58:54] Connected to server at localhost:8080
Type messages to send. Type 'quit' to exit.
> Hi from Go!
> Server: Echo: Hi from Go!
quit
[2025-10-18 18:59:05] Disconnected from server.
```

With a solid understanding of creating TCP clients, we can now turn our attention to UDP, exploring how to handle connectionless communication in Go.

Developing a UDP server

UDP provides a lightweight, connectionless transport service suitable for applications that can tolerate data loss in exchange for reduced overhead and latency. Applications using UDP must implement their own reliability mechanisms *if needed*, with common UDP applications including DNS queries, live video streaming, online gaming, and network management protocols. Developing a UDP server in Go leverages the handy `net` package. Unlike TCP, UDP does not require establishing a persistent connection; the server begins by creating a `net.UDPAddr` for the desired port, and then calls `net.ListenUDP("udp", &addr)` to start listening. The server can receive messages using `conn.ReadFromUDP(buffer)`, which returns both the data and the address of the sender, and can respond with `conn.WriteToUDP(response, clientAddr)`. By combining these calls in a loop, the server can handle multiple incoming datagrams, echoing data back to clients or generating dynamic responses such as timestamps or random numbers. In this case, when a client sends a message, the server replies with a random number and the current date and time.

The first part of `main()` from `ch08/udpServer.go` initializes the UDP server:

```go
func main() {
    if len(os.Args) != 2 {
        fmt.Println("Usage: go run udp_server.go <port>")
        return
    }
    port := os.Args[1]
    addr := net.UDPAddr{
        Port: mustParsePort(port),
```

```
        IP:   net.ParseIP("0.0.0.0"),
    }
    conn, err := net.ListenUDP("udp", &addr)
    if err != nil {
        fmt.Println("Error starting UDP server:", err)
        return
    }
    defer conn.Close()

    fmt.Printf("UDP server listening on port %s...\n", port)
    buffer := make([]byte, 1024)
    rand.Seed(time.Now().UnixNano())
```

If provided, the code retrieves the port number from the command line and constructs a `net.UDPAddr` structure, specifying the listening address (`0.0.0.0`) so that the server accepts connections from any network interface; if you want to use a specific network interface, you should use that here. The `mustParsePort()` helper function ensures that the provided port is a valid one. Next, the program calls `net.ListenUDP()` to create a UDP socket bound to that address and port. If this operation fails, it reports the error and exits; otherwise, it defers closing the socket to ensure cleanup when the program terminates. Once the server is successfully listening, it prints a confirmation message and allocates a 1 KB buffer to store incoming datagrams. Finally, it seeds the pseudo-random number generator using the current time in nanoseconds, preparing the program to generate random values later in the communication loop.

The main loop of the UDP server, which completes the `main()` function implementation, continuously waits for incoming datagrams from clients and responds to each message with a random number and the current time:

```
    for {
        n, clientAddr, err := conn.ReadFromUDP(buffer)
        if err != nil {
            fmt.Println("Error reading from client:", err)
            continue
        }
        fmt.Printf("Received %d bytes from %s: %s\n", n, clientAddr,
string(buffer[:n]))
        randomNum := rand.Intn(1000)
        currentTime := time.Now().Format(time.RFC1123)
        response := fmt.Sprintf("Random: %d | Time: %s\n", randomNum, currentTime)
        _, err = conn.WriteToUDP([]byte(response), clientAddr)
```

```
        if err != nil {
            fmt.Println("Error sending response:", err)
        }
    }
}
```

Inside the for loop, the call to `conn.ReadFromUDP(buffer)` blocks until a client sends data. When a message is received, the function returns the number of bytes read (`n`), the client address (`clientAddr`), and any potential errors. If an error occurs while reading, the program logs it and continues listening without crashing. Otherwise, it prints the received data along with the client IP address and port. After logging the incoming message, the server generates a random integer between `0` and `999` using `rand.Intn(1000)` and retrieves the current system time formatted according to the `time.RFC1123` standard. It then constructs a response string containing both the random number and the timestamp. Finally, the server sends this response back to the same client using `conn.WriteToUDP()`. If an error occurs while sending the response, it is reported, but the loop continues running so the server can handle further requests.

The server uses a fixed-size buffer (1,024 bytes) to receive incoming datagrams. In UDP communication, each call to `ReadFromUDP()` reads a single datagram into the provided buffer. If the datagram is larger than the buffer, the excess bytes are truncated and discarded by the OS. In practice, developers choose a buffer size that comfortably accommodates the expected message size or design their protocol so that messages fit within a known limit. For many simple UDP protocols, a small, fixed buffer is sufficient, but production systems often use larger buffers or explicitly document the maximum datagram size they support.

The next step is about testing the UDP server. As we did for the TCP server, we are going to use the handy `nc(1)` utility for testing. After running the UDP server, issue the following command on a different Unix terminal:

```
$ nc -u localhost 1234
Hi!
Random: 529 | Time: Mon, 20 Oct 2025 20:57:06 EEST
```

The `ch08/udpServer.go` is going to generate the following output:

```
$ go run ch08/udpServer.go 1234
UDP server listening on port 1234...
Received 4 bytes from [::1]:55475: Hi!
```

The example confirms that the UDP server is correctly receiving datagrams and replying to the sender. Now that we have a working UDP server capable of receiving and responding to datagrams, it is time to develop the corresponding UDP client.

Developing a UDP client

A client starts establishing a communication endpoint with `net.DialUDP("udp", nil, serverAddr)`. Once set up, the client can send messages to the server using `conn.Write([]byte(message))` and receive responses with `conn.Read(buffer)` or `conn.ReadFromUDP(buffer)`. Since UDP is connectionless, each send or receive operation is independent, allowing the client to exchange datagrams quickly without the overhead of maintaining a persistent connection, making it ideal for lightweight, low-latency messaging. The example code can be found in the `main()` function of `ch08/udpClient.go`:

```
func main() {
    if len(os.Args) != 3 {
        fmt.Println("Usage: go run udp_client.go <host> <port>")
        return
    }
    host := os.Args[1]
    port := os.Args[2]
    address := net.JoinHostPort(host, port)

    // Resolve the UDP address
    serverAddr, err := net.ResolveUDPAddr("udp", address)
    if err != nil {
        fmt.Println("Error resolving UDP address:", err)
        return
    }

    // Create a UDP connection to the resolved address
    conn, err := net.DialUDP("udp", nil, serverAddr)
    if err != nil {
        fmt.Println("Error connecting to server:", err)
        return
    }
    defer conn.Close()
```

The program begins by validating that exactly two command-line arguments are provided: the target host and port. These are extracted from `os.Args` and then combined into a single `"host:port"` string using `net.JoinHostPort()`, which ensures proper formatting for both IPv4 and IPv6 addresses. This combined string is then passed to `net.ResolveUDPAddr("udp", address)`, which resolves the hostname to an actual IP address and returns a `*UDPAddr` structure containing the numeric port, IP, and optional IPv6 zone. Resolving the address explicitly is important when you need precise control over the UDP endpoint, such as when creating a server or using `net.DialUDP()` directly. After resolving the address, the program calls `net.DialUDP("udp", nil, serverAddr)` to create a UDP connection to the remote server. The `nil` argument allows the OS to automatically assign a free local port for the client. This returns a `*UDPConn`, which provides a convenient interface for sending and receiving datagrams. The `defer conn.Close()` statement ensures that the connection is properly closed when the function exits, preventing resource leaks even if an error occurs later. The rest of `main()` comes with the following code — this is where the client sends the message:

```
    message := "request"
    fmt.Printf("Sending message to %s: %s\n", address, message)
    _, err = conn.Write([]byte(message))
    if err != nil {
        fmt.Println("Error sending message:", err)
        return
    }

    buffer := make([]byte, 1024)
    // Prevent blocking forever
    conn.SetReadDeadline(time.Now().Add(5 * time.Second))
    n, _, err := conn.ReadFromUDP(buffer)
    if err != nil {
        fmt.Println("Error receiving response:", err)
        return
    }
    fmt.Printf("Server response: %s\n", string(buffer[:n]))
}
```

After establishing the UDP connection, the client prepares to send the `"request"` string and writes it to the server using `conn.Write([]byte(message))`. Even though UDP is connectionless under the hood, the `*UDPConn` returned by `net.DialUDP()` allows the program to send datagrams to the resolved server address without specifying it on each send. To receive a response, the program creates a buffer and calls `conn.ReadFromUDP(buffer)`, which reads an incoming datagram and returns the address of the sender. To prevent indefinite blocking if the server does not respond, the client sets a read deadline using `conn.SetReadDeadline(time.Now().Add(5 *` `time.Second)`). Once data is received, the client slices the buffer up to the number of bytes read and converts it to a string for display.

Run `ch08/udpClient.go` on your machine to interact with the UDP server:

```
$ go run ch08/udpClient.go localhost 1234
Sending message to localhost:1234: request
Server response: Random: 169 | Time: Mon, 20 Oct 2025 20:58:54 EEST
```

The line `Sending message to localhost:1234: request` confirms that the message was transmitted. The last line of the output shows the server response.

Let us take a close look at `net.ResolveUDPAddr("udp", address)`. The function is used in Go to translate a human-readable network address, such as `"localhost:9000"` or `"192.168.1.5:8080"`, into a `*net.UDPAddr` structure. In practice, you need `net.ResolveUDPAddr()` whenever you want *explicit control* over the local or remote endpoint of a UDP connection. For example, a UDP server that listens for incoming datagrams must bind to a specific address and port using `net.ListenUDP()`, which requires a `*net.UDPAddr` as input. Similarly, a client that uses `net.DialUDP()` to send messages to a fixed destination must also pass a resolved `*net.UDPAddr` for the remote host. In both cases, calling `net.ResolveUDPAddr()` first is essential because these lower-level functions operate directly on socket-level addresses rather than higher-level abstractions. However, in many simpler situations, such as when writing a lightweight client that only sends a few UDP packets, you do not need to call `net.ResolveUDPAddr()` yourself. The higher-level `net.Dial("udp", address)` function automatically performs address resolution internally. It returns a `net.Conn` object that you can use immediately for reading and writing, without worrying about the underlying socket details. In short, use `net.ResolveUDPAddr()` when you need low-level access to socket parameters, want to bind to specific interfaces, or are working directly with `net.DialUDP()` or `net.ListenUDP()`. Skip it when you only need a quick, convenient UDP connection and are fine letting Go handle the resolution internally through `net.Dial()`.

The same principle applies to TCP connections. The `net.Listen("tcp", ":8080")` function we have used in `ch08/concTCP.go` is a convenient, high-level way to create a TCP server. It automatically performs address resolution, binds to the given port on all available interfaces, and starts listening for incoming connections. Internally, it calls `net.ResolveTCPAddr()` to handle the low-level details. For more control over socket behavior, such as binding to a specific IP address or configuring IPv4 versus IPv6 behavior, you can instead use `net.ListenTCP("tcp", addr)`, where `addr` is a `*net.TCPAddr` obtained from an explicit call to `net.ResolveTCPAddr()`. In short, `net.Listen("tcp", ":8080")` is the preferred choice for simplicity and general use, while `net.ListenTCP("tcp", addr)` is useful in specialized situations where you need direct control over the socket or address configuration.

Modern systems generate valuable insights through metrics such as connection counts, data throughput, packet drops, and latency — all of which help developers diagnose performance issues and optimize networked applications. In the next section, you will see how to gather these metrics programmatically and prepare them for export to monitoring tools such as Prometheus. In *Chapter 9, Creating Web Services*, you will learn how to read them back!

Collecting TCP/IP metrics

By collecting information such as the number of active connections, listening sockets, packet counts, and connection states, developers can monitor the health, throughput, and responsiveness of their systems. For example, a sudden spike in established TCP connections may indicate increased user traffic, a misbehaving client, or even the early stages of a denial-of-service attack. Similarly, tracking these metrics alongside CPU or memory usage can help operators detect unusual load patterns and decide whether to scale resources or investigate potential issues.

In Go, these metrics can be accessed programmatically through libraries that interface with the OS networking stack, allowing applications to expose real-time data for analysis and monitoring tools such as Prometheus. This section explores how to gather and interpret TCP and UDP statistics from within Go programs, providing the foundation for building *observability* into network services and diagnosing performance or connectivity issues effectively. The list of possible TCP/IP metrics you can collect is virtually endless. From packet loss, retransmission rates, and connection durations to latency distributions and error counts, the specific metrics that matter most depend on your needs. In this section, we present a small, representative example to illustrate how metric collection works in practice. As a developer, you should identify the aspects of network behavior that are most relevant to your system — whether it is throughput, reliability, or response time — and design your own monitoring strategy accordingly. The key is not to collect everything, but to collect what provides actionable insight. Just to be 100% clear: In the presented setup, the role of the Go program is to *expose* metrics, not to store them. It collects TCP and UDP statistics and makes them available via an HTTP endpoint in a format that Prometheus can scrape. Prometheus, in turn, is responsible for periodically requesting this data, storing it efficiently in its time-series database, and making it available for querying and visualization. This separation of responsibilities ensures that the metrics server remains lightweight and focused on gathering and exposing metrics, while Prometheus handles the actual collection, storage, retention, and aggregation of the data over time.

There exist several external packages that make it easy to export application metrics to Prometheus. The most widely used is `prometheus/client_golang`, which provides a comprehensive toolkit for instrumenting Go programs. The package provides collectors for gathering runtime statistics, including memory usage, garbage collection, and network activity, as well as an HTTP handler (`promhttp.Handler()`) that exposes a `/metrics` endpoint for Prometheus to scrape. Go programs can also implement the `prometheus.Collector` interface to create custom collectors for application-specific metrics.

We are going to present the Go program that collects TCP/IP metrics (`ch08/metrics/getMetrics.go`) in chunks. The first code snippet is the following — this is where the Go program defines Prometheus metrics for monitoring TCP and UDP network activity using the `prometheus/client_golang` library:

```
package main

import (
    "log"
    "net/http"
    "time"

    "github.com/prometheus/client_golang/prometheus"
    "github.com/prometheus/client_golang/prometheus/promhttp"
    "github.com/shirou/gopsutil/net"
)

// TCP metrics
var (
    tcpEstablished = prometheus.NewGauge(prometheus.GaugeOpts{
        Name: "tcp_established_connections",
        Help: "Number of TCP connections in ESTABLISHED state",
    })
    tcpListen = prometheus.NewGauge(prometheus.GaugeOpts{
        Name: "tcp_listen_connections",
        Help: "Number of TCP sockets in LISTEN state",
    })
    tcpOther = prometheus.NewGauge(prometheus.GaugeOpts{
        Name: "tcp_other_connections",
        Help: "Number of TCP connections in other states",
    })
)

// UDP metrics
var (
```

```
    udpListening = prometheus.NewGauge(prometheus.GaugeOpts{
        Name: "udp_listen_sockets",
        Help: "Number of UDP sockets currently listening",
    })
)

func init() {
    prometheus.MustRegister(tcpEstablished, tcpListen, tcpOther, udpListening)
}
```

The code imports standard Go packages for logging, HTTP handling, and timing, as well as two external libraries: `prometheus/client_golang` for exposing metrics and `gopsutil/net` for gathering network statistics. The program declares four Prometheus **gauge** metrics: three for TCP connections (`tcpEstablished`, `tcpListen`, and `tcpOther`) and one for UDP sockets (`udpListening`). A gauge represents a single numerical value that can go up or down, making it ideal for tracking quantities such as the number of active connections or sockets. Each metric includes a name and a help description, which are displayed by Prometheus when scraping data from the `/metrics` endpoint. The `init()` function plays a special role in Go. It is automatically executed before the `main()` function, and it does not need to be explicitly called. In this program, `init()` registers all the defined metrics with the Prometheus client library using `prometheus.MustRegister()`. This ensures that the metrics are ready to be collected as soon as the program starts. In this case, the use of `init()` simplifies the setup by automatically initializing the metric registry before any other logic runs, which is a common pattern in Go programs that expose Prometheus metrics.

The next part presents the `updateTCPMetrics()` function, which is responsible for collecting and updating Prometheus metrics related to active TCP connections:

```
func updateTCPMetrics() {
    conns, err := net.Connections("tcp")
    if err != nil {
        log.Printf("Error reading TCP connections: %v", err)
        return
    }
    var est, listen, other float64
    for _, c := range conns {
        switch c.Status {
        case "ESTABLISHED":
            est++
        case "LISTEN":
```

```
            listen++
        default:
            other++
        }
    }

    tcpEstablished.Set(est)
    tcpListen.Set(listen)
    tcpOther.Set(other)
    log.Printf("TCP metrics updated: EST=%v LISTEN=%v OTHER=%v\n", est, listen,
other)
}
```

`updateTCPMetrics()` starts by calling `net.Connections("tcp")`, which retrieves a list of all current TCP connections on the system, including their states (such as `ESTABLISHED` or `LISTEN`). If this call fails, an error message is logged, and the function returns early. The function then iterates over each connection, examining its `Status` field to categorize it as either `ESTABLISHED`, `LISTEN`, or another state. It keeps separate counters for each category— `est`, `listen`, and `other` — incrementing them as appropriate. After scanning all connections, these values are assigned to the corresponding Prometheus gauge metrics (`tcpEstablished`, `tcpListen`, and `tcpOther`) using their `Set()` methods. Finally, a log entry prints the updated metrics, confirming that the data has been collected and exported successfully for monitoring by Prometheus. Similarly, the `updateUDPMetrics()` function is used for collecting UDP metrics:

```
func updateUDPMetrics() {
    conns, err := net.Connections("udp")
    if err != nil {
        log.Printf("Error reading UDP connections: %v", err)
        return
    }

    // UDP doesn't have a "state", so we just count active sockets
    udpListening.Set(float64(len(conns)))
    log.Printf("UDP metrics updated: LISTEN=%v\n", len(conns))
}
```

The code begins by calling `net.Connections("udp")` to obtain a list of all currently active UDP sockets. If an error occurs during this call, the function logs the error and exits without updating the metrics. Unlike TCP, UDP does not maintain connection states such as `ESTABLISHED` or

`LISTEN`. Because of that, the function simply counts the number of active UDP sockets by taking the length of the `conns` slice. This count is then assigned to the Prometheus `udpListening` gauge using the `Set()` method, reflecting the total number of open UDP sockets on the system. Finally, a log entry records the updated value, providing feedback that the UDP metrics have been successfully refreshed and are ready to be scraped by Prometheus. Lastly, the `main()` function is what connects all components:

```
func main() {
    // Periodically update metrics
    go func() {
        for {
            updateTCPMetrics()
            updateUDPMetrics()
            time.Sleep(5 * time.Second)
        }
    }()

    // Expose metrics for Prometheus
    addr := "0.0.0.0:9100"
    log.Printf("Metrics server listening on %s\n", addr)
    http.Handle("/metrics", promhttp.Handler())
    log.Fatal(http.ListenAndServe(addr, nil))
}
```

The `main()` function serves as the entry point for the metrics collection service. It begins by launching a goroutine that continuously updates the TCP and UDP metrics at regular intervals. Inside the goroutine, the program calls `updateTCPMetrics()` and `updateUDPMetrics()` in sequence, then pauses for five seconds using `time.Sleep()` before repeating the cycle. This ensures that the Prometheus metrics remain current without blocking the main execution thread. After starting the background metrics updater, the function sets up an HTTP server to expose the collected data — you will learn more about the use of the HTTP protocol in Go in *Chapter 9, Creating Web Services*. The server listens on all network interfaces at port `9100`, a common choice for Prometheus exporters, and registers a `/metrics` endpoint handled by `promhttp.Handler()`. This handler automatically formats and serves the metrics in the text-based exposition format expected by Prometheus. Finally, the program calls `http.ListenAndServe()` as previously explained. Now that the metrics server is functional and ready to expose TCP and UDP data for Prometheus, the next step is to containerize the application. By packaging it into a Docker container, we make deployment simpler.

Containerizing the server

Creating a Docker image for the server packages the Go application and its dependencies into a lightweight container, allowing the TCP server to run consistently across different environments. By defining a Dockerfile, you can specify how to build the Go binary, copy it into a minimal base image, and configure the container to start the server automatically. Containerizing the server not only simplifies deployment and scaling but also ensures that the application behaves the same way everywhere, independent of the host system's configuration. We begin this section with the Dockerfile for creating the Docker image for `ch08/metrics/getMetrics.go`:

```
# Use Go 1.25 (or your preferred version)
FROM golang:1.25-alpine
WORKDIR /app

# Copy Go modules
COPY go.mod go.sum ./
RUN go mod download

# Copy source code
COPY getMetrics.go .

# Build the metrics server
RUN go build -o getMetrics getMetrics.go
EXPOSE 9100
CMD ["./getMetrics"]
```

The process starts from the lightweight `golang:1.25-alpine` base image, which includes the Go toolchain and a minimal Linux environment. The `WORKDIR /app` instruction sets the working directory inside the container, so all subsequent commands operate within `/app`. Next, the Dockerfile copies the Go module files (`go.mod` and `go.sum`) into the container and runs `go mod download` to fetch all dependencies. This step is optional if no Go modules are used, but it helps leverage Docker's layer caching to avoid re-downloading dependencies unnecessarily on rebuilds. Then, the `getMetrics.go` file is copied into the container with the `COPY getMetrics.go .` command. The `RUN go build -o getMetrics getMetrics.go` instruction compiles the Go source file into a binary named `getMetrics`. The `EXPOSE 9100` command documents that the container listens on port `9100` for incoming connections, allowing Prometheus or other clients to connect. Finally, the `CMD ["./getMetrics"]` instruction specifies the default command to run when the container starts, which launches the metrics server.

The Dockerfile shown here builds and runs the Go server in a single image for simplicity and clarity. In production environments, developers often use multi-stage builds to reduce the final image size. In such setups, the Go code is compiled in one build stage using a full Go toolchain image, and only the resulting binary is copied into a smaller runtime image. This approach produces leaner containers and reduces the attack surface while keeping the build process reproducible.

With the metrics server collecting and exposing data, the next step is to store and manage these TCP/IP metrics. This responsibility falls to Prometheus, which automatically scrapes the server's `/metrics` endpoint at regular intervals, storing the collected data for analysis, visualization, and long-term monitoring.

Storing TCP/IP metrics

In this example, Prometheus is responsible for collecting and storing the TCP/IP metrics exposed by our Go server. The server publishes its metrics over an HTTP endpoint, and Prometheus periodically scrapes this endpoint using its *pull-based* model, recording the values as time-series data. Once stored, these metrics can be queried to observe connection behavior over time or visualized using tools such as **Grafana**, allowing us to analyze how the server and the underlying system behave under load.

Here is the Prometheus configuration file (`prometheus.yml`), which defines how and how often it should collect metrics from monitored targets:

```
global:
  scrape_interval: 5s

scrape_configs:
  - job_name: "go_metrics_server"
    static_configs:
      - targets: ["tcp_metrics:9100"]
```

At the top, the `global` section sets a scrape interval of 5 seconds, meaning that Prometheus will attempt to collect metrics from all configured targets every 5 seconds. The `scrape_configs` section defines individual scraping jobs. In this case, there is a single job named `"go_metrics_server"`, which groups together the targets associated with the Go metrics server. Under `static_configs`, the `targets` list specifies the endpoint to scrape. Here, `tcp_metrics:9100` refers to the Go metrics container by its Docker Compose service name and the port where it exposes metrics. Prometheus will make HTTP requests to `http://tcp_metrics:9100/metrics` at the configured interval, collecting real-time metrics from the Go server for storage, querying, and visualization.

With the Go metrics server ready and Prometheus configured to scrape its data, the next logical step is to run both services as Docker containers, which ensures a consistent and reproducible environment.

Running Prometheus and the Go server as Docker images

We will run both the Go metrics server and Prometheus inside Docker containers using a single `docker-compose.yaml` file. This approach simplifies deployment by defining all services, ports, and configurations in one place. Instead of manually running multiple containers with long command-line options, Docker Compose allows you to start, stop, and manage the entire monitoring setup with a single command — making it ideal for testing, development, or even lightweight production environments. We are going to need a `docker-compose.yaml` file with the following contents:

```
services:
  tcp_metrics:
    build: .
    container_name: tcp_metrics
    ports:
      - "9100:9100"
    restart: unless-stopped

  prometheus:
    image: prom/prometheus:latest
    container_name: prometheus
    volumes:
      - ./prometheus.yml:/etc/prometheus/prometheus.yml:ro
    ports:
      - "9090:9090"
    restart: unless-stopped
    depends_on:
      - tcp_metrics
```

This `docker-compose.yaml` file defines two services that work together. The `tcp_metrics` service builds the Go metrics server from the current directory and exposes port `9100` so Prometheus can scrape the metrics endpoint. The `prometheus` service runs the official Prometheus image, loading its configuration from the local `prometheus.yml` file and exposing port `9090` to access the Prometheus web interface. The `depends_on` directive ensures that the metrics server is started before Prometheus begins scraping data. Execute `docker-compose up` from inside `ch08/metrics/`. The last lines of the output should be similar to the following:

```
$ cd ch08/metrics
$ docker-compose up
...
tcp_metrics  | 2025/10/21 05:56:03 TCP metrics updated: EST=0 LISTEN=2 OTHER=0
tcp_metrics  | 2025/10/21 05:56:03 UDP metrics updated: LISTEN=1
tcp_metrics  | 2025/10/21 05:56:08 TCP metrics updated: EST=1 LISTEN=2 OTHER=0
tcp_metrics  | 2025/10/21 05:56:08 UDP metrics updated: LISTEN=1
```

Now, here is the tricky part. As everything runs on Docker images, for the metrics to change, we must do something from inside the Docker image! Run the following command, which lets you step inside your running container (`tcp_metrics`) and interact with it as if it were its own mini Linux machine:

```
$ docker exec -it tcp_metrics sh
```

Now, if you execute `nc -l 8080` in the provided shell, the TCP metrics are going to change. Similarly, if you execute `nc -u -l 8080`, the UDP metric is going to change as we have a new UDP server listening on port `8080`:

```
tcp_metrics  | 2025/10/21 05:57:19 TCP metrics updated: EST=1 LISTEN=2 OTHER=0
tcp_metrics  | 2025/10/21 05:57:19 UDP metrics updated: LISTEN=2
tcp_metrics  | 2025/10/21 05:57:24 TCP metrics updated: EST=1 LISTEN=2 OTHER=0
tcp_metrics  | 2025/10/21 05:57:24 UDP metrics updated: LISTEN=2
```

Put simply, the Go code used to collect TCP/IP metrics is meant to be integrated into the actual systems or services you want to monitor. In a real-world deployment, you would typically embed the metrics-gathering logic directly into your running applications or infrastructure components so that Prometheus can scrape live data from them. Running the metrics collector in its own standalone Docker container serves only as a simple and self-contained example.

This concludes the chapter, where we explored how to develop TCP/IP applications, monitor TCP/IP activity, expose metrics to Prometheus, and containerize everything for a complete, automated monitoring setup.

Summary

In this chapter, we explored how to build networked programs that communicate over TCP and UDP. You learned how to create servers and clients, handle connections concurrently, and gather useful insights about network behavior. These concepts form the foundation for building more sophisticated systems that operate over the web.

In the next chapter, we will move from TCP and UDP programming to the higher-level HTTP protocol, learning how to design, implement, and expose web APIs in Go. This transition marks an important step — from managing low-level network communication to building complete, production-ready web services. You are also going to learn how to read data from Prometheus, which is not as simple as it looks!

Exercises

1. Change the code in `ch08/concTCP.go` to use `net.ListenTCP("tcp", addr)`.
2. Create a Docker image for `ch08/concTCP.go`. Use a client to connect to it.
3. Change `ch08/metrics/getMetrics.go` so that the port number is given as a command-line argument.
4. If you are feeling brave, use Grafana to visualize the Prometheus metrics.
5. Make `ch08/udpClient.go` to accept the message from the command line.
6. Add signal handling to `ch08/udpServer.go`.

Additional resources

- `gopsutil`: The `psutil` library for Go: `https://github.com/shirou/gopsutil`
- Prometheus: `https://prometheus.io/`
- Grafana: `https://grafana.com/`

Scan the QR or visit the link to subscribe for free.

`https://packt.link/deep-engineering-newsletter`

9

Creating Web Services

Go's simplicity and strong performance make it an excellent choice for developing web services — especially since its built-in `context` package provides a clean way to manage request lifecycles, cancellations, and timeouts across distributed systems. With its powerful `net/http` package and efficient concurrency model, you can go from handling a single HTTP request to running a complete web service in just a few lines of code. Rather than enforcing strict concurrency control, the `context` package provides a lightweight and flexible way to *pass signals* across goroutines. It is up to your code to cooperate by listening to these signals and respecting time limits when appropriate. In this chapter, we explore how to create and manage HTTP servers and clients, build a proxy server, and learn how to profile and monitor web applications for performance insights. You will also put these skills into practice by developing a simple yet functional note-taking REST API server and client, and finally, you will learn how to read data from Prometheus.

This chapter covers the following:

- Using the `net/http` package and profiling and testing web applications
- The `context` package
- Creating a Proxy server
- Creating and using a note-taking web service
- Reading data from Prometheus

Let us begin by discussing the powerful and handy `net/http` package.

The net/http package

The `net/http` package is a powerful and high-level library for building web clients and servers. What sets it apart is its integration with Go's concurrency model: handlers run in lightweight goroutines, allowing simple, safe and efficient concurrent processing of multiple requests. It provides the foundational components necessary for handling HTTP requests and responses. It abstracts much of the *underlying complexity of TCP networking*, letting developers focus on building HTTP-based applications efficiently and concisely. At its core, `net/http` enables you to set up HTTP servers using the `http.ListenAndServe()` function and handlers that satisfy the `http.Handler` interface. It also provides a default `ServeMux` multiplexer and a convenient way to define routes using `http.HandleFunc()`. On the client side, it includes the `http.Client` and `http.Request` types, which support sending requests, managing connections, setting headers, handling cookies, and following redirects. Internally, it uses goroutines and channels to handle multiple requests concurrently. It also supports TLS out of the box, via `http.ListenAndServeTLS`, which simplifies secure communication. In summary, the lifecycle of a request in the `net/http` package follows a straightforward pattern: the server receives an HTTP request, the appropriate handler processes it, and the handler generates a response that is returned to the client. Now, let us put that knowledge into practice by building a simple HTTP server and enhancing it with middleware.

Creating a simple HTTP server with middleware

Creating a simple HTTP server in Go is straightforward thanks to the `net/http` package. With just a few lines of code, you can spin up a web server that listens on a given port, routes incoming requests, and responds with dynamic or static content. This section walks you through the basics of setting up a server, defining handlers, and serving responses, giving you the foundation needed to build more complex web applications.

> **Note**
>
> In small programs, simple route registrations like the ones shown here are usually sufficient. As applications grow, developers often organize routes into groups or separate router modules or adopt routing libraries such as Chi (`https://go-chi.io/`) to support features such as middleware chains and parameterized paths. This structure helps keep large APIs maintainable as the number of endpoints increases.

Before diving into handlers and routes, it is important to understand **middleware functions**. A **Middleware function** is a powerful yet simple concept that allows you to *inject extra behavior into your HTTP server* without changing the core logic of your handlers. For example, a logging middleware can automatically print each incoming request method, path, and client address, giving you real-time insight into how your server is being used. Other common uses include authentication, rate limiting, panic recovery, or measuring request duration. What makes middleware particularly elegant in Go is that it is just a function returning another `http.HandlerFunc()`, which keeps the code composable, readable, and easy to experiment with. Even on a small teaching server, adding a middleware can immediately demonstrate how web servers in the real world manage cross-cutting concerns, helping you understand that the flow of an HTTP request is more than just a simple *call and respond* process. Our sample HTTP server is going to support several endpoints to showcase the routing code, as well as a middleware function. The root route (/) serves as a welcome page, returning a friendly message to confirm that the server is running. A `/time` endpoint can demonstrate generating dynamic responses by returning the current server time. To show how query parameters work, an `/echo` route accepts a `msg` parameter (for example, `/echo?msg=hello`) and sends it back to the client, while a `POST /echo` variant echoes data sent in the request body. A `/headers` endpoint can return the client's HTTP request headers, providing insight into the metadata exchanged in HTTP communication. Finally, a `/health` route can serve as a minimal health-check endpoint, responding with a simple `"OK"` to confirm service availability. Let us begin presenting our HTTP server (`ch09/simpleHTTP.go`) by explaining `writeJSON()`, which is designed to simplify sending JSON responses back to the client. The `writeJSON()` function takes two parameters: `http.ResponseWriter`, which represents the HTTP response that will be sent back to the client, and a generic `data` value of type `interface{}`, which can hold any Go data structure. The function first sets the `Content-Type` header of the response to `application/json`, clearly indicating to the client that the data being returned is in JSON format. It then creates a new JSON encoder with `json.NewEncoder(w)` and immediately calls its `Encode()` method to serialize the `data` value into JSON and write it directly to the response body.

Here is the *middleware function* (`loggingMiddleware()`) used in the program that demonstrates a common middleware pattern in Go web servers: it wraps an existing handler to add behavior before and after the main request is processed. In this case, it logs the request details before calling the wrapped handler and reports the duration after the handler completes:

```
func loggingMiddleware(next http.HandlerFunc) http.HandlerFunc {
    return func(w http.ResponseWriter, r *http.Request) {
        start := time.Now()
        fmt.Printf("[%s] %s %s\n", r.Method, r.URL.Path, r.RemoteAddr)
        next.ServeHTTP(w, r)
        fmt.Printf("Completed in %v\n", time.Since(start))
    }
}
```

This function accepts another handler, next, as an argument and returns a new `http.HandlerFunc` that performs logging before and after executing the wrapped handler. Last, it calls `next.ServeHTTP(w, r)` to *pass control to the actual handler*, ensuring that the main request processing still occurs. After the handler finishes, the middleware calculates and prints how long the request took to complete.

Here are three of the handler functions of the HTTP server:

```
func handleRoot(w http.ResponseWriter, r *http.Request) {
    fmt.Fprintln(w, "Welcome to the Go Web Service!")
}

func handleTime(w http.ResponseWriter, r *http.Request) {
    now := time.Now().Format(time.RFC3339)
    writeJSON(w, map[string]string{"time": now})
}

func handleEchoQuery(w http.ResponseWriter, r *http.Request) {
    msg := r.URL.Query().Get("msg")
    if msg == "" {
        msg = "No message provided"
    }
    writeJSON(w, map[string]string{"echo": msg})
}
```

These three handler functions illustrate the foundation of how the `net/http` package handles different types of HTTP requests. The server defines a small set of handler functions that demonstrate different response styles. The `handleRoot()` handler returns a simple welcome message for the root path (/), acting as a basic landing page and confirming that the server is reachable. In contrast, `handleTime()` produces a structured response: it obtains the current time with `time.Now()`, formats it using the ISO 8601 standard (`time.RFC3339`), and sends it to the client as JSON via the `writeJSON()` helper, reflecting a common pattern in API-style services. Query parameter handling is introduced by `handleEchoQuery()`, which reads the `msg` value from the request URL using `r.URL.Query().Get("msg")` and echoes it back to the client. If no message is provided, it defaults to `"No message provided"`. The function then returns the message as a JSON object, echoing the input back to the client. Next, here are the remaining handler functions:

```
func handleEchoPost(w http.ResponseWriter, r *http.Request) {
    defer r.Body.Close()
    var body map[string]interface{}
    if err := json.NewDecoder(r.Body).Decode(&body); err != nil {
        http.Error(w, "Invalid JSON body", http.StatusBadRequest)
```

```
        return
    }
    writeJSON(w, map[string]interface{}{"echo": body})
}
func handleHeaders(w http.ResponseWriter, r *http.Request) {
    headers := make(map[string][]string)
    for k, v := range r.Header {
        headers[k] = v
    }
    writeJSON(w, headers)
}
func handleHealth(w http.ResponseWriter, r *http.Request) {
    fmt.Fprintln(w, "OK")
}
```

These three handlers extend the server capabilities by introducing JSON body parsing, header inspection, and a health check endpoint, which are features that are commonly found in production services. The `handleEchoPost()` function handles HTTP `POST` requests that send JSON data in the request body. It begins with `defer r.Body.Close()` to ensure the request body is properly closed after processing, preventing resource leaks. It then declares a body variable as a generic map to hold the decoded JSON data. The `handleHeaders()` function provides a way to inspect incoming HTTP request headers. It creates a new map and iterates over `r.Header`, which stores all request headers as key-value pairs. Each header key and its list of values are copied into the new map, and the result is returned as a JSON object. This endpoint is *useful for debugging and understanding what information clients send along with their requests.* Finally, the `handleHealth()` function serves as a lightweight health check endpoint. It simply writes `"OK"` to the response, signaling that the server is operational. Health checks like this are typically used by load balancers, orchestration systems, or monitoring tools to verify that a service is running correctly.

The `main()` function implementation provides a clear and complete example of how to initialize an HTTP server in Go, as it configures routing, applies middleware, allows flexible configuration, and starts the server loop:

```
func main() {
    port := "8080"
    if len(os.Args) > 1 {
        port = os.Args[1]
    }

    mux := http.NewServeMux()
```

```
    mux.HandleFunc("GET /", loggingMiddleware(handleRoot))
    mux.HandleFunc("GET /time", loggingMiddleware(handleTime))
    mux.HandleFunc("GET /echo", loggingMiddleware(handleEchoQuery))
    mux.HandleFunc("POST /echo", loggingMiddleware(handleEchoPost))
    mux.HandleFunc("GET /headers", loggingMiddleware(handleHeaders))
    mux.HandleFunc("GET /health", loggingMiddleware(handleHealth))

    fmt.Printf("Starting server on http://localhost:%s\n", port)

    if err := http.ListenAndServe(":"+port, mux); err != nil {
        panic(err)
    }
}
```

The `main()` function initializes and starts the Go web server. It creates a `ServeMux` multiplexer and registers all routes (`/`, `/time`, `/echo`, `/headers`, `/health`) using method-aware routing patterns introduced in Go 1.22. Each handler is wrapped with `loggingMiddleware()`, ensuring that every request is logged along with its execution time. For example, the `/echo` endpoint registers separate handlers for `GET` and `POST` requests, allowing the routing system to dispatch requests directly to `handleEchoQuery()` or `handleEchoPost()` without manual method checks. Finally, the server begins listening on the configured port using `http.ListenAndServe()`, which blocks the main goroutine while processing incoming requests concurrently. This setup illustrates the typical flow of a Go web service: *requests arrive at the server, the multiplexer selects the appropriate handler based on the method and path, and the handler generates the response.*

Run `ch09/simpleHTTP.go` on your machine to test its operation. Now, interact with it using `curl(1)` on a different terminal window:

```
$ curl http://localhost:8080/
Welcome to the Go Web Service!
$ curl http://localhost:8080/time
{"time":"2025-10-25T21:01:10+03:00"}
$ curl "http://localhost:8080/echo?msg=HelloWorld"
{"echo":"HelloWorld"}
$ curl "http://localhost:8080/echo"
{"echo":"No message provided"}
$ curl -X POST http://localhost:8080/echo \
     -H "Content-Type: application/json" \
     -d '{"user":"Mihalis","language":"Go"}'
{"echo":{"language":"Go","user":"Mihalis"}}
```

```
$ curl -H "X-Demo: true" http://localhost:8080/headers
{"Accept":["*/*"],"User-Agent":["curl/8.7.1"],"X-Demo":["true"]}
$ curl http://localhost:8080/health
OK
```

The first command calls the root endpoint (/), confirming that the server is running. The second command queries `/time`, which responds with the current system time, encoded as JSON. The next two requests interact with the `/echo` endpoint using the `GET` method: one passes a message (`msg=HelloWorld`), which is echoed back in JSON form, while the other omits the parameter and receives `"No message provided"`. The following example switches to the `POST` method; the server parses and echoes this data back as structured JSON. The `/headers` endpoint shows how incoming HTTP headers are handled — it returns a JSON object listing all request headers, including the custom `"X-Demo"` header. Finally, the `/health` endpoint provides a simple health check, responding with `"OK"`, confirming that the server is operational and responsive. The server output was the following:

```
$ go run ch09/simpleHTTP.go
Starting server on http://localhost:8080
[GET] / [::1]:51439
Completed in 32.542µs
[GET] /time [::1]:51440
Completed in 513.042µs
[GET] /echo [::1]:51441
Completed in 170.541µs
[GET] /echo [::1]:51442
Completed in 78.042µs
[POST] /echo [::1]:51443
Completed in 305µs
[GET] /headers [::1]:51446
Completed in 193.375µs
[GET] /health [::1]:51447
Completed in 36.875µs
```

Each line logs the HTTP method, path, client address, and how long the server took to process the request — demonstrating that the server successfully responded to multiple endpoints with very low latency.

Overall, this example illustrates the core workflow of a Go web service: requests arrive at the server, the multiplexer routes them to handlers, middleware records request activity, and handlers generate responses. Just as Go makes it easy to build servers, the `net/http` package also provides a powerful and flexible API for creating HTTP clients, which is presented in the next subsection.

Creating an HTTP client

An HTTP client allows your program to send requests to web servers, retrieve responses, and process data such as JSON, HTML, or plain text. In this section, we explore how to create a simple HTTP client, send requests, and work with responses, equipping you with the tools to interact programmatically with web services and APIs. The presented HTTP client shows how to interact with web servers of any kind, handle responses, send JSON payloads, and add HTTP headers. *However, what an HTTP client should always do is understand the rules of the server so that it can successfully interact with it.* We are going to begin the presentation of `ch09/httpClient.go` by looking at the `getRequest()` function implementation, which performs a simple HTTP `GET` request to a given URL and prints out the response:

```
// Helper function for making GET requests and printing responses
func getRequest(url string) {
    resp, err := http.Get(url)
    if err != nil {
        fmt.Println("Error:", err)
        return
    }
    defer resp.Body.Close()
    fmt.Printf("[GET] %s\nStatus: %s\n", url, resp.Status)
    body, _ := io.ReadAll(resp.Body)
    fmt.Print("Response:", string(body))
}
```

The `getRequest()` function uses `http.Get()`, which handles creating a request, opening a connection, and reading the response. After checking for errors, the function ensures that the response body is properly closed using `defer resp.Body.Close()`. It then prints the request type and target URL, followed by the HTTP status code. Finally, it reads the response body using `io.ReadAll()` and displays it as plain text. This function is perfect for testing endpoints such as `/`, `/time`, or `/health`.

The `postJSON()` function extends the pattern used in `getRequest()` by sending structured JSON data with `http.Post()`, demonstrating how to encode Go data into JSON and set the `Content-`

Type header. Finally, getWithHeaders() shows how to include custom HTTP headers, a common need for APIs requiring authentication tokens or additional client metadata:

```
func getWithHeaders(url string, headers map[string]string) {
    req, err := http.NewRequest(http.MethodGet, url, nil)
    if err != nil {
        fmt.Println("Error creating request:", err)
        return
    }
    for k, v := range headers {
        req.Header.Set(k, v)
    }
    client := &http.Client{}
    resp, err := client.Do(req)
    if err != nil {
        fmt.Println("Error:", err)
        return
    }
    defer resp.Body.Close()
    fmt.Printf("[GET with Headers] %s\nStatus: %s\n", url, resp.Status)
    body, _ := io.ReadAll(resp.Body)
    fmt.Print("Response:", string(body))
}
```

getWithHeaders() *manually constructs a new request* with http.NewRequest(), allowing fine-grained control over headers and methods, before iterating through the provided headers map and attaching each key-value pair using req.Header.Set(). The request is executed using an http.Client, giving you the ability to customize behavior such as timeouts or redirects if needed. Once the response is received, it prints the request type, status, and body contents. This function is particularly useful when testing the /headers endpoint of the server, as it allows you to verify that the server properly reads and echoes back custom headers. The main() function ties everything together – here is its example code:

```
func main() {
    server := "http://localhost:8080"
    if len(os.Args) > 1 {
        server = os.Args[1]
    }
    fmt.Printf("Connecting to server: %s", server)
    getRequest(server + "/")
```

```
    getRequest(server + "/time")
    getRequest(server + "/echo?msg=GoProgramming")
    postJSON(server+"/echo", map[string]interface{}{
        "user": "Mihalis",
        "lang": "Go",
    })
    getWithHeaders(server+"/headers", map[string]string{
        "X-Client": "GoHTTPClient",
        "X-Demo":   "true",
    })
    getRequest(server + "/health")
}
```

The code begins by setting a default server address (`http://localhost:8080`), but if the user provides a command-line argument, that value is used instead. It then calls the other helper functions in sequence to interact with all available endpoints of the web service. This includes sending basic `GET` requests to `/` and `/time`, using both `GET` and `POST` requests for `/echo`, adding headers for `/headers`, and finally checking the `/health` route.

Now, while `ch09/simpleHTTP.go` is running, run `ch09/httpClient.go` on your machine:

```
$ go run ch09/httpClient.go
Connecting to server: http://localhost:8080[GET] http://localhost:8080/
Status: 200 OK
Response:Welcome to the Go Web Service!
[GET] http://localhost:8080/time
Status: 200 OK
Response:{"time":"2025-10-24T17:33:33+03:00"}
[GET] http://localhost:8080/echo?msg=GoProgramming
Status: 200 OK
Response:{"echo":"GoProgramming"}
[POST] http://localhost:8080/echo
Status: 200 OK
Response:{"echo":{"lang":"Go","user":"Mihalis"}}
[GET with Headers] http://localhost:8080/headers
Status: 200 OK
Response:{"Accept-Encoding":["gzip"],"User-Agent":["Go-http-client/1.1"],"X-
Client":["GoHTTPClient"],"X-Demo":["true"]}
[GET] http://localhost:8080/health
```

```
Status: 200 OK
Response:OK
```

For each request, the HTTP client logs the HTTP method, target URL, response status, and returned data — confirming that it can perform `GET` and `POST` requests, send headers, and correctly parse responses from various endpoints of the web service.

Before we move on, let us take a step back and look at how our web service performs under the hood. Building features is only part of the story — understanding how efficiently they run is just as important. In the next section, we will learn how to enable profiling for HTTP servers and use `go tool pprof` to see what is happening.

Profiling HTTP applications

Profiling HTTP applications is an essential practice for understanding how your Go web services perform under real-world conditions. By systematically measuring metrics such as request latency, throughput, memory allocation, goroutine usage, and CPU consumption, you can identify performance bottlenecks and inefficiencies in your code or infrastructure. Go provides robust built-in tools, including the `pprof` package, which allows you to capture detailed CPU and memory profiles, and the `net/http/pprof` package, which exposes runtime profiling data via HTTP endpoints. To add profiling support to our Go HTTP server or service, we only need a few small but powerful changes. First, we import the `net/http/pprof` package *anonymously* (using `_ "net/http/pprof"`). This automatically registers a collection of profiling endpoints under `/debug/pprof/`, giving us access to runtime metrics such as CPU usage, memory allocation, goroutines, and blocking events. You can list all currently registered profiles using the `pprof` package, as presented in the `main()` function implementation of `ch09/availableProfiles.go`:

```
func main() {
    for _, p := range pprof.Profiles() {
        fmt.Println(p.Name())
    }
}
```

Running `ch09/availableProfiles.go` generates the following output:

```
$ go run ch09/availableProfiles.go
allocs
block
goroutine
heap
```

```
mutex
threadcreate
```

The `allocs` endpoint (`/debug/pprof/allocs`) reports information about all past memory allocations since the program started. The `block` endpoint (`/debug/pprof/block`) captures stack traces of goroutines that were blocked, typically waiting for synchronization primitives such as channels, `sync.Mutex` or `sync.Cond`. The `goroutine` endpoint (`/debug/pprof/goroutine`) provides a snapshot of all currently running goroutines and their stack traces. The `heap` endpoint (`/debug/pprof/heap`) shows information about memory that is currently in use. The `mutex` endpoint (`/debug/pprof/mutex`) collects stack traces showing where locks (`sync.Mutex` or `sync.RWMutex`) are contended. Last, the `threadcreate` endpoint (`/debug/pprof/threadcreate`) displays stack traces of where new operating system threads were created. The six profiles you saw are the always-available runtime profiles, and the CPU profile (`profile`) *only exists when you explicitly trigger a sampling session.*

Back to profiling the HTTP server now. Next, we need to start a secondary HTTP server —typically on port `6060` — in a *separate goroutine*. This allows the profiling interface to run independently of the main web service, ensuring that performance monitoring does not interfere with normal request handling. Once these two changes are in place, you can access the profiling data through your browser (`http://localhost:6060/debug/pprof/`) or analyze it using the `go tool pprof` command. These minimal modifications give developers deep visibility into the server behavior, making it much easier to identify performance bottlenecks and optimize resource usage. The relevant code can be found in `ch09/profileHTTP.go`. The important code can be found inside `main()` – it launches a background goroutine that starts an HTTP server using the `net/http/pprof` package:

```
go func() {
    fmt.Println("Profiler starting http://localhost:6060/debug/pprof/")
    if err := http.ListenAndServe("localhost:6060", nil); err != nil {
        fmt.Println("pprof server error:", err)
    }
}()
```

The `go func() { ... }()` line executes an anonymous function as a goroutine, allowing it to run concurrently with the main HTTP server that is going to start in a while. Inside the function, a message is printed to the console to indicate that the profiler is active and where it can be accessed. Then, `http.ListenAndServe("localhost:6060", nil)` starts the HTTP server on port `6060` that exposes the profiling endpoints. The `nil` handler means that the default `http.DefaultServeMux` is used, which has already been configured by importing the `net/http/pprof` package elsewhere in the program. If an error occurs while starting or running the profiler server, it is printed to the console.

We are now ready to collect data with the help of Apache `ab(1)`, which is an HTTP server benchmarking tool that creates traffic to a web server. First, run `ch09/profileHTTP.go` on a terminal window. Next, run `go tool pprof -seconds=30 http://localhost:6060/debug/pprof/profile` to collect a 30-second CPU profile and then view it interactively. Immediately after that, on a different terminal, run something such as `ab -n 5000000 -c 10 "http://localhost:8080/echo?msg=test"` to create traffic to the web server. The output from `go tool pprof` should look similar to the following:

```
$ go tool pprof -seconds=30 http://localhost:6060/debug/pprof/profile
Fetching profile over HTTP from http://localhost:6060/debug/pprof/profile?
seconds=30
Please wait... (30s)
Saved profile in /Users/mtsouk/pprof/pprof.profileHTTP.samples.cpu.008.pb.gz
File: profileHTTP
Type: cpu
Time: 2025-11-04 00:50:05 EET
Duration: 30.15s, Total samples = 42.65s (141.45%)
Entering interactive mode (type "help" for commands, "o" for options)
(pprof)
```

The output confirms that the Go CPU profiler successfully collected performance samples while your HTTP server was running. It shows which parts of the program consumed the most CPU time, including time spent on system calls and Go runtime operations, and can indicate concurrent activity across multiple logical CPU cores due to goroutines running in parallel. The profiler stores this data locally, which can later be analyzed using `go tool pprof` to generate reports, inspect function-level CPU usage, and visualize call graphs. This information helps identify performance bottlenecks and optimize critical code paths. For a full guide to exploring and interpreting profiles, you should refer to the official documentation at `https://pkg.go.dev/net/http/pprof`. Executing the `top` command on the interactive shell summarizes where the CPU spent its time during the profiling session:

```
$ (pprof) top
Showing nodes accounting for 41.07s, 96.30% of 42.65s total
Dropped 267 nodes (cum <= 0.21s)
Showing top 10 nodes out of 116
```

```
      flat  flat%   sum%           cum   cum%
    19.31s 45.28% 45.28%        19.32s 45.30%  syscall.syscall
     7.80s 18.29% 63.56%         7.80s 18.29%  runtime.kevent
     4.64s 10.88% 74.44%         4.64s 10.88%  runtime.pthread_cond_wait
     3.27s  7.67% 82.11%         3.27s  7.67%  runtime.usleep
     2.93s  6.87% 88.98%         2.93s  6.87%  runtime.pthread_cond_signal
     1.97s  4.62% 93.60%         1.97s  4.62%  syscall.syscall6
     0.76s  1.78% 95.38%         0.76s  1.78%  runtime.pthread_kill
     0.24s  0.56% 95.94%         0.24s  0.56%  runtime.madvise
     0.08s  0.19% 96.13%         0.25s  0.59%  runtime.scanobject
     0.07s  0.16% 96.30%         1.25s  2.93%  runtime.gcDrain
```

The report shows that out of a total of 42.65 seconds of sampled CPU time, 41.07 seconds (96.3%) are accounted for by the top functions, while the remaining nodes each consumed very little time and were dropped from the display. The `flat` column shows the amount of time spent directly in each function, while the `cum` column shows the cumulative time including calls to other functions. Here, the largest single consumer is `syscall.syscall`, which took 19.31 seconds or 45.28% of total time, indicating that a significant portion of the program execution involves system calls. The next largest contributors are `runtime.kevent` (7.8s, 18.29%) and `runtime.pthread_cond_wait` (4.64s, 10.88%), reflecting time spent waiting on kernel-level events or condition variables, typical in network I/O and synchronization. Other functions, such as `runtime.usleep` and `runtime.pthread_cond_signal`, also indicate waiting or signaling among goroutines. Lesser contributors, such as `runtime.madvise` and `runtime.gcDrain`, suggest occasional memory management and garbage collection activity. This output indicates that most CPU time during this profiling period is consumed by the runtime and OS-level operations related to I/O and goroutine scheduling, rather than the application's own computation, which is typical for an HTTP server that spends much of its time waiting for requests.

After exploring how to measure the performance characteristics of a web service through profiling, the next logical step is to ensure that it behaves correctly. In the following section, we shift our focus from performance analysis to *testing HTTP applications,* where we verify that each endpoint produces the expected results.

Testing HTTP applications

Testing HTTP applications is slightly different from testing regular functions because you are dealing with network interactions, request handling, and structured responses. Instead of directly calling functions and checking return values, you *simulate HTTP requests* and inspect the resulting responses — including status codes, headers, and body content. This approach lets you verify that your handlers, routes, and middleware all work together as intended, without actually running a full server. The `net/http/httptest` package provides everything you need to perform these realistic yet lightweight HTTP tests efficiently – this is illustrated in `ch09/profileHTTP_test.go`, where the `TestEndpoints()` function is a unit test written in Go using the `testing` package, designed to verify the behavior of multiple HTTP endpoints of the server:

```
func TestEndpoints(t *testing.T) {
    tests := []struct {
        method       string
        path         string
        expectString string
        body         []byte
    }{
        {"GET", "/", "Welcome to the Go Web Service!", nil},
        {"GET", "/time", `"time":`, nil},
        {"GET", "/echo", `"echo":"No message provided"`, nil},
        {"POST", "/echo", `"echo":{"msg":"hello"}`, []byte(`{"msg":"hello"}`)},
        {"GET", "/headers", `"User-Agent"`, nil},
        {"GET", "/health", "OK", nil},
    }

    for _, tt := range tests {
        rr := executeRequest(t, tt.method, tt.path, tt.body)
        if rr.Code != http.StatusOK {
            t.Errorf("%s %s: expected status 200, got %d", tt.method, tt.path,
rr.Code)
        }

        if !strings.Contains(rr.Body.String(), tt.expectString) {
            t.Errorf("%s %s: expected body to contain %q, got %q", tt.method,
tt.path, tt.expectString, rr.Body.String())
        }
    }
}
```

The code first defines a slice of anonymous structs called `tests`, where each struct specifies four fields: the HTTP method (`method`), the URL path to request (`path`), a string expected to appear in the response body (`expectString`), and an optional request body (`body`) for methods such as `POST`. The test data includes `GET` requests for the root path `/`, the `/time` endpoint, the `/echo` endpoint (with and without a query message), the `/headers` endpoint, and the `/health` endpoint, as well as a POST request to /echo with a JSON payload. The function then iterates over each test case using a for loop. For each test case, it calls executeRequest(), a helper function that constructs an httptest.Request and passes it through the appropriate handler wrapped in loggingMiddleware(). The returned ResponseRecorder captures the server response. The test first checks whether the HTTP status code returned is 200 OK; if not, it reports an error with t.Errorf() showing the method, path, expected status, and actual status. Next, it verifies that the response body contains the expected string, which ensures the endpoint behaves as intended. If the expected content is missing, another error is reported, showing the actual response body. This approach allows multiple endpoints to be tested systematically in a single function while keeping the tests concise and readable. Now, execute the tests on your machine to get an output similar to the following:

```
$ cd ch09
$ go test -v profileHTTP_test.go profileHTTP.go
=== RUN   TestEndpoints
[GET] / 192.0.2.1:1234
Completed in 23.208µs
[GET] /time 192.0.2.1:1234
Completed in 353.542µs
[GET] /echo 192.0.2.1:1234
Completed in 3.792µs
[POST] /echo 192.0.2.1:1234
Completed in 28.084µs
[GET] /headers 192.0.2.1:1234
Completed in 6.208µs
[GET] /health 192.0.2.1:1234
Completed in 3.25µs
--- PASS: TestEndpoints (0.00s)
PASS
ok      command-line-arguments    (cached)
```

The last line of output confirms that all test cases passed successfully, and the results were retrieved from the *build cache* since no code changes required recompilation.

In practice, testing HTTP services in Go follows a straightforward workflow: create or configure the handler under test, simulate an HTTP request using the httptest utilities, and then validate the response produced by the handler. This pattern allows developers to verify endpoint behavior without running a full server, making tests fast, reliable, and easy to automate.

Now that you have seen how to test, profile, and measure the performance of Go web services, it is important to consider another key aspect of building reliable servers: *managing the lifecycle of requests*. In real-world systems, requests may need to be canceled, timed out, or coordinated with other operations such as database queries or external API calls. Go addresses this challenge through the `context` package, which provides a standardized way to propagate cancellation signals, deadlines, and request-scoped values across API boundaries.

The context package

Imagine you and your friends are playing a game where you must do different tasks — such as running, jumping, or solving puzzles. Someone is holding a stopwatch and says, *"You only have 2 minutes!"*. When the time is up, everyone must stop, no matter what they are doing. Introduced in Go 1.7 and essential for building robust concurrent applications, the `context` package enables you to gracefully handle timeouts, implement cancellation patterns, and pass request metadata through call chains. For example, if your program is waiting for a slow website, the context can say, *"Time is up, stop waiting!"*. Or, if the user closes the app, the context tells all running parts to stop working, so nothing is left hanging. In simple terms, `context` helps programs stay organized and stop work when it is no longer needed, just like a coach blowing a whistle to end the game. Strictly speaking, the `context` package in Go provides a standardized way to carry deadlines, cancellation signals, and request-scoped values across API boundaries and between goroutines. By creating a tree-like hierarchy of contexts that can be canceled independently or together, it helps prevent resource leaks and allows for clean shutdown of long-running operations, making it indispensable for HTTP servers, database operations, and any scenario where you need to coordinate the lifecycle of concurrent processes. Through `context.WithCancel()`, `context.WithTimeout()`, or `context.WithDeadline()`, you can derive new contexts that automatically cancel operations when a condition is met — such as a timeout or explicit cancellation. While this example demonstrates interaction between a client and server, the same pattern applies broadly in distributed systems: microservices, internal APIs, message queues, or any architecture with multiple downstream components. Contexts allow services to propagate cancellation and deadlines through a chain of calls, ensuring that work stops promptly when no longer needed and resources are used efficiently. This makes context indispensable not just for local goroutines but for coordinating work across modern, concurrent, and distributed Go applications. Here is a code example (`ch09/useContext.go`) that illustrates the `context` package:

```
func doWork(ctx context.Context) {
    for {
        select {
        case <-ctx.Done():
            fmt.Println("Work canceled:", ctx.Err())
```

```
            return
        default:
            fmt.Print("Working... ")
            time.Sleep(500 * time.Millisecond)
        }
    }
}

func main() {
    ctx, cancel := context.WithTimeout(context.Background(), 2*time.Second)
    defer cancel() // Always call cancel to release resources
    fmt.Println("Starting work")
    doWork(ctx)
    fmt.Println("Finished")
}
```

In this example, the `main()` function creates a context with a two-second timeout using `context.WithTimeout()`. The `doWork()` function simulates a continuous task by printing `"Working..."` in a loop. Inside the loop, it uses a `select` statement to listen for `ctx.Done()`, which signals when the context is canceled — either due to the timeout or an explicit cancellation. Once the context is done, `doWork()` stops gracefully and prints the cancellation reason. This pattern is directly applicable to HTTP handlers and downstream calls: by passing a context through your request handling chain, you can ensure that long-running operations, database queries, or external API requests are automatically canceled when the client disconnects or a timeout occurs, preventing wasted resources and improving service responsiveness.

Now, imagine you are playing the game we described earlier, but this time each player has a badge showing their name and team color. Whenever they pass through different game stations, the people running the stations can look at the badge to know who the player is and what team they belong to. That is what the *key–value feature* of the `context` package does; it lets you attach little bits of information to the context. Then, when the context is passed around your program, any function can check those *"badges"* to learn more about what is going on. Here is such a code example as presented in `ch09/keyValContext.go`:

```
func main() {
    // Create a base context
    ctx := context.Background()

    // Derive a new context with key-value data
    ctx = context.WithValue(ctx, "userID", 42)
```

```
    ctx = context.WithValue(ctx, "role", "admin")
    processRequest(ctx)
}

func processRequest(ctx context.Context) {
    userID := ctx.Value("userID")
    role := ctx.Value("role")
    if userID != nil && role != nil {
        fmt.Printf("Processing request for user %v with role %v\n", userID, role)
    } else {
        fmt.Println("Missing user information in context")
    }
}
```

This example starts by creating a base context with `context.Background()`. Then, two key–value pairs are attached using `context.WithValue()`, where `"userID"` and `"role"` serve as keys. These values are stored within the new context and can be safely passed down the call chain. The `processRequest()` function receives the context and retrieves the stored values using `ctx.Value(key)`. In practice, this pattern is useful for carrying request metadata — such as authentication details, trace IDs, or configuration settings — throughout your application without changing every function signature. Run `ch09/keyValContext.go` on your machine:

```
$ ch09/keyValContext.go
Processing request for user 42 with role admin
```

You might ask, *"Why not use a structure instead?"*, which is a valid question. You absolutely can use a structure instead of storing data in a `context`, and in many cases, that is actually better. The main reason to use `context.WithValue()` is for request-scoped data that should *travel automatically across function calls* — for example, a user ID that follows a web request through middleware, handlers, and database calls. However, using a `struct` is often clearer when the data belongs logically to your application, not to the *context* of the request. For example, configuration data, database connections, or large objects should live in well-defined structs, not in `context`. Think of it like this: a `struct` is your backpack (you decide what to carry and when), while a `context` is like a shared clipboard that travels with a task so everyone can jot down quick notes about the request.

The last use of context is going to be related to the HTTP protocol, as presented in `ch09/httpContext.go`, which contains the following example code that shows how context helps prevent long-running or stuck operations from wasting resources:

```
func slowOperation(ctx context.Context) (string, error) {
    select {
    case <-time.After(3 * time.Second):
        return "Operation completed successfully!", nil
    case <-ctx.Done():
        return "", ctx.Err()
    }
}

func handler(w http.ResponseWriter, r *http.Request) {
    // Create a new context with a 2-second timeout
    ctx, cancel := context.WithTimeout(r.Context(), 2*time.Second)
    defer cancel()

    result, err := slowOperation(ctx)
    if err != nil {
        http.Error(w, fmt.Sprintf("Request canceled: %v", err),
http.StatusRequestTimeout)
        return
    }

    fmt.Fprintln(w, result)
}

func main() {
    http.HandleFunc("/", handler)
    fmt.Println("Server running on http://localhost:8080")
    http.ListenAndServe(":8080", nil)
}
```

This web server listens on port `8080` and handles incoming HTTP requests. Inside the handler, it creates a child context with a two-second timeout using `context.WithTimeout()`. Then it calls `slowOperation()`, which simulates a task that takes three seconds to finish. Because the timeout is shorter than the operation, the context's `Done()` channel triggers first, and the handler returns an HTTP 408 (Request Timeout) response. In a real web service, you might use the same idea to cancel database queries, API calls, or background jobs when the client disconnects or the timeout expires. Now that you understand how to manage cancellations, deadlines, and request-scoped data with the `context` package, let us move on to something more practical: *building a proxy server*.

Creating a proxy server

A **proxy server** is an intermediary system that sits between a client (such as a web browser) and a target server, handling requests and responses on behalf of the client. Instead of connecting directly to the destination, the client sends its request to the proxy, which then forwards it to the intended server, retrieves the response, and passes it back to the client. This extra middle step can serve many purposes: improving security by hiding client IP addresses, controlling access to resources, caching frequently requested data for faster responses, filtering or modifying traffic, and even monitoring network activity. In essence, a proxy server acts as a controlled gateway, giving you the ability to inspect, manipulate, or optimize the flow of network communication. Creating a proxy server is a classic exercise in systems programming that offers a hands-on way to explore how data flows between clients and servers, how connections are managed, and how protocols such as HTTP can be intercepted, analyzed, and modified on the fly. The proxy implementation is found in `ch09/httpProxy.go` – we are going to explain its most important components without presenting any code here; feel free to look at the code while reading this.

Due to the Proxy length, we will discuss its architecture conceptually; consult the source code for full implementation details. The `Proxy` structure encapsulates all state and dependencies, including the TCP listener, a logger for runtime messages, a quit channel for system signals and a `WaitGroup` to track active client sessions. The `NewProxy()` function constructs the server, setting up the listener, a prefixed logger, and a cancellable `context.Context` that responds to OS signals such as `SIGINT` or `SIGTERM`. Once initialized, the `Start()` method enters the main event loop: it accepts incoming client connections, handing each to a separate goroutine for concurrent handling via `handleClient()`. The loop monitors the context for cancellation and distinguishes normal shutdowns from errors. The `Shutdown()` method ensures a clean exit by closing the listener and waiting for all active goroutines to finish, logging a confirmation once complete. This design — combining context cancellation and `WaitGroup` synchronization — provides a robust mechanism for graceful, coordinated shutdowns while keeping all server state encapsulated within the `Proxy` type.

Each client connection is handled by `handleClient()`, which manages the full lifecycle: accepting the connection, processing the request, and shutting down cleanly. The function parses the incoming HTTP request, sanitizes it, and either forwards it to the target server or establishes a `CONNECT` tunnel for HTTPS. Responses are relayed back to the client and data copying in both directions is managed concurrently using goroutines with a shared `context.WithCancel()`, ensuring that when one side closes, all related operations terminate gracefully. Read deadlines and header sanitization protect the server while bridging raw TCP streams with structured HTTP traffic efficiently.

With all that information in mind, run `ch09/httpProxy.go` on your machine and then issue the `curl -x http://127.0.0.1:8080 https://www.mtsoukalos.eu/` command to test it. The generated output should be similar to the following:

```
$ go run ch09/httpProxy.go
[PROXY] 2025/10/31 10:04:32 httpProxy.go:49: Proxy server starting on :8080
[PROXY] 2025/10/31 10:05:36 httpProxy.go:94: Accepted connection from
127.0.0.1:59035
[PROXY] 2025/10/31 10:05:36 httpProxy.go:112: Client 127.0.0.1:59035 requested
CONNECT //www.mtsoukalos.eu:443
[PROXY] 2025/10/31 10:05:36 httpProxy.go:176: Handling HTTPS CONNECT for
www.mtsoukalos.eu:443 from 127.0.0.1:59035
[PROXY] 2025/10/31 10:05:37 httpProxy.go:221: CONNECT tunnel closed for
www.mtsoukalos.eu:443 from 127.0.0.1:59035
^C[PROXY] 2025/10/31 10:10:17 httpProxy.go:72: Shutting down proxy server...
[PROXY] 2025/10/31 10:10:17 httpProxy.go:76: Proxy server shut down gracefully.
[PROXY] 2025/10/31 10:10:17 httpProxy.go:58: Listener closed - stopping accept
loop.
```

The logs illustrate the **accept–handle–shutdown lifecycle**: accepting client connections, processing HTTP/HTTPS requests (including `CONNECT` tunnels) and shutting down cleanly. Each log line captures timing, client addresses, and actions, giving a clear view of the proxy's runtime behavior. The last three lines of the output are created after pressing *Ctrl* + *C* on the terminal.

Now that you have seen how to create a proxy server that forwards and filters requests, it is time to take a step further and build something of your own. In the next section, we will develop a complete web service from scratch — one that defines its own routes, handles JSON data, and responds to clients directly instead of relaying traffic.

Developing a web service

Developing a web service builds on the same foundations as creating an HTTP server, but takes the concept further by structuring your server to provide data and functionality over HTTP in a consistent, machine-readable format. Typically, this means exposing endpoints that respond with JSON, allowing clients to interact with your application programmatically. Using the `net/http` package, you can easily define routes, implement request handlers, and return structured responses. Carefully designing your web services is essential because good design establishes the foundation for reliability, scalability, and maintainability. A well-thought-out design clarifies how your service will handle requests, manage resources, and recover from errors long before any code is written. This planning helps you define clear APIs, choose the right data formats, and establish consistent naming and routing conventions that make your service easier for others to use and extend. It also allows you to identify performance bottlenecks early, ensuring that your service can scale smoothly as traffic grows. Just as importantly, good design helps you separate concerns and concepts — keeping business logic, network handling, and data persistence distinct — which simplifies debugging and testing.

The following example illustrates a complete Go web service that ties together many of the ideas we have discussed. Think of this as the chapter's centerpiece: a concrete demonstration of how Go's HTTP handling, routing, and JSON responses can be combined in practice. So, we will focus on the essential steps for building a **note-taking web service**, including setting up routes, handling different HTTP methods, and sending JSON data back to clients. The note-taking web service is a simple, RESTful API designed primarily for teaching purposes. It allows users to create, read, update, and delete notes, each of which consists of an *ID*, *title*, and *content*. The server exposes the following endpoints: `POST /notes` to create a new note, accepting a JSON body with title and content; `GET /notes` to list all notes, with an optional `?title=` query parameter for filtering by title; `GET /notes/{id}` to retrieve a specific note by its ID; `PUT /notes/{id}` to update an existing note with new title and content; and `DELETE /notes/{id}` to remove a note. Optional middleware-style logging prints request method, URL, status, and duration. The most interesting part of it is the implementation of the `main()` function, as found in `ch09/notes/server/server.go`:

```
func main() {
    loadNotes()

    mux := http.NewServeMux()

    // /notes routes
    mux.HandleFunc("GET /notes", loggingMiddleware(listNotesHandler))
    mux.HandleFunc("POST /notes", loggingMiddleware(createNoteHandler))

    // /notes/{id} routes
    mux.HandleFunc("GET /notes/", loggingMiddleware(getNoteHandler))
    mux.HandleFunc("PUT /notes/", loggingMiddleware(updateNoteHandler))
    mux.HandleFunc("DELETE /notes/", loggingMiddleware(deleteNoteHandler))

    fmt.Println("Starting note-taking server on http://localhost:8080")
    if err := http.ListenAndServe(":8080", mux); err != nil {
```

```
        panic(err)
    }
}
```

The code begins by calling `loadNotes()` to read any existing data. It then creates a `ServeMux` and registers each route using the new method-prefixed syntax, wrapping all handlers with `loggingMiddleware()` to record requests and processing times. The `/notes` routes handle the full collection, using `listNotesHandler()` for `GET` requests and `createNoteHandler()` for `POST` requests. The `/notes/` routes operate on individual notes identified by ID, supporting `GET`, `PUT`, and `DELETE` operations via `getNoteHandler()`, `updateNoteHandler()`, and `deleteNoteHandler()`. Finally, the server prints a startup message with its address and begins handling requests with `http.ListenAndServe()`, using the configured `ServeMux`. Behind the scenes, `loadNotes()` and `saveNotes()` synchronize the in-memory notes map with the JSON file, while `writeJSON()` ensures consistent JSON responses with appropriate headers and encoding. With all the information in mind, let us try executing the note server:

```
$ cd ch09/notes/server
$ go run server.go
Starting note-taking server on http://localhost:8080
```

After running the server process, let us test it with the following `curl(1)` commands:

```
$ curl -X POST http://localhost:8080/notes \
  -H "Content-Type: application/json" \
  -d '{"title": "First Note", "content": "This is my first note."}'
{"id":2,"title":"First Note","content":"This is my first note."}
$ curl -X GET http://localhost:8080/notes
[{"id":1,"title":"Shopping","content":"Buy milk"},{"id":2,"title":"First
Note","content":"This is my first note."}]
$ curl -X DELETE http://localhost:8080/notes/1
$ curl -X GET http://localhost:8080/notes/1
Note not found
```

The first command inserts a note, and the second command gets a list of the existing notes, whereas the third command deletes the note we inserted earlier. The last command verifies the deletion of the note. The generated output at the terminal window of the server is going to look as follows:

```
[POST] /notes [::1]:60169
Completed in 405.958µs
[GET] /notes [::1]:60170
Completed in 79.292µs
[DELETE] /notes/1 [::1]:60172
Completed in 235.583µs
[GET] /notes/1 [::1]:60173
Completed in 5.333µs
```

This output confirms that the server handled different operations (creating, listing, deleting, and retrieving notes) correctly and responded with very low latency.

Another technique for testing the server is writing a separate Go program to do so. In our case, the program is `ch09/notes/testServer.go`. We are going to present the important code in multiple chunks, starting with the `createNote()` function, which demonstrates how a Go client can send JSON data to a REST API using a `POST` request:

```
func createNote(title, content string) error {
    note := Note{Title: title, Content: content}
    data, _ := json.Marshal(note)

    resp, err := http.Post(baseURL+"/notes", "application/json",
bytes.NewBuffer(data))
    if err != nil {
        return fmt.Errorf("error creating note: %w", err)
    }
    defer resp.Body.Close()
    if resp.StatusCode != http.StatusCreated {
        return fmt.Errorf("create note failed with status: %s", resp.Status)
    }
    fmt.Println("Created new note successfully!")
    return printJSON(resp.Body)
}
```

The code begins by constructing a `Note` struct from the given `title` and `content` and then *serializes this struct into JSON* using `json.Marshal()`. The resulting *byte slice* is wrapped with `bytes.NewBuffer()` so it can be sent as the request body. The function then calls `http.Post()` to send the data to the /notes endpoint, specifying "application/json" as the content type to indicate that the payload is JSON. If an error occurs during the request, it returns a descriptive wrapped error. After ensuring the response body is closed with `defer resp.Body.Close()`, the function checks whether the server responded with a `201 Created` status, which confirms that the note was successfully added. If not, it returns an error describing the failed status. When the request succeeds, it prints a confirmation message and calls `printJSON()` to display the server JSON response in a readable format.

The remaining functions in the program follow a similar structure and logic to `createNote()`: they build an HTTP request, send it to the appropriate endpoint, check the response status, and handle the JSON data accordingly. Each function, however, targets a different HTTP method and purpose. For example, `listNotes()` sends a `GET` request to retrieve all notes, `getNote()` fetches a specific note by ID, `updateNote()` uses a `PUT` request to modify an existing note, and `deleteNote()` issues a `DELETE` request to remove a note. Despite these differences, they all share the same core approach: constructing the request, processing the response, and providing user-friendly feedback.

Next, we are going to try the utility while the server is running:

```
$ go run ch09/notes/testServer.go
. . .
Created new note successfully!
{
  "content": "This is the first note.",
  "id": 3,
  "title": "First note"
}
...
Listing all notes:
[
  {
    "content": "This is the first note.",
    "id": 3,
    "title": "First note"
  },
...
]
get note failed with status: 404 Not Found
update note failed with status: 404 Not Found
Deleted note with ID 2 successfully.
```

```
Listing all notes:
[
  {
    "content": "This is the first note.",
    "id": 3,
    "title": "First note"
  },
  {
    "content": "This is the second note.",
    "id": 4,
    "title": "Second note"
  }
]
```

The output shows the step-by-step interaction between the sample client and the note-taking HTTP server. The client first creates two new notes successfully, as indicated by the `Created new note successfully!` messages, each followed by a JSON representation of the new note returned by the server (the output is abbreviated for clarity). The IDs (3 and 4) show that previous notes existed in the database file (`notes.json`), so the counter continues from there. When the client lists all notes, the server responds with an array of three entries — two newly created notes and an older note with ID 2. The subsequent `get note failed with status: 404 Not Found` and `update note failed with status: 404 Not Found` messages mean that the client tried to retrieve and update a note with ID `1`, but no such note exists on the server. Next, the client successfully deletes the note with ID `2`, as confirmed by `Deleted note with ID 2 successfully`. Finally, when listing all notes again, the response correctly shows only the remaining two notes — IDs 3 and 4 — confirming that the deletion was processed and persisted by the server.

The modular test Go code we just wrote for interacting with the note-taking server can be directly transferred into a Cobra-based CLI program with minimal changes. Each function — `listNotes()`, `getNote()`, `createNote()`, `updateNote()`, and `deleteNote()` — encapsulates a single REST operation and handles both HTTP errors and success responses. By reusing these same functions inside Cobra commands, we separate the HTTP logic from the command-line interface logic, making the code cleaner, easier to maintain, and more reusable. This technique is highly effective for building CLI clients: you can first test all API interactions in a standalone Go program, then simply plug those functions into Cobra command handlers. It ensures that your HTTP interactions are correct before adding CLI-specific concerns. So, this is what we will present next!

Developing a client for the web service

In this section, we will build a command-line client for the note-taking service using *Cobra* and *Viper* that can interact with the RESTful web service. It exposes intuitive commands corresponding to the supported endpoints: `list` to retrieve all notes, with an optional `--title` filter; `create` to add a new note by specifying `--title` and `--content`; `get` to fetch a note by its ID; `update` to modify an existing note's title or content; and `delete` to remove a note. In order to create a skeleton of the command-line client, you should execute the following commands:

```
$ cd ch09/notes/client # Create the directory if it does not exist
$ go mod init notecli
$ ~/go/bin/cobra init
$ ~/go/bin/cobra add list
$ ~/go/bin/cobra add get
$ ~/go/bin/cobra add add
$ ~/go/bin/cobra add update
$ ~/go/bin/cobra add delete
```

After the last command, the structure of the directory should look as follows:

```
$ tree
.
├── cmd
│   ├── add.go
│   ├── delete.go
│   ├── get.go
│   ├── list.go
│   ├── root.go
│   └── update.go
├── go.mod
├── go.sum
├── LICENSE
└── main.go
2 directories, 10 files
```

After that, we are ready to start implementing the commands by working with the files found in the `cmd` directory.

Implementing the commands

In this section, we focus on the two most important parts of the Cobra-based note client: the `root.go` and `add.go` files. The `root.go` file defines the main command of the CLI application and serves as the entry point for all subcommands, setting up global flags and configuration. The `add.go` file, on the other hand, implements the functionality for creating a new note through the command line, using the same HTTP client logic we developed earlier. The remaining command files — `get.go`, `list.go`, `update.go`, and `delete.go` — follow the same overall structure and logic as `add.go`. Each defines a Cobra command with its own `Run()` function that interacts with the note-taking server using HTTP requests. The only difference lies in the specific HTTP method and endpoint they target: `get.go` retrieves a single note, `list.go` lists all notes, `update.go` modifies an existing note, and `delete.go` removes one. This consistent design makes the code easy to extend with new commands if needed. Here is the example code of `cmd/root.go`:

```
package cmd

import (
    "fmt"
    "os"

    "github.com/spf13/cobra"
)

var baseURL string
var rootCmd = &cobra.Command{
    Use:   "notescli",
    Short: "A CLI client for the Go note-taking web service",
    Long: `notescli communicates with a running note-taking HTTP server to
create, list, update, and delete notes.`,
}

// Execute runs the root command.
func Execute() {
    if err := rootCmd.Execute(); err != nil {
        fmt.Println(err)
        os.Exit(1)
    }
}

func init() {
```

```
    rootCmd.PersistentFlags().StringVar(&baseURL, "url", "http://localhost:8080",
"Base URL of the note server")
}
```

The `root.go` file defines the foundation of the utility. It first declares a global `baseURL` variable to store the address of the running note-taking server, which can be customized by the user. The `rootCmd` variable is a Cobra command representing the top-level CLI command, `notescli`. It includes a short description for quick help and a longer description explaining the overall purpose of the CLI: interacting with the Go note-taking HTTP server to create, list, update, and delete notes. The `Execute()` function is the entry point that runs the root command and exits the program with an error code if execution fails. Finally, the `init()` function (a special function that is automatically executed before `main()`) sets up a *persistent flag*, `--url`, allowing users to override the default server URL. All subcommands, such as `add` or `delete`, are attached to this root command, inheriting the base URL flag and forming the structure of the CLI.

Next, here is the example code of `cmd/add.go`:

```
package cmd

import (
    "bytes"
    "encoding/json"
    "fmt"
    "net/http"

    "github.com/spf13/cobra"
)

type Note struct {
    ID      int    `json:"id"`
    Title   string `json:"title"`
    Content string `json:"content"`
}

var addCmd = &cobra.Command{
    Use:   "add",
    Short: "Add a new note",
    RunE: func(cmd *cobra.Command, args []string) error {
        note := Note{Title: title, Content: content}
        data, _ := json.Marshal(note)
```

```
        resp, err := http.Post(baseURL+"/notes", "application/json",
bytes.NewBuffer(data))
        if err != nil {
            return fmt.Errorf("error creating note: %w", err)
        }
        defer resp.Body.Close()

        if resp.StatusCode != http.StatusCreated {
            return fmt.Errorf("server returned: %s", resp.Status)
        }
        fmt.Println("Note created successfully!")
        return nil
    },
}

var title, content string

func init() {
    rootCmd.AddCommand(addCmd)
    addCmd.Flags().StringVarP(&title, "title", "t", "", "Note title")
    addCmd.Flags().StringVarP(&content, "content", "c", "", "Note content")
    addCmd.MarkFlagRequired("title")
    addCmd.MarkFlagRequired("content")
}
```

The code defines a `Note` struct to match the JSON structure expected by the server, with fields for `ID`, `Title`, and `Content`. The `addCmd` variable is a Cobra command configured to run when the user invokes `notescli add` (or `go run main.go add`). Its `RunE` function is executed for the command: it creates a `Note` using the `title` and `content` flags, marshals it into JSON and sends it to the server via an HTTP `POST` request to the `/notes` endpoint. If the request fails or the server responds with a status other than `201 Created`, it returns an error. Otherwise, it prints a success message. The `init()` function registers `addCmd` as a subcommand of the root command and defines two *required* flags, `--title` (or `-t`) and `--content` (or `-c`), ensuring the user must provide both values to create a note.

We can now interact with the note-taking server as follows:

```
$ go run main.go add -t "Book Idea" -c "Write about Go middleware"
Note created successfully!
$ go run main.go list
```

```
[3] First note - This is the first note.
[5] Book Idea - Write about Go middleware
[4] Second note - This is the second note.
$ go run main.go get 1
Error: server returned: 404 Not Found
$ go run main.go get 3
[3] First note - This is the first note.
$ go run main.go update 3 -t "Updated title" -c "Improved note content"
Note updated successfully!
$ go run main.go delete 3
Note deleted successfully.
```

Having explored how to build a Go-based web service and interact with it via a command-line client, we now turn our attention to monitoring: in the next section, we will learn how to *read metrics from Prometheus.*

Reading data from Prometheus

Reading data from Prometheus involves interacting with one of the most popular monitoring and time-series databases in modern systems. Prometheus communicates primarily over HTTP: applications expose metrics at a path (usually `/metrics`) that Prometheus scrapes at regular intervals, and Prometheus provides an HTTP API that allows clients to query its time series database using PromQL (**Prometheus Query Language**). This API supports retrieving raw metrics, aggregated statistics, and metadata. To explore these capabilities with our Go utility, we first need some sample metrics — let us create them in the next section.

Creating sample data for Prometheus

In this subsection, we will create sample metrics and push them to Prometheus so that we have meaningful values to retrieve later using `ch09/Prometheus/sampleData.go`. The program is designed to simulate realistic Prometheus metrics and optionally push them to a Pushgateway, which is a component of the Prometheus monitoring ecosystem designed for scenarios where your application cannot be scraped directly by Prometheus, but it can also run without any server. It begins by defining global configuration variables — `pushURL`, `interval`, and `backfillDays` — which are set through command-line flags in the `init()` function, while also seeding the random number generator to ensure varied simulation values. Three metric types are defined as Go structs: `cpuMetric` for CPU usage by core and mode, `memMetric` for memory usage by type, and `httpMetric` for HTTP request counts by handler, method, and status code. In the `main()` function, initial metric slices for CPU, memory, and HTTP requests are populated with example values. The program then calls `backfillMetrics()`, which repeatedly generates metrics and updates their values to mimic historical data. This historical backfill does not use timestamps in the metric output, keeping the metrics compatible with the Pushgateway. Metric generation is handled by the `generateMetrics()` function, which builds Prometheus-compliant payloads as a `byte` buffer, iterating over each metric slice and formatting it with labels and values. The `pushMetrics()` function attempts to send this payload to the configured Pushgateway URL via an HTTP `POST`, returning an error if the server is unreachable or responds with a non-2xx status code. We create updated metrics using `updateMetrics()`, which simulates realistic patterns: CPU values follow day/night sinusoidal cycles with small random noise, memory values slowly fluctuate with a sinusoidal trend, and HTTP requests exhibit random bursts to mimic traffic spikes.

It is now time to try the utility using the Prometheus Docker image, which can be executed using `ch09/Prometheus/docker-compose.yaml`:

```
$ cd ch09/Prometheus
$ docker-compose up
. . . Lots of output
```

After that, you are ready to run `ch09/Prometheus/sampleData.go`:

```
$ go run ch09/Prometheus/sampleData.go --push-url http://localhost:9091/metrics/
job/testjob --backfill-days 7
Starting realistic simulation for 7 days...
Backfill progress:   4% (100/2016 steps)
. . .
Backfill progress:  99% (2000/2016 steps)
Backfill complete. Exiting.
```

This output shows that `sampleData.go` is simulating and pushing Prometheus metrics for a seven-day period. It tracks progress in steps, reporting completion percentages as it backfills historical data and confirms when the process finishes successfully.

With our sample metrics now flowing into Prometheus, it is time to put them to use. In the next section, we will build a Go utility that connects to Prometheus, retrieves metric data, and presents it in a readable, structured way.

Implementing the utility

With our sample data in place, we can now focus on writing the Go utility that connects to Prometheus, sends queries, and reads back the metrics we created. Here are the most important parts of `ch09/Prometheus/readProm.go`, starting from its structures:

```
type InstantResponse struct {
    Status string `json:"status"`
    Data   struct {
        Result []struct {
            Value []interface{} `json:"value"`
        } `json:"result"`
    } `json:"data"`
    Error     string `json:"error"`
    ErrorType string `json:"errorType"`
}
type RangeResponse struct {
    Status string `json:"status"`
    Data   struct {
        Result []struct {
            Values [][]interface{} `json:"values"`
        } `json:"result"`
    } `json:"data"`
    Error     string `json:"error"`
    ErrorType string `json:"errorType"`
}
```

`InstantResponse` and `RangeResponse` are designed to model the JSON responses returned by the Prometheus HTTP API. The `InstantResponse` struct corresponds to the output of an *instant Prometheus query* (`/api/v1/query`). It contains a `Status` field to indicate whether the query succeeded or failed, a nested `Data` struct with a `Result` slice holding the query results – each result contains a `Value` field represented as a slice of `interface{}`. The `Value` slice typically holds two elements: the timestamp of the sample and the actual metric value, though it is typed generically as `interface{}` because JSON numbers or strings may appear. Similarly, `RangeResponse` models the JSON returned by a *range query* (`/api/v1/query_range`). It also contains a `Status` field and a nested `Data` struct, but its `Result` slice contains a `Values` field, which is a two-dimensional slice of `interface{}` (`[][]interface{}`). Each inner slice represents a `[timestamp, value]` pair, and the outer slice represents a sequence of samples over the requested time range. These structs allow Go programs to unmarshal Prometheus query responses directly into *strongly typed data structures* while still handling the dynamic nature of JSON numeric and string types.

Next, let us see the implementation of `listMetrics()`, which is designed to query a running Prometheus server and print all available metric names:

```
func listMetrics(baseURL string) {
    api := fmt.Sprintf("%s/api/v1/label/__name__/values", baseURL)
    resp, err := http.Get(api)
    if err != nil {
        fmt.Fprintf(os.Stderr, "Querying metric names: %v\n", err)
        os.Exit(1)
    }
    defer resp.Body.Close()
    body, _ := io.ReadAll(resp.Body)
    var result struct {
        Status string   `json:"status"`
        Data   []string `json:"data"`
    }
    if err := json.Unmarshal(body,&result); err != nil || result.Status !=
"success" {
        fmt.Fprintln(os.Stderr, "Invalid Prometheus response.")
        os.Exit(1)
    }

    sort.Strings(result.Data)
    fmt.Println("Metrics:")
    for _, name := range result.Data {
        fmt.Println(" -", name)
    }
}
```

The implementation starts by constructing the API URL for fetching metric names using the special Prometheus label endpoint `__name__/values`, which returns all metric identifiers in the database. The function then performs an HTTP `GET` request to this endpoint and checks for errors, immediately exiting with an error message if the request fails. After receiving a response, it reads the full body and attempts to parse it as JSON into a temporary struct with `Status` and `Data` fields. The `Data` field is a slice of strings, each representing a metric name. If parsing fails or the status returned by Prometheus is not `"success"`, the function prints an error and exits. Once the metric names are successfully retrieved, the function sorts them alphabetically to make the output more readable. Finally, it prints the list of metrics to standard output, prepending each name with a dash for clarity.

We are now ready to start using `ch09/Prometheus/readProm.go`, beginning with `--list`:

```
$ go run readProm.go --url http://127.0.0.1:9090 --list
Metrics:
. . .
 - go_threads
 - http_requests_total
 - node_cpu_seconds_total
 - node_memory_bytes
 - process_cpu_seconds_total
 - process_max_fds
 - process_network_receive_bytes_total
 - process_network_transmit_bytes_total
 - process_open_fds
 - process_resident_memory_bytes
. . .
 - scrape_duration_seconds
 - scrape_samples_post_metric_relabeling
 - scrape_samples_scraped
 - scrape_series_added
 - up
```

The metrics we created are `http_requests_total`, `node_cpu_seconds_total`, and `node_memory_bytes`. Next, let us see the contents of `node_cpu_seconds_total`:

```
$ go run ch09/Prometheus/readProm.go --url http://localhost:9090 --metric
node_cpu_seconds_total
2025-11-05T19:15:53+02:00  0.154915
2025-11-05T19:16:53+02:00  0.154915
2025-11-05T19:17:53+02:00  0.154915
. . .
```

The `--metric node_cpu_seconds_total` flag specifies that you want to query the CPU time metric, which is a counter that tracks the cumulative number of seconds the CPU has spent in various modes since the system started. Let us now be more specific and query specific labels from `node_cpu_seconds_total` with the help of `--labels`:

```
$ go run ch09/Prometheus/readProm.go --url http://127.0.0.1:9090 --metric
node_cpu_seconds_total --labels cpu=0,mode=idle
2025-11-05T19:15:53+02:00  0.154915
2025-11-05T19:16:53+02:00  0.154915
2025-11-05T19:17:53+02:00  0.154915
. . .
```

The `--labels cpu=0,mode=idle` flag is crucial because `node_cpu_seconds_total` is a *multi-dimensional metric* that has multiple label combinations. Without label filters, you would get data for all CPUs (`cpu=0`, `cpu=1`, `cpu=2`, etc.) and all CPU modes (`idle`, `user`, `system`, `iowait`, etc.), which could be overwhelming. By specifying these labels, you are telling the program you only want data for CPU number `0` (the first CPU core) when it is in `idle` mode. The program transforms this comma-separated list into Prometheus's query language syntax, converting it to `{cpu="0",mode="idle"}` and appending it to the metric name to create `node_cpu_seconds_total{cpu="0",mode="idle"}`, which is a complete query. Next, let us see the use of `--start` and `--end` in action for filtering the output based on time and date:

```
$ go run ch09/Prometheus/readProm.go --url http://127.0.0.1:9090 --metric
node_cpu_seconds_total --start 2025-11-01T00:00:00Z --end 2025-11-05T21:00:00Z
2025-11-05T19:16:00+02:00  0.154915
2025-11-05T19:17:00+02:00  0.154915
2025-11-05T19:18:00+02:00  0.154915
. . .
```

The `ch09/Prometheus/readProm.go` utility demonstrates the practical application of Go for building monitoring and observability tools. By providing a simple command-line interface to the Prometheus API, it enables quick data exploration and ad hoc queries without requiring the web UI or complex PromQL knowledge.

This chapter demonstrated how to build, test, and profile Go web services, covering HTTP routing, middleware, request handling, and integration with tools such as Prometheus. The examples emphasized best practices for logging, context-based cancellation, and concurrency, providing a solid foundation for writing reliable and efficient web services.

Summary

In this chapter, you have seen how Go's simplicity and strong standard library make it a first-class choice for web development. You started by understanding the `net/http` and `context` packages — the essential building blocks for networked applications — and advanced through creating proxy servers and profiling web workloads. Then, by developing a complete note-taking web service and a command-line client, you experienced firsthand how Go's design encourages clarity, reusability, and performance. You even learned how to read data from Prometheus!

With the skills you have gained in this chapter, you now understand how Go handles networking, concurrency, and communication between systems — all fundamental ideas in computer science. In the next chapter, we will shift gears and explore something even more ambitious: *writing your own programming language*. This journey will take you beneath the surface of the tools you have been using so far and into the world of *parsers*, *lexers*, and *interpreters*. By building a small language from scratch, you will see how programming languages translate human-readable instructions into the logic that computers can execute — and in doing so, you will deepen your understanding of how all code, including Go itself, truly works.

Exercises

1. Change the code of `ch09/simpleHTTP.go` to support signal handling.
2. The note-taking server stores its data in a JSON file. Modify it to store the data in a SQLite3 database! Next, modify it to store the data in XML format!
3. Change the name of the metrics in `ch09/Prometheus/sampleData.go` and read the new metrics using `ch09/Prometheus/readProm.go`.
4. Change `ch09/notes/server/server.go` to accept the port number as a command-line argument.

Additional resources

- The `ab` tool: `https://httpd.apache.org/docs/2.4/programs/ab.html` (Apache HTTP server benchmarking tool)
- Visit `https://prometheus.io/docs/prometheus/latest/querying/basics/` to learn more about PromQL.
- The `net/http/pprof` documentation: `https://pkg.go.dev/net/http/pprof`
- The `context` package documentation: `https://pkg.go.dev/context`

Get this book's PDF version and more

Scan the QR code (or go to `packtpub.com/unlock`). Search for this book by name, confirm the edition, and then follow the steps on the page.

UNLOCK NOW

Note: Keep your invoice handy. Purchases made directly from Packt don't require an invoice.

Part 3

Applications

The final part of the book is dedicated to the synthesis of your skills through the development of sophisticated, practical tools. We begin by constructing a custom programming language, SMALL, and extending it with advanced features to demonstrate how Go can be used to build complex, domain-specific systems. The focus of the remaining chapters shifts toward specialized data analysis and systems utilities, covering the mathematics and implementation of time series data mining. The section concludes with the creation of a high-performance indexer for UNIX files, applying the durability and concurrency principles discussed throughout the book. By completing these applications, you will have moved from theoretical knowledge to the craftsmanship required to engineer professional-grade systems that are durable, observable, and efficient.

This part of the book includes the following chapters:

- *Chapter 10, Writing a Programming Language*
- *Chapter 11, Adding New Features to SMALL*
- *Chapter 12, Time Series Distances*
- *Chapter 13, Time Series Data Mining*
- *Chapter 14, Creating an Index for UNIX Files*

10

Writing a Programming Language

Up to this point, we have explored the systems programming capabilities of Go, focusing on how to manipulate raw byte streams, carefully manage memory, and interact with the operating system. Building a programming language from scratch is the natural culmination of these concepts. There is no better way to understand core principles such as syntax trees, scope, and evaluation strategies than by building a programming language from scratch. In this chapter, we will construct the three pillars of an interpreter: a lexer to transform raw text into tokens, a parser to structure those tokens into a tree, and an evaluator to execute the code. The simplicity, the strong standard library, and the excellent tooling make Go an ideal choice for building interpreters or compilers from scratch. The name of our programming language is **SMALL**, and, in this chapter, we are going to create its first, minimal version, which we will enrich in *Chapter 11, Adding New Features to SMALL*.

This chapter covers the following topics:

- Defining the syntax of SMALL
- The components of a programming language: Lexer, parser, and evaluator
- Implementing SMALL and executing SMALL code

Let us now begin with why creating a programming language is good.

Why create a new programming language?

Creating your own programming language is a powerful way to deepen your understanding of how computers interpret and execute code as it forces you to bridge the gap between high-level ideas and machine-level operations. Beyond the educational value, a custom language can often solve domain-specific problems more elegantly than general-purpose languages, offering a concise and expressive way to describe computations. For instance, regular expressions and SQL are classic domain-specific languages that allow developers to parse complex text patterns or query databases far more succinctly than equivalent routines written in C or Go.

Before we can build the parser, we must first establish the blueprint of our language by formally defining the syntax and grammar rules of SMALL.

Defining the syntax of SMALL

To formally define the structure of our language, we use **Extended Backus–Naur Form (EBNF)**. EBNF is a standard notation in computer science used to describe the syntax of programming languages with mathematical precision. Unlike natural language, which can be ambiguous, EBNF defines exactly which sequences of characters constitute a valid program, making it the ideal blueprint for building parsers and compilers. SMALL is defined as a minimal, C-like language focused on expression evaluation. Its syntax encompasses the essential building blocks of programming — including variable binding, arithmetic, block scoping, and control flow — governed by the following formal rules:

```
Program        = { Statement } ;
Statement      = LetStatement
               | ReturnStatement
               | ExpressionStatement
               | IfStatement
               ;

LetStatement    = "let" Identifier "=" Expression ";" ;
ReturnStatement = "return" Expression ";" ;
ExpressionStatement = Expression ";" ;
IfStatement = "if" Expression Block [ "else" Block ] ;
Block           = "{" { Statement } "}" ;

Expression      = Equality ;
Equality        = Relational { ("==" | "!=") Relational } ;
Relational      = Addition { ("<" | ">" | "<=" | ">=") Addition } ;
Addition        = Multiplication { ("+" | "-") Multiplication } ;
Multiplication  = Primary { ("*" | "/") Primary } ;

Primary         = Number | String | Identifier
                | "(" Expression ")"
                ;
```

```
Identifier      = Letter { Letter | Digit | "_" } ;
Number          = Digit { Digit } ;
String          = "\"" { Character | Escape } "\"" ;
Letter          = "a"..."z" | "A"..."Z" ;
Digit           = "0"..."9" ;
Escape          = "\\\"" ;
```

At the highest level, a program is simply a sequence of statements, each taking one of several forms. Statements may declare a variable using `let`, return a computed value, evaluate a standalone expression, or express conditional logic with `if` and an optional `else` branch. Expressions themselves are built from a hierarchy of operators, with equality comparisons at the widest layer, followed by relational operators such as < and >=, then the + and - arithmetic operators, and finally, multiplication and division, which bind most tightly. The most fundamental components of an expression include **identifiers**, **numeric literals**, **string literals**, or another expression wrapped in parentheses. Identifiers begin with a letter or underscore and may continue with digits, and numbers consist of one or more digits. Strings are wrapped in double quotes and allow embedded escaped quotes using `\"`. This grammar, therefore, describes a compact but expressive language capable of variable binding, arithmetic computation, conditional branching, and nested expression evaluation. The specification provides a blueprint for the parser: how to recognize constructs, determine operator precedence, and evaluate code in a structured and predictable way. Based on the definition of the SMALL language, we can tell whether a given program is valid or invalid. This is not always an easy task for a human, but it is always easy for a computer.

You may notice that comments are excluded from the EBNF grammar. This is intentional because comments can appear almost anywhere in source code; including them in the grammar would require adding optional comment rules between nearly every token, making the grammar large and hard to read. Instead, comments are treated as trivia and handled entirely by the lexer, which skips them in the same way it skips whitespace. As a result, the parser operates on a clean stream of tokens, focused solely on syntax.

The formal grammar provides a static blueprint of SMALL, detailing exactly what constitutes a valid program. To turn this theoretical specification into a working interpreter, we must build the machinery that processes it. This transformation occurs in three distinct stages. First, the lexer breaks the raw source text into a stream of meaningful tokens. Next, the parser organizes those tokens into the hierarchical structures defined by our EBNF rules. Finally, the evaluator traverses that resulting structure to execute the underlying logic. By examining these components in sequence, we can see exactly how abstract characters on a screen become concrete computations.

The components of a programming language

A programming language is built from several key components that work together to transform human-readable code into executable behavior. The **lexer** (or **tokenizer**) reads raw source text and breaks it into meaningful units called **tokens**. The **parser** then takes these tokens and organizes them according to the language's grammar, producing an **Abstract Syntax Tree (AST)** that represents the program's structure. The **semantic analyzer** checks that the program makes logical sense — verifying types, variable usage, and scope rules. Once validated, the **interpreter** or **compiler** takes over: an interpreter walks the AST to execute it directly, while a compiler translates it into another language or machine code for later execution. Around these core stages, additional components — such as the runtime system, garbage collector, or standard library — provide memory management and built-in functionality. Together, these layers form the complete machinery that allows code to move from abstract syntax to concrete computation.

The lexer is the first stage in turning raw source code into something a computer can understand. Its job is to scan the input text character by character; recognize patterns such as keywords, identifiers, and symbols; and convert them into a structured sequence of tokens that the parser can process. In essence, the lexer transforms a messy stream of characters into the clean, well-defined vocabulary of your programming language.

The lexer

A **lexer** (short for **lexical analyzer**), also known as a **tokenizer**, is the first concrete processing stage of a programming language implementation. Building on its role of supplying the parser with tokens, the lexer operates by scanning the source code character by character, skipping over whitespace and comments. Based on the current character, it decides which token to construct: letters trigger the reading of identifiers or keywords, digits form numeric literals, and quotation marks initiate string literals with proper handling of escape sequences. For operators, the lexer performs limited lookahead to distinguish between single-character symbols and multicharacter operators, such as `==`, `!=`, `<=`, or `>=`. Each recognized element is emitted as a structured token, providing the parser with a clean, unambiguous stream of syntactic input.

While the machinery of a lexer is generic — reading input, tracking positions, and skipping whitespace — the definitions are highly language-specific. Keywords, operator precedence, comment syntax, and literal formats differ from one language to another. In this sense, a lexer is a combination of a generic scanning engine and specific grammatical rules, providing the flexible foundation needed to build an interpreter for SMALL.

Now, let us see the actual implementation of the lexer, saved as `ch10/lexer.go`, which we are going to present in multiple code snippets, starting with the program preamble. This portion of the code defines the **token system** that both the lexer and parser rely on to understand source code:

```
package main

import (
    "fmt"
)

type TokenType string
const (
    // Special tokens
    TokenEOF     TokenType = "EOF"
    TokenIllegal TokenType = "ILLEGAL"

    // Identifiers + literals
    TokenIdent  TokenType = "IDENT"
    TokenNumber TokenType = "NUMBER"
    TokenString TokenType = "STRING"

    // Keywords
    TokenLet    TokenType = "LET"
    TokenIf     TokenType = "IF"
    TokenElse   TokenType = "ELSE"
    TokenReturn TokenType = "RETURN"

    // Operators
    TokenAssign   TokenType = "="
    TokenPlus     TokenType = "+"
    TokenMinus    TokenType = "-"
    TokenAsterisk TokenType = "*"
    TokenSlash    TokenType = "/"
    TokenEqual    TokenType = "=="
    TokenNotEqual TokenType = "!="
    TokenLE       TokenType = "<="
    TokenGE       TokenType = ">="
    TokenLT       TokenType = "<"
    TokenGT       TokenType = ">"

    // Delimiters
    TokenSemicolon TokenType = ";"
```

```
    TokenLParen     TokenType = "("
    TokenRParen     TokenType = ")"
    TokenLBrace     TokenType = "{"
    TokenRBrace     TokenType = "}"
)
```

The program begins by declaring `TokenType`, a string-based type that represents different categories of language elements. Following this, a collection of constants enumerates every token the lexer may produce — from basic categories such as `IDENT`, `NUMBER`, and `STRING` to reserved keywords such as `LET`, `IF`, `ELSE`, and `RETURN`. Included are operators such as +, -, *, and / as well as comparison operators such as >=, <=, and !=, assignment (=), and punctuation and structural symbols such as semicolons, braces, and parentheses. Special tokens such as `EOF` and `ILLEGAL` mark the termination of input or unexpected character sequences. Consider the following example code:

```
let x = 10;
let msg = "Hello \"world\"!";
if x >= 10 {
    return x + 5;
}
if x != 5 {
    return msg;
}
```

The lexer begins by reading the first character of the input. It skips over any whitespace or comments until it encounters the `let` keyword. Recognizing that `let` matches a reserved keyword, it produces a `TokenLet` token. Immediately after, it reads the identifier `x` as a `TokenIdent`, followed by the assignment operator, =, as `TokenAssign`. When it reaches `10`, it reads the entire sequence of digits and returns a `TokenNumber` value. The semicolon at the end is recognized as a `TokenSemicolon`. Moving to the next line, the lexer identifies `msg` as an identifier, as well as the assignment operator, =, and then reads a full string literal, `"Hello \"world\"!"`, as a `TokenString`, carefully handling the escaped quote inside the string. For the conditional `if x >= 10` statement, the lexer produces `TokenIf` for the keyword, `TokenIdent` for `x`, and `TokenGE` for the `>=` operator, followed by `TokenNumber` for `10` and `TokenLBrace` for the opening brace. Inside the block, it reads `return` as `TokenReturn`, `x` as `TokenIdent`, `+` as `TokenPlus`, and `5` as `TokenNumber`, concluding the statement with a `TokenSemicolon`. On encountering the second `if` statement, it similarly produces `TokenIf`, `TokenIdent` for `x`, `TokenNotEqual` for `!=`, and `TokenNumber` for `5`, opening a new block with `TokenLBrace`. Finally, the `return msg;` statement is tokenized as `TokenReturn`, `TokenIdent`, and `TokenSemicolon`, followed by the closing brace, `TokenRBrace`. By processing the input sequentially, handling whitespace, comments, and multicharacter operators, this lexer converts the entire source code into a well-structured stream of tokens, ready for parsing or interpretation.

The next code snippet introduces the `Token` and `Lexer` structures, which form the foundation of how raw text becomes structured data:

```
type Token struct {
    Type    TokenType
    Literal string
}
type Lexer struct {
    input        string
    position     int
    readPosition int
    ch           byte
}
func NewLexer(input string) *Lexer {
    l := &Lexer{input: input}
    l.readChar()
    return l
}
func (l *Lexer) readChar() {
    if l.readPosition >= len(l.input) {
        l.ch = 0
    } else {
        l.ch = l.input[l.readPosition]
    }
    l.position = l.readPosition
    l.readPosition++
}
```

The `Token` type is simple but essential. It stores two pieces of information: `Type`, which identifies the kind of token, and `Literal`, which holds the exact text extracted from the source code. The `Lexer` component reads characters from the input and transforms them into tokens. It tracks the text being scanned (`input`), the current reading location (`position`), and the next character to be read (`readPosition`), along with a stored variable, `ch`, which holds the character currently being examined. The `NewLexer()` constructor initializes a lexer with input code, then calls `readChar()` to load the first character. The `readChar()` function advances through the input one byte at a time, setting ch to 0 when the end of the input is reached. By incrementing both position and readPosition, the lexer can efficiently move forward while always keeping the next character accessible.

After that, we present peekChar(), which implements look-ahead capability in the lexer, allowing it to examine the next character without advancing through the input stream:

```
func (l *Lexer) peekChar() byte {
    if l.readPosition >= len(l.input) {
        return 0
    }
    return l.input[l.readPosition]
}
```

The method checks whether readPosition — the index of the next unread character — has gone past the end of the input. If it has, then it returns 0, a null byte often used to signal the end of the file. Otherwise, it simply returns the character located at readPosition, leaving the lexer's current reading position unchanged. This ability to *peek ahead* is particularly useful when identifying multicharacter tokens such as ==, !=, <=, or >= because the lexer can verify the character following the current one before deciding how to classify the token.

Next is the NextToken() method, which implements the main logic of the lexer. If you have time to read just a single function from a lexer implementation, make it this one. The first portion of NextToken() demonstrates how the lexer reads individual characters, decides what token type they represent, and constructs a Token value accordingly:

```
func (l *Lexer) NextToken() Token {
    l.skipWhitespace()
    var tok Token

    switch l.ch {
    case '=':
        if l.peekChar() == '=' {
            ch := l.ch
            l.readChar()
            tok = Token{Type: TokenEqual, Literal: string(ch) + string(l.ch)}
        } else {
            tok = Token{Type: TokenAssign, Literal: string(l.ch)}
        }
```

The `NextToken()` method starts by skipping over whitespace, ensuring that only meaningful characters are considered. It then examines the current character to decide what kind of token to produce. For example, when it encounters =, it checks whether the next character forms a two-character equality operator (==) or is simply an assignment (=). This lookahead ensures the lexer correctly distinguishes between single-character and multicharacter operators, producing the appropriate token for the parser to consume.

In the next part of the `NextToken()` method, the lexer follows the same pattern used for = to handle operators that may consist of one or two characters:

```
case '!':
    if l.peekChar() == '=' {
        ch := l.ch
        l.readChar()
        tok = Token{Type: TokenNotEqual, Literal: string(ch) + string(l.ch)}
    } else {
        tok = Token{Type: TokenIllegal, Literal: string(l.ch)}
    }
case '<':
    if l.peekChar() == '=' {
        ch := l.ch
        l.readChar()
        tok = Token{Type: TokenLE, Literal: string(ch) + string(l.ch)}
    } else {
        tok = Token{Type: TokenLT, Literal: string(l.ch)}
    }
```

When encountering `!`, the lexer again checks the next character with `peekChar()`. If the following character is =, the two together form the `!=` (not equal) operator. In this case, `readChar()` advances the input, and the lexer builds a `TokenNotEqual` with the literal `!=`. However, if there is no = after the exclamation mark, the character does not correspond to any valid operator defined for this language, so it is marked as `TokenIllegal`. This acts as a safeguard against unexpected or unsupported input. The same procedure is then applied to <, another operator that may appear alone or as part of a compound token. If the next character is =, the combined operator `<=` represents "less than or equal to," so the lexer produces a `TokenLE`. Otherwise, a standalone `<` is recognized as a simple "less than" operator and returned as `TokenLT`.

This next piece of `NextToken()` continues the same branching structure to recognize additional operators, delimiters, and literal types:

```
case '>':
    if l.peekChar() == '=' {
        ch := l.ch
        l.readChar()
        tok = Token{Type: TokenGE, Literal: string(ch) + string(l.ch)}
    } else {
        tok = Token{Type: TokenGT, Literal: string(l.ch)}
    }
case '+':
    tok = Token{Type: TokenPlus, Literal: string(l.ch)}
case '-':
    tok = Token{Type: TokenMinus, Literal: string(l.ch)}
case '*':
    tok = Token{Type: TokenAsterisk, Literal: string(l.ch)}
case '/':
    if l.peekChar() == '/' {
        l.readChar()
        l.skipComment()
        return l.NextToken()
    } else {
        tok = Token{Type: TokenSlash, Literal: string(l.ch)}
    }
case ';':
    tok = Token{Type: TokenSemicolon, Literal: string(l.ch)}
case '(':
    tok = Token{Type: TokenLParen, Literal: string(l.ch)}
case ')':
    tok = Token{Type: TokenRParen, Literal: string(l.ch)}
case '{':
    tok = Token{Type: TokenLBrace, Literal: string(l.ch)}
case '}':
    tok = Token{Type: TokenRBrace, Literal: string(l.ch)}
case '"':
    tok.Type = TokenString
    tok.Literal = l.readString()
case 0:
    tok = Token{Type: TokenEOF, Literal: ""}
```

The code first handles the > character, which, like <, may appear alone or as part of a compound operator. If `peekChar()` sees an = character following it, the lexer combines them into the >= operator and returns a `TokenGE`. If not, the single > becomes a `TokenGT`. After that, the lexer processes arithmetic operators one by one: + becomes `TokenPlus`, - becomes `TokenMinus`, and * becomes `TokenAsterisk`. Each is a simple one-character token, so no look-ahead logic is required. The / character is more interesting because it plays two roles. If the next character is also /, the lexer recognizes a single-line comment. It consumes the second slash using `readChar()`, skips characters until the end of the line via `skipComment()`, and then recursively calls `NextToken()` to resume the lexing process normally. However, if a slash stands alone, it is returned as the division operator, `TokenSlash`. After operators are processed, the lexer moves on to punctuation and grouping symbols (;, (,), {, and }), each mapped to its corresponding token type. When encountering a double quote, the lexer knows it is starting a string literal. It sets the token type to `TokenString` and uses `readString()` to capture all characters up to the closing quote. Finally, if the character reads as `0`, which indicates the end of input, the lexer emits a `TokenEOF`, signaling that no further tokens are available. The final part of `NextToken()` handles everything that does not fall under the `switch` cases:

```
    default:
        if isLetter(l.ch) {
            literal := l.readIdentifier()
            return Token{Type: lookupIdent(literal), Literal: literal}
        } else if isDigit(l.ch) {
            return Token{Type: TokenNumber, Literal: l.readNumber()}
        } else {
            tok = Token{Type: TokenIllegal, Literal: string(l.ch)}
        }
    }
    l.readChar()
    return tok
}
```

When the current character is a letter or underscore, the lexer reads an entire identifier or keyword using `readIdentifier()`, then checks with `lookupIdent()` whether it should be a language keyword token or a generic identifier. If the character is a digit, it collects a numeric sequence via `readNumber()` and returns it as a number token. Any unrecognized character is flagged as `TokenIllegal`. After producing the token, the lexer advances its position to ensure the next call continues correctly.

Next, there is a set of helper methods, starting with skipWhitespace():

```
func (l *Lexer) skipWhitespace() {
    for l.ch == ' ' || l.ch == '\t' || l.ch == '\n' || l.ch == '\r' {
        l.readChar()
    }
}
func (l *Lexer) skipComment() {
    for l.ch != '\n' && l.ch != 0 {
        l.readChar()
    }
}
func (l *Lexer) readIdentifier() string {
    start := l.position
    for isLetter(l.ch) {
        l.readChar()
    }
    return l.input[start:l.position]
}
func (l *Lexer) readNumber() string {
    start := l.position
    for isDigit(l.ch) {
        l.readChar()
    }
    return l.input[start:l.position]
}
func (l *Lexer) readString() string {
    l.readChar() // skip opening quote
    start := l.position
    for l.ch != '"' && l.ch != 0 {
        if l.ch == '\\' && l.peekChar() == '"' {
            l.readChar() // skip escape char
        }
        l.readChar()
    }
    s := l.input[start:l.position]
    l.readChar() // skip closing quote
    return s
}
```

This group of methods provides the utility work that powers token scanning. `skipWhitespace()` advances through spaces, tabs, and newlines until a non-whitespace character appears, ensuring the lexer ignores formatting and only returns meaningful tokens. Similarly, `skipComment()` consumes characters until it reaches a newline or the end of the input — allowing the language to support // comments naturally by skipping them entirely during tokenization. When the lexer encounters an identifier or a keyword, `readIdentifier()` records where the word begins and continues reading as long as the characters are alphabetic or underscores. It then slices that substring out of the original input and returns it unchanged. `readNumber()` operates in a similar manner, except it consumes only digits, producing number literals such as `42` or `1000`. The `readString()` manages string handling. After consuming the opening quotation mark, it walks forward until it finds the matching closing quote, also accounting for escaped characters such as \". When the terminating quote is found, the substring representing the string literal is returned and the lexer moves forward and continues scanning the rest of the program.

The next two helper functions act as simple character classifiers, which are essential for breaking input text into meaningful tokens:

```
func isLetter(ch byte) bool {
    return 'a' <= ch && ch <= 'z' || 'A' <= ch && ch <= 'Z' || ch == '_'
}
func isDigit(ch byte) bool {
    return '0' <= ch && ch <= '9'
}
```

The `isLetter()` function determines whether a given byte represents an alphabetic character, allowing both uppercase and lowercase letters as well as the underscore character. This is what makes identifiers such as `myVar`, `_hidden`, or `Message` valid variable names within the language. Meanwhile, `isDigit()` provides an equally focused check for characters `'0'` through `'9'`, enabling the lexer to distinguish numbers from other forms of input. This final helper function is responsible for distinguishing general identifiers from reserved keywords in the language:

```
func lookupIdent(ident string) TokenType {
    switch ident {
    case "let":
        return TokenLet
    case "if":
        return TokenIf
    case "else":
        return TokenElse
```

```
    case "return":
        return TokenReturn
    default:
        return TokenIdent
    }
}
```

When the lexer reads a sequence of letters and extracts it as a potential identifier, it passes that string into `lookupIdent()`, which checks whether it matches one of the language's predefined keywords: `let`, `if`, `else`, or `return`. If a match is found, the function returns the corresponding `TokenType`, ensuring the parser later interprets the token correctly. If no match exists, the identifier is treated as a user-defined name, such as a variable or function, and the function returns `TokenIdent`.

Last, we present the implementation of the `main()` function, which serves as a simple demonstration of how the lexer processes source code and produces a stream of tokens:

```
func main() {
    input := `
    // Sample program with strings and operators
    let x = 10;
    let msg = "Hello \"world\"!";
    if x >= 10 {
        return x + 5;
    }
    if x != 5 {
        return msg;
    }
    `

    lexer := NewLexer(input)
    for tok := lexer.NextToken(); tok.Type != TokenEOF; tok = lexer.NextToken() {
        fmt.Printf("%+v\n", tok)
    }
}
```

This `main()` function begins by defining a multiline string containing a small program with variable declarations, string literals, arithmetic, comparison operators, and two `if` statements — enough variety to exercise different parts of the lexer. The program text is passed to `NewLexer`, which initializes a fresh lexer instance prepared to scan through the input character by character. The heart of the function is a loop that repeatedly calls `lexer.NextToken()`, retrieving the next token each time until it eventually returns a token of type `TokenEOF`, signaling the end of the input. Each retrieved token is then printed using `fmt.Printf()`, with `%+v` ensuring that both the token's type and literal value are shown.

Run `ch10/lexer.go` on your machine to see its output:

```
$ go run ch10/lexer.go
go run ch10/lexer.go
{Type:LET Literal:let}
{Type:IDENT Literal:x}
{Type:= Literal:=}
{Type:NUMBER Literal:10}
{Type:; Literal:;}
{Type:LET Literal:let}
{Type:IDENT Literal:msg}
{Type:= Literal:=}
{Type:STRING Literal:Hello \"world\"!}
{Type:IF Literal:if}
{Type:IDENT Literal:x}
{Type:>= Literal:>=}
{Type:NUMBER Literal:10}
{Type:{ Literal:{}
{Type:RETURN Literal:return}
{Type:IDENT Literal:x}
{Type:+ Literal:+}
{Type:NUMBER Literal:5}
{Type:; Literal:;}
{Type:} Literal:}}
{Type:IF Literal:if}
{Type:IDENT Literal:x}
{Type:!= Literal:!=}
{Type:NUMBER Literal:5}
{Type:{ Literal:{}
{Type:RETURN Literal:return}
{Type:IDENT Literal:msg}
{Type:; Literal:;}
{Type:} Literal:}}
```

The output you see is the stream of tokens produced by the lexer as it scans the source code from left to right. Each line represents a single token, showing both its type (such as `LET`, `IDENT`, `NUMBER`, or `IF`) and the literal text taken directly from the input program. The lexer begins by identifying variable declarations such as `let x = 10;`, breaking them down into their component tokens: the `let` keyword, the identifier `x`, the assignment operator, `=`, the numeric literal `10`, and the terminating semicolon. It continues with `let msg = "Hello \"world\"!";`, recognizing the `STRING` token and safely capturing the escaped quotation marks inside the literal. As it moves into the conditional logic, the lexer emits tokens for the `if` keyword, identifiers, comparison operators such as `>=` and `!=`, numeric literals, and the braces that define block scopes. Inside each block, it identifies return statements and arithmetic operators such as `+`, ensuring every syntactic element is represented as a token.

The next logical step is to make our tool more flexible by allowing it to read and analyze code supplied from external files rather than embedded strings.

Reading code from external files

We are going to modify `ch10/lexer.go` to make it read program from external files – the name of the new version is `ch10/lexerFile.go`. What is important in this modified version is the implementation of `main()` as the remaining code stays the same. Here is the `main()` implementation of `ch10/lexerFile.go`, which shifts the lexer from working with hardcoded code to processing real source files provided by the user:

```
func main() {
    if len(os.Args) < 2 {
        fmt.Println("Usage: lexer <sourcefile>")
        os.Exit(1)
    }
    filename := os.Args[1]
    data, err := os.ReadFile(filename)
    if err != nil {
        fmt.Printf("Error reading %s: %v\n", filename, err)
        os.Exit(1)
    }

    input := string(data)
    lexer := NewLexer(input)
    for tok := lexer.NextToken(); tok.Type != TokenEOF; tok = lexer.NextToken() {
        fmt.Printf("%+v\n", tok)
    }
}
```

The code begins by checking whether a filename was supplied on the command line; if not, it prints a short usage message and exits to prevent running without input. When a filename is provided, `os.ReadFile()` loads the entire file into memory, and any read error is reported clearly before the program terminates. The source code is converted into a string and passed to `NewLexer()`, which initializes the lexer with the external source code. As in `ch10/lexer.go`, the function loops through tokens produced by `NextToken()`, printing each one until the lexer emits an EOF token.

Let us now try `ch10/lexerFile.go` using the contents of `ch10/lexer.code`:

```
$ cat ch10/lexer.code
// Sample program
let x = 10;
if x >= 10 {
    return x + 5;
}
if x != 5 {
    return msg;
}
```

First, let us see how this program is produced by the EBNF grammar of the programming language, without including the comment. To create the corrected program using the provided EBNF grammar, the parser begins at the root `Program` rule, which expects a sequence of `Statement` items. The first item matches the `LetStatement` rule. This generates the literal `let` token, followed by an `Identifier` generated as "x", the assignment operator, and an `Expression` that descends through the hierarchy (`Equality -> Relational -> Addition -> Multiplication`) to find a `Primary Number 10`. The statement concludes with the mandatory semicolon. The second item is identified as an `IfStatement`, which begins with the `if` keyword. `Expression "x >= 10"` is parsed using the `Relational` rule, which handles the greater-than-or-equal-to operator between two `Addition` terms. After that, the grammar requires a `Block`. This starts with `{` and contains a nested `Statement`, specifically a `ReturnStatement`. This inner statement consists of the `return` keyword, an `Expression "x + 5"` (matched via the `Addition` rule), and a semicolon. The block then closes with `}`. The final item is another `IfStatement`. It follows the same structure: the `if` keyword and `Expression "x != 5"`. Unlike the previous condition, this one is matched by the `Equality` rule because of the `!=` operator. After the closing parenthesis, a new `Block` is created using `{`. Inside, the `ReturnStatement` returns `msg`. In this context, `msg` is parsed as an `Identifier` (a string of letters) found within the `Primary` rule options. The block closes with `}`, completing the statement sequence and the program. Now, let us feed `ch10/lexerFile.go` with `ch10/lexer.code`:

```
$ go run ch10/lexerFile.go ch10/lexer.code
{Type:LET Literal:let}
{Type:IDENT Literal:x}
{Type:= Literal:=}
{Type:NUMBER Literal:10}
{Type:; Literal:;}
{Type:IF Literal:if}
{Type:IDENT Literal:x}
{Type:>= Literal:>=}
{Type:NUMBER Literal:10}
{Type:{ Literal:{}
{Type:RETURN Literal:return}
{Type:IDENT Literal:x}
{Type:+ Literal:+}
{Type:NUMBER Literal:5}
{Type:; Literal:;}
{Type:} Literal:}}
{Type:IF Literal:if}
{Type:IDENT Literal:x}
{Type:!= Literal:!=}
{Type:NUMBER Literal:5}
{Type:{ Literal:{}
{Type:RETURN Literal:return}
{Type:IDENT Literal:msg}
{Type:; Literal:;}
{Type:} Literal:}}
```

As the output demonstrates, the lexer successfully translates the raw source text into a structured sequence of tokens. Notice that all formatting, such as spaces and newlines, has been completely discarded, leaving only the grammatically significant components. The output also highlights the lexer's ability to differentiate between user-defined variables, such as the identifier `x`, and reserved language keywords, such as `let`, `if`, and `return`. Furthermore, multicharacter relational operators, including `>=` and `!=`, are correctly recognized as single, unified tokens rather than fragmented symbols. By isolating the character-level analysis into this dedicated lexical phase, we guarantee that the subsequent parsing stage receives a clean, predictable stream of data, allowing the parser to focus entirely on structural grammar rather than textual artifacts.

As soon as the lexer has transformed raw characters into a clean stream of tokens, the next stage of the pipeline can begin. The parser takes over from here, consuming those tokens and organizing them into a meaningful syntactic structure.

The parser

A parser is a core component of a compiler or interpreter that analyzes source code according to the language's grammar and transforms a linear sequence of tokens into a structured representation, typically an AST. While the lexer is responsible for identifying individual tokens, the parser determines how those tokens relate to one another syntactically, capturing the hierarchical structure of the program.

In this implementation, we use a **Pratt parser** — a compact, top-down parsing technique particularly well suited to expression-heavy languages. Rather than encoding operator precedence through an extensive set of grammar rules, Pratt parsing associates parsing behavior directly with tokens. Each token may define a prefix function (describing how it starts an expression) and/or an infix function (describing how it combines with a left-hand expression). The parser advances through the token stream by recursively parsing expressions while comparing the precedence, or binding power, of the next token against the current context. Parsing continues only while the upcoming token binds more tightly, which naturally enforces correct operator grouping. This approach makes operator precedence an explicit, data-driven property of the language rather than an implicit feature of the grammar. For example, when parsing the expression `1 + 2 * 3`, the parser recognizes that * has a higher binding power than +. As a result, it groups `2 * 3` into a subexpression before combining it with `1`, producing an AST that reflects the intended mathematical structure. This mechanism avoids backtracking and complex grammar hierarchies while remaining easy to extend, as adding a new operator requires only defining its precedence and associated parsing functions. The AST nodes and the `Program` struct are a direct structural reflection of the EBNF grammar defined earlier. Each non-terminal in the grammar corresponds to one or more concrete AST node types, while the `Program` node represents the grammar's top-level production. Where the grammar describes what forms are syntactically valid, the AST provides a concrete, in-memory representation of those forms, preserving hierarchy and order so later stages — such as semantic analysis or evaluation — can operate on the program structure directly.

The parser handles this logic by dividing the world into two types of interactions: **prefix** and **infix. Prefix positions** are how expressions start. When the parser is expecting a new expression, it looks for things that can stand alone or start a phrase: a number (5), a variable name (x), a unary operator (`-5`), or a grouped expression, such as `(5)`. **Infix positions** are how expressions continue. Once a "left side" is established, the parser looks for an operator that bridges it to a "right side" (such as +, ==, or <). The parsing loop creates a rhythm: find a starter (prefix), then look for a joiner (infix), then recurse to find the next starter. This recursive "ping-pong" between functions allows the parser to handle expressions of infinite complexity and depth, such as `x + y * (z - 10) / a`, simply by following the trail of precedence. Finally, the parser wraps these complex expressions inside **statements**, which act as the containers for logic. The logic here is much simpler: it looks at the very first token of a line to decide what to do. If it sees `let`, it knows to build a variable declaration box. If it sees `return`, it builds a return box. If it sees `if`, it builds a conditional flow box. It effectively puts the "math" (expressions) inside these "boxes" (statements). This separation of concerns — simple statement matching on the outside, complex precedence logic on the inside — is what makes this parser design both robust and easy to extend. If you wanted to add a `while` loop later, you would simply add a new `Statement` container; the complex expression parsing logic would remain exactly the same.

Let us now present the important parts of `ch10/parser.go`, without including the functionality of the lexer, which is also embedded in the parser code – you cannot have a parser without a lexer, and you cannot have an evaluator without a parser and a lexer.

Before we can parse tokens, we need a structure to hold them. The AST represents the logical structure of our program. Unlike the linear list of tokens produced by the lexer, the AST is hierarchical. We start by defining the fundamental interfaces that every node in our tree must satisfy:

```
type Node interface {
    TokenLiteral() string
    String() string
}
type Statement interface {
    Node
    statementNode()
}
type Expression interface {
    Node
    expressionNode()
}
type Program struct {
    Statements []Statement
}
func (p *Program) TokenLiteral() string {
    if len(p.Statements) > 0 {
        return p.Statements[0].TokenLiteral()
    }
```

```
    return ""
}
func (p *Program) String() string {
    var b strings.Builder
    for _, s := range p.Statements {
        b.WriteString(s.String())
        b.WriteString("\n")
    }
    return b.String()
}
```

The Node interface is the base for everything in our tree; it requires methods to retrieve the literal token value and a string representation for debugging. We explicitly distinguish between a `Statement` (which performs an action, such as `let x = 5;`) and an `Expression` (which produces a value, such as `x + 5`). The `Program` struct serves as the root node of our AST, containing a slice of `Statements` that represent the entire source file. The `String()` methods allow us to recursively print the AST back into code syntax, which is invaluable for testing if our parser is working correctly.

Next, we define the structs for the specific statements our language supports. `LetStatement` and `ReturnStatement` are the most critical. Notice how `LetStatement` binds an identifier (`Name`) to an expression (`Value`):

```
type LetStatement struct {
    Token Token // 'let'
    Name  *Identifier
    Value Expression
}

func (ls *LetStatement) statementNode()       {}
func (ls *LetStatement) TokenLiteral() string { return ls.Token.Literal }
func (ls *LetStatement) String() string {
    if ls.Value == nil {
        return fmt.Sprintf("let %s = ;", ls.Name.String())
    }
    return fmt.Sprintf("let %s = %s;", ls.Name.String(), ls.Value.String())
}

type ReturnStatement struct {
    Token       Token // 'return'
```

```
    ReturnValue Expression
}
```

Each struct holds the original token (for debugging and error reporting) and pointers to the child nodes.

With our tree defined, we build the (Pratt parser) Parser struct. This requires the parser to store not only the current tokens but also a registry of parsing functions associated with token types:

```
type (
    prefixParseFn func() Expression
    infixParseFn  func(Expression) Expression
)

type Parser struct {
    l *Lexer
    curToken  Token
    peekToken Token
    errors []string
    prefixParseFns map[TokenType]prefixParseFn
    infixParseFns  map[TokenType]infixParseFn
}

func NewParser(l *Lexer) *Parser {
    p := &Parser{
        l:      l,
        errors: []string{},
    }
    p.prefixParseFns = make(map[TokenType]prefixParseFn)
    p.infixParseFns = make(map[TokenType]infixParseFn)
    // register prefix parse fns
    p.registerPrefix(TokenIdent, p.parseIdentifier)
    p.registerPrefix(TokenNumber, p.parseIntegerLiteral)
    p.registerPrefix(TokenString, p.parseStringLiteral)
    p.registerPrefix(TokenMinus, p.parsePrefixExpression)
    p.registerPrefix(TokenLParen, p.parseGroupedExpression)
    p.registerPrefix(TokenIf, p.parseIfExpression)

    // register infix parse fns
    for _, t := range []TokenType{
        TokenPlus, TokenMinus, TokenSlash, TokenAsterisk,
```

```
        TokenEqual, TokenNotEqual, TokenLT, TokenGT, TokenLE, TokenGE,
    } {
        p.registerInfix(t, p.parseInfixExpression)
    }

    // read two tokens, so curToken and peekToken are set
    p.nextToken()
    p.nextToken()
    return p
}
```

The code begins by establishing the fundamental architecture of a Pratt parser through the definition of two specific function types: `prefixParseFn` and `infixParseFn`. These types represent the two ways a token can behave within an expression. `prefixParseFn` is triggered when a token appears at the beginning of an expression (such as a number, an identifier, or a unary operator such as -) and it returns a constructed `Expression` node. `infixParseFn` is triggered when a token appears between two existing expressions (such as + or *); uniquely, it accepts an argument representing the `Expression` found to its *left*, allowing it to combine that left-hand side with what follows to form a new tree node. The `Parser` struct itself acts as the state container, holding a reference to the `Lexer`, a list of errors, and two distinct token buffers: `curToken` (the token currently being analyzed) and `peekToken` (the lookahead token used to make parsing decisions). Crucially, the struct also holds the `prefixParseFns` and `infixParseFns` maps, which serve as the dispatch tables that link specific `TokenType` types to their corresponding parsing functions.

The `NewParser()` function serves as the constructor and initialization hub, where the static grammar rules are dynamically wired into the parser instance. After initializing the maps, the code explicitly registers the parsing logic for every supported token. Prefix functions are registered for terminals such as identifiers, numbers, and strings, as well as for structural tokens such as the left parenthesis (for grouped expressions) and keywords such as `if`. Simultaneously, a loop iterates through all binary operators, such as arithmetic symbols and comparison operators, registering them to use the generic `parseInfixExpression()` method. Finally, the constructor prepares the parser for operation by calling `nextToken()` twice. This ensures that `curToken` holds the first valid token of the program and `peekToken` holds the second, setting the stage for the parsing loop to begin immediately.

The entry point for parsing is `ParseProgram()`. It iterates through the token stream until it hits `EOF`, delegating the heavy lifting to `parseStatement()`:

```
func (p *Parser) ParseProgram() *Program {
    program := &Program{}
    program.Statements = []Statement{}

    for p.curToken.Type != TokenEOF {
        stmt := p.parseStatement()
        if stmt != nil {
            program.Statements = append(program.Statements, stmt)
        }
        p.nextToken()
    }
    return program
}

func (p *Parser) parseStatement() Statement {
    switch p.curToken.Type {
    case TokenLet:
        return p.parseLetStatement()
    case TokenReturn:
        return p.parseReturnStatement()
    default:
        return p.parseExpressionStatement()
    }
}
```

`parseStatement()` acts as a high-level switch. If the current token is `let`, it knows to parse a variable declaration. If it is `return`, it parses a return statement. Anything else is assumed to be an `ExpressionStatement` (such as `x + 5;` sitting on its own line).

The `parseLetStatement()` method is responsible for enforcing the syntactic structure of a variable declaration, ensuring that the tokens follow the specific `let <identifier> = <expression>;` pattern. It uses `expectPeek()` to ensure the tokens appear in the correct order (`let -> identifier -> assign -> expression`):

```
func (p *Parser) parseLetStatement() *LetStatement {
    stmt := &LetStatement{Token: p.curToken}
    if !p.expectPeek(TokenIdent) {
```

```
        return nil
    }

    stmt.Name = &Identifier{Token: p.curToken, Value: p.curToken.Literal}

    if !p.expectPeek(TokenAssign) {
        return nil
    }

    // move to expression
    p.nextToken()
    stmt.Value = p.parseExpression(LOWEST)
    // optional semicolon
    if p.peekTokenIs(TokenSemicolon) {
        p.nextToken()
    }
    return stmt
}
```

The function begins by initializing a `LetStatement` node using the current token (which is known to be `let` because of the dispatch logic in the caller). It then employs the `expectPeek()` helper method to assert that the next token is a valid identifier. This helper is crucial: if the expectation is met, it advances the token stream automatically; if not, it records an error and aborts the function immediately to prevent parsing a malformed statement. Once the identifier is successfully captured and stored in the `Name` field, the function asserts the presence of an assignment operator (=). With the structure validated, the parser advances past the equals sign and hands control over to `parseExpression()` to generate the `Value` node. Crucially, it passes `LOWEST` precedence to this call, ensuring that the expression parser consumes the entire right-hand side of the assignment, regardless of the operators involved, as in `let x = 1 + 2 * 3`. Finally, the method checks for a terminating semicolon; if one is present — which is standard for this grammar — it consumes the token to leave the stream in a clean state for the next statement.

Next, we have the Pratt expression parser, which manages the recursive construction of the AST based on token types and their relative binding powers. Instead of a mess of nested `if` statements, `parseExpression()` uses the precedence maps we set up earlier:

```
func (p *Parser) parseExpression(precedence int) Expression {
    prefix := p.prefixParseFns[p.curToken.Type]
    if prefix == nil {
        p.errors = append(p.errors, "no prefix parse function for
```

```
"+string(p.curToken.Type))
        return nil
    }
    leftExp := prefix()

    for !p.peekTokenIs(TokenSemicolon)&&precedence< p.peekPrecedence() {
        infix := p.infixParseFns[p.peekToken.Type]
        if infix == nil {
            return leftExp
        }
        p.nextToken()
        leftExp = infix(leftExp)
    }
    return leftExp
}
```

The logic proceeds in two distinct phases: establishing a base node and then optionally extending it. The function begins by inspecting the current token to identify a "prefix" unit— the starting point of any valid expression (such as an identifier, `x`, a number, `5`, a unary operator, `-`, or an opening parenthesis). It retrieves the associated function from the `prefixParseFns` map; if no such function exists, the parser recognizes an invalid syntax error and aborts. Otherwise, it executes the function to create the initial `leftExp` node, which serves as the anchor for whatever comes next. Once the "left side" is established, the function enters a loop that embodies the core of the operator-precedence logic. It repeatedly examines the next token (`peekToken()`) to decide whether the expression should grow. This loop continues only as long as the next token is not a semicolon (which would end the statement) and, importantly, possesses a precedence value higher than the precedence argument passed into the current call. This comparison is what enforces the order of operations; the parser effectively asks, "Is the upcoming operator *stronger* than the one I am currently handling?" If the answer is yes, the parser retrieves the corresponding infix function, advances the token stream, and recursively updates `leftExp` by wrapping it inside a new structure (for example, turning the node x into the node `x + 5`). This cycle repeats until the next operator is too weak to bind to the current expression, at which point the fully constructed AST node is returned.

Next, we look at how binary operations are handled. The `parseInfixExpression()` function is called when an operator sits between two expressions:

```
func (p *Parser) parseInfixExpression(left Expression) Expression {
    expr := &InfixExpression{
        Token:    p.curToken,
```

```
        Left:     left,
        Operator: p.curToken.Literal,
    }
    prec := p.curPrecedence()
    p.nextToken()
    expr.Right = p.parseExpression(prec)
    return expr
}
```

The `parseInfixExpression()` method serves as the structural pivot for handling binary operations, transforming a linear sequence of tokens such as `1 + 2` into a hierarchical tree node. This function is triggered only after the parser has successfully processed a left-hand operand (passed into the function as the `left` argument) and has identified the current token as an infix operator. The method begins by constructing a new `InfixExpression` AST node, anchoring it with the current operator token (such as + or *) and attaching the existing `left` expression as its first child. This step effectively "wraps" the previous node, making it a sub-component of this new, larger expression. The critical logic of the Pratt parsing algorithm occurs in the subsequent lines, where the function determines the boundaries of the right-hand operand. It first retrieves the precedence level of the current operator using `p.curPrecedence()` — a numerical value indicating how strongly this operator binds to its arguments. After advancing the token stream past the operator, the function recursively calls `parseExpression()` to generate the `Right` child node. Crucially, it passes the current operator's precedence into this recursive call. This acts as a "binding power" threshold: the inner `parseExpression()` call will continue to consume tokens for the right side only so long as it encounters operators with a *higher* precedence than the current one. This ensures that in an expression such as `1 + 2 * 3`, the right side correctly parses as `2 * 3` (because * beats +), maintaining the correct mathematical order of operations.

After that, we present the `parseIfExpression()` method, which is responsible for capturing the branching logic of the program:

```
func (p *Parser) parseIfExpression() Expression {
    expr := &IfExpression{Token: p.curToken}
    // support both styles: if (cond) { ... } or  if cond { ... }
    if p.peekTokenIs(TokenLParen) {
        p.nextToken() // advance to '('
        p.nextToken() // advance to first token of condition
        expr.Condition = p.parseExpression(LOWEST)
        if !p.expectPeek(TokenRParen) {
            return nil
```

```
        }
    } else {
        p.nextToken()
        expr.Condition = p.parseExpression(LOWEST)
    }

    // expect '{'
    if !p.expectPeek(TokenLBrace) {
        return nil
    }
    expr.Consequence = p.parseBlockStatement()

    // optional else
    if p.peekTokenIs(TokenElse) {
        p.nextToken() // move to 'else'
        // allow 'else { ... }' only
        if !p.expectPeek(TokenLBrace) {
            return nil
        }
        expr.Alternative = p.parseBlockStatement()
    }
    return expr
}
```

The code begins by creating an `IfExpression` node and immediately addresses the syntax of the condition itself. Uniquely, this implementation is designed to be flexible, supporting both C-style syntax with parentheses (`if (x > 5)`) and a cleaner, Go-like syntax without them (`if x > 5`). It achieves this by peeking at the next token; if an opening parenthesis is detected, the parser consumes the surrounding parentheses while parsing the expression inside. If not, it simply proceeds directly to parsing the expression. In either scenario, `parseExpression(LOWEST)` is utilized to capture the full logic of the condition. Once the condition is processed, the parser enforces the presence of an opening brace, `{`, and delegates the parsing of the `Consequence` body to `parseBlockStatement()`. Finally, the method checks for an optional `else` token; if present, it enforces another block structure to populate the `Alternative` field, allowing for complete if-else control flow.

This flexibility reflects the design goals of SMALL: keeping the language compact and readable, reducing boilerplate where possible, and making it easier for programmers to write clear, concise conditional logic without being constrained by rigid syntactic requirements.

The `parseBlockStatement()` method serves as the container logic for grouped sequences of code, such as the conditional arm of an `if` statement:

```
func (p *Parser) parseBlockStatement() *BlockStatement {
    block := &BlockStatement{Token: p.curToken}
    block.Statements = []Statement{}

    // move into first token of block
    p.nextToken()

    for !p.curTokenIs(TokenRBrace) && !p.curTokenIs(TokenEOF) {
        stmt := p.parseStatement()
        if stmt != nil {
            block.Statements = append(block.Statements, stmt)
        }
        p.nextToken()
    }

    return block
}
```

The primary job of the function is to encapsulate a list of statements within a defined scope, delimited by curly braces. The method begins by initializing the `BlockStatement` node and consuming the opening brace, {, to enter the block's interior. It then enters a loop that continues processing tokens until it encounters either a closing brace, }, or the end of the file— a safety check to prevent infinite loops in malformed code. Inside this loop, it repeatedly delegates to the high-level `parseStatement()` method, aggregating the resulting nodes into the block's `Statements` slice. Once the closing brace is reached, the populated block node is returned, effectively treating the entire sequence of statements as a single, cohesive syntactic unit.

Both `peekPrecedence()` and `curPrecedence()` act as the navigational instruments for the Pratt parser, translating raw token types into numerical binding powers that determine the order of operations:

```
// These helpers are required for the Pratt parser to compile
func (p *Parser) peekPrecedence() int {
    if prec, ok := precedences[p.peekToken.Type]; ok {
        return prec
    }
    return LOWEST
```

```
}

func (p *Parser) curPrecedence() int {
    if prec, ok := precedences[p.curToken.Type]; ok {
        return prec
    }
    return LOWEST
}
```

Although nearly identical in implementation, they serve distinct roles. Both functions query the global `precedences` map to retrieve the integer value associated with a specific token type — returning the specific level for operators (such as `SUM` or `PRODUCT`) or defaulting to `LOWEST` if the token is not an operator. The distinction lies in their focus: `peekPrecedence()` allows the parser to look ahead at the upcoming token to decide whether it should continue extending the current expression (asking, "Is the next operator stronger than what I am holding?"), while `curPrecedence()` is used once an operator is consumed to establish the "floor" precedence for the right-hand side of the expression. We are now ready to use our parser. Execute the following on your machine:

```
$ go run ch10/parser.go ch10/lexer.code
=== Pretty-printed AST ===
Program
  LetStatement: x
    IntegerLiteral: 10
  ExpressionStatement
    IfExpression
      Condition:
        InfixExpression: >=
          Identifier: x
          IntegerLiteral: 10
      Consequence:
        BlockStatement
          ReturnStatement
            InfixExpression: +
              Identifier: x
              IntegerLiteral: 5
  ExpressionStatement
    IfExpression
      Condition:
        InfixExpression: !=
```

```
        Identifier: x
        IntegerLiteral: 5
    Consequence:
      BlockStatement
        ReturnStatement
          Identifier: msg
```

When the ParseProgram() function is called, the parser initializes an empty Program struct and enters a loop that continues until it encounters the EOF token. It begins by examining the first token, let. The parseStatement switch case identifies this as a TokenLet and delegates control to parseLetStatement(). This function verifies that let is followed by an identifier (x) and an assignment operator (=). It then calls parseExpression() to handle the value on the right side. The expression parser identifies 10 as an integer literal and returns it. The statement concludes by consuming the semicolon, and the resulting LetStatement node is appended to the program's list of statements. Next, the parser encounters the if token. Since TokenIf is not explicitly a let or return token, parseStatement() defaults to calling parseExpressionStatement(). This triggers parseExpression(), which looks up the prefix function registered for TokenIf, pointing to parseIfExpression(). Inside this function, the parser checks whether the next token is an opening parenthesis. Seeing x instead of (, it executes the logic for the optional parentheses style. It parses the condition x >= 10 by identifying x, recognizing >= as an infix operator, and recursively parsing 10. Once the condition is built, the parser enforces the presence of an opening brace, {, and calls parseBlockStatement(). This recursively enters a new parsing loop for the code inside the braces, creating a ReturnStatement for return x + 5; before closing the block when it hits }. Finally, the parser processes the second if block (if x != 5) using the exact same logic. It creates another ExpressionStatement containing an IfExpression. The condition x != 5 is parsed using the infix parser for the not-equal operator. The block is processed recursively, generating a ReturnStatement that holds the msg identifier. Once the closing brace, }, of this second block is consumed, the parser advances, sees the EOF token, and terminates the loop, returning the fully constructed Program object containing these three main statements.

With the AST successfully constructed, we will now turn to the evaluator, which breathes life into our static data structure by traversing the nodes and executing the logic defined within.

The evaluator

An evaluator is the component responsible for executing the parsed program. It takes the AST produced by the parser and computes its meaning by walking the tree and performing the operations described by each node. Rather than compiling the program into machine code, the evaluator functions as a tree-walking interpreter, recursively visiting nodes to produce results at runtime. Evaluation begins at the root `Program` node and proceeds through top-level statements in order. To preserve program state, the evaluator maintains a *runtime environment* — a map that stores variable bindings as they are introduced. When a variable declaration is encountered, the evaluator first evaluates the associated expression and then stores the resulting value in the environment under the variable's name. Later references to that identifier retrieve the stored value, allowing data to flow across statements and blocks.

Control flow is handled by evaluating conditional expressions. When an `if` expression is reached, the evaluator computes its condition and determines which block to execute based on truthiness: integers are considered true unless they are zero, and strings are true unless they are empty. The selected block is then evaluated as a nested sequence of statements. Return statements are handled through a dedicated return object that signals early termination of evaluation. When such an object is encountered, execution of the current block stops immediately, and the return value is propagated upward through the call stack until it reaches the top level. This mechanism ensures that `return` behaves as an explicit control flow escape, even when nested inside conditional blocks. Literal expressions — such as integers and strings — form the base cases of evaluation. They are directly converted into internal runtime objects and serve as the fundamental data values upon which all other computations are built.

First, let us present the logic behind the evaluator implementation as found in `ch10/evaluator.go`. The execution flow begins in `main()`, which initializes a new variable scope by calling `NewEnv()` and passes the parsed `Program` node to the `Eval()` function. `Eval()` acts as the central dispatch mechanism, utilizing a type switch to determine the specific behavior for each `Node` implementation. When handling the root `Program` or a nested `BlockStatement`, `Eval()` iterates through the slice of statements, recursively calling itself for each one; inside this loop, it checks whether the result is a `ReturnValue` object to determine whether it should halt execution and return the unwrapped value immediately. For specific statement types, `Eval()` delegates logic accordingly: processing a `LetStatement` triggers a recursive call to `Eval()` for the value, followed by a call to `env.Set()` to bind the result to the identifier name. A `ReturnStatement` results in `Eval()` computing the inner expression and wrapping it in a `ReturnValue` struct. When `Eval()` encounters `IntegerLiteral` or `StringLiteral` nodes, it instantiates and returns corresponding `Integer` or `String` objects, which satisfy the `Object` interface by implementing `Type()` and `Inspect()`. The `Identifier` nodes trigger a call to `env.Get()` to retrieve stored values. Control flow is managed within the `IfExpression` case, where `Eval()` computes the condition and passes the result to `isTruthy()`; depending on the Boolean returned, `Eval()` is then recursively called on either the `Consequence` or `Alternative` block.

With this architectural overview in place, we will now turn to the concrete implementation. Since the evaluator's primary job is to generate and manipulate values, we must first define what a "value" actually is within our interpreter. So, we begin with the object system, which defines how Go represents and categorizes the dynamic data types of our language:

```
type ObjectType string
const (
    IntegerObj = "INTEGER"
    StringObj  = "STRING"
    NullObj    = "NULL"
    ReturnObj  = "RETURN"
)

type Object interface {
    Type() ObjectType
    Inspect() string
}
```

The code begins by defining `ObjectType` as a `string` alias, paired with a set of constants such as `IntegerObj` and `StringObj`. These constants serve as a rigid enumeration of every valid data type the interpreter understands, preventing typos and ensuring that type-checking (e.g., verifying whether a variable is an integer) relies on consistent, predefined labels. The list also includes `ReturnObj`, a special internal type used not for user data but to manage control flow when exiting functions. The center of this architecture is the `Object` interface, which acts as a universal container for all runtime values. Because Go is statically typed, this interface allows the interpreter to treat disparate Go structs polymorphically as a single type. Any struct that wishes to be used as a value in our language must satisfy this contract by implementing two methods: `Type()`, which returns one of the defined constants to identify the object's category, and `Inspect()`, which returns a formatted string representation of the value, primarily used for printing results to the console or debugging. Following that, let us see the implementation of `Integer`:

```
type Integer struct{ Value int64 }
func (i *Integer) Type() ObjectType { return IntegerObj }
func (i *Integer) Inspect() string {return fmt.Sprintf("%d", i.Value)}
```

The `Integer` struct itself serves as a wrapper around a raw Go `int64`, allowing the native machine integer to be treated as a generic `Object` within our interpreter's memory. To fulfill the interface contract, it defines the `Type()` method, which returns the specific `IntegerObj` constant; this allows the evaluator to easily identify this object as a number when performing type checks before arithmetic operations. The `Inspect()` method provides the string representation of the value, utilizing `fmt.Sprintf()` to convert the internal numerical data into text, ensuring it can be displayed correctly.

After that, let us see the implementation of `isTruthy()`, which serves as the logic bridge between the interpreted language's data types and Go's native control flow, specifically to support conditional statements such as `if-else`:

```
func isTruthy(obj Object) bool {
    switch obj {
    case nil:
        return false
    }
    switch i := obj.(type) {
    case *Integer:
        return i.Value != 0
    case *String:
        return i.Value != ""
    case *Null:
        return false
    default:
        return true
    }
}
```

Since SMALL does not include a dedicated Boolean type, `isTruthy()` defines "truthiness" based on the presence or value of data. The function begins with a defensive check to ensure the passed `Object` interface is not `nil`; if it is, the function immediately returns `false` to prevent runtime panics. Following this safety check, the function utilizes a type switch to determine the underlying type of the object and applies specific rules: for `*Integer` objects, any non-zero value is treated as true, whereas `0` is false. For `*String` objects, any non-empty string is considered true. The specific `*Null` object type is explicitly defined as `false`. Finally, a `default` case ensures that any other valid object type not explicitly handled (which would fall into the default block) is treated as true, ensuring that the evaluation logic remains robust as new types are added. Next, let us see how an environment is defined:

```
type Env struct {
    store map[string]Object
}
```

```
func NewEnv() *Env {
    return &Env{store: make(map[string]Object)}
}
func (e *Env) Get(name string) (Object, bool) {
    obj, ok := e.store[name]
    return obj, ok
}
func (e *Env) Set(name string, val Object) Object {
    e.store[name] = val
    return val
}
```

The `Env` struct represents the interpreter's runtime environment, serving as the memory system where variable bindings are stored and retrieved. Rather than exposing a raw Go map directly, we encapsulate it within a struct; this abstraction not only organizes the code but also prepares the architecture for future features, such as nested scopes. The underlying storage, defined as `store`, maps variable names (strings) to their corresponding runtime values (`Object`). The `NewEnv()` constructor is responsible for initializing this internal map, ensuring that the environment is ready for use immediately upon creation. The `Get()` and `Set()` methods provide the standard interface for interacting with this memory. `Set()` is triggered by variable declarations, assigning a computed value to a specific identifier in the map. Conversely, `Get()` retrieves these values using Go's "comma OK" idiom. This return signature is critical for error handling as it allows the evaluator to distinguish between a valid variable and one that has not been defined, preventing runtime panics when the code references an unknown identifier. By encapsulating storage behind `Get()` and `Set()`, the evaluator remains decoupled from the underlying implementation, interacting with the environment only through a simple, well-defined interface.

The `Eval()` function acts as the central dispatch hub for the interpreter, utilizing a large type switch to determine the execution logic for every possible node type in the AST. Let us look at its full implementation in parts, starting with the following code snippet:

```
func Eval(node Node, env *Env) Object {
    switch n := node.(type) {

    // Statements
    case *Program:
        return evalProgram(n, env)
    case *BlockStatement:
        return evalBlockStatement(n, env)
```

The func Eval(node Node, env *Env) Object function signature highlights its recursive nature: it takes any AST node and the current memory environment as input and returns a computed runtime Object. Inside, the logic relies on a type switch (switch n := node.(type)) to dynamically dispatch execution to the correct handler based on the specific node type. In this initial code, switch handles the structural containers of the language. case *Program matches the root of the AST, triggering evalProgram to execute the top-level statements sequentially. Similarly, case *BlockStatement matches nested sequences of code — such as those found inside if statement braces — and delegates them to evalBlockStatement(). While these two cases may look similar, distinguishing them allows the interpreter to handle scope and control flow (such as return statements) differently at the top level versus inside nested blocks.

case *ExpressionStatement addresses lines of code that consist solely of an expression, such as a solitary function call or an arithmetic operation:

```
case *ExpressionStatement:
    return Eval(n.Expression, env)
```

Because the parser wraps these expressions in a statement container to fit the language's grammar, the evaluator must unwrap them first. This case simply extracts the underlying n.Expression and recursively calls Eval() on it, passing the current environment, env, forward. The result of that inner evaluation is then returned directly, allowing the program to compute values or trigger side effects even when they are not assigned to variables. Next, we have the case *LetStatement block, which handles variable declaration and assignment, acting as the bridge between static syntax and runtime memory:

```
case *LetStatement:
    val := Eval(n.Value, env)
    if isError(val) {
        return val
    }
    env.Set(n.Name.Value, val)
    return val
```

The process is strictly ordered: before a variable can be stored, its value must be computed. Therefore, the code first calls Eval() recursively on the right-hand-side expression (n.Value), reducing potentially complex logic (such as let x = 5 * 5;) down to a single result. It immediately follows this with an error check (isError(val)); if the right-hand-side evaluation failed (for example, a division by zero), the process halts and the error is returned immediately, preventing the environment from being corrupted with invalid data. Once a valid result is confirmed, `env.Set()` is invoked to bind the computed object to the variable's identifier in the environment map, effectively "saving" the state for future lookups. After that, `case *ReturnStatement` implements the logic for halting execution and passing data back to the caller:

```
case *ReturnStatement:
    val := Eval(n.ReturnValue, env)
    if isError(val) {
        return val
    }
    return &ReturnValue{Value: val}
```

Like variable assignment, the process begins by evaluating the expression associated with the `return` keyword, reducing it to a final concrete object. After a standard error check to ensure validity, the critical step occurs. Instead of returning the raw value directly, the evaluator wraps it inside a `ReturnValue` struct. This wrapper acts as a unique signal to the interpreter's control loop; it allows upstream functions — specifically the block evaluator — to distinguish between a normal computed value (which allows the loop to continue to the next line) and a return signal (which interrupts the flow and exits the current scope immediately).

The `case *IntegerLiteral` and `case *StringLiteral` blocks represent the base cases of the evaluation process — the leaves of the AST where execution hits raw data. Unlike expressions that require computation, literals are values that are already fully resolved:

```
case *IntegerLiteral:
    return &Integer{Value: n.Value}
case *StringLiteral:
    return &String{Value: n.Value}
```

Here, the job is simple but crucial: it converts the static AST nodes produced by the parser into dynamic runtime objects. It takes the raw native Go values (such as `int64` or `string`) stored in the AST nodes and wraps them in their corresponding `Integer` or `String` structs. This transformation ensures that these simple values satisfy the `Object` interface, allowing them to flow seamlessly through the rest of the system, ready to be stored in variables or used in arithmetic operations. Next, the `case *Identifier` block handles variable resolution, which occurs whenever the code references a named variable (such as using `x` in `x + 5`):

```
case *Identifier:
    return evalIdentifier(n, env)
```

Unlike literals, which carry their own value, identifiers are merely pointers to data stored elsewhere. Therefore, this case delegates the task to the `evalIdentifier()` helper function, passing along the current environment, env. This triggers a lookup process where the interpreter searches the memory map for the variable name, effectively retrieving the runtime value that was previously bound to it.

The code in the `case *PrefixExpression` block manages unary operations, where an operator precedes a single operand (such as `-5` or `!true`):

```
case *PrefixExpression:
    right := Eval(n.Right, env)
    if isError(right) {
        return right
    }
    return evalPrefixExpression(n.Operator, right)
```

The evaluation strategy is strictly right to left: the interpreter must first determine the value of the operand before it can modify it. To achieve this, the code recursively calls `Eval()` on `n.Right`. This step is crucial because the operand itself might be a complex expression, such as `-(5 + 5)`, and it must be reduced to a concrete runtime object first. After validating that this sub-evaluation did not produce an error, the code delegates the final step to `evalPrefixExpression()`. This helper function takes the resolved object and the operator symbol, applying the specific logic — such as numeric negation — to produce the final result.

The `case *InfixExpression` block manages binary operations, which constitute most arithmetic and logical comparisons, such as `5 + 5` or `x > 10`:

```
case *InfixExpression:
    left := Eval(n.Left, env)
    if isError(left) {
        return left
    }
    right := Eval(n.Right, env)
    if isError(right) {
        return right
    }
    return evalInfixExpression(n.Operator, left, right)
```

Because an operator requires two concrete values to function, the evaluator must perform a recursive "depth-first" reduction. It systematically evaluates the left operand first, followed by the right operand. Crucially, error checking is performed immediately after each step; if the left side produces an error, execution stops before the right side is even touched. Only when both operands have been successfully resolved into runtime objects are they passed to the `evalInfixExpression()` helper, which performs the actual calculation based on the operator.

The `switch` concludes with `case *IfExpression`, which delegates the logic for branching control flow to `evalIfExpression()`:

```
    case *IfExpression:
        return evalIfExpression(n, env)
    }
    return nil
}
```

This keeps the main dispatch loop clean while allowing the specific handler to determine whether to execute the `Consequence` or `Alternative` block based on the condition. Finally, the function ends with a catch-all `return nil`. This serves as a safety mechanism; if the evaluator encounters an AST node type that it does not recognize or has not been programmed to handle, it gracefully returns `nil` rather than causing a runtime panic.

Next, let us explain `evalInfixExpression()`, which serves as a specialized type dispatcher for binary operations and is responsible for enforcing the language's typing rules before any actual computation occurs:

```
func evalInfixExpression(operator string, left, right Object) Object {
    // Check if both operands are integers
    if left.Type() == IntegerObj && right.Type() == IntegerObj {
        return evalIntegerInfixExpression(operator, left, right)
    }
    // Handle String concatenation
    if left.Type() == StringObj && right.Type() == StringObj {
        return evalStringInfixExpression(operator, left, right)
    }
    return &Null{}
}
```

Since the language is dynamically typed, the evaluator does not know in advance whether it is being asked to add two numbers, concatenate two strings, or attempt an invalid operation. Therefore, `evalInfixExpression()` acts as a gatekeeper, inspecting the `Type()` of both the left and right operands to ensure they are compatible. The logic prioritizes integer arithmetic, first checking whether both operands are of type `IntegerObj`. If they match, the specific operator and values are handed off to the `evalIntegerInfixExpression()` helper. If that check fails, the function attempts to handle text manipulation by verifying whether both operands are `StringObj`, delegating to `evalStringInfixExpression()` if a match is found. Crucially, if the operands are mismatched — such as trying to add an integer to a string — or if the types are unsupported, the function falls through to the end and returns a `&Null{}` object. This design effectively treats type errors or invalid combinations as undefined values rather than crashing the program. Last, let us explain `evalIntegerInfixExpression()`:

```
func evalIntegerInfixExpression(operator string, left, right Object) Object {
    leftVal := left.(*Integer).Value
    rightVal := right.(*Integer).Value
    switch operator {
    case "+":
        return &Integer{Value: leftVal + rightVal}
    case "-":
        return &Integer{Value: leftVal - rightVal}
    case "*":
        return &Integer{Value: leftVal * rightVal}
    case "/":
        return &Integer{Value: leftVal / rightVal}
    // Comparisons return 1 or 0 because we don't have Booleans
    case "<":
        return nativeBoolToInteger(leftVal < rightVal)
    case ">":
        return nativeBoolToInteger(leftVal > rightVal)
    case "==":
        return nativeBoolToInteger(leftVal == rightVal)
    case "!=":
        return nativeBoolToInteger(leftVal != rightVal)
    default:
        return &Null{}
    }
}
```

The `evalIntegerInfixExpression()` function performs the actual computational heavy lifting for integer operations. Since the `Object` interface hides the underlying data, the function begins by "unwrapping" the operands using Go type assertions (`.(*Integer).Value`). This extracts the raw `int64` values so that native Go math can be applied. The core logic is contained in a `switch` statement that segregates operations into two categories: arithmetic and comparison. For standard math operators such as + and *, the function computes the result and immediately re-wraps it in a new `Integer` object. However, the comparison logic (such as `<` or `==`) reveals a specific design constraint of this language: the absence of a dedicated Boolean type. Instead of returning `true` or `false`, the function delegates to `nativeBoolToInteger()`, which maps the result of the comparison to a numerical value — returning `1` for true and `0` for false — ensuring the result remains compatible with the rest of the interpreter's integer-based logic.

We now have our first working version of SMALL, a minimal yet expressive language. It supports variables, arithmetic and relational expressions, strings, and flexible `if-else` statements, all while enforcing proper operator precedence. Its simplicity makes it an ideal example for exploring lexing, parsing, AST construction, and evaluation without unnecessary complexity. With the evaluator in place, the core architecture of our interpreter is fully realized. The pipeline now flows seamlessly from end to end: the lexer converts raw source text into a structured stream of tokens, the parser groups those tokens into a hierarchical AST, and the evaluator recursively traverses that tree to execute the underlying logic. With all that in mind, let us use our language!

Using SMALL

We present and run two short SMALL programs to make sure that everything works as expected, starting from a program that calculates the absolute difference between two numbers, defined inside the code:

```
$ cat ch10/absDiff.code
let a = 10;
let b = 25;
if a > b {
    return a - b;
}

// Since a is not greater than b, we subtract a from b
return b - a;
$ go run ch10/evaluator.go ch10/absDiff.code
=== Program Result ===
15
```

The output of this program is `15`. Since a (`10`) is not greater than b (`25`), the evaluator skips the `if` block and proceeds to the final line, calculating `25 - 10`.

Next, we have a program that checks whether a number is positive, negative, or zero:

```
$ cat ch10/sign.code
let x = -5;
if x > 0 {
    return "Positive";
}
if x < 0 {
    return "Negative";
}
return "Zero";
$ go run ch10/evaluator.go ch10/sign.code
=== Program Result ===
Negative
```

The program outputs `"Negative"` because variable `x` is initialized to `-5`, causing the interpreter to bypass the first conditional but enter the second `if x < 0` block. Once inside, the `return` statement triggers an immediate halt to the execution flow, ensuring the final fallback value of `"Zero"` is ignored.

These initial programs confirm that our architectural design is sound. The components we constructed — the lexer, parser, and evaluator — now operate as a cohesive runtime environment. While SMALL currently possesses a minimal feature set, this robust foundation proves the viability of our execution pipeline, setting the stage for the more advanced language features we will implement next.

Summary

By combining our Pratt parser with a recursive tree-walking evaluator, we have successfully transformed a static collection of Go structs into a programming language. We have moved beyond simple text processing to capture the semantics of variable binding, arithmetic, and conditional logic, proving that the interpreter can not only understand the structure of code but meaningfully execute it. However, our language currently exists in a limited scope; while it can calculate and decide, it lacks fundamental capabilities such as functions, Boolean values, and `for` loops, as well as support for assignments. All of these, as well as writing tests, are going to be implemented in the next chapter!

Exercises

1. Execute `ch10/ifElse.code` on your machine.
2. SMALL has support for `Integer`, which internally is an `int64` value. Add a new data type named `Int32`, which will be an `int32` value.

Additional resources

- Operator precedence parser: `https://en.wikipedia.org/wiki/Operator-precedence_parser`

11

Adding New Features to SMALL

In our initial implementation of **SMALL**, we established the fundamental architecture of an interpreter. We built a lexer to digitize raw text into a stream of tokens, a Pratt parser to organize those tokens into a mathematically sound abstract syntax tree, and a tree-walking evaluator to execute the resulting logic. While this minimal feature set proved the viability of our execution model, a language restricted to simple arithmetic and static conditionals is limited in its practical utility. To transform SMALL from a theoretical exercise into a capable programming tool, we must now expand its expressive power.

Adding new features to a programming language, such as SMALL, is more than just a technical exercise; it is also a process driven by the desire to evolve, adapt, and better serve the needs of its users. By the end of this chapter, you will have moved beyond simple calculations to building a language that can execute simple algorithms, understand true and false conditions, support functions, and verify its own correctness through a comprehensive suite of automated tests.

This chapter covers the following topics:

- Why dowe need to extend a programming language
- New features in SMALL
- Implementing the updated version of SMALL
- Writing tests for SMALL

Why do we need to extend a programming language

Extending a simple programming language enhances its utility without sacrificing the simplicity that makes it accessible. A minimal base offers a low barrier to entry but often lacks the abstractions required for complex domains such as web development or systems programming. By strategically introducing libraries, syntactic sugar or built-in features, we bridge this gap. This enables developers to write concise, maintainable code, allowing the language to adapt to new paradigms while preserving the stable foundation users rely on.

New features in SMALL

The updated **SMALL** introduces several powerful features that make it more expressive and practical for programming. First, it adds support for assignments. Next, it supports Boolean values with the `true` and `false` literals, along with logical operators such as `!` (not), `&&` (and), and `||` (or), allowing for complex conditional expressions and control flow. SMALL now includes built-in functions, specifically, `print()` for displaying values and `println()` for printing values followed by a newline, making debugging and output straightforward. You can define your own functions using the `func` keyword, with parameters and return values. Additionally, we added `for` loops with initialization, condition, and post expressions. The language also enhances string handling by supporting escape sequences such as `\n` for newline and `\t` for tab, allowing formatted text output.

The first EBNF snippet of the updated SMALL establishes the foundational structure of the language:

```
<program>               ::= { <statement> }
<statement>             ::= <let-statement>
                          | <return-statement>
                          | <expression-statement>
                          | <if-statement>
                          | <for-statement>
                          | <function-declaration>
<let-statement>         ::= "let" <identifier> "=" <expression> ";"
<return-statement>      ::= "return" <expression> ";"
<expression-statement>  ::= <expression> ";"
```

The hierarchy begins with `<program>`, which is defined as a collection of zero or more `<statement>` nodes (indicated by the curly braces, `{ }`). This rule allows a source file to be empty or to contain an infinite sequence of commands. The `<statement>` rule itself functions as a high-level "dispatcher," explicitly listing the valid grammatical constructs the parser recognizes: variable bindings (`let`), flow control (`return`, `if`, and `for`), function definitions, and standalone expressions. The snippet then details the syntax for three fundamental statement types, all of which enforce a termination rule using a semicolon (`;`). The `<let-statement>` defines variable binding; it strictly requires the `let` keyword, a valid identifier name, an assignment operator (`=`), and a resulting expression. The `<return-statement>` handles function exits, consisting of the `return` keyword followed immediately by the expression to be returned. Finally, the `<expression-statement>` allows values or function calls (such as `call()` or `x + 5`) to stand alone as complete statements, provided they are terminated by a semicolon.

The next segment defines the core control structures and scoping mechanisms:

```
<if-statement>          ::= "if" <expression> <block> [ "else" <block> ]
<for-statement>    ::= "for" <let-statement> <expression> ";" <expression> <block>

<function-declaration>  ::= "func" <identifier> "(" [ <parameters> ] ")" <block>

<parameters>            ::= <identifier> { "," <identifier> }
<block>                 ::= "{" { <statement> } "}"
```

The `<if-statement>` rule describes conditional logic, requiring the `if` keyword followed immediately by a conditional expression and a mandatory block of code to execute if the condition is `true`. The grammar allows for an optional `else` clause (denoted by the square brackets, `[ ]`), which provides an alternative block of code for `false` conditions. Central to these structures is `<block>`, defined as a sequence of zero or more statements enclosed within curly braces, `{ }`, creating a new local scope for variable execution. The `<for-statement>` rule codifies the iterative capabilities of SMALL, enforcing a strict C-style loop structure. It begins with the `for` keyword, followed by a `<let-statement>` for initialization, a condition expression, an explicit semicolon separator, and finally, an update expression before the loop body. Simultaneously, the `<function-declaration>` rule outlines how reusable logic is defined: using the `func` keyword, a specific identifier name, and a parenthesized list of `<parameters>`. These parameters are defined as a comma-separated list of identifiers, allowing the function to accept dynamic input before executing its associated block.

The next snippet illustrates the topmost layer of the expression hierarchy-making assignment as the operation with the lowest binding power in the grammar:

```
<expression>            ::= <assignment-expression>
<assignment-expression> ::= <identifier> "=" <assignment-expression>
                          | <logical-or-expression>
```

The `<expression>` rule now serves as the gateway to mutable state, delegating immediately to `<assignment-expression>`. This represents a fundamental shift: expressions can now produce side effects. By defining assignment recursively — an identifier and equals sign followed by another `<assignment-expression>` — we enable right-associativity. This structure allows the parser to handle chained assignments, such as a = b = 5, naturally, processing them from right to left. If no assignment pattern is matched, the grammar falls through to <logical-or-expression>, handing control to the standard operator hierarchy.

The next snippet defines the hierarchy of logical and relational operations, establishing the specific operator precedence that governs how Boolean conditions are evaluated. The structure imposes a strict layering where operators defined *lower* in the list bind more tightly than those above them:

```
<logical-or-expression> ::= <logical-and-expression> { "||" <logical-and-
expression> }
<logical-and-expression>::= <equality-expression> { "&&"<equality-expression> }
<equality-expression>    ::= <comparison-expression> { ("==" | "!=") <comparison-
expression> }
<comparison-expression> ::= <term> { ("<" | ">" | "<=" | ">=") <term> }
```

This hierarchy defines logical and relational operations, using a layered structure to enforce standard operator precedence. By nesting the rules, the grammar ensures that operators defined *lower* in the chain bind more tightly. Relational comparisons (<, >) are resolved first, followed by equality checks (==), logical AND (&&), and finally, logical OR (||). This ordering allows composite conditions such as x <10&&y> 5 to be evaluated intuitively without requiring explicit parentheses.

The next segment of the EBNF grammar establishes the rules for arithmetic operations and the fundamental atomic units of the language, strictly enforcing standard mathematical precedence:

```
<term>                   ::= <factor> { ("+" | "-") <factor> }
<factor>                 ::= <unary> { ("*" | "/") <unary> }
<unary>                  ::= [ "!" | "-" ] <primary>
<primary>                ::= <integer>
                           | <string>
                           | <boolean>
                           | <identifier>
                           | <function-call>
                           | "(" <expression> ")"
```

The arithmetic subset mirrors this layered approach to enforce the standard order of operations. The <term> rule handles addition and subtraction, composed of <factor> nodes that handle multiplication and division. This nesting ensures that multiplication binds tighter than addition automatically (e.g., parsing 1 + 2 * 3 correctly). Descending further, <unary> handles prefix operators such as negation (-) and logical NOT (!), giving them precedence over binary arithmetic. Finally, `<primary>` defines atomic values — literals, identifiers, and function calls — along with parenthesized expressions, which provide the mechanism to manually override these precedence rules.

The grammar continues with more rules:

```
<function-call>         ::= <builtin-function-call> | <user-function-call>
<builtin-function-call> ::= ("print" | "println") "(" [ <arguments> ] ")"
<user-function-call>    ::= <identifier> "(" [ <arguments> ] ")"
<arguments>             ::= <expression> { "," <expression> }
<boolean>               ::= "true" | "false"
```

The `<function-call>` rule serves as a branching point, separating invocations into two distinct categories: built-in operations and custom function execution. The `<builtin-function-call>` rule hardcodes the syntax for input/output operations, strictly recognizing the `print` and `println` keywords followed by a parenthesized list of arguments. This is structurally distinct from the `<user-function-call>` rule, which allows any valid `<identifier>` — representing a variable bound to a function definition — to be invoked in the same manner. Both types rely on the `<arguments>` rule, which defines a flexible, comma-separated list of expressions, ensuring that functions can accept dynamic inputs ranging from simple literals to complex calculations. Finally, the `<boolean>` rule provides the foundational truth values for the language's conditional logic, strictly limiting valid Boolean literals to the `true` and `false` keywords.

Last, at the foundational lexical level, the grammar defines the atomic rules for constructing names and literals, ensuring consistent tokenization of the source code:

```
<identifier>            ::= letter { letter | digit | "_" }
<integer>               ::= digit { digit }
<string>                ::= '"' { <character> | <escape-sequence> } '"'
<escape-sequence>       ::= "\" ("n" | "t" | "\"" | "\\" )
```

The `<identifier>` rule enforces standard variable naming conventions by requiring that every name begin with a letter. Following this initial character, the rule permits a mixed sequence of zero or more letters, digits, or underscores, effectively distinguishing user-defined names from numeric literals while allowing for descriptive *snake_case* naming styles. The `<integer>` rule is straightforward, strictly defining a number as a contiguous sequence of one or more digits. Finally, the `<string>` rule handles text literals by demanding they be enclosed within double quotes. This rule incorporates a sub-definition for `<escape-sequence>`, which allows the parser to recognize and correctly interpret special formatting characters — specifically, newlines (`\n`), tabs (`\t`), literal quotes (`\"`), and backslashes (`\\`) —that would otherwise break the string's delimiters or structure. With that information in mind, we are ready to present the implementations of the lexer, the parser, and the evaluator for the updated version of SMALL.

Implementing the updated version of SMALL

We now move from definition to implementation, using our expanded grammar as the blueprint. The new syntactic rules for control flow map directly to extensions in the *parser*, while the introduction of variable assignment necessitates a stateful *evaluator* to manage mutable environments. We begin this process by upgrading the *lexer* to support the new tokens and precise error tracking required for these features.

The lexer

We are now going to talk about the modified lexer code. Apart from the changes in SMALL, the most fundamental difference lies in how the input source code is stored and accessed. The original lexer stored the input as a raw `string` and accessed characters using `byte` indexing. In Go, indexing a `string` returns a `byte`, not a character. This means if the source code contained any multi-byte `UTF-8` characters, the lexer would read them incorrectly, splitting a single character into multiple invalid bytes. The new version of the lexer converts the input into a `[]rune` slice upon initialization. By reading from a rune slice, the lexer handles characters safely, ensuring that `position` and `readPosition` always align with logical characters rather than raw memory bytes. Let us now see the implementation of `NewLexer()` that shows the explicit type conversion of the input string into a slice of runes (`[]rune(input)`):

```
func NewLexer(input string) *Lexer {
    l := &Lexer{input: []rune(input)}
    l.readChar()
    return l
}
```

The critical update to `NextToken()` resolves a synchronization issue where the lexer aggressively consumed characters. Because helper methods such as `readString()` fully consume their respective tokens (including the closing quote), the original implementation's default behavior of advancing the input again caused the lexer to skip the character immediately following a string. We have adjusted the logic to respect the cursor position established by these helpers, ensuring that subsequent delimiters — such as semicolons or closing parentheses — are accurately detected rather than swallowed. With the lexical analysis layer now stabilized, we turn our attention to the parser.

The parser

The updated parser introduces a significant structural improvement by redefining *variable assignment* from a simple statement to a fully-fledged expression. In the original design, assignments were rigid statements that could not return a value or be nested, which made constructs such as C-style `for` loops (specifically, the update clause, `i = i + 1`) syntactically impossible. By implementing `AssignExpression` and registering the `=` token with its own precedence level, the parser now allows assignments to occur anywhere an expression is valid. Additionally, the expression scanning logic has been tightened to resolve a *greedy consumption* bug; it now explicitly peeks for closing parentheses, `)`, during infix parsing to ensure that arguments in nested function calls are delimited correctly, preventing the parser from erroneously absorbing tokens that belong to the enclosing scope. We begin updating the parser to support the latest SMALL enhancements by defining the following constants:

```
const (
	_ int = iota
	LOWEST
	ASSIGN
	LOGICAL
	EQUALS
	LESSGREATER
	SUM
	PRODUCT
	PREFIX
	CALL
)
```

The provided code block establishes the hierarchy of operator precedence for the parser, essentially defining the strict *order of operations* that governs how the language understands mathematical and logical expressions. By using Go's `iota` identifier (a predeclared constant generator used within `const` blocks to create a sequence of related, auto-incrementing integer values without manual numbering), the code automatically assigns strictly increasing integer values to each constant, starting from `LOWEST` (assigned `1`, since the `0` value is skipped with `_`) up to `CALL` (assigned `9`). This numerical progression represents **binding power**: operators with higher values bind more tightly to their operands than those with lower values. For example, because `ASSIGN` is placed near the bottom of the list with a value of 2, it has very low binding power, ensuring that in a statement such as `x = 1 + 2`, the parser evaluates the addition (which has a higher precedence) before attempting the assignment. Conversely, `CALL` is placed at the top of the list, ensuring that function invocations such as `myFunc(a)` are evaluated before any surrounding arithmetic or logical operations. This specific ordering — placing logical comparisons below sums and sums below products — is what enforces standard mathematical rules, such as multiplication happening before addition, within the structure of your programming language. But this definition of constants is not enough. We need a structure to support it:

```
var precedences = map[TokenType]int{
    TokenAssign: ASSIGN,
    TokenOr:      LOGICAL, TokenAnd: LOGICAL,
    TokenEqual: EQUALS, TokenNotEqual: EQUALS,
    TokenLT: LESSGREATER, TokenGT: LESSGREATER,
    TokenLE: LESSGREATER, TokenGE: LESSGREATER,
    TokenPlus: SUM, TokenMinus: SUM,
    TokenSlash: PRODUCT, TokenAsterisk: PRODUCT,
    TokenLParen: CALL,
}
```

The `precedences` map serves as the operational bridge between the theoretical hierarchy defined in the previous `const` block and the parser's actual decision-making logic. While the `const` block establishes the abstract ranking of binding powers, the map applies those rankings to concrete language tokens. By associating specific tokens, such as `TokenPlus` with the `SUM` constant or `TokenAsterisk` with `PRODUCT`, this data structure allows the parser to instantaneously look up the "weight" of any operator it encounters. This relationship enables the Pratt parsing algorithm to dynamically decide whether to continue extending the current expression or to stop and group terms, enforcing the grammatical rules defined by the integer constants.

The `parseExpression()` method acts as the recursive engine of the Pratt parser, orchestrating AST construction through two distinct phases: **prefix handling** and **infix extension**. First, the function establishes a "base" expression by evaluating the current token as a prefix — handling simple literals, identifiers, or unary operators (such as negation). This phase determines the left-hand side of any potential operation. Once established, the parser enters the infix phase, a loop that extends this base into larger structures. If the next token has a higher binding power, it is consumed as an infix operator (such as + or *), wrapping the existing expression into a binary operation or function call. This dual-phase approach allows the parser to seamlessly handle complex, nested logic while adhering to the strict order of operations defined by the grammar. (See `ch11/upParser.go` for implementation details.)

In the updated parser, we have also enhanced the functionality of the Lexer by incorporating column and line tracking into the error reporting mechanism. Instead of halting with a vague failure, the parser extracts the `Line` and `Col` fields from the offending token to construct detailed error messages. This integration ensures that if the structural logic defined in `parseExpression()` fails to match the input, the interpreter can pinpoint the exact coordinate of the discrepancy, allowing the user to fix syntax errors quickly without guessing where the problem lies. This position tracking logic is concretely implemented within the `readChar()` function of the lexer.

Next, we present the handling of the newly introduced `for` statement:

```
func (p *Parser) parseForStatement() *ForStatement {
    stmt := &ForStatement{}
    p.nextToken()
    if !p.curTokenIs(TokenLet) {
        p.errors = append(p.errors, "for loop must start with let")
        return nil
    }
    stmt.Init = p.parseLetStatement()
    p.nextToken()
    stmt.Condition = p.parseExpression(LOWEST)
    if !p.expectPeek(TokenSemicolon) {
        return nil
    }
    p.nextToken()
    stmt.Update = p.parseExpression(LOWEST)
    if !p.expectPeek(TokenLBrace) {
        return nil
    }
    stmt.Body = p.parseBlockStatement()
    return stmt
}
```

The code begins by enforcing a syntactic requirement: every loop must commence with an explicit variable declaration via the `let` keyword, ensuring that the loop counter is properly initialized within the local scope. Once this initialization is processed, the parser advances to the termination condition, treating it as a standard expression followed by a mandatory semicolon separator. The function then parses the update clause; this step leverages the architectural shift that treats assignments as expressions, allowing the parser to validly accept variable updates — such as incrementing a counter — directly within the loop header. Finally, the method verifies the presence of an opening brace before handing control over to the block parsing logic to capture and structure the executable body of the loop.

With the source code now successfully transformed into an AST, the interpreter shifts its focus from structural analysis to runtime execution.

The evaluator

The primary goal of the updated evaluator is to introduce mutable state, transforming the language from a purely functional design to one capable of imperative control flow. Originally, variables defined via `let` were immutable, rendering constructs such as counting loops impossible. To resolve this, we extend the `Environment` with an `Update()` method that recursively modifies existing values within the scope chain. This mechanism powers the new `*AssignExpression` handler, which commits changes to memory. Consequently, this infrastructure enables `*ForStatement` to execute a standard C-style lifecycle: initializing state once, repeatedly checking conditions, and applying updates across iterations.

Let us begin our code presentation with the `Update()` method, which serves as the engine for mutable state:

```
func (e *Environment) Update(name string, val Object) (Object, bool) {
    if _, ok := e.store[name]; ok {
        e.store[name] = val
        return val, true
    }
    if e.outer != nil {
        return e.outer.Update(name, val)
    }
    return nil, false
}
```

The logic of `Update()` begins by inspecting the current environment's `store`; if the specified variable `name` is found locally, the method immediately overwrites it with the new `val` and returns `true` to indicate success. However, if the variable is absent locally, the function checks for the existence of an `outer` (enclosing) environment. If one exists, it recursively delegates the update request up the chain, allowing the change to propagate to parent scopes — a feature critical for closures where an inner function must modify a variable defined in an `outer` block. If the recursion reaches the top level without finding the identifier, the method returns `false`, signaling that the user is attempting to assign to an undeclared variable.

After that, we present the `*AssignExpression` case implementation inside `Eval()`, which defines how the interpreter handles assignment expressions, such as `x = 10`, which are crucial for mutable state:

```
case *AssignExpression:
    val := Eval(node.Value, env)
    if isError(val) {
        return val
    }
    if _, ok := env.Update(node.Name.Value, val); !ok {
        return newError("identifier not found for assignment: %s",
node.Name.Value)
    }
    return val
```

Assignment evaluation strictly enforces valid state transitions before modifying memory. First, the right-hand side is evaluated; any runtime errors (such as *division by zero*) propagate immediately, halting execution. Next, the environment attempts to update the variable, raising a *not found* error if the identifier was never declared. On success, the state is modified in place, and the value is returned, allowing the assignment to function as an expression within larger statements.

Next, we move into the `evalForStatement()` function that orchestrates the execution of the `for` loop that closely mimics the behavior of a standard C-style `for` loop:

```
func evalForStatement(fs *ForStatement, env *Environment) Object {
    loopEnv := NewEnclosedEnvironment(env)
    if fs.Init != nil {
        if err := Eval(fs.Init, loopEnv); isError(err) {
            return err
        }
    }
    for {
        if fs.Condition != nil {
            cond := Eval(fs.Condition, loopEnv)
            if isError(cond) {
                return cond
            }
            if !isTruthy(cond) {
                break
            }
```

```
        }
        res := Eval(fs.Body, loopEnv)
        if res != nil && (res.Type() == RETURN_VALUE_OBJ || res.Type() ==
ERROR_OBJ) {
            return res
        }
        if fs.Update != nil {
            if err := Eval(fs.Update, loopEnv); isError(err) {
                return err
            }
        }
    }
    return NULL
}
```

The code begins by establishing a new, enclosed scope (`loopEnv`) to ensure that any variables initialized within the loop, such as a counter, remain local and do not pollute the outer environment. The `NewEnclosedEnvironment()` function is responsible for creating a new, local scope that maintains a reference to an existing `outer` environment. This structural link allows the interpreter to resolve variables by first checking the immediate local scope and then recursively searching up the chain if the identifier is not found, effectively implementing closure support. The function then proceeds to the initialization phase, executing the setup statement — typically, a variable assignment such as `let i = 0` — and immediately checking for any errors that might abort the process. Once the environment is primed, the function enters an infinite Go loop to drive the iteration cycle. In each pass, it first evaluates the termination condition; if this condition resolves to `false`, the loop breaks immediately, ceasing execution. If the condition holds `true`, the loop executes its body. Crucially, the evaluator checks the result of this body execution for *return values* or *errors*. This check allows a `return` statement nested deep within a loop to correctly bubble up and exit the entire function, rather than just the current iteration. Finally, the function executes the update clause (e.g., `i = i + 1`), modifying the loop variable in place before the cycle repeats. If the loop completes naturally without returning a value, the function returns `NULL`.

With the interpreter internals fully implemented, the language is complete. So, we shift our focus from how the language works to writing representative SMALL programs. The representative programs that follow are not merely syntax tests; they are designed to demonstrate the real-world capabilities of the interpreter you have just built. By writing and executing these scripts, we validate that our lexer, parser and evaluator work seamlessly in concert to solve actual computational problems.

Using the language

This section explores the practical capabilities of the updated SMALL language by implementing more powerful algorithms that were previously impossible.

First, we will execute the following code that shows Booleans in action:

```
$ cat ch11/booleans.usm
print("--- Boolean Logic Example ---");
println("");

let isDay = true;
let isRaining = false;

print("Is it day? ");
println(isDay);

print("Is it raining? ");
println(isRaining);

// Logical AND
if (isDay && isRaining) {
    println("Look for a rainbow.");
} else {
    println("No rainbow right now.");
}

// Logical OR and NOT
if (!isRaining || isDay) {
    println("You can probably go for a walk.");
}

// Comparisons
let x = 10;
let y = 20;

print("10 < 20 is: ");
println(x < y);

print("10 == 20 is: ");
println(x == y);
```

```
print("10 != 20 is: ");
println(x != y);
$ go run ch11/upEval.go ch11/booleans.usm
--- Boolean Logic Example ---
Is it day? true
Is it raining? false
No rainbow right now.
You can probably go for a walk.
10 < 20 is: true
10 == 20 is: false
10 != 20 is: true
```

The output confirms that the interpreter correctly stores and retrieves Boolean literals (`true` or `false`) and successfully utilizes them to drive conditional branching. The final three lines validate the evaluator's ability to process relational expressions such as `10 < 20`.

Now, let us try the following program, which shows that SMALL can handle recursion:

```
$ cat ch11/factorial.usm
func factorial(x) {
    if (x == 0) {
        return 1;
    } else {
        return x * factorial(x - 1);
    }
}

let result = factorial(10);
print("Factorial of 10 is: ");
println(result);
$ go run ch11/upEval.go ch11/factorial.usm
Factorial of 10 is: 3628800
```

The script defines a factorial function that calls itself, progressively reducing the problem size (`x - 1`) until it reaches the base case (`x == 0`). The successful execution of this logic demonstrates that the evaluator correctly manages the call stack, creating a fresh, isolated `Environment` for every single function invocation to prevent variable collisions. The final output (`3628800`) confirms that the arithmetic logic is sound.

Last, let us explore `for` loops:

```
$ cat ch11/loops.usm
print("--- Standard For Loop Example ---");
println("");

let sum = 0;
for let i = 0; i < 5; i = i + 1 {
    print("Index: ");
    print(i);
    sum = sum + i;
    print(" -> Sum so far: ");
    println(sum);
}

println("");
print("Final Total: ");
println(sum);
$ go run ch11/upEval.go ch11/loops.usm
--- Standard For Loop Example ---
Index: 0 -> Sum so far: 0
Index: 1 -> Sum so far: 1
Index: 2 -> Sum so far: 3
Index: 3 -> Sum so far: 6
Index: 4 -> Sum so far: 10

Final Total: 10
```

The script demonstrates the classic accumulator pattern, initializing a `sum` variable and progressively modifying it within a loop structure. The output confirms that the interpreter correctly handles the full lifecycle of the loop: initializing the `i` counter to zero, evaluating the `i < 5` condition before every pass, executing the body to update the running total, and correctly applying the `i = i + 1` increment after each iteration.

The SMALL language has evolved from a simple calculator into a system capable of complex state management. However, this power comes with increased risk; the introduction of mutable variables and iterative control flow opens the door to subtle bugs involving scope leakage and pointer mismanagement that manual verification simply cannot catch. To ensure that these features are robust, we must shift our focus from implementation to systematic validation.

Writing tests for SMALL

We construct a comprehensive test suite to validate that basic language features, variable assignments, and nested loops work as expected. Although we did not present lots of Go code for the updated language implementation, we show and explain the code of each testing function, starting with `TestEvalIntegerExpression()`, which validates the interpreter's core arithmetic capabilities by employing a table-driven testing strategy:

```
func TestEvalIntegerExpression(t *testing.T) {
    tests := []struct {
        input    string
        expected int64
    }{
        {"5", 5},
        {"10", 10},
        {"-5", -5},
        {"-10", -10},
        {"5 + 5 + 5 + 5 - 10", 10},
        {"2 * 2 * 2 * 2 * 2", 32},
        {"-50 + 100 + -50", 0},
        {"5 * 2 + 10", 20},
        {"5 + 2 * 10", 25},
        {"20 + 2 * -10", 0},
        {"50 / 2 * 2 + 10", 60},
        {"2 * (5 + 10)", 30},
        {"3 * 3 * 3 + 10", 37},
        {"3 * (3 * 3) + 10", 37},
        {"(5 + 10 * 2 + 15 / 3) * 2 + -10", 50},
    }

    for _, tt := range tests {
        evaluated := testEval(tt.input)
        testIntegerObject(t, evaluated, tt.expected)
    }
}
```

The function defines a comprehensive suite of test cases within a slice of structures. These cases progress in complexity from simple literals and prefix negation to intricate expressions that mix addition, subtraction, multiplication, and division. The test suite includes expressions with mixed operators and explicit parentheses — such as `2 * (5 + 10)` versus `5 + 2 * 10`— to verify that the parser and evaluator correctly enforce standard mathematical operator precedence and grouping rules. For each entry in the table, the function iterates through the list, executes the interpreter via the `testEval()` helper, and asserts that the resulting object matches the expected value using `testIntegerObject()`.

Next, we have `TestEvalBooleanExpression()`, which verifies the interpreter's ability to handle logical values and relational operators:

```
func TestEvalBooleanExpression(t *testing.T) {
    tests := []struct {
        input    string
        expected bool
    }{
        {"true", true},
        {"false", false},
        {"1 < 2", true},
        {"1 > 2", false},
        {"1 < 1", false},
        {"1 > 1", false},
        {"1 == 1", true},
        {"1 != 1", false},
        {"1 == 2", false},
        {"1 != 2", true},
        {"true == true", true},
        {"false == false", true},
        {"true == false", false},
        {"true != false", true},
        {"(1 < 2) == true", true},
        {"(1 < 2) == false", false},
        {"(1 > 2) == true", false},
        {"(1 > 2) == false", true},
    }

    for _, tt := range tests {
        evaluated := testEval(tt.input)
        testBooleanObject(t, evaluated, tt.expected)
    }
}
```

The set of test cases covers three distinct categories of Boolean operations: direct Boolean literals (`true` or `false`), integer comparisons (<, >, ==, or `!=`) and Boolean equality checks, while paying attention to edge cases.

After that, we have `TestIfElseExpressions()`, which verifies the interpreter's conditional control flow logic, ensuring that the `if` and `else` constructs correctly route execution based on the truth value of their conditions:

```
func TestIfElseExpressions(t *testing.T) {
    tests := []struct {
        input    string
        expected interface{}
    }{
        {"if (true) { 10 }", 10},
        {"if (false) { 10 }", nil},
        {"if (1) { 10 }", 10},
        {"if (1 < 2) { 10 }", 10},
        {"if (1 > 2) { 10 }", nil},
        {"if (1 > 2) { 10 } else { 20 }", 20},
        {"if (1 < 2) { 10 } else { 20 }", 10},
    }

    for _, tt := range tests {
        evaluated := testEval(tt.input)
        integer, ok := tt.expected.(int)
        if ok {
            testIntegerObject(t, evaluated, int64(integer))
        } else {
            testNullObject(t, evaluated)
        }
    }
}
```

Unlike the previous tests, this function utilizes an `interface{}` (equivalent to any) for the expected result field, allowing the test table to accommodate both integer return values (when a block is executed) and `nil` (representing the `NULL` object returned when a condition fails without an alternative branch). We check three distinct behaviors: standard Boolean branching, the "truthiness" of non-Boolean values (e.g., treating the integer `1` as `true`), and the correct execution of `else` blocks when the initial condition is `false`. The function confirms that the evaluator correctly selects the consequence block or the alternative block or returns `NULL` when no path is valid.

Next, we have `TestReturnStatements()`, which is designed to verify the ability to prematurely terminate execution and return a value to the caller:

```
func TestReturnStatements(t *testing.T) {
    tests := []struct {
        input    string
        expected int64
    }{
        {"return 10;", 10},
        {"return 10; 9;", 10},
        {"return 2 * 5; 9;", 10},
        {"9; return 2 * 5; 9;", 10},
        {
            `
            if (10 > 1) {
                if (10 > 1) {
                    return 10;
                }
                return 1;
            }
            `,
            10,
        },
    }

    for _, tt := range tests {
        evaluated := testEval(tt.input)
        testIntegerObject(t, evaluated, tt.expected)
    }
}
```

The test suite begins by confirming that a `return` statement correctly evaluates its accompanying expression — whether it is a simple integer literal such as `10` or a calculation such as `2 * 5`. The tests also check for "dead code" handling; inputs such as `return 10; 9;` ensure that the interpreter strictly halts processing immediately after the `return`, ignoring any subsequent statements. The final test case escalates the complexity by embedding a `return` statement inside nested `if` blocks.

Next, we have `TestLetStatements()`, which validates variable binding and retrieval within the interpreter's environment:

```
func TestLetStatements(t *testing.T) {
    tests := []struct {
        input    string
        expected int64
    }{
        {"let a = 5; a;", 5},
        {"let a = 5 * 5; a;", 25},
        {"let a = 5; let b = a; b;", 5},
        {"let a = 5; let b = a; let c = a + b + 5; c;", 15},
    }

    for _, tt := range tests {
        testIntegerObject(t, testEval(tt.input), tt.expected)
    }
}
```

The test cases in `TestLetStatements()` are structured to ensure that the `let` keyword correctly associates an identifier with a value and that this value can be subsequently accessed. We verify three key behaviors: direct assignment of literals (e.g., binding `5` to `a`), the evaluation of expressions prior to binding (e.g., calculating `5 * 5` before storing the result), and the ability to define new variables based on the values of existing ones (e.g., `let b = a`).

Here is a testing function (`TestAssignments()`) that verifies that `Environment.Update()` is working correctly:

```
func TestAssignments(t *testing.T) {
    tests := []struct {
        input    string
        expected int64
    }{
        {"let a = 5; a = 10; a;", 10},
        {"let a = 5; a = a + 10; a;", 15},
        {"let a = 5; let b = 10; a = b; a;", 10},
        {"let a = 5; a = a * 2; a = a + 5; a;", 15},
    }

    for _, tt := range tests {
```

```
        testIntegerObject(t, testEval(tt.input), tt.expected)
    }
}
```

This test confirms that a variable's value can be modified after its initial declaration. The test cases progress from simple reassignment to more complex, self-referential updates such as `a = a + 10`. This specific case is crucial because it proves that the evaluator correctly retrieves the current value from the environment, performs the calculation, and then successfully commits the new value back to the same memory address.

Here is a more complex testing function for testing loops:

```
func TestForLoops(t *testing.T) {
    tests := []struct {
        input    string
        expected int64
    }{
        // Standard counting loop
        {
            `let sum = 0;
            for (let i = 0; i < 5; i = i + 1) {
                sum = sum + 1;
            }
            sum;`,
            5,
        },
        // Using the loop index in calculation
        {
            `let sum = 0;
            for (let i = 0; i < 4; i = i + 1) {
                sum = sum + i;
            }
            sum;`,
            6, // 0 + 1 + 2 + 3
        },
```

The first test case targets the fundamental mechanics of a counting loop, verifying that the interpreter can initialize a counter (`i = 0`), repeatedly evaluate a condition (`i < 5`), execute a body that updates an external variable (`sum`), and perform a post-iteration update (`i = i + 1`).

This specific test ensures that the loop runs exactly five times. The second test case introduces a higher level of complexity by actively using the loop index, `i`, within the body's calculation.

The remaining code of the `TestForLoops()` testing function is the following:

```
        // Double nested Loop
        {
            `let sum = 0;
            for (let i = 0; i < 2; i = i + 1) {
                for (let j = 0; j < 2; j = j + 1) {
                    sum = sum + 1;
                }
            }
            sum;`,
            4,
        },
        // Loop with return (Early Exit)
        {
            `func() {
                for (let i = 0; i < 10; i = i + 1) {
                    if (i == 5) {
                        return i;
                    }
                }
                return -1;
            }();`,
            5,
        },
    }

    for _, tt := range tests {
        testIntegerObject(t, testEval(tt.input), tt.expected)
    }
}
```

The first scenario employs a *double nested loop,* where an inner loop runs to completion for every single iteration of the outer loop. This test is critical for verifying that the evaluator correctly manages multiple, distinct `Environment` instances simultaneously, ensuring that the inner loop's counter (`j`) does not conflict with the outer loop's counter (`i`) and that both can modify the shared `sum` variable. The expected result of `4` confirms that the inner body executed exactly `2×2` times. The final test case introduces a sophisticated *early exit* scenario by wrapping a `for` loop inside an immediately invoked function expression. It tests that SMALL can handle a `return` statement triggered deep within a loop's body. Instead of completing all 10 iterations, the loop monitors the `i == 5` condition and, upon matching, executes a `return`. This test validates that the `ReturnValue` object correctly bubbles up through the loop mechanism.

Next, we present `TestClosuresAndScoping()`, which validates the interpreter's implementation of closures:

```
func TestClosuresAndScoping(t *testing.T) {
    //
    // Verifies that Update() correctly walks up the scope chain
    input := `
    let newAdder = func(x) {
        func(y) { x + y };
    };
    let addTwo = newAdder(2);
    addTwo(2);
    `
    testIntegerObject(t, testEval(input), 4)
}
```

The test script defines `newAdder`, a higher-order function that takes an argument, `x`, and returns a new anonymous function, `func(y)`. Critically, this inner function references `x`, a variable that exists only in the outer function's scope. When `newAdder(2)` is called, it returns a closure where `x` is permanently bound to 2. The subsequent call, `addTwo(2)`, executes this inner function with `y=2`. The successful result of 4 proves that the inner function correctly retained access to `x` from its parent environment long after the parent function finished executing, confirming that the scope chain lookup (via `NewEnclosedEnvironment`) is functioning correctly.

Last, we have `TestOuterScopeMutation()`, which verifies that a function can produce side effects outside its own local boundary:

```
func TestOuterScopeMutation(t *testing.T) {
    // Verifies that a closure can modify a variable in the outer scope
    input := `
    let global = 10;
    let modifier = func() {
        global = 20;
    };
```

```
    modifier();
    global;
    `

    testIntegerObject(t, testEval(input), 20)
}
```

A `global` variable is defined in the top-level scope, and a closure modifier is created with the specific intent of changing that variable's value from `10` to `20`. This test is critical because it distinguishes between *shadowing a variable* (creating a new local version) and *mutating* one. The successful result of `20` confirms that when `modifier()` is executed, the interpreter correctly traverses the environment chain, locates the original definition in the outer scope, and updates the value in place.

Let us now execute the tests:

```
$ go test -v ch11/upEval_test.go ch11/upEval.go
=== RUN   TestEvalIntegerExpression
--- PASS: TestEvalIntegerExpression (0.00s)
=== RUN   TestEvalBooleanExpression
--- PASS: TestEvalBooleanExpression (0.00s)
=== RUN   TestIfElseExpressions
--- PASS: TestIfElseExpressions (0.00s)
=== RUN   TestReturnStatements
--- PASS: TestReturnStatements (0.00s)
=== RUN   TestLetStatements
--- PASS: TestLetStatements (0.00s)
=== RUN   TestAssignments
--- PASS: TestAssignments (0.00s)
=== RUN   TestForLoops
--- PASS: TestForLoops (0.00s)
=== RUN   TestClosuresAndScoping
--- PASS: TestClosuresAndScoping (0.00s)
=== RUN   TestOuterScopeMutation
--- PASS: TestOuterScopeMutation (0.00s)
PASS
ok      command-line-arguments  (cached)
```

Each of the nine test functions executed without error, resulting in a distinct `PASS` status for every case. This result is particularly significant for the newly introduced architecture; the success of

`TestAssignments()` and `TestForLoops()` definitively proves that the updated `Environment` and `Eval` logic can now handle mutable variables and iterative cycles correctly.

Beyond their primary role in verification, the testing functions serve as an invaluable form of living documentation for the features of SMALL. Each test case effectively acts as an executable specification, providing concrete, unambiguous examples of how to utilize complex constructs such as mutable assignments, C-style `for` loops, and closure scopes. For a developer seeking to understand the precise syntax required to initialize a loop or the expected behavior of a `return` statement nested within an `if` block, the test suite offers a definitive reference that is guaranteed to be accurate. Unlike static manuals, which may drift out of sync with the code base, tests should remain true to the implementation, making them the ultimate source of truth for the language's capabilities.

Summary

With the latest updates, SMALL has become a much more expressive and practical programming language. To ensure the reliability of these new features, we created a comprehensive suite of unit tests for the updated evaluator. These tests specifically target the nuances of variable scoping, nested loop execution, and the correct propagation of `return` statements, ensuring that the interpreter not only runs code but does so with predictable and stable behavior.

With the SMALL interpreter now fully operational and capable of executing iterative algorithms, we have established a mechanism to define logic through code. However, in the real world, logic is rarely abstract; it operates on data, and that data often arrives in continuous, time-stamped streams. Having built a tool to process instructions, we now turn our attention to processing information itself. The next chapter leaves the domain of compiler theory to tackle time series distances.

Exercises

1. Write a `for` loop in the updated SMALL and execute it.
2. Write a program that finds the biggest of three numeric variables.
3. Try to add the *square root function* to SMALL. You will have to change the grammar first to help you during implementation.

Additional resources

- *How we found a bug in Go's arm64 compiler* (Cloudflare blog post): `https://blog.cloudflare.com/how-we-found-a-bug-in-gos-arm64-compiler/`
- The prep package: `https://github.com/pijng/prep`

Get this book's PDF version and more

Scan the QR code (or go to `packtpub.com/unlock`). Search for this book by name, confirm the edition, and then follow the steps on the page.

UNLOCK NOW

Note: Keep your invoice handy. Purchases made directly from Packt don't require an invoice.

12

Time Series Distances

Constructing an interpreter in the previous two chapters illustrated how software parses and evaluates abstract linguistic structures. This chapter shifts focus from language design to data analysis, specifically addressing the temporal dimension of information processing. Time series data — sequences of data points put in time order — is ubiquitous in financial markets, IoT sensor networks and system metrics. We will begin by exploring the mathematical foundations of measuring similarity between temporal sequences, implementing algorithms such as Euclidean distance and **Dynamic Time Warping (DTW)** to quantify how *close* two series are. By the end of this chapter, we will have transformed these theoretical concepts into a reusable Go toolkit, applying it directly to real data to solve practical problems such as finding the nearest neighbor within a large dataset.

Finally, the chapter concludes by working with **TigerBeetle**, a high-performance distributed database designed for financial accounting. To understand why a specialized database such as TigerBeetle is necessary, we must first look at the friction inherent in building financial systems on general-purpose databases. In a traditional setup using PostgreSQL or MySQL, the concepts of *accounts, transfers,* and *double-entry bookkeeping* do not exist natively; they are abstractions that you, the application developer, must build from scratch using tables, rows, and heavy transaction logic. This approach forces you to manage row locking manually to prevent race conditions and to write complex queries just to calculate simple balances. As your dataset grows, the database struggles to maintain performance while strictly enforcing the consistency required for financial data, often leading to slow queries or, worse, subtle concurrency bugs that corrupt the ledger.

This chapter covers the following topics:

- Introduction to time series
- Time series distances
- Creating a Go package

- Finding the nearest neighbor of a time series
- Using TigerBeetle for financial accounting

Let us now begin with a pedagogical story.

If you only work for money, you will become miserable

The title says it all. Do not work for money only. When you also work for something greater, you might find happiness in what you do. Of course, we must have money to live decently, and few people work for pleasure only. However, the truth is somewhere in the middle. You should always remember how funny and entertaining it is to solve tricky problems with code. The feeling of achievement is a great performance booster. *You should always try to find ways to make your jobs exciting, innovative, and meaningful.* Everything is a matter of how we prioritize what we do. Some people prefer a relatively boring job – nobody prefers a completely boring job – whereas others want to create innovative software and hardware and be at the edge of technology. Just think about Apple and the late Steve Jobs. If it were not for him, we might not have the iPhone right now! In practice, this means that we should always spend some time reflecting on how we feel about our current job and the tasks at hand. Sometimes, the solution to a relatively boring job is to start a side project. Other times, the solution is to start searching for a different job, even if that means that we must design and create that job on our own! If you want to take it to the next level, close your eyes and imagine that you currently have 1,000,00 euros, or US dollars, or UK pounds. What would you do with your life? What would you change? What would you do the same? Would you choose the same lifestyle? Would you stay in the same house, country, or city? Would you hang out with the same people? Answer all these questions truthfully, and then arrange your habits and your actions according to the things that you want to change. Usually, the issue is not with money but with the way we approach life. For me, such an area of experimentation and research is *time series*, which is the subject of this chapter.

Introduction to time series

A **time series** is a sequence of data points indexed in temporal order, typically measured at successive, evenly spaced intervals. Time series arise naturally in many domains — finance, weather forecasting, signal processing, and system monitoring — where understanding how values evolve over time is crucial. Unlike static datasets, time series carry the added dimension of temporal dependency, making analysis both more powerful and complex. Tasks such as smoothing, forecasting, anomaly detection, and pattern matching depend on recognizing trends, seasonality, and noise within the sequence. These same structural characteristics also determine how we measure similarity between time series, which leads directly to the study of distance metrics later in this chapter.

The first task we need to do is to be able to read a time series from a compressed file.

Reading time series

Reading compressed plain text files efficiently is essential to avoid unnecessary memory usage and slow processing times. As time series can contain lots of data, it is a common practice to keep them in a compressed format. A very common format is *GZIP*, which is what we are going to use here. The function that does the reading is as follows and can be found in `ch12/readTS.go`:

```
func readGzipTimeSeries(path string) ([]float64, error) {
    file, err := os.Open(path)
    if err != nil {
        return nil, err
    }
    defer file.Close()

    gr, err := gzip.NewReader(file)
    if err != nil {
        return nil, err
    }
    defer gr.Close()

    var values []float64
    scanner := bufio.NewScanner(gr)
    for scanner.Scan() {
        line := scanner.Text()
        if line == "" {
            continue
        }

        val, err := strconv.ParseFloat(line, 64)
        if err != nil {
            return nil, fmt.Errorf("invalid float: %s", line)
        }
        values = append(values, val)
    }
    if err := scanner.Err(); err != nil {
        return nil, err
    }
    return values, nil
}
```

The `readGzipTimeSeries()` function implements a streaming data pipeline designed to handle compressed input efficiently. Rather than loading the entire file into memory, it chains standard library components: the `os.Open()` function acquires the file handle, which is immediately wrapped by `gzip.NewReader()` to perform transparent, on-the-fly decompression. This decoded stream is then consumed by a `bufio.Scanner()` function, allowing the function to process the time series data line by line. Inside the scanning loop, the code applies a strict validation filter — skipping empty lines and using `strconv.ParseFloat()` to convert valid text into 64-bit floating-point numbers — ensuring that the final slice contains only clean, numerical data or returns a specific parsing error.

Let us now try `ch12/readTS.go` on our machines using the sample time series found in `ts`:

```
$ go run ch12/readTS.go ts/ts1.gz
Successfully read 1000 values from ts/ts1.gz
First value: -0.000000
Last value:  0.100000
```

The output confirms the integrity of the data pipeline: the program successfully decompressed and parsed `1,000` values from the GZIP stream. By explicitly printing the first data point (`-0.000000`) and the last (`0.100000`), we verify that the file was read completely from start to finish without truncation or offset errors – a corrupted archive might prematurely trigger an **end-of-file** (**EOF**) condition, silently passing a partial dataset to the application.

The next step is about creating a utility program that allows us to get statistical information about the time series read – this kind of program can help us understand the data we are dealing with before doing any actual processing.

Getting information about a time series

Understanding a time series begins with extracting meaningful information from its data points. In this section, we focus on methods for analyzing a time series to uncover its statistical properties, such as mean, variance, and autocorrelation. We are not going to go into too many details about the implementation of `ch12/statsTS.go`. At this stage, our primary focus is on the practical application of these statistical tools rather than the mechanical derivation of the formulas themselves. What really matters is the structure that holds the information:

```
type Statistics struct {
    Count    int
    Min      float64
    Max      float64
    Mean     float64
```

```
        Median   float64
        Q1       float64
        Q3       float64
        StdDev   float64
        Skewness float64
        Kurtosis float64
}
```

The `Statistics` struct serves as a comprehensive data container designed to capture the distributional properties of a time series in a single object. Now, let us try it:

```
$ go run ch12/statsTS.go ts/ts1.gz
Metric     Value
------     -----
Count      1000
Min        -0.2000
Q1 (25%)   0.0000
Median     0.0000
Q3 (75%)   0.1000
Max        0.3000
Mean       0.0350
StdDev     0.0866
Skewness   1.1931
Kurtosis   1.4474
```

The metrics reveal a time series that is positively skewed (`Skewness: 1.1931`). This is confirmed by the mean (`0.0350`) being higher than the median (`0.0000`), indicating that while most data points are clustered near zero (as seen by `Q1` and `Median` both being `0.0000`), there is a long "tail" of positive values pulling the average up. The positive kurtosis (`1.4474`) further suggests a "leptokurtic" distribution, meaning the data has heavier tails than a standard normal distribution; in financial terms, this implies a higher likelihood of outliers or extreme values (reaching up to a max of `0.3000`) than one would expect from a purely random bell curve.

While statistical summaries and reduction techniques allow us to characterize individual datasets in isolation, the true power of time series analysis emerges when we compare time series values against one another. By defining a mathematical "distance" between two signals, we transform isolated values into a relative map, enabling us to cluster similar behaviors and isolate anomalies that deviate from the norm. In the next section, we explore time series distances, the fundamental metrics that make these comparative insights possible.

Time series distances

A time series distance metric is a quantitative measure that calculates the similarity or dissimilarity between two time series. These metrics are used in various applications, including time series analysis, pattern recognition, and **machine learning** (**ML**), to quantify temporal relationships and patterns within sequences of data points. The goal is to numerically express how close or different two time series are in terms of their shapes, trends, or overall behaviors.

About the Euclidean distance

The **Euclidean distance** is the most straightforward and intuitive way to measure the difference between two time series of equal length. It treats each time series as a point in a high-dimensional space, where each dimension corresponds to a specific timestamp. The distance is then calculated as the square root of the sum of the squared differences between corresponding values. This is the familiar distance formula from geometry, extended into the temporal domain. Despite its simplicity, Euclidean distance is powerful when the time series are aligned in time and similar in shape. It is fast to compute, easy to understand, and works well as a baseline for comparison. However, it is also sensitive to noise, time shifts, and differences in scale. Still, it serves as a fundamental building block in time series analysis, providing a clear starting point before exploring more flexible or robust alternatives. The Euclidean distance has another major drawback. It can only work with vectors of the same length. So, when having to deal with vectors of different lengths, we have two choices: either cancel the operation or use the length of the smaller vector in both vectors, which is the approach we are going to follow here.

Now that you have seen how the Euclidean distance measures similarity (or dissimilarity), let us shift to a different perspective, which is the Chebyshev distance.

About the Chebyshev distance

The **Chebyshev distance**, also known as the maximum metric, is a measure of similarity between two sequences that focuses on their largest individual difference rather than the overall accumulation of differences. Unlike the Euclidean distance, which computes the square root of the sum of squared differences across all corresponding points, the Chebyshev distance considers only the maximum absolute difference between corresponding elements in two time series. This makes it particularly sensitive to the largest deviation at any single point, which can be useful when extreme values or spikes are more significant than cumulative variations. Compared to the Euclidean distance, it provides a complementary perspective, highlighting the worst-case pointwise difference rather than the overall magnitude of differences. For the Chebyshev distance to work, the two time series should have the same length.

With that in mind, let us learn about the Manhattan distance, which takes a more balanced approach.

About the Manhattan distance

The *Manhattan distance*, also known as the city-block distance, is another common metric for comparing time series. Unlike the Euclidean distance, the Manhattan distance measures the sum of the absolute differences between corresponding elements in two sequences. In other words, it treats the distance as the total taxicab distance you would travel along a grid to move from one series to the other. Compared to the Euclidean distance, it is more robust to outliers because it does not square differences and it emphasizes the cumulative absolute deviation rather than the straight-line distance, providing a complementary way to quantify similarity between time series. Again, for the Manhattan distance to work, the two time series should have the same length.

Next, we present the **Longest Common Subsequence Similarity** (**LCSS**) distance, which takes a slightly different perspective. Instead of counting edits, LCSS measures how much of two sequences match. Let us learn more about it.

About LCSS

The **LCSS distance** is a similarity measure designed for comparing time series or sequential data while being tolerant of noise, gaps, and temporal misalignments. Unlike the Euclidean distance, which computes strict point-to-point differences, LCSS focuses on identifying the longest subsequence of matching points between two sequences, where two points are considered a match if their absolute difference is within a given threshold epsilon. Points that do not match are effectively ignored, making LCSS robust against local distortions and outliers. This property makes LCSS useful when working with noisy or incomplete time series, where slight temporal shifts or missing data could otherwise distort similarity measures such as the Euclidean or Manhattan distances. The resulting distance is derived from the ratio of matched points to the overall sequence length. In that sense, a higher LCSS value indicates greater similarity between the sequences. However, when converted into a distance metric, it is typically defined as 1 minus that similarity, meaning lower distance values correspond to higher similarity. It is a matter of definition that you should keep in mind when using LCSS. Next, we present the powerful DTW distance.

About DTW

Dynamic Time Warping (DTW) is an algorithm used to measure the similarity between two time series that may vary in speed or timing. Unlike Euclidean distance, which compares the *i-th point* of one series strictly to the *i-th point* of another, DTW allows for a non-linear alignment of the series. This means it can "warp" the time axis, compressing or stretching sections of the sequences to find the optimal match between their features. For example, if you have two audio recordings of the same word spoken at different speeds — one slow and drawled, the other fast and clipped — Euclidean distance would fail because the peaks of the sound waves would not align. DTW, however, would stretch the faster signal to match the slower one, correctly identifying them as the same word.

The primary advantage of DTW is its robustness to temporal distortions. It is the gold standard for comparing time series where the "shape" of the data matters more than the exact timestamp of every peak and trough. This makes it exceptionally useful in domains such as speech recognition, gesture recognition, and financial pattern matching, where events often happen in the same order but not necessarily at the exact same speed. Furthermore, unlike many other distance metrics, DTW can natively compare time series of different lengths without needing to truncate data or perform complex interpolation beforehand, as the warping mechanism naturally handles the length discrepancy.

However, DTW comes with significant drawbacks, the most prominent being its *computational cost*. Because it requires filling out a full cost matrix, the time complexity is `O(n×m)`, which becomes prohibitively slow for very long time series or large datasets. Additionally, DTW can sometimes be "too" flexible; without constraints, it might warp a series so aggressively that it matches a straight line to a complex pattern by mapping a single point in one series to hundreds of points in the other (a singularity). To mitigate these issues, practitioners often apply global constraints such as the Sakoe-Chiba band or the Itakura parallelogram, which limit how far the warping path can deviate from the diagonal, reducing search space and preventing pathological warping.

Next, we present a distance that takes a different approach.

About MPdist

MPdist is a recently developed distance measure derived from the **Matrix Profile**, designed to assess the similarity between two time series by examining the similarity of their constituent subsequences rather than comparing entire sequences globally. Unlike DTW or Euclidean distance, which attempt to align the full length of one series to the other, MPdist acknowledges that real-world data is often messy; two series might represent the same underlying behavior but contain significant sections of noise, gaps, or irrelevant anomalies. MPdist solves this by effectively breaking both series into small, overlapping windows and asking, *How well do the snippets of time series A fit into time series B and vice versa?* The mechanism relies on computing the Matrix Profile, which is a vector that stores the distance to the nearest neighbor for every subsequence. Specifically, MPdist calculates the "AB-join" (finding the best match in series B for every subsequence in A) and the "BA-join" (finding the best match in A for every subsequence in B). These two sets of nearest-neighbor distances are combined into a single list. Instead of summing or averaging these distances, MPdist takes the value at a specific percentile (typically the 5th percentile) of this combined list. This means the metric explicitly discards the worst 95% of the matches, focusing entirely on how well the best matching shared substructures align. The primary advantage of MPdist is its extraordinary robustness. Because it ignores the majority of non-matching data, it is nearly immune to spikes, dropouts, wandering baselines, or large sections of "garbage" data padded at the beginning or end of a recording. If a recognizable heartbeat pattern exists within a noisy signal, MPdist will identify the similarity and report a low distance, whereas Euclidean distance would be overwhelmed by the noise and report a high distance. However, this robustness comes with the drawback of computational intensity. Calculating the full Matrix Profile requires performing a nearest-neighbor search for every single subsequence, which is computationally expensive ($O(n^2)$).

When selecting distance measures for time series analysis, computational complexity becomes a critical consideration, particularly as sequence lengths increase. Simple point-to-point distance functions such as Euclidean, Manhattan, and Chebyshev operate in linear `O(n)` time, making them extremely fast even for sequences with millions of data points. In contrast, dynamic programming-based measures such as LCSS require `O(n×m)` computations, where `n` and `m` are the lengths of the two time series being compared. This quadratic complexity means that while these sophisticated measures can capture temporal shifts and non-linear alignments that simple distances miss, they become prohibitively slow for large datasets — comparing two sequences of 10,000 points each requires 100 million operations rather than just 10,000. The trade-off between computational accuracy and speed often necessitates the use of approximation techniques such as windowing constraints, sampling strategies, or processing only representative subsequences, allowing practitioners to balance the need for meaningful similarity measures against practical time and memory limitations. Due to these complexity issues, we often create summaries of time series.

Creating a summary of a time series

Time series summarization involves various techniques designed to reduce the volume of data while preserving its essential characteristics. By computing distances on these summarized forms rather than the raw, high-resolution data, we drastically reduce the number of floating-point operations required for every comparison.

In this subsection, we describe three distinct methods: **Piecewise Aggregate Approximation (PAA)**, *Random Sampling*, and *Stepping*. The logic behind PAA involves partitioning the time series into equal-sized segments and representing each section by its average value. To maintain accuracy, the segmentation process ensures that data points are distributed as uniformly as possible across all segments, preventing the distortion that would occur if the final segment were left disproportionately large due to uneven division. Random Sampling takes a different approach by selecting a specific number of data points by chance. However, the critical logic here is that while the selection of indices is random, the retrieval of values allows for strictly preserving their chronological order; this ensures that the overall shape and temporal trend of the time series remain intact rather than being shuffled into meaningless noise. Finally, Stepping (or decimation) reduces the dataset by systematically retaining every *k-th* data point and discarding the rest. Unlike PAA, which synthesizes a new value through averaging, Stepping acts as a periodic filter that preserves exact snapshots of the original data without modification.

Each approach offers a specific trade-off between computational speed and structural accuracy. PAA generally provides the highest fidelity by averaging data segments to preserve the overall trend, though it requires slightly more processing time to calculate those means. Stepping offers a much faster alternative by systematically extracting every *k-th* data point, which is highly efficient but risks aliasing or missing narrow, high-frequency peaks. Finally, Random Sampling prioritizes maximum execution speed over accuracy by arbitrarily selecting points, an approach primarily suitable for massive datasets where only a rough approximation of the underlying distribution is required.

Next, we are going to create a package that includes time series distances as well as the time series summarization methods and host it on GitHub.

Creating a Go package

In this section, we will bundle these algorithms into a dedicated Go package, structuring the code base to cleanly separate distance calculations from data reduction methods. This transition from ad hoc code to a formal library not only improves maintainability and testing but also creates a portable toolkit that can be seamlessly imported into other projects or published for the wider Go community. For that, we need a practical way of working locally without the friction of publishing to a remote repository for every minor change. To achieve this, we will utilize **Go workspaces**.

Working with workspaces

Workspaces can be very handy during development because they allow you to work locally with your Go packages. After you finish developing and testing them, you can publish them on GitHub or any other similar service to make them available to the world. In our case, the GitHub repository will be `https://github.com/mactsouk/tslib`. However, we have some work to do first, starting with setting up a workspace environment:

```
$ cd ch12
$ mkdir wspace
$ cd wspace
$ mkdir tslib
$ cd tslib
$ go mod init github.com/mactsouk/tslib
$ cd ..
```

In this first phase, we have created a space for the Go module. Next, we should continue by creating a space for the application module that uses the Go module – notice that so far, we have no Go code:

```
$ mkdir app
$ cd app
$ go mod init app
$ cd ..
$ go work init ./tslib ./app
```

At this point, we are ready to begin populating our files – after that, the structure of the workspace folder is going to be as follows:

```
$ .
├── app
│   ├── go.mod
│   └── main.go
├── go.work
└── tslib
    ├── distances.go
    ├── go.mod
    └── summarize.go

3 directories, 6 files
```

The two most interesting files are `go.work` and `main.go`, which are presented next, starting with `go.work`, which is automatically generated:

```
go 1.25.5

use (
    ./app
    ./tslib
)
```

We'll continue with `app/main.go`:

```
package main

import (
```

```
    "fmt"

    // Because of go.work, this imports from ../tslib
    "github.com/mactsouk/tslib"
)
```

At this point, there is no `github.com/mactsouk/tslib` instance created, but the code works due to workspaces! We continue with the `main()` function implementation:

```
func main() {
    ts1 := []float64{1, 2, 3, 4, 5, 6, 7, 8, 9, 10}
    ts2 := []float64{1, 2, 3, 5, 5, 6, 7, 8, 9, 12}
    fmt.Println("--- Time Series Library Test ---")
    fmt.Printf("Series A: %v\n", ts1)
    fmt.Printf("Series B: %v\n\n", ts2)

    fmt.Println("1. Lock-Step Measures:")
    euc := tslib.EuclideanDistance(ts1, ts2)
    fmt.Printf("  Euclidean: %.4f\n", euc)
    man := tslib.ManhattanDistance(ts1, ts2)
    fmt.Printf("  Manhattan: %.4f\n", man)
    che := tslib.ChebyshevDistance(ts1, ts2)
    fmt.Printf("  Chebyshev: %.4f\n", che)
    fmt.Println()

    fmt.Println("2. Elastic Measures:")
    dtw := tslib.DTW(ts1, ts2, 2)
    fmt.Printf("  DTW (w=2): %.4f\n", dtw)
    lcss := tslib.LCSS(ts1, ts2, 2, 1.0)
    fmt.Printf("  LCSS (d=2, eps=1.0): %.4f\n", lcss)
    mpd := tslib.MPdist(ts1, ts2, 3)
    fmt.Printf("  MPdist (w=3): %.4f\n", mpd)
}
```

There is nothing special about the `main()` function, which is constructed as usual. At this point, running `main.go` from inside the app folder generates the following output:

```
$ go run main.go
--- Time Series Library Test ---
Series A: [1 2 3 4 5 6 7 8 9 10]
```

```
Series B: [1 2 3 5 5 6 7 8 9 12]

1. Lock-Step Measures:
  Euclidean: 2.2361
  Manhattan: 3.0000
  Chebyshev: 2.0000

2. Elastic Measures:
  DTW (w=2): 3.0000
  LCSS (d=2, eps=1.0): 0.1000
  MPdist (w=3): 0.0000
```

The output makes sure that everything works as expected. The only thing that is left is documentation! *Do not forget about documentation*, which is presented next.

Documenting the package

Clear documentation is the bridge between a well-designed package and the developers who use it. We are not going to document everything, just `tslib/summarize.go`. The `Stepping()` function of the package is going to look as follows:

```
// Stepping (also known as Decimation) reduces the time series by keeping
// only every 'step'-th data point. For example, a step of 2 keeps every
// second point.
//
// This is the fastest summarization method but it is prone to
// "aliasing," where high-frequency features (like sharp spikes)
// falling between steps are completely lost.
//
// Parameters:
//   - data: The input time series slice.
//-step:Theintervalatwhichtosamplepoints(mustbe> 1).
//
// Returns a new slice containing the decimated time series.
func Stepping(data []float64, step int) []float64 {
    ifstep<= 1 {
        return data
    }
    var result []float64
    for i := 0; i < len(data); i += step {
        result = append(result, data[i])
    }
```

```
    return result
}
```

The documentation identifies this function as an implementation of *decimation*, a technique that reduces dataset size by systematically retaining only every *k-th* element. It flags this as the *fastest summarization method* available since it avoids complex math such as averaging but explicitly warns of *aliasing* risks: high-frequency features such as sudden spikes that fall between steps will be lost. Finally, the parameter section clarifies usage constraints, noting that the step interval must be greater than one and confirming that the function returns a new, distinct slice rather than modifying the original data in place.

How to see the documentation

By adding those specific comments (starting with `//`) directly above your functions, you have integrated your documentation into the standard Go ecosystem. The most immediate way to use this documentation is through your code editor or IDE. When you are writing code in `main.go` and you hover your mouse cursor over `tslib.Stepping()` or `tslib.RandomSampling()`, a pop-up window will appear displaying the text you wrote, including parameter descriptions and warnings about aliasing or data loss. This allows you to understand the behavior of the library without ever needing to leave your current file or open the library source code. For a more comprehensive view, you can use the go doc command-line tool, which is installed with Go. This tool prints documentation directly to your terminal, which is helpful for quick lookups. If you are inside your `app` directory, you can simply type `go doc tslib` to see a summary of the entire package and the list of available functions. To read the specific details for a single function, you can run a command such as `go doc tslib.PAA`. This will output the full function signature followed by the documentation text, formatted neatly for reading in the console. Let us try that:

```
$ cd app
$ go doc tslib.Stepping
package tslib // import "github.com/mactsouk/tslib"

func Stepping(data []float64, step int) []float64
    Stepping (also known as Decimation) reduces the time series by
    keeping only every 'step'-th data point. For example, a step
    of 2 keeps every second point.

    This is the fastest summarization method but it is prone
    to "aliasing", where high-frequency features (like sharp spikes)
    falling between steps are completely lost.
```

```
    Parameters:
      - data: The input time series slice.
      - step: The interval at which to sample points (must be > 1).

    Returns a new slice containing the decimated time series.
```

Finally, you can view your documentation as a fully rendered web page, similar to the official Go standard library documentation. To do this, you first install the documentation server by running `go install golang.org/x/tools/cmd/godoc@latest`. Once installed, you run `godoc -http=:6060` in your terminal. This starts a local web server that generates HTML documentation for every Go package on your machine. You can then open your web browser to `http://localhost:6060/pkg/github.com/mactsouk/tslib` (or your specific module path), where you will see your comments transformed into a professional documentation site, complete with clickable links to source code and navigable indexes.

Our time series library is now fully implemented. However, it currently exists only on our local machine, limiting its utility to just this one project. To make these tools reusable across our future applications and accessible to the wider Go community, we need to distribute them properly.

Publishing the Go package on GitHub

The final step is publishing the Go package for the world to use it! First, execute the following commands:

```
$ git init
Initialized empty Git repository in /Users/mtsouk/go/src/github.com/mactsouk/
goSP2/ch12/wspace/tslib/.git/
$ git add .
$ git commit -m "Initial release"
[main (root-commit) 6f1b704] Initial release
 4 files changed, 433 insertions(+)
 create mode 100644 distances.go
 create mode 100644 distances_test.go
 create mode 100644 go.mod
 create mode 100644 summarize.go
```

At this point, *you should create the desired repository* (`tslib`), which in my case, and based on my own GitHub login name, is `git@github.com:mactsouk/tslib`. Next, run the following:

```
$ git remote add origin git@github.com:mactsouk/tslib.git
$ git push -u origin main --force
```

```
Enumerating objects: 6, done.
Counting objects: 100% (6/6), done.
Delta compression using up to 14 threads
Compressing objects: 100% (5/5), done.
Writing objects: 100% (6/6), 3.89 KiB | 3.89 MiB/s, done.
Total 6 (delta 0), reused 0 (delta 0), pack-reused 0 (from 0)
To github.com:mactsouk/tslib.git
 + 359469c...447270d main -> main (forced update)
branch 'main' set up to track 'origin/main'.
```

Have in mind that `--force` overrides the standard safety mechanisms of distributed version control. By default, Git refuses to push changes if the remote repository contains commits that do not exist in your local history, ensuring that no data is accidentally lost. Appending `--force` bypasses this check entirely, instructing the remote server to discard its current timeline and unconditionally replace it with your local branch history.

The last commands are needed for versioning the Go package:

```
$ git tag v0.1.0
$ git push origin v0.1.0
Total 0 (delta 0), reused 0 (delta 0), pack-reused 0 (from 0)
To github.com:mactsouk/tslib.git
 * [new tag]         v0.1.0 -> v0.1.0
```

Once the tag is pushed, other developers can use this specific version by running `go get github.com/mactsouk/tslib@v0.1.0`. We are almost there! We still need to test whether the published package can be accessed or not. So, we are going to create a new folder inside `ch12` and use the external package from there by copying `./app/main.go`:

```
$ mkdir test
$ cd test
$ cp ../wspace/app/main.go .
$ go mod init
go: creating new go.mod: module github.com/mactsouk/goSP2/ch12/test
go: to add module requirements and sums:
    go mod tidy
$ go mod tidy
go: finding module for package github.com/mactsouk/tslib
go: downloading github.com/mactsouk/tslib v0.1.0
```

```
go: found github.com/mactsouk/tslib in github.com/mactsouk/tslib v0.1.0
$ go run main.go
```

Congratulations! Let us now benchmark the distances to understand their performance.

Benchmarking the distances

While theory can tell us about algorithmic complexity or sensitivity to certain data characteristics, *only careful benchmarking reveals how these distances behave under real-world conditions*. All benchmarking code can be found in `distances_test.go`. While being inside `ch12/wspace/tslib`, run the following command:

```
$ go test -bench=.
goos: darwin
goarch: arm64
pkg: github.com/mactsouk/tslib
cpu: Apple M4 Pro
BenchmarkEuclidean-14        4659560             235.6 ns/op
BenchmarkManhattan-14        5098916             236.4 ns/op
BenchmarkChebyshev-14        1393040             874.6 ns/op
BenchmarkDTW-14                 1573          762658 ns/op
BenchmarkLCSS-14                1370          867052 ns/op
BenchmarkMPdist-14               759         1573517 ns/op
PASS
ok      github.com/mactsouk/tslib    9.468s
```

The benchmark results illustrate a dramatic performance divide between simple lock-step metrics and complex elastic measures. Euclidean and Manhattan distances are exceptionally fast, executing in roughly 236 nanoseconds, as they rely on simple, linear arithmetic that the CPU can easily optimize. However, Chebyshev distance is nearly four times slower (875 nanoseconds). In contrast, the elastic measures operate on a completely different time scale, running 3,000 to 6,000 times slower than the linear metrics. DTW and LCSS require roughly 0.8 milliseconds because they must construct computational grids to handle temporal warping. MPdist is the most expensive algorithm at 1.57 milliseconds; despite utilizing the 14 cores of the Apple M4 Pro for parallel processing, the sheer volume of calculating nearest neighbors for every possible subsequence makes it the heaviest computational task in the library.

While benchmarking time series distances highlights the importance of computational efficiency when analyzing trends and patterns, using the distances for identifying the nearest neighbor of a time series is what the entire chapter is all about.

Finding the nearest neighbor of a time series

It is now time to put the distances to work. The task at hand is computing the *nearest neighbor* of a time series, and we are going to create a command-line utility for it named `findNN.go`. As expected, execute the following commands first:

```
$ cd ch12/NN
$ go mod init
$ go mod tidy
```

Then, use the utility on the time series from the `ts` folder:

```
$ go run findNN.go ../../ts/ts1.gz ../../ts/ts2.gz ../../ts/ts3.gz ../../ts/
ts4.gz ../../ts/ts5.gz ../../ts/ts6.gz ../../ts/ts7.gz ../../ts/ts8.gz
[ts1.gz] Euclidean: ts2.gz (4.07) | Manhattan: ts2.gz (92.20) | Chebyshev: ts2.gz
(0.40) | DTW: ts2.gz (56.50) | LCSS: ts2.gz (0.50) | MPdist: ts2.gz (0.00)
[ts2.gz] Euclidean: ts1.gz (4.07) | Manhattan: ts1.gz (92.20) | Chebyshev: ts1.gz
(0.40) | DTW: ts1.gz (56.50) | LCSS: ts1.gz (0.50) | MPdist: ts1.gz (0.00)
[ts3.gz] Euclidean: ts4.gz (7795.33) | Manhattan: ts4.gz (205474.85) | Chebyshev:
ts4.gz (695.44) | DTW: ts4.gz (92894.48) | LCSS: ts4.gz (0.38) | MPdist: ts4.gz
(45.63)
[ts4.gz] Euclidean: ts3.gz (7795.33) | Manhattan: ts3.gz (205474.85) | Chebyshev:
ts3.gz (695.44) | DTW: ts3.gz (92894.48) | LCSS: ts3.gz (0.49) | MPdist: ts3.gz
(45.63)
[ts5.gz] Euclidean: ts6.gz (5038.21) | Manhattan: ts6.gz (159052.49) | Chebyshev:
ts6.gz (189.94) | DTW: ts6.gz (159052.49) | LCSS: ts1.gz (1.00) | MPdist: ts6.gz
(682.55)
[ts6.gz] Euclidean: ts5.gz (5038.21) | Manhattan: ts5.gz (159052.49) | Chebyshev:
ts5.gz (189.94) | DTW: ts5.gz (159052.49) | LCSS: ts1.gz (1.00) | MPdist: ts5.gz
(682.55)
[ts7.gz] Euclidean: ts6.gz (9957.01) | Manhattan: ts6.gz (306561.56) | Chebyshev:
ts6.gz (444.90) | DTW: ts6.gz (806376.60) | LCSS: ts1.gz (1.00) | MPdist: ts8.gz
(49834.96)
[ts8.gz] Euclidean: ts5.gz (60746.66) | Manhattan: ts5.gz (1920758.36) |
Chebyshev: ts5.gz (1980.04) | DTW: ts5.gz (2783352.08) | LCSS: ts1.gz (1.00) |
MPdist: ts5.gz (40166.55)
```

A clear pattern of mutual pairings emerges immediately: `ts1.gz` and `ts2.gz` identify each other as closest, as do the `ts3-ts4` and `ts5-ts6` pairs. The bond between `ts1` and `ts2` is particularly strong, evidenced by an MPdist score of `0.00`, implying that their subsequence structures are effectively identical.

The results also highlight how *different metrics "see" data differently*. For `ts7.gz`, the lock-step metrics (Euclidean, Manhattan) and global elastic metrics (DTW) identify `ts6.gz` as the nearest neighbor, likely because they align well in roughly the same global timeframe. However, MPdist disagrees, identifying `ts8.gz` as the closest match. This indicates that while `ts7` might align with `ts6` generally, it shares more specific local shapes (motifs) with `ts8`, a relationship that only a subsequence-based metric could detect. Finally, the LCSS results for files `ts5` through `ts8` reveal a configuration issue. The distance of `1.00` represents zero similarity (a complete mismatch), and the listing of `ts1.gz` as the neighbor is simply a default fallback artifact because no valid match was found. This occurred because the data values in `ts5-ts8` are massive (distances in the millions), so the default matching threshold (epsilon) was too strict to detect any "common" points between them. In such a case, using a normalization method might help.

We now shift our focus from analyzing noisy sensor signals to managing precise transactional history. Fundamentally, a financial ledger is simply a *time series of immutable events* — a strictly ordered sequence of deposits and withdrawals where history cannot be altered, only appended. To handle this rigorous requirement, we will introduce TigerBeetle, a specialized database designed to handle money correctly by default. While not marketed as a general-purpose time series engine such as InfluxDB or Prometheus, TigerBeetle is built entirely around this temporal nature. It allows you to query not just the current balance, but exactly what the balance was at any past timestamp, transforming the database from a static storage engine into a temporal system that can perfectly reconstruct the state of the world at any previous point in time.

Using TigerBeetle for financial accounting

TigerBeetle is a reliable, fast, and highly available database for *financial accounting*. In other words, it stores values, which can be considered a time series. In this section, we are only going to show how to work with TigerBeetle in Go – *experimenting* with new technologies and software is an integral part of what it means to be a good developer.

TigerBeetle represents a paradigm shift by elevating financial primitives to the system level. It is not a general-purpose store trying to do everything; it is a purpose-built engine designed specifically to track value. By embedding the logic of double-entry accounting directly into the database kernel, it eliminates the need for the developer to reinvent the wheel. When you send a transfer to TigerBeetle, the engine itself ensures that money cannot be created or destroyed and that debits match credits, enforcing integrity constraints that a standard SQL database leaves entirely up to the application layer. This specialization allows it to strip away the overhead of SQL parsing and generic transaction management, resulting in performance capabilities that generic databases simply cannot match. Beyond raw performance, TigerBeetle is important because it illustrates the power of safety-critical engineering and deterministic design. The database is built on a "shared-nothing" architecture and utilizes advanced Linux kernel features such as `io_uring` to bypass standard operating system bottlenecks, demonstrating how modern software can be optimized to saturate hardware limits. Furthermore, its development process relies on deterministic simulation, a technique where the database is fuzz-tested against simulated years of chaotic network failures to prove its reliability before it ever reaches production. We begin by presenting the `docker-compose.yaml` file used for running TigerBeetle. The first part of it is the following:

```
services:
  # Init container: Formats the data file
  tigerbeetle-init:
    image: ghcr.io/tigerbeetle/tigerbeetle:latest
    security_opt:
      - seccomp:unconfined
    cap_add:
      - IPC_LOCK
    ulimits:
      memlock:
        soft: -1
        hard: -1
entrypoint:>
      sh -c "if [ ! -f /data/0_0.tigerbeetle ]; then
      ./tigerbeetle format --cluster=0 --replica=0 --replica-count=1 /data/
0_0.tigerbeetle;
      echo 'Formatted data file.';
      else echo 'Data file already exists.'; fi"
    volumes:
      - ./data:/data
```

The `tigerbeetle-init` service acts as a transient setup utility, responsible solely for preparing the environment before the main database starts. It pulls the official TigerBeetle image but uses a custom `entrypoint` script instead of the default server command. This script checks for the existence of the data file (`0_0.tigerbeetle`) in the mounted volume; if the file is missing, it executes the `format` command to initialize a new single-replica cluster (`cluster 0, replica 0`). This prevents the main server from failing or accidentally overwriting existing data on restart, ensuring that a valid storage file is always available. This initialization step requires specific system privileges to function correctly, mirroring the requirements of the main server. The `security_opt: - seccomp:unconfined` directive disables Docker's default security filter, allowing the container to make advanced system calls such as `io_uring` that are essential for the TigerBeetle storage engine. Additionally, `cap_add: - IPC_LOCK` grants the permission to lock memory, and the `ulimits` section removes the limit on locked memory (`memlock: -1`). These settings ensure that TigerBeetle can perform direct I/O and manage memory pages without interference from the operating system's swapping mechanism, even during this brief formatting phase. The `volumes` section maps a local `./data` directory to `/data` inside the container, ensuring that the formatted file persists on the host machine after this `init` container exits. The remainder of the `docker-compose.yaml` file comes with the following contents:

```
# Main container: Runs the server
tigerbeetle:
  image: ghcr.io/tigerbeetle/tigerbeetle:latest
  depends_on:
    tigerbeetle-init:
      condition: service_completed_successfully
  security_opt:
    - seccomp:unconfined
  cap_add:
    - IPC_LOCK
  ulimits:
    memlock:
      soft: -1
      hard: -1
  command: start --addresses=0.0.0.0:3000 /data/0_0.tigerbeetle
  ports:
    - "3000:3000"
  volumes:
    - ./data:/data
```

The `tigerbeetle` service defines the main database server, which takes over once the initialization phase is complete. To enforce this strict ordering, the configuration uses a `depends_on` block with the `service_completed_successfully` condition. This ensures that Docker will not attempt to boot the main server until the `tigerbeetle-init` container has finished its task and exited with a success code. Without this coordination, the server would likely crash immediately upon startup because it would be looking for a data file that does not yet exist. This service mirrors the security and resource configuration of the initialization container, applying `seccomp:unconfined`, `IPC_LOCK`, and unlimited memory locking. While the `init` container needed these permissions simply to format the file, the main server requires them to sustain its high-performance runtime guarantees. These settings allow the TigerBeetle engine to utilize `io_uring` for asynchronous I/O and to pin its memory pages to RAM, preventing the operating system from swapping active data to disk, which would introduce unacceptable latency spikes. Finally, the service executes the `start` command to launch the database process. It is configured to listen on `0.0.0.0:3000`, making the database accessible from outside the container, and it points to the `/data/0_0.tigerbeetle` file that was just created. The `ports` section maps the container's internal port `3000` to the host's port `3000`, allowing your Go programs running on your local machine to connect. The `volumes` mount is identical to the one used in the `init` step, ensuring that the persistent storage created in the previous step is visible and writable by the running server.

Let us now learn how to connect to TigerBeetle using Go code. First, however, you should execute `docker-compose up` for TigerBeetle to start.

Connecting to TigerBeetle

We present a small Go program that allows you to connect to TigerBeetle and make sure that everything works as expected. The code of `ch12/tb/connect.go` is the following:

```
package main

import (
	"log"
	"os"

	tb "github.com/tigerbeetle/tigerbeetle-go"
	"github.com/tigerbeetle/tigerbeetle-go/pkg/types"
)

func main() {
	client, err := tb.NewClient(types.ToUint128(0),
[]string{"127.0.0.1:3000"})
	if err != nil {
		log.Printf("Error creating client: %s", err)
		os.Exit(1)
	}
	defer client.Close()
	log.Println("Successfully connected to TigerBeetle!")
}
```

The program begins by importing two packages from the standard library (`log` and `os`). Next, it imports the official TigerBeetle SDK, which is aliased as `tb` to simplify function calls (`github.com/tigerbeetle/tigerbeetle-go`). After that, the `pkg/types` sub-package is imported to access specific data structures — most importantly, the 128-bit integers that are native to the database's binary protocol. Inside the `main()` function, the core logic revolves around the `tb.NewClient()` method, which initializes the connection using two parameters. First, `types.ToUint128(0)` specifies the cluster ID, which must strictly match the `--cluster=0` flag used when you formatted and started your Docker container, ensuring the client attempts to talk to the correct cluster instance. Second, the `[]string{"127.0.0.1:3000"}` address slice points the client to the local loopback interface on port `3000`, which is the host port exposed by your Docker configuration. If the program connects successfully to the TigerBeetle instance, a success message is logged to the console, confirming that the Go application is properly configured and ready to perform actual transactions. Let us see how to run `ch12/tb/connect.go`:

```
$ cd ch12/tb
$ go mod init
$ go mod tidy
$ go run connect.go
2025/12/30 07:10:29 Successfully connected to TigerBeetle!
```

So, we are good to go! Let us now learn how to write data to TigerBeetle.

Writing data to TigerBeetle

The first task is writing data to TigerBeetle, which is performed by `ch12/tb/writer.go`. Here is the `main()` function implementation, starting with the connection details:

```
func main() {
    client, err := tb.NewClient(types.ToUint128(0), []string{"127.0.0.1:3000"})
    if err != nil {
        log.Printf("Error creating client: %s", err)
        os.Exit(1)
    }
    defer client.Close()
```

The next code snippet initializes the data structures required to create new accounts in the TigerBeetle database:

```
    // --- Step 1: Create Accounts ---
    accounts := []types.Account{
```

```
        {
            ID:     types.ToUint128(1),
            Ledger: 1,
            Code:   1,
        },
        {
            ID:     types.ToUint128(2),
            Ledger: 1,
            Code:   1,
        },
    }
```

The program prepares to execute a batched operation using the defined slice of `types.Account` objects, which is central to TigerBeetle's high-performance design because sending multiple accounts in a single request minimizes network overhead. Inside the struct, the `ID` field is assigned a 128-bit integer using `types.ToUint128()`, a necessary conversion because TigerBeetle uses 128-bit IDs natively to support global uniqueness across massive datasets. The `Ledger` field acts as a namespace or partition — ensuring that accounts can only transact with others in the same ledger (e.g., keeping USD separate from EUR) — while the `Code` field serves as a user-defined category, allowing you to tag accounts as specific types such as `Assets`, `Liabilities`, or `Equity` for your application's logic. In this specific example, the value `1` is simply a *magic number* that the developer has decided to represent a specific category.

The following code snippet handles the actual submission of the account creation request and the interpretation of the results:

```
accountErrors, err := client.CreateAccounts(accounts)
if err != nil {
    log.Fatalf("Fatal network error creating accounts: %s", err)
}

for _, err := range accountErrors {
    if err.Result == types.AccountExists {
        log.Printf("Account at %d exists.", err.Index)
    } else {
        log.Printf("Error at %d: %s", err.Index, err.Result)
    }
}
fmt.Println("Accounts 1 and 2 are ready.")
```

The call to `client.CreateAccounts(accounts)` is the moment the data actually leaves your Go application and travels to the TigerBeetle server. It returns two distinct types of errors: a standard Go `err` instance and a specialized slice called `accountErrors`. The first check, `if err != nil`, is looking for failures such as the server being offline or the network connection dropping, which would prevent the entire batch from being processed; in such cases, the program logs a fatal message and exits. The `for` loop that follows handles more granular, logic-level errors. *Because TigerBeetle is designed for high-throughput batching, it does not fail the whole request just because one account in the batch has a problem.* Instead, it processes what it can and returns a list of specific errors for the items that failed. The loop iterates through these `accountErrors` instances to check the `Result` code. The specific check for `types.AccountExists` is a common pattern in idempotent systems: it tells the application, "This isn't a failure. The account is already there." This allows the program to safely rerun the initialization code without crashing. Any other error code indicates a genuine problem (such as an invalid ledger ID), which is logged specifically with its index, so you know exactly which account in the batch was rejected. Finally, if the code reaches the `print` statement, it means the application has confirmed that the accounts were either just created or already existed, and it is safe to proceed.

The next code block executes the core financial operation – moving values between accounts using a double-entry transfer:

```
transfers := []types.Transfer{
    {
        ID: types.ToUint128(100),
        DebitAccountID:  types.ToUint128(1),
        CreditAccountID: types.ToUint128(2),
        Amount:          types.ToUint128(100),
        Ledger:          1,
        Code:            1,
    },
}
transferErrors, err := client.CreateTransfers(transfers)
if err != nil {
    log.Fatalf("Fatal network error creating transfer: %s", err)
}
for _, err := range transferErrors {
    log.Printf("Error at index %d: %s", err.Index, err.Result)
}
if len(transferErrors) == 0 {
    fmt.Println("Transfer of 100 units successful.")
```

```
    }
}
```

The code begins by constructing a slice of `types.Transfer` objects, where each transfer represents an atomic transaction. Inside the struct, we assign a unique ID (`100`) to the transaction itself; this is crucial for idempotency, ensuring that if you accidentally send the same request twice due to a network retry, the database will recognize the ID and refuse to execute it a second time. The direction of funds is defined by the `DebitAccountID` (the source, account 1) value and the `CreditAccountID` (the destination, account 2) value, while the `Amount` field specifies the quantity of units to move. The `Ledger` field is set to `1` to match the accounts we created earlier; if this did not match, the database would reject the transfer to prevent cross-ledger contamination. Once the transfer object is defined, the code submits it to the server using `client.CreateTransfers()`. As with the account creation step, the error handling is split into two layers. The first check guards against total system failures, such as network disconnects. The second layer involves iterating through `transferErrors`. The final check, `len(transferErrors) == 0`, serves as definitive confirmation that the money has successfully moved, allowing the program to print the success message with confidence that the ledger is now updated.

Execute `writer.go` on your machine to put data into TigerBeetle:

```
$ go run writer.go
Accounts 1 and 2 are ready
Transfer of 100 units successful.
```

Before continuing with the Go code that reads the data we just put in, we are going to manually connect to the TigerBeetle REPL and read the data. Executing the following commands on your machine will give you similar output:

```
$ docker exec -it tb-tigerbeetle-1 ./tigerbeetle repl --cluster=0 --addresses=3000
2025-12-30 05:12:12.586Z info(message_bus):
255674976222256274120386543367805976220: on_connect: connected to=0
2025-12-30 05:12:13.138Z warning(client): 255674976222256274120386543367805976220:
on_reply: slow request, request=0 op=10 size=512 register time=608ms
TigerBeetle CLI Client 0.16.67+2398229
  Hit enter after a semicolon to run a command.
  Ctrl+D to exit.

Examples:
  create_accounts id=1 code=10 ledger=700 flags=linked|history, id=2 code=10
ledger=700;
```

```
  create_transfers id=1 debit_account_id=1 credit_account_id=2 amount=10
ledger=700 code=10;
  lookup_accounts id=1;
  lookup_accounts id=1, id=2;
  get_account_transfers account_id=1 flags=debits|credits;
  get_account_balances account_id=1 flags=debits|credits;
> lookup_accounts id=1, id=2;
{
  "id": "1",
  "debits_pending": "0",
  "debits_posted": "100",
  "credits_pending": "0",
  "credits_posted": "0",
  "user_data_128": "0",
  "user_data_64": "0",
  "user_data_32": "0",
  "ledger": "1",
  "code": "1",
  "flags": [],
  "timestamp": "1767071480728374065"
}
{
  "id": "2",
  "debits_pending": "0",
  "debits_posted": "0",
  "credits_pending": "0",
  "credits_posted": "100",
  "user_data_128": "0",
  "user_data_64": "0",
  "user_data_32": "0",
  "ledger": "1",
  "code": "1",
  "flags": [],
  "timestamp": "1767071480728374066"
}
```

The output serves as definitive proof that the Go program successfully executed the double-entry transfer, reflecting the raw state of the two accounts on the TigerBeetle ledger. The most critical fields for verification are `debits_posted` and `credits_posted`. TigerBeetle differs from traditional databases by not storing a single "current balance" field; instead, it tracks the cumulative total of values sent and received. For account 1, the `debits_posted` value of `100` confirms that it was the source of the transfer, matching the `DebitAccountID` value you specified in your code. Since it has received no funds, its net balance is effectively negative `100` relative to its starting point. Conversely, account 2 shows a `credits_posted` value of `100`, confirming it was the destination account and now holds a positive balance of 100 units. You will also notice that the `debits_pending` and `credits_pending` fields are both zero. This is the expected behavior for a standard transfer such as the one you performed. These fields are reserved for two-phase commits, a pattern used in payment systems where funds must be authorized or "held" before they are finally captured — similar to a pending credit card charge at a hotel or gas station. Because your transfer was executed as a single, immediate action, the funds bypassed this pending state entirely and were written directly to the posted ledgers. The metadata fields, specifically `ledger` and `code`, confirm that the accounts were created within the correct partitions. The `ledger` value of `1` acts as a namespace, ensuring that these accounts interact only with others in the same ledger, *which prevents accidental transfers between different currencies or unrelated systems.* As discussed earlier, the `code` value of `1` reflects the user-defined category you assigned, which in a real-world application would likely represent a specific account type, such as a checking or savings account. The user data fields remain at zero because no external metadata, such as a foreign key to a SQL user table, was attached during creation. Finally, the system fields provide the immutable context for the account's state. The `timestamp` field represents the exact nanosecond relative to the Unix epoch when the account was last modified, governed by the cluster's internal logic to ensure a strictly ordered history of events. The `flags` field is empty, indicating that no special constraints were applied to these accounts. Had you enforced rules such as `debits_must_not_exceed_credits` to prevent overdrafts, those flags would appear here as active constraints on the account's behavior.

Next, let us see the Go program that reads data from TigerBeetle.

Reading the data back

Having successfully executed our transactions, the final and most critical step in the accounting life cycle is to query the database and verify that our ledger reflects the precise state of balances we expect. The `main()` implementation of `ch12/tb/reader.go` begins as follows:

```
func main() {
    client, err := tb.NewClient(types.ToUint128(0), []string{"127.0.0.1:3000"})
    if err != nil {
        log.Printf("Error creating client: %s", err)
        os.Exit(1)
    }
    defer client.Close()
```

As before, this is the code for connecting to the TigerBeetle instance. The rest of the code is the following:

```
    ids := []types.Uint128{
        types.ToUint128(1),
        types.ToUint128(2),
    }
    accounts, err := client.LookupAccounts(ids)
    if err != nil {
        log.Fatalf("Could not lookup accounts: %s", err)
    }
    fmt.Println("--- Account Balances ---")
    for _, acc := range accounts {
        fmt.Printf("Account ID: %s\n", acc.ID)
        fmt.Printf("  Ledger: %d\n", acc.Ledger)
        fmt.Printf("  Credits Posted: %s\n", acc.CreditsPosted)
        fmt.Printf("  Debits Posted:  %s\n", acc.DebitsPosted)
        fmt.Println("------------------------")
    }
}
```

The core logic starts by defining a slice of 128-bit integers using `types.ToUint128(1)` and `types.ToUint128(2)`. So, instead of querying one account at a time, we prepare a batch of IDs (in this case, for account 1 and account 2) to fetch them all in a single network round-trip. The actual retrieval is performed by `client.LookupAccounts(ids)`, which sends the batch request to the server. If this operation encounters a network or protocol error, `log.Fatalf()` terminates the program immediately. If successful, the function returns a slice of `Account` structs containing the current ledger state. The code then iterates over these results using a `range` loop, printing key details to the console. Inside the loop, the output focuses on fields that confirm the double-entry accounting logic. It prints the account ID to identify the record and the ledger ID to verify that the account is in the correct partition. Most importantly, it displays `CreditsPosted` and `DebitsPosted`. Unlike traditional databases that might just show a "balance" column, TigerBeetle explicitly tracks the total money received (`credits`) and total money sent (`debits`) separately. This allows the developer (and the user) to verify not just the final net position, but the history of movement that led there.

Running `ch12/tb/reader.go` produces the following output:

```
$ go run reader.go
--- Account Balances ---
```

```
Account ID: 1
  Ledger: 1
  Credits Posted: 0
  Debits Posted:  64
-----------------------
Account ID: 2
  Ledger: 1
  Credits Posted: 64
  Debits Posted:  0
-----------------------
```

Account 1 shows `Debits Posted: 64`, indicating that it was the source of the funds (money leaving the account), while account 2 shows `Credits Posted: 64`, identifying it as the recipient (money entering the account). Perfect!

The logic behind adopting a specialized tool is that when the underlying infrastructure natively guarantees deterministic execution and **fault tolerance (FT)** at scale, the surrounding application code becomes dramatically simpler, faster, and inherently more resilient.

Summary

In this chapter, we successfully bridged the gap between raw algorithmic theory and data processing. We began by demystifying time series analysis, implementing fundamental distance metrics to quantify similarity and structuring this logic into a modular, reusable Go package. This foundation allowed us to solve the practical problem of nearest-neighbor search. Finally, we contextualized these analytical skills within the demanding realm of financial technology by introducing TigerBeetle, demonstrating how a purpose-built database can enforce strict ledger immutability and performance.

The next chapter is about time series data mining, the systematic process of uncovering meaningful patterns, relationships, and structures within time series data.

Exercises

1. Change `ch12/tb/connect.go` so that the server address as well as the port number are both given as command-line arguments.
2. Make `./NN/findNN.go` a concurrent utility!
3. Implement z-normalization for the distances of the `tslib` package.

Additional resources

- TigerBeetle: `https://tigerbeetle.com/`
- The Go package for working with TigerBeetle can be found at the following URL: `https://github.com/tigerbeetle/tigerbeetle/tree/main/src/clients/go`
- The TigerBeetle documentation: `https://docs.tigerbeetle.com/`

13

Time Series Data Mining

Time series data mining is the process of discovering useful patterns, relationships, and structures within data that change over time. In practice, it involves techniques for classification, clustering, anomaly detection, forecasting, and motif or shape discovery in sequences of numeric values collected over regular intervals — such as sensor readings, stock prices, log file analytics, system metrics, service metrics or network metrics. The selection of an appropriate metric is often an essential step in all data mining tasks. This choice depends on the nature of the data and the characteristics of the patterns one is trying to capture. Different metrics may be more suitable for different applications and types of time series data. Modern approaches use a combination of distances with different weights for each distance or allow a machine learning model to decide which distance gets a higher priority.

However, as we scale these mining operations to handle massive datasets, the intense data processing generates substantial memory churn and demands high levels of concurrency. The performance of our analytical tools thus becomes tightly coupled to the mechanical efficiency of the Go runtime. To bridge the gap between algorithmic design and system performance, this chapter extends beyond data mining to explore the Green Tea garbage collector, illustrating how memory reclamation behaves under heavy allocation pressure. We then conclude by examining Go's advanced observability features, specifically Goroutine metrics and the Goroutine leak profile, to provide the diagnostic tools necessary for resolving the concurrency bottlenecks that frequently arise in large-scale data applications.

This chapter covers the following:

- Classification, clustering, and outlier detection
- The Green Tea garbage collector
- Goroutine metrics
- Goroutine leak profile

We are going to use the Go package that we created in the previous chapter, as time series data mining depends on time series distances. What differs among the three data mining tasks is the way a distance is used. We begin with classification.

Classification

Time series classification is a supervised learning task where the goal is to assign a discrete label or category to a given time series. The **k-Nearest Neighbors (kNN)** classifier is one of the simplest yet most effective algorithms for time series classification, operating on the intuitive principle *that similar data points likely share the same label.* The **Leave-One-Out Classification** (similarity search) utility that we are going to implement operates by treating every time series in your dataset as an unknown query to find its single most authentic match among the remaining labeled files. Before any comparison begins, the program Z-normalizes all data to ensure that differences in amplitude or offset do not distort the results, allowing the algorithm to focus purely on the shape of the signal. Instead of relying on a single distance metric, which might be biased, it calculates six different distances (Euclidean, Manhattan, Chebyshev, DTW, LCSS, and MPdist) for every pair. It then ranks the potential neighbors from 1 to N for each metric and computes a final "consensus" score by summing these ranks, *applying double weight to elastic measures such as DTW and MPdist.* This weighted rank aggregation ensures that the identified NN is robust, satisfying both rigid alignment and flexible shape matching criteria. Having solidified our understanding of the underlying principles, we can now assemble these components into a cohesive implementation. The source code that follows serves as the final synthesis of our architectural decisions, bridging the gap between theoretical design and a functioning system.

Classification implementation

The classification utility (`ch13/classification.go`) is presented in multiple code snippets, starting with the preamble of the program:

```
package main

import (
	"flag"
	"fmt"
	"log"
	"math"
	"os"
	"path/filepath"
	"runtime"
	"sort"
	"strings"
```

```
    "sync"
    "text/tabwriter"

    "github.com/mactsouk/tslib"
)

// Weights for the metrics
const (
    WeightLockStep = 1.0
    WeightElastic  = 2.0
)

type DistanceResult struct {
    Filename   string
    Values     map[string]float64
    Ranks      map[string]int
    FinalScore float64
}

// Struct to store the final decision for each file
type MatchDecision struct {
    Query    string
    Neighbor string
    Score    float64
    Ranks    map[string]int // Store ranks for display
}
```

The diversity of the `import` block signals a transition from a simple utility to a more robust, CLI-driven application. Most notable is the inclusion of the `flag` package, which facilitates a more sophisticated parameter strategy. This approach, combined with `text/tabwriter`, demonstrates a commitment to a professional user experience, ensuring that complex data is presented in a clean, aligned, and human-readable format. However, the logic relies on the external `github.com/mactsouk/tslib` package. Following the imports, the program defines the rules and data structures that drive its decision-making process. The `WeightLockStep` and `WeightElastic` constants are configuration parameters that explicitly bias the algorithm; by assigning a higher weight (`2.0`) to elastic measures, the program declares that finding a match in "shape" (via DTW or MPdist) is twice as important as finding a match in raw alignment (via Euclidean distance). `DistanceResult` is used during the calculation phase to hold the raw distance values and calculated ranks for a single candidate file. Once the best candidate is identified, the relevant information is put into `MatchDecision`, a summary structure that captures the query, its chosen neighbor, and the final score.

Next, we present the first part of `main()`, which includes the program parameters:

```
func main() {
    window := flag.Int("w", 20, "Window size for elastic metrics")
    targetLen := flag.Int("L", 0, "Target length (0=disabled)")
    summaryMethod := flag.String("S", "paa", "Summarization method")
    flag.Parse()

    files := flag.Args()
    if len(files) < 2 {
        log.Fatal("Need at least 2 files to perform comparisons.")
    }
```

The `flag` package defines three primary command-line switches that allow the user to tune the analysis: `-w` sets the *window size* constraint for elastic metrics such as DTW to limit the search space; `-L` defines a target length for dimensionality reduction, allowing large datasets to be compressed for speed; and `-S` selects the specific summarization algorithm to perform that compression. If fewer than two files have been provided, the program will terminate execution with a fatal error log.

Next, we print the active program parameters:

```
    fmt.Println("--------------------------------------------------")
    fmt.Println("        LOOCV Time Series Similarity")
    fmt.Println("--------------------------------------------------")
    fmt.Printf("Config: Window=%d, SummaryLen=%d, Method=%s\n", *window,
*targetLen, *summaryMethod)
    fmt.Printf("Input:  %d files\n", len(files))
    fmt.Println("--------------------------------------------------")
```

This code block ensures that the user can verify exactly which settings are being applied and helps prevent wasted compute time on misconfigured runs.

The next section handles the preprocessing phase of the time series pipeline:

```
    fmt.Print("Loading and processing data... ")
    dataMap := make(map[string][]float64)
    for _, f := range files {
        raw := loadAndProcess(f, *targetLen, *summaryMethod)
```

```
        norm := zNormalize(raw)
        dataMap[f] = norm
    }
    fmt.Println("Done.")

    metrics := []string{"Euclidean", "Manhattan", "Chebyshev", "DTW", "LCSS",
"MPdist"}

    var decisions []MatchDecision
    lookup := make(map[string]string)
    fmt.Println("Calculating distances (Parallel)...")
```

The code begins by iterating through every input file to perform two key transformations: loading the raw data and then applying z-normalization, which is necessary for more accurate pattern recognition. The processed data is then stored in `dataMap` for fast, repeated access. Following the data preparation, the code defines the `metrics` slice, explicitly listing the six distance algorithms that will be used to judge similarity. It also initializes the `decisions` slice and the `lookup` map, which serve as the central repositories for the results; these structures will later enable the program to not only report individual nearest neighbors but also to efficiently detect "mutual groups" (symmetric pairs).

The code block that follows implements the core *Leave-One-Out* comparison engine, utilizing a concurrent design to handle computationally expensive metrics:

```
    for _, queryFile := range files {
        queryTS := dataMap[queryFile]
var results []*DistanceResult
        var mu sync.Mutex
        var wg sync.WaitGroup
        sem := make(chan struct{}, runtime.NumCPU())

        for _, candidateFile := range files {
            if queryFile == candidateFile {
                continue
            }

            wg.Add(1)
            go func(candFile string) {
                defer wg.Done()
                sem <- struct{}{}
                defer func() { <-sem }()
```

```
            candTS := dataMap[candFile]
            dists := make(map[string]float64)

            dists["Euclidean"] = tslib.EuclideanDistance(queryTS, candTS)
            dists["Manhattan"] = tslib.ManhattanDistance(queryTS, candTS)
            dists["Chebyshev"] = tslib.ChebyshevDistance(queryTS, candTS)
            dists["DTW"] = tslib.DTW(queryTS, candTS, *window)
            dists["LCSS"] = tslib.LCSS(queryTS, candTS, *window, 0.5)
            dists["MPdist"] = tslib.MPdist(queryTS, candTS, *window)

            res := &DistanceResult{
                Filename: candFile,
                Values:   dists,
                Ranks:    make(map[string]int),
            }
            mu.Lock()
            results = append(results, res)
            mu.Unlock()
        }(candidateFile)
    }
    wg.Wait()
```

The outer loop iterates through the file list, designating one time series at a time as the "query" (`queryTS`). Before examining potential matches, the program sets up synchronization via a `sync.WaitGroup` and a buffered channel (`sem`) sized to the number of CPU cores. This channel acts as a semaphore, restricting the number of simultaneous calculations to match hardware capacity, preventing the system from spawning thousands of threads and crashing due to memory exhaustion. Inside the inner loop, the program iterates through all other files (*candidates*), skipping the query itself to avoid a trivial self-match. For every candidate, it launches a goroutine to perform the heavy lifting. This goroutine calculates the six distinct similarity metrics in isolation. The results are packaged in a `DistanceResult` struct.

The next code snippet implements the **Weighted Rank Aggregation** algorithm, which serves as the decision-making core of the program:

```
    for _, m := range metrics {
        sort.Slice(results, func(a, b int) bool {
            return results[a].Values[m] < results[b].Values[m]
        })
        for rank, res := range results {
            res.Ranks[m] = rank + 1
```

```
            }
        }

        for _, res := range results {
            score := 0.0
            score += float64(res.Ranks["Euclidean"]) * WeightLockStep
            score += float64(res.Ranks["Manhattan"]) * WeightLockStep
            score += float64(res.Ranks["Chebyshev"]) * WeightLockStep
            score += float64(res.Ranks["DTW"]) * WeightElastic
            score += float64(res.Ranks["LCSS"]) * WeightElastic
            score += float64(res.Ranks["MPdist"]) * WeightElastic
            res.FinalScore = score
        }

        sort.Slice(results, func(a, b int) bool {
            return results[a].FinalScore < results[b].FinalScore
        })
        best := results[0]
        decisions = append(decisions, MatchDecision{
            Query:    queryFile,
            Neighbor: best.Filename,
            Score:    best.FinalScore,
            Ranks:    best.Ranks,
        })
        lookup[queryFile] = best.Filename
    }
```

As *raw distance values from different metrics are mathematically incompatible*, the code normalizes them by converting values into ranks. It iterates through each of the six metrics individually, sorting the entire list of candidates based on their raw distance for that specific metric. Once sorted, every candidate is assigned a rank from 1 to N (where 1 represents the closest match for that metric). This transforms the heterogeneous distance values into a uniform ranking scale that can be safely compared and combined.

Once the rankings are established, the code proceeds to calculate a composite `FinalScore` for every candidate. It iterates through the results and computes a weighted sum of the ranks assigned in the previous step. *Lock-step* metrics such as Euclidean and Manhattan are multiplied by `WeightLockStep`, while "elastic" metrics such as DTW and LCSS are multiplied by `WeightElastic`. Finally, the list of candidates is sorted one last time based on this aggregated score. The candidate with the lowest score is declared the winner, and its details are stored in the `decisions` list and `lookup` map for the report.

The next code snippet handles the presentation layer of the application, converting the complex internal results into a structured, human-readable table:

```
fmt.Println("\n--- Nearest Neighbor Report ---")
w := tabwriter.NewWriter(os.Stdout, 0, 0, 3, ' ', 0)
// Header
fmt.Fprintln(w, "Query\tNeighbor\tScore\tRank Breakdown")
fmt.Fprintln(w, "-----\t--------\t-----\t--------------")

for _, d := range decisions {
    qShort := filepath.Base(d.Query)
    nShort := filepath.Base(d.Neighbor)

    rankStr := fmt.Sprintf("LockStep: Euc(#%d) Man(#%d) Cheb(#%d) | Elastic:
DTW(#%d) LCSS(#%d) MPdist(#%d)",
        d.Ranks["Euclidean"], d.Ranks["Manhattan"], d.Ranks["Chebyshev"],
        d.Ranks["DTW"], d.Ranks["LCSS"], d.Ranks["MPdist"])

    fmt.Fprintf(w, "%s\t%s\t%.1f\t%s\n", qShort, nShort, d.Score, rankStr)
}
w.Flush()
```

The code utilizes the `text/tabwriter` package, which is designed to create elastic text columns; by writing tab-separated strings to this writer, the program ensures that the columns (`Query`, `Neighbor`, `Score`) align perfectly regardless of how long the filenames are. The code sets up the writer to output to the terminal (`os.Stdout`) with a padding of 3 spaces between columns for readability. Inside the loop, the program iterates through the `MatchDecision` structs. It uses `filepath.Base()` to strip away long directory paths, leaving only the concise filenames. After that, `rankStr` is constructed to provide full transparency as it details exactly how the chosen neighbor performed across every individual metric. Finally, the `w.Flush()` command is executed to calculate the necessary column widths and physically write the aligned buffer to the screen.

This final logic block performs a post-processing analysis to identify *Mutual Nearest Neighbors*, which is often the strongest signal of a true relationship in time series mining. The goal is to find symmetric pairs: instances where File A identifies File B as its best match and File B simultaneously identifies File A as its best match, which can be useful for eliminating false positives caused by generic patterns that happen to sit near the statistical average of the dataset — a common issue known as the *hubness problem*:

```
    fmt.Println("\n---Mutual Nearest Neighbors (Symmetric Groups)---")
    printed := make(map[string]bool)

    foundGroup := false
    for _, d := range decisions {
        fileA := d.Query
        fileB := d.Neighbor

        if lookup[fileB] == fileA {
            key1 := fileA + fileB
            key2 := fileB + fileA
            if !printed[key1] && !printed[key2] {
                fmt.Printf("%s  <-->  %s\n", filepath.Base(fileA),
filepath.Base(fileB))
                printed[key1] = true
                printed[key2] = true
                foundGroup = true
            }
        }
    }
    if !foundGroup {
        fmt.Println("No symmetric pairs found.")
    }
    fmt.Println()
}
```

The code iterates through the `decisions` list, retrieving the neighbor (`fileB`) for each query (`fileA`). After that, it checks the `lookup` map to see if `lookup[fileB] == fileA`. To prevent duplicate output, the program uses a `printed` map to track pairs that have already been displayed. It constructs composite keys (`fileA + fileB` and `fileB + fileA`) to represent the unique relationship. If a symmetric relationship is confirmed and has not been printed yet, it outputs the pair with a `<-->` indicator and marks both permutations as seen. Finally, a `foundGroup` flag tracks if any such pairs were discovered; if the loop completes without finding a single mutual match, a message (`"No symmetric pairs found"`) is displayed to confirm the analysis ran correctly but yielded no strong clusters.

The next helper function implements Z-normalization, which ensures that similarity comparisons focus purely on the shape of the signal rather than its amplitude:

```
func zNormalize(data []float64) []float64 {
    if len(data) == 0 {
        return data
    }
    sum := 0.0
    for _, v := range data {
        sum += v
    }
    mean := sum / float64(len(data))
    sqDiffSum := 0.0
    for _, v := range data {
        diff := v - mean
        sqDiffSum += diff * diff
    }
    stdDev := math.Sqrt(sqDiffSum / float64(len(data)))
    if stdDev == 0 {
        stdDev = 1.0
    }
    result := make([]float64, len(data))
    for i, v := range data {
        result[i] = (v - mean) / stdDev
    }
    return result
}
```

The function operates in three clear passes. First, it iterates through the input slice to calculate the *arithmetic mean* by summing all values and dividing by the count. Second, it computes the *variance* by summing the squared differences between each point and that mean, then taking the square root to find the standard deviation. If the standard deviation is zero (which happens if the time series is a flat line), it defaults to 1.0 to prevent a *division by zero* panic. Finally, it allocates a new slice and populates it by applying the formula to every data point, returning the normalized sequence ready for analysis.

Last, we have another helper function:

```
func loadAndProcess(path string, length int, method string) []float64 {
    raw, err := tslib.ReadGzipTimeSeries(path)
    if err != nil {
```

```
        log.Fatalf("Error reading %s: %v", path, err)
    }
    if length <= 0 {
        return raw
    }
    switch strings.ToLower(method) {
    case "paa":
        return tslib.PAA(raw, length)
    case "random":
        return tslib.RandomSampling(raw, length)
    case "step":
        return tslib.Stepping(raw, length)
    default:
        return raw
    }
}
```

The code begins by calling `tslib.ReadGzipTimeSeries()` to read and decompress the raw floating-point data from a GZIP-encoded file; if this operation fails, the program logs a fatal error and terminates immediately to prevent cascading failures. Once the raw data is loaded, the function checks the `length` parameter. If `length` is zero or negative, it bypasses all processing and returns the full, raw dataset. However, if a target length is specified, the function enters a `switch` statement to select the appropriate downsampling algorithm based on the user's method flag. Let us now try the utility:

```
$ cd ch13
$ go run classification.go -L 100 ../ts/ts1.gz ../ts/ts2.gz ../ts/ts3.gz ../ts/
ts4.gz ../ts/ts5.gz ../ts/ts6.gz ../ts/ts7.gz ../ts/ts8.gz
go: downloading github.com/mactsouk/tslib v0.1.0
------------------------------------------------
       LOOCV Time Series Similarity
------------------------------------------------
Config: Window=20, SummaryLen=100, Method=paa
Input:  8 files
------------------------------------------------
Loading and processing data... Done.
Calculating distances (Parallel)...

--- Nearest Neighbor Report ---
Query    Neighbor   Score   Rank Breakdown
```

```
-----    --------   -----   --------------
ts1.gz   ts2.gz     17.0    LockStep: Euc(#1) Man(#1) Cheb(#3) | Elastic: DTW(#1)
LCSS(#4) MPdist(#1)
ts2.gz   ts1.gz     25.0    LockStep: Euc(#2) Man(#3) Cheb(#6) | Elastic: DTW(#1)
LCSS(#5) MPdist(#1)
ts3.gz   ts4.gz     15.0    LockStep: Euc(#1) Man(#1) Cheb(#1) | Elastic: DTW(#4)
LCSS(#1) MPdist(#1)
ts4.gz   ts3.gz     15.0    LockStep: Euc(#1) Man(#1) Cheb(#3) | Elastic: DTW(#1)
LCSS(#1) MPdist(#3)
ts5.gz   ts3.gz     30.0    LockStep: Euc(#7) Man(#5) Cheb(#6) | Elastic: DTW(#2)
LCSS(#2) MPdist(#2)
ts6.gz   ts2.gz     21.0    LockStep: Euc(#2) Man(#2) Cheb(#1) | Elastic: DTW(#2)
LCSS(#4) MPdist(#2)
ts7.gz   ts8.gz     9.0     LockStep: Euc(#1) Man(#1) Cheb(#1) | Elastic: DTW(#1)
LCSS(#1) MPdist(#1)
ts8.gz   ts7.gz     9.0     LockStep: Euc(#1) Man(#1) Cheb(#1) | Elastic: DTW(#1)
LCSS(#1) MPdist(#1)

--- Mutual Nearest Neighbors (Symmetric Groups) ---
ts1.gz  <-->  ts2.gz
ts3.gz  <-->  ts4.gz
ts7.gz  <-->  ts8.gz
```

The most obvious result is the perfect pairing of `ts7` and `ts8`, which achieved the minimum possible score of `9.0`. This score indicates that they ranked #1 across every single metric. Two other strong, symmetric groups emerged: `ts1` paired with `ts2` and `ts3` paired with `ts4`. These are *Mutual Nearest Neighbors*. `ts1` ranked `ts2` as its #1 neighbor in Euclidean, DTW, and MPdist metrics. Similarly, `ts3` and `ts4` formed a tight core, with `ts4` ranking `ts3` as #1 in almost every category. The most interesting insights come from the "outlier" files, `ts5` and `ts6`. `ts5` is a classic example of an **elastic match**. Its Euclidean rank was terrible (#7), meaning it does not look like `ts3` at all when overlaid directly. However, its elastic ranks (DTW #2) were high, suggesting `ts5` is a time-shifted or stretched version of the `ts3` and `ts4` group. Conversely, `ts6` identified `ts2` as its neighbor, but `ts2` preferred `ts1`.

While classification relies on predefined labels to categorize data, we now shift to clustering to handle datasets where structural patterns are not yet known. So, we introduce a specialized clustering utility designed to partition data.

Clustering

Time Series Clustering is an unsupervised learning technique where the objective is to partition data (time series in our case) into distinct groups or "clusters" such that sequences within the same group are highly similar to each other while being significantly different from those in other groups. Unlike classification, there are no pre-defined labels; the algorithm must discover the underlying structure of the data on its own, making it invaluable for exploratory data analysis — such as identifying common usage patterns in server logs or categorizing stock movements.

Clustering methodology

The **K-Means Clustering** utility organizes your time series into *k* distinct groups by iteratively refining the center point, or *centroid*, of each cluster. The process begins by randomly selecting *k* files to serve as the initial centroids. In the assignment phase, the program uses parallel processing to compare every time series against these centroids, assigning each file to the cluster with the closest center (*typically using Euclidean distance*). Once all files are assigned, the update phase calculates the new centroid for each cluster by computing the mathematical average of all its members. This cycle of assignment and update repeats until the clusters stabilize and no files change groups. This implementation relies on summarization techniques such as PAA to ensure that all time series are of equal length, a mathematical requirement for calculating a valid average centroid.

Clustering implementation

For the clustering implementation, we are going to present the `main()` function only as the remaining code is analogous to the classification utility. We begin the presentation of `main()` with the following code snippet:

```
func main() {
    k := flag.Int("k", 2, "Number of clusters")
    iter := flag.Int("iter", 10, "Maximum iterations")
    targetLen := flag.Int("L", 0, "Target length")
    summaryMethod := flag.String("S", "paa",    "Summarization method")
    seed := flag.Int64("seed", 0, "Random seed (0 for current time)")
    flag.Parse()

    files := flag.Args()
    if len(files) < *k {
        log.Fatal("Error: Number of files must be greater " +
            "than number of clusters (k).")
    }
```

The `main()` function begins by defining the command-line parameters. We define `k` to specify the target number of clusters and `iter` to impose a restriction on the K-Means refinement loop, preventing infinite execution if convergence is slow. Command-line flags are provided for the target compressed length (`L`) and the summarization strategy (`S`), which defaults to PAA. A `seed` flag is also included to support reproducible research; by manually setting this, users can force deterministic output, whereas a default value of 0 signals the program to use the current time. The code verifies that the number of input files is at least equal to `k`, as it is mathematically impossible to partition data into more groups than the data available.

The next section implements a *transparency layer* for the application, ensuring that the user's runtime choices are explicitly confirmed before any complex processing begins:

```
// --- 0. Print Active Parameters ---
fmt.Println("------------------------------------------")
fmt.Println("       K-Means Time Series Clustering")
fmt.Println("------------------------------------------")
fmt.Printf("Config: Clusters(k)=%d, MaxIter=%d\n",    *k, *iter)
fmt.Printf("Summary: Length=%d (0=Full), Method=%s\n",
    *targetLen, *summaryMethod)
fmt.Printf("Input:  %d files\n", len(files))
fmt.Println("------------------------------------------")
```

The next snippet handles the *Data Ingestion* phase. We iterate through the list of provided filenames, passing each to the `loadAndProcess()` helper function:

```
// 1. Load ALL Data (Serial I/O)
fmt.Print("Loading data... ")
var data [][]float64
var fileNames []string
for _, f := range files {
    ts := loadAndProcess(f, *targetLen, *summaryMethod)
    data = append(data, ts)
    fileNames = append(fileNames, f)
}
fmt.Println("Done.")
```

The results are then aggregated into two parallel slices: `data`, which holds the processed floating-point time series, and `fileNames`, which preserves the original identity of each series for later reporting. This way, we ensure that the subsequent K-Means clustering algorithm has immediate, low-latency access to the dataset, trading initial memory usage for faster iterative calculations later.

The next section enforces the strict geometric requirements of the K-Means algorithm:

```
// 2. Validate Data Consistency
if len(data) == 0 {
    log.Fatal("Error: No data loaded.")
}
expectedLen := len(data[0])
for i, ts := range data {
    if len(ts) != expectedLen {
        log.Fatalf("Error: Inconsistent time series "+
            "length at index %d (%s): "+
            "expected %d, got %d",
            i, fileNames[i], expectedLen, len(ts))
    }
    if len(ts) == 0 {
        log.Fatalf("Error: Empty time series "+
            "at index %d (%s)",
            i, fileNames[i])
    }
}
fmt.Printf("Validated: All %d time series have length %d\n",
    len(data), expectedLen)
```

As Euclidean distance calculations are only defined between vectors of identical dimensions, the code must guarantee that our dataset forms a perfect mathematical rectangle — N time series of exactly length M. The code establishes the first loaded file as the *baseline truth* and then validates every subsequent series against this standard. So, we prevent the algorithm from attempting impossible comparisons later, transforming potential runtime crashes into clear, actionable error messages about data inconsistency.

The next code snippet establishes the stochastic foundation of the K-Means algorithm, which relies heavily on random initialization:

```
// 3. Initialize Random Number Generator
var rng *rand.Rand
if *seed == 0 {
    rng = rand.New(rand.NewSource(time.Now().UnixNano()))
} else {
    rng = rand.New(rand.NewSource(*seed))
```

```
    fmt.Printf("Using random seed: %d\n", *seed)
}
```

The logic offers two distinct modes of operation controlled by user input: *non-deterministic* (default) and *deterministic*. By default (`seed == 0`), the generator is seeded with the current nanosecond, ensuring a unique sequence of random numbers for every run. However, if a specific seed is provided, the code locks the generator to that value, guaranteeing that the exact same sequence of "random" choices is made every time. This reproducibility is vital for debugging and scientific validation, allowing you to consistently replay a specific clustering scenario.

The next section executes the critical first step of the K-Means algorithm: selecting the initial centers of our clusters. Instead of creating synthetic points, the logic employs a Forgy initialization strategy, which randomly selects `k` actual data points from the existing dataset to serve as the starting centroids:

```
// 4. Initialize Centroids (Random initialization)
centroids := make([][]float64, *k)
perm := rng.Perm(len(data))
for i := 0; i < *k; i++ {
    centroids[i] = make([]float64, expectedLen)
    copy(centroids[i], data[perm[i]])
}

assignments := make([]int, len(data))
for i := range assignments {
    assignments[i] = -1 // Initialize to unassigned
}
```

The initial centers are achieved by generating a random permutation of indices (`rng.Perm`) and picking the first `k` items, ensuring no duplicates are selected. We then `copy()` these chosen time series into a dedicated `centroids` slice to prevent modifying the original data during subsequent calculations. Finally, we prepare an `assignments` slice to track which cluster each time series belongs to, initializing all values to `-1` to represent a clean slate state before the first iteration begins.

The next code snippet executes the *assignment step* (or *expectation phase*) of the algorithm, where the geometric structure of the clusters begins to form:

```
// 5. K-Means Loop
fmt.Println("--------------------------------------------")
```

```
for it := 0; it < *iter; it++ {
    changes := 0

    // --- Step A: Assignment (Serial - no race conditions)
    for i := 0; i < len(data); i++ {
        ts := data[i]
        bestCluster := -1
        minDist := math.Inf(1)

        for cIdx, center := range centroids {
            d := tslib.EuclideanDistance(ts, center)
            if d < minDist {
                minDist = d
                bestCluster = cIdx
            }
        }

        if assignments[i] != bestCluster {
            assignments[i] = bestCluster
            changes++
        }
    }
```

For every time series, the code performs a comprehensive search to find its NN among the current *k* centroids. It calculates the Euclidean distance to each center, tracking the minimum value to determine the optimal group. The logic monitors stability by comparing the new cluster index against the previous iteration; if a time series switches allegiance, the `changes` counter is incremented. This allows us to detect when the system has converged to a stable state.

The next code block implements the *update step* (or *maximization phase*), where the algorithm recalculates the geometric center of each cluster:

```
    // --- Step B: Update Centroids ---
    emptyClusterCount := 0
    for cIdx := 0; cIdx < *k; cIdx++ {
        sum := make([]float64, expectedLen)
        count := 0

        for i, a := range assignments {
            if a == cIdx {
                for j := 0; j < expectedLen; j++ {
```

```
                    sum[j] += data[i][j]
                }
                count++
            }
        }

        if count > 0 {
            // Update centroid with average
            for j := range sum {
                centroids[cIdx][j] = sum[j] /
                    float64(count)
            }
        } else {
            // Handle empty cluster: reinitialize
            // with random data point
            emptyClusterCount++
            randomIdx := rng.Intn(len(data))
            copy(centroids[cIdx], data[randomIdx])
            fmt.Printf("  Warning: Cluster %d empty, "+
                "reinitialized with random "+
                "point\n", cIdx)
        }
    }
```

For every group, the code aggregates the vectors of all assigned members, summing their values element by element and dividing by the count to derive the new *mean centroid*. A critical feature of this implementation is its robust *empty cluster strategy*: if a centroid effectively *dies* because no data points were assigned to it (often happening when *k* is too high or initialization was poor), the logic detects this zero-count state and forcefully reinitializes the orphan centroid with a new random data point. This *reboot* mechanism prevents the algorithm from collapsing into fewer than *k* clusters and gives the stray centroid a second chance to find a meaningful grouping in the next iteration.

The next code snippet provides real-time telemetry on the clustering process and enforces the *convergence criteria*:

```
    fmt.Printf("Iteration %d: %d reassignment(s)",
        it+1, changes)
    if emptyClusterCount > 0 {
        fmt.Printf(" (%d empty cluster(s) "+
            "reinitialized)", emptyClusterCount)
```

```
        }
        fmt.Println()
        if changes == 0 {
            fmt.Println("Converged (no changes).")
            break
        }
    }
```

At the end of every iteration, the code reports the "volatility" of the system by printing the number of reassignments; high numbers indicate active learning, while low numbers suggest the clusters are settling. It also explicitly flags if any empty clusters were "rebooted," alerting the user to potential instability in the value of *k* or the initialization. The code also implements an *early stopping* mechanism: if the `changes` counter hits zero, it confirms that the centroids have stabilized and the system has mathematically converged, allowing the loop to break immediately rather than wastefully running out the remaining iterations.

This final code block is responsible for translating the internal state into a human-readable summary of the discovered patterns:

```
    // 6. Print Results
    fmt.Println("------------------------------------------")
    fmt.Printf("--- Final Clusters (k=%d) ---\n", *k)
    for cIdx := 0; cIdx < *k; cIdx++ {
        var members []string
        for i, a := range assignments {
            if a == cIdx {
                members = append(members,
                    filepath.Base(fileNames[i]))
            }
        }
        if len(members) > 0 {
            fmt.Printf("Cluster %d (%d members): %s\n",
                cIdx, len(members),
                strings.Join(members, ", "))
        } else {
            fmt.Printf("Cluster %d (0 members): <empty>\n",
                cIdx)
        }
    }
    fmt.Println("------------------------------------------")
}
```

The logic iterates through each of the `k` clusters, performing a linear scan of the `assignments` slice to aggregate the specific files that belong to that group. We strip away full directory paths using `filepath.Base()`, using only the essential filenames in a temporary slice to have a cleaner output. These members are then concatenated into a single comma-separated string, allowing the program to output a concise report for each cluster that includes its ID, the total count of members, and the specific list of files.

Based on the clustering methodology, let us try our utility:

```
$ cd ch13
$ go run clustering.go -k 3 -L 100 ../ts/ts1.gz ../ts/ts2.gz ../ts/ts3.gz ../ts/
ts4.gz ../ts/ts5.gz ../ts/ts6.gz ../ts/ts7.gz ../ts/ts8.gz
go: downloading github.com/mactsouk/tslib v0.1.0
-------------------------------------------
       K-Means Time Series Clustering
-------------------------------------------
Config: Clusters(k)=3, MaxIter=10
Summary: Length=100 (0=Full), Method=paa
Input:   8 files
-------------------------------------------
Loading data... Done.
Validated: All 8 time series have length 100
-------------------------------------------
Iteration 1: 8 reassignment(s)
Iteration 2: 2 reassignment(s)
Iteration 3: 0 reassignment(s)
Converged (no changes).
-------------------------------------------
--- Final Clusters (k=3) ---
Cluster 0 (2 members): ts3.gz, ts4.gz
Cluster 1 (5 members): ts1.gz, ts2.gz, ts5.gz, ts6.gz, ts7.gz
Cluster 2 (1 members): ts8.gz
-------------------------------------------
```

The iteration log offers a clear view of the algorithm's convergence behavior. In the first pass, every single item (8 reassignments) moved, which is expected given the random initialization. However, the system stabilizes rapidly: by iteration 2, only two items needed adjustment, and by iteration 3, the `changes` counter hit zero, triggering the *early stopping* mechanism we implemented. This suggests that for this specific dataset and `k=3`, the clusters are distinct and well-separated. The final grouping reveals an interesting insight: while cluster 1 captures most of the files (suggesting a common "normal" behavior), cluster 2 contains a single member, `ts8.gz`. In a data mining context, this singleton cluster suggests that `ts8.gz` is a statistical outlier or a unique signal type compared to the rest of the batch. The appearance of a singleton cluster serves as a perfect segue into outlier analysis, as it demonstrates how clustering algorithms naturally isolate anomalous data points that deviate significantly from the norm.

Outlier analysis

Outlier detection, often referred to as **anomaly detection**, focuses on *identifying data points that deviate significantly from the general consensus or expected behavior of the dataset.* In the context of time series, an outlier is not a single value but an entire sequence that is "shaped" differently — such as a sensor that flatlines while others oscillate or a heartbeat that skips a rhythm.

The *outlier detection* utility we are going to implement identifies anomalies by measuring how isolated a time series is relative to its neighborhood. The fundamental metric here is the "outlier score," defined as the average distance between a file and its `k` nearest neighbors; a high score indicates that even the file's closest matches are significantly different from it. When running in its default "unified" mode, the program calculates this isolation score using all six distance metrics simultaneously. Because raw distances vary wildly in scale (e.g., thousands for Manhattan versus fractions for MPdist), the utility converts these raw scores into ranks (where rank 1 is "normal" and rank N is "most outlier"). It then combines these ranks into a final weighted score, allowing it to robustly flag files that are consistently outliers across multiple mathematical definitions of similarity.

For the presentation of the outlier analysis implementation, we are going to skip the `import` block as well as the `loadAndProcess()` helper function and start with the constants and the structures of the program:

```
const (
    WeightLockStep = 1.0
    WeightElastic  = 2.0
)

// Result for a single file in "ALL" mode
type CompositeResult struct {
    Filename    string
    RawScores   map[string]float64 // Map[Metric] -> AvgDist
    Ranks       map[string]int     // Map[Metric] -> Rank
    FinalScore  float64
}
```

```
// Result for single metric mode
type SimpleResult struct {
    Filename string
    Score    float64
}
```

This code establishes the data structures for a flexible *ensemble outlier detection* system. As before, the logic prioritizes elastic measures over lock-step measures. So, an anomaly detected by DTW is considered more significant or trustworthy than one found by simple geometric distance. The `CompositeResult` struct is the backbone of the "ALL" mode, which aggregates insights from multiple algorithms. Instead of storing a single number, it maintains a detailed ledger: `RawScores` preserves the actual distance values for normalization, while `Ranks` tracks how each specific metric ordered the files. In contrast, the `SimpleResult` struct provides a lightweight container for standard, single metric runs where such aggregation complexity is unnecessary.

The `main()` function acts as the central orchestrator for the application, parsing command-line flags to determine whether to run a specific metric or the composite `ALL` mode. It manages the data loading pipeline, dispatches the appropriate analysis routines — calculating distances or aggregating ranks — and formats the final outlier report. Rather than dissecting every line of this high-level coordination logic here, we encourage you to examine the full source code to see how the flag parsing and error handling are wired together to support the ensemble analysis.

We continue with the first part of `runCompositeMode()`, which establishes the foundation for ensemble analysis, acting as the setup phase before the heavy computation begins:

```
func runCompositeMode(files []string,
    data map[string][]float64, k, window int) {
    metrics := []string{"Euclidean", "Manhattan", "Chebyshev",
        "DTW", "LCSS", "MPdist"}

    // Store raw scores for everyone
    // results[filename].RawScores["Euclidean"] = 50.4
    results := make(map[string]*CompositeResult)
    for _, f := range files {
        results[f] = &CompositeResult{
            Filename:  f,
            RawScores: make(map[string]float64),
            Ranks:     make(map[string]int),
        }
    }
```

```
    fmt.Println("Calculating ALL metrics (Parallel)...")
```

Initially, the code defines the list of algorithms that will "vote" on which time series are outliers. The code then iterates through the input file list to pre-allocate a `CompositeResult` structure for every item. Next, it initializes the internal `RawScores` and `Ranks` maps. By creating these maps upfront, we ensure that when the parallel workers start returning data, they have a safe, non-nil destination to record their findings, preventing runtime panics during the concurrent aggregation.

Next, the code executes the core ensemble ranking logic:

```
    // Calculate one metric at a time to simplify ranking
    for _, m := range metrics {
        scores := computeScoresForMetric(files, data, m, k,
            window)

        // Store raw scores
        for _, s := range scores {
            results[s.Filename].RawScores[m] = s.Score
        }

        // Rank: Ascending Score = Least Outlier = Rank 1
        // High Score = Most Outlier = Rank N
        sort.Slice(scores, func(i, j int) bool {
            return scores[i].Score < scores[j].Score
        })

        for rank, s := range scores {
            // Rank 1 = smallest distance (most normal)
            // Rank N = largest distance (most outlier)
            results[s.Filename].Ranks[m] = rank + 1
        }
    }
```

Instead of trying to compare raw values directly, where a Euclidean distance of `50.0` might be small but a DTW distance of `50.0` might be huge, the code normalizes everything through ranking. For each metric in the list, it first computes the raw outlier scores for every file. It then sorts these scores in ascending order, effectively converting absolute floating-point numbers into relative integer ranks. The file with the smallest distance (most "normal") gets rank 1, while the file with the largest distance (most "anomalous") gets rank N. This transformation allows us to fairly combine results from mathematically distinct algorithms (such as MPdist and Manhattan) into a single, unified judgment later.

The next code snippet implements the *weighted rank aggregation* logic, transforming the individual rankings from six different algorithms into a single *outlier score*:

```
// Compute Final Weighted Score
var finalBox []*CompositeResult
for _, r := range results {
    wSum := 0.0
    wSum += float64(r.Ranks["Euclidean"]) *
        WeightLockStep
    wSum += float64(r.Ranks["Manhattan"]) *
        WeightLockStep
    wSum += float64(r.Ranks["Chebyshev"]) *
        WeightLockStep

    wSum += float64(r.Ranks["DTW"]) * WeightElastic
    wSum += float64(r.Ranks["LCSS"]) * WeightElastic
    wSum += float64(r.Ranks["MPdist"]) * WeightElastic
    r.FinalScore = wSum
    finalBox = append(finalBox, r)
}
```

For every file in the dataset, the code sums the ranks assigned by each metric but applies weights to them based on the values of `WeightElastic` (2.0) and `WeightLockStep` (1.0). The resulting `FinalScore` represents a weighted confidence level: The higher the number, the more strongly the ensemble believes the file is an anomaly.

The final code block handles the presentation of the information:

```
// Sort by Final Score Descending (Biggest Outlier first)
sort.Slice(finalBox, func(i, j int) bool {
    return finalBox[i].FinalScore >
        finalBox[j].FinalScore
})

fmt.Println("\n--- Composite Outlier Report " +
    "(Weighted Ranks) ---")
w := tabwriter.NewWriter(os.Stdout, 0, 0, 3, ' ', 0)
```

```
    fmt.Fprintln(w, "Rank\tFilename\tComposite Score\t"+
        "Top Metric Contributors (Rank)")
    fmt.Fprintln(w, "----\t--------\t---------------\t"+
        "------------------------------")

    for i, r := range finalBox {
        // Create a quick summary of where this file
        // ranked highest e.g. "DTW(#8) MPdist(#8)"
        contribs := getTopContributors(r.Ranks)
        fmt.Fprintf(w, "%d\t%s\t%.1f\t%s\n", i+1,
            r.Filename, r.FinalScore, contribs)
    }
    w.Flush()
}
```

The logic sorts the aggregated results in descending order, placing the file with the highest weighted score — the definitive *biggest outlier* — at the top of the list. The code employs a `tabwriter` to format the text into perfectly aligned columns. This report prioritizes explainability: alongside the composite score, it lists the "top metric contributors." This context is vital for the analyst, as it reveals why a file was flagged, allowing for a nuanced understanding of the anomaly's nature.

The `runSingleMode()` function implements the straightforward single metric mode for outlier detection, allowing the user to isolate the performance of a specific algorithm:

```
// --- Mode 2: Standard Single Metric ---
func runSingleMode(files []string, data map[string][]float64,
    metric string, k, window int) {
    scores := computeScoresForMetric(files, data, metric, k,
        window)

    // Sort Descending (High dist = Outlier)
    sort.Slice(scores, func(i, j int) bool {
        return scores[i].Score > scores[j].Score
    })

    fmt.Printf("\n--- Outlier Detection Report "+
        "(Metric: %s) ---\n", metric)
    fmt.Println("Rank  Filename            " +
        "Outlier Score (Avg Dist)")
    fmt.Println("----  --------            " +
```

```
        "------------------------")
    for i, s := range scores {
        fmt.Printf("%-4d  %-14s  %.4f\n", i+1, s.Filename,
            s.Score)
    }
}
```

The code begins by delegating the heavy lifting to `computeScoresForMetric()`, which returns a raw list of outlier scores based on the chosen distance measure. The core logic then sorts these results in descending order, placing the file with the highest average distance at the top of the list. Finally, the function generates a tabular report to standard output, ranking every file from "most anomalous" to "most normal" based on its score.

The `computeScoresForMetric()` function implements a *parallelized* k-Nearest Neighbor (k-NN) density estimator:

```
func computeScoresForMetric(files []string,
    data map[string][]float64, metric string,
    k, window int) []SimpleResult {
    results := make([]SimpleResult, len(files))
    var wg sync.WaitGroup

    for i, currentFile := range files {
        wg.Add(1)
        go func(idx int, fname string) {
            defer wg.Done()
            currentTS := data[fname]
            distances := make([]float64, 0,
                len(files)-1)

            for _, otherFile := range files {
                if fname == otherFile {
                    continue
                }
                otherTS := data[otherFile]
                d := 0.0
                switch strings.ToLower(metric) {
                case "dtw":
                    d = tslib.DTW(currentTS, otherTS,
                        window)
                case "mpdist":
```

```
                d = tslib.MPdist(currentTS,
                    otherTS, window)
            case "lcss":
                d = tslib.LCSS(currentTS, otherTS,
                    window, 0.5)
            case "manhattan":
                d = tslib.ManhattanDistance(
                    currentTS, otherTS)
            case "chebyshev":
                d = tslib.ChebyshevDistance(
                    currentTS, otherTS)
            default:
                d = tslib.EuclideanDistance(
                    currentTS, otherTS)
            }
            distances = append(distances, d)
        }

        sort.Float64s(distances)
        sum := 0.0
        for j := 0; j <k&&j< len(distances); j++ {
            sum += distances[j]
        }
        avg := sum / float64(k)
        results[idx] = SimpleResult{fname, avg}
    }(i, currentFile)
  }
  wg.Wait()
  return results
}
```

Instead of processing the dataset sequentially, the logic employs a **fan-out concurrency pattern**: it spawns a dedicated goroutine for every file in the input list. This is critical for performance, especially when using computationally expensive "elastic" metrics such as DTW or MPdist, as it allows the heavy mathematical lifting to be distributed across all available CPU cores. Inside each worker goroutine, the code calculates the distance between its assigned file and every other file in the dataset using the specific algorithm dispatched by the `switch` statement. Once these pairwise comparisons are complete, the distances are sorted to find the "neighborhood." The outlier score is the average distance to the *k* nearest neighbors. This approach is statistically robust: a file is only flagged as an outlier if it is significantly distant from all its closest matches, effectively measuring the local density around that data point. Finally, the function demonstrates a high-performance memory pattern. By pre-allocating the `results` slice and passing a unique index (`idx`) to each worker, the code allows every goroutine to write its output directly to a reserved memory slot. This design eliminates the need for mutex locks during the aggregation phase. Let us try our utility to find irregular time series:

```
$ cd ch13
$ go run outlierDetection.go -L 100 -metric MPdist ../ts/ts1.gz ../ts/ts2.gz ../
ts/ts3.gz ../ts/ts4.gz ../ts/ts5.gz ../ts/ts6.gz ../ts/ts7.gz ../ts/ts8.gz
--------------------------------------------
       Time Series Outlier Detection
--------------------------------------------
Metric: MPdist
Config: Window=20 (Elastic only)
Config: Neighbors(k)=1
Summary: Length=100 (0=Full), Method=paa
Input:  8 files
--------------------------------------------
Loading data... Done.
Validated: All 8 time series have length 100

--- Outlier Detection Report (Metric: MPdist) ---
Rank  Filename        Outlier Score (Avg Dist)
----  --------        ------------------------
1     ../ts/ts8.gz    7711.6151
2     ../ts/ts7.gz    1046.8263
3     ../ts/ts5.gz    703.7211
4     ../ts/ts6.gz    703.7211
5     ../ts/ts3.gz    117.8607
6     ../ts/ts4.gz    117.8607
7     ../ts/ts1.gz    0.1068
8     ../ts/ts2.gz    0.1068
```

This output confirms that the MPdist algorithm has successfully identified the structure of our dataset. The configuration section validates that our dimensionality reduction pipeline is active, compressing the raw inputs into 100-point PAA vectors before analysis. The results table provides two distinct insights. First, `ts8.gz` is the definitive outlier. Its score is nearly an order of magnitude higher than the next candidate, indicating that its subsequences are fundamentally unlike anything else in the collection. Second, the *identical scores for pairs of files* strongly suggest that the dataset consists of duplicate or near-duplicate signal pairs. The algorithm correctly matched each file to its "twin" (its nearest neighbor, `k=1`), resulting in identical distances for both members of the pair.

The effectiveness of outlier detection — particularly when processing millions of data points — is fundamentally constrained by the runtime ability to handle high-frequency memory allocations and deallocations. In CPU-intensive data mining workloads, the competition for processing power between the analytical algorithms and the Go memory management can often lead to "stop-the-world" pauses that degrade throughput. Such CPU-intensive Go programs would take full advantage of the new, improved garbage collector called *Green Tea*. The updated GC minimizes the latency penalties that typically plague parallel data processing by offloading more of the marking and sweeping work to background threads. This ensures that most CPU cycles are dedicated to the actual outlier analysis rather than overhead management, maintaining consistent performance even as the volume of analyzed data scales.

Trying the Green Tea garbage collector

Starting with Go 1.26, the **Green Tea garbage collector** is enabled by default. The Green Tea GC replaces the traditional object-by-object "graph flood" mark phase with a page-centric approach: *rather than scanning each object one at a time through pointers, Green Tea treats entire memory pages as units of work.* It enqueues pages instead of individual objects, tracks two bits per object (a *seen* bit and a *scanned* bit) within each page, and thus can process large contiguous runs of objects in memory order. By doing so, it improves locality (reducing cache misses and main-memory stalls) and reduces the overhead of work queues and pointer chasing. The result is fewer CPU stalls, lower GC cost per cycle, and significantly better performance on modern hardware.

To demonstrate the architectural improvements of the Green Tea GC, we need a program that specifically targets the *mark phase*, which is the part of the cycle where the GC traverses memory to find live objects. The Green Tea advantage lies in CPU cache locality. The old GC (Go 1.25 and earlier) chased pointers individually, often causing "cache misses" (waiting for data to be fetched from RAM). Let us illustrate the Green Tea GC using the `ch13/greenTea.go` sample program – feel free to look at its code.

This program (`ch13/greenTea.go`) is designed as a GC "Torture Test," specifically engineered to exploit the mechanical weaknesses of a mark-and-sweep collector. The core logic relies on creating a "hostile" memory layout using the `Node` struct. By adding a `[64]byte` payload, the code pads each node to match the size of a standard CPU cache line. This prevents the CPU from fetching multiple nodes in a single memory request (spatial locality), forcing a slow fetch from main RAM for every single step of the traversal. Furthermore, the use of a linked list instead of a contiguous slice is a deliberate choice to force "pointer chasing." To verify the list is alive, the GC cannot simply scan a block of memory; it must sequentially read the address of node A to find node B, making parallel scanning difficult and maximizing the time spent in the "mark" phase.

First, the program builds a persistent chain of 5,000,000 nodes that stays in memory forever (the "live set"). Then, it enters a loop that allocates and discards 50,000,000 temporary objects. This churn rapidly fills the heap, triggering the GC repeatedly. The trap is that every time the GC wakes up to clean the temporary mess, it is obligated to verify that the massive live set is still in use. This forces the collector to re-scan the cache-unfriendly linked list repeatedly, amplifying the overhead of every cycle. The final line, `_ = root`, acts as a "keep-alive" anchor, preventing the compiler's escape analysis from optimizing the entire structure away and defeating the purpose of the test.

> **Note**
>
> The Green Tea GC may be disabled by setting `GOEXPERIMENT=nogreenteagc` at build time, but this option is expected to be removed in Go 1.27. However, this is enough for our experiments using Go 1.26.

Now, let us try `ch13/greenTea.go` with the two different garbage collectors:

```
$ GOEXPERIMENT=nogreenteagc go run ch13/greenTea.go
1. Setup: Building the massive Live Set (Linked List)...
2. Benchmark: Starting allocation churn...

--- Results ---
Total Wall Time:     12.197584ms
Total GC Cycles:     111
Total GC Pause:      3.662998ms
Avg Time per Cycle: 109.888µs
$ go run ch13/greenTea.go
1. Setup: Building the massive Live Set (Linked List)...
2. Benchmark: Starting allocation churn...

--- Results ---
Total Wall Time:     11.552917ms
Total GC Cycles:     114
Total GC Pause:      3.362327ms
Avg Time per Cycle: 101.341µs
```

The results demonstrate that the Green Tea GC is providing a measurable performance boost for your specific workload. When running with the default settings, the application achieved a total wall time of roughly `11.55ms` and a total GC pause of `3.36ms`. In contrast, explicitly disabling the Green Tea GC resulted in a slower wall time of `12.20ms` and a longer total pause of `3.66ms`. This represents an approximate 8% reduction in pause times and a 5% improvement in overall execution speed. The legacy GC, unable to distinguish between old and new data effectively, is forced to re-scan a significant portion of those 5 million old objects during every cycle to verify they are still in use. The Green Tea GC, however, applies the generational hypothesis: it identifies that the linked list has survived multiple cycles and promotes it to an *old generation*. By doing so, it can ignore this stable memory during minor collections and focus its scanning efforts almost exclusively on the *young generation* — the temporary churn objects. This allows it to complete each cycle faster, explaining why it could afford to run slightly more cycles while still finishing the total workload more quickly.

While an optimized garbage collector ensures that memory management does not throttle our data mining performance, true production-readiness requires more than just raw speed— it demands visibility. As we scale our parallel analysis across thousands of concurrent tasks, understanding the scheduler behavior becomes just as vital as managing its memory footprint. This bridge between execution and observation is essential; if we cannot measure how our goroutines are being utilized, we cannot truly validate the performance gains provided by the runtime. To address this, Go 1.26 introduces enhanced goroutine metrics, providing a standardized way to observe the lifecycle and health of concurrent tasks in real time. This shift from internal runtime optimization to external observability allows us to verify that our processing remains efficient and that our system is not suffering from subtle bottlenecks or goroutine leaks that even a fast GC couldn't fix.

New in Go 1.26: Goroutine metrics

The release of Go 1.26 addresses a long-standing blind spot in the Go observability ecosystem: *deep, runtime-level introspection of Goroutine behavior.* With the expanded capabilities of the `runtime/metrics` package, developers now have direct, low-overhead access to the scheduler's internal accounting, allowing them to visualize not just how many goroutines are running, but what they are doing — whether they are runnable, blocked on I/O, or sleeping — in real time. Here is the relevant example code:

```
package main

import (
    "fmt"
    "runtime/metrics"
    "time"
)

func main() {
```

```
    go func() { time.Sleep(10 * time.Second) }()
    go func() {
        for {
            // Busy Loop to force "Running" state
            if false {
                break
            }
        }
    }()
descs := []metrics.Sample{
        {Name: "/sched/goroutines/runnable:goroutines"},
        {Name: "/sched/goroutines/running:goroutines"},
        {Name: "/sched/goroutines/waiting:goroutines"},
        {Name: "/sched/goroutines/syscall:goroutines"},
    }

    metrics.Read(descs)
    fmt.Println("Go 1.26 Scheduler State Breakdown:")
    for _, sample := range descs {
        if sample.Value.Kind() == metrics.KindUint64 {
            fmt.Printf(" - %-35s : %d\n",
                sample.Name, sample.Value.Uint64())

        }
    }
}
```

The code logic is divided into two phases: setup (creating specific traffic) and measurement (sampling the runtime). First, the `main()` function spawns two distinct goroutines to artificially populate different scheduler states. One goroutine executes `time.Sleep()`, immediately entering the *waiting state* as it pauses execution. The second goroutine enters a tight `for` loop (a "busy wait"), forcing itself into the *running state* and consuming CPU cycles. This deliberate setup ensures that when we snapshot the system, the metrics will show a diverse mix of activity rather than just an idle runtime. The second phase involves constructing a *sampling request*. The code defines a slice of `metrics.Sample` structs, specifying exactly which data points it wants to retrieve. Finally, `metrics.Read(descs)` performs the atomic read of these values directly from the runtime internal counters. The program then iterates through the results, checking the value type

(`KindUint64`) and printing a formatted report. Running `ch13/goMetrics.go` on a macOS M4 Pro machine generates the following kind of output:

```
$ go run ch13/goMetrics.go
Go 1.26 Scheduler State Breakdown:
  - /sched/goroutines/runnable:goroutines : 1
  - /sched/goroutines/running:goroutines : 3
  - /sched/goroutines/waiting:goroutines : 4
```

The single runnable goroutine represents a unit of work that is fully prepared to execute but is currently sitting in a queue, waiting for an available logical processor to pick it up. The three running goroutines indicate that the application is actively utilizing parallelism, executing code simultaneously across multiple OS threads at this exact moment. Finally, the four waiting goroutines are currently paused in the `_Gwaiting` state; they have voluntarily surrendered control to the scheduler while awaiting an external event, such as file I/O, a timer expiration, or a channel operation. The absence of output for `/sched/goroutines/syscall:goroutines` on macOS occurs because `time.Sleep()` is managed by the Go runtime internal timer heap and the OS event notification system (`kqueue`), which places the goroutine in the *waiting* state, not the *Syscall* state.

In the context of our forthcoming discussion on *goroutine leaks*, this *waiting* category is the most critical to monitor: while a constant number is normal, a value that grows indefinitely is the definitive signature of leaked goroutines accumulating in the background. To bridge the gap from detection to diagnosis, we now turn to a powerful new experimental feature that identifies the exact origin of these stalled workers.

New in Go 1.26: Goroutine leak profile

The `GOEXPERIMENT=goroutineleakprofile` feature introduces a powerful diagnostic tool designed to solve one of the most persistent challenges in concurrent programming: *identifying the origin of a goroutine leak.* Traditionally, debugging a stalled application involves dumping stack traces, which only reveal where a goroutine is currently blocked rather than the business logic that spawned it. This new profile fundamentally shifts the focus from the symptom to the cause by tracking the creation site of goroutines. When enabled during the build process, the runtime statistically samples go statements and records the stack trace of the parent at the exact moment of spawn. By targeting the `goroutineleak` endpoint with `pprof`, you can retrieve a report of all sampled goroutines that are still active, providing a heap profile for execution threads. This is particularly valuable for the parallel processing patterns we implemented earlier; if your application fails to exit cleanly, this profile can pinpoint exactly which loop or handler function is responsible for the lingering workers. Instead of guessing which channel operation hangs, you get a direct pointer to the line of code that initiated the leak, allowing for rapid remediation of complex concurrency bugs.

To see the leak profile tool in action, we are going to use `ch13/goLeakProfile.go`. This program intentionally constructs a deadlock scenario to showcase how the new profile pinpoints the exact creation site of the leaked goroutine. The program illustrates a classic concurrency pitfall known as an **orphan worker leak**. The architecture relies on a strict one-to-one synchronization: for every image in the input list, the `Process()` method spawns a worker goroutine that is contractually obligated to perform a blocking send into an unbuffered results channel. The critical logical flaw is in the consumer loop, which reads these results. When it encounters the specific `corrupted.jpg` error case, the function executes an immediate `return`, abruptly terminating the consumer side of the relationship without draining the remaining messages. The leak occurs because the communication channel is unbuffered. In Go, sending to an unbuffered channel requires an active receiver to be ready at that exact moment; if the receiver is missing, the sender blocks indefinitely. Once `Process()` returns early due to the error, the remaining workers effectively wake up to find their receiver gone. They attempt to send their completion status, but with no one left to listen, they hang forever at that line, consuming memory and runtime resources until the entire program terminates. If you were to analyze this situation with a standard stack trace, you would only see these workers stuck at a generic `runtime.chansend()` operation, which tells you that they are blocked but not why they exist. The `goroutineleak` profile transforms this debugging process by ignoring the blocking call and instead pointing to the creation site: the go `func` line inside the `Process()` loop. This clarifies that the leak is not a random system hang but a specific failure of the `Process()` function to clean up the resources it allocated before exiting.

Now execute `ch13/goLeakProfile.go` with `GOEXPERIMENT=goroutineleakprofile`:

```
$ GOEXPERIMENT=goroutineleakprofile go run ch13/goLeakProfile.go
Processing images...
image processing failed: ERROR: corrupted.jpg
* * * Some worker goroutines are now leaked!

--- Goroutine Leak Profile ---

Detected leaked goroutines!

goroutine 1 [running]:
runtime/pprof.writeGoroutineStacks({0x1005fac58, 0xaae41902020})
    /opt/homebrew/Cellar/go/1.26.0/libexec/src/runtime/pprof/pprof.go:819 +0x6c
```

```
runtime/pprof.writeGoroutineLeak({0x1005fac58, 0xaae41902020}, 0x2)
    /opt/homebrew/Cellar/go/1.26.0/libexec/src/runtime/pprof/pprof.go:806 +0xe0
runtime/pprof.(*Profile).WriteTo(0x1005fac58?, {0x1005fac58?, 0xaae41902020?},
0x1e?)
    /opt/homebrew/Cellar/go/1.26.0/libexec/src/runtime/pprof/pprof.go:408 +0x144
main.main()
    /Users/mtsouk/go/src/github.com/mactsouk/goSP2/ch13/goLeakProfile.go:97 +0x388

goroutine 22 [chan send (leaked)]:
main.(*ImageProcessor).Process.func1({0x10050132d, 0xa})
    /Users/mtsouk/go/src/github.com/mactsouk/goSP2/ch13/goLeakProfile.go:30 +0xe0
created by main.(*ImageProcessor).Process in goroutine 1
    /Users/mtsouk/go/src/github.com/mactsouk/goSP2/ch13/goLeakProfile.go:20 +0x78

goroutine 23 [chan send (leaked)]:
main.(*ImageProcessor).Process.func1({0x100501337, 0xa})
    /Users/mtsouk/go/src/github.com/mactsouk/goSP2/ch13/goLeakProfile.go:30 +0xe0
created by main.(*ImageProcessor).Process in goroutine 1
    /Users/mtsouk/go/src/github.com/mactsouk/goSP2/ch13/goLeakProfile.go:20 +0x78
```

The critical diagnostic information follows under the `Goroutine Leak Profile` header. Here, the runtime identifies two specific goroutines (IDs 22 and 23) with the explicit status `[chan send (leaked)]`. This tag distinguishes them from standard waiting goroutines, signaling that the GC has determined they are blocked on a channel operation that can never proceed because the receiving end is unreachable. The profile provides a dual-layer stack trace for each leaked entity, offering a complete lifecycle view. The top section points to line 30 (`goLeakProfile.go:30`), which corresponds to the blocking send operation `p.results <- ...`. This confirms where the execution halted.

However, the most significant technical value lies in the `created by` section at the bottom. It pinpoints line 20 (`goLeakProfile.go:20`) inside `main.(*ImageProcessor).Process` as the spawning point. This definitively attributes the leak to the loop iterating over the image slice, proving that the error handling logic failed to account for the concurrent workers created at that specific location. Note that `goroutine 1 [running]` appears in the profile, not as a leak but as the active goroutine executing the `pprof.WriteTo` call itself.

By diving into the mechanics of the Green Tea garbage collector and the new `goroutineleakprofile`, we learned that high-performance analysis requires us to be as disciplined with our system resources as we are with our algorithms. You now possess the tools to not only discover hidden insights in massive datasets but to build the robust, leak-free Go applications necessary to bring those insights to production.

Summary

In this chapter, we explored the core ideas of time series data mining, focusing on how to uncover hidden patterns and relationships in data. We saw that finding these insights depends on choosing the right way to measure similarity, whether using simple distance checks or more flexible, elastic methods. But even the best math needs a solid program to run it. That is why we dove into the practical side of Go, examining how the Green Tea garbage collector manages memory and how to track goroutine metrics to keep performance high. We also learned how to use goroutine leak profiles to catch invisible bugs that can slow down your system. At the end of the day, building effective data mining tools requires balancing these two skills: understanding the data algorithms and mastering the Go runtime that powers them.

In the next chapter, we will shift our focus from the data inside the file to the metadata that describes it. We will build a high-performance indexing engine in Go that crawls your file system, stores the structure in an efficient data format, and allows for instant queries.

Exercises

1. We demonstrated how `GOEXPERIMENT=goroutineleakprofile` can catch a deadlock, but fixing it is the goal. So, take `goLeakProfile.go` and modify `ImageProcessor` to use a buffered channel sized to match the number of inputs (`make(chan string, len(images))`). Rerun the profile to confirm that even with the early return triggered by the error, the remaining workers can exit gracefully without leaking.
2. Run `go run ch13/goLeakProfile.go` without using `GOEXPERIMENT=goroutineleakprofile`.

Additional resources

- The `https://github.com/golang/go/blob/master/src/runtime/chan.go` file shows the implementation of the `runtime.chansend()` private function.
- Go 1.26 release notes: `https://go.dev/doc/go1.26`
- The Green Tea garbage collector: `https://go.dev/blog/greenteagc`

- GopherCon 2025 – Advancing Go Garbage Collection with Green Tea: https://www.youtube.com/watch?v=gPJkM95KpKo
- Detecting goroutine leaks with DTrace: https://gaultier.github.io/blog/detecting_goroutine_leaks_with_dtrace.html

Get this book's PDF version and more

Scan the QR code (or go to packtpub.com/unlock). Search for this book by name, confirm the edition, and then follow the steps on the page.

UNLOCK NOW

Note: Keep your invoice handy. Purchases made directly from Packt don't require an invoice.

14

Creating an Index for Unix Files

At the heart of any operating system lies an invisible structured labyrinth of files and directories, silently housing our code, data, logs, and projects. As systems programmers, we rarely pause to consider that this hierarchy, which we so casually navigate, is not just a technical abstraction but a mirror of human cognition. Our minds crave order. Faced with overwhelming complexity, we instinctively seek patterns, maps, and indexes. We do not just want to store data — we want to *find it, understand it* and *connect it*. An index can transform chaos into clarity, converting raw structure into searchable knowledge. From a different perspective, indexing files is an exercise in epistemology — the study of knowledge. What do we need to know about a file or directory? What makes that information retrievable and meaningful? The decisions you make while designing an index — what to record, how to categorize, which metadata to preserve — are all reflections of deeper assumptions about purpose, access, and utility.

Technically speaking, this chapter explores how to traverse Unix filesystems and how to construct meaningful indexes that can power everything from file search utilities to metadata-driven applications. You will learn to walk directory trees and store structured file information coming from multiple computers efficiently and precisely.

This chapter covers the following topics:

- Understanding binary trees
- Understanding radix trees
- Creating a filesystem index service
- Creating a command-line client

As Aristotle said, *"The purpose of knowledge is action, not knowledge."* This reminds us that learning has little value if it is not applied. Action transforms that knowledge into something alive and meaningful. For example, understanding algorithms or data structures in theory is important, but their true worth emerges when we use them to solve real-world problems — optimizing a search engine, securing a system, or designing reliable software.

The connection between a conceptual data structure and a real-world file indexer lies in the need for efficient retrieval. A simple list of filenames is easy to create, but becomes prohibitively slow as the number of files grows into the thousands. By utilizing binary trees, we transform a linear search into a logarithmic one, allowing the indexer to navigate massive amounts of file metadata with minimal effort. In this context, studying the elegance of a tree structure is not just an academic exercise — it is the engineering foundation that ensures our search results remain near-instantaneous, regardless of the size of the directory we are indexing. Knowledge prepares us to design these structures; action fulfills it as we implement them to make our application truly performant.

Understanding Binary Trees

A **binary tree** is a hierarchical data structure in which each node has at most two child nodes, commonly referred to as the *left* and *right* child. It is one of the most widely used data structures in computer science because it organizes data in a way that makes searching, inserting, and deleting efficient. In a **binary search tree** (**BST**), a special type of binary tree, the left subtree contains values less than the parent node, whereas the right subtree contains values greater than the parent. This structure allows operations such as search and insertion to be performed in *O(log n)* time on average, making binary trees a foundation for implementing efficient storage systems, databases, compilers, and many algorithms. Implementing a binary tree will help you understand its operation better – this knowledge is going to be used when we talk about radix trees. To support the construction of our indexing engine, we will leverage the improved `new()` function introduced in Go 1.26. This enhancement allows us to allocate and initialize our binary tree nodes in a single step, providing a cleaner and more performant way to build the search hierarchy.

A sweet improvement to new()

Go 1.26 updated the built-in `new()` function to accept expressions, merging memory allocation and initialization into a single step. Previously, `new(T)` only zero-initialized memory, forcing developers to use separate assignment statements or temporary variables to establish initial values. With this update, the compiler infers the type from the provided value, allocates the necessary storage on the heap, initializes it, *and returns the pointer immediately*. You can see `new()` in action in `ch14/newNew.go`:

```
package main

import (
```

```
    "fmt"
)

type ServerConfig struct {
    Port    *int    `json:"port"`
    Enabled *bool   `json:"enabled"`
    Name    *string `json:"name"`
}

type User struct {
    ID   int
    Role string
}

func main() {
    config := ServerConfig{
        Port:    new(8080),
        Enabled: new(true),
        Name:    new("API Server"),
    }

    admin := new(User{
        ID:   1,
        Role: "admin",
    })

    fmt.Printf("Config: %s running on port %d (Enabled: %t)\n",
        *config.Name, *config.Port, *config.Enabled)
    fmt.Printf("User: %v\n", admin)
}
```

The program defines a `ServerConfig` struct where `Port`, `Enabled`, and `Name` are pointers; this is a standard pattern used to *distinguish between* a zero value (such as port `0`) and a missing configuration (`nil`). Inside `main()`, the code initializes these fields inline using the new syntax: `new(8080)` and `new(true)`, which creates a pointer to a specific value immediately rather than just allocating zeroed memory. The difference lies in what `new()` accepts as an argument. In all previous versions of Go, `new()` accepted a *type* such as `new(int)`, which would allocate memory, set it to the zero value of the type (`0`), and return a pointer. To achieve what this code does in older versions, a developer was forced to declare a temporary variable such as `p := 8080` and then take its memory address (&p) or use helper functions, which cluttered the local scope with transient variables. Execute `ch14/newNew.go` on your machine:

```
$ go run ch14/newNew.go
Config: API Server running on port 8080 (Enabled: true)
User: &{1 admin}
```

In the first line, you see the plain values `API Server`, `8080`, and `true` because the code explicitly dereferenced the pointers using the * operator. In the second line, you see the standard Go representation of a pointer to a struct.

With that in mind, let us present the implementation of a binary tree in Go as found in `ch14/binaryTree.go`, starting with the definition of the binary tree itself and its nodes:

```
type Node struct {
    Value int
    Left  *Node
    Right *Node
}

type Tree struct {
    Root *Node
    mu   sync.RWMutex
}
```

The code defines the fundamental structures for a *thread-safe BST*. The `Node` struct acts as the atomic unit of the data structure, encapsulating the data payload (`Value`) and the structural links (`Left` and `Right`) that define the tree's recursive hierarchy.

By using pointers for the children, the structure allows for the dynamic growth of the tree, where a `nil` pointer signifies a leaf node or an empty path. This recursive definition is the standard approach for creating self-referential data structures, enabling algorithms to traverse depth or breadth by following memory addresses. The `Tree` struct serves as the public entry point. Rather than exposing the `Node` pointers directly, `Tree` wraps the `Root` pointer alongside a `sync.RWMutex` instance. The logic behind including a reader-writer mutex specifically, rather than a standard mutex, is to optimize for a common access pattern in databases and caches where "reads" (searches) vastly outnumber "writes" (insertions or deletions). This decision allows multiple goroutines to traverse the tree simultaneously without blocking each other, while still ensuring that any modification obtains an exclusive lock to prevent data races, balancing safety with high-throughput performance.

Next, we show the code for the `Insert()` method as well as the `insert()` helper method:

```
func (t *Tree) Insert(value int) {
    t.mu.Lock()          // Exclusive lock for writing
    defer t.mu.Unlock() // Unlock after insertion

    if t.Root == nil {
        t.Root = new(Node{Value: value})
    } else {
        t.Root.insert(value)
    }
}

func (n *Node) insert(value int) {
    if value <= n.Value {
        if n.Left == nil {
            n.Left = new(Node{Value: value})
        } else {
            n.Left.insert(value)
        }
    } else {
        if n.Right == nil {
            n.Right = new(Node{Value: value})
        } else {
            n.Right.insert(value)
        }
    }
}
```

The separation of node insertion into two distinct methods — a public method on the `Tree` struct and a private recursive helper on the `Node` struct — decouples concurrency control from algorithmic traversal. The public `(t *Tree) Insert()` method is primarily responsible for establishing the correct execution context for the operation: it acquires the `t.mu.Lock()` function to ensure that the entire insertion sequence is atomic and thread safe. By handling the lock at the `Tree` level, we guarantee that the mutex is acquired exactly once per operation, avoiding the performance overhead and potential deadlocks of recursive locking. Additionally, this method handles the structural edge case where the tree is empty (`t.Root == nil`), a state that a node-level method cannot easily resolve since no nodes exist yet to receive the call. Once the safety and initial state are established, the logic delegates to the private `(n *Node) insert()` method, which acts as the recursive engine. This method focuses on the binary search algorithm: comparing values to the current node and traversing down the `Left` or `Right` pointers. It is here that the actual memory modification occurs, utilizing the new Go 1.26 `new(Node{...})` syntax to allocate and link new nodes directly into the structure. So, the `Tree` struct manages locks and root existence, whereas the `Node` struct manages the logic and links, preventing the mixing of synchronization primitives with recursive business logic. In the same style, here we have `Search()` and `search()`:

```
func (t *Tree) Search(value int) bool {
    t.mu.RLock()           // Shared lock for reading
    defer t.mu.RUnlock() // Unlock after reading
    return t.Root != nil && t.Root.search(value)
}

func (n *Node) search(value int) bool {
    if n == nil {
        return false
    }
    if value == n.Value {
        return true
    } else if value < n.Value {
        return n.Left.search(value)
    } else {
        return n.Right.search(value)
    }
}
```

The search implementation mirrors the architectural pattern of insertion but diverges critically in its concurrency model to optimize for read-heavy workloads. Instead of the exclusive lock used previously, this method employs `t.mu.RLock()` (*read lock*). Once the shared lock is acquired, the public method performs a quick existence check — immediately returning `false` if the tree is empty — before delegating to the recursive helper. The internal logic leverages the sorted nature of the BST to achieve logarithmic time complexity: it compares the target `value` instance against the current node, returning `true` on a match or recursively descending into the `Left` or `Right` child based on whether the target is smaller or larger. The last set of methods is for printing the tree in three different ways:

```
func (t *Tree) InOrder() {
    t.mu.RLock()
```

```
    defer t.mu.RUnlock()
    fmt.Print("InOrder Traversal: ")
    inOrder(t.Root)
    fmt.Println()
}

func inOrder(n *Node) {
    if n == nil {
        return
    }
    inOrder(n.Left)
    fmt.Printf("%d ", n.Value)
    inOrder(n.Right)
}

func (t *Tree) PreOrder() {
    t.mu.RLock()
    defer t.mu.RUnlock()
    fmt.Print("PreOrder Traversal: ")
    preOrder(t.Root)
    fmt.Println()
}

func preOrder(n *Node) {
    if n == nil {
        return
    }
    fmt.Printf("%d ", n.Value)
    preOrder(n.Left)
    preOrder(n.Right)
}

func (t *Tree) PostOrder() {
    t.mu.RLock()
    defer t.mu.RUnlock()
    fmt.Print("PostOrder Traversal: ")
    postOrder(t.Root)
    fmt.Println()
}
```

The necessity for three distinct traversal strategies arises because visiting a node has radically different utility depending on when it occurs relative to the node's structural dependencies. While all three methods visit every node exactly once, the timing dictates the algorithm's application. We use *in-order traversal* when the semantic value of the data is paramount; for a BST, this is the only strategy that linearizes the hierarchy into a sorted sequence, flattening the tree into a human-readable list. However, when the structure itself is the critical data, we turn to *pre-order*. By processing the root before its subtrees, this traversal generates a serialization stream that can be read back sequentially to reconstruct the exact original shape of the tree — a requirement for network transmission or disk persistence where the hierarchy must be preserved. *Post-order* is the algorithm of dependency resolution and cleanup. By deferring the processing of a node until after its children are complete, it ensures that we never operate on a parent until its dependencies are resolved. This bottom-up approach is indispensable for systems tasks such as safe memory deallocation (deleting children before the parent) or directory size calculations, where a folder's total size cannot be known in advance.

With all that in mind, execute `ch14/binaryTree.go` on your machine:

```
$ go run ch14/binaryTree.go
[Insert] 13
[Insert] 14
. . .
[Insert] 8
[Insert] 6
InOrder Traversal: 1 3 4 6 7 8 10 13 14
PreOrder Traversal: 3 1 13 8 4 7 6 10 14
PostOrder Traversal: 1 6 7 4 10 8 14 13 3
[Search] 2 -> false
[Search] 15 -> false
[Search] 7 -> true
[Search] 13 -> true
```

Lines beginning with `[Insert]` refer to the insertion of nodes based on the values stored as `values := []int{8, 3, 10, 1, 6, 14, 4, 7, 13}`. These lines appear out of numerical order because multiple goroutines are racing to acquire the lock; this confirms that the Go scheduler is managing execution non-deterministically, yet `sync.Mutex` successfully serialized every write to prevent data corruption. The `InOrder` list is perfectly sorted `(1 3 4...)`, validating that the binary search property (`Left < Root < Right`) was maintained throughout the concurrent insertions. The `PreOrder` sequence starting with 3 reveals the tree topology, indicating that 3 was the first node successfully locked and established as the root. The `PostOrder` traversal output (1

`6 7 4 10 8 14 13 3`) reveals the dependency structure of the tree. In this mode, the root is always the last element printed because the algorithm strictly processes children before their parents (`Left` -> `Right` -> `Root`). This specific sequence tells us that `1` and `6` are leaf nodes (or at least the bottom-most nodes in their respective subtrees) because they appear first. We can deduce that `7` is the parent of `6` (or `6` is the left child of `7`), `4` is the parent of `7`, and so on, cascading all the way up to `3`, which is the absolute root of the tree. This bottom-up ordering is exactly what you would use if you needed to delete the tree safely, ensuring you free the memory for leaves `1` and `6` before you ever touch root `3`. Finally, the `[Search]` results confirm that the read-lock (`RLock`) logic works correctly, accurately finding existing nodes such as `7` and `13` while returning `false` for values such as `2` and `15`.

While binary trees organize data by splitting values into two branches at each node, *radix trees*— also known as *prefix trees* or *compact tries*— take a different approach. Instead of comparing entire values at each step, radix trees store and *compare common prefixes* of keys, making them particularly efficient for scenarios involving strings, prefixes, or hierarchical data such as IP addresses. In a binary tree, each node decides to go left or right based on comparisons, whereas in a radix tree, traversal follows shared segments of a key, potentially skipping multiple characters or bits in a single step. This makes radix trees highly space-efficient when many keys share common prefixes and faster for operations such as prefix matching. Understanding these differences will help you see why radix trees are often preferred in applications such as routing tables, search engines, and autocompletion systems, where prefix-based lookups outperform traditional BSTs. In the next section, we create an implementation of a radix tree in Go.

Understanding Radix Trees

A **radix tree**, also known as a **compact prefix tree** or **Patricia trie**, is an efficient data structure for storing strings with shared prefixes. It reduces memory by merging single-child nodes. The following radix tree plot visually represents a compact prefix tree built from the words go, gone, good, `gopher`, god, `golf`, `golden`, `galaxy`, `game`, and `gamma`. At the very top, the tree starts with an empty string node `""`, which connects to a single child node labeled g, because all words begin with the letter g. This node branches into several distinct paths based on the next letters that follow in each word.

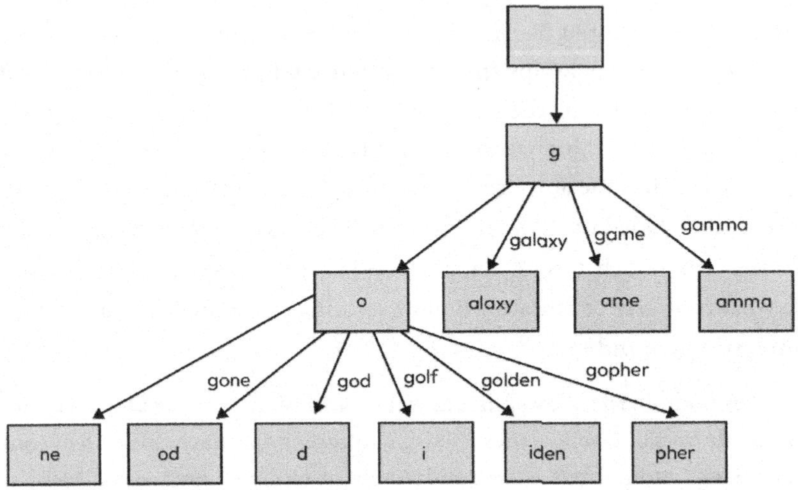

Figure 14.1 – A radix tree

One major branch is from g to o, covering all words that begin with go — specifically, go, gone, good, `gopher`, god, `golf`, and `golden`. From the o node, the tree splits into several shorter prefixes: `ne` for gone, `od` for good, `pher` for `gopher`, `d` for god, `l` for `golf`, and `lden` for `golden`. Each of these nodes is marked as a terminal node in the tree, indicating the end of a complete word. Aside from the go branch, the `g` node also branches to `alaxy`, representing the word `galaxy`; to `ame`, representing `game`; and to `amma`, representing `gamma`. These nodes do not branch further because no other words in the dataset share their prefixes beyond that point, and they are also marked as terminal nodes. The structure of the plot reflects the compactness of a radix tree. Instead of storing one character per node as in a traditional trie, this tree compresses linear chains of nodes into single nodes containing substrings. For example, instead of representing `game` as four separate nodes (`g → a → m → e`), the tree uses one edge from g to `ame`, which is more space-efficient and faster for lookups.

This radix tree is particularly effective for prefix-based lookups and space-efficient storage, making it a useful structure for systems programming tasks such as file path resolution, command autocompletion, or configuration key lookup. Let us now look at the most important parts of our radix tree implementation (`ch14/radixTree.go`), starting with the structures that support it:

```
type Node struct {
    prefix   string
    children []*Node
    isWord   bool
```

```
}

type RadixTree struct {
    root *Node
}
```

The logic of the radix tree centers on the `Node` struct, which stores a `prefix` string rather than a single character. This design implements *path compression*, whereby sequences of nodes with single children are merged into a single edge, significantly reducing the tree height and memory footprint for sparse datasets. The `children` slice manages branching paths, allowing the tree to split where prefixes diverge, while the `isWord` Boolean serves as a guard. This flag distinguishes between nodes that represent complete, valid keys and internal nodes that exist solely as structural bridges to longer words. The `RadixTree` struct acts as the public handle for the entire structure, encapsulating the `root` pointer. This separation allows the `RadixTree` struct to manage tree-wide concerns — such as locking or handling an empty tree state — without interfering with the recursive logic of individual nodes. A new radix tree is created as follows:

```
func NewRadixTree() *RadixTree {
    return new(RadixTree{
        root: new(Node{}),
    })
}
```

The `NewRadixTree()` function serves as the constructor for the data structure, ensuring that it is initialized in a valid, usable state. The use of `new()` makes sure that the tree is a *heap-allocated*, persistent structure ready for immediate use.

The `Insert()` method orchestrates the logic of path compression, ensuring that the tree remains compact by storing string segments rather than individual characters:

```
func (tree *RadixTree) Insert(word string) {
    current := tree.root
    for {
        var child *Node
        var i int
        var j int
        for _, c := range current.children {
            j = commonPrefixLength(word, c.prefix)
            if j > 0 {
                i = j
```

```
                child = c
                break
            }
        }

        if child == nil {
            newNode := new(Node{prefix: word, isWord: true})
            current.children = append(current.children, newNode)
            return
        }

        if i < len(child.prefix) {
            splitNode := new(Node{
                prefix:   child.prefix[i:],
                children: child.children,
                isWord:   child.isWord,
            })

            child.prefix = child.prefix[:i]
            child.children = []*Node{splitNode}
            child.isWord = false
        }

        word = word[i:]
        if word == "" {
            child.isWord = true
            return
        }
        current = child
    }
}
```

The algorithm iterates through the tree, comparing the input string against existing edge prefixes to identify the longest shared path. Unlike a standard binary tree, where insertion is a simple matter of finding a `nil` pointer, a radix tree often requires structural mutation of existing nodes. When the input string shares only a partial prefix with a child node, the algorithm performs an *edge split*: it truncates the current node to the shared prefix and pushes the remaining characters into a new child node, inserting a new fork in the road without breaking the existing hierarchy. If no common prefix is found among the children, the logic identifies a completely new branch and appends a new node using the `new()` syntax. If the algorithm consumes the entire input string while traversing, it marks the terminating node as a valid word. This logic ensures that the tree depth is determined by the distinctiveness of stored keys rather than their length.

The `Search()` method implements the retrieval logic for the radix tree, designed to verify the existence of a specific string with maximum efficiency:

```
func (tree *RadixTree) Search(word string) bool {
    current := tree.root

    for {
        var child *Node
        var i int
        for _, c := range current.children {
            if strings.HasPrefix(word, c.prefix) {
                child = c
                break
            }
            i = commonPrefixLength(word, c.prefix)
            if i > 0 {
                return false
            }
        }

        if child == nil {
            return false
        }

        if len(word) == len(child.prefix) {
            return child.isWord
        }

        word = word[len(child.prefix):]
        current = child
    }
}
```

Unlike a standard search that might compare the target string character by character against a list, this algorithm traverses the tree structure, consuming the search word in chunks that match the compressed prefixes stored in the nodes. The process is iterative: at each current node, it scans the children to find one whose stored prefix completely matches the beginning of the remaining search string. The logic handles three distinct outcomes during this traversal. If a child's prefix matches the start of the search word, the algorithm consumes that portion of the word and descends deeper into the tree. If it finds a child that shares some characters but not the full prefix, it immediately knows the word does not exist in the tree because the path diverges at that point. Finally, if the algorithm successfully consumes the entire search word and lands exactly on a node boundary, it checks the `isWord()` flag; this ensures that finding a prefix returns `false` if only the longer word was inserted.

The `StartsWith()` method implements the logic for prefix matching, a feature distinct from exact word retrieval and essential for applications such as autocomplete or predictive text:

```
func (tree *RadixTree) StartsWith(prefix string) bool {
    current := tree.root

    for {
        var child *Node
        for _, c := range current.children {
            if strings.HasPrefix(prefix, c.prefix) {
                child = c
                break
            }
            if strings.HasPrefix(c.prefix, prefix) {
                return true
            }
        }
        if child == nil {
            return false
        }
        if len(prefix) <= len(child.prefix) {
            return true
        }
        prefix = prefix[len(child.prefix):]
        current = child
    }
}
```

While the code shares the traversal mechanism of `Search()`, its success condition is significantly broader: it does not require the `isWord` flag to be set, nor does it require the tree path to end exactly where the input string ends. The algorithm traverses the nodes, consuming the input prefix in chunks that match the compressed edges of the tree. If the algorithm encounters a node whose stored string is longer than the remaining search prefix (e.g., searching for "`auto`" and hitting a node storing "automobile"), it immediately returns true. This works because the existence of the longer path logically proves that the shorter prefix exists within the tree. Conversely, if the search prefix is longer than the current node, the algorithm continues descending. If the navigation can successfully trace the entire length of the input string without diverting from the tree structure, the method confirms that the prefix is valid, regardless of whether it stops mid-edge or at a node boundary. I encourage you to consult the accompanying repository for the full source code and use this foundation to extend the tree yourself. True mastery of systems programming comes not just from understanding the happy path, but from wrestling with edge cases of memory management and structural maintenance.

Execute ch14/radixTree.go on your machine:

```
$ go run ch14/radixTree.go
Search("go"): true
Search("gone"): true
Search("god"): false
Search("gob"): false
Search("gopher"): true
Search("zeb"): false
Search("zebra"): true
StartsWith("go"): true
StartsWith("gop"): true
StartsWith("zeb"): true
StartsWith("x"): false
```

The Search("zebra") instance returns true because it is a stored key, whereas Search("zeb") returns false. Even though "zeb" exists physically in memory as part of the compressed path to "zebra", it was never explicitly inserted as a key, so its isWord flag remains false. However, the StartsWith results ignore this sentinel flag, returning true for inputs such as "zeb", "go", and "gop". The negative results demonstrate the tree's efficiency in early rejection: as soon as the path diverges, the search aborts immediately.

Having dissected the low-level mechanics of the radix tree, we now turn to a domain where its specific strengths — prefix compression and hierarchical storage — are indispensable: indexing a filesystem. This transition is naturally bridged by the way filesystems themselves are structured; since directory paths and common file tokens often share long, repetitive prefixes, the radix tree allows us to store thousands of similar entries by only recording their unique suffixes. By utilizing this structure for our indexer, we can significantly reduce the memory footprint required to map search terms back to their original file locations, ensuring the application remains lightweight even when tracking a vast directory hierarchy.

Creating a filesystem index service

With radix trees understood, we are ready to build a complete file index service. The tree structure you just learned becomes the search engine, and the insert and search operations become index operations. However, first, we need to understand the architecture of the service.

The server architecture follows a strict separation of concerns where the server operates as a passive, **high-availability** (**HA**) engine, while the client functions as the active driver of intent. The server initializes the radix tree and **Write-Ahead Log** (**WAL**) once, then enters an infinite loop accepting TCP connections and dispatching request handlers based solely on the incoming JSON `Op` code (`"index"`, `"search"`, etc.). It has no concept of a "scan" or "watch" session; it merely reacts to individual atomic messages. The intelligence regarding workflow resides entirely in the client. It is the client binary that parses user-specified command-line arguments to determine its personality for the session, translating these distinct high-level behaviors into standardized protocol streams that the server consumes. With the theoretical foundation laid, we turn our attention to the practical implementation of the index server. While a raw path lookup is useful, a truly powerful filesystem index allows us to search by partial names or keywords found anywhere within a file path — finding `/var/log/nginx/error.log` simply by querying `"nginx"` or `"error"`. To achieve this, our logic does not just store the full path string; instead, it performs tokenization. The `tokenize()` function splits a file path into meaningful semantic units based on delimiters such as slashes, dots, and underscores. For example, `src/main/server_test.go` yields `src`, `main`, `server`, `test`, and go tokens. Each of these tokens is then inserted individually into our in-memory `Trie` structure. The server iterates over the characters of each token and creates new branches as necessary. This approach transforms the search experience; rather than requiring an exact prefix match of the full path, a user can query any fragment of the filename, and the `Trie` structure will efficiently locate every file containing that token, regardless of where it resides in the directory hierarchy.

The provided server implementation is a robust, concurrent, in-memory search engine designed for distributed filesystem indexing. Its core capabilities include the following:

- **Token-based inverted indexing**: Unlike a standard key-value store, the server breaks file paths into searchable tokens. This allows for flexible queries where users can find files by matching any component of their path (e.g., searching `"config"` locates both `/etc/config` and `/app/config.json`).
- **High-performance in-memory storage**: The index is held entirely in RAM using a custom `Trie` (*prefix tree*) structure. This ensures that search operations are extremely

fast, typically requiring only a few pointer traversals proportional to the length of the search query, rather than the number of stored files.

- **Durability via WAL**: To prevent data loss during restarts or crashes, the server implements a `Journal` system. Every state-changing operation (*index* or *delete*) is serialized to disk in an append-only file (`server.wal`) before modification. On startup, we reconstruct the entire in-memory index from this history file without the overhead of a database.
- **Concurrency and thread safety**: The server is engineered for parallel access. It employs a `sync.RWMutex` instance to allow multiple search requests to execute simultaneously without blocking, while ensuring that *index* and *delete* operations obtain exclusive access to maintain data integrity.
- **JSON-RPC over TCP**: The communication layer uses a lightweight, custom JSON protocol over raw TCP. This allows for simple integration with various clients while supporting keep-alive connections for continuous interaction.

With all this in mind, we proceed with the implementation of the index server.

The server code

We begin the implementation details by presenting the structures of the server:

```
type Message struct {
    Op    string `json:"op"`
    Host  string `json:"host,omitempty"`
    Path  string `json:"path,omitempty"`
    Query string `json:"query,omitempty"`
}

type Response struct {
    Status  string         `json:"status"`
    Results []string       `json:"results,omitempty"`
    Stats   map[string]int `json:"stats,omitempty"`
    Total   int            `json:"total_files,omitempty"`
    Message string         `json:"message,omitempty"`
}

type Node struct {
    Children map[string]*Node
    Files    []string // Stores "Host:Path" strings
}
```

```
type Journal struct {
    file *os.File
    mu   sync.Mutex
}

type Server struct {
    Root     *Node
    Registry map[string]bool
    Stats    map[string]int
    Total    int
    Journal  *Journal
    mu       sync.RWMutex
}
```

The protocol layer establishes a standardized communication boundary through the `Message` and `Response` structures. By utilizing a single `Message` schema for all client interactions, the design multiplexes various operations — such as indexing, searching, and querying statistics — through the `Op` field. The strategic use of JSON `omitempty` tags minimizes network payload size, ensuring that a simple status request does not transmit uninitialized string fields. Similarly, the `Response` struct provides a unified envelope capable of carrying simple status acknowledgments, arrays of search results, or complex statistical maps back to the connected client. The core of the search engine resides in the `Node` and `Server` structures. The `Node` struct forms the backbone of an inverted index implemented as a trie; its `Children` map provides paths for character sequences, while the `Files` slice accumulates the exact `Host:Path` identities of any files containing that token. To manage the global state, the `Server` struct anchors this trie at its root and maintains a `Registry` map. The logic behind the `Registry` map is to act as a fast deduplication filter, preventing the system from uselessly re-indexing files that have already been processed. It also tracks the distributed system's scale using the `Stats` map and the `Total` integer. To ensure data durability across crashes, the `Journal` struct binds an active `os.File` pointer to a `sync.Mutex` instance. This coupling guarantees that concurrent indexing requests are strictly serialized when written to the underlying append-only log, preventing interleaved data corruption on disk. Finally, the `Server` struct wraps its entire state in a `sync.RWMutex` instance, allowing search operations to traverse the index concurrently without blocking, while acquiring an exclusive lock only when new files arrive and structural mutations are required.

The `OpenJournal()` function initializes the persistence layer by configuring the underlying file descriptor specifically for an *append-only WAL*. This design ensures *durability* by committing every state change to disk before it is reflected in the volatile, in-memory index. The logic behind this sequential, append-only approach is to provide a reliable *recovery* mechanism; should the system crash or lose power, the application can reconstruct its internal state by replaying journal entries in order. By prioritizing this "write-first" protocol, we bridge the gap between high-speed RAM and persistent storage, ensuring that once an operation is acknowledged, it remains resilient against system failure:

```
func OpenJournal(filename string) (*Journal, error) {
    f, err := os.OpenFile(filename, os.O_APPEND | os.O_CREATE | os.O_WRONLY, 0644)
    if err != nil {
        return nil, err
    }
    return &Journal{file: f}, nil
}
```

The function logic relies on a precise combination of bitwise flags passed to `os.OpenFile()` to establish the correct operational semantics. The `os.O_APPEND` instance guarantees that all new indexing events are sequentially written to the very end of the file, whereas `os.O_CREATE` automatically creates a new journal file if one does not already exist. Last, restricting the descriptor with `os.O_WRONLY` makes sure that the active journaling mechanism only records state changes and never reads them. The logic behind this constraint is rooted in the **principle of least privilege (PoLP)**: by stripping the ability to read, we ensure that the active journaling process remains a producer of data, never a consumer. This prevents a class of logical errors where a faulty write routine might inadvertently read stale or partial data from the journal and use it to corrupt the in-memory index.

Next, the `WriteEvent()` method ensures that every state modification is safely recorded to the WAL:

```
func (j *Journal) WriteEvent(msg Message) error {
    j.mu.Lock()
    defer j.mu.Unlock()
    data, err := json.Marshal(msg)
    if err != nil {
        return err
    }
    if _, err := j.file.Write(append(data, '\n')); err != nil {
        return err
    }
    return j.file.Sync()
}
```

As the server processes requests concurrently across multiple goroutines, the function immediately acquires a mutual exclusion lock (`j.mu.Lock()`) as concurrent writes to a single file descriptor without synchronization will interleave byte streams, resulting in irreversible data corruption. By marshaling the `Message` structure into JSON, the code creates a serialized representation of the event. Then, we append a newline character to the byte slice before issuing the `Write()` system call. This simple framing technique structures the file as a **JSON Lines (JSONL)** document. This design decision allows the server's recovery mechanism to read the log line by line sequentially, cleanly separating independent events during the replay phase.

The `Close()` method provides a controlled shutdown of the journaling subsystem:

```
func (j *Journal) Close() error {
    j.mu.Lock()
    defer j.mu.Unlock()
    return j.file.Close()
}
```

Although releasing a file descriptor might seem like a trivial operation, we acquire a mutual exclusion lock before invoking the underlying operating system call because if the server begins its shutdown sequence while active workers are simultaneously attempting to append new events, terminating the file descriptor unilaterally would cause those concurrent writes to fail or potentially panic the application.

The `NewServer()` function serves as the constructor for the application, arranging the transition from a cold start to a fully operational, consistent state before any network traffic is accepted:

```
func NewServer(journalPath string) *Server {
    j, err := OpenJournal(journalPath)
    if err != nil {
        panic(fmt.Sprintf("Failed to open journal: %v", err))
    }

    s := &Server{
        Root:     &Node{Children: make(map[string]*Node)},
        Registry: make(map[string]bool),
        Stats:    make(map[string]int),
        Journal:  j,
    }

    // Replay history immediately upon creation
    s.replayJournal(journalPath)
```

```
    return s
}
```

The code begins by securing the persistence layer via `OpenJournal()`; if this physical file operation fails, the function immediately issues a `panic` response. Silently proceeding without a functional journal will compromise the system core durability guarantees, making a *fail-fast* approach the only safe alternative to prevent silent data loss. Once the journal file descriptor is safely acquired, the constructor allocates the `Server` struct, using `make()` to initialize the `Root` node's children, the `Registry` map, and the `Stats` map. This explicit allocation establishes a clean, non-nil foundation in memory, preempting potential runtime panics when concurrent workers later attempt to insert data. The most critical architectural decision within this initialization block is the synchronous invocation of `s.replayJournal()` immediately before the function yields control. By executing the history replay sequentially upon creation, the code ensures that the volatile in-memory *radix tree* is completely reconstructed from the append-only log before the `Server` instance is returned to the `main` routine. This synchronization guarantees that connecting clients will never query an incomplete, partially loaded index, maintaining the illusion of uninterrupted, persistent memory across server reboots.

The `replayJournal()` method functions as the bootstrap mechanism for the server state, translating the append-only disk log back into a highly structured in-memory trie. The logic behind this reconstruction is to decouple slow, durable writes from fast, ephemeral queries, allowing the system to benefit from both. By sequentially processing each log entry, this mechanism ensures that the in-memory index is restored to a state identical to the one held before the shutdown, effectively turning a flat file back into a sophisticated search structure upon every boot. This reconciliation of disk-based durability with memory-based performance is what allows the server to remain both resilient to failure and optimized for near-instantaneous search:

```
func (s *Server) replayJournal(path string) {
    file, err := os.Open(path)
    if err != nil {
        if os.IsNotExist(err) {
            return
        } // No journal yet, that's fine
        panic(err)
    }
    defer file.Close()

    fmt.Println("Replaying journal to restore index...")
    scanner := bufio.NewScanner(file)
    count := 0
```

```
    start := time.Now()

    for scanner.Scan() {
        var msg Message
        iferr:=json.Unmarshal(scanner.Bytes(),&msg); err != nil {
            continue
        }
        if msg.Op == "index" {
            s.IndexInternal(msg.Host, msg.Path)
        } else if msg.Op == "delete" {
            s.DeleteInternal(msg.Host, msg.Path)
        }
        count++
    }
    fmt.Printf("Restored %d events in %v. Total files: %d\n", count,
time.Since(start), s.Total)
}
```

The logic explicitly accounts for a cold start by gracefully returning if the journal file does not exist, acknowledging that a new server has no history to load, while strictly panicking on any other filesystem error to prevent starting with an inaccessible but existent log. By using `bufio.Scanner`, the routine processes the file sequentially, line by line, perfectly complementing the newline-delimited JSON format established during the writing phase. This streaming approach ensures memory efficiency, preventing the system from exhausting RAM regardless of how large the historical journal grows. Furthermore, if a specific line is corrupted and fails to unmarshal, the loop uses `continue` to skip the malformed entry rather than halting the entire restoration, prioritizing maximum data recovery over strict termination. Crucially, the routing logic directly invokes `IndexInternal()` and `DeleteInternal()` rather than their public, thread-safe counterparts. Because this replay occurs strictly within the constructor, the memory structures are guaranteed to be free from concurrent access. Bypassing the mutex locks during this phase eliminates unnecessary overhead, allowing the server to ingest thousands of historical events at maximum speed.

The `tokenize()` function acts as the lexical analyzer for our search engine, transforming raw, OS-specific file paths into a normalized stream of semantic keywords:

```
func tokenize(path string) []string {
    cleanPath := strings.ReplaceAll(path, "\\", "/")
    return strings.FieldsFunc(cleanPath, func(r rune) bool {
        return r == '/' || r == '.' || r == '_' || r == '-'
```

```
    })
}
```

The logic begins by sanitizing the input environment, using `strings.ReplaceAll()` to unconditionally convert Windows-style backslashes to Unix-style forward slashes. This critical normalization step ensures that the underlying search index remains platform-agnostic, preventing identical files on different operating systems from creating divergent tree structures. Following this homogenization, the code delegates the actual segmentation to `strings.FieldsFunc()`. By providing a custom evaluation function that returns `true` for slashes, dots, underscores, and hyphens, the algorithm explicitly defines the boundaries of a word within the context of a filesystem. This decision strips away structural noise — such as directory delimiters or file extensions — and fractures compound filenames such as `server_test.go` into independent, highly searchable tokens such as `server`, `test`, and `go`. By aggressively discarding these punctuation marks rather than indexing them, the function guarantees that the resulting trie remains compact and strictly focused on the core vocabulary of the user's data.

The `IndexInternal()` method integrates a new file path into the index without acquiring locks, delegating thread safety to the caller:

```
func (s *Server) IndexInternal(host, path string) {
    fullID := fmt.Sprintf("%s:%s", host, path)

    if s.Registry[fullID] {
        return
    }
    s.Registry[fullID] = true
    s.Stats[host]++
    s.Total++

    tokens := tokenize(path)
    for _, token := range tokens {
        if len(token) < 2 {
            continue
        }
        token = strings.ToLower(token)

        node := s.Root
        for _, char := range token {
            charStr := string(char)
            if node.Children == nil {
```

```
                node.Children = make(map[string]*Node)
            }
            if _, exists := node.Children[charStr]; !exists {
                node.Children[charStr] = &Node{Children: make(map[string]*Node)}
            }
            node = node.Children[charStr]
        }
        exists := false
        for _, f := range node.Files {
            if f == fullID {
                exists = true
                break
            }
        }
        if !exists {
            node.Files = append(node.Files, fullID)
        }
    }
}
```

The code first synthesizes a *unique identifier combining the host and path,* querying the `Registry` map to immediately discard pre-existing entries and prevent duplicate processing. After updating global statistical counters, the algorithm tokenizes the path, discarding fragments shorter than two characters and *normalizing the rest to lowercase* to ensure case-insensitive queries. For each valid token, the logic traverses the trie character by character, dynamically allocating maps and child nodes only when a specific branching path is absent. Upon reaching the terminal node of a token, the unique file identifier is appended to the internal slice of the node, verifying it does not already exist to guarantee absolute uniqueness at the leaf level.

The `DeleteInternal()` method acts as the inverse of the indexing operation, removing a file's presence from both the global tracking maps and the trie:

```
func (s *Server) DeleteInternal(host, path string) {
    fullID := fmt.Sprintf("%s:%s", host, path)

    if !s.Registry[fullID] {
        return
    }
    delete(s.Registry, fullID)
    s.Stats[host]--
    if s.Stats[host] <= 0 {
```

```
            delete(s.Stats, host)
        }
        s.Total--

        tokens := tokenize(path)
        for _, token := range tokens {
            if len(token) < 2 {
                continue
            }
            token = strings.ToLower(token)

            node := s.Root
            for _, char := range token {
                if next, ok := node.Children[string(char)]; ok {
                    node = next
                } else {
                    node = nil
                    break
                }
            }

            if node != nil {
                newFiles := make([]string, 0)
                for _, f := range node.Files {
                    if f != fullID {
                        newFiles = append(newFiles, f)
                    }
                }
                node.Files = newFiles
            }
        }
    }
```

The code verifies the file existence within the `Registry` map; if the file is unknown, it immediately returns. This early exit allows the server to safely ignore redundant deletion requests. Upon proceeding, the global state is aggressively pruned. The file is removed from the registry, and the global counter is decremented. The logic surrounding `s.Stats` checks if a host's file count has reached zero. If so, the host key is entirely deleted from the map, preventing a memory leak of stale hostnames over the lifetime of a long-running server. Once the global state is reconciled, the function tokenizes the path and traverses the trie for each valid token. The traversal logic is strictly read-only: it attempts to walk the character path but breaks early if an edge is missing, acknowledging that the token is already absent. When the traversal successfully reaches the terminal node, the code must remove the `fullID` element from the node's `Files` slice. Because Go slices are backed by contiguous arrays, removing an element from the middle can be complex. Instead of shifting elements in place, the logic makes a deliberate, defensive memory decision: it allocates a completely new slice (`newFiles`), iterates over the existing entries, and appends only those that do not match the deleted file. By reassigning `node.Files` to this new slice, the GC is left to reclaim the old backing array, ensuring a clean and safe removal without risking off-by-one errors or mutating an array that might currently be read by a concurrent search operation.

The explicit lack of thread safety in these internal methods is a deliberate architectural decision rooted in the separation of concerns. In concurrent programming, modifying shared state — such as the `Registry` map, `Stats` counters, or dynamically allocated tree nodes — requires strict synchronization to prevent race conditions. If two network requests arrive simultaneously and attempt to update the `Registry` map without coordination, the Go runtime will detect the concurrent map write and immediately terminate the program with a fatal panic. Similarly, if one goroutine attempts to read the `node.Files` slice while another is reallocating its backing array during an append or delete operation, the system will read corrupted, partially overwritten memory. However, burying mutex locks deep inside these internal traversal functions would be a fundamental design mistake. The server must guarantee transaction atomicity: an incoming event must be serialized to the disk journal and applied to the in-memory radix tree as a single, indivisible operation. If `IndexInternal()` and `DeleteInternal()` managed their own internal locks, a concurrent network request could theoretically interleave its execution in the microscopic window between the journal write completing and the memory update beginning, permanently breaking the synchronization between disk and RAM. By intentionally leaving these core data-structure manipulations lock-free, the architecture forces the outer layer of the program to manage concurrency. This design dictates that the public-facing caller must acquire a single, comprehensive lock to secure the entire server state, execute the journal write, perform the memory update, and only then release the lock, ensuring absolute consistency.

The public `HandleIndex()` and `HandleDelete()` methods represent the synchronization boundary of the index server, protecting volatile internal data structures from the unpredictability of concurrent network requests:

```
// Public Methods (Thread-Safe)
func (s *Server) HandleIndex(host, path string) {
    s.mu.Lock()
    defer s.mu.Unlock()
    s.Journal.WriteEvent(Message{Op: "index", Host: host, Path: path})
```

```
    s.IndexInternal(host, path)
}

func (s *Server) HandleDelete(host, path string) {
    s.mu.Lock()
    defer s.mu.Unlock()
    s.Journal.WriteEvent(Message{Op: "delete", Host: host, Path: path})
    s.DeleteInternal(host, path)
}
```

The logic dictates that both functions immediately acquire an exclusive write lock on the server's central `sync.RWMutex` instance. This exclusive lock ensures that only one goroutine can mutate the server state at any given moment. Once exclusive access is secured, the sequence of operations implements a strict Write-Ahead Logging protocol. The architectural design enforces that the system must first serialize its intent by writing the event to the disk via `s.Journal.WriteEvent()`. Only after this write operation completes does the execution proceed to mutate the in-memory structure using `IndexInternal()` or `DeleteInternal()`. Enclosing both the disk I/O and the memory update within a single mutex lock achieves true transactional atomicity. To any concurrent search request waiting to read the tree, these two distinct physical steps appear as a single, indivisible state transition, guaranteeing that the persistent disk journal and the in-memory index remain perfectly synchronized across the lifetime of the process.

The `HandleSearch()` function executes thread-safe prefix queries against the in-memory trie:

```
func (s *Server) HandleSearch(query string) []string {
    s.mu.RLock()
    defer s.mu.RUnlock()
    node := s.Root
    for _, char := range strings.ToLower(query) {
        if next, ok := node.Children[string(char)]; ok {
            node = next
        } else {
            return nil
        }
    }

    var results []string
    seen := make(map[string]bool)
    var collect func(*Node)
    collect = func(n *Node) {
```

```
        for _, file := range n.Files {
            if !seen[file] {
                results = append(results, file)
                seen[file] = true
            }
        }
        for _, child := range n.Children {
            collect(child)
        }
    }
    collect(node)
    sort.Strings(results)
    return results
}
```

The algorithm traverses the tree using the lowercased query; if any character path diverges, it returns `nil` immediately, an early-exit optimization that minimizes unnecessary computation. Upon locating the terminal node of the prefix, a recursive `collect` closure performs a depth-first search across all descendant branches to aggregate matching files. A `seen` map acts as a deduplication filter during this traversal, ensuring unique entries. Finally, the collected slice is sorted alphabetically, guaranteeing deterministic output.

Next, the `HandleStats()` method provides a thread-safe window into the global state of the index cluster:

```
func (s *Server) HandleStats() (int, map[string]int) {
    s.mu.RLock()
    defer s.mu.RUnlock()

    statsCopy := make(map[string]int)
    for k, v := range s.Stats {
        statsCopy[k] = v
    }
    return s.Total, statsCopy
}
```

The method logic guarantees that the internal statistics are not actively being mutated by an indexing or deletion operation while they are being queried. The most critical design decision in this function is the explicit allocation of `statsCopy` and the subsequent manual iteration over the `s.Stats` map. Because maps in Go are implicitly reference types, returning `s.Stats` directly would pass a pointer to the caller, leaking a reference to the server-protected internal memory. If the lock were then released and a concurrent write operation modified the original map while the client handler was reading the returned reference to encode the JSON response, the Go runtime would instantly detect a concurrent map read-write race and panic, terminating the server. By explicitly copying each key and value into a *newly allocated, isolated map*, the function guarantees that the caller receives a safe, immutable snapshot of the system health at that exact moment. The `Total` integer, being a primitive value type, is safely copied by default upon return.

The `handleConnection()` function implements a lightweight **remote procedure call** (**RPC**) system:

```
func handleConnection(conn net.Conn, server *Server) {
    defer conn.Close()
    decoder := json.NewDecoder(conn)
    encoder := json.NewEncoder(conn)

    for {
        var msg Message
        iferr:=decoder.Decode(&msg); err == io.EOF {
            return
        } else if err != nil {
            return
        }
        switch msg.Op {
        case "index":
            server.HandleIndex(msg.Host, msg.Path)
            encoder.Encode(Response{Status: "ok"})
        case "delete":
            server.HandleDelete(msg.Host, msg.Path)
            encoder.Encode(Response{Status: "deleted"})
        case "search":
            results := server.HandleSearch(msg.Query)
            encoder.Encode(Response{Status: "ok", Results: results})
        case "stats":
            total, breakdown := server.HandleStats()
            encoder.Encode(Response{Status: "ok", Total: total, Stats: breakdown})
        }
    }
}
```

The design treats the TCP socket as a continuous stream rather than a series of discrete, fully buffered payloads, which is implemented by wrapping the connection with `json.NewDecoder()` and `json.NewEncoder()`. This decision enables persistent keep-alive connections; an infinite `for` loop allows a single client agent to send thousands of indexing events over one session without the latency overhead of repeatedly establishing new network handshakes. Within this loop, the error handling isolates `io.EOF` to recognize a normal exit condition from the client, while using `defer conn.Close()` to guarantee that the underlying file descriptor is reclaimed regardless of how the loop terminates. The `switch` block examines the `Op` string of the decoded message to route the operation to the appropriate thread-safe server method, isolating the network parsing layer from the complexities of the concurrency and storage layers we discussed previously.

What is missing is the `main()` function implementation, which mainly reads the command-line parameters and begins the server – feel free to look at the implementation details. With all the preceding information in mind, let us perform a simple server interaction to make sure that it works.

Using the service

Let us now execute the server process:

```
$ cd ch14/index
$ go run server.go
Replaying journal to restore index...
Restored 0 events in 47.542µs. Total files: 0
Running on port 8080 (PID: 88872)
Press Ctrl+C to shutdown.
```

At this point, we do not have a client implementation, so we are going to interact with the server using `nc(1)`. The sample interaction is the following:

```
$ echo '{"op": "index", "host": "web-01", "path": "/var/log/nginx/error.log"}' |
nc localhost 8080
{"status":"ok"}
```

This manual interaction elegantly demonstrates the architectural flexibility of using *standard JSON over raw TCP*. Because the interface is completely decoupled from the client implementation language, any tool capable of writing a correctly formatted string to a network port can act as an active agent in this distributed indexing system.

A robust server is only half of a complete system; it requires an equally capable interface to translate human intent into actionable network requests. So, let us now develop the missing piece, which is the command-line client for the service.

Creating a command-line client

Rather than a simple messenger, this client will function as an autonomous agent — capable of walking directory trees, watching for live file modifications, and formatting distributed search results into human-readable output, thereby transforming our raw JSON protocol into a practical, composable tool. However, first, we are going to discuss an essential Go package, `fsnotify`, and explain why it is needed.

About fsnotify

The `github.com/fsnotify/fsnotify` library is a Go library that provides a unified, cross-platform interface for receiving real-time filesystem notifications. Under the hood, operating systems monitor file changes using entirely different mechanisms: Linux uses `inotify`, macOS uses `kqueue` or `FSEvents`, and Windows relies on `ReadDirectoryChangesW`. Writing a program that supports all these distinct system calls manually would require maintaining separate, complex code bases for each operating system. The `fsnotify` library abstracts this complexity away, delivering consistent event data regardless of whether the application is running on a Windows server, a MacBook, or a Linux container. Without an event-driven library such as `fsnotify`, your client would be forced to repeatedly scan every single file in the directory tree — perhaps every few seconds — comparing the current state to the previous state to detect changes. This approach, known as *polling*, causes high CPU usage and constant disk I/O even when absolutely nothing is changing, and it introduces a lag between when a file is created and when it appears in the index. Instead of constantly asking *Did anything change?*, the client registers its interest with the operating system kernel and essentially goes to sleep, consuming near-zero resources. When a user creates, deletes, or renames a file, the OS kernel immediately wakes the application with a specific event. This allows the indexer to react instantly to changes, updating the central server milliseconds after a file is modified, while remaining lightweight enough to run in the background without impacting performance.

The first thing we need to understand in the client code is the Go structures used:

```
type Message struct {
    Op    string `json:"op"`
    Host  string `json:"host,omitempty"`
    Path  string `json:"path,omitempty"`
    Query string `json:"query,omitempty"`
}
```

```
type Response struct {
    Status  string          `json:"status"`
    Results []string        `json:"results,omitempty"`
    Stats   map[string]int `json:"stats,omitempty"`
    Total   int             `json:"total_files,omitempty"`
    Message string          `json:"message,omitempty"`
}
```

Communication between the client and the server is governed by a strict, formalized protocol, defined by the `Message` and `Response` structures. By *mirroring the exact data definitions found in the server implementation,* the client guarantees symmetric encoding and decoding across the network boundary. Next, we have the `getMachineID()` function, which establishes a persistent, unique identity for the client across multiple executions:

```
func getMachineID() string {
    idFile := ".agent_id"
    content, err := os.ReadFile(idFile)
    if err == nil {
        return strings.TrimSpace(string(content))
    }

    fmt.Println("First run detected. Generating unique Agent ID...")
    bytes := make([]byte, 4)
    if _, err := rand.Read(bytes); err != nil {
        panic(err)
    }

    hostname, _ := os.Hostname()
    if hostname == "" {
        hostname = "unknown"
    }
    hostname = strings.ReplaceAll(hostname, ":", "_")
    fullID := fmt.Sprintf("%s-%s", hostname, hex.EncodeToString(bytes))
    os.WriteFile(idFile, []byte(fullID), 0644)
    return fullID
}
```

The code first attempts to read a cached identifier from a local `.agent_id` file. If this file exists, the client reuses the identity, maintaining continuity for its previously indexed files. During the initial run, the function generates a new identifier by combining the hostname with four cryptographically random bytes. Appending this random hexadecimal suffix ensures uniqueness even if multiple clients execute on distinct machines sharing identical default hostnames. The code explicitly sanitizes the hostname by replacing colons with underscores; this is a critical structural defense as the server's internal registry relies on the colon as the precise delimiter between the host and the file path. Finally, this newly minted identity is committed to disk for all future network operations.

Next, we have the `runScan()` function that implements the bulk ingestion mechanism of our client, designed to recursively discover and transmit local files to the central index:

```
func runScan(args []string) {
    fs := flag.NewFlagSet("scan", flag.ExitOnError)
    dir := fs.String("dir", ".", "Directory to scan")
    server := fs.String("server", "localhost:8080", "Server address")
    fs.Parse(args)
    machineID := getMachineID()
    absDir, _ := filepath.Abs(*dir)

    fmt.Printf("Connecting to %s as '%s'...\n", *server, machineID)
    conn, err := net.Dial("tcp", *server)
    if err != nil {
        fmt.Printf("Connection error: %v\n", err)
        os.Exit(1)
    }
    defer conn.Close()

    encoder := json.NewEncoder(conn)
    decoder := json.NewDecoder(conn)
    fmt.Printf("Scanning paths in %s...\n", absDir)
    count := 0
    start := time.Now()

    err = filepath.WalkDir(absDir, func(path string, d os.DirEntry, err error)
error {
        if err != nil {
            return nil
        }
        if d.IsDir() {
            return nil
        }
```

```
            msg := Message{Op: "index", Host: machineID, Path: path}
            if err := encoder.Encode(msg); err != nil {
                return err
            }
            var resp Response
            iferr:=decoder.Decode(&resp); err != nil {
                return err
            }
            count++
            if count%1000 == 0 {
                fmt.Printf("\rIndexed %d files...", count)
            }
            return nil
        })

        fmt.Printf("\nDone. Sent %d paths in %v.\n", count, time.Since(start))
    }
```

The code begins by defining a subcommand-specific `FlagSet` instance, isolating the `dir` and `server` arguments from the rest of the application. Before initiating network traffic, the code proactively resolves the target directory to its absolute path using `filepath.Abs()`. This is an important normalization step as it ensures that executing the client from different relative working directories does not result in the same file being indexed under multiple, divergent path strings on the server. Once the client identity and absolute path are established, a single, persistent TCP connection is dialed. The client avoids the latency overhead of performing a new network handshake for every individual file by wrapping this socket with `json.Encoder()` and `json.Decoder()` functions before the traversal begins.

To explore the local filesystem, the implementation relies on `filepath.WalkDir()`. This modern standard library function is intentionally chosen over the older `filepath.Walk()` function because it provides an `os.DirEntry` instance to the callback, bypassing the need to execute costly `os.Stat()` system calls on every item just to ascertain its type. The callback logic explicitly ignores directories, as our inverted index is solely concerned with tracking terminal file endpoints. For each discovered file, the client constructs an `index` message, serializes it across the wire, and synchronously waits to decode the server acknowledgment. Finally, to provide immediate feedback without producing thousands of lines of terminal noise, the routine utilizes a carriage return (`\r`) to update the progress counter in place.

After that, we have `runWatch()`, which transforms the client from a batch processor into a process capable of maintaining real-time synchronization with the central index:

```
func runWatch(args []string) {
    fs := flag.NewFlagSet("watch", flag.ExitOnError)
    dir := fs.String("dir", ".", "Directory to watch")
    server := fs.String("server", "localhost:8080", "Server address")
    fs.Parse(args)
    machineID := getMachineID()
    absDir, _ := filepath.Abs(*dir)
    conn, err := net.Dial("tcp", *server)
    if err != nil {
        panic(fmt.Sprintf("Cannot connect to server: %v", err))
    }
    defer conn.Close()
    encoder := json.NewEncoder(conn)
    watcher, err := fsnotify.NewWatcher()
    if err != nil {
        panic(err)
    }
    defer watcher.Close()

    fmt.Printf("Setting up watchers for %s...\n", absDir)
    dirCount := 0
    err = filepath.Walk(absDir, func(path string, info os.FileInfo, err error)
error {
        if err != nil {
            return nil
        }
        if info.IsDir() {
            dirCount++
            return watcher.Add(path)
        }
        return nil
    })
    if err != nil {
        fmt.Println("Error walking path:", err)
    }
    fmt.Printf("Watching %d directories on machine '%s'.\n", dirCount, machineID)
```

The initialization phase mirrors the `scan` command, parsing domain-specific flags, resolving the absolute directory path to ensure canonical naming, and dialing a persistent TCP connection to the server. The pivotal addition here is the integration of the `fsnotify` library. The critical logic to observe resides in the `filepath.Walk()` implementation. Because standard operating system notification APIs do not inherently monitor directory trees recursively, the client cannot simply attach a watcher to the root folder. Instead, it must manually traverse the entire filesystem hierarchy at startup, explicitly registering a discrete watch on every discovered directory using `watcher.Add(path)`. By maintaining a dedicated watch on each directory node, the client guarantees that file creations, deletions, or modifications anywhere within the target tree will reliably trigger an event, keeping the remote server precisely mirrored with local disk activity.

While `watcher.Add(path)` provides a straightforward interface for monitoring filesystem events, it is not an infinite resource. On Unix systems, the kernel manages these events through mechanisms such as `inotify`, which are constrained by system-wide limits — most notably, `fs.inotify.max_user_watches`. This parameter defines the maximum number of directories a single user can monitor to prevent a single process from monopolizing kernel-side memory. In a large-scale file indexer, recursively attaching to every subdirectory can quickly exhaust these limits, especially when encountering deeply nested structures such as `node_modules` or `.git`. If the limit is reached, the application may fail to register new watches, leading to an index that is silently incomplete and no longer reflects the true state of the filesystem. To resolve this, the indexer must adopt a more discerning approach to resource allocation. The most effective strategy is the implementation of exclusion patterns. The logic behind this decision is that not all files are created equal; ephemeral build artifacts, caches, and third-party dependencies rarely require the overhead of real-time monitoring. By allowing the user to define a "blacklist" of patterns, the indexer can skip these high-density, low-value directories during the recursive walk. This preserves the limited supply of kernel watches for the source code and configuration files that truly define the project state. This modification is left as an exercise for the reader.

The heartbeat of the active watcher resides in an infinite loop that multiplexes channel communication using the `select` statement. By listening concurrently to both the `Events` and `Errors` channels provided by the `fsnotify` library, the client remains responsive to the operating system without blocking CPU execution while waiting for disk activity:

```
for {
    select {
    case event, ok := <-watcher.Events:
        if !ok {
            return
        }
```

```
            absPath, _ := filepath.Abs(event.Name)

            if event.Op&fsnotify.Create == fsnotify.Create {
                info, err := os.Stat(absPath)
                if err == nil && info.IsDir() {
                    watcher.Add(absPath)
                    fmt.Printf("[NEW DIR] %s\n", absPath)
                } else {
                    fmt.Printf("[INDEX] %s\n", absPath)
                    encoder.Encode(Message{Op: "index", Host: machineID, Path:
absPath})
                }
            }

            if event.Op&fsnotify.Remove == fsnotify.Remove ||
event.Op&fsnotify.Rename == fsnotify.Rename {
                fmt.Printf("[REMOVE] %s\n", absPath)
                encoder.Encode(Message{Op: "delete", Host: machineID, Path:
absPath})
            }

        case err, ok := <-watcher.Errors:
            if !ok {
                return
            }
            fmt.Println("Watcher error:", err)
        }
    }
}
```

The logic handling a `Create` event contains a mechanism for maintaining absolute synchronization over time. Because standard OS watchers do not automatically cascade their monitoring into newly created subdirectories, the client must intervene. When a creation event arrives, the program immediately uses `os.Stat()` to inspect the new physical entity on the disk. If the new item is indeed a directory, the program actively registers it via `watcher.Add()`, dynamically expanding the monitoring net to catch any subsequent files created inside it. Conversely, if the item is a standard file, the client formats an `index` message and streams it directly to the server. Similarly, the logic groups `Remove` and `Rename` operations together under a single response branch. From the perspective of our simple inverted index, a file that is renamed or moved is effectively removed from its original known path. Therefore, both filesystem events trigger a straightforward `delete` message to the server, ensuring the remote index sheds stale data and perfectly mirrors the current state of the local distribution.

The remaining code of the client implementation consists primarily of standard boilerplate for flag parsing, TCP dialing, and the JSON encoding loop for the implementation of the remaining commands. The architecture relies on these simple, composable parts to achieve complex distributed behavior. I encourage you to examine the full source code in the repository to see the complete assembly.

Let us now try the client from a macOS machine, which also runs the server process:

```
$ cd ch14/index
$ go run client.go scan -dir . -server localhost:8080
First run detected. Generating unique Agent ID...
Connecting to localhost:8080 as 'M4.local-65335ee4'...
Scanning paths in /Users/mtsouk/go/src/github.com/mactsouk/goSP2/ch14/index...

Done. Sent 6 paths in 713.667µs.
$ go run client.go search -q mod -server localhost:8080
Found 1 results:
 [M4.local-65335ee4] /Users/mtsouk/go/src/github.com/mactsouk/goSP2/ch14/index/
go.mod
$ go run client.go stats
========================================
      Distributed Index Status
========================================
 Total Files Indexed : 7
 Active Agents       :
----------------------------------------
 M4.local-65335ee4          : 6 files
 web-01                     : 1 files
----------------------------------------
```

Everything works as expected. Let us now try the client from a remote Linux machine:

```
$ cd ch14/index
$ go run client.go scan -dir /var/log -server m4:8080
First run detected. Generating unique Agent ID...
Connecting to m4:8080 as 'think-fe023adf'...
Scanning paths in /var/log...

Done. Sent 87 paths in 865.102812ms.
```

```
$ go run client.go stats -server m4:8080
========================================
       Distributed Index Status
========================================
 Total Files Indexed : 94
 Active Agents       :
----------------------------------------
 M4.local-65335ee4          : 6 files
 think-fe023adf             : 87 files
 web-01                     : 1 files
----------------------------------------
```

Now, let us test the `fsnotify` functionality:

```
$ cd ch14/index
$ go run client.go watch -dir .
Setting up watchers for .../go/src/github.com/mactsouk/goSP2/ch14/index
Watching 1 directories on machine 'M4.local-65335ee4'.
[INDEX] /Users/.../go/src/github.com/mactsouk/goSP2/ch14/index/watchME
[REMOVE] Users/.../go/src/github.com/mactsouk/goSP2/ch14/index/watchME
```

The `Watching 1 directories` log entry indicates that only the root directory was found; if subdirectories existed, the `filepath.Walk()` logic would have registered each one with the `fsnotify` engine, incrementing this count accordingly. The subsequent log entries represent real-time reactions to physical file manipulations.

Great! Both the server and the client are working as expected.

While our implementation currently relies on a single, append-only journal for persistence, the release of Go 1.26 introduces a more flexible approach to system observability through the ability to direct log output to multiple targets simultaneously. Such a capability might ensure that a server can remain highly transparent to operators while keeping its core indexing logic focused and performant.

New in Go 1.26: log to multiple targets

Go 1.26 comes with native support for fan-out logging through the new `slog.NewMultiHandler()` constructor, simplifying complex operational telemetry. The logic behind this feature is to allow a single logging event to be distributed across multiple handlers — such as a local file for persistent auditing and a network-based dashboard for real-time monitoring — without complicating the core application code. In a production system, this is vital; it ensures that a critical failure, such as an exhausted `inotify` limit, is simultaneously recorded for historical analysis and instantly visible to the operations team. By composing these handlers into a single logical logger, we can maintain high-fidelity observability across the entire life cycle of our indexer, ensuring the system remains transparent and manageable under heavy load. Here is the relevant code, as found in `ch14/multiLog.go`:

```
package main

import (
	"log/slog"
	"os"
)

func main() {
	jsonH := slog.NewJSONHandler(os.Stdout, nil)
	textH := slog.NewTextHandler(os.Stderr, &slog.HandlerOptions{
		Level: slog.LevelError,
	})

	multi := slog.NewMultiHandler(jsonH, textH)
	logger := slog.New(multi)
	logger.Info("App starting", "version", "1.26")
	logger.Error("Database down", "db", "primary")
}
```

This program demonstrates the new Go 1.26 `slog.NewMultiHandler()` feature as it configures a single logger to send data to two different destinations (standard output and standard error) simultaneously, while applying different formatting and filtering rules to each stream. This is a common operational pattern where you want a complete machine-readable record of all events for debugging, but only want to see critical human-readable alerts for errors. The logic begins by initializing two distinct handlers. The first, `jsonH`, is a JSON handler writing to `os.Stdout`. Since no specific options are provided (`nil`), it defaults to logging everything at `Info` level and above. The second handler, `textH`, is a text handler writing to `os.Stderr`. This handler is initialized with a `slog.HandlerOptions()` struct setting the level to `slog.LevelError`, which means that it completely ignores any log messages below the `Error` severity (such as `Debug` or `Info`), ensuring that the error stream remains quiet unless something goes really wrong. The core of the program is the call to `slog.NewMultiHandler(jsonH, textH)`, which creates a unified handler that acts as a broadcaster. When `logger` receives a record, it passes it to this multi-handler, which then forwards the record to both `jsonH` and `textH` independently. Each child handler then applies its own logic. This simplifies the application code significantly; the rest of the program only needs to interact with the single logger object, oblivious to the complex routing happening underneath.

Now, try `ch14/multiLog.go` on your machine – you should get the next kind of output:

```
$ go run ch14/multiLog.go
{"time":"2026-02-14T21:13:42.822921+02:00","level":"INFO","msg":"App
starting","version":"1.26"}
{"time":"2026-02-14T21:13:42.823131+02:00","level":"ERROR","msg":"Database
down","db":"primary"}
time=2026-02-14T21:13:42.823+02:00 level=ERROR msg="Database down" db=primary
```

When `logger.Info("App starting"...)` is called, the multi-handler dispatches it to both destinations. The `jsonH` handler accepts it and writes a JSON line to standard output. However, when `logger.Error("Database down"...)` is called, both `jsonH` and `textH` process it as it meets the `Error` requirement.

The `NewMultiHandler()` function enables the architectural decoupling of logging. It allows you to maintain a verbose, machine-readable audit trail while simultaneously providing a high-priority, human-readable stream for critical errors. This ensures that observability requirements remain isolated from the core application logic.

This program does not just end the current chapter but the entire book! Thank you for choosing this book, and I hope that you enjoyed it as much as I enjoyed writing it!

Summary

In building an index of files and directories, we have done more than automate traversal or collect metadata. We have given form to the formless. What began as a recursive walk through system paths became a deeper exploration into how we organize, access, and relate to information. Technically, we leveraged concurrency, file I/O primitives, and filesystem interfaces to tame a potentially massive, nested space. On a deeper level, we exercised our human need to catalog, to reduce the unknown to the known, to make the silence of a machine speak in terms we understand. Putting it in another way, *indexing* is an assertion of control over impermanence: files may come and go, directories may change shape, but the act of recording their presence — even temporarily — is an effort to preserve meaning in a system designed for change.

As you close this final chapter and return to your terminal, remember that the knowledge you have acquired here is more than just syntax — it is a continuous invitation to build systems that are as maintainable as they are powerful. As you move beyond these pages to architect your own systems, remember that the true power of a language such as Go lies in its ability to stay out of your way. Software engineering is a continuous dialogue between the abstract logic of the programmer and the physical constraints of the machine. By respecting both, you ensure that your code is not just a collection of statements but a lasting piece of craftsmanship that stands the test of scale and time. The Go runtime is ready, the standard library is sharper than ever, and the path forward is clear; *the rest is up to you*!

Exercises

1. Change the code of the index client to use Cobra for the supported commands, as we learned in *Chapter 9, Creating Web Services*.
2. Implement node deletion for `ch14/binaryTree.go`.
3. Implement node deletion for `ch14/radixTree.go`.
4. Include the functionality of `ch14/multiLog.go` in the index server.
5. As a final exercise, consider modifying the `tokenize()` function found in `ch14/index/server.go` to support *exact filename matching*. The current logic is designed for keyword discovery, which is why searching for `go.mod` fails while searching for go succeeds; the dot acts as a structural boundary that fragments the filename into two separate tokens. To bridge this gap, you should update the indexing logic to treat the full, original filename as a primary token alongside the individual fragments produced by the current tokenizer. Implementation-wise, you might look at the `filepath.Base()` function to extract the terminal filename from the path and ensure it is added to the `tokens` slice without being subjected to character-based splitting.

Additional resources

- *Go-Release-Cycle*: `https://go.dev/wiki/Go-Release-Cycle`
- *Using go fix to modernize Go code*: `https://go.dev/blog/gofix`
- Creating an arena allocator: `https://mcyoung.xyz/2025/04/21/go-arenas/`
- *Building a Corruption-Proof Write-Ahead Log in Go*: `https://unisondb.io/blog/building-corruption-proof-write-ahead-log-in-go/`
- Go keeps evolving, and data structures get faster – look at *Faster Go Maps with Swiss Tables*: `https://www.youtube.com/watch?v=aqtIM5AK9t4`
- SIMD operations package: `https://pkg.go.dev/simd/archsimd`
- Go dependency analysis toolkit: `https://github.com/loov/goda`

15

Unlock Your Exclusive Benefits

Your copy of this book includes the following exclusive benefits:

DRM-Free PDF Version

Download DRM-free PDF and ePub copies of this book.

7-Day Packt Library Access

Get 7-day unlimited access to 8,000+ books and videos. No credit card required.

Available for first-time Packt+ trial users only.

Next-Gen Reader Access

Read this book on Packt Reader with progress sync, dark mode and note-taking.

Follow the guide below to unlock them. The process takes only a few minutes and needs to be completed once.

Unlock this Book's Free Benefits in 3 Easy Steps

Step 1

Keep your purchase invoice ready for *Step 3*. If you have a physical copy, scan it using your phone and save it as a PDF, JPG, or PNG.

For more help on finding your invoice, visit `https://www.packtpub.com/en-us/unlock?step=1`.

> Note
>
> **Note**: If you bought this book directly from Packt, no invoice is required. After *Step 2*, you can access your exclusive content right away.

Step 2

Scan the QR code or go to `packtpub.com/unlock`.

On the page that opens (similar to *Figure 15.1* on desktop), search for this book by name and select the correct edition.

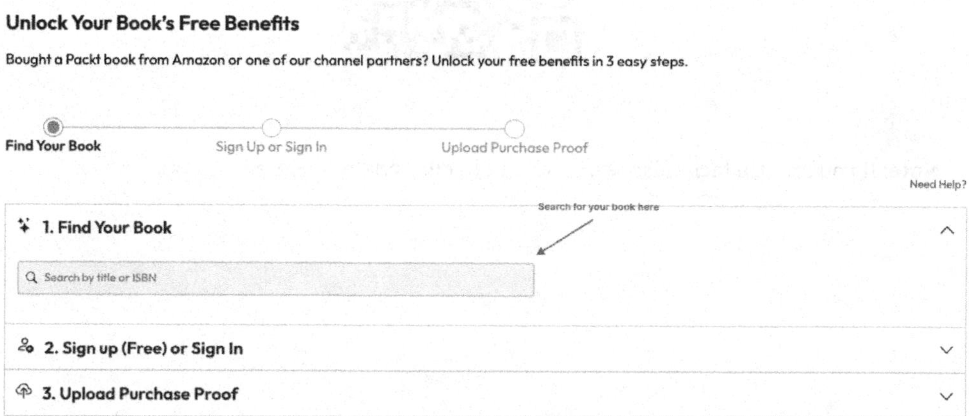

Figure 15.1 - Packt unlock landing page on desktop

Step 3

After selecting your book, sign in to your Packt account or create one for free. Then upload your invoice (PDF, PNG, or JPG, up to 10 MB). Follow the on-screen instructions to finish the process.

Need Help

If you get stuck and need help, visit `https://www.packtpub.com/unlock-benefits/help` for a detailed FAQ on how to find your invoices and more. This QR code will take you to the help page.

Note

Note: If you are still facing issues, reach out to `customercare@packt.com`.

Other Books You May Enjoy

If you enjoyed this book, you may be interested in these other books by Packt:

Mastering Go

Mihalis Tsoukalos

ISBN: 9781805127147

- Learn Go data types, error handling, constants, pointers, and array and slice manipulations through practical exercises
- Create generic functions, define data types, explore constraints, and grasp interfaces and reflections
- Grasp advanced concepts like packages, modules, functions, and database interaction
- Create concurrent RESTful servers, and build TCP/IP clients and servers
- Learn testing, profiling, and efficient coding for high-performance applications
- Develop an SQLite package, explore Docker integration, and embrace workspaces

Learning Zig

Alex Rios

ISBN: 9781835085127

- Find out how to maintain low-level control over system resources
- Set up a Zig development environment across different operating systems
- Organize maintainable projects with proper structure and build systems
- Implement error handling using Zig's unique approach to managing failures
- Leverage Zig's standard library effectively for everyday programming tasks
- Build applications that use files, external libraries, and C code
- Cross-compile and package Zig applications for multiple platforms

Packt is searching for authors like you

If you're interested in becoming an author for Packt, please visit `authors.packt.com` and apply today. We have worked with thousands of developers and tech professionals, just like you, to help them share their insight with the global tech community. You can make a general application, apply for a specific hot topic that we are recruiting an author for, or submit your own idea.

Subscribe to Deep Engineering

Join thousands of developers and architects who want to understand how software is changing, deepen their expertise, and build systems that last.

Deep Engineering is a weekly expert-led newsletter for experienced practitioners, featuring original analysis, technical interviews, and curated insights on architecture, system design, and modern programming practice.

Scan the QR or visit the link to subscribe for free.

Share your thoughts

Now you've finished *Practical Systems Programming in Go*, we'd love to hear your thoughts! Scan the QR code below to go straight to the Amazon review page for this book and share your feedback or leave a review on the site that you purchased it from.

https://packt.link/r/1806112191

Your review is important to us and the tech community and will help us make sure we're delivering excellent quality content.

Index

A

Abstract Syntax Tree (AST) **368**
add.go file **351**
anomaly detection **487**
arrays **3, 22, 23**
atomic counters **255**
automatic dereferencing **68**

B

Bellman-Ford algorithm **275**
basename(1) utility
  implementing 42 – 44
benchmarking **172**
  ch04/jsonReflection.go 173 – 176
  file copying 215 – 217
  Go code 172, 173
  PGO gains 176
  profiling applications 176 – 178
binary tree **506**
buffered channels **104 - 108**

C

CPU profiling **193**
CRUD operations **284**
Chebyshev distance **440**
Coordinated Universal Time (UTC) **172**
callback function **239**
capturing groups **33**
ch01/basename.go
  testing 167, 168
ch04/jsonReflection.go
  benchmarking 173 – 175
channels **4, 91, 99**
  buffered channels 104 – 108
  data exchanging 102 – 104
  goroutines, timing out with 108 – 110
  monitor goroutines 116 – 118
  select statement 99, 100
  signal channels 115
  unbuffered channels 104 – 108
  worker pools, implementing 110 – 114
classification utility **468**
  implementing 468 – 478
clustering **479**
  implementation 479 – 486
  methodology 479
cobra package **39**
comma ok idiom **49**
command-line arguments **35**
  working with 35 – 38
command-line client
  creating 535
compact prefix tree **513**
compiler **368**
concurrent matrix multiplication **127**
connection string **287**
constants **9**
constraint **163**
context package **339 - 342**
custom generic constraint **163**
cyclic imports **8, 39**

D

DNS issues **298**
Dijkstra algorithm **275**
  implementing 275 – 279
Docker image
  using, for PostgreSQL 288, 289
Dynamic Time Warping (DTW) algorithm **435, 441, 442**
data
  reading, from Prometheus 354
data types **8**
  constants 9
  numeric data types 10 – 12
  printing values 10

private 9
public 9
runes 12 – 15
strings 12 – 15
strings.Builder 16 – 18
variables 9

database reports
creating 290 – 294

dates and times
working with 170 – 172

dd(1) utility
creating, in Go 255 – 257

deadlocks **119, 129 - 132**

device ID (Dev) **250**

directory trees
traversing 231 – 235

dynamic programming (DP) **271**

E

Euclidean distance **440**

Extended Backus-Naur Form (EBNF) **366**

embed package **236**

empty directories
finding, with utility 239, 240

empty interface **154**
uses 155 – 159

empty structs **79**

end-of-file (EOF) condition **438**

error handling **18 - 22**

error values **19**

F

fault tolerance (FT) **464**

file I/O operations **183**

file copying **215**
benchmarking 215 – 217

file path existence
checking 185

file systems **223**

files reading **186, 187**
buffered and unbuffered reading, benchmarking 192
buffered and unbuffered reading, profiling 192 – 197
buffered reading 190, 191
character by character reading 199 – 201
file seeking 187, 188
line by line reading 197, 198
unbuffered reading 189, 190
word by word reading 198, 199

files writing **201**
buffer size, benchmarking in buffered writing 214, 215
buffered and unbuffered writing, benchmarking 213
buffered writing 212, 213
files, appending to 205, 206
logging to files 207 – 211
new files, creating 202 – 204
system logging 207 – 211
unbuffered writing 211

filesystem index service
creating 520
server code 521 – 534
using 534

fsnotify library **535 - 543**

functions **27 - 29**
iterator functions 29 – 31

G

G-M-P model **147**

GOGC environment variable **140 - 142**

GOMAXPROCS **148**
effects 148 – 151

Go **3**
advantages 4, 5
interfaces 5
misconceptions 137 – 139
versus C 5, 6
versus Rust 5, 6
versus Zig 5, 6

Go 1.26
Goroutine leak profile 499 – 501
Goroutine metrics 497 – 499
logging, to multiple targets 543 – 545

Go code
benchmarking 172, 173
running 6 – 8
testing 166, 167

Go garbage collector (GC) **139**

Go package
creating 444

distances, benchmarking 451
documentation, viewing 448, 449
documenting 447, 448
publishing, on GitHub 449 – 451
workspaces, working with 444 – 447

Go program execution process 136, 137

Go scheduler 92, 147, 148

Go server
running, as Docker images 318, 319

Go utility
implementing, in Prometheus 356 – 359

Grafana 317

Green Tea garbage collector 495 - 497

garbage collection 139

gauge metrics 313

generic containers 165

generic function 163

generics 163 - 165

goroutines 4, 91, 92
creating 93, 94
sync.WaitGroup, for goroutine synchronization 95 – 97
timing out, with channels 108 – 110
WaitGroup.Go 98

H

Hamiltonian cycle 271

Held-Karp algorithm 271

hash tables 47

I

idempotency 97

identifiers 367

infinite loop 299

infix positions 383

inode number (Ino) 250

interfaces 154
empty interface 154

interpreter 368

io/fs package 230

iterator functions 29 - 31

J

JSON data
benchmarking 261 – 263
converting to XML 264 – 266
json/v2 version 266 – 268
storing, in SQLite3 database 285, 286
stream of records, working with 260, 261
working with 260

JSON marshaling 74

json/v2 version 266 - 268

K

k-Nearest Neighbors (kNN) classifier 468

L

Leave-One-Out Classification utility 468

Longest Common Subsequence Similarity (LCSS) distance 441

last-in, first-out (LIFO) 96

lazy sweeping 139

lexer 368

linked list 85

M

MPdist 442

Manhattan distance 441

Matrix Profile 442, 443

machine learning (ML) 440

make() memory allocation 153

maps 47, 48
using 48 – 56

mark-and-sweep collector 139

matrix multiplication 125 - 128

memory leaks 143
goroutines 145 – 147
pointers and references 143 – 145

memory profiling 193

middleware functions 324
simple HTTP server, creating with 324 – 329

min-heap 276, 277

modules 6, 165, 166

monitor goroutine pattern 116 - 118

multiple channels
handling, with select statement 100

mutex 123

N

naive brute-force approach 271
namespace isolation 77
nc(1) (Netcat) utility 300
nested anonymous structs 76
net/http package 323
new() function
improvement 506 – 513
new() memory allocation 153
non-concurrent TCP server 298
non-generic approach 164
numeric data types 10 - 12
numeric literals 367

O

orphan worker leak 500
outlier analysis 487 - 495
outlier detection 487

P

Patricia trie 513
Piecewise Aggregate Approximation (PAA) 443, 444
PostgreSQL 286
Docker image, using for 288, 289
working with 286, 287
Pratt parser 383
Profile-Guided Optimization (PGO) 151, 152, 176
PromQL (Prometheus Query Language) 354
Prometheus
data reading 354
Go utility, implementing 356 – 359
running 318, 319
sample data, creating 354, 355
packages 6, 165
parallelism 91
parser 368
pattern matching 31
pointer arithmetic 5
pointers 84 - 89
polymorphism 72, 159
prefix positions 383
prepared statement 282
pretty-printed JSON 175
principle of optimality 271
priority queue (PQ) 276
profiling applications 176 - 178
programming language
extending 409
proxy server
creating 343, 344

R

race conditions 120 - 124
radix tree 513 - 519
reflection 159, 160
structures, inspecting with 160 – 163
regular expressions 31
using 31 – 35
representative workload 177
root.go file 351
runes 12 - 15

S

SMALL 365, 409
code reading, from external files 380 – 382
evaluator 395 – 405, 418 – 420
lexer 368 – 379, 414
new features 410 – 413
parser 383 – 395, 415 – 417
programming language components 368
syntax 366, 367
tests, writing for 424 – 433
updated language, implementing 421 – 423
updated version 414
using 405
SQLite3 280
external Go modules, using 280
interactions, demonstrating 280 – 284
JSON data, storing in 285, 286
select statement 99, 100
multiple channels, handling with 100 – 102
semantic analyzer 368
setgid 250
setuid 250
short variable declaration syntax 66

signal channels **115**
signals **223**
simple HTTP server
- creating, with middleware 324 – 329
- HTTP applications, profiling 333 – 336
- HTTP applications, testing 336 – 338
- HTTP client, creating 330 – 333

single file
- copying, into multiple directories 251 – 254

singly linked list **85**
slice of runes **200**
slice of strings **198**
slices **3, 23**
slicing **24 - 26**
statements **384**
static assets
- embedding, in Go binaries 236 – 238

stderr **184**
stdin **184**
stdout **184**
sticky **250**
string literals **367**
strings **12 - 15**
strings.Builder **16 - 18**
struct embedding **59, 69**
struct pointers **68**
struct tags **57, 264**
structures **47, 57 - 81, 84**
- inspecting, with reflection 160 – 163

submatches extraction **33**
sweep phase **139**
symbolic link **248**
sync.WaitGroup **95**
synctest package **168, 169**

T

TCP client
- developing 302 – 305

TCP server
- concurrency, developing 301, 302
- developing 298 – 300
- testing 300, 301

TCP/IP metrics
- collecting 311 – 315
- Go server, running as Docker images 318, 319
- Prometheus, running 318, 319
- server, containerizing 316, 317
- storing 317, 318

TigerBeetle **435, 453**
- connecting to 456, 457
- data, reading 462 – 464
- data, writing 457 – 461
- for financial accounting 453 – 456

Time Series Clustering **479**
Transmission Control Protocol/ Internet Protocol (TCP/IP) **297**
table-driven test **168**
testing, Go code **166, 167**
- ch01/basename.go 167, 168
- synctest package 168, 169

text-processing task
- space-to-tab conversion 218
- tab-to-space conversion 217, 218

time series **436 - 439**
- classification 468
- data mining 467
- nearest neighbor, finding 452, 453
- reading 437, 438
- summarization 443

time series classification **468**
time series distances **440**
- Chebyshev distance 440
- Dynamic Time Warping (DTW) 441, 442
- Euclidean distance 440
- LCSS distance 441
- Manhattan distance 441
- MPdist 442, 443

token system **369**
tokenizer **368**
tokens **368**
traveling salesman problem (TSP) **259**
- sample graphs, creating 269 – 271
- solving 268, 269
- traveling salesman algorithm, implementing 271 – 275

tree(1) utility
- creating 240 – 251

type assertion **157, 165**
type inference **9**
type switch **157**

U

UDP client
developing 308 – 310

UDP server
developing 305 – 308

UNIX file system
file information, obtaining 229, 230
file types, differentiating 227 – 229

UNIX signals **223**
handling 224 – 227

unbuffered channels **104 - 108**

V

variables **9**

viper package **38**

W

WaitGroup.Go
goroutines 98

Weighted Rank Aggregation algorithm **472**

Wireshark **298**

wc(1) utility
developing 219, 220

web service
client, developing 350
commands, implementing 351 – 353
developing 344 – 349

weighted directed graph **269**

weighted graph representation **269**

which(1) utility
implementing 39 – 42

work stealing **148**

worker pools
implementing 110 – 114

workspaces **153**

write barrier **140**

Z

zero value initialization **66**

Made in the USA
Monee, IL
16 September 2026

63035042R00326